Theodore Friend

INDONESIAN DESTINIES

THE BELKNAP PRESS OF
HARVARD UNIVERSITY PRESS
CAMBRIDGE, MASSACHUSETTS, AND LONDON, ENGLAND
2003

Library of Congress Cataloging-in-Publication Data

Friend, Theodore
Indonesian destinies / Theodore Friend.
p.   cm.
Includes bibliographical references.
ISBN 0-674-01137-6 (alk. paper)
1. Indonesian—Politics and government—20th century.   I. Title.

DS644.F69   2003
959.803—dc21   2002043937

For our children,
Tad, Pier, and Timmie,
with love

Men are dangerous not only because they have unlimited appetites and unlimited yearning for power, but because they are creatures with dreams; and their extravagant dreams turn into nightmares if they seek to realize them in history.

Reinhold Niebuhr, *The Structure of Nations and Empires*

PREFACE

I aim here to convey to the lay reader an idea of "Indonesia" and what it has become in its first half century as a nation state. That requires trying to supply proportions among forces, momentum of events, flavor of leading characters, limits of successes, and reasons for failures. Also to convey the smells of the past: sometimes rarified aromas; too often, bloody reek.

I began this work after my wife, Elizabeth, recovered from high-dose chemotherapy for high-risk breast cancer. She was not only courageous but understanding of me: that after twenty-one years of administration, fulfilling as they were, I was free of office life. As an independent scholar, I was eager to comprehend Indonesia better and to help others do so. I had written a comparative study of Indonesia and the Philippines under Japanese occupation, which required reaching back into the Dutch and American colonial policy to understand the revolution that followed in one case and semi-colonial restoration in the other. Now I wished to come forward from the Indonesian revolution to the beginning of the twenty-first century. And, this time, to write for the educated layperson who might care to understand Indonesia with me. In doing so I have made clear in the notes my debts to specialists in various fields—to scholars of several nations and to journalists and NGO writers who have also enriched the study of Indonesia for everyone.

I began this commitment just before the Asian financial crisis struck in 1997 and turned Indonesia from crouching tiger to spastic dragon. I conclude with Sukarno's eldest daughter as president, a title her father still formally held when, in 1967–68, I first did research in Indonesia.

To know what is happening with the nation requires immersion in Jakarta and elite politics. But I also focus on other places: Yogyakarta, older and more stable than the capital; and Minangkabau, to the west, a matrilineal society and strongly Muslim. Timor to the east, with its split colonial heritage, half Dutch and half Portuguese, becomes a special theme because of international attention to the Indonesian annexation and, finally, relinquishment of East Timor. I give Toraja, high in the hills of South Sulawesi, special note not only for its topographic beauty and anthropological uniqueness but as an example of other enclaves of culture in the archipelago that continue on their own course.

The years 1997–2002 get relatively strong weight in the book because they bring to a head numerous crises that were suppressed in the long Suharto era. I dwell on several individual Indonesians of no special prominence because they illustrate ordinary lives with grace under pressure, and because I like them. I believe that the gravity of history is not ultimately centered in the nation state or its armies or corporations or criminal organizations but in the human soul. This may mark me, in the eyes of *realpolitikers,* as an idealist, but that does not trouble me. I would rather look realistic to private persons who ask themselves about the ground of being, or "what really matters?"

The deeds of a few Americans get special attention, too. In them, my purpose is to help citizens of the third largest country in the world to understand the peoples of the fourth largest, and vice versa. And through the dynamics attending these individuals, the better to engage English readers of any nation, any culture, in the adventure of trying to live intelligently in Indonesia.

I allow myself occasionally to appear in the narrative, not out of importance but out of vulnerability. I hope that limited use of such a voice may help make this book, as some of its readers see it, a distinct genre of history and personal witness. I grew up as a polite child of bourgeois Calvinist parents in industrial Pittsburgh—then (not now) a smog-blighted, depression-ridden city. Indonesia has been a great exploration for me, and a revelation of much that is other and different, better and worse than the place of my birth.

I am grateful not only to Indonesia for my continuing education but to many individuals who helped in various ways. John Bresnan, Donald Emmerson, and Adam Schwarz encouraged me to re-enter the field. Early in my seven recent research trips to Indonesia, staff members of the Indonesian Institute of Science (LIPI), the Center for Strategic and International Studies (CSIS), the Center for Information and Development Studies (CIDES), and the American Embassy helped me build interview schedules. Later I generated my own, in the end aided by Ms. Cornelia Paliama.

For other help and hospitality, I should especially note Iwan Jaya Azis, Gordon Bishop, Wayne Forrest, Jeffrey Hadler, Dennis Heffernan, Yuli Ismartono and John McBeth, Marla Kosec and Bernie Scher, Keith Loveard, John McGlynn, Suryani and Faizal Motik, Rudy Pesik, Kohar Rony,

Mohamad Sobary, Suryo Sulisto, and Norma, Renée, and Alan Zecha. For their expert professional advice I am grateful to Dr. Robert Bernstein on public health, Alden Brewster on debt in emerging market economies, Dr. Rachel Ehrenfeld on corruption, Professor Douglas Fuller on ecology and fire, and Alberto Hanani on Indonesian entrepreneurship. Translations from Japanese are by Komori Akiko. Translations from Indonesian are mine except where otherwise noted. The Tripod library system of Swarthmore, Bryn Mawr, and Haverford Colleges was especially helpful on interlibrary loans.

The United States–Indonesia Society (USINDO) produce stimulating programs in Washington, DC, which have been indispensable to me. I am especially grateful to its president, Paul Cleveland, its founders, Edward and Allene Masters, and their staff. Two of their trustees, former Ministers Mohamad Sadli and Emil Salim, are recognized often in the pages that follow. My affiliation with the Foreign Policy Research Institute in Philadelphia carries no stipend but provides splendid colleagues for discussing international affairs. Interns at the Institute gave bibliographic, computer, and conversational help: Nandini Deo, Carmen Jardaleza, Deborah Landres, Aaron Ratner, Leo Wise, and Corina Zappia. So did Nancy Ameen, Trudy Kushner, and Katie Gonos. The Board of FPRI gave me the equivalent of one roundtrip ticket to Jakarta. My overseas research, otherwise financed from pensioner savings, fortunately concluded before the American bubble burst in 2001–02.

The trustees of the Dillon Fund, chaired by Mrs. Douglas Dillon, generously supported by grant the production of the illustrations in this book. I honor them and the international vision of the founder of the Fund, Mr. C. Douglas Dillon. The amateur photographers, professional photojournalists and artists, photo-archivists, and other experts who have enriched this work visually are separately thanked for their help, and where possible credited adjacent to the images they provided.

Aid not specified here is not forgotten. The most vital help is implicitly recognized in the narrative, or explicitly in the list of persons interviewed in the essay on Sources. I cannot express fully enough my gratitude to those who have told me their stories and views. I absolve them completely from my own errors of fact, perception, or judgment. For these I take full responsibility and welcome discourse toward any corrections that should prove necessary.

Readers of the manuscript in late drafts have helped make it shorter and better: Don Emmerson, Tad Friend, William B. Goodman, and Frederick A. Terry, Jr. Three anonymous expert readers of the submitted version gave it the benefit of their searching critiques. Shellie Wilensky Camp, who sings in seven languages, rendered my pencil into type through her skill on a word processor. Bill Goodman and Polly Young-Eisendrath gave me the courage to attempt the project in the first place. Michael Aronson, as my editor, was a wise motivator, commentator, and guide. He and many others at Harvard University Press have made this the most professional and pleasurable experience in publication I have ever enjoyed. Susan Wallace Boehmer, who edited the manuscript, knows how both to embolden voice and to humble tone. She culled prose and called plays for a splendid team, including Marianne Perlak, the book's designer, as the project moved toward production. Philip Schwarzberg did the map; Marcia Carlson the index.

My wife, Elizabeth, endured my absences and moments of dementia in realizing this project. All I write is in debt to her. It makes me especially happy to dedicate this book to the children we raised together.

Theodore Friend
Villanova, Pennsylvania
March 1, 2003

CONTENTS

PROLOGUE:
THE LARGEST MUSLIM NATION

"Now we are free," Nur smiles. "And in an explosion of participation." He looks to Omi for confirmation. She is his wife, aide, and interlocutor; his anima, conscience, and constant companion. She, the wide-eyed one, nods. Her eyes are very round and her face pale for a Javanese. She looks startled by the world she sees, but trusting nonetheless.

We are in Nur's office at Paramadina, the young Islamic university he founded, having been a major voice of civil Islam in Indonesia since his own student days. It is late October 1998. We are looking back on what brought about Suharto's resignation as President, after thirty-two years in power. Indonesia is still in turmoil. In sixteen months its per capita income has dropped by half. The number of people in poverty has doubled or tripled, depending on how you count. Many are hungry. Riot breaks out in city after city, town after town. People die, are injured, are dispossessed. Women are raped, and children go homeless. But still there is hope in *reformasi:* reform.

Nurcholish Madjid is one of the hopeful. He helped to bring an end to Suharto's presidency. He knows that many people, many forces, converged to make that happen. But he played a clear and conscious part in the story, and he wants to tell it. "You are going to see Cak Nur?" my taxi driver had asked as I gave him my destination. He referred to the rector by his public nickname, pronouncing it affectionately "Chock Noor." "He should run for President." Nur laughs now as I tell him that. "I would get one vote only . . . the vote of Omi." She smiles. Nur is a stocky, dignified man in his late fifties, of benign bearing. His voice is mild but deeply musical, his lips full and sensuous, his complexion ruddy brown. A thick shock of hair reveals very little gray, and bushy eyebrows project over deep-set eyes—eyes harder to read than Omi's but clear and steady nevertheless. He wants to tell his story.

"I was always 'softly critical,'—that is, not using his name." Even now he does not utter the word Suharto. "I couched my criticisms in general and social science language. Now my essays are collected and published (he gave the English translation of their title as *Dialogue of Openness*), including my urging that we demand real opposition parties . . . I said Indonesia should *experiment* with democracy. Without error, we don't know what's right. Without trying we won't know what works." Nur credits his conviction on this point to his experiences as an Eisenhower Fellow in the United States in 1990, and especially to free-ranging seminar discussions among the fellows, mid-career professionals in many fields. The openness, pluralism, and pragmatism of the American experiment seemed to affect all of his comrades. Without his ever saying so to them or to his hosts, it sank in deeply with Nur.

He spread his views on return, and kept spreading them. Unaggressively. Threatening no one, embarrassing no one. Then in 1997 Indonesia descended rapidly into compound crisis. Massive forest fires spread ecological disaster; prolonged drought precipitated an agricultural catastrophe. The Indonesian rupiah plummeted; the stock market crumbled. Corporate insolvencies everywhere, small business strangulations, economic suffering for everyone.

The Deafness of Suharto

In March 1998, Nur recalls, "ABRI people"—armed forces leaders—began coming to his house privately, notably Lieutenant General Susilo Bambang Yudhoyono, chief of staff for social and political affairs. They wanted quietly to vent the question, "What shall we do?"

Following the secret conversations, Nur and several like-minded thinkers received invitations to the ABRI headquarters at Cilangkap, a large, squarish, sterile campus south of Jakarta. They found to their surprise a lecture hall filled with attentive generals trying to conceal their worry; trying not to betray themselves with ill-advised comments to colleagues; trying to see if a solution would articulate itself in a seminar without any of them being held responsible for it.

Nur was prepared with a plan. He voiced it. It rested on a silent, shared historical image as premise. Thirty-five years before, Sukarno had obtained the title "President for Life," meaning that power could be transferred only by force. In 1965, after the communists botched a revolution for the third time (previously in 1926 and 1948), violence was guaranteed, and the outcome was the opposite of what the activists had intended: army control, led by Suharto. Rivers of blood created lasting dread.

Change, this time, must be different. It is time, Nur said, for this president to make a public speech apologizing for his mistakes and errors of policy that contributed to the crisis. He must yield his financial gains and call upon the people to cooperate in economic recovery. By his personal example of returning wealth to the nation he could renew his moral power to lead. At the same time he should renounce any future intention to run again and should curtail the new seventh term just conferred on him by advancing the time of the next election. He should do so by means of an immediate general session of Parliament. There, his graceful exit scenario should be accompanied by legislation completely reforming the political laws and creating a social safety net through effective use of International Monetary Fund and World Bank aid. All of this must begin at once, Nur said—bringing the great shared fear to the surface—so that the Indonesian people would avoid any major trauma resembling 1965–66, when half a million were killed. It is necessary, Nur concluded, for Indonesia to learn how to transfer power *peacefully,* and to begin now.

Nur remembers the reactions of the generals: a kind of collective sigh of relief at seeing a sensible path. A low buzz of assent—yes, there is a way, this is the way. And then, from one officer, a loud and anguished puzzlement: "But who is going to *tell* him?!?"

That frustrated cry encapsulates the history of Indonesian democracy. And it suggests the coiled and rusted spring that is the Indonesian military. Some of these men were old enough to remember easy toleration of an entrepreneurial military by the only previous president in national history. President Sukarno had liked to grin and quip, "Britannia rules the waves, but Indonesia waives the rules." But Suharto had gone far beyond Sukarno in dispensing power franchises and allowing a deprofessionalized military to become dependent on his sultanic favor. No one knew what changing the Suharto game would lead to. Some of the generals had reason to fear untrammeled democratic inquiries, for in the service of Suharto they had suppressed demonstrations or hunted down activists in ways violating human rights. Other generals were uncompromised by either corruption or brutality, but all of them—*all*—owed their rank to Suharto, who had steadily, almost stealthily, absorbed the power to promote into his own hands. Who, indeed, would tell this president that his time was up? Even in a democracy, that job is not easy. It takes a tough man and an intimate relationship, such as Alexander Haig's with Richard Nixon.

Nur Madjid himself had avoided Suharto for thirty years because of his maltreatment of Natsir, a devout Muslim prime minister of the Sukarno era. Eventually Nur would be summoned to the palace for advice. But his gentle counsel was not the pivot of change. Only riot and the threat of still worse violence would finally drive Suharto from office.[1]

So who was going to tell him? To whose voice, to what signs, to which manifestations of power would Suharto actually listen? In those uncertainties lay enfolded eras of Indonesian history and the myriad complexities of its culture.

Human Geography and Layers of History

The succession crisis of 1997–98 contained a global question as well. Could a nation with three quarters as many Muslims as all the Arab countries combined become the world's third largest democracy? For anyone using compact European nation states as a standard, Indonesia is extraordinarily diffuse and diverse. Its population is more than three quarters as large as that of the United States but lives on less than one fifth of America's total land area. Indonesia's stretch of islands, if superimposed end-to-end on the Atlantic Ocean, would more than span the distance from New York City to Lisbon. In reality, they run from above Australia's northernmost point well into the Indian Ocean. Through the Strait of Malacca (which narrows to 1.5 miles near Singapore) and the other straits in Indonesian waters passes more than half the world's shipping, including most of the oil to Japan and Korea from the Middle East, and much to the United States.

Bisected by the equator and lying mostly below it, Indonesia's climate is tropical: hot and humid, with little variation in temperature because of warm surrounding waters. The highlands are cooler. In western Indonesia a dry season can be expected from June to September and a rainy season from December to March. El Niños and their aftermaths can produce serious exaggerations of both seasons.

A chain of seismic activity runs west to east, Sumatra through Java (south of, and excluding, Kalimantan) out through all of Nusa Tenggara. Earthquakes and volcanic eruptions have been frequent in recorded history along this extended string of islands, themselves the creation of volcanoes. In a different plane, a zoogeographic line divides marsupials to the east from the elephants (now extinct) to the west. Starting between Bali and Lombok, it runs northeasterly through the Lombok Strait and Makassar Strait, passing west of Sulawesi and east of the Philippines. "Wallace's line" was named for a solitary collector without a university education who found Sulawesi and Maluku to be living laboratories of nature. In 1858, in a malarial fever and flash of illumination, Alfred Russel Wallace formulated a short essay that contained the theory of evolution through natural selection over which Charles Darwin had been laboring for twenty years and had not yet published; the two men presented their work in a joint paper to the Linnean Society of London in July of that year.

The zoological south-north line and the seismic west-east line may be imagined to intersect just east of Bali, an arbitrary center of the physical features of Indonesia. There are about 17,500 islands in the entire archipelago, but more than nine tenths of their surface is on five of them. In descending order of size they are Kalimantan (80 percent of the area of Texas), Sumatra (a little bigger than California), Irian Jaya (almost exactly California's area), Sulawesi (equal to the state of Washington), and Java. A lean and tattered kidney bean the size of Louisiana, Java is the center of Indonesia's population and politics. Its people are almost as numerous as the Japanese, but they live in an area one third the size of Japan. Java's density in human numbers, unparalleled on any major world island, is of mighty consequence to history and the future.

The discovery of Java Man in 1891 points to a hominid presence perhaps 1.8 million years ago. First signs of human intervention in the environment can be dated back nine thousand years. The current inhabitants of the country can be seen as diverse mixtures of two general stocks from ancient migrations: Melanesians—dark-skinned, round-eyed, curly haired; and Austronesians—with skin colors from pale ochre to burnt sienna, oval eyes, and straight hair. Although no anthropological Wallace line bisects Indonesia, Melanesians are mostly found east of this divide and Austronesians to the west. Many Indonesians blend features of both.

The nation has no official system of ethnic identification, and it is easier to label a foreigner—Chinese or Western or Arab—than Indonesians themselves. The largest ethnic group is Javanese, comprising 45 percent of the population. Sundanese make up 14 percent; Madurese and coastal Malays are 7.5 percent each. The other quarter of the population is composed of a large number of ethnic groups, minorities, or self-styled indigenous peoples. Counting the languages of the archipelago is even more arbitrary than counting its ethnic groups. Over two hundred Austronesian and over one hundred and fifty Melanesian languages exist and can be grouped in larger clusters because of fairly recent descent from common ancestors.[2]

Indonesia, then, is ancient, tropical, crowded, and agricultural. A typical rural landscape features cultivated wet rice lands *(sawah)* ringed with palm and banana trees. Modern urban Indonesia is thick with mosques and malls. The country barely knew the transfer of culture that carried Chinese science and technology, Arab and Indian mathematics to Europe in the period 1000–1500. It is still trying to absorb the globalization of the period 1500–2000 that has poured from the North Atlantic eastward and southward. In

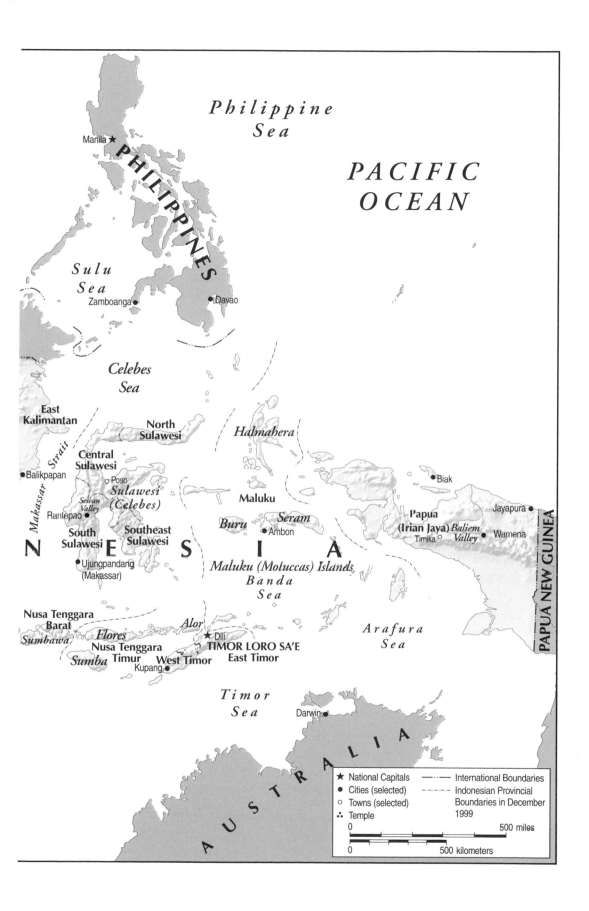

any case, it must be understood from the inside out, not from the outside in.

Layers of cultural sedimentation predated the arrival of Islam and Western colonialism. In Central Java, the Sailendra dynasty sponsored the construction of the massive Buddhist monument Borobudur roughly 780–833 in the Common Era (CE). Hindu monuments, such as Prambanan, arose nearby soon after, and Java absorbed Sivaism into its Buddhism in a distinctive manner that persists today. The kingdom of Srivijaya, also Hindu-Buddhist, developed a porous maritime empire dominating the Strait of Malacca and hence the China-India trade, but it declined by the eleventh century. The widest ambit of any Hindu-Buddhist power center was reached in the fourteenth century, when the kingdom of Majapahit claimed empire from its East Javanese base through Sumatra to the Malay peninsula.

The port city of Melaka displaced Majapahit's control and was briefly one of the great cities of the world until conquered by the Portuguese in 1511. Melaka was the first major state in Southeast Asia to convert to Islam. In contrast to the Hindu-Buddhist states, which each insisted it was the center of a hierarchical world, the God of the new creed was "everywhere," and its believers were "equal."

Travelers and merchants found appeal in this geographically and socially mobile religion and spread it steadily throughout Indonesia. Islam advanced more by trade than by sword. The strongest Indonesian state to endorse it was Mataram, which by the early seventeenth century encompassed more of Java than any previous kingdom. But it was soon in ragged contest with the Netherlands East India Company (VOC), a private commercial vehicle of the Dutch Republic and a military-mercantile competitor with other European powers throughout the archipelago and all of Asia. After dissolution of the VOC, the Dutch government in the Indies fought numerous wars against indigenous resistance. Even after imperial consolidation in the early twentieth century, the Netherlands East Indies consisted of a loose system of garrisons and administrative divisions, direct and indirect. The Dutch political police tracked nationalist, communist, and Islamic movements as threats to their rule.

Western imperial power affected culture everywhere in the archipelago to different degrees, through weapons, technology, education (discriminating and stingy), and example (good and bad). But underlying cultures persisted. Hindu-Buddhist influence is still seen today when a Javanese military officer requires a prisoner to touch his forehead to his warden's knee. Orthodox Islam is manifest in the prostration of worshippers, head bowed toward Mecca in daily prayers. Syncretic Islam (affected by Hindu-Buddhism, especially in East and Central Java) can be discerned in the acknowledgment of a *guru* or superior by kissing his hand and pressing it to one's heart or forehead.

Ways of classifying Indonesian varieties of Islam are readily disputed, however. What was once seen as a Hindu-Buddhist underlay of Islam is now more properly called Sufi, to stress the historical percolation of mystical Islam into Javanese culture and literature—a process intensified in the 1980s and 1990s by middle- and upper-class explorations of neo-Sufism.[3] At the same time, neo-Orthodoxy has also reached Indonesian Islam, affecting it with scriptural literalism and restricted behavior. A further look into the subject after September 11, 2001, sobers those who have discerned abundant "civil Islam" in Indonesia, swelling with democratic promise.[4] A degree of uncivil Islam has also raised its head. Minority movements work daily trying to install Islamic law in the constitution or to repel and suppress Western cultural influences; and a few adopt violent methods. These headline-grabbing events, however, should not obliterate our consciousness of pre-Islamic centuries of Javanese sensibility expressed through sculptural triumphs "in which gods have human faces and royalty wear divine attributes."[5] At a folk level, and even in the inner consciousness of many sophisticates, such images and attitudes still thrive.

Even pagan traditions endure. Men of the Dani tribe, Stone Age inhabitants of the highlands of central Papua, may greet one another with a light grasp of the other person's testicles, as a reminder of their mutual vulnerability. Whatever one may think about the proper behavior of parliaments, markets, and civil society, one must concede that this Dani gesture is both democratic and transparent.

While Indonesia is fixed in relation to the equator—one third above, and two thirds below it—nearly all else is fluid. Its per capita income has risen from the UN category of "lower" to "lower middle" and fallen back again. Its constitution has been spare and elastic enough to accommodate almost any form of government. With the dissolution of the Soviet Union, it has become the fourth most populous country in the world, after China, India, and the United States. But can it become and remain what many aspire to have it be—a stable democracy with plural institutions and free expression?

Democracy functions best when its citizens share a sense of common interest, even if the content of that interest is disputed. This ideal of commonweal, in turn, flourishes best when it rests on a common identity. Indonesia's national motto, "Bhinekka Tunggal Ika," translates from Sanskrit roots into a sentiment akin to "E pluribus unum"—"from many, one." In this book I will look repeatedly at tensions in Indonesia between the one and the many: many layers of history, many regions, religions, languages.[6]

Borobudur

The massive Buddhist monument near Yogyakarta dates from before 800 (Common Era). UNESCO and international philanthropy restored it in the late 1970s, as a site for steady visits by Indonesian tourists and international travelers. It was bombed (and repaired) in reaction to the killings of Muslim protesters in Tanjung Priok (North Jakarta) by the Suharto regime in 1984.

1. BUDDHA AT DAWN, with the volcano Mt. Merapi in the distance. (Marla Kosec)

2. THE KING OF THAILAND (foreground) is received for a Buddhist ceremony in February 1959, at an upper level of the sacred monument. His host, Sultan Hamengku Buwono IX (rear, center), is in military uniform. (Arsip Nasional)

3. STUPAS OF BOROBUDUR in early morning light. (Marla Kosec)

4. HO CHI MINH, president of North Vietnam (center, in white), is led on a tour around the base of Borobudur in March 1959. (Arsip Nasional, Jakarta Selatan)

Even conflicts of race—as found in the prejudice of many mainstream Javanese and Sumatrans against those with darker skin or frizzy hair or those who live close to nature, including the Melanesians east of Bali all the way to Irian Jaya and the natives of Kalimantan. Added to this are continuing debates, even after "reform," over the proper roles of the military and the police.

In modern Indonesia, deep-rooted corruption, a high incidence of violence, and an absence of effective modern law unhappily reinforce one another.[7] All, nonetheless, coexist with gentle demeanor, grace of movement, prevalence of tradition (including *adat,* customary law), generous hospitality, and beauty of arts and artifacts. Indonesia seeks its way as a culture of cultures, a community of communities. One of the most vast and various countries of our time, it goes on adapting itself selectively to the fast-moving world around it. Without any nearby enemy, it can choose to ignore the presumptions of the great world when these demands seem brazen or unfitting. Its worst enemy is usually itself.

Tone, Spirit, and Split-Level Values

Westerners have their own tensions, contradictions, and inconsistencies. Not to mention hypocrisies, some of which appeared to endanger, early in the new millennium, America's vaunted systems linking law and transparency with productivity. New symbols of corporate greed and collusive laxity echoed the 1920s and the 1890s. Crashes of American systems, however, have been followed by critical review and repair. An awareness of when inconsistency can be crippling drives the system and its individuals toward self-renewal.

Americans are underaware, however, of ways in which semi-assimilated Western values affect other cultures. No one has analyzed this better than Jaime Bulatao, who discerns in the Philippines a "split-level Christianity," in which the inconsistency of Christian belief with pagan, tribal, or traditional habits either is not perceived or is suppressed in consciousness or simply "forgotten." It is not felt as hypocritical; both systems coexist without guilt. Christian worship occurs alongside cheating in class, infidelity to a spouse, policemen raking in protection money, businessmen buying politicians, politicians buying soldiers, and so forth, until and unless an authority pierces the mask, arousing shame to a calamitous level.[8]

Such split-level phenomena—"coexistence within the same person of two or more thought-and-behavior systems which are inconsistent with each other"—are, in various ways, worldwide. They may even be conceived as a core part of "illiberal democracy" as defined by Fareed Zakaria—democracy in its troubled forms around the world, where free elections indeed exist as the inescapable essence of democracy, but other public virtues are lacking: rule of law and separation of powers; accountability of the government to the people; autonomy of individuals, as expressed through freedom of speech, assembly, religion, and property. "If a democracy does not preserve liberty and law, that it is a democracy is a small consolation," he writes.[9]

Without in any degree detracting from Indonesia's uniqueness and vibrancy, I suggest that the country suffers from just such a stressed and delaminated value system in at least three areas: split-level democracy, split-level free enterprise, and split-level Islam. From these fundamental separations in both the larger culture and individual psychology arise the difficulties Indonesians have experienced in welding constitutional liberalism to democracy, and thereby guaranteeing it. As an opening illustration, I submit the remarks of an observer engaged in Indonesia across half a century; and thereafter I let the evidence in this book speak for itself.

Clifford Geertz arrived in Jakarta in 1952 as the so-called October 17th Affair hit its peak. A civil war was threatened or pretended, but after declamatory feints, menacing public gestures, and pseudo-resolutions, the crisis was dampened down. Not just on this occasion but often, such *peristiwa* (incidents or affairs) have become a style of public life, "leaving a silence where deliberation, the life-blood of a popular government, should be." Geertz elsewhere speaks of a Javanese tendency, on both a cultural and emotional level, toward a life made up half of unfelt gestures and half of ungestured feeling. This suggests a core problem in Indonesia distinct from that in the Philippines but similar in that split-level characteristics tend to disable public life and may promote disintegration in private lives. However that may be, *peristiwa*—"affairs" instead of deliberations—exemplify "everything we hopelessly lump together as tone, or tradition, or spirit, or the inward shape of things, [which] contrives to hang on, as obstinate as geography, as lingering as climate, rendering the whole—'Indonesia'—familiar, continuous, puzzling, and original."[10]

Indonesia puzzles Indonesians themselves. "Tell us, Dr. Friend"—a retired civil servant proud of being able, he said, to dream and to make love in English, addressed me at a hush in a small reception—"Tell us how can such a gentle and lovable people as we be so murderous to each other?" I could not tell him. When I repeated the question later to a former cabinet member, he hastened to contradict it, by citing a "Chinese admiral" who centuries ago described the people living in the islands now called Indonesia as "killers who like to test their new knives on each other."[11] He seemed to wish to reverse the energy of the question and to ask, "How can such violent peoples produce such refined cultures?" In the history that follows, I hope that readers may find their own ways between questions so differently posed, and the dynamic evidence to begin shaping their own answers.

SUKARNO

INDONESIA:
THE DEVOURING NURTURER

One hundred years after the first president of Indonesia was born, his daughter became its fifth president. One of the greatest political assets of Megawati Sukarnoputri, elected in July 2001, is her father's legacy. His record is ragged but inescapable. Dispute will persist about his contributions to Indonesia and the distractions he presented to his nation. For a large proportion of the Indonesian population, however, there is no debate. Their collective memory, rounded and softened, is of Sukarno as revolutionary nationalist and man of the people, a lovable source of their national identity. Megawati, as his eldest daughter, enjoys the momentum of those attributes, along with projected expectations unique to herself: the patient mother, succorer to a suffering people, and restorer of unity to a nation again badly torn, as in her father's era.

To evoke the great range of character and characteristics of this nation that lives so markedly in the world of myth, I turn to a symbolic pairing whose source is Indian mythology, transformed by centuries of Javanese history. The pairing is of Durga, who stands for power, destruction, rage at man, and Umayi, who represents all that is gentle, feminine, and beautiful. Durga appears in old Javanese sculptures as a many-weaponed warrior, female, adamant, Amazonian in her fearlessness (see Figure 33 in Chapter 6). Umayi, not captured in stone, represents the soft, submissive, and creative side of the same mighty character. Both are consort to the great god Siva. Umayi is his sweet and domestically fulfilled spouse; but by an ancient curse she is always transformable into her angry and vengeful opposite, Durga, with her appetite for war.[1]

All his life Sukarno courted Indonesia as Umayi. He charmed and won her. She was faithful to him; and he, in his fashion, despite his petty mortal passions, was faithful to her. But in the end Sukarno had to face the reality that he was playing games with the gods. Eventually, the curse emerged, and Umayi was transformed into the dreadful Durga. Sukarno's rule went down, and with it the lives of half a million Indonesians. The romantic who had aroused the masses was reduced to an isolated, weeping wreck.

Megawati Sukarnoputri's womanhood makes her potentially a full expression of the binary character Durga/Umayi. Which Indonesia she will invoke is a function of her inner person, her circle of advisors, the vortex of Indonesian politics, and the typhoons of international affairs. Whether she will arouse an Indonesia more affirming than destroying, or one more devouring than nurturing, is history yet to be made.

Of Mandalas and the Perfume of Ten Million Flowers

Significant kingdoms existed in Java a millennium before the Dutch began to prevail. The great Buddhist monument of Borobudur near Yogyakarta, erected in the eighth century CE, as well as the Shivaite temple at Prambanan of the late ninth century, not far away, are remarkable displays of royal spending for sacred and political purposes. But there were no "empires" in a boundaried and bureaucratic sense.

The largest radial phenomena of Southeast Asian regional history are best called mandalas—a Sanskrit word that still suggests sacred geometry but, in the view of Oliver Wolters, conveys "a particular and often unstable situation in a vaguely definable geographical area without fixed boundaries, and where smaller centers tended to look in all directions for security." Mandalas could expand and contract like concertinas. Angkor at its grandest radiated influence from Cambodia through modern Thailand to the Malay peninsula and parts of southern Vietnam, enlarging and collapsing accordion-like: a mandala marked by "cliques, factions, personalities, clientage and patronage." The great carvings on the forty square miles of its surviving monuments convey a richly textured social life, military clashes with neighbors, and above all the sacred nature of its kingship, which presumed that it expressed the universe in microcosm. But despite court eulogies to the ruler and claims of unlimited sovereignty, "the Sanskrit tongue was chilled to silence at 500 metres" from the throne. There was little evidence of protracted lineage descent in dynasty. Likewise little of extended spatial control, as distinct from the amassing—in the more effective mandala centers—of political and commercial intelligence about what went on within its imagined circumference, which was overlapped by other influences radiating from other centers.[2]

Southeast Asia was a polycentric landscape-seascape, dotted with royal centers and connected trading ports but without a Genoa or Venice or any city states commercially expansive in the European sense. Far less, after

1500, were there indigenous mercantile empires evolving in the Portuguese-Dutch-French-British style and sequence.[3]

What is now called Indonesia had, in Anthony Reid's description, a "robust pluralism often coexisting with exalted Indic ideas of kingship."[4] Indeed, the more autonomous the area—Bugis and Balinese to the east of Java, Minangkabau to the west—the greater the king's impulse to assert the charisma of lineage and the magic of royal language. The Minangkabau rulers, in their letters and seals, proclaimed world-mightiness on a par with China and Constantinople, as legatees of Alexander the Great and as *khalif,* or deputy of God on earth—strike you dead if you doubt or disagree. Such cosmic claims puzzled Europeans, who were accustomed at home to better-monied monarchs with larger armies to back up their ambitions. But the Minang sovereigns knew their limits. Aside from the occasional civil war, they respected the local autonomies of their own subregional organizations of clans. Their edicts of power were not assertions of real domination but a language of inclusion for other Sumatrans, and later a language of resistance against the Dutch.[5]

A mandala in its full religio-political sense was developed most pronouncedly in Java, where the king, recognizing all the center-fleeing instincts of his realm, would seasonally go out to reinforce the center-seeking, or at least the center-recognizing, forces. His way was to show the flag and display the splendors of the court, receive homage, collect tribute, examine ferries, bridges, and roads, check land registers, cultivate elders, and conduct surveillance. He visited family shrines and local holy places, confirmed charters of holy foundations, mediated disputes among land users, distributed favors. So "Javaneseness" grew.

In the mid-fourteenth century an extended Javanese expansion effort succeeded, with an affluence and impact that most nearly resemble ancient Angkor for regional power. This new, most mighty of early Javanese mandalas was called Majapahit. It came to an end in the early fifteenth century after a five-year war between the ruler and his brother-in-law, ripped apart for lack of an orderly succession.[6]

Majapahit reached well into the areas that the Dutch would later labor for centuries to conquer. For modern Indonesian nationalists of several kinds, it became a symbol of past greatness.[7] Sukarno evoked it in nation-building, and Suharto, his army, and his court ideologues employed it to expand and consolidate his state. One moment, one monument, will suggest Majapahit at its influential zenith as a "trading power with military clout" and with the imperial pretensions that inspired Sukarno.[8] It also symbolizes the moral nadir of Suharto's Indonesia, when its exercise of state power suggested mafia and mob murder far more than mandala.

The moment occurs a century and a half before Europeans penetrated the Pacific. The monument, inscribed in 1370 and erected in West Sumatra, speaks of the nature of Majapahit. Seven tons of sculpted stone, fifteen feet high, manifest Adityavarman as god-king. The historical person Adityavarman, as an adventurous young man, was either delegated by his Javanese king, or went prospecting as a prince, to bring west and central Sumatra under the sway of Majapahit, almost a thousand miles eastward. To the great tribe called Minangkabau he brought troops enough to conquer them and panache enough to erect a statue to his glory, to the eminence of his court of origin, and to the god of that court. That god was—in the language of Schnitger, the Dutch archaeologist who used three hundred coolies to transport the statue out of the jungle for public display—worshipped by the Bhairavas, or Terrible Ones, "a mystic sect of demonic Buddhism," one with Shivaite elements, which had originated in eastern Bengal perhaps eight centuries before.

The statue itself was "a terrifying figure" representing Adityavarman "with a knife and skull in his hands, serpents twined about his ankles, wrists, upper arms, and in his ears, standing on a recumbent human body, which in turn rests upon a pedestal of eight huge grinning skulls." In his hairdress sits the Buddha of the East. A flaming halo encircles his head. The Bhairavas "sought their highest bliss in mystic union with their supreme god" and attained it by drinking blood as heavenly wine, which inspired the faithful to ecstatic dances. They invoked the appearance, in pillars of smoke, of the flame-haired Mahakala, lord of cemeteries, destroying all earthy ties.

According to the inscription, Adityavarman "was initiated as a god . . . enthroned alone on a heap of corpses, laughing diabolically and drinking blood, while his great human sacrifice was consumed in flames, spreading an unbearable stench, which, however, affected the initiated as the perfume of ten million flowers."[9]

To the question, why did the modern Indonesian nation state tolerate just two men at its apex across fifty years, historic examples of god-kings may be a partial answer. But not one that absolves modern leaders of modern responsibilities. Sukarno as poetic romanticist, a mixture of South Pacific D'Annunzio and indigenous mystagogue, was smart enough to dress his presumptive divinity in democracy. Suharto was more provincial and atavistic. He wore a formal smile and specialized in armed force. What smelled like perfume to him we can only guess.

For centuries before Europeans arrived, Islamic infusions had been propelled by commerce and emissaries from Arabia. Islam penetrated coastal communities through traders, and internal court cities through the mystical teachings of Sufis. Evidence exists of a Muslim dynasty in thirteenth-century North Sumatra. Military technology and ideology eventually combined in Islamic sultanates strong enough to break with pluralist social patterns and proclaim a higher unity. But even the sultanate of Mataram in Central Java was "one" only from 1620 to 1660. At other times the island was marked by wars among dozens of kings or princes.

The Netherlands required centuries to unify Indonesia in their own fashion: first for mercantilist advancement of trade and then for nineteenth-century motives of geographic empire. After 1830 the Javanese courts ceased to struggle and, as Merle Ricklefs says, became "ritual establishments and generally docile clients of the Dutch." The Minangkabau were finally subjugated in the Padri War of 1821–1838. Batak resistance was not finally crushed until 1895. Balinese independence ended in the period 1906–1908, when royal families at odds with the Dutch ritually purified themselves for death, women and children included. Dressed in white and armed with lances and krises, they stormed against Dutch guns, pausing only to kill their own wounded, and continued their suicidal protest until virtually all— over a thousand members of royalty—were dead. Aceh warred fiercely against the Dutch from 1873 until 1912. In the minds of some Acehnese, their struggle for independence has never ceased.

Once they secured power throughout their Netherlands East Indies, the Dutch systematically rid the islands of slavery, widow-burning, head-hunting, cannibalism, piracy, and internecine wars.[10] After 1910 they were able to install the most centralized state power ever felt in Southeast Asia, "more centralised and absolutist than the Netherlands itself or any European constitutional state of the same period."[11] The capital was Batavia, now called Jakarta. With only 16,000 officers and men, augmented by 26,000 hired native troops, they completed their conquest with a ratio of one imperial arms-bearer to nearly a thousand subjects.[12]

How could so few succeed over so many? The answer: because only a handful of mandalas had to be overcome, each caring little about the others or knowing nothing of them. The Dutch brought a layer of assiduous modernity to political vacuums strung throughout a vast archipelago. Geographically disconnected and culturally discordant but now administratively centralized, the Netherlands East Indies was for the length of one human generation the first comprehensive empire that region had ever known. Yet, along with a taste for "progress" among the elite, the Dutch imparted to Indonesians of every kind one great resource they had never had before: a common enemy. That gift cannot be overvalued. Once the Indonesians ex-

5. ADITYAVARMAN AS GOD-KING. This fourteenth-century ruler of
Minangkabau in West Sumatra is here portrayed as the Bhairava Buddha—
the supreme figure of a death cult analogous to certain forms of Sivaism on
Java. (National Museum, Jakarta / Sidup Damiri; author's collection)

6. ROYAL PALACE OF THE MINANGKABAU. This twentieth-century reconstruction in traditional Minangkabau style uses multiple tiered gables and upswept ridge lines and walls profusely incised with floral carvings. From the center of their kingdom, at Pagaruyung, Adityavarman's successors proclaimed descent from Alexander the Great. As late as the nineteenth century, a Minangkabau king described himself as a Qur'anic "image for mankind." (Tara Sosrowardoyo/INDOPIX)

pelled the Western imperialists, they discovered that they no longer had a threatening external enemy. They would find no substitute as powerful as their hatred of the Dutch.

Sukarno and the Western Imperial Era

Sukarno was born the year England's Queen Victoria died: 1901. He spent all his mature life trying to overthrow the imperial era that she stood for, the era that Dutch monarchs represented with gentility, their civil servants with bureaucracy, their police with brutality. He entered the world in the year the British prevailed over Dutch-descended Calvinists in South Africa to end the Boer War. In that same year, troops from the United States finally quelled the Filipino revolutionaries who had launched a war for independence against Spain in 1896. When Sukarno died in 1970, the Portuguese were still in East Timor and the "Vasco da Gama Epoch" in world history was not yet finished.[13]

Sukarno's father was from Java and his mother from Bali—a marriage so unusual at the turn of the century that Sukarno suggests it was seen as a "calamity." His grandfather and father bore the title *Raden,* lord, indicating membership in Java's aristocratic official class, the *priyayi.* His mother, he claimed, was the daughter of the Hindu priestly class of Bali, the *Brahmana.* Whether or not the latter is true, an intercultural and unorthodox marriage (of a Muslim theosophist with a Hindu-Buddhist) is a complex source from which an unusual boy and man would spring. He was named Kusno Sosro Sukarno, but by common Javanese practice he dropped the first two names early in his life. He was thereafter simply Sukarno.

Can Sukarno's claims to high birth be reconciled with his protestations of minimal means? "Like David Copperfield," he declared in his autobiography, "I was born amidst poverty and grew up in poverty. I did not own shoes. I did not bathe in water from a tap. I did not know about forks and spoons."[14] His family could not even buy a firecracker for festival days, a deprivation that seems especially to have marked Sukarno, who expressed himself throughout his life with explosive metaphor and extended political fireworks. "We were so poor we could barely eat rice once a day." Every day his mother pounded unhusked *padi* (unpolished rice), which could then be mixed with chopped corn and "other edibles."[15]

Is this a tale shaped for Americans, who love stories of leaders with log-cabin (or palm-thatch) origins? Not wholly. To be both a lord and as hungry as a peasant was not a contradiction in the Netherlands East Indies. There, the family of a teacher partook of the common poverty. Under Dutch rule, in the late Victorian period, rice plus nonpreferred staples allowed Javanese an estimated daily supply of about 1650 calories—low by any standards and threatening chronic malnutrition in some parts of the population. When the Japanese arrived in 1942, Indonesians were poorer in rice consumption than when Sir Thomas Raffles and the English left, after their brief occupation, in 1815.[16]

Sukarno could fairly claim both an elevated birth, for presumed natural leadership, and experience of mass poverty, for presumed democratic fellowship. While technically *priyayi* class, he could also claim real affinities with both the *santri* (the white ones), educated Muslims, and the *abangan* (the red ones), animists and syncretists of popular tradition, close to the earth. He was from highly populous Java—that key island where the Hindu-Buddhist kingdoms had been centered for a millennium, before Islam prevailed. And with a mother from Bali, he could lay claim to understanding the people of the outer islands, the other half of the Indonesian population.

Sukarno could draw naturally on traditions in which the ruler radiated magical power through the court into the realm, which, in analog to the cosmos, was kept in balance by mystical contemplation of its sacred and powerful king. At the same time, he soaked up any part of the modern world that newspaper and, later, radio could bring him. He was seething with inchoate ambitions, bursting with instabilities, boiling over with energies of revolution, which were, to him, volcanic, natural, just. Sukarno learned how to synthesize to gain power and how to syncretize to keep it. Nature, nurture, and imperial pressure made him an eloquent simplifier.

As a schoolboy Sukarno learned the names of all the stops on the Netherlands railway lines, from Friesland to Belgium—and would recite them to charm displaced Dutchmen after independence. But organizations were being formed that would suggest a new identity—a new "Indonesian" identity, long before the Dutch would tolerate use of the word. Sarekat Islam (Islamic Union) arose in 1912 and unnerved the colonials by soon claiming two million members. The solidarity among Islamic villagers lay in their shared hostility to the Chinese, the *priyayi*, and the Dutch.[17]

Sukarno was sent by his family to room at the house of the leader of Sarekat Islam, Haji Omar Said Tjokroaminoto, in Surabaya. There, he read, he says, of the deeds of Washington, Jefferson, and Lincoln; "my boyhood was spent worshipping America's founding fathers." Ever eclectic, Sukarno also imbibed Beatrice and Sidney Webb; Mazzini, Cavour, Garibaldi; Marx, Engels, Lenin; Voltaire, Rousseau, and Jean Jaures, "the grandest orator in French history."[18] The Indian philosopher Vivekananda, who walked from village to village in moral regeneration of India, also affected him; he had been the sensation of the first World Congress of Religions in Chicago in 1893. Vivekananda gave Sukarno a perambulatory example and a maxim: "Don't make your head a library. Put your knowledge into action."[19]

Among Tjokroaminoto's associates were early communists Musso and Alimin, founders in 1920 of the Partai Kommunis Indonesia (PKI) or Indonesian Communist Party. Sukarno would be close to it, merge it in his thinking. NASAKOM, his guiding acronym of 1960 onward (*NASionalisme, Agama* [religion] and *KOMunisme*), can be traced back to the emergence, in his childhood and youth, of Sarekat Islam and the PKI.

By the time Sukarno was twenty, his mind was stocked with rebellion, and he found that he could rouse an audience. On July 4, 1927, he organized the Partai Nasional Indonesia (PNI), the Indonesian National Party. Response to his message, independence *now,* "brought with it the greatest joy I have ever known. To intoxicate the masses until they were heady with the wine of inspiration was all I lived for. To me this was elixir . . . I wax lyrical. I literally am overcome and this is transmitted to my listeners."[20]

His listeners included the Dutch police. Confinement naturally followed, and often. But while free, Sukarno made his convictions graphic, individualized, popularly accessible. Marhaen, a young Sundanese independent farmer, supporting a wife and four children on less than an acre of inherited land, became Sukarno's symbol for "a little man with little ownership, little tools, sufficient to himself," a nonexploitative individual, symbol of unconscious Indonesian socialism in operation. Sarinah, the unmarried servant girl with whom Sukarno had shared a narrow cot in his childhood, was "the greatest single influence of my life. She slept with us, lived with us, ate what we ate, but she got no wage whatsoever . . . Sarinah taught me to love people, masses of people . . . 'You must love the small people. You must love humanity.'" Having drunk in his own influences, he was ready to be a fountain of inspiration to others. "Sukarno, the Great Ear of the Indonesian people, became Bung [Brother] Karno, the tongue of the Indonesian people."[21]

But what good is a teeming mind and a gifted tongue in jail, where one confronts the stupid faces of Dutch guards and watches "coprisoners go mad sexually." Forbidden access to political books, he "began to probe Islam . . . [and] devour the Koran."[22] Sukarno's life from the end of 1929 until early 1942 was a succession of arrest, detention, trial, conviction; solitary confinement, successful foreign intercession, release; brief arousal of the people by speechifying under surveillance; rearrest, conviction, encagement; banishment to the island of Flores; intellectual wasting, stir-craziness, malaria; transfer to more healthful isolation in South Sumatra. The Dutch accrued thousands of pages of notes on him and prosecuted him under a peculiarly Dutch colonial law against "sowing seeds of hate" (which is still in effect in post-Suharto Indonesia). They removed him from any place where he might broadcast his ideas and banished him to desolate outposts where he would languish in silence; and even there, in his places of rustication, had him followed by bicycle at sixty meters.

Sukarno could not endure it. In 1934 he wrote the governor general promising cooperative behavior if he were released. Satisfied that Sukarno's spirit was broken, the Dutchman denied the request.[23] The plea was pathetic; its denial ruthless. Sukarno in his autobiography makes no mention of his cry of supplication. Nor, given his customary tone of aggressive bravado, would one expect him to. But there it is: a whining correspondence that suggests a streak of weakness. Did Nehru in his eleven imprisonments, or Gandhi in all his own, ever yield to such a tone? Did Nelson Mandela ever compromise his dignity with the white Afrikaans? Sukarno, who later enjoyed the title Bearer of the Message of the People's Suffering, was not superlative at enduring suffering himself. The redeeming side of this characteristic was that he did not like to inflict it either. Unlike Suharto, who would not hesitate to kill.

Japan's Holy War for Greater East Asia

In 1929 Sukarno, like his nationalist comrade Mohammad Hatta, foresaw a Pacific war and the opportunity that a Japanese advance on Indonesia might present.[24] Suddenly, in February 1942, the Japanese were there. The Dutch marched, bussed, and trucked Sukarno three hundred kilometers to Padang, on the coast of Sumatra, to keep him their prisoner. Then they abruptly abandoned him so as to rescue themselves.

The Japanese had their own files on Sukarno, and they approached him with respect. They wanted to use him to organize and pacify the Indonesians. Sukarno wanted to use the Japanese to free Indonesia. Mutually suspicious, differently needful, calculating in their courtesies, they worked out their bargain of collaboration. Sukarno romanticized the moment in speeches during the war. When he talked with Colonel Fujiyama, high in Bukitinggi, the core city of Minangkabau country, "The Lord be praised, God showed me the way; in that valley of the Ngarai I said: Yes, Independent Indonesia can only be achieved with Dai Nippon . . . For the first time in all my life, I saw myself in the mirror of Asia."[25]

Sukarno's first administrative act, he acknowledges, was to gather 120 prostitutes as "volunteers" to be penned in a special camp for service to Japanese soldiers. He congratulated himself on simultaneously enhancing the women's income, sating the lust of the invaders, and thereby protecting virtuous Minangkabau maidens.[26]

By the time he reached Java, the masses, by word of mouth, were awake to him. His nationalist comrades, attuned to his character, were alert to protect his autonomy. Several banded together to offer money for housing, a car, and a modest stipend so that he need not rely on the Japanese. But he declined the offer, confident that he could extract more from the invaders than they could squeeze from him.[27]

Indonesia's two other key nationalists chose different routes, according to their values. Both Mohammad Hatta and Sutan Sjahrir were, like a disproportionately high number of early leaders, ethnically Minangkabau. Both were Dutch-educated, which further distinguished them from the Java-bound Sukarno. The two had shared internal exile on the island of Banda Neira, but they approached politics differently. Hatta was deeply Muslim by training and conviction, scholarly by inclination, and coldly severe when angered. His careful demeanor, spectacles, and disciplined style gave him the aspect of a man torn between the monastery and the insurance business. He committed himself to celibacy until Indonesia became independent.

Whereas Hatta evoked respect, Sjahrir worked with charm and enthusiasm. While Hatta always wore the *pici*, the black Muslim cap adopted as a badge of nationalism, Sjahrir never covered his wavy locks. He smiled readily, argued strenuously. Friends likened him to the *cabé*, hot pepper. In 1949 during capture and isolation by the Dutch on Lake Toba in Sumatra, Sjahrir had to live for months in the same house with Sukarno, who remembered his insults years afterward. Once, in response to Sukarno's loud singing of Johan Strauss in English while taking a bath, Sjahrir yelled, "Shut your mouth!"—in Dutch.[28]

Sjahrir was secular in the style of European democratic socialists. He married a Dutchwoman, divorced her after independence, and in 1951 wed a tall, beautiful, cultured Javanese. During the war he kept as far away as possible from the Japanese while building up a cell of *pemuda* (political youth) devoted to study and clandestine listening to overseas radio. Hatta, while semi-engaged with the Japanese, insisted enough on his independent dignity to provoke the *Kenpeitai*, Japan's brutal military police, to plot his assassination by auto accident—a plan not in the end attempted.[29]

In contrast with Hatta and Sjahrir, Sukarno spent the war years rousing the masses in collaboration speeches whose mythological allusions and Javanese metaphors allowed him to serve two aims at once: stoking nationalism and stroking the Japanese as "liberators" of Asia. Sukarno said later that independence was the end and collaboration the means. He intervened to save the lives of several individual nationalists who had dared too much. But he took no step to protect Dr. Muchtar, who was wrongly tortured and executed for the deaths of thousands of labor conscripts, who were actually either victims of faulty Japanese inoculations or subjects of demonic medical experiments.[30] Throughout the war, Sukarno continued to engage prostitutes for the Japanese army, so as to protect the chastity of more fortunate women, and defended himself against the charge of pimping for conquerors.

Sukarno conceded that on a massive scale he helped the Japanese enroll labor conscripts, called *sukarela* in Indonesian or *romusha* in Japanese. These words, translated into English as "volunteers," come through as grossly ironic. Sukarno made the speeches; Sukarno picked up the tools and was photographed as an example of a man unafraid of labor. The total number of *romusha* ran into the millions; those transported overseas were perhaps a quarter of a million; those who died away from home and family were tens, and conceivably hundreds, of thousands.[31] Sukarno was lastingly ashamed of it all.

> They died in foreign lands. Often they were treated as inhumanly as the prisoners of war with whom they were shackled side by side to build the notorious Burma Road . . . Yes, yes, yes, I knew they'd travel in airless box-cars packed in thousands at a time. I knew they were down to skin and bone. And I couldn't help them.
>
> In fact it was I—Sukarno—who sent them to work . . . I shipped them to their deaths. Yes, yes, yes, yes, I am the one . . . It was horrible. Hope-less.
>
> And it was I who gave them to the Japanese. Sounds terrible, doesn't it? . . . Nobody likes the ugly truth.[32]

The barbarity of the Japanese practice, and the shamefulness of Sukarno's involvement, are overwhelming. But he bought political gains, Sukarno says. In September 1944 Indonesians were granted permission to sing their national anthem, "Indonesia Raya," and to fly their red and white national flag alongside the Japanese. They were granted permission to form the Chuo Sangi In, a civilian body advisory to the Japanese Military Government. True. But the strategic reasons for these concessions were the deaths of Japanese soldiers in General MacArthur's island-hopping across the Pacific and the deaths of Japanese civilians in air raids on industrial cit-ies. Sukarno never realized that. He knew only vaguely of the progress of the war, relying far too heavily on Japanese intentions and information. He need not have traded a huge number of lives of poor Indonesian laborers for the flag and anthem. These concessions would have come anyway dur-ing imperial military retreat. The Philippines received them much earlier, despite their guerrilla resistance against the Japanese in many provinces.

Constitution, Pancasila, Proclamation

When the Japanese military finally let an Investigatory Committee for Indo-nesian Independence meet in May 1945, it was not as a mother to indepen-dence, they cautioned, "but as a midwife." Sukarno replied that "Indepen-dence seems like a marriage," and across nine days he led the hammering out of a pre-nuptial contract, the constitution of 1945. Its compromises be-tween centralists and federalists, between Muslims and followers of other religions and secularists, were imperfect—how could they be otherwise?—and have troubled Indonesian political discourse for over half a century.[33] They will continue to do so. The true accomplishment was to cobble an agreement that would hold together a system of archipelagoes involving five major islands and over 17,000 smaller ones, with a combined land area three times that of Texas, strung out across a distance wider than the continental United States. The new Indonesia would comprise several major ethnic groups and speakers of hundreds of different languages. Rather than unity, there could have been many Lone Star States; there might have been a theocracy. The temptation toward Indonesian imperial expansion was ever present, though without the military power to express it. Common sense and Sukarno forestalled disunity, at least for a time.

Sukarno electrified the assembly with a speech on the philosophy of the constitution. The contents of that speech would become as important as the constitution itself, and an essential element in nation-building. He called

7. CONSTITUTION OF 1945. The constitution hammered out under Japanese occupation dissatisfied strong elements, which still seek adoption of Muslim law. But concepts from the American revolution provided valuable rallying cries and international advertising points—as on this Jakarta building in October 1945. (Gift of Niels Douwes Dekker/author's collection)

it the *Pancasila* (pronounced pahnt·jah·*see*·lah), meaning the five principles. This distillate of his years of fomentation, action, and reflection in prisons consisted of: (1) nationalism; (2) humanity (neither humanism nor humanitarianism but a nationalism embedded in internationalism; a recognition that all humankind bears common characteristics); (3) democracy (based not on a plurality of votes, but on the deeply ingrained Indonesian custom of deliberation to consensus); (4) social justice; and (5) belief in one Supreme Being. Sukarno showed how these five principles could be reduced to three: socio-nationalism, socio-democracy, and belief in one God; and how the three could be simplified to one, a *gotong-royong* (mutual help) state, all for one and one for all.[34]

Sukarno's tour de force ensured that the cobblers of independence would stitch together something wearable. He had essentially taken the three principles on which Sun Yat-sen based the Chinese Republic of 1911—nationalism, democracy, and the people's livelihood—and added to them global humanity and a hospitable monotheism. Elementary globalism was inescapable in 1945 and essential for international recognition of the new state. Belief in one Supreme Being was the only way to articulate a common ground for Muslims of all kinds, Christians (trinitarian though they might be), Hindus (whether triune in the sense of Brahma/Vishnu/Shiva or polytheistic), Buddhists, and animists. Sukarno's political vision looked backward in order to spring forward into the unknown. The job was done too quickly, perhaps. But Indonesia had a constitution ready before it declared its independence.

The proclamation of independence finally came on August 17, 1945, two days after the emperor of Japan announced surrender. Sukarno was kidnapped by radical youth trying to force him to premature and extreme action (which abduction he wrongly blamed on Sjahrir), but he faced them down and returned to Jakarta. He gathered nationalist confreres and internationalist Japanese officers and with Hatta crafted a two-sentence statement on school paper with a borrowed pen. In the morning, sleepless and fevered—his malaria had returned—Sukarno read it out in a ceremony shared with Hatta. An Indonesian captain trained by the Japanese ran a flag up a length of bamboo stuck in the soil of Sukarno's front yard. A piece of white cloth with a piece of red, sewn together by his wife Fatmawati. There was no band. Those present sang "Indonesia Raya."[35]

The Soft Revolution

Indonesia was not prepared for peace to break out. Nor was it really ready to wage revolutionary warfare. The peoples of the Netherlands East Indies

8. PROCLAMATION OF INDEPENDENCE. For a rare moment, Mohammad Hatta takes center stage in the improvised ceremony of August 17, 1945. Behind him stands Sukarno. In the background are Japanese and Indonesian military officers. Hatta, the original vice president, would resign in 1956. His criticisms would grow so pronounced (likening Sukarno to Mephistopheles in Goethe's *Faust*) that the president would have him silenced from 1960 to 1965. (Gift of Niels Douwes Dekker/author's collection)

had suffered tremendous human losses in Japan's Holy War for the Liberation of Asia. They felt their hunger and weakness; they resented their servitude; they sensed their opportunity. But what to do now? And how?

Two power vacuums defined the situation: one around Indonesia and the other within it. No "victorious" foreign force would enter Indonesia for weeks, and then it would be small numbers of British as surrogates for the battered, disorganized Dutch, who were not able to return in military numbers until early in 1946. Meanwhile, the Japanese were obliged both to lay down their arms and to preserve order—contradictory requirements that some solved by passing arms to Indonesians they had trained to further "Asian liberation." Meanwhile, their countrymen at home in Japan were beginning to learn for the first time in their history what it meant to be a conquered people.[36]

Within Indonesia, Sukarno, Hatta, and Sjahrir stood at the head of an enthused but flimsy nationalist government, focused in Java where focused at all, rarely and loosely in contact with other islands. Against them—convinced neither of the 1945 constitution as organic law nor of Sukarno's Pancasila as a guiding principle—were forces that had worried the Dutch for decades and would worry the new republic for decades more: communists and Islamic extremists.[37] Both would break into competitive rebellion in 1948 before the republic achieved transfer of sovereignty: the communists in central Java, the Darul Islam in western Java and the outer islands.

One wonders what might have ensued if General MacArthur had had his way and fought with Allied troops into Java in 1944–45. Many more Japanese, Javanese, and American dead, certainly. Swifter international brokering of Indonesian independence, very likely. Eventual eruption of communist and Islamist armed insurgency against the new republic, inescapable nonetheless. That MacArthur did not get his way saved American lives. And because no American blood was ever shed there, ordinary American citizens barely know where Indonesia is. But Americans understand little more of the Philippines or Vietnam despite tens of thousands of Americans having died in each country. To an American aberration in the Philippines (the war of 1898, the humiliation of 1941–42, and the liberation of 1944–45) and to the willed tragedy of Vietnam (1961–1975), few would wish to have added needless mortalities in Indonesia.

At the strategic conference in Hawaii in mid-1943, the joint chiefs and President Roosevelt confined MacArthur to an island-hopping strategy that would leave the large number of Japanese forces in the Netherlands East Indies isolated, thereby reducing American casualties. MacArthur, at first, did as told, hitting Luzon and Manila full force. Then he backtracked for a four-month series of unauthorized landings in the central and southern Philippines and Borneo—contrary to his Hawaii conference orders but fulfilling to his heroic ego. MacArthur lusted still to liberate Java, but the joint chiefs finally drew a restraining line.[38]

Mountbatten, meanwhile, committed a minimal number of British troops to replace the Dutch, themselves pulverized by the European war and paralyzed by Nazi occupation. Finding themselves in the strange position of defending the Netherlands' flag, the British exchanged heavy losses with Indonesian revolutionaries in Surabaya between November 10 and 20, 1945. They pulled out as soon as they could, preferring to die for old Queen Victoria's empire rather than the new Queen Wilhelmina's.

Mountbatten himself, like MacArthur, never set foot in Indonesia. He became viceroy of India, while MacArthur installed himself as the surrogate emperor of Japan. During all this, Indonesia idled on a vast rackety engine, low on fuel, with many hands grabbing for the steering wheel. Battle had not devastated Java or any other island in 1944–45, but four years of war had emaciated its people. Hunger, disease, lack of medical attention, merciless use of *romushas,* and executions had produced, at an outer estimate, three million dead in Java alone.[39]

The Japanese let their Javanese collaborators ponder how to distribute fearful insufficiencies. Meanwhile, Field Marshal Terauchi's Seventh Army staff determined on a merciless parasitic stripping of what is now Indonesia, Malaysia, and Singapore. On May 19, 1944, they defined as regional policy for Japanese commanders to feed their soldiers as well as they could, and as a corollary "to maintain the natives' standard of living at the lowest possible level." This policy held in Indonesia for another fifteen months, as an equivalent of the old samurai saying, "Don't let them live, don't let them die."[40] More revealing even than face-slappings, tortures, summary beheadings, and extra-judicial executions, this order conveyed the unwritten but relentless Japanese conviction that the Indonesians were a lesser people, to be treated as servants, to be used like slaves.

A leading physician of that era remembered the garbage trucks on daily rounds in Jakarta, picking up the bodies.[41] The then young writer Pramoedya Ananta Toer later recalled a scene of desperately hungry people ignoring human dead on the road and fighting each other to get a bloated chicken floating down the river.[42] In that way the occupation crisis of 1942–1945 was more grimly quiet, more generally devastating than the politico-economic crisis of 1965–66. And both were far more Malthusian in depth and pervasiveness than the complex multiyear financial crisis that began in 1997.

Revolution and a power vacuum followed.[43] Sukarno orated to Java while arguing with Hatta and Sjahrir on how to proceed politically. Japanese-trained Indonesian officers prevailed over those trained by the Dutch in organizing a national army against the Netherlands' return. The self-created army elected as its commander a thirty-year-old former schoolteacher who had become a battalion leader under the Japanese: the slim, prim, tubercular Sudirman. In him were strangely blended samurai discipline, Marxist disposition, and raw courage. He would steadfastly lead even when his disease so weakened him, later, that he had to be carried by palanquin.

A photograph of the meeting that elected him conveys the new army's "cowboy" irregularity and desperado quality. It would continue to behave, as at its birth, independently from the nationalist government or any institution that government might create. The army was, to some degree, an association of volunteer militias—a few levels more advanced than provincial "struggle organizations," the followings of local prophets, bands organized

9. LEADERS OF THE FIRST INDONESIAN ARMY. In the postwar anarchy, Sukarno announced an army, but it could not agree on strategy or tactics. This first meeting in Yogyakarta, on November 11, 1945, brings together division commanders from Java and Sumatra, to which some come armed with samurai swords. In a "crazy . . . cowboy . . . revolutionary" meeting, they elect a commander-in-chief, Sudirman, and a defense minister, Sultan Hamengkubuwono IX, who attends in a made-up general's outfit. (Ipphos Photo Archive)

by *jagos* (cocks-of-the-walk), and gangs of thugs. Against all these, the Dutch, on return, were too weak to prevail but strong enough to resist being thrown out. The revolution had to be won by persuasion in New York, Washington, and other cities overseas, as well as fought in pockets of Java and other islands of Indonesia.

A sporadic four-year military struggle was punctuated by two diplomatic interventions. One was brokered by the British late in 1946, but the Dutch, just as unhappy with it as the republic was, claimed it was violated and launched a "police action," to which, in mid-1947, international reaction was negative. The UN Security Council promoted another negotiation, on the U.S. Navy ship *Renville,* ratified in January 1948. Believing the republic to be weakened both by Islamic and communist insurgencies, the Dutch opportunistically and defiantly launched a second police action in December

10. CONDEMNED TO DEATH. Seven prisoners have been convicted by a revolutionary tribunal. Bound by rope to one another, they are led under armed guard to dig their own graves before execution. Note the loudspeakers in the crowd. Hasty proceedings, or none, and public executions are common for those accused of antirevolutionary acts. (Gift of Niels Douwes Dekker / author's collection)

1948. They captured Yogyakarta, imprisoned Sukarno, Hatta, Sjahrir, and others, and produced further negative international reaction.

Meanwhile, the Cold War radiated to other continents. Several communist uprisings in Southeast Asia in 1946 are traceable to a Soviet shift toward support of armed struggle in Asia, struggles that prevailed differently in China, North Korea, and Vietnam, while eventually failing elsewhere. One of the failures was in Indonesia. From mid- to late September 1948, Indonesian communists under Musso seized and held Madiun, east of Yogyakarta. They intended it as a rallying center for revolt against "Sukarno-Hatta, the slaves of the Japanese and America." That was one of three great miscalcu-

lations by elements in the Indonesian Communist party—the first had occurred in 1927 and a third would transpire in 1965—who judged these moments ripe for proletarian uprising. Republican forces won back Madiun,
killed Musso, and crushed the rebellion. So ended a perilous distraction
from their anticolonial revolution and a mortal threat to its success.

Now the Indonesian nationalists could be seen as allies in the Cold War—
a transfiguration never possible for the Vietnamese nationalist movement,
which was always led by communists. But the Dutch were allies of the
United States in Europe, which was for three years a controlling consider-
ation. Anticommunism in Europe was more important to the States than
anticolonialism in Asia, until the Netherlands launched its second police action in December 1948, taking Yogyakarta by force. As international con-

11. CHINESE-INDONESIANS PROTEST MURDERS. Murders and other atrocities, chiefly in the area of Tangerang, West Java, during the second quarter of
1948 arouse protests from Chinese Indonesians, aimed at getting international attention. (Douwes Dekker Collection/Kroch Library, Cornell University)

sciousness shifted against the Dutch, the State Department dithered elegantly on what to do.

The New York Times pointed out that since the end of the war the United States had provided the Netherlands more than a billion dollars in Marshall Plan aid, military equipment, Export-Import Bank credits, and credits for the purchase of war surplus supplies. Meanwhile, the Dutch had spent almost half that sum maintaining their armed forces in Indonesia. Other data supported the gathering argument that the United States was financing a senile and ineffectual imperialism. From Congress, especially among Republicans, from churches, and from NGOs, key voices rose and joined in on the Indonesian side.

In April 1949 the new secretary of state, Dean Acheson, at last pushed the embarrassed Hollanders into the negotiations earlier recommended by the UN Security Council, which until then the Dutch defied. The Netherlands eventually conceded a "United States of Indonesia," to which it transferred sovereignty on December 27, 1949, with immediate recognition by the United States. Many of the "federal" states of Indonesia were Dutch-sponsored attempts to cling to their influence. But magnetized by the new republic, they soon dissolved themselves to join it.[44] On the fifth anniversary of his proclamation of independence, August 17, 1950, Sukarno ecstatically proclaimed the Republic of Indonesia as a unitary state.

Early in the century, the Dutch had put their seal on the conquest of Indonesia with fewer than 42,000 armed men against a population of 37 million. Now, in a nation of perhaps twice that number, they failed to retake control with troops more than four times the size of the original force of conquest.[45] The reasons lie far less in tactical analysis or applied force ratios than in the strategic suction of global war. In three and a half years it swept away from most of the world map the underpinnings of classic Western empire and its chief imitator, the Japanese empire. The archipelago that stretched from the Indian Ocean to the South Pacific had now as its sovereign claimant the Republic of Indonesia.

B. M. Diah, one of the leading young revolutionary nationalists, later became a prominent journalist and publisher. From an interview with Diah in 1983, I am grateful for the phrase by which, in the context of anticolonial struggles, he described the 1945–1949 period: "the soft revolution."[46] It was a revolution chiefly of attrition, in which the Indonesians would use their own new confidence and will power, guerrilla tactics, Dutch exhaustion, and international opinion slowly to win, with as few losses as possible in face-to-face battle.

Sukarno remembers independence finally achieved far more thrillingly than independence first proclaimed:

12. ARMY OF STUDENT ACTIVISTS. Such *pemuda* as these (political youth of the revolution against the Dutch) would inspire two successor generations: protesters allied with the army against Sukarno in 1966; and protesters arrayed against the army, Suharto, and Habibie in 1998. (Ipphos Photo Archive)

Millions upon millions flooded the sidewalks, the roads. They were crying, cheering, screaming " . . . Long live Bung Karno . . . " They clung to the sides of the car, the hood, the running boards. They grabbed at me to kiss my fingers.

Soldiers beat a path for me to the topmost step of the big white palace. There I raised both hands high. A stillness swept over the millions. "*Alhamdulillah*—Thank God," I cried. "We are free."[47]

'Mitro, 'Darpo, and Mattie Fox vs. the State Department

Sutan Sjahrir, the young prime minister of the revolutionary republic, had sent the even younger Dr. Sumitro Djojohadikusumo to New York in mid-1947 as trade and financial representative plenipotentiary. A Central Javanese aristocrat with a Dutch doctorate in economics, Sumitro would re-

main a prominent voice in national affairs until his death in 2001, when a
critic observed that he had a "D'Artagnan complex," always believing himself better than the Three Musketeers, or anyone else. But he cooperated
effectively with the team built up around him, which came to include
Soedarpo Sastrosatomo and Soedjatmoko Mangundiningrat, sons of Central Javanese *priyayi* and medical student activists, whose imprisonment and
torture by the Japanese had completed their revolutionary motivation.

This handful of Indonesian diplomats came to rely on a boy-wonder of
American business, still in his thirties. Matthew Fox involved himself in late
1947 to accelerate Indonesian independence and would become an emblem of the complex forces and feelings to which Americans may subject
themselves when they merge their personal fortunes with the destiny of Indonesia.

Mattie Fox was an usher in a Racine, Wisconsin, movie theater at the age

13. INDONESIAN DELEGATES TO THE UNITED NATIONS. Members of the
first Indonesian delegation to the UN, in 1948, are technically "observers," but in
practice they are influential. Sutan Sjahrir (front, center) leads them. Around him,
clockwise from the left: Soedjatmoko, Sumitro Djojohadikusumo, Charles Thambu.
Haji Agus Salim, white-bearded, leans into the center. Soedarpo Sastrosatomo
would later join them. (Courtesy of the Indonesian Embassy, Washington, DC)

of nine, and by the age of twenty-five was executive vice president of Universal Studios, which he saved from bankruptcy and made profitable. After the war, Joseph P. Kennedy telephoned Fox to ask for help with his son, who had been shaken up by experience with a PT boat in the Pacific and needed "his clock cleaned." Would Mattie, with his connections to cinema's female talent, help him out? Mattie arranged a month-long visit to Hollywood for young Jack Kennedy to enjoy its horological wonders.

Prominent business executives who vetted Mattie for investment purposes often "fell in love" with him and bet on him. One concluded that he was always in debt and yet completely trustworthy. Another said, "What a bank account is to other people, a telephone is to Mattie." Still another opinion: "Mattie was a genius at selling the future for money in the present."[48] Fox's greatest venture made him "the power behind the creation of subscription television." He began to shape a cable system with electronic means of charging subscribers for viewing specific programs, and men like Sol Hurok, Walter O'Malley, and Horace Stoneham signed up behind him. Fox was not only right about pay TV but foresaw purely commercial channels selling goods directly and, forty years before it happened, the first American election through electronic ballot-casting, in the Arizona Republican primary of 2000. Fox died of a heart attack in 1964. Home Box Office began to succeed a decade later.[49]

Robert Nathan chaired mobilization by the War Production Board under President Franklin D. Roosevelt. Fox worked for him "on scrap iron and rubber. He was terrific on stuff like that. He didn't have to know much . . . [except that] rubber stretched . . . He was terribly energetic, more of a talker than a listener . . . I couldn't use him on price control and wage restraints [because] Mattie was not a conceptualizer. But what an operator! He'd scream and get results. He'd sink in his teeth and wouldn't let go. Bite and bite and bite!"

Short, fat, balding, ugly, Mattie married a former Miss America, Yolande Betbeze from Alabama. Nathan was impressed with her intelligence and stability. "This beautiful woman would go to bed and he'd be up gambling half the night . . . A wasted talent . . . He could have been rich . . . He had *seichal*. That's a Yiddish word meaning 'smarts.'" A sigh suggested the difference between "smarts" and wisdom. "After the war he was always probing about Indonesia with me. It had *resources*. So I was able to help him understand the thing . . . It was hard to see where it was going."[50]

Even for Indonesians, hard to see. "But I have no experience of the States," Sumitro had protested to Sjahrir. "Nobody does," the prime minister replied. Sumitro had to smuggle some rubber and vanilla for enough foreign exchange to make his trip. Yet how to get into the States on a passport not recognized *de jure?* He befriended a secretary in the American Consulate in Singapore, who gave him a special affidavit enabling a visa for trade. "She pitied me. Pity is a powerful emotion, especially in a woman."[51]

On arrival Sumitro had no contacts and no cash. One American ship trying to break the blockade around Indonesia was confiscated by the Dutch. Another shipper succeeded in bringing goods to New York but apparently did not pay the Republic. Sumitro cancelled its contract.[52] He engaged the New York firm of Delson, Levin and Gordon without fee, who in turn enrolled the Washington lawyer-lobbyist Joseph Borkin, also for the attraction of the cause and without compensation. Not everyone jumped at the opportunity to help Indonesia, however. The entrepreneur Milton Reynolds answered, "I would promote a pen that wrote underwater, but that crazy I am not!"[53]

Borkin, who knew Mattie Fox through television, brought Sumitro to him late in 1947. Sumitro was impressed with Fox. "He was a genius . . . He took a political interest, he saw the commercial potential. He said, 'Look, chum, we need a way to contact big financiers. It will look like my monopoly. But I won't hold you to the contract.'"[54] Thus met two supremely skilled operators, one of whom, Sumitro, would become a rare man to serve in both the Sukarno and Suharto cabinets. Fox was in turn impressed with Sumitro as a European-trained economist, so he obtained the Indonesians their first bank credit—for $80,000 on his own guarantee. They formed the American-Indonesian Corporation (AIC) in January 1948—in effect an all-purpose government agent, to which Fox then advanced $250,000 as working funds, while also loaning the revolutionary government $100,000 in cash plus other expense money. All of this, including a 51:49 split on voting rights for Fox, as required by American corporation law (in Delaware), was cleared with the U.S. Department of State, and, after revisions, with the Indonesian revolutionary government. "Fox was engaged in a great gamble, that no one else would take on."[55] His continuing advances enabled the Indonesians to finance a series of small diplomatic offices around the world.

In New York, "I lived on five hundred dollars a month," Sumitro recalls. "We had one car for three people. Everything was shoestring." Fox's generosity allowed the frail worldwide advocacy network to get moving. In return the Indonesians eventually allowed him to trade them some textiles and gave him the first automobile assembly plant in Indonesia, as well as a license for a Chrysler agency. Small returns. "A very decent fellow . . . an operator. Always with liquidity problems," Sumitro smiled, "too many projects. But he's really *human.*"[56]

Ideological intensity, emotional affinity for the underdog, speculative appetite for financial gains if the AIC could be made to work—all of it drove Fox, with his stupendous energy. But the Dutch blockade of the Indies and the State Department's European bias made the AIC a losing business proposition from the start. And the eventually-sovereign government of Indonesia did little to help it become a winner in the end. Fox persisted against the odds, for devotion to a cause, new friends, and love of the game. He put a total of at least $895,000 of his own money into the effort, an amount that fifty years later might have the purchasing power of at least $10 million.[57]

Traditionalists in the State Department summoned Fox to tell him that he was wrecking American foreign policy and threatening Europe with a fall to communism. They withdrew his passport so he could not make a planned trip to Indonesia.[58] The revolutionary nationalists' victory over the communist rebels at Madiun strengthened the Indonesian political case. But they were militarily weakened. The Dutch, defying their truce agreement, made ready for another attack. Their plans were so transparent that Sukarno asked Fox to find a large plane to airlift his republican cabinet out of the country. Fox and Sumitro told State Department officials of the situation, but they "passed it off as another Fox movie plot."[59]

Meanwhile, to help repay Fox's advances, Sumitro and Sudarpo were trying to bring out confiscated Dutch gold bars kept in the revolutionary republic's Central Bank reserve in Yogyakarta—"under trusteeship," as Sumitro put it. The head of the bank was his father, a close friend of Hatta, now the premier. They got Hatta's permission.[60]

On December 17, 1948, the Dutch submitted an onerous and complicated proposal to Premier Hatta and demanded a reply in eighteen hours. On the 18th, Fox's big transport plane arrived in Jakarta. President Sukarno suddenly decided, however, not to leave that way but to await the arrival from India of Premier Nehru's personal aircraft. Sukarno had asked Nehru for arms, which he declined; then asylum, which he would provide. So Fox's transport was instead loaded, swiftly and secretly the night of the 18th, with small heavy boxes of gold instead of people, and flown through Manila. There Carlos Romulo (Philippine representative to the UN and later president of its Assembly), whom Sumitro had earlier befriended, helped him get it through his country to the United States.

At 5:30 AM on December 19 the Dutch began to strafe and storm Yogya. By the end of the day they held as prisoners the entire cabinet of the Republic. Netherlands authorities had delayed Nehru's plane in Singapore. So the gold flew out safely in Fox's transport, the original get-away plane, while the Indonesian leaders were captured.[61] For eight months thereafter, the guerrilla army command were effectively in charge of government, with a lasting impact on their own concept of the military's national role and their sometimes disdainful views of civilian leaders.[62]

Their New York-Washington operatives meanwhile, in their spare and curious, youthful and zealous ways, were flourishing. Fox's gold-carrying transport hopped across the Pacific and landed finally in New Jersey. Sudarpo recalls: "Mattie had good connections with the AFofL, CIO, automobile workers . . . and the mafia." "*Fabulous* connections," he added, mentioning men he met through Mattie and their project: Arthur Goldberg, Walter Reuther, Clark Clifford. Mattie told him, "'Darpo, you should know, this is rough stuff." He meant that respectable as the front men were, the activities they abetted were less so. Sumitro remembers that some of the gold was sold in Mexico. Sudarpo is clear that the key operative was Val D'Auvray, "the prototype of an adventurer." "Statewise, I am a Basque," said D'Auvray, despite his French name. Sudarpo's face lights up with rhetorical questions and their answer. "How would you think to transport gold bars this way? Federal offense! The greasing of palms? How? Whom? Val D'Auvray did it."[63] The amount realized, in the account by Alex Shakow (who later became the first, youngest, and only director of the Peace Corps in Indonesia), was $500,000.[64] The money helped climax the triumph of Indonesia's anticolonial advocacy in both the United States and the United Nations. Sudarpo went over the records with Soedjatmoko when his friend became ambassador in Washington in 1967. They both marveled, not only at what had been accomplished but what had been risked.[65]

Among the Dutch goods seized by the revolutionaries from the Japanese was the state opium and salt monopoly, with lots of raw opium in warehouses in Jakarta next to the university's medical school. The overseas operatives of the republic got authority from Hatta to sell the opium in Singapore and Bangkok, where it was easy to get foreign exchange for it. The minister of finance set up a trading company run by two Acehnese, who smuggled it out through Medan and Phuket. Money realized for arms was kept in Bangkok, a major trading post for weapons. The rest went to New York to help continue financing the republic's various offices for making their case to the world.[66]

That case was easier now. The story of the republic began to sail in American media, and to sell in Congress and the UN against the Dutch: annual American aid to the Netherlands now approximated the cost of maintaining Dutch armed forces in Indonesia. It took another year, but now Indonesian diplomatic momentum was positive.[67] Fox helped Sumitro's delegation establish a New York office at 40 Wall ("Crazy boys on Wall Street!"). He made the deepest impression on Sudarpo, who was later inspired to go into business—a highly contrary, even "contaminating" pursuit for a Central Javanese *priyayi* to follow. "If someone wouldn't like Mattie, it was race prejudice. I met people like that . . . They say, 'Sudarpo, you cannot be friends with kikes.' It was the first time I heard that word." Sudarpo marveled at Fox's Art Deco penthouse on Park Avenue, his friendship with Hubert Humphrey, his whole modus operandi. "Mattie, where do you make your money?" "Here and there."

Reflecting on it all, Sumitro later saw the advocacy of Indonesian independence as a story financed by vanilla and quinine, gold and opium, and Mattie Fox: a success of "guts and luck." Sudarpo personalized it more: "Fox! This is a fabulous man!! A man of his background, with projects like this!!" Basically he got paid back. But he didn't make any money. He had borrowed it all and could very well have wound up bankrupt.[68] Where Sumitro made calculations as an economist, Sudarpo was sympathetic to Fox as an ally and as an inspiring businessman.

Fox wanted to follow through after independence, through corporations

14. SUKARNO RECEIVING ADULATION. A famous French photographer catches Sukarno in 1949 as, celebrated by his people, he begins emerging to internationally recognized stature. (Henri Cartier-Bresson/Magnum Photos)

in which he would contribute a portion of the working capital and hold a management contract. Transport, textiles, rubber, and paper manufacture were his priority areas. Indonesians would be given full experience and responsibility, and after ten years complete ownership—a private training and development program, the very antithesis of colonialism. Fox's Indonesian Service Corporation, conceived to these ends, quickly prospered. But after little more than a year, according to Alex Shakow, "Indonesia requested that Fox sell its share to the Government, which he did at the original investment cost level." Fox had hoped that a university would be named after him. But he found no honor—just suspicion of private enterprise and ignorance of his role in the revolutionary struggle. "Even old friends, such as Sumitro, had little use for him in the changed circumstances." Fox might have felt betrayed, but he was not a complainer. His efforts had surely accelerated independence by months or even years. His good offices and financial advances achieved in part that goal to which MacArthur's forces were never applied. But, according to Shakow, "Fox left Indonesia a disappointed and frustrated man."[69]

Mattie swallowed his personal defeat and turned to other ventures, blazing on in charm and daring and speculative debt, living on a surcharge of imagination. He had married a Miss America but he died in the bed of another woman. He fell in love with the Indonesian Revolution, but its transformation, the sovereign republic, rejected him. Mattie Fox was the first American to experience in depth how Indonesia, the beautiful Umayi, can manifest herself as the stony Durga.

2

GUIDED CHAOS

Making Indonesia was not easy. Once made, it was neither cohesive nor secure. Life for most of its citizens was economically precarious. Now that the far-flung empires of NATO states were dissolving, Indonesia could suppress Dutch influence, and its president could voice the glory of a new country. But pride alone could not guide it.

Sukarno inherited a civil service that had little of the professional esprit that the British had imparted to India. The educational system was meager in size and stilted in standards, combining the worst of Javanese insularity with the limited horizons of a small European power. New and pressing questions now faced Sukarno. How could hungry Indonesians be fed? How could order and mutual tolerance be sustained among religions and ethnicities? Could regions be held accountable to central authority other than by force? Exploring these questions will help us understand how Sukarno finally arrived at an animal he called "guided democracy"—a tiger that would finally throw and then devour its rider.

Those assembling the new Indonesian nation did not lack vision. But they did lack resources, sometimes even food and medicine; often money. They lacked security and fought for it as guerrillas. The young leaders lacked managerial experience because of their own non-business heritage; and they lacked knowledge of governing, because of the Dutch insistence on a dichotomy for the educated: one could be a clerk with dwarf responsibilities or a politician under police surveillance—that was it.

Above all, perhaps, Indonesian leaders lacked agreement. Where there was a will, there were many contending ways. The wonder, in retrospect, is how their agreements-to-disagree still survive, more than half a century later, as the connective tissue of nationhood.

Tracking the Indonesian idea of democracy will illustrate the problem. The word "democracy" (Dutch: *democratie*) entered the Sumatran vocabulary among adventurous and educated Minangkabau in 1906. It was a far

easier notion for Minangs to embrace than for most Javanese, with their hierarchical sense of order and subliminal belief in a sacred Hindu-Buddhist
kingship, their history of murderously competitive sultanates and enerva-
tion by generations of submission to Dutch colonial society—which had its
own bourgeois and aristocratic preoccupations with status and control. The
Dutch had layered the social cake with themselves the top tier, "foreign
orientals" the middle, and "natives" the bottom.

Sir Thomas Raffles, a century and a half before, had found himself
preaching democracy to the Javanese. But to the Sumatrans he preached order. There, down-river sovereigns would pay lip service to up-river sultans
and then do what they pleased, while in Pagaruyung the supreme ruler of
the Minangkabau continued a fiction of expecting fealty in mainland Southeast Asia while extracting the reality from the neighboring Bataks. The
Bataks, in their own local government, were just as free-wheeling as local
Minangs.

From such a history came an elementary and diffuse recognition of "democracy" as meaning (1) progress (either within or beyond *adat,* customary
law); (2) social equality; and (3) emancipation or training for self-rule in a
modern nation state.[1] The last was offered by the Dutch in minimal ways.
Haji Agus Salim, Minang and national Muslim leader, likened representation in the Volksraad after 1918 as a *komedi omong* (talking movie, or comic
"talkie"). He was more concerned that Islam prevail over communism in
the Indonesian national movement.

Leading nationalists in the 1920s downplayed cultural and religious progress, and pushed democracy as *kerakyatan*—"people-ness," or even "masses-
ness," a vague sort of empowerment. Mohammad Hatta gave that notion
fuller form, using organic Minangkabau life as a model, with its deliberation to consensus, peaceful mass protest against injustice, and ethic of mutual help. From this to an "iron law of history" was a jump, but Hatta tried
it. He said that national unity, independence, and democracy would culmi-
nate in freedom, leaving only the question whether it "would be gained by
blood and tears or by peaceful means."[2]

Sukarno stressed power-formation and mass-action so pronouncedly
that his party dissolved when he went to jail. But he kept his focus throughout the Japanese period. In the constitutional debates of 1945 Hatta sided
with him against excessive individualism and in favor of a concept of the
state as a father-substitute, integrally ordering society and all of its groups,
parts, and members. There remained, as usual, differences between them.
Hatta insisted on a "state that manages" rather than a "power state" with
the "cadaver discipline" of Russia and Germany. The leaders' compromise
took the form of three articles concessionary to Hatta and to the Minang

constitutionalist Mohammad Yamin. Those articles guaranteed the rights of the citizen (1) to dignified life and work; (2) to organization, assembly, and expression; and (3) to worship.[3] When the constitution was revised for the brief Republic of the United States of Indonesia (RUSI) in 1949, it enormously expanded Hatta's kinds of articles on rights. The provisional constitution of 1950, for the unitary Republic of Indonesia, simply copied that expansion. So Hatta prevailed.

But Sukarno grumbled. The issue persisted (and persists). As head of state, Sukarno thought the concept of individual rights was wrong. He also deeply regretted having let Hatta sign and issue Vice Presidential Proclamation Number Ten on November 15, 1945, allowing the free formation of political parties. By 1956 he was calling parties a "serious mistake." "Let us bury them, bury them, bury them," he urged.[4]

A second major issue bedeviled the original three constitutions in their five years of gestation and revision and continues to haunt Indonesia today. In Western terms, it is fundamentally a church/state question—which of course cannot be formulated in Muslim terms except as a unity of church and state in submission to Islam. In the 1945 debates, Sukarno's Pancasila speech, although brilliant, did not provide earnest Muslims with a fully acceptable foundation for the state. They wished to add seven key words in Indonesian, reducible to five in English: "Muslims must follow Islamic law."

Hatta, a far more devout Muslim than Sukarno, had agreed to include those words in a compromise preamble to the constitution made under Japanese auspices, known as the Jakarta Charter. But Hatta took the initiative to delete those words from the constitution for parliamentary ratification the very day after independence, August 18, 1945. He consulted influential Muslims, who consented to their removal in order "to prevent the splitting of the nation."[5] As a result, the Jakarta Charter remained unchartered. Not one of the three constitutions—1945, 1949, or 1950—adopted shariah law, as many earnest Muslims wished. All those documents make a concession to Islam in retaining Dutch-originated family courts over marriage, inheritance, and divorce. But none takes the further giant step of a Pakistan, far less of a Saudi Arabia.

How integral is an "integral" state? Neither Sukarno nor Hatta thought an Islamic state would work. The next most corporative idea was a Pancasila state. Sukarno's efforts on its behalf were for a long time curbed by Hatta, with his strong strain of democratic management and individual rights. But Hatta would, in the end, be foiled by the failure of elections, the squabble of parties, and a squalor of society that seemed to call for one man's wisdom: an authoritarian savior. Javanese history richly prophesies the Just King *(Ratu Adil),* and Sukarno gladly adopted the role. That solu-

tion, power "integralized" in the president's hands, would in the end transform democracy's terrible clutter into autocracy's horrible chaos.

The National Election of 1955

Trouble abounded, but elections beckoned. Free exercise of the franchise
would clear the air of conflict, clear the decks for action. It took several
years of planning, but Indonesia did produce, on September 29, 1955, under
its sixth government in five years, its first general election. Nobody could
know that it would be its last genuinely competitive national contest until
forty-four years later.

Indonesian society in 1955, compared to that at the last moment of full
Dutch power, 1942, had more schools and readers, more bicycles and travelers, more brick houses and lighting, more sports and participation in organizations, and much more national pride. Indonesians were displacing
foreigners in various leadership roles and learning new poise and ease.
Throughout society, where the economy allowed, a new "white-shirt style
of life of the government official and the student" was rapidly gaining adherents, according to the Australian expert Herbert Feith. But there was
much cause for shame and disappointment: snobbery in the elite, ostenta-
tion in the newly rich, corruption among government servants; beggars in
the cities, large numbers of unemployed and underemployed, insecurity in
many regions, conflict everywhere.[6]

So casting ballots would have cleansing in it: to replace rascals, even to
cast out demons. There were no soldiers or police needed at the polls.
Voters arrived early, in their best clothes. Women came in advanced stages
of pregnancy, and babies were born at polling places. Solemnity prevailed.
"Uncanny quietness, broken only by whispering" reflected the impact of
the long campaign. It was a "national ceremonial." All but about six percent
of registered voters used the franchise.

There were defects, of course. PKI youth with knives and truncheons
had collected signatures and thumbprints for front organizations.[7] In Central Java, a later prominent civil servant recalls, villagers assembled to hear
how to cast their first ballot, as explained by Masyumi representatives. After
Masyumi left, the PKI came in and asked if the villagers understood the
procedures.

"Yes, we do."

"OK. Now vote PKI."[8]

In general the villagers voted their moral or financial indebtedness: to
their religious leaders or village chief or head of the village guard; to their
landowner or their creditor or their senior kinsman. "The greatest freedom

of choice," as Feith saw it, "was a function of competing obligations; but that was free enough."[9] Voting was part of independence. The average Indonesian hoped it would make independence better.

The results were interesting but inconclusive. The phenomenon of *aliran* prevailed. The word means "stream" and suggests a current carrying peoples along in it with a variety of shared values and associations—a clear nationwide mode of behavior at the time, and since.[10] A more exact word for the political impact of this conduct, however, might be "channels." Distinct beliefs cut deep and separated people, and the difficulty of *transaliran* dialogue suggested ruts in thinking habits. The streams did not converge in one mighty, if muddy, river. The *aliran*, furthermore, were a downcutting, as distinct from an uplifting, metaphor of society. Unlike "pillarization," which until about 1970 was the prevailing trope for Dutch religious politics, *aliran*, singular or plural, did not suggest a common roof.

Four parties won nearly 80 percent of the otherwise widely splintered vote: PNI (Nationalist Party), 22.3 percent; Masyumi ("modernist" Muslims), 20.9 percent; Nahdlatul Ulama (NU; "traditionalist" Muslim), 18.4 percent; PKI (Communist Party) 16.4 percent. The sharpest constitutional cleavage was between the PNI, which just acknowledged "the One Deity" and argued for Pancasila as the basis of the state, and Masyumi, which demanded a state based on Islam. The sharpest cleavage in religious practice was between Masyumi (textualists; urban and outer-island in nature and provenance) and NU (syncretist, rural, and largely Javanese). A more extreme cleavage existed between religious believers in all parties and the PKI, with its atheism and redistributionist agenda.[11]

In 1955 Indonesians found political identities for themselves, but they did not find a responsive government. Those political identities were still partly traceable four and a half decades later, but they certainly had not generated a nation state by sincerity of popular will. What, indeed, could have been expected? The Dutch had collected pre-capitalist mandalas under its imperial keeping but spent 50 percent of Indonesian revenues on maintenance of its own civil service and military. Japanese victory and defeat led to anarchy in 1945, during which the state almost disappeared. And what eventually defeated the Dutch was not a republican state but a loose tessellation of political and military organizations motivated by a vision of a free nation.

Given these antecedents, Benedict Anderson writes, "Parliamentary democracy survived in Indonesia until about 1957 simply because no other form of regime was possible."[12] There was no coherent civil bureaucracy, nor truly professionalized armed forces; clearly, no dominant political party. With a state so ill-defined, Sukarno intensified his projection of a romanticized nation to a hungry society.

Why were the elections of 1955 not the redemptive and galvanizing event hoped for by democratically-minded Indonesians? In retrospect, it seems astonishingly early, by any standard of developing Asia, to have expected a surge of democratic process. The Philippines had set a precarious example, after half a century of imitation of America, but it would slump into autocracy from 1972 to 1986 under Ferdinand Marcos. South Korea, Taiwan, and Thailand were not even on the horizon of expectation in producing the new middle classes who would, from the 1970s into the 1990s, lead sustained drives for democratization.[13] Even by 1999, Indonesia had the smallest middle class in the region, and the weakest politically, not to mention a business class frail in its social responsibility and a working class feeble in consciousness and expressive power. The high expectations of the general election of 1955 were simply premature; and even those of 1999 would be excessive for their time. We need, in fact, to clear the election of 1955 of responsibility for the disorders of ensuing years. It barely established a popular toehold for parliamentary democracy. Other factors of that time were fatal to it.

The Revolt of Darul Islam

In 1928 the Muslim Brotherhood was founded in Egypt to advance the idea of "Islamic modernity." That meant opposition to European modernity, with its compartmentalized discourses on politics, religion, society, and culture. Wrongly fractionated dialogues must be reassembled under the holy unity of Islam. By 1954 the Brotherhood posed such a threat to Nasser's Egypt that he had its leaders jailed, exiled, or hanged. But it sprang back, most recently in both legal and violent confrontations with Mubarak's government from 1992 to 1997. The ideas and organization of the Muslim Brotherhood also radiated to many other countries in the late twentieth century.[14]

Violent Islamism in Indonesia at first took a very different form. Syncretic and idiosyncratic, Darul Islam was an expression of its Javanese leader, S. M. Kartosoewiryo. When finally captured after a dozen years on the move, he had to sit still for the camera: a slight, aging man with tousled gray-white hair; broad brow, and high forehead emphasizing a pointed chin, large ears, and big, startled eyes.[15] This man, whose revolt would cause 40,000 Indonesian deaths, was born in 1905 in a quiet town on the Solo River, between Central and East Java. His father was a middleman in the Dutch government's controlled distribution of ready-for-use opium. The son was sent to the best Dutch schools open to "natives." He did not have the status for access to European-style secondary and higher education but

15. IMAM WITH FORKED SWORD. A mosque in Banten, West Java, about 1950, indirectly suggests the spirit of Darul Islam and the Islamic National Army. They would fight for an Islamic state until they were finally suppressed in the early 1960s. (P. Wessing, Douwes Dekker Collection/Kroch Library, Cornell University)

was gifted enough to attend a school for "Javanese doctors," the graduates of which were not treated as equals of Dutch counterparts. After one year he was expelled for political activity.

Several years after the young Sukarno had served in a similar capacity, Kartosoewiryo worked as Haji Omar Said Tjokroaminoto's private secretary—at a time when Tjokro's Sarekat Islam was being overshadowed by Sukarno's PNI, was losing its radical leftist cadres to the PKI, and was being forced to compete with new Islamic organizations—Muhammadiyah and NU. From the marginalized Sarekat Islam, Kartosoewiryo adopted mixed religious and political activity. He studied the Qu'ran in Dutch. Lack of Arabic kept him from *haj* (holy pilgrimage) and international contact. He became a "dedicated Sufist," mainly influenced by local *kiais,* venerated teachers of Islam, including his father-in-law. His form of mystical learning estranged him from modernists, but his personality and way of life fitted him for popular rural support and a disposition to rebellion. He carried magical swords of victory and prosperity, named Ki Dongkol and Ki Rompang.

For a while Kartosoewiryo followed Haji Agus Salim in a pre-war Gandhian devotion to *swadeshi* and *hijrah* (self-reliance and repudiation of colonial structure), linking Hindu tradition with Islamic tradition in a comfortable Central Javanese way that was suspicious of urban life and colonial style. His Gandhism, transitory and opportune, then gave way to *jihad,* or holy struggle.

Dutch proclamation of martial law after the German invasion of the Netherlands in 1940 precluded all open political activity, but not before Kartosoewiryo, increasingly independent, opened his own training institute. He taught Dutch language, astrology, and dogmatics of the Oneness of God. The East Indies political police jailed him briefly on suspicion of pro-Japanese espionage. The Japanese thought him unimportant, but he gave some time to the guerrilla training movements they sponsored and played the role of chief religious teacher to boys of Hizbullah and Sabilillah, Islamic militias loosely authorized late in the war.

In 1945, attempts to secure Japanese arms by both the new national army and irregulars gave clues as to what could follow. Those who wanted a communist state staged a mistimed, disastrous rebellion at Madun in 1948. Kartosoewiryo, who wanted an Islamic state, took advantage the same year of a power vacuum in West Java to launch Darul Islam—"the world of Islam." He enlisted Islamic guerrillas to fight the Dutch and afterward the secular, hence profane, republic.[16] The struggle in various manifestations would go on into the early 1960s.

From his intensive study of West Java, one careful scholar sees Javanese Darul Islam as a group whose formation was based on traditional, non-ideological village bonds, with Kartosoewiryo the unique authority figure: an urban Javanese leading Sundanese peasants, not only an Islamic *imam* but a mystic and a Just Prince. In Kartosoewiryo's idea of a Muslim corporatist state, all government offices would be held by orthodox Muslims, thus excluding Sukarno from the highest office and all secular nationalists from any office. But this was theory. The prior necessity was *jihad,* in a form of absolute Islamic war and siege.[17]

Outside Java lay a richer assembly of motivations. Some were socio-economic: the undermining of traditional elites through association with colonial rule; the dislocation of the rural poor caused by new commercial agriculture; the creation of a rootless migrant labor force; the disappearance of previous attitudes of "shared poverty," combined with a fearful recognition of how capital markets soaked up surplus without plowback for the poor.

Some causes were circumstantial: irregulars competed for arms and power with the TNI (Indonesian National Army) or, brusquely demobilized from it, took up arms against the republic. The new Jakarta central government appeared both hegemonic over provincial autonomy and parasitic with regard to export earnings. Religious factors fused and intensified other causes. Muslim ideals, once used to resist the infidel colonizer, were now trained on ruling Indonesians and deficient co-religionists. Darul Islam lacked textual purity, but it promised a Just King who would bring an imminent era of peace and prosperity.[18] A brief sorting of regions, characters, and years of conclusion of the revolt conveys its nature, extent, and variety (Table 1). That these areas of rebellion were only loosely connected did not mitigate their threat to the new national republic.

The cost in lives of stamping out Darul Islam is estimated at 40,000, far more than died fighting the Dutch. Karl Jackson writes, "In 1961, Kartosoewiryo had a vision that the road to the Islamic state would be covered by mounds of corpses."[19] He exhorted his followers to kill all men, women, and children who did not actually assist them. But the vise was already tightening against him. The army, required to send prisoners to Jakarta, tired of having Masyumi officials release them on the way and so began sending their heads, with bodies arriving later. Sukarno banned the Masyumi party in 1960 and thus weakened Islamists within it. The army developed a tactic of driving entire village populations up the mountains where Darul Islam detachments were hiding and, after drawing reluctant fire, replying with superior force. They also kept negotiations open with terms that included honorable surrender. Kartosoewiryo, who had called

Table 1. Rebellion of Darul Islam: Provincial Dynamics

Province	Prominent features and causes	Year of conclusion
West Java	Territorial autonomy; Islamic jihad under an Imam Mahdi, mixed with Javanese Just Prince millennarianism	1962
Central Java		1955
South Sulawesi	Discriminatory demobilization of former guerrillas by the TNI	1965
South Kalimantan	Underestimation of local achievements in struggle for independence	1963
Aceh	Religious inspiration combined with traditional opposition to incursive central government	Compromise 1957; last rebels surrender 1962

for the killing of Sukarno, was wounded in April 1962 (no longer "invincible") and captured in June.

Sukarno recalled that in the 1920s in Bandung, "we lived, ate, and dreamed together." But he signed the order for Kartosoewiryo's execution by firing squad in September. "It was not an act of satisfaction. It was an act of justice." Sukarno believed that there was room in modern Java, and all Indonesia, for only one Just Prince. In fact, personality cults were easily launched. Sukarno's, through NASAKOM, appealed broadly to nationalism, all religions, and ideals of social progress. Kartosoewiryo's became narrowly that of an Islamic jihadist redeemer. From captivity he somehow managed to pass on his torch to David Bevreueh, a prominent Islamic militant from Aceh, for future transmission.[20]

Nonalignment and Regional Rebellions

Sukarno's search for a place in world history expressed itself in a timely way with his Bandung Conference of non-aligned nations in 1955. In that year, the shriller voices of the Cold War were subsiding. The Geneva summit appeared to resolve the French phase of war in Indochina; the Soviet Union and Japan opened peace negotiations; the United States and China had avoided seemingly imminent conflict in the Taiwan Straits.

Opposing positions were nonetheless fixed. The Southeast Asia Treaty Organization (SEATO) stood as a sign of American policy to contain and deter communism throughout the world. President Dwight D. Eisenhower, in lighting the national Christmas tree in December 1954, articulated his sometime-crusader world view by casting "grave doubt . . . upon the validity of neutralistic argument." His secretary of state, John Foster Dulles, a Presbyterian moralist, thought that next to atheistic communism, neutralism was the worst of sins. In June 1956 he called it a pretense "that a nation can best gain safety for itself by being indifferent to the fate of others . . . an obsolete conception, and, except under exceptional circumstances, . . . immoral and short-sighted."

The other side was courting neutrals. The Soviets had led their Eastern European bloc, along with China, into buying rice from neutralist Burma during its crisis of 1953–54, in exchange for bloc commodities and technical services. This allowed Burma to compete effectively with the United States, which had become the world's third largest rice exporter. China was even more active with neutralists than the Soviets, identifying with their desires for a period of peace in order to concentrate on nation-building.[21]

The Afro-Asian Conference in Bandung of April 18–25, 1955, brought together twenty-nine delegations, thirteen of them headed by prime ministers. As host, Sukarno declared that together "we can mobilize what I have

16. SUKARNO AS ASIAN-AFRICAN LEADER. Sukarno, in 1950, introduces President Sekou Touré of Guinea to a Javanese classical dancer. In 1955, at Bandung, he would host the first major Asian-African conference, with Nehru and Chou En-lai attending. Most of the twenty-nine powers present would agree on non-alignment in the cold war. (Gift of Amb. Ilen Suryanegara/author's collection)

called the *Moral Violence of Nations* in favor of peace." His hospitality committee organized a call-girl service for the benefit of delegates. Some American State Department wits, with a racial snobbery characteristic of the
times, referred to the event as the "Darktown Strutters Ball."[22] But nothing
could detract from the fact that Indonesia had brought together the largest
non-Western conference of the postwar period.

Its major arguments were over alignment in defensive pacts versus non-
alignment. When Nehru criticized SEATO, Carlos Romulo of the Philippines memorably replied that pact membership conserved resources, while
India and Pakistan were putting half their budgets into military prepara-
tions. On communist imperialism, the absent Soviets got some chastise-
ment, but (aside from a Thai who pointed to subversion from the north) no
one criticized the Chinese, skillfully and gracefully represented by Chou
En-lai. He emerged as the preeminent personality of the conference, as
Nehru's homilies and India's self-assumed role as mother-in-law to the
world became wearisome. Bandung was perhaps the high point of China's
diplomacy of regional brotherhood, which was thereafter overshadowed by
domestic concerns or ensnared in specific conflicts. In the conference principles finally adopted, non-alignment prevailed.

Sukarno's stature was greatly enhanced by the conference.[23] But his effu-
sive neutralism, he knew, needed further explaining, and in the following
year he got himself invited to the United States for a state visit. For Sukarno
as an insatiable cosmophage, and for Indonesia as a leader of world neutralism, the Bandung Conference was an unrepeatable act. An attempt to celebrate and advance the cause ten years later was ill-attended and flat. Indonesia's year of leading globally was 1955; 1965 would be The Year of Living
Dangerously.

Tension between Indonesia's regions and the center, a troubling theme
from the national revolution, thickened into impasse in the late 1950s and
then curdled into rebellion in four areas: West, North, and South Sumatra
and Sulawesi. Bitterness lingered from military reorganizations that had dis-
membered units of fighters against the Dutch and not only had left regional
units feeling dishonored but had left families living in wretched conditions.[24] And sharp resentments arose at General Nasution's moves as chief
of staff to transfer long-established regional commanders. On November
15, 1956, such feelings boiled over in the Army Staff and Command School
in Bandung, in an attempted coup by Colonel Zulkifli Lubis, deputy chief
of staff, against Nasution and Prime Minister Ali Sastroamidjojo. For that
moment, Nasution and Ali kept the ship of state from capsizing.[25] But successive regional uprisings followed and continued to rock it.

Had the four regional epicenters of turbulence been better coordinated,
the outcome might have been different. But as so often happens in Indone-

17. SUKARNO WITH THE EISENHOWERS. President Sukarno as guest of honor of President and Mrs. Eisenhower at an affair of state, Mayflower Hotel, Washington, D.C., May 18, 1956. The year after this occasion, Eisenhower would accept the flawed recommendations of John Foster Dulles and his brother Alan to try to destabilize Sukarno's government, as being increasingly influenced by communists. (Courtesy of Eisenhower Fellowships, Philadelphia, PA)

sia, a congruity of angers did not produce coordination of actions. The uprisings are schematically summarized in Table 2.[26]

These regions shared a sense that they were realizing too little from their exports and were in effect helping to feed Java. All had contributed to the strength of the Masyumi party in the 1955 election, which topped the polls in most provinces but came in fourth in Java and was stymied in national maneuvering. All had reasons to be disappointed with the prospects of reform when Vice President Hatta chose to resign on December 1, 1956.

Once Indonesia had proclaimed independence, Hatta, with Bung Karno as marriage broker, at last took a young bride in November 1945. He presented her a book on Great Democracy and was happy in marriage until death.[27] But Sukarno's thrust toward authoritarian centralization grew too

Table 2. Regional Rebellions: Leaders and Outbreaks

Region	Leaders[a]	Initial move for power
West Sumatra	Col. Ahmad Husein	December 20, 1956
North Sumatra	Col. Maludin Simbolon	December 22, 1956
South Sumatra	Lt. Col. Barlian	Mid-January 1957
Sulawesi	Lt. Col. "Ventje" Sumual	March 2, 1957

a. Interviews with some of these, and other survivors, enrich the narrative of Kenneth Conboy and James Morrison, *Feet to the Fire: CIA Covert Operations in Indonesia, 1957–1958* (Annapolis, MD: Naval Institute Press, 1999).

much for the Minang democrat. Hatta did not wish to "remain wedded" to Sukarno.[28] By resignation he preserved his integrity, but the action inevitably led to further weakening of national focus.

Regional commanders, especially outside Java, had been plagued with how to feed, clothe, and equip their troops. Many had resorted to private business, sometimes in cooperation with civilians, even to opening up trade links through Singapore.[29] General Nasution did not criticize these operations per se—could not do so sincerely, in view of a recognized paucity of help from the national government—but the corollary growth in commanders' regional autonomy worried him. He struck at it by transfers. The rebellions this action helped to inflame were not, however, solely in defense of regional business operations. Nor were they indeed profoundly separatist in ultimate aim.

These rebels, unlike Darul Islam, did not wish to create a totally new society. They strongly wished to make national policy more sensitive to their regional political economies. The limited nature of their goals draws the apt description of "half-hearted rebellion."[30] There was plenty of ethnic and regional sentiment to fuel it but never the mass mobilization necessary to make it explosive. Within six months the uncoordinated rebellions hit their separate high points and began slowly to recede. Eventually they led to about 30,000 deaths.[31] This, taken together with the cumulative 40,000 deaths in the Darul Islam rebellions (then still ongoing), suggests how painfully rent was the fabric of Indonesian nationality in the late 1950s. All of which was badly understood and grossly mishandled in policy launched in Washington, D.C.

The Dulles Brothers

The Dulles brothers, John Foster and Allen, were an ambitious, highly motivated pair with a high family standard to live up to: both their maternal uncle and maternal grandfather had been secretary of state. Their father was a leading Presbyterian pastor in New York City who had the family play Bible games on Sundays and wished his sons to follow his career. But neither was willing to be poor, and both wound their way to their mother's family's side in profession, John Foster through corporate law and the younger Allen through the foreign service and intelligence. In the Eisenhower presidency, as secretary of state and as director of the Central Intelligence Agency, they became the most powerful pair of brothers for the longest time ever to stand at the apex of American foreign policy. Overthrowing Mossadegh in Iran in 1953 and Arbenz in Guatemala in 1954 may have made them feel not only right but omnipotent.[32] Indonesia, in 1958, would teach them their limitations. For John, the ideologist, the lesson would be that not all the world could be converted and mobilized; for Allen, the operator, it would be that not all could be subverted and manipulated.

Secretary of State Dulles made his view on Indonesia privately clear as early as October 1953, in dispatching Hugh S. Cumming, Jr. as ambassador there: "As between a territorially united Indonesia which is leaning and progressing toward Communism and a breakup of that country into racial and geographical units, I would prefer the latter as furnishing a fulcrum which the United States could work later to help them eliminate Communism in one place or another, and then in the end, if they so wish arrive back again at a united Indonesia."[33]

With this mindset at the top, the outbreak of regional rebellions generated astonishingly hyperbolic reporting from the CIA. Allen Dulles told the National Security Council on March 14, 1957, that "only the island of Java remains under the control of the Central Government. The armed forces of all the outlying islands have declared their independence of the Central Government in Jakarta."[34] Cumming, now back in Washington, submitted a "Special Report on Indonesia" six months later from an ad hoc interdepartmental committee to the NSC. In it he laid down a two-track policy recommendation: overt—unruffled normal continuity; and covert—advancing the chances for a government as vigorously anti-communist as possible.[35] This policy was pursued even in the absence of full consensus in Washington, with covert delivery of weapons to Sumatra, of which then Ambassador John Allison was kept in the dark. His own sage opinion was ignored: "premature or too vigorous insistence on an *anti*-Communist government may prevent the establishment of a *non*-Communist government." When he grew aware that he was being bypassed, Allison offered to resign and retire. Instead, he was "sent into exile" as ambassador to Czechoslovakia.[36]

Washington, in the grip of the Dulles brothers, stepped up aid to Sumatra and, with more effect, to Sulawesi, until a sudden reversal in mid-1958.

American aircraft, flying from American bases in the Philippines, were bombing targets in eastern Indonesia in support of PRRI-Permesta, the acronym for the combined rebellions.[37] A B-26 bomber piloted by Alan Pope was shot down over Ambon on May 18, 1958. Washington pretended he was a soldier of fortune, but the trove of documents he carried proved his employ by the CIA. In 1960 an Indonesian military jury sentenced Pope to death by firing squad. The CIA spent a year practicing with a new invention, the Skyhook, to lift him by B-17 out of his prison courtyard.[38] Diplomacy spared them the further embarrassment of probable failure. Sukarno enjoyed keeping Pope as evidence of American perfidy. But in 1962, when the Kennedys helped him secure the return of Indonesia's easternmost province, Irian Jaya, from the Dutch, he let the prisoner go.

Cover blown, Foster and Allen Dulles changed heart and abandoned the rebel cause. The rebels were not doing so well anyway. Within days Washington began selling rice to Jakarta, issuing export licenses for aircraft parts, and advancing measures for an economic development loan for the Sumatra north-south highway.[39]

The CIA had already wasted a million dollars trying to influence the Indonesian national election in 1955. In the fall of 1957, Allen Dulles had signed, "with his usual flourish," a voucher for $10 million to support the regional rebellions. But within a year, the project was a fiasco. One of its key managers, Frank Wisner, went into severe depression and shot himself dead in 1965—another brilliant preppy Ivy Leaguer in the CIA whose soul was "slowly consumed by the moral ambiguities of a 'life in secrets.'"[40] Allen Dulles lost interest in Indonesia. Intelligence was no fun any more—too bureaucratic. His brother died of cancer in mid-1959, but not before retreating from anti-neutralism in Indonesia to his still more basic anti-communism.

Mounting concern over arms delivery to Jakarta from the Soviet bloc—a third of a billion dollars worth for 1958 through August 1959—stimulated American transfers of virtually cost-free military equipment in the same period at a value exceeding that of the Soviets. This action tipped the procurement policies of Indonesia's army in favor of the West, though not those of the navy and air force, which had suffered losses as a result of the first Dulles policy.[41]

The regional rebels felt the loss of American covert aid. Worse for them, they had never made effective connection among themselves, although Sumitro, ubiquitous as a conspirator and international fundraiser during this period, tried hard to fashion the links.[42] In the end Permesta leaders tried to kill, or killed, each other. Sumitro remembers his own motivations as innate rebelliousness, distrust of the communists, and defiance of

Sukarno, who wanted to co-opt him in his cabinet. As for the CIA, with whom Sumitro dealt in Sumatra: "Bay of Pigs, deja vu!"[43] Ignorant tech-fanciers, politically clumsy.

Heavy commotion and high confusion in elite politics moved Sukarno to postpone the national elections scheduled for 1959. This nondemocratic act was cheered by official Washington, for it eliminated the only road readily available to a growing PKI power—parliamentary takeover.[44] A phase of secret American policy that began in ignorant ideologism had reversed itself upon embarrassing discovery and then concluded in classic arms competition with the Soviets. Overt Machiavellianism replaced the covert form.

The Army and Guided Democracy

The Indonesian army was born of mixed traditions and contradictory trainings, or none. Fervor for independence unified all elements. But a combination of scarce resources, regional tensions, and an unclear constitutional role has produced energies along the whole spectrum of indiscipline: preoccupation with profit-making business, dereliction of duty, insubordination, and mutiny. Yet a coup, in the sense of directly seizing power, never. Perhaps they were restrained by pride in their origins as a "people's army." Perhaps by raw fear of unpopularity.

Three kinds of soldier made up the heart of the Army of the Republic of Indonesia, whose name was changed in mid-revolution (1947) to the Indonesian National Army (TNI). From Peta, the Japanese-trained officer corps, came the largest number of officers. But those of the Koninklijke Nederlandsche Indische Leger (KNIL), soldiers earlier trained by the Dutch, also provided an invaluable source of men experienced in arms. And from the society at large sprang up all kinds of *laskar* and struggle groups—fighters with various orientations and motivations. Not regular soldiers but youths willing to put their lives on the line for a democratic republic, or a communist republic, or an Islamic republic.

Y. B. Mangunwijaya exemplified the young patriot volunteer fighting for his nation's freedom. But the army's arbitrary killings and burnings moved him, after the struggle, to study for the priesthood. He had been recruited by Colonel Suharto, who benefited from both Dutch and Japanese training. Much later, as Romo Mangun, the mature priest and social critic, he would castigate the hyper-orderliness and ruthlessness which came from Japanese examples and the "Indonesian samurai."[45]

Among more classic students of imperial teachers was Sudirman, from Peta, a former schoolteacher whose passion and courage got him (barely) elected commander of the army by a meeting of officers, at a time when

18. REUNION OF REVOLUTIONARY VETERANS. Weapons-carrying veterans of
the Diponegoro Division gather in Semarang, North Central Java, on October 25,
1958. Nationalist fervor at this time is strong enough to defeat the regional rebellions in Sumatra and Sulawesi. (Arsip Nasional, Jakarta Selatan)

the government had no idea how to form and direct a military. Like the Japanese who taught him, Sudirman as supreme military commander did not
consider his office subordinate to the cabinet but chose to report directly
and only to the president as commander-in-chief. Finally, in 1949, sick and
secluded on a pallet in Sobo, a village in South Central Java, he directed resistance to the Dutch and reported to no one. The cabinet and Sukarno had
been captured.[46]

Abdul Haris Nasution had also been trained as a schoolteacher and used
his training to write on the eighty-year Dutch war for independence from
Spain concluding in 1648. He became a cadet of the Royal Military Academy and rose during the revolution to commander of the (West Java)
Siliwangi Division (1946), then commander for all Java (1948), and, for the
first of many years, chief of staff of the army (1949). As a handsome and
studious young Batak Muslim, aspiring to responsibility, he strained to resolve a tension between his mother's desire that he join the *ulama* (doctors
of Islamic law) and his grandfather's example as an expert in *pencak* (an Indonesian form of judo). In choosing a military path, he carried with him a

simplicity, frugality, and incorruptibility that even in mature years brought on the taunting nickname of "dominee" (minister of the Dutch Reformed Church).

In contrast to the East and Central Javanese preoccupation with *ksatriya* (knightly) heroism, reinforced by Japanese warrior spirit, Nasution thought strategically and tactically, as well as in organizational and legal terms. What good is spirit without discipline? Struggle without system? Such thinking enabled him eventually to become a military statesman. But he never forgot the "primeval frenzy and . . . merciless cruelty" of revolutionary fighting, feeling sympathy both for those who expressed it and those who suffered it. "One morning a young woman fighter halted her horse before the door, dismounted and put the severed head of a Gurkha officer in front of me on the table together with his ribbons. I felt sorry for this brave young man with his sympathetic face, who had become a victim of a political upheaval far away from home and which did not concern him. The woman . . . was called Susilowati. She sometimes escorted my car sitting on the mudguard."[47]

Sudirman and Nasution shared mutual respect but differed on policy and style. Sudirman's views on struggle as the only strategy, battle as the supreme tactic, paralleled those of the communist Tan Malaka. As commander and as a "politician in uniform," he was inclined to disobey the government in moments of its weakness or excessive reliance on diplomacy.[48] Nasution opted for neutrality in early party politics, but he felt, with Sudirman, a disdain of civilian government—with its dithering, bickering failure to seize strategic opportunities. He saw guerrilla warfare as total war, nationalism as a uniting concept, and "unity of command" as utterly vital to winning war and sustaining nationhood.[49]

Does global comparison really support the claim that Nasution's military achievements justify his being seen as "one of the foremost trailblazers of guerrilla warfare"?[50] Or should he be remembered critically as the founder in 1954 of a "non-party" party, IPKI, which fathered a youth movement, Pemuda Pancasila, now famous for decades of thuggism?[51] In any case, Nasution presented himself consistently both as a constitutionalist and a defender of Pancasila. To the end he was proud of American observers' compliments on his "crack Siliwangi division," and the slang English adjective still burst from his tongue like a shot fifty years later. His patient, teacherly, sardonic humor came through in a reply to snipers he set up to pick off Dutch soldiers traveling on a crowded highway. They asked, in effect, "How do we tell our guys from theirs?" And Nasution answered, "Ours are the people who are poorly dressed."[52]

Military-civilian relations were a constant problem. After the Dutch captured Yogya at the end of 1948, revolutionary authority was transferred to Minister Syafruddin Prawiranegara in Sumatra. He brought to bear the Western principle of military subordination to civilian authority, and Nasution in Java upheld him against obdurate officers who insisted that they served not a state army but a people's army. Nasution, Dutch-trained, had difficulties with East and Central Javanese officers who were Japanese-trained and loyal first to Sudirman, who was not only hard to reach but had his own approach to the war for freedom, independent of Sukarno-Hatta.[53] Even after defeat of the communist rebellion in Madiun, Sudirman created an intelligence body, staffed by followers of the communist Tan Malaka, to spy on civilian democratic socialists. And he issued an order that the National Army, Darul Islam, and communist fighters work and fight together against the Dutch. Left wing *laskar* or right wing *laskar,* all were his "sons," as commander of the armed forces.[54]

Sudirman's precarious health and his precious view of his responsibilities came into high focus when the civilian government, with the help of international pressure, achieved a cease-fire on August 1, 1949. Sukarno asked Sudirman and Nasution to see him at the palace in Yogya, now abandoned for good by the Dutch. He asked their cooperation as negotiations with the Netherlands proceeded. Sudirman insisted that military resistance continue, to maximize their advantage in a fluid situation. Otherwise, he repeatedly asked to be released from his position. In Nasution's account, Sukarno finally countered: "If the leaders of the TNI resign because of this, we as the president and the supreme commander will also resign."

"Silence. Tears in the president's eyes. Tears in Sudirman's eyes . . . Tears came also from my eyes."

Sudirman prepared an undated letter of resignation. He gave Nasution a chance to read his request for discharge, with its allusion to the deaths of other soldiers from the "mental stress" known in the army as "spiritual suicide." Nasution finally persuaded him not to send it, stressing that national and organizational unity required accepting a bad strategy.[55] Within half a year Indonesia was free and Sudirman was dead.

Such a legacy in civilian-military struggle does not disappear. In 1952 the civilian Parliament stepped in for a prolonged attack on government defense and security policies, in a crisis which came to a head in October. The army had only reluctantly accepted responsibility for internal security as a major part of its role, a policing task that naturally undermined its cherished self-image as a people's liberation army.

The scolded military was being housed at per capita expenditures one-fifth of the old KNIL, with health and welfare outlays one-tenth as large. Only 60 percent of its weapons were battle worthy. Its share of the national budget was far less than half that of Burma, Thailand, and the Philippines, and yet Nasution as technocrat loyally proposed reducing it further in conformity with national constraints.[56]

Aroused by the military in mid-October, 30,000 people roamed the streets of Jakarta, briefly occupied Parliament, and massed in front of the palace to demand dissolution of the legislature. Lieutenant Colonel Kemal Idris, who loathed Sukarno, had his tank turrets trained on the palace, waiting for further orders, which never came. The officers who went to see Sukarno the next morning (Nasution in the background, not wholehearted) came, as one of them remembered, "like children . . . to their father" and spoke "with tears in their eyes."[57] Sukarno was able to send them away without committing to anything, just as he had with the demonstrators the day before. Firepower was not threatened. Petitioning was the point. Parliament was the target. No coup was in conception. This was the delegation of a pressure group against an unelected legislature and its unjustified censures of the army.

They did not win their points. Sukarno himself instigated revolts in three of seven army divisions—astounding evidence of quasi-anarchy, leaderly arrogance, and indifference to consolidation of institutions. A key aim of reforms proposed by Nasution, to transform the TNI into a conscript army, was rejected. The 80,000 Nasution had professionally slated for discharge was softened to 50,000. The transient prime minister suspended Nasution himself. The army remained underfunded, overaged, and substandard in skill; "discipline had reached a pitiful low."[58] Clifford Geertz, who first arrived in Jakarta during this October 17 Affair, saw it, half a century later, as "prophetic and paradigmatic"—a staged *peristiwa* with predictable oppositions, repetitive persona, semi-resolutions, and failures of resolution—a "curious avoidance of definitive outcome."[59]

Three years later a mismanaged defense sector and rancorous civil/military relations led the army to reassert, in an Order of the Day, its functions in the national struggle. This time it won popular assent and brought down the existing cabinet. But again, no coup was intended or plotted. "Rather, it was an act of insubordination . . . [like] an industrial dispute" in which affected principals serve notice of intended opposition. As in 1952, no force was directly threatened, but mutual mistrust of civilian and military leaders deepened.[60]

Further events thickened the plot. Late in 1956 Sukarno came back from a visit to China, where Mao's one-party state appealed to him; and he used his public oratory more frequently to try to smother diseased bourgeois democracy and to replace parties with "functional groups." The regional revolts of 1957–58 precipitated the thinking of Nasution, by now restored to office, in a convergent direction. He wanted a return to the constitution of 1945. This would put Sukarno at the helm of the executive, make the president clearly responsible for administrative and government affairs, and eliminate the rapid turnover of prime ministers thrown out by the legislature.

But the proposal to return from the 1950 liberal constitution to the 1945 corporative constitution had to go through Parliament in a constitutional way. That, of course, reawoke the explosive debate over the Jakarta Charter, dear to the more Mecca-minded Muslims. Masyumi members of the Assembly persuaded Nahdlatul Ulama members to join them in blocking the 1945 constitution, as carrying Indonesia further away from realizing an Islamic state, or even one properly Muslim in morality. A two-thirds vote was needed for passage. Only four-sevenths was obtained. Sukarno sat out the impasse, went traveling overseas, returned to consort and cooperate with Nasution, whom he needed but neither liked nor trusted. Then on July 5, 1959, Sukarno resolved the long crisis in a way satisfactory to Nasution and himself. He dissolved the constituent assembly and promulgated the 1945 constitution by presidential decree.[61] Guided democracy, long forecast, and pre-advertised by Sukarno, had arrived. Now Sukarno was legitimizing an integralistic constitution as its father, instead of having a liberal constitution legitimize him as its figurehead.[62]

Sukarno had relied on the TNI to put down regional revolts. Now he had his eye on "liberating" West Irian from the Dutch and would need them for that. As an anti-institutionalist but a macro-nationalist, if he needed one organization, it should be an armed one. He could not rely on parties and wild parliamentary instability. He could rely on the TNI because Nasution was a legalist rather than a power-hungry praetorian. As for the army, it needed Sukarno to legitimize its advance into government—into legislative bodies and almost all state agencies; into administering the law and managing the economy under the enormous powers of martial law, which had been declared in 1957.[63]

Nasution's vision of the Indonesian soldier as a partner of the people, however, was still viable. While out of office, he had written *Fundamentals of Guerrilla Warfare*. Ten years before volumes on counter-insurgency became an international industry, his was uniquely comprehensive on how to overthrow a stronger power and how, as a new establishment, not to be overthrown. Indonesia had "spooked" the Dutch with its unpredictable guerrilla war and the threat of it, its scorched-earth strategy, and the pressures of international politics. Indonesia had seen the Japanese theory of "decisive battle" and "final victory" to be a humiliating illusion. Better to bleed the enemy slowly into defeat.

Guerrilla analogies with China (where communists were triumphant in the 1949 civil war) and with Vietnam (where civil war was still ongoing) applied to "winning the hearts and minds of the people." But those wars had been fratricidal, whereas Indonesia's struggle against a foreign foe was "a war of brothers who never lost their ferocity." Since independence, Nasution wrote, we have had to confront guerrillas fighting against the republic. It was vital to remember our own lessons and avoid Dutch errors. Fight insurgents with their own weapons. Split them from their popular base by emphasizing political, psychological, and economic activities. Employ a mobile, flexible offense. "The guerrillas we [now] confront are given the opportunity to manifest the spirit of region and religion by becoming partners, even as we increase our strikes against them."[64]

Indonesians did not have the means, Nasution admitted, even to pay and equip the equivalent of one division of American troops. Obviously unable to defend all of a far-flung territory, they had to organize regionally, saturating the effort with the "five senses" of the anti-guerrilla movement. Every *desa* must watch and report to the commander of operations. The people must be urged again and again to the fullest self-motivation. Every soldier must be a "pioneer of ideological war."[65]

Nasution directly contradicted Western orthodoxy that an army "must be non-political" with injunctions that the Indonesian army "must be revolutionary . . . constitutional . . . an instrument of the state." The soldier "truly has to plant himself in the middle of politics with both feet . . . Politico-ideological consciousness is a source of inner spiritual strength."[66]

The fighting principles articulated by Nasution, while sacked by Sukarno from 1952 to 1955, proved effective against regional secessions and against Darul Islam in the 1950s through the early 1960s. Even after Nasution's death in 2000, the army still needed the experienced insights of his youth. But somewhere in the interim it so lost that spirit that it operated with militia gangs instead of turning guerrilla opponents into partners. It seemed to remember not the "People's Army with the Soldier of 1945 as its core" but a romantic phrase of the dying General Sudirman, which Nasution invoked when he was restored as commander-in-chief late in 1955. In his last message Sudirman described the TNI as the "only national property of the Republic."[67] This self-glorifying phrase could and would be used in the future to justify numberless prerogatives. It led easily to praetorian corporatism.

Sukarno and Nasution, in the 1959 promulgation of guided democracy, had prevailed over a battlefield of exhausted representative principles and persons. But their merger of interests was imperfect. Sukarno did not understand the army or control it. While he resented them, they resented him for "donning phantasy uniforms with five stars on his shoulders and loaded with medals."[68] As for the military sharing responsibility for government policies—Nasution's "middle way"—it might prevent attempted coups, but it invited corruption.

More important still: whoever governed Indonesia still had to address the economic and political phenomena that had brought him to the dissatisfying apex of integralistic power. In the late 1950s economic deficits were running from 8 to 30 percent of current receipts; inflation was moving at a gallop; international lenders were being evaded for repayment. Infrastructure left by the Dutch—roads and shipping, irrigation and flood control, forestry projects—was deteriorating. Confiscation of Dutch firms and assets had led to desirable Indonesianization but undesirable inefficiencies. Get-rich-quick banks had appeared and would disappear. Credits were being obtained through political influence, for projects without commercial viability. Too many on the edge of new wealth, or in its grip, were drawn to prestigious consumption.

Regional rebellions had been quelled without vanquishing banditry in the provinces and without far-sighted development of regional autonomy. The bureaucracy was growing at 10 percent a year. In government, power-scramble and patronage-management were stultifying progress. Ideological antagonism was on the rise, the press was increasingly politicized, and civil liberties were being undermined.[69] The army was struggling to be independent of civilian leadership, and the PKI was snuggling under presidential protection. Within the new "guided democracy" were hiding two directly contradictory and irreconcilable visions, neither one democratic: guardianship by the military and dictatorship of the proletariat.

3

EGO, VOICE, VERTIGO

A great man leading a giant nation under grueling conditions, Sukarno attracted to himself six would-be assassins, seven wives of different standing, and numerous other bed partners. After long imprisonment under the Dutch, a stretch as cheerleader for the Japanese, and several years as a president locked in coalition politics—a *formateur* of governments—Sukarno wanted to break free and move around. He had never traveled out of Indonesia until he was flown to Tokyo in 1944, an astonished provincial, to shake the emperor's hand. Having brought the Afro-Arab-Asian world to Bandung in 1955, Sukarno set out to rectify his insularity with a trip to Mecca and Cairo.

Then, in May 1956, the United States. He loved Hollywood. He adored American department stores and industrial productivity—thousands of auto workers' cars parked outside Detroit factories. He took his son to Disneyland and addressed Congress. He listened to John Foster Dulles tell him "Neutralism is immoral." He found President Eisenhower ignorant of Asian political feeling, but at a state dinner he exchanged radiant smiles with Ike and Mamie. Sukarno pushed onward to Western and Eastern Europe, Russia, China, and home after almost four months. His "Bury the Parties" speech followed. World travel had encouraged his autocratic leanings.

In 1959 Sukarno again circled the globe, his fourth foreign trip in four years. Indonesia was still under the "National State of War and Siege" that General Nasution had urged him to declare two years before, but Sukarno kept away from Indonesia for more than two months. On his return, Nasution urged him to implement the 1945 constitution by presidential decree. Sukarno did so on July 5, 1959. In a weak and weary nation, few protested, except ex-comrades like Hatta and Sjahrir.[1] Them, he would silence. Now the constitution would mean whatever Sukarno said it meant.

When he returned to the United States on an unofficial visit in 1960,

Sukarno claimed that Eisenhower humiliated him by keeping him waiting too long outside his office. In fact, the delay arose because Sukarno, unannounced, had brought the PKI leader, Aidit, along with him. Eisenhower aides were scurrying about to warn him of his unplanned hospitality to a major communist. The President chose to welcome the whole delegation. Sukarno said Eisenhower deliberately insulted him, but he himself had brought on the situation by mischievous confrontation.[2] Presidency was theater for him.

But not always play. In November 1957 Sukarno had survived a grenade attack while leaving his son's primary school. Eleven died and dozens were injured. This was the first of five failed assassination attempts over the next few years, of which the most spectacular was a strafing of the presidential palace from the air in 1960. A sixth time, Sukarno believed he stopped a grenade thrower in Makassar with a glance that shook his nerve. He was convinced that in all his life "there's been a Supreme Power guarding, guiding and protecting me."[3] That conviction began to color his charismatic view of his own role and to promote an arrogant belief that only Sukarno knew the true course for Indonesia.

At the heart of this confidence, figuratively and practically, was his third wife, Hartini. Sukarno began an affair with her in 1953, when she was the wife of an oil official. His prime minister at the time urged him to keep her as a mistress to spare the country and himself the problems of disturbing his marriage with Fatmawati. But Sukarno loved Hartini's intelligence and sophistication, which seemed to meet the growing demands of his responsibility. In the opinion of others, her courtesan tact and wiles fed his hungry ego. They married in 1955. Fatmawati was "bitterly angry . . . [and] stormed out of the *istana* [Istana Merdeka = Freedom Palace (the "White House")]. That was her individual choice," said Sukarno, "not mine." Living in the suburbs, she remained married to him and kept the position of Ibu Negara, Mother of the Nation.[4]

Sukarno saw both wives as "devout Moslems well aware of our holy laws. And they understand. Or should, anyway." By the same autobiographical statement, he attempted to educate the non-Muslim reader to his sacred options. But his childhood friends the Tjokroaminoto brothers saw through him. "As soon as Sukarno took a second wife, we knew he'd take the full [Qu'ranic] limit of four." There began his loss of *pamor,* said his ex-brothers-in-law: he lost his luster and nobility, his edge and integrity, bit by bit.[5]

Hartini was Sukarno's second wife simultaneously but was actually his fourth chronologically. The first, when he was 21 and she 16, was Utari, eldest child of his mentor and benefactor Haji Omar Said Tjokroaminoto.

Sukarno says he did it out of sympathy and respect for the father, recently widowed; and, out of delicacy and concern for the girl, he kept it a *kawin gantung*, "hanging marriage," that is, unconsummated. All that is credible. But "it didn't work out." Young Karno fell in love with an older married woman, Inggit, who believed that he had a great destiny and who enriched his field of dreams. So with three formal dismissals to Utari, Karno returned her to her father. He exchanged a teenage wife for a divorced woman twelve years older than he. Inggit would endure all his imprisonments and share his banishments but could not bear him a child.

In the Japanese period Sukarno fell in love with Fatmawati. She was 17; Inggit by this time was nearly 53. "I was still young, vital, in the prime of life. I wanted children . . . I wanted gaiety." He offered Inggit "topmost position . . . thus retaining all the honor associated with this while I exercise my religious and civil rights and take a second wife to continue my name." Inggit refused for two years; then she accepted divorce rather than a shared household. In 1944 Fatmawati bore a son to a joyful Sukarno, who was now 43. Guntur ("Thunder"), the first of their five children, was followed by Megawati, the first daughter.

Sukarno realized that his conflict of loves was an inverse repetition of what had happened two decades before. He had then divorced a young wife for an older one; now an older wife for a much younger one. But he rationalized it with the dialogue between Arjuna, the hero of the *Mahabharata* and of Javanese puppet plays, with the deity Krishna:

Arjuna: Where are you?

Krishna: I am in the winds. I am present in the water. I am the moon. I . . . am even in the smile of the girl who fascinates you.

Sukarno (arguing with himself): . . . Then if I love the beautiful smile of the beautiful girl and if that smile is God's reflection and He created this beautiful girl and I but appreciate His handiwork, then why is it a sin to want to take her?[6]

On such mythic inspiration, with rationales from *hadith,* Sukarno pulled off his third major marriage bargain, this time without divorce. Fatma would leave the palace but never yield the title Ibu Negara. Hartini moved in, toughened and inspired Sukarno's political character, and bore him two more children in his late fifties. But a day came when she, having expanded her own political horizons, allowed a women's convention to consider a motion designating her Mother of the Nation. Sukarno, learning of it, broke off his business, rushed to the meeting hall, took Hartini out of it, and ordered her dispatched to Bogor.[7] In this cool and beautiful hill resort she created her own kind of court. Although Hartini was prohibited from attending state functions with Sukarno and from entering the palace in Jakarta, she built a web of access around Sukarno that made her his first wife in influence, if not in name.

Others entered Sukarno's complement of legal Islamic wives. Dewi, the alluring Japanese bar girl whom he met in Tokyo in 1959, became his third wife. She still seized her occasional place in the international gossip columns four decades later, once for slashing the face of an Osmena woman, descendant of a leading Filipino political family, at an Aspen, Colorado, cocktail party. Hariati became number four. Then Yurike Sanger, a Eurasian, became a fifth wife, unrecognized by the State because Sukarno had exceeded the four-wife limit in Muslim law, to which he had once been attentive.

Sukarno's edifice of marriages would collapse in the end. Dewi bore him a daughter but left him before he was deposed and secured a divorce early in 1970. Hariati also divorced him. Yurike Sanger had never married him under Muslim law. Even Fatmawati eventually ended her marriage. She said to Shimizu, the ebullient wartime Japanese interpreter who had been Sukarno's informal switchboard to the military, "Big Daddy can build a nation, but he can't form his own character."[8]

In the end, of the seven women Sukarno bound to him in his varying concepts of sacred love, Hartini was his only remaining partner. Perhaps she gave him his sharpest politico-erotic focus as leader of what, in his autobiography, he jokingly called the sexiest nation in the world.[9] But Sukarno's last trip to Europe stirred dismal rumors of a Czech prostitute who was contemptuous of his performance; and far more dangerous than waning prowess, Sukarno began to lose his political balance and timing.[10] In the end, only Hartini clung to him in his shame, just as she had basked in his glory.

Sukarno as Expansionist

Thinking big is a way to outwit imperialism, but it can become a route toward imperialism itself. Sukarno always thought grandly. As early as the constitutional debates held during Japan's occupation, he envisioned independent Indonesia as inheriting a big slice of the Japanese Greater East Asia Co-Prosperity Sphere. Mohammad Yamin, an aggressive Minangkabau lawyer, served as his *pujangga,* court historian and chronicler, entrusted with keeping and elaborating the state myth. Together, their concepts converged in giving birth to a romantic vision of Muslim and Malay unity as part of meta-Indonesian togetherness. They imagined national community beginning with the Netherlands Indies, including West New Guinea, enhanced by adding Portuguese Timor and British North Borneo and Malaya. Such a concept embraced opportunistic anthropology and historic anomalies. Hatta and Haji Agus Salim took an opposing stand: seize the former territory of the Dutch and let others decide for themselves. Sukarno-Yamin won the vote, 39 to 27. But postwar deployment of Allied forces tilted the reality to settle on the Hatta-Salim side.[11]

These facts did not quiet Sukarno's imagination, however. West Irian (Western New Guinea), a territory the size of California, remained with the Dutch. Indonesians who differed on tactics were united in wanting it "back." A nation fighting PRRI-Permesta rebels until mid-1961 and the last of the Darul Islam rebels until 1962 was not, however, in a position to take it by force. But after the Dulles brothers' debacle in Sumatra-Sulawesi, Sukarno began effectively to play Cold War blackmail. General Nasution had tried for additional military equipment on a trip to Washington in 1960. No luck. But in the Kremlin, Khrushchev embraced him. By the end of 1962 Indonesia received from Russia an estimated $1.3 billion in military assistance. American military aid was less than one fourteenth that amount. Economic assistance was equal from the two sides, around half a billion dollars each, but different in nature. The American program was aimed at stabilizing the economy, while the Russian program was pointed at more publicizable projects, such as a giant sports stadium.

Although the Sverdlov class cruiser received from the Soviets was not suitable for Indonesian needs, or accompanied with spare parts and expertise, Sukarno pushed the heavy Soviet hardware—modern fighters, long-range bombers, new ships—to branches of the service he trusted more than the army.[12] The army, blooded by victories over rebels and whetted with real equipment, posed a threat to Sukarno's own aim, which was to galvanize Indonesia with revolutionary irridentism—a motive intimately suited to his style and calculated to enhance his power.

In December 1961 Sukarno created a Supreme Operations Command for the liberation of Irian, with himself as commander. Nasution wished to be commander of all the armed forces, but Sukarno soon reduced him to minister of defense and security while replacing him as army chief of staff with Major General Yani. Now a major general, Suharto was put in charge of a Mandala Command for the actual fighting in Irian.

Sukarno made Omar Dhani air vice-marshal, head of the air force. He became an ally of the president and the PKI against the leaders of the army. The PKI itself used the Irian campaign to increase its influence and membership. By the end of 1962 it was the largest communist party in any non-communist nation, with more than 2 million members. The PKI peasant front had 5.7 million members; its labor front had 3.3 million; its youth front and its women's movement each claimed 1.5 million more.[13] The membership of Lekra, its intellectual front, would claim 100,000 members, with the distinguished novelist Pramoedya Ananta Toer one of its strongest voices against "bourgeois" mentality among thinking Indonesians. Years later, Pramoedya would say that John Steinbeck and William Saroyan were great models for him.[14] Their influence is discernible in his writing, but in this period he went beyond literary populism to class polemic.

The army meanwhile was professing interest in sound administration, economic stability, and the avoidance of social unrest. They accompanied these aims with increased budget requests and justified them by the concept of "civic mission" (*dwifungsi,* or two-fold responsibility). Nasution wanted army units to support provincial development projects, which in practice meant militarized civil administration (and what looks like mission distortion to a Western professional military mind). To the end of his life, however, Nasution saw his *dwifungsi* as intended "to fulfill the revolution."[15] The same rationale overcame any soldierly hesitation of the army over the West Irian dispute and over the confrontation of Malaysia which followed. Each provided the Indonesian army an opportunity to play a special role in national life and to get a large budget allotment.

In net effect, the PKI was behind Sukarno in his expansionism with their Communist vision of social revolution, and the army was behind him with their praetorian vision of national revolution. Both were associated with him in attacking the last nearby holdings of Dutch imperialism; and each was deeply, mortally suspicious of the other.

With Indonesian infiltration and guerrilla action testing the Netherlands in West Irian, the United States reentered the picture. Dutch casualties were relatively few, but the Netherlands government early realized that they could hold on only by earnest and protracted jungle warfare. Nehru's India, after all, had just taken back Goa and other remaining Portuguese enclaves after failed negotiations. West Irian was incomparably larger. Unwilling, perhaps, to undergo a long replay of 1945–1949, with anguishing losses for an antique cause, the Dutch acceded to American mediation.

John F. Kennedy, the new President supporting the secret talks, knew that compromise "will inevitably be unsatisfactory in some degree to both sides (indeed we have deliberately let ourselves be placed in this exposed position to give both sides someone else to blame)."[16] He would soon learn how volatile Sukarno could be—and how obstinate Luns, the Dutch foreign minister. The American ambassador, Howard Jones, whose task it was to overcome the Dulles fiasco in Sukarno's mind, attended many of Bung Karno's semipublic functions in the palace—what might be called salons, for their variety of company and conversation, except that they took place early in the morning, after breakfast. Kennedy followed Jones's advice and that of his own National Security Council, over the objections of the Dutch, the CIA, and Australian Prime Minister Menzies, who described to him Indonesia's position on Irian Jaya as "the substitute of brown colonialism for white colonialism."[17]

When Sukarno, on yet another world tour in April 1961, came to Washington, Kennedy broke tradition to meet him at the airport. At the visit's end, he helicoptered him back and, having found Sukarno delighted with the presidential craft, asked if he would like one. Sukarno was thrilled.[18] Kennedy had overcome the image of Eisenhower's inhospitability, but his attentions did not alter Bung Karno's fundamental goals.

Indonesia went ahead with its military pressure. President Kennedy sent his brother Robert to Jakarta to solicit entry into negotiations without preconditions. He also asked Sukarno to release Allen Pope, sentenced to death for bombing Ambon nearly four years prior. While in Washington Sukarno had hinted at freeing him, but now he offered to release Pope only in return for American pressure on the Dutch. Businessmen who deal with the Javanese remark on their tendency to bait and switch, but Attorney General Kennedy, unused to this style, blew his stack. Anger got him nowhere, however, and Ambassador Jones later apologized for him.

By July 1962 negotiations were languishing. Suharto's Mandala Command was ready for a major military strike, with airplanes, warships, task force, and coffins at the ready in the hospital ship. President Kennedy at this point "scared the living daylights out of Soebandrio," Indonesia's foreign minister, and at the same time "wrote a flowery appeal," persuasively, to Sukarno.[19]

At the United Nations on August 15, 1962, both parties signed an agreement on West Irian. The Dutch transferred it to interim UN administration on October 1, for turnover to Indonesia by May 1, 1963. By the end of 1969 Jakarta would hold an "act of free choice" in Irian to see if its people wished, or did not, to integrate with Indonesia. There existed no Papuan nationalism sufficient yet to contest the "consensual" ritual with which the Indonesian government went on to absorb what became Irian Jaya.

A serious political scientist studying the conflict over this "worthless area" from the Dutch point of view found that "Holland's involvement in the bitter struggle . . . was not prompted by Dutch objective interests at all, but wholly and exclusively by its emotional commitment."[20] Indeed, the first great discoveries of copper there by Freeport MacMoRan, an American firm, did not happen until the late 1960s. But now, in the twenty-first

19. SUKARNO AGAINST "NEO-COLONIALISM." Rising to his favorite theme, Sukarno gnashes his teeth and claws the air at Kota Baru, Irian Jaya, on May 4, 1963. Having just taken over this giant province from the Dutch, he proceeds in July to declare as a battle cry, "Crush Malaysia." In 1965 he would withdraw Indonesia from the UN. (AP/Wide World Photos)

century, Indonesia—the underdog power befriended by John F. Kennedy—is regarded by many Papuans as an imperial power taking away the value of their own mineral inheritance, with Freeport's help.

The Kennedy administration had an action plan for Indonesia—emergency food, spare parts, technical assistance, with grants and loans heavily weighted toward education. Plus a Peace Corps presence, about which Sukarno overcame his hesitation because of Kennedy's personal interest. But the logic of "continuing revolution," such as Mao's or Sukarno's, is always to continue. In September 1962, even before the Kennedy action plan was approved, Soebandrio announced in Singapore Indonesia's aversion to the British plan to federate into "Malaysia" its remaining colonies—Singapore, Sarawak, North Borneo (Sabah), and Brunei—along with independent Malaya. Early in 1963, despite official American reassurances of Britain's sincerity in decolonizing, Sukarno told a mass rally, "I now officially declare that Indonesia opposes Malaysia." In English he added, "We are being encircled. We do not want to have neo-colonialism in our vicinity." Soebandrio then christened the policy "confrontation" *(konfrontasi)*. To packed stadiums in months ensuing, Sukarno stirred popular blood with the slogan "Crush Malaysia!" (Ganyang Malaysia).[21]

Why try to crush a neighbor when Indonesia itself had only recently averted crumbling? Sukarno wished to divert a populace short on bread with another gladiatorial circus. He put forward more elegant reasonings through Soebandrio: Malaysia was a corrupt, subversive neo-colonial artifact; it was not in the Afro-Asian revolutionary mold; its leadership was stained by the aristocratic character of the Brits who had fashioned it.

The PKI flourished in this atmosphere of anti-imperial radicalism. In grotesquely agreeable convergence with these anti-Malaysia energies were the perceived interests of the army: a new Malaysia would strengthen the Chinese, hence the People's Republic of China (PRC), in the region, whereas opposing Malaysia was an opportunity to continue strengthening military budgets and influence.

From the Philippines came a brief attempt at triangular regional synergy in solving border problems and damping flashpoints. But President Diosdado Macapagal's Maphilindo (Malaya, Philippines, Indonesia) provided, in the long run, little more than a tasty acronym. The tensions in the region were too high. In Singapore, a riot sparked in a Muslim procession to celebrate Maulud, the Prophet's Birthday, on July 21, 1965, left 22 dead and nearly 500 injured.[22] Less than three weeks later, Tunku Abdul Rahman announced the expulsion of Singapore from the Federation of Malaysia. Even the dauntless, massively stoic Lee Kuan Yew gave way to tearful anguish before the television cameras, trying to explain the failure of a merger of Chinese and Malay peoples connected by geography and economics and history.[23]

Now the old Sukarno-Yamin romantic anthropology about fellow Malays was tested with the new Sukarno-Soebandrio antifeudal ideology. The low point of brotherhood and the highest point of anxiety came in early September 1964, after the drop of about a hundred Indonesian troops in the central mountain spine of the southern peninsula of Malaya: mostly para-commandos, with about ten Malaysian Chinese defectors, including two young women. The aim apparently was to set up a jungle camp to attract local Chinese plantation workers into defection and fan the embers of the earlier communist insurrection. The effort lacked food and maps, and flopped in execution. General Nasution admitted that "volunteers" had been entering Borneo and Malaya for some time. He rationalized their presence: "For the volunteers, national boundaries do not exist. Their boundaries are political ones."[24] But the British too, Indonesians insisted, were infiltrating agents and weapons into Sumatra, Kalimantan, and Sulawesi and violating air space.

Indeed, Britain brought air and naval forces in Singapore to the edge of a retaliatory attack on Indonesia. Their warships moved in Indonesian waters. Air raid precautions were instituted in Jakarta. The government announced a new form of martial law, with emergency powers in the president. Sukarno, with astonishing aplomb or bizarre irresponsibility, flew off toward the Cairo Conference, more than two weeks before it was due to commence, making stops along the way. The crisis in the Sunda Straits slowly passed, but not before a Foreign Office spokesman had hinted that Britain might follow the war-enabling precedent set by President Lyndon Johnson in the Tonkin Gulf several weeks before.

Indonesian military efforts thereafter subsided, but slowly. In March 1965 about eighty Indonesian regulars landed twenty-three miles northeast of Singapore, won an initial engagement, but were soon defeated. The Indo-

20. DEAD INDONESIAN PARATROOPER. Sukarno's "confrontation" with Malaysia includes dropping paratroops in to foment resistance against its allegedly feudal and neo-colonial government. They are quickly mopped up by Malaysian soldiers, as shown here in Labis, Johore State, on September 3, 1964. (UPI, John Fairfax Publications, Sydney/Corbis Images, NYC)

nesians did not, for some reason, test Malaya's east coast and apparently never made efforts to use the remnants of the Malayan Communist Party to stir up trouble in the tribes of the northern border with Thailand. Indonesia spent some weeks defending itself in the Security Council of the UN later in the year, repeating its now highly vigorous "anticolonial" argument. It lost, 9–2. A Russian veto eased its embarrassment.[25]

Sukarno meanwhile had another domestic political crisis to solve. An avalanche of Sukarnoism had been launched by left and socialist leaders like Adam Malik and anticommunist officers in the armed services, in order to rally forces against the PKI and to picture them as using Sukarno to cloak their very different purposes. The PKI and the left of the PNI responded bitterly with charges of splitting the nation and undermining NASAKOM unity. Sukarno, in a decisive surprise, tilted against the Sukarnoists. He received the Chinese Foreign Minister Chen Yi as a visitor at a time when China allowed talk about providing Indonesia with an atomic bomb.

When the UN opened in 1965, it was known that Malaysia was to take a seat on the Security Council on an earlier split-term sharing agreement with Czechoslovakia. On January 7, 1965, without full discussion among his ministers, Sukarno announced the withdrawal of Indonesia from the United Nations—the first nation ever formally to exit UN membership.

Acting on impulse and then adjusting opportunistically was part of Sukarno's style. But by turning the wheel of revolution so far to the left, he had only China now as a major ally. He had alienated many of the nations drawn to the Bandung Conference in 1955. Indonesia was no longer nonaligned but strangely arrayed with what Sukarno now called the "Jakarta-Pnomh Penh-Hanoi-Peking-Pyongyang axis." This lengthy locution tried to avoid the appearance of being hitched only to China's wagon.[26]

Such an axis worried the American government just the same. The British had abandoned Singapore and sent no troops to Vietnam. Indeed, they met Sukarno's confrontation in a "subaltern's and platoon sergeant's war" with understrength troop units, never dropping a single bomb on Borneo, "while the United States was plastering Vietnam with bombs, napalm, and defoliant." Later events would prove British tactics to be adequate and its strategy correct. Rather than a watershed, America's war in Vietnam would turn out to be an appalling waste of lives and resources. The real heart of Southeast Asia, with an approaching pivotal crisis, was Indonesia.[27]

Pride, Class, Race, and the Failure of Entrepreneurship

Under the red and white flag of the unitary Republic, the Indonesian economy, isolated by war and revolution in the decade 1939–1949, was dead

calm. Gross domestic product (GDP) was lower in 1950 than in 1939, and
the manufacturing share of it had declined. Because Indonesia had only a
tiny indigenous class of entrepreneurs and no domestic capital markets—
unlike India of the 1950s—domestic business people could not buy out controlling interests in foreign firms, or at least gain representation on their
boards.[28]

To kick the economy into action, should Indonesia encourage entrepreneurship? The new minister of trade and industry, Sumitro Djojohadikusumo, had trained in the Netherlands and was familiar with the United
States. He saw the need for indigenous builders of businesses to compete
with the Chinese and the expatriate firms which dominated much of what
there was of manufacturing, transport, financial services, wholesale and retail trade. His Economic Urgency Plan aimed to begin by developing small
industries to produce import substitutes and reduce dependence on foreign
trade, to restrict certain markets to indigenous sellers, and to provide capital assistance to home-grown enterprises. As he recalled thirty years later,
the goal "was to try to set up a counter-force to Dutch interests . . . I
thought that if you gave assistance to ten people, seven might turn out to
be parasites but you might still get three entrepreneurs."[29]

It did not work out. His colleague in the cabinet, Minister of Finance
Sjafruddin Prawiranegara, argued that his plan was too nationalistic, that
changes in ownership and control would have to come more slowly and
naturally. But he was not Sumitro's worst opposition. A widespread fundamental mistrust tied capitalism of any kind to colonialism. Sukarno
made the most of that naive hostility. When in November 1957 the UN
first denied the Indonesian motion on the future of West Irian, the Indonesian government proceeded to take over Dutch companies and expel Dutch
nationals. This expropriation without compensation not only led to a decline in output but made Indonesia a pariah to Western investors for a full
decade.[30]

Sumitro in the meantime exercised his "personal option of rebellious
character."[31] President Sukarno invited him into his cabinet, but Sumitro,
mistrusting the communist clique drawing closer to the president, fled Jakarta and linked up with Sjafruddin in leadership of the regional revolts of
the late 1950s. Only in 1967, rehabilitated by the Suharto government,
would he be able, as minister of industry and trade, to father a new investment law and improve the entrepreneurial climate.

Meanwhile Sukarno, who had argued for the unity of nationalism, Islam,
and Marxism as early as 1926, in 1960 proclaimed that triad as NASAKOM
(Nationalisme, Agama, Kommunisme)—a putative doctrine of state that
anesthetized efforts at economic analysis and policy thinking.[32] Revolution-

ary national pride would continue to belittle individual business effort and resent international investment.

These antibusiness developments did not deter Soedarpo Sastrosatomo, who would become an internationally trusted business leader. No cramped Javanese gravity for him. His smile was spontaneous and stunning—big white teeth clamped shut but lips curling wide open in a cartoon-like mirth. At a revered age he wore two gold rings: on his left hand a big green stone, and on his right a big red one. He had steadily applied a simple lesson from Mattie Fox: try it, see if it works.

As the young son of court-connected *priyayi* in Yogya, Soedarpo had rejected efforts to make an obedient civil servant of him. The transforming experience was driving with an elder brother, a regional doctor, to a clinic south of Cirebon. They were late. A Dutch assistant resident was going slowly in front of them on a narrow road. The doctor ordered his driver to honk the horn and pass, and the Dutch car finally yielded. That night the regent summoned Soedarpo's brother at the local club and told him of the assistant resident's complaint that "he had been forced to eat dust."[33] Soedarpo's brother replied, "If you share his opinion, I resign." Soedarpo himself vowed to work for an independent Indonesia and to be a doctor.

The experience of working with Mattie Fox redirected his sights toward business. He had to contend with his own class's conceits that being a *priyayi* meant security, prestige, pension, "and being sought by would-be mothers-in-law." Businessmen were stereotyped as Eurasians or Dutch sons of sugar factory engineers. They were *saudagar,* meaning merchants, traders, dealers of minimal entrepreneurial dimension, all the way down to batik traders, "third class people" who lived in a special quarter. Children of *saudagar* rode bikes to school and carried their books on their backs—"coolie work," as seen by children of *priyayi,* who did not transport books but were chauffeured to school. The famous Professor Supomo, in his inaugural university lecture, focused on a presumptive principle of *adat* law: *Never talk about money, not even to a debtor.* His fastidious attitude was for the socially, financially secure. Supomo's wife was a granddaughter of the sultan of Yogya. Soedarpo vowed with other nationalist youth never to fall into the titular trap, by which the Dutch, with nominal honors and medals, subordinated indigenous aristocracy to foreign royalty. For those who went that route the young activists had a term of contempt in Dutch: *kontlikker.*

At the age of thirty, after working with Fox, Soedarpo in 1950 was a counselor in the new Indonesian Embassy in Washington. How to put Indonesia onto the mental maps of Americans? Show them, in the words of his intimate friend Soedjatmoko, that "we are not just people who came out of the trees." He organized traveling exhibits of the great painter Affandi and arranged a cross-country tour of batik with Saks Fifth Avenue. When a jealous boss confined his style, he got invited back to Jakarta for "consultations," where Hatta, the foreign minister, gave him a ticket to travel around all Indonesia for the first time and power to pick his own successor (in the end, a young talent from far-off Makassar). "Meanwhile, from what I've seen of the United States and of Indonesia . . . I felt *opportunities galore!* The world is wide open!"

Mattie Fox asked him to consider managing his Zorro Corporation of Indonesia (*zorro* means fox in Spanish), which he had set up to bring pepper to the United States and which then had contracts to represent RCA, Remington, and, best of all, Willys Overland Jeeps. Willys had responded to his argument that "these young nationalists will rule Indonesia," whereas GM and Ford had not. With Mattie as the contact, Soedarpo in 1948 had met William Taylor of Bankers Trust, who told him to rent a deposit box and "use a false name so the Dutch can't get you." From Taylor he learned escrow and arbitrage. "This is when I was exposed to business, why I thought I could be a success."

First he served Zorro as CEO. Then he set up Soedarpo Company to manage Isthmian Shipping Lines. Fearful Dutch owners saw that they could ride the wave by letting him manage it, replacing Dutch employees with Indonesians. Fox, meanwhile, sent Val D'Auvray out to transfer all the accounts from Zorro to Soedarpo because Zorro's chief operating officer was drinking and womanizing three quarters of the time. When Sukarno in 1957 broke relations with the Netherlands, Remington Rand, which owned UNIVAC and used a Dutch distributor, shifted that as well to Soedarpo, an avant-garde entrepreneur.

"Corruption?" Soedarpo told me, "It started being bad when the military take over Dutch businesses. They just ask 'Where is house? Car?' If we did it correctly, we would never have had national bankruptcy in 1964." But it was another "fruits of the revolution situation" as in 1950: eat the fruit, plant no seed, develop no orchard.[34]

The military threatened Soedarpo: unless he gave them a controlling interest, he would not get a license to export. He saved himself by going to Hashim Ning, a Chinese friend of Sukarno's, to do the trading. One of the military persisted in trying to force him out of business. But Sukarno, who had known Soedarpo since his wartime days as a student activist, said, "This is a real businessman. We need him. You hurt him, you're out . . . He doesn't fit the system, but he's doing no harm."[35] So Soedarpo, having prevailed over *priyayi* class prejudice to become a businessman, survived hypernationalism by Indonesianizing his and others' holdings on his own initiative. A gain endangered, this time by NASAKOM, he survived because Sukarno had fond memories of him as a revolutionary youth. But even he, as a *pribumi* or native son, needed a Chinese connection to do so. The arrangements, styled as "Ali-Baba," indigenous plus Chinese, would become even more common in the Suharto decades.

All the preconditions of a sophisticated capitalism, arguably, have been lurking in Southeast Asia, including Indonesia, since world market capitalism began unfolding in the region through colonial regimes in the nineteenth century.[36] If creative arrangements between "state" and "Chinese" could accelerate such development, capitalism should have flowered easily. Indigenous bureaucrats and immigrants as joint entrepreneurs need nothing fancy in order to synergize: telephones, conference tables, and a mutual appetite for back-scratching will suffice.

Then why did so little happen in Indonesia until the late twentieth century? Because nationalist ideology tended to be autarchic. And the *pribumi* business it looked to favor was shriveled by *priyayi* values in the courts and bureaucracies, which looked on commerce with disfavor. Muslim traders (*santri*) were an exception, but they were not yet drawn to more elaborate forms of capitalism. The only internationalist ideologies availed of were Marxism, which proved repeatedly, and then terminally, counterproductive; and Sukarno's NASAKOM, an inedible hardtack.

One must focus then on the Chinese in Indonesia, long an underlying entrepreneurial asset. They have always been a small minority, sometimes a persecuted minority. By 1961 they had never been more than 2.5 percent of the population. And even at the end of the twentieth century, when they had grown to about six million in number, they were no more than 2.8 percent of the population.[37]

So few; what's the problem? Cannot forty people tolerate one among them who is different? The nature of that difference was the crux of the issue. The Chinese, on average, were more literate and more prosperous than other Indonesians. The Chinese were seen as having no "homeland," unlike Bataks or Bugis and other *pribumi*. They were alleged to be urban, clannish, disloyal, economically dominant, expert in bribery and smuggling. They were additionally suppressive of indigenous entrepreneurship, averse to Islam, oppressive of the masses.

Neighboring nations assimilated Chinese more fully. In the Philippines, there was no mega-bureaucracy and there were no pariah capitalists. The social and business elite had strong Chinese mestizo strains, born of nineteenth-century alliances of old partly-Hispanic landed families. And American entrepreneurial ideology flowed in on everybody. In Thailand the indigenous elite managed over time to cultivate business through bureaucracy without excessive snobbery regarding commerce or crippling prejudice regarding race.[38]

Those two countries dramatize by contrast the influence that the Dutch had upon Indonesia. They were the first to mount a Chinese massacre, killing perhaps 10,000 in 1740, because the East India Company feared a plot against themselves.[39] But far more lasting was the hierarchic stratification with which the Dutch rigidified Indonesian society: Europeans on top, foreign Orientals in the middle, and natives (the Dutch term *Inlanders* had both derogatory denotations and connotations of contempt) at the bottom. Stuck in the middle tier underneath Japanese and Arabs in the ever-proliferating Dutch system of discrimination, the Chinese were nevertheless ranked above indigenous Indonesians for centuries, because the Dutch needed them as traders, tax collectors, and financiers-for-hire.[40] Envy and resentment were predictable among those natives from whom the Chinese extracted taxes and collected debts.

By the late 1950s the proportion of Chinese-Indonesians born in Indonesia was nearly 80 percent. A majority of them were at least third generation. A significant number could trace their lineage back twelve generations, and some even further, all the way to the Majapahit era. But during the national revolution they fell between the Dutch anvil and the revolutionary hammer. Where Republican forces were in retreat or carrying out scorched earth policies, the Chinese were in danger of violence.[41]

The worst recorded incidents were within several months of the return of Dutch forces. Tangerang, not far from the capital, generated grievous specific reports during six weeks of 1946, concluding in totals of 1,085 killed and 213 missing, while 15,300 people were counted as having safely fled to Jakarta.[42] Photographs convey the rage of perpetrators and the pain of their targets: sexless figures hacked and burned beyond recognition, solo, in pairs, and trios; buried in mass graves. A boy perhaps ten or twelve years old, his face contorted, fire blisters like tears on his swollen cheeks, which are puffed up as if trying to expel his swollen tongue. Figures in burned houses lie in the last spasms of death. A girl on her side, knees drawn up, modestly holds a piece of burnt tarpaper across her breast. She appears to smile like a sylph; her eyes are innocent as a fountain statue.[43] Such records continue through Dutch police and military reports as late as September 1947.[44]

In 1956 two rich and able young Chinese men of Indonesian citizenship got into separate public altercations which led to mobbing and destruction of their businesses. One got a year and a half sentence in jail and the other seven (for blackmail), while no action was taken against the rioters. The Assa'at movement against Chinese business was launched at that time by a prominent *santri* and former minister of the interior. It quickly intensified. A head tax on aliens followed in 1957. Far more onerous was a ban on retail trade by aliens outside the major capitals. This regulation struck so hard at the rural and small town niches carved out by Sino-Indonesian merchants that an exodus to China of over 100,000 soon followed.[45]

Sukarno's government, however, as part of its precarious balancing of powers, sought an accommodation with "domestic foreign capital" among the progressive funds and forces needed for the nation. A nationality law accordingly tried to separate citizens from aliens. In 1964 Sukarno even described the national capitalist class—still chiefly Sino-Indonesian—as a "pillar of the revolution." Many Chinese were proud to mobilize their capital—or their collective identity gathered in a political organization called Baperki—for development. Even if they were extorted, ostensibly for the state, these Chinese were relieved that imperialism and neo-colonialism were the major enemies, and not themselves. But that was an illusory security. Too close association with any form of power—the Dutch, the Sukarno bureaucracy, or the Suharto family —has always ended with painful backlash for the Chinese-Indonesian community.

"To Hell with Your Aid!"

In the early and mid-1960s, from the coils of Sukarno's ignorance and convictions, his ever-expansive egoism, his irresponsible obscurantism, sprang a bold and disastrous logic of "continuing revolution."

Indonesia's agricultural productivity had fallen so short of the country's needs that Sukarno urged his people to eat not rice but corn (distinctly second-level, to most Indonesian tastes), in order to save foreign exchange, since Indonesia had become a significant importer of rice. Crumbling infrastructure was evident everywhere, without adequate plans or available funds for repair. Inflation broke into a gallop, reaching 640 percent in 1966. International borrowing, ambitious in extent and dubious in impact, reached $2.1 billion by 1965. Anticipated export earnings could not even service the debt.[46]

Sukarno's increasing reliance on the West for borrowing and on his own East Asian Marxist axis for political inspiration was so contradictory that something had to snap. With an incongruity that would have been comic if it had not been bitterly serious, Sukarno decided to attack not borrowing but *giving*. To a major donor, the United States, he finally said, "To hell with your aid!" Sometimes he clarified that he meant aid with strings attached, sometimes he did not. He enjoyed hitting a big target, with simplistic defiance, and then repeating himself.

Review of Sukarno's mythology may help illuminate his lapse into a magico-mantraism that was more an attempt to hypnotize his people than to lead them. The figures of *wayang* stories, the Indonesian narrative epic that evolves from the Mahabharata and the Ramayana, gave Sukarno great evocative power, especially among his Javanese audiences. Lord Bima, one of five warrior-hero brothers, appears to have dominated his mind in his student years—a courageous figure with a bold style, truthful and blunt, prepared to rebuke the gods. Sukarno indeed appeared like Bima to Indonesian aristocrats. He was rough *(kasar)* rather than refined *(halus),* a basic distinction of style, class, taste, even morality among those for whom harmoniousness *(kecocokan)* was the prevailing ethic.[47] Needless to say, for the Dutch and British and Malaysians, his confrontative tactics felt rough indeed.

Wayang Purwa evolved wholly unlike Aesop's Fables, short stories ending in pithy maxims. *Wayang* versions of small parts of the Indonesian epic can run all night long until sunrise. Its core is not didactic morality but a philosophic ambiguity, a stay-the-course stoicism with a tender respect for likeable villains and, above all, a loving regard for flawed heroes. Sukarno, in his *Autobiography,* does not mention Bima. There, his warrior brother of choice is Gatotkaca, his "favorite hero," who "only wants to do good," whose enormous resilience allows him to spring back from defeat and disaster and at last to slay the demon. Just as often he mentions Arjuna, the brother who stands for self-control—a quality he cultivated successfully as nationalist underdog and prisoner but in the end squandered as imperialist eminence and dissipate.[48]

During the Japanese occupation, Sukarno had played upon the (non-*wayang*) myth of Joyoboyo, a meta-historic king of Java who prophesied that a yellow people from the north would come to free the kingdom from demons and then would themselves be displaced. The Japanese liked the first part of the myth but not the last. The *Kenpeitai*—the Japanese military police, counter-intelligence, and torture experts—used belief in the Joyoboyo prophecy as one of several test questions of those suspected of hypernationalism or disloyalty to the emperor. It testifies to Sukarno's skill as orator and his subversive daring how often, especially toward the end of the war, he invoked Joyoboyo, trusting in Shimizu or other sympathetic interpreters to soften the message for his Japanese audience.[49] After that foreshadowing was done, and events cooperated in fulfillment, he never used this prophecy again.

Sukarno the nationalist prophet began as accusatory in an Old Testament finger-pointing sense, attributing all Indonesian error and suffering to the Dutch. He went on to summoning the people under an even more drastically exploitative regime, the Japanese, because he could see national opportunity beckoning. He maintained his rallying voice during and after the national revolution, while Hatta, Sjahrir, and others were prime ministers and strategists. And finally, without dropping the condemnatory style against real or imagined imperial intrusions or losing his summoning fervor (all too often a call to sacrifice without pointing out a clear path of action), he loaded in a strong strain of revelation—a body of his own ideas intended to equip, arouse, and ennoble the Indonesian people. In this he distinguished himself among Asian leaders by fabricating a national ideology, Pancasila—a task to which Ghandi and Nehru were not called, the former preoccupied with exemplary personal morality, the latter inhibited by Cantabridgian sophistication. Neither were Mao Zedong nor Ho Chi Minh moved in such a direction; both were inheritors of Marx-Leninism, the first employing it in a Machiavellian reshaping of society at great cost of lives, the second in the pragmatics of sustained Indo-China wars, with another tremendous death toll.

The most distinctive Sukarno, in some ways, was the leader of guided democracy, who rode from decree to decree, using the speeches of August 17 each year to celebrate independence, reveal national destiny, and elaborate continuing revolution. With Pancasila and NASAKOM as strategic unifying themes, he rolled out tactical variations.

His assumption that the people relied on him as master and oracle came to verge on the ridiculous. On August 17, 1963, he spoke in the new Soviet-financed stadium called Gelora Bung Karno, the Turbulence of Bung Karno. The name suggested his favorite metaphors, of thunder and lightning, of volcanic fire and lava flow, of the people's spirit, gleaming, burning, exploding. "I am not . . . speaking as President Mandatory or as President/Prime Minister, as President/Supreme Commander—I speak here as the Extension of the Tongue of the People of Indonesia—as President Great Leader of the Revolution . . . Everything invisible in my body seethes; my thoughts overflow . . . the stars in the heavens are not high enough."[50]

The Indonesian revolution is "identical with the social conscience of man," a telescoping of history, "a summing up of many revolutions in one generation."[51] He castigated reactionaries, subversives, counter-revolutionaries. He called, in effect, for Indonesian Stakhanovites—solving economic difficulties by dramatic personal increases in production. "I am not an economist . . . I am not a business technician. I am a revolutionary, and I do what is right for an economic revolutionary."[52]

21. MEGAWATI AND SUKARNO IN HIS GLORY. Sukarno, fully bemedaled and berib-boned, with riding crop, appears in 1963 with his eldest daughter, Mega-wati, then age sixteen. In this year, parliament bestows on Sukarno the title "President for Life"—a title it strips from him just three years later, in March 1966. (Ipphos Photo Archive)

In his "Multicomplex Revolution," he could embrace all facets of life, endorse any program he wished, warn against false psychologies, and, as ever, war against imperialism. Watch out for farmer-phobia, worker-phobia, above all NASAKOM-phobia, lest they weaken counter-imperial resolve. In a single page he interjected Dutch, French, English, and Arabic phrases to emphasize his point that imperialism is not just expansion of territory by force of arms but peaceful penetration by economic and political subtlety. Thus he displayed an early and passionate neo-Marxism in the sense of alerting his countrymen on all fronts, in all sectors, against letting foreign influence weaken Indonesia, like a soft cake of fermented soybean.[53]

By 1963 Sukarno was aiming for the stars with a slingshot. In his speech of August 17, 1964, he surpassed even himself in romantic zealotry. From the early twentieth-century Italian poet-nationalist D'Annunzio he took as his theme "The Year of Living Dangerously." Now was the time to realize a romantic, dynamic, dialectical mass revolution. Sukarno invoked as comrades in arms, among others, Nasser, Ben Bella, Sekou Toure, Jomo Kenyatta; Ayub Khan, Ne Win, Kim II Sung; Sihanouk, Ho Chi Minh, and Mao Zedong—an incongruous collection of praetorians, autarchs, mercurians, aging revolutionaries, and personality-cult populists. His stress on the artistic and romantic led him far beyond Mao's "Let the Hundred Flowers Bloom" to a sentimental Indonesian expressionism—cherishing individual flowers such as jasmine and the rose and specifying weeds that would not be allowed to grow. He urged a return to Indonesian culture against foreign influences: implicitly, the ever-present shadow of Hatta and Sjahrir (despite their being under house arrest), with their European educations, and explicitly the fear of American mass culture and media penetration.[54]

He enlarged his NASAKOM themes to embrace "all ethnic groups, all religions, all political factions, all faiths." Accept all distinctive features of Bataks, Chinese, Arabs, Balinese, Irianese, and others as positive and blend them into one family, the Indonesian nation. He urged that Indonesia import no more rice and that it achieve self-sufficiency on the model of North Korea. In light of the North Korean famine of the late 1990s, this remark now looks more myopic than it was then. South Korea at the time, in the economists' cliché, was a basket case.

Sukarno urged a "spiritual revolution" that would make ordinary large industry irrelevant. His models appeared to be Japanese wartime "inspiriting" *(bersemangat)* toward triumph of mind over matter and Mao's Great Leap Forward. He was apparently indifferent to the disasters that attended those two adventures. He tried to validate himself with a dismissal of American materialism (using an unidentified Thoreauvian-sounding source) as leading to loss of inner meaning and to "virtual despair."

Sukarno warned strenuously against the American "advisers" in Vietnam, who were really neo-imperial guerrillas like the British in Malaysia. Indonesian sympathies should be with the North Vietnamese fight to the death against imperialism. And Indonesia should take note of the fate of the president of South Vietnam, Ngo Dinh Diem—assassinated late in 1963, just as dispensable as the deposed Syngman Rhee of South Korea. Here Sukarno switched into English, followed by his own idiomatic translation into Indonesian: "paper tissues which one uses once and then throws away."[55]

Already Sukarno had associated himself with Prince Sihanouk of Cambodia in saying to imperialist handouts, "Go to hell with your aid!"[56] He returned to the theme with a dismissal of the United States as once, but no longer, "the Centre of an idea." Now its behavior made it lumpable with

Disraeli, Bismarck, Gambetta, Mussolini, and Hitler as outside the "Universal Revolution of Man." Sukarno charged the United States with waging
"psy-war" against Indonesia, with rumors of its disintegration and word
that this month or that month Sukarno will be overthrown by coup or will
no longer be there. "No Sir!" He broke into English again. "Go to hell with
your 'Indonesia going to economic collapse.' *Go to hell!*" Indonesia is not going to fold up. For the fourth time in his speech: *"Go to hell!"*[57]

Sukarno meanwhile ordered or allowed pressure on the United States Information Service (USIS) and Peace Corps volunteers and American diplomats like that earlier put on the Dutch and British. At the same time he was
dictating engrossingly candid (and defectively inventive) memoirs which
were also a charming public relations piece for the American public. Yes, he
appreciated the Peace Corps and medical volunteers and the eradication of
malaria in Java and Bali. No, Indonesia does not want free grant aid. Yes, we
are grateful for the $600 million dollars of help from the United States.
"However, American aid is NOT free . . . It is a system of borrowing and
paying back." And its motives are hypocrisy: get back the interest, develop
good markets, and prevent communism.

"I am not asking America to give money . . . All I have really wanted
from America was friendship . . . Maybe she didn't see how our revolution
paralleled hers. OK, America . . . Don't try to win my heart. But don't try to
break it either . . . Why did your senators do it in open speeches killing me?
Don't publicly treat Sukarno like a spoiled child by refusing him any more
candy unless he's a good boy because Sukarno has no choice but to say,
'The hell with your aid.'" He accepted responsibility for beginning the
name-calling. But Sukarno "thunders only at those he loves. I would adore
to make up with the United States of America. I once even made love with
a girl who had hurt my feelings . . . Oh, America, what is the matter with
you? Why couldn't you have been my friend? I would love to have been
yours."[58]

In his speech "The Year of Living Dangerously" and in his autobiography
Sukarno may be seen at his extremes of romantic aggressiveness and of political seductiveness, inflaming his constituency to unite them and wooing
his adversary to indulge him. Even as he proclaims that Indonesia will not
ambruk, or disintegrate, he sounds desperately embattled and falling apart.

Using elements of his 1963 speech, particularly on "Bearers of the Message of the People's Sufferings," one distinguished analyst sees in Sukarno
"the language of revolution brought under control."[59] I believe, however,
that Sukarno's language of revolution shot grossly out of control, in a dangerous reciprocity with the neglected, unguided economy. The worse the
sufferings of the Indonesian people became, the more eloquently and comprehensively he ranted about revolution. Sukarno needed to feed his peo-

ple. But instead of filling their stomachs, he tried to inflame their imaginations with *wayang* heroes from the mythic past and cumbersome intellectuality about continuing revolution.

Perhaps his successor, Suharto, could be judged adversely for the opposite: cultivating full bellies and empty spirits. In any case, one who suffered house arrest and surveillance under both leaders expressed judgment of Sukarno graphically. Mochtar Lubis, chiefly an essayist, went to paint and canvas for satire. The eyes and the rest of the countenance of the Great Leader of the Revolution are dwarfed by a huge dark open mouth, dazzling teeth, and idiot pink tongue.[60]

Until 1949, and even after, Sukarno did master the language and imagery of revolution. Certainly not beyond 1959. Toward the end, his ideology became infected with auto-idolatry. "I am NASAKOM," he said in 1963. "Sukarno *is* the *people*," he says in the autobiography which followed.[61] In such self-absorption he grew disastrously out of touch with the message whose dynamic he sympathetically invoked but whose pandemic his rule worsened—the People's Suffering.

The Short Sweet Life of the Peace Corps

Indonesia did not want the Peace Corps. But Sukarno felt he owed President Kennedy something for his help in squeezing the Dutch out of Irian Jaya in 1962. Sargent Shriver, first director of the Peace Corps, flew over to negotiate it and was bombarded by Sukarno's staff with questions about Hollywood and Marilyn Monroe. They had mistaken him for another Kennedy in-law, Peter Lawford. Shriver was fobbed onto Soebandrio, the strongly China-leaning foreign minister, who shunted him to an aide, who got the thing done in an Indonesian way.

"Peace Corps" did not translate well into Indonesian, so they became "Development Volunteers." The original plan, that two hundred university faculty be sent, was shot down in mutual fear as too political. The final agreement was that they be coaches. Even that turned out to be political, as Sukarno not only pulled out of the UN but out of the 1964 Olympics, for which he substituted his own Games of the New Emerging Forces. Eventually the young American deputation of volunteers grew to fifty, scattered widely over Indonesia. Forty-nine were instructors in sport. One in English was absorbed into the Foreign Ministry and put to work improving translations of its anti-American polemics.

The first thirty volunteers was the only group to meet with President Kennedy at the Rose Garden of the White House, several months before his assassination. Fresh from the London School of Economics with a doctorate in economic assistance was Alex Shakow, as acting director at age twenty-six. He opened the Peace Corps office in Indonesia. Less than three years later he would close it. There were many causes of anxiety. Coaches sometimes had to be guarded against the PKI with bared bayonets, an incongruous implementation of the Sukarno-Kennedy personal agreement. But no one was hurt, and not a single volunteer went home early. That was "rare," says Shakow, whose task was to maintain contact with the Ministry of Sport, define all jobs, and keep tabs on the volunteers.

One of the volunteers, assigned to Semarang in track, looked to Shakow like a beach bum. He thought this guy, Bob Dakan, would fail. Too laidback, lazy. And surrounded in Semarang by graffiti: "Beware of Bob's smile"; "Crush the Peace Corps." Shakow looks back, smiling fondly about a friend: "My judgment of his potential was so far off!"[62] Dakan knew how to roll with the punches, go with the flow; he learned how to meet Javanese impassivity with Stanford dignity, and communist assaults with California cool.

The PKI, Dakan found, was ready for them, alleging in advance that they were all CIA agents. He recruited for national teams in basketball, boxing, and volleyball, timed track and field events, and helped coaches coach. The best basketball players, he found, were in schools funded by mainland Chinese: they were stronger kids, getting better food. He went after them, even though the Ministry of Sport was more interested in *pribumi* players. As he cultivated and coached his athletes, he traveled all over central Java and saw people dying of hunger in Japara, Wonogiri, Demak, and Kudus; others, coming to Semarang to beg, were dying in the streets.

There were demonstrations against America. After September 1964 rocks were thrown at Dakan as he rode his motorbike without a helmet. Once at the invitation of his athletes he went to a performance of Chinese dancers. The show was interrupted with an announcement that a CIA agent was in the hall. Some of his boxers protected him, pulled him out on a Vespa, and got him home. Ambassador Howard Jones called all volunteers to Jakarta, concerned that no one be hurt on his watch. What did they really need and want? They answered, "A hot shower."

The harshest moment for Dakan was seeing some of his own athletes among the forces arrayed against him. "The PKI came to the house one afternoon, right into my room, and walked me down the street, into the governor's office, asking me to leave town." Shakow remembers it as a "demand that he be sent home." But Dakan stayed. They all stayed. Many made lifelong friendships. Many were the only Americans ever seen or known in their areas. They were good kids, doing no harm. Dakan laughs, "We gave the PKI heartburn . . . just stumbling around in Bahasa, being nice guys."[63]

Dakan fell in love with a champion swimmer. He saw her playing basket-ball barefoot on a cement floor. She was tall, with a Dutch mother. Her father was a major PKI official in Central Java. Maya was nineteen; and like other Javanese youth, though forbidden to dance, she was interested in Western parties and styles. Yet "Indonesian identity" was Sukarno's watchword. Boys with pants legs too tight were apprehended by police; if they couldn't get a bottle up the pants legs, they cut them off. Girls with pouffed hair would be reprimanded; men with long hair would have it shaved. Coca-Cola was banned. Old Coke bottles were used for indigenous carbonated drinks. "I wasn't a big party-goer," Maya remembers, "and not a dancer at all. And there was Bob, everybody expecting him to do the twist. But he couldn't. He's not a dancer, and he couldn't sing cowboy songs."

Bob recalls, "For Americans it was difficult to date. We had reputations like sailors." He just watched Maya ride by on her 49 cc two-seat motorcycle, the largest allowed. Then he heard she had an accident, a concussion; she was in the Catholic hospital. He looked for a present. As a low civil servant in the Ministry of Sport, Bob's salary was eleven dollars a month. All he could manage to give was his last package of chewing gum and some fresh-picked lilies. He visited her, woozy in the hospital, a girl who spoke Dutch at home, Indonesian in the classroom, Javanese everywhere else, and no English. Her friends snickered, "You have a boyfriend who gives you funeral flowers."

Maya went on to college in Yogya. Bob drove his motorcycle three hours each way every weekend to visit a Peace Corps friend. His American idea of a date was impossible. "We were 'londo,' which was Javanese slang for Dutch, or 'whitey.'" They went to movies with six friends. On group motorcycle trips, they carried the cycles over the rivers on their backs. "The only time to be alone with Maya was on a twenty minute run down the hard, flat beach."

For Maya, it was a strange environment for romance. "Bob would tell me about surfing. Why would anyone want to be on a board in the water? Indonesians don't like it, they're afraid of it . . . If you insist on swimming, at least don't wear a green bathing suit. All the Javanese expected Nyai Loro Kidul, Queen of the Southern Sea, to eat you up . . . or the sharks."

USIS libraries and American books were being burned in Surabaya, Yogya, Medan. The State Department thought Ambassador Jones "too soft on Sukarno" and sent out, on review of the mission, the grim-lipped Ellsworth Bunker, multicompetent and icy as a banker. One clear decision that ensued was to withdraw the Peace Corps, which action was completed by June 1965. USIS and the Agency for International Development (AID) were also closed down. Dakan's two years had already ended in April. As a

Peace Corps volunteer he could not marry. He went off to work on refugee relief in the hills of Laos, exchanging letters with Maya. Her mother was discouraging her from marriage. Her father did not want to lose a daughter to an alleged CIA agent.

Maya finally obtained a student passport to study in Holland. All letters were being held and checked, because it was now "post-coup" and Indonesia was in murderous turmoil. But Bob managed a phone call from Vientiane in Indonesian, to meet Maya's plane in Bangkok. By rowboat, train, and plane he made it in three days from the hills of Laos. He missed Maya by fifteen minutes.

He quit his job in Laos and pushed on to Holland. Maya's father had been in China, celebrating the communist revolution, when the coup struck in Jakarta. He proceeded to the Netherlands instead of home. Still lacking consent from her father, Bob and Maya married there on December 29, 1965, at a wedding attended by no parents.[64] Bob Dakan went on to stellar work for AID in the Philippines, Africa, Nepal, Pakistan, and elsewhere, including a return to Indonesia. He and Maya raised two daughters, one eventually a Peace Corps volunteer.

I asked Dakan what his Peace Corps experience meant to him, in addition to his marriage and family. "It gave me a different set of eyes . . . America is so rich, so powerful . . . But it makes me cringe at the arrogance with which our government makes our case . . . the present president, secretary of state, and all [at that time, speaking of Clinton, Albright, and Gore]."

Was he ever aware of any CIA attempts to infiltrate the Peace Corps? "No, I wasn't. I don't think there were any. The military attaché, when I was in Jakarta, wanted information on the port in Semarang. I said what port? It was mostly mud. The fishing boats anchored way out. Now, of course, it's much more developed."[65]

The Peace Corps was not an instrument of foreign policy and was not corrupted by foreign policy. But as private citizens the volunteers were effective informally. Why hasn't the Peace Corps ever returned to Indonesia? Many American ambassadors have encouraged the Republic to ask for that. But the Indonesian government thinks they have enough of their own underemployed college grads. They have their own volunteers for a rural development program and do not want to give the impression of using Americans to do things they could do themselves.[66]

Living Dangerously, Dying Suddenly

Sukarno's independence day speech of August 1964, "The Year of Living Dangerously," contributed to the atmosphere of terror that followed over a year later. His diatribes contained little in concrete policy for the economic-financial crisis. His nation-building rhetoric was so familiar that only his anger came through. And his central theme was an invitation to political gamblers.

Deprivations and tensions had been growing for several years. By late 1964 they were touching depths not felt for two decades, since the worst of the Japanese occupation in 1944–45, the years of bottomless misery in modern Indonesia's history.[67] Like his Japanese mentors in the spasms of their own approaching disaster, Sukarno redoubled his efforts as he lost sight of his goal. Triumph of the will over the materialism of the enemy is a dangerous slogan, particularly when one's listeners are hungry for life's necessities; when the allotment of provisions raises questions about whose will is actually governing, and how fairly. Sukarno's speeches could not much longer mask worsening insecurities for ordinary Indonesians. They looked around and could not see any "imperialist" enemy. But they might look with fear and hatred upon a neighbor living only meters away.

The per capita income of Indonesia, already low, had been falling since 1958. By 1965 it was below the level of 1940, in the then-continuing world depression. People do not, of course, eat statistics. But there were stagnant overall rice yields from 1960 all the way through 1967, aggravated by very poor rainfalls in Java in alternate years (1961, 1963, 1965, and 1967). By 1961 the manufacturing labor forces in Indonesia showed a demonstrable absolute decline, "entirely due to a decline in female employment from over one million in 1930 to only 500,000 in 1961." Compounding effects of this atrophy of manufactures was a rapid deterioration in the terms of trade after 1959.

Sukarno did nothing effective about any of these problems. He allowed quick-yielding rehabilitation projects and increased government investment in "prestige" construction projects with low yields, both of which impacts were quickly exhausted.[68] On top of these trends had been superimposed greater expenditures for the armed forces to meet three security crises: provincial rebellions, West Irian annexation, and *konfrontasi* Malaysia, the latter two of which were Sukarno-generated.

The purchasing power of wages and salaries dropped sharply over a decade, and even those with steady jobs might find themselves destitute.[69] Even if the data of rural Java and rural Indonesia looked egalitarian compared with South Asia or Latin America, political and emotional polarization were evident there, if not as a result of Sukarno's own populist rhetoric then in consequence of his encouragement of the Communist Party.

Public finance had gotten way out of hand in 1961, with the effect that estimated (because unpublished) actual deficits in 1964 were almost quadru-

ple the size of projected deficits, and equal in volume to total actual revenue for that year. How long can a government continue to spend twice
what it takes in? Not surprisingly, rates of increase were shooting up, on a
semi-logarithmic scale, for money supply, retail price of cheap rice, consumer price index, black market rate of the rupiah, and weighted index
numbers of nineteen foodstuffs in the Jakarta free market. The last, from a
base of 100 in 1953, by late 1965 shot well beyond 10,000.[70]

Technically these increases did not amount to exponential inflation such
as Germany had suffered in the 1920s and China in the 1940s, which were
arguably major propellants of Nazism in the first case and communism in
the second. That is only to say that inflation was not yet feeding on itself.
But from 1961 through 1964 it was feeding on nearly everything else. The
volume of money and the cost of living doubled every twelve months, and
by the last weeks of 1965 "prices were doubling within a few weeks."[71]

A government so overextended loses its credibility not only with external
creditors but with its own citizens. Indonesia was suffering a series of simultaneous vicious circles. Falling exports led to falling imports of capital
goods, which resulted in falling production. In consequence, government
reserves sank, deficits soared, and inflation spiked, all of which in turn ac-
centuated the foregoing debilitations and exaggerations, thus increasing ve-
locity of circulation of money, hoarding, and speculation. Inflation even appeared in the size of the cabinet, which swelled from 43 ministers in 1959 to
90 by 1965. "Consensus" in such a context offered no real consent, let alone
resolution of basic policy conflicts.

Sukarno had no idea how to get these phenomena under management.
With them, in fact, came the atrophy of controls and the impossibility for
businessmen and fixed income employees to lead a completely honest life.
Gross administrative inefficiency, demoralization, and cynicism followed.
To misery was added bizarre incongruity. Those from societies with better
distribution could barely believe the luxuries enjoyed by a few and deprivation suffered by the many. The social acceptance of national billionnaires at
the palace was a sign of premature and grotesque *embourgeoisement,* preceding rather than following economic development.[72]

By 1964–65, despite all Sukarno's talk about socialization, Indonesia was
becoming thoroughly *laissez-faire,* with the corollary of hypercorruption.[73]
This was obviously not Sukarno's intention but the perverse consequence
of his own failures of leadership, which he could not recognize, name, analyze, or change.

Despite a squatter riot in Kediri in 1961, anti-Chinese riots in Java and
Northern Sumatra in 1963, and many "unilateral actions" for "land reform"
led by the PKI in 1964–65, the question has been asked why there was no

"popular uprising." The question is wrongly conceived, I believe, but the answers to it are interesting just the same: (1) The government had access to overwhelming military force; (2) the PKI was interested in gaining power *without* provoking a massive strategic conflict; (3) indigenous fatalism and other cultural factors inhibited direct challenge to authority; (4) Indonesia's food problems were not on the same order as China's or India's, because of more productive soil and more equable climate; (5) Indonesia's inflation was not yet exponential; and (6) the weakness of the debilitated and starving is often less dangerous than the frustrations of the decently fed.[74]

All of these factors are correctly observed as facts. But they overlook a compounded social reality: the convergence of multiple deprivations and disappointments over time can produce an extremely high level of political flammability. Too many inequities, instabilities, and vulnerabilities for too long make for an overstressed people. Then repressed private compulsions can explode in acute and unpredictable ways. Even the obedient will finally raise their fists. Even the hungry will cut others' throats. Even the disregarded will find a momentary surge of power in crowd identity and anonymous violence.

Many Indonesians rose, indeed, although not "up" in the sense of against top authority. Indonesians in 1965–66 would enact a mass political murder, partly orchestrated but better understood as a vast popular irruption. What is uncontrolled too long leads to the uncontrollable. And what is too easily categorized in retrospect as Suharto's blood-letting should be understood as also caused by the blind raptures of Sukarno's leadership, and by the boiling over of Sukarnoism.

MASS MURDER

Killings were the central fact of Indonesian political life for half a year after September 30, 1965. They were not genocidal, but they were a politicide: attacks on communists—actual, alleged, and suspected. The mass murder was systematic and horrible.[1] How and why did it begin? Who did what to whom? How many died? With what impacts on national consciousness?

The late Sukarno years went far beyond the sentimentality of "shared poverty" to the raw fact of unshareable fears. Widespread deprivation, the historian Onghokham recalls, was accompanied by a strange social excitation, a charismatic clash of norms that he remembers through two extraordinary phenomena. One was the case of a wealthy woman who, on a shopping expedition, complained that her *becak* driver had overcharged her. The argument unresolved, she chose to take it to court. For the hearing, hundreds of trishaw drivers rallied around their comrade. When she went to the session, she was trailed by more than a half mile of thin, grim, leg-muscled men peddling their vehicles and chanting slogans of class exploitation. Newspapers featured the story, with its unmistakable indication of who saw whom as an enemy of the people.

Of far greater dimension was the rural equivalent of this *becak* solidarity. The PKI organized a campaign against the "Seven Devils of the Desa"— roughly "villains of the villages." The seven included almost every identifiable village official or functionary. In late 1963 the PKI launched a "unilateral action" campaign to justify seizures of land by its villagers. Violence naturally followed, especially in East Java, and also in Bali, Central and West Java, and North Sumatra.

Proletarian arousal predictably evokes counter-alert. Ong noted in the same period an extraordinary fervor mounting in the NU, down to its grade schools. This mostly rural and syncretic Muslim organization had a different concept of who might be enemies of the people—notably cadres of the PKI, intermixed in communities everywhere in Java. To identify the danger

22. BUNG KARNO AND A MAY DAY MARCH. The Communist Party of Indonesia raises the image of Sukarno in the company of Marx, Engels, Lenin, and Stalin in Yogyakarta on May 1, 1947. (Gift of Niels Dowes Dekker/author's collection)

and ward off infection, the NU held patriotic meetings and marches. Every day became the equivalent of the Fourth of July, with its Bible waving and flag-strutting—only it was the Qur'an and the red and white Indonesian flag brandished against an immediate enemy: atheistic communism, with its hammer and sickle banner. Eloquent schoolchildren were put on display, rehearsed to motivate their fellows and elders. Some, with extraordinary gifts of impromptu eloquence, led marches to counter-intimidate godless *becak* drivers and to win other lost souls. Often, the poor preaching to the poor. In Ong's well-stocked historical imagination, "It began to look like a children's crusade."[2]

Beyond these layers of class antagonism and culture war were calculations, by serious professionals, of relative armed strength. The PKI had been demanding a "fifth force" since 1964: an "armed people" in addition to the forces of ABRI (Angkatan Bersenjata Republik Indonesia)—the army, navy, marines, and police. In a speech early in 1965, the PKI leader, D. N. Aidit, called for the arming of five million workers and ten million peasants to carry on the war against Malaysia. Chou En-lai came to Indonesia in April for the tenth anniversary of the Bandung Conference and, according to Sukarno, offered arms for the purpose of creating the fifth force. The president, in turn, praised the defense systems of China and North Vietnam for their prominent use of guerrillas. He urged his army commanders to study the fifth force proposal and submit their plans to him.

Perhaps Sukarno only intended to continue balancing internal adversaries by hints of ideology and glints of purpose. He never came to the point of requiring ABRI to accept a fifth force. Nor did he openly arm the PKI, although the air force under Omar Dhani in July began giving short training courses to PKI civilians, and the air vice-marshal himself was later alleged to have flown to Peking in August to negotiate a secret small-arms deal.[3] But Sukarno's experience should have told him that he had created an atmosphere in which threats and feints, even without plans, could produce a *peristiwa*.

George Benson, a huge, smiling Philadelphia Catholic and West Pointer, was concluding three years as military attaché at the American Embassy. During that term he lunched at the German Club, perhaps twenty times in all, with friends in top echelons of the Indonesian military. Frequently he responded to their urgings to ask the commander of Kostrad (the Army Strategic Reserve Command), whose headquarters was near the American Embassy, to join them. Usually General Suharto was reading a magazine, no papers on his desk. Invariably he would answer, in bad English, to Benson's bad Bahasa, "Ibu said I have to be home early today." His excuse: the missus won't let me.

"When I left in July '65," Benson remembers, Lieutenant General Yani, minister/commander of the army, invited him to lunch with three key colleagues and asked him, "What are you going to say to the Pentagon?" Benson answered, "I'm just going to say everything's been going down the tubes for three years. Sukarno and the PKI have the initiative." Three points came back at him fast. One from Major General Parman (first assistant). "I'm only three to five hours behind the PKI. I know what happens in any sensitive meeting." Parman went on to acknowledge that the PKI knew they were penetrated and had organized a small select group for ultra-sensitive strategizing. Two points from Yani himself: "We have 120 battalion commanders, and we appointed them all. They are dependable." Furthermore: "We *have the guns,* and we have kept guns out of their hands. So if there's a clash, we'll wipe them out."

On the night of September 30, Yani was visited by some of his own men with a warning report. But he dismissed them and then "died of his overconfidence," as Benson sees it.[4] Parman also would die that night. Whatever intelligence leads he had, either they, or his understanding of them, fatally lagged behind the moment.

The Movements and the Moment

To understand the circumstances of September 30/October 1, 1965, it does not help to look for a single mastermind, or to single out a master cabal. Reconstruction must be speculative. But to help simplify a power struggle in the midst of national misery, we may speak of four activist groups.

(1) *The palace circle:* At its center were Sukarno and his suave, adroit foreign minister, Soebandrio. The watchword from the top was "steer to the left." Closer ties to communist China were central to their strategy.

(2) *The council of generals:* Opposing the palace circle was the council of generals. General Yani and his closest advisors surely met to go over more than the promotions and appointments that they acknowledged managing together. They knew they were in a vital struggle with the PKI, and they certainly did not intend to be on the short side of a deadly resolution.

(3) *The politburo:* Sympathetic to the palace but fired up with its own designs was the politburo. At its core, the five PKI leaders, D. N. Aidit at the helm, sometimes considered themselves saviors of the people, like the five mythical Pendawa brothers. None of them survived, nor did any strategic plan of theirs. Such a paper would have been unlikely anyway, given suspicions, jeopardy, and a tendency in all groups toward tactical-reactive thinking. They knew they were being infiltrated and invigilated. They, or some of them, took ultra-sequestered council among themselves. Numerous previous actions suggest that they felt they were prevailing with their anti-imperialist slogans and policies. Eccentric as those were to mainline Marxist theory, eclectic as their exponents chose to be to survive in Javanese dynamics, they did believe that history was with them. At least the inertia of the semi-decade was with them. They had more to gain from patience than precipitancy; they should have remembered the disastrously premature communist initiatives of 1926 and 1948. Even so, they believed that historical inevitability needs nudges. Their mass popularity, including their own padded and redundant numbers, apparently helped convince them that this was the moment for a special push.

(4) *The progressive officers:* This group may have helped the communists believe so. Executions later obliterated some of the officers. Torture, extorted confessions, and recantations darkened others' memories, and no planning document survives to enlighten us as to their evaluation of assets or precise purposes. Their actions, led by Lieutenant Colonel Untung, a battalion commander of the palace guard, seem overconfident, inconsistent,

politically immature. But they are not the first group of colonels so to behave in modern world history.

Beyond these four groups stood Major General Suharto, the ultimate
outsider, commander of Kostrad, to which elite battalions of infantry brigades were assigned as required. He had no affinity with Sukarno nor any
special Islamic conviction at that time with which to oppose him. He despised disorder. He prized opportunity; but making way for himself financially had, years earlier, brought General Yani down on him. So no affinity
there either. The only principal of ensuing events with whom Suharto
talked on the night of September 30 was Colonel Abdul Latief, in the hospital where Suharto was preoccupied with attending to his son Tommy, who
had been scalded by burning soup.

The Indonesian public learned by radio after 7 AM on October 1 that

23. MASS GATHERING OF PKI. D. N. Aidit, their paramount leader, addresses the
45th anniversary gathering of the Communist Party of Indonesia on May 23, 1965.
Just before the events of September 30, the PKI claimed 27 million members for the
party and its mass organizations—the largest such entity in any country without a
formal Communist government. (Ipphos Photo Archives)

something extraordinary was afoot. The announcement was from the September 30th Movement (Gerakan September Tigapuluh; later labeled negatively as Gestapu, or neutrally as G30S). They had arrested members of the council of generals, who, they said, were sponsored by the CIA and had been preparing to carry out a coup during the assembly of regional detachments scheduled for October 5, Armed Forces Day. President Sukarno and his policies were safe under the G30S's protection. Among other announcements that followed during the afternoon was one by Air Force commander Dhani, putting the air force behind "all progressive-revolutionary movements."

At about 9 PM, however, a brief speech by General Suharto of Kostrad announced that six generals, including the army commander, had been kidnapped by a "counter-revolutionary movement." He himself had taken over command of the army, which together with the navy and police would crush the September 30th Movement. Suharto issued an ultimatum to Halim Air Force Base, the headquarters of G30S, at which were gathered Sukarno, Dhani, Aidit, and others. They evacuated and dispersed. Suharto took control of the base after dawn on October 2.

Of the seven infantry battalions in Central Java, five were under rebel command by October 1. They were overcome by Suharto's forces in a short while. Suharto's veiled and successful command to Sukarno to leave Halim on October 1, and Sukarno's obedience to it, changed all power relationships that had existed during "guided democracy." All contending forces, however, including Suharto's, avowed that they were protecting President Sukarno and the Indonesian Revolution.

Six generals had died by bayonet or bullet. Plus a lieutenant, aide to General Nasution; a nearby policeman; and, after several days, the mortally wounded Irma, five-year-old daughter of Nasution. Her father escaped death by climbing over a wall and falling with a broken ankle into the garden of the Iraqi ambassador. Nasution had sharp differences with Yani but was aghast to learn the next morning of Yani's death, among others. He wrote an order to "free" Sukarno, to put Major General Suharto in charge of all operations, and to inform the people of the "true facts."[5] This frantic attempt to regain initiative from an unclear power position was symptomatic of a universal confusion that was slow to clarify itself. Muddled pronouncements and patriotic rallying cries by radio from the G30S movement were followed, contradicted, and silenced by announcements directed by Suharto's headquarters. The latter included incendiary lies that the rebels had gouged out the generals' eyes and had castrated them in the presence of Gerwani, the PKI women's movement. From Kostrad headquarters, overlooking Merdeka Square from the east, Suharto could control the presidential palace on the north of the square, the radio station on the west, and telecommunications on the south. Soon he controlled all of Java.[6]

The Indonesian military, in its twenty years of turbulence, had gone through rebellions, mutinies, unauthorized initiatives, passive resistance to authority, and multifarious political in-fighting, but it had never experienced cold-blooded murder among its own leaders.[7] Now, in a national atmosphere of deprivation, escalating fear, and mutual mortal suspicion, murder of one's neighbor would become for months a way of life.

Who Started It?

The first apparently new word in many years on "what really happened" is from Colonel Abdul Latief, released in 2000 after thirty-five years in prison. Actually, Latief's defense document, a strongly aggressive one, is twenty-two years old. Only after thirteen years in prison was he tried for being part of the September 30th Movement. In his defense he made two historic accusations. First, that he had briefed Suharto himself on the plot of the "council of generals" to overthrow Sukarno and on the September 30th Movement's plans to take preventive action. A Cornell-based master of Southeast Asian languages and cultures, Ben Anderson, adopts this line as true. He interprets Latief to mean that Suharto deliberately let the movement start operations without previously reporting its activities to his superiors, Nasution and Yani. The reason: to let his rivals at the top of the command chain be eliminated.

This interpretation credits Suharto with cold-blooded calculation, which, in general, is apt enough. Latief may have indeed underestimated Suharto's guile. Perfect timing in a proactive sense, however, is highly implausible to attribute to anyone in those circumstances. To the degree that he suggests that Suharto made everything go his way, Anderson strains credulity. Latief's second accusation follows on the first: that the "real council of generals" threatening the president was not those surrounding Yani and Nasution—a group too contradictory and vague to have existed—but was the group surrounding Suharto, which later came to power. But the post hoc fallacy is evident here.

Latief's endurance under terrible treatment was admirable; and, under trial, his accusatory courage about G30S killings was remarkable. Yet all that was new in 2000 was his response to the question from Ben Anderson, "How did you feel on the evening of October 1?" "I felt I had been betrayed."[8] But so did everybody else. Each prime figure identifying the national interest with himself could have been actually betrayed from several directions at once. Whatever was said between Latief and Suharto at the hospital on September 30, it was not pivotal. Suharto was a loner. He was not one of Yani's inner circle. He may have been silently critical or even contemptuous of Sukarno, but he voiced nothing about it. He did not plot with anybody, in the sense of drawing strength from a clique. He smiled with everybody. He was therefore not on the list of anti-Sukarno, anti-PKI activists seized by the September 30th Movement. Latief may with justification feel that Suharto was two-faced. But to listen and nod and to keep one's own counsel was a good way to survive.[9]

Most of the years Latief spent in prison, Anderson spent barred from Indonesia, a country to which he had devoted brilliant and loving study. Suharto's minions did not like his view that September 30/October 1 was just "an internal army affair." For them, Anderson's point of view was too similar to that of the PKI, expressed, for instance, by its number two leader, Njoto, to Japanese journalists on October 20, 1965—a protective rationale that said, as at Madiun in 1948, nobody here but us chickens, while it was clear they were foxing the coop.[10]

What of the opposite view: the later official position of Suharto and the army that the PKI masterminded the events of that night? Their accusatory motive was to discredit the PKI and wipe out its influence in Indonesia, while supplying post facto justification of army-incited or army-assisted murders of communists. Despite the unhappy analogy with 1948, there is nothing approaching proof that the military activists led by Colonel Untung were primarily motivated or manipulated by PKI leaders. These progressive officers were very possibly buzzing among themselves on any or all of these motivating themes: puritan revulsion at the lifestyle of Yani and his group, proletarian sympathy for the condition of the poor, and professional ambition, not uncommon among colonels, to do better what their superiors were doing badly.

At the far end of strained possibility is the view that President Sukarno himself engineered the wiping out of men who stood between himself and the goals of NASAKOM. Only one uncorroborated and inconsistent witness holds this opinion. Sukarno's failure to attend the funeral of the generals was seen as a major political mistake but does not of itself implicate him in their murder. By errors of policy and perspective he had helped produce the crisis, and he made many mistakes during the crisis itself. The worst of these was going to Halim Air Force Base with Aidit and Dhani. Any one of his wives would have been better and less compromising company on that night; and Dewi continues to complain and grieve that it was not she. She did talk him out of going to Madiun, which would have been utterly damning.[11] Sukarno was about to fire Yani, and possibly he had often wished Nasution dead. He was indeed a plotter by character. But he was not a killer. As a leader, he had sown obscurantism. Now he reaped deadly confusion.

In a situation of mutually intense suspicion among four activist groups, the progressive officers, in order to preempt the expected move of the council of generals, launched their own initiative, encouraged by, or pulling along, the politburo. If that were to be called a preventive coup d'etat, then what followed from Suharto, successfully, was a counter-preventive coup d'etat.[12] The irony is that the least "active" of the principals, Suharto, prevailed.

Jakarta, Java, and much of Indonesia then went into a giant social spasm. Sukarno and most of his ideas wound up on the ash heap of history. Aidit's five PKI leaders, instead of becoming midwives to the future, left their followers as widows. Those whom the Marxists believed should bear the pain and pay the "overhead of historical progress" instead became its landlords and contractors. Everyone's relationship to anyone who partook of the national macro-tension was now changed.

The simplest summary of what followed across months is that the army and the armed elements of NU (Ansor) and of the Nationalist Party (PNI Youth) led a zealous population, or a merely willing or fearfully compliant one, in wiping out the PKI. The first full-scale massacre of communists was in Aceh in early October. Muslim leaders orchestrated it, with the army making some attempts to moderate their fury. In West Java, as few as 10,000 may have been killed, but where communism was more deeply entrenched the fatalities were enormous. In Central Java the balance of power was extremely precarious, and five battalions there supported the September 30th Movement. In East Java civilians took the lead in attacking the PKI, as the struggle continued to move eastward. In Bali, finally, massacres ran out of hand, as they had in Aceh. They were not expressly condoned by the military in Jakarta.[13] Just the same, local military support within Bali was fully evident in logistics and in spirit.[14]

Sukarno spoke of the coup attempt as "a ripple in the ocean of the revolution." He remonstrated, pleaded, and appointed an investigatory commission; but his anguish for nation and people was largely ineffective. He made the large tactical mistake of claiming that communist "sacrifices in Indonesia's struggle for freedom were greater than the sacrifices of other parties and other groups." Again and again men of diverse motives evoked Sukarno's name as Father and Leader, while their deeds eroded his power. "Sometimes I feel that I am being farted upon, brothers."[15]

Earlier in 1965, Aidit had said, "Politics continues to move to the left, but stomachs move to the right."[16] Now Aidit was on the move to rally and restrain the PKI, then to save his own life. He encountered great difficulties establishing contact with PKI activists in Central Java. He tried to travel back to Jakarta, as a Sukarno minister without portfolio, to attend a cabinet meeting in early October, but he could get no transport. Njoto, a politburo comrade and fellow minister, attended, was arrested on leaving the palace, and was later shot.

General Suharto summoned the commander of the fourth infantry brigade of Kostrad, Colonel Yasir Hadibroto, and dispatched him with a unit to Central Java to "deal with" Aidit. To track their prey they used Aidit's personal bodyguard, who reestablished contact with the unsuspecting Aidit and escorted him to his last hiding place, in a village not far from Solo. There, Yasir's men arrested him on November 22. A major from Semarang drove down to suggest detention while they informed Suharto. Yasir feigned agreement, put the major in front of a convoy, and then eluded it. He ordered his men to strap Aidit up, stand him in front of a well, and shoot him dead. They threw the body down the well, covered it with leaves, burnt them, and planted banana trees over the site.

When the major found out, he said, "That's terrible. Someone will have to answer for this." "Why?" Yasir responded. "He's been dealt with. This is a time of war, isn't it?" Yasir went to Yogya two days later for a meeting with Suharto, described the whole operation to him, and asked, "Is this what you meant when you said we should 'deal with' him?" Suharto smiled and said nothing.[17]

Blood-Letting

Ali Al-Gadri, over eighty, stands erect, with a glinting eye and sharply defined chin, lips, and, particularly, nose. He is descended from chiefs of the Arab community in Surabaya, was an associate of Sjahrir in the revolution, became ambassador to Burma. Ali went into business in the 1950s, and in 1957, when the Sukarno government confiscated all Dutch assets, was assigned the largest Dutch commercial property in Surabaya. From November 1965 he remembers seeing forty to fifty people kneeling before a long trench two meters deep, which they had been forced to dig. They remained passive while a hundred people shot, stabbed, or clubbed them to death. Ali is still amazed. With those odds they could have tried fleeing or died fighting. But they meekly took their deaths.

"Nrima," says his old friend Norma Zecha. "The Javanese way. *Accept.*" She recalls those days. "Our guard, our front door porter . . . was such a nice man, he was so nice to my little son. But that time? He went to my mother and asked permission at night to go out and join the killing . . . Otherwise, they would call him a communist . . . He would come home, his

sword wet with blood . . . They are *fanatik,* the Muslims here. They do what their *ulama* tell them. They do it exactly as they are told."[18]

Norma remembers when the terror began in Pasuruan, an hour east of Surabaya, with an announcement from the central mosque, an elegant white and green structure, the gift of Ali Al-Gadri's grandfather. The announcer demanded to know of the Muslim men in the community if they were really men, or only women. They could show which by killing communists, or by refusing to do so. The killing lasted for about two weeks. At the factory chaired by Norma's husband, instigators posted lists of "communists" to be killed. He intervened in some cases. But when the worker who had taught Norma to play guitar asked for his intercession, her husband was in Jakarta. Learning that, he said goodbye, he would not see her again. They killed him, cut off his head, and stuck it on a pole outside the factory. "All he had done was play guitar for the communist cultural group, Lekra."

A watchman at the factory had incurred enemies. He was not political at all, but he was a marked man. One day he appeared at Norma's house and ran in. "It was the first time I actually *smelled* fear in a human being." He tried to hide under their Confucian altar. "I told him get out of there . . . He had a gun with him. He said he would take a few of them with him."

"I had had enough. I called up the local military commander. I told him to get over here and stop this! What kind of an army officer was he if he couldn't stop this killing? Pretty soon he screeched into the compound with four armed men. They took the watchman away . . . for safety, and next day he made a speech against the killing. Later he told my husband I was a vicious woman when I got mad . . . I had been calm for two weeks, but I broke down the next day."

One of the killing places was right across the street in a big field with a graveyard at one end, including the Kwie family grave. Previously, the area had been seized by the military and built up in commercial ways. The Muslim leaders told Norma to keep her little children at the back of the house, so they would not see or hear things. But nobody could escape the tension. Norma's daughter, nearing forty, tells her she still has nightmares about those times. "The bodies, a lot of them, were dumped in the river," Norma says. "A friend of mine didn't believe it, but she went and looked and saw them. Epidemics started. The bodies floated out to the ocean. People refused to eat seafood for a long time. They didn't know what they could catch, or what they would think, or feel like."[19]

Clifford Geertz had first been to Pare, in easternmost Central Java, in 1952. Reflecting on over four decades of anthropology, he concludes, "It is necessary . . . to be satisfied with swirls, confusions, inconstant connections;

clouds collecting, clouds dispersing. There is no general story to be told, no synoptic picture to be had."[20] He went back to Pare in 1971, and from a retired Nationalist Party leader got a vivid recollection of the killings six years before.

"Everyone here was terrified. A Communist leader's head was hung up in the doorway of his headquarters. Another's was hung on the footbridge in front of his house with a cigarette stuck between his teeth. There were legs and arms and torsos every morning in the irrigation canals. Penises were nailed to telephone poles. Most of the killing was by throat cutting and stabbing with bamboo spears . . . I myself am as anti-Communist as I always was. But the real hatred, the murdering and the being murdered, was a matter between Muslim militants and Communist ones. Sukarno people, like me, were, in the end, really just bystanders. Like, in the end, Sukarno himself." In 1986, Geertz again returned to Pare. This time, he found "a commercialization of town life at least as pervasive, and nearly as obsessive, as its politicization once had been. Buying and selling . . . replaced getting ready for doomsday as the dominant preoccupation of just about everyone."[21]

In Jakarta a prominent journalist remembers a female university student coming to him in tears. Her own classmates, male and female, were determining who was communist among them and exterminating them. The journalist does not remember any advice that he had offered for the situation.[22] There was, perhaps, mutual consolation in speaking about, and listening to, descent into inhumanity in arbitrary, sudden, and final ways.

The blood-letting proceeded to Bali. Between December 1965 and early 1966 an estimated 80,000 people, roughly five percent of the population, were killed.[23] In the minds of Western tourists and armchair travelers, there still exists an image of Bali —created in the 1930s by Margaret Mead, Gregory Bateson, Miguel Covarrubias, Walter Spies, and Colin McPhee—as an enchanted land of aesthetes at peace with themselves and with nature. From confluent friendships of anthropologist, psychiatrist, journalist, choreographer, and musicologist arose charming images of social harmony that survive seven decades later.[24]

Geoffrey Robinson, as a discerning historian of modern Bali, dismisses political and journalistic accounts tinged with such exoticism. It is too easy to fuse the Balinese PKI who dressed in white burial robes and serenely faced death with the suicidal royal family who, also dressed in white and purified, resisted the Dutch in 1906 and 1908, and with its smaller repetition of 1946 during the revolution. Robinson insists on the primary importance of the "political economy of violence" developed in the twentieth century.[25] He quotes Colonel Sarwo Edhie on a distinction between Central Java,

24. BALINESE VILLAGE FROM THE AIR. This pre-1950 shot captures an enduring image of wet rice fields, a Balinese Hindu temple complex as the heart of the
village, and rooftops of houses and palm trees. Such apparent calm would be shattered by the killing of tens of thousands of Balinese Communists in 1965–66. (Gift
of Niels Douwes Dekker/author's collection)

where "I was concerned to encourage people to crush the Gestapu," and
Bali, where eagerness to crush was so great that the military had to prevent anarchy. Bringing order meant ensuring that only PKI were killed,
and killed systematically. That required logistics, and Robinson documents
them. He affirms that "in this context of cultivated anticommunist hysteria,
the fuses of Bali's historical conflicts over land, politics, religion and culture
were easily ignited."[26]

   In demystifying Bali and showing its dark side, Robinson succeeds so
powerfully that he undermines the force of his efforts also to convict
Suharto and the army of "orchestrating" the killings and to demonstrate
American "complicity" in the massacre. His own evidence makes clear that
Suharto's army was involved in channeling the killings away from anarchy

and in supporting them logistically to their grim conclusion. But the army did not need to conceive, compose, or score the murders in Bali, let alone orchestrate them entirely. They began there, as elsewhere, spontaneously. They increased, as elsewhere, with propaganda's incitation from many directions, including from a Jakarta that was now in new hands. They involved, as elsewhere, PNI-backed gangs and NU-affiliated Ansor groups. Additive here, however, and basic to Bali, was the awakening of Balinese Hindus. The leader, Ida Bagus Oka, told them: "There can be no doubt [that] the enemies of our revolution are also the cruelest enemies of religion, and must be eliminated and destroyed down to the roots."[27]

A body floating down the river may be seen by many people. What if some of them are counting, and several of them are reporting? Then one dead person becomes many. Bodies dumped in isolated forests, and pelted by tropical rain in the acidity of decaying plant material in a year or two may not even be bones. Then many dead people become none. A close count of the Indonesian killings of 1965–66 was difficult from the beginning, and impossible at the end. In the first score of years after that enormous social convulsion, thirty-nine serious estimates of the dead were attempted. They ranged all the way from 78,000 (too early; Sukarno commissioned the report for the sake of stabilizing his tottering regime) to 2,000,000 (also too early, probably reflecting the traumatized fear among communists who were the chief target of the killings). Ben Anderson, who generated an estimate of 200,000 in 1966, by 1985 adopted a range of 500,000 to 1,000,000. Between his first lower bound and his last upper one run the varying figures of the others.[28]

When empirical evidence is lacking—bodies are gone and any documents are unlikely to have survived—all is guesswork, or at worst, political argument. The United States Embassy, with no eyewitnesses, at the time came up with a consensus estimate of 300,000.[29] The ambassador many years later regretted transmitting that figure, which he regarded as too high and as indirectly influenced by the pressures of journalistic appetite. My own instinct has been to use a median guess of a half million dead, within a range that could be a quarter million lower or higher. Robert Cribb, in his latest study, reminds us that of the "fear, anger, sorrow and despair that surge . . . through the bodies of those who know they are to die soon . . . cold statistics tell us nothing."[30]

To survive as a communist also involved fear, anger, sorrow, and despair. Amnesty International in 1977 numbered political prisoners—PKI cadres and others trained in or suspected of involvement in party affairs—at "about one million." The Indonesian government, between 1981 and 1990, gave figures of between 1.6 and 1.8 million former prisoners "at large" in

25. COMMUNISM SALUTES FEUDALISM. Marching Communists in Bali on April 4, 1948, honor the nobleman Sukawati, president of the Dutch-sponsored "State of East Indonesia." Lieutenant Governor General Van Mook would regret resurrecting Balinese rajas like Sukawati—"a bunch of expensive racing dogs—quite useless." (Geoffrey Robinson, *The Dark Side of Paradise*, p. 175; photograph gift of Niels Douwes Dekker/author's collection)

society.[31] Together, the numbers of the executed and the incarcerated, probably over two million, convey a massive and systematic campaign of extermination, suppression, and stigmatization. After the first months of frenzy, those with tenuous involvement had little reason to fear for their lives or freedom. But neither they nor fellow citizens of different convictions could ever forget or ignore the fact that Indonesia went through a political detoxification campaign of savage momentum and sweeping proportions, with vigilance afterward sustained for three decades. To have a PKI parent, an Indonesian political scientist said to me, was the local equivalent of original sin. In Toraja, far from the center of national political action and not a place of regional PKI convulsions, chance conversation thirty years after the killings could still identify someone who was once involved with the communists, or someone descended from such a person.[32]

However many communists or their sympathizers were killed, some must surely have died on the other side. But the fifth force had never possessed weapons, and there is no plausible evidence of an armed PKI coup, as distinct from a power play at the top that unrealistically relied on the air force and sympathetic units of the army. A few PKI surely defended themselves, and there was certainly occasional mortality among their attackers. But aside from the monument to the generals killed on that first night, I am aware of no gravestones of heroes who "died valiantly in the extermination of the Communist threat of 1965–66."

Any real accounting would also have to acknowledge that "some mistakes were made" and "some different matters were also resolved." A myth gained momentum in the American press, briefly repeated in the *New York Times* in 1998, that the main targets were the Indonesian Chinese. Not true. The main targets were communists. But the Sukarno-Soebandrio outreach to Peking in foreign policy did not make things easier for Chinese in Indonesia. And, in a time when political scores were being lethally settled, some Chinese were probably killed so that the debts owed them could be forgotten.

These were not, it is well to remember, bureaucratic killings over a period of years. No worldview governed, as under the bizarre convictions promulgated by Hitler and Pol Pot. No typewriters chattered to document the realization of the great Third Reich or the Khmer Rouge purification plans. There are no chambers full of skulls, as in many provinces of Cambodia. No cartons were filled with human hair or teeth extracted for their metal fillings, as in the relentlessly commercial pursuits of the Nazis. There is precious little, nearly nil, by way of photographic evidence, again unlike those two other regimes, whose pedantry nearly equaled the dimensions of their sadism. What may have been recorded on film the army later purged from the files of news agencies. That left just a lot of people dead and gone forever. Unmarked.[33] Not unmourned, yet not ceremonially memorialized, for that would have drawn suspicion on the mourners.

A hesitant search has begun for mass graves by genetic and spiritual survivors of the era, but little that is systematic has to my knowledge yet been identified. This was a pre-modern economy, not able to afford such luxuries as gas chambers. The killings were mostly face to face, one by one; very often the killers and the killed knew each other well. A strangely intimate frenzy of murder. The army sometimes tried to make it easier in Bali by trucking people from village A to village B, and vice versa, so that one need not slit one's neighbor's throat.

Was the United States Complicit in Mass Murder?

In the light of the Dulles brothers' debacle of the decade previous, and covert interventions of the United States against anti-American governments elsewhere during the Cold War, it is reasonable to inquire what role the United States played in the critical events of 1965–66 in Indonesia.[34]

In 1957 the U.S. government had missed the chance to mediate on West Irian, an initiative recommended by Ambassador John Allison. Instead, the United States deeply damaged its own credibility with its military intervention and attempted destabilization of Sukarno's regime in 1957–58. To clean up its mess, the State Department sent as ambassador Howard Palfrey Jones, a man of acute intelligence, humane values, and patient good will. To win Sukarno's friendship back for the United States, he spent seven unflagging years, the longest service ever of any American ambassador to Indonesia. He failed. Worse, his personal rapport with Sukarno obscured from him his own lack of success. Still worse, by accepting Sukarno's taunts and belittlings in semi-public gatherings and by not walking out of Sukarno's "to hell with your aid" speech, he appeared to many Indonesians and international observers to have become a political panderer to the Great Leader of the Revolution.[35]

When finally Jones was replaced by Marshall Green in late July 1965, American influence, too long unfocused from Washington, too long dissipated in Jakarta, was nearly nil. General Nasution was counseling the United States "to stand aside while the Indonesians iron out their difficulties."[36] On the morning of October 1, 1965, Embassy personnel reacted with genuine surprise to what was going on and did not begin to get a grip on it for several days.[37] One of the staff blurted out to a local counterpart "Who's Suharto?"—a gaffe that would be long treasured by Indonesian sophisticates as a sign of irremediable American ignorance about their country.[38] It was also a tangible, if trivial, sign of America's noninvolvement in what happened that night.

The harder question is about degree of involvement in what followed. The American Embassy, top to bottom, approved of the shift of power and, in keeping with Cold War strategy, supported the army in its encouragement of popular retaliation upon the communists. But the limits of American influence must be borne in mind. The allegation that "U.S. officials . . . had two months to prevent a full-scale massacre in Bali, but made no effort to do so" is an interesting theoretical challenge.[39] But it defies the pragmatics of the era to imagine an American government, ever more deeply and fatally involved in fighting communists in Indochina, willing and able to save communists in Bali.

A more troubling issue is that of information exchange. Whatever hit lists were compiled during that period would be unlikely to have survived. The PKI, certainly, had its own lists. In the particularly jealous righteousness of those who owned the term "proletariat," it readily defined its class adversaries as "enemies of the people" and therefore opponents of the forces of history.

The surviving ABRI leadership is known to have compiled lists. Colonel George Benson recalls the key role of General Panggabean, a Batak Protestant who had fought against the Dutch and the Darul Islam revolt. He was made "responsible for purging the ranks of the Armed Forces of Communist sympathizers." In 1969 he became commander of Kopkamtib (Operational Command for the Restoration of Security and Order) and was promoted to commander of ABRI and minister of defense and security, serving from 1973 to 1978. The precondition for his ascent was success in 1965–66. Panggabean proudly explained his promotion checklist: was the man a good soldier? was he a good nationalist? was he a believer (as proper to Pancasila, the five principles) in the Divine Being? Three checks were reassuring. But an atheistic communist was not going to get that third check. A good Muslim or a good Christian would get it. Such was the political filter for an army in crisis. Panggabean went on in the 1980s to be a propagator of Pancasila.[40]

Purging the whole society, of course, was a far larger task than purging the army. There can be little doubt that elements of the army had been compiling lists of potential adversaries, particularly in the light of PKI's promotion of a fifth force. PKI membership rolls, when not already known, could be bought, stolen, or captured. And where national rolls were imprecise, local knowledge was likely to be detailed. So ABRI leadership, shocked by murders in its top echelons, began moving into a national response with ready assistance from many elements in society.

Through September 1965, under siege, the American Embassy staff had been ready to burn its own files if necessary; but after October it was ready to share some of them. Without question, a maximum number of 5,000 names was collected by Robert Martens, a sovietologist and PKI expert in the Embassy's political section, who passed them on to Kim Adhyatman, then aide to Adam Malik, later foreign minister and vice president. From Malik they went to "Suharto's people." In 1990 Kathy Kadane, a journalist, conducted aggressive interviews with Ambassador Marshall Green, subsequent Ambassador Edward Masters, and former Deputy Chief of Mission

Jack Lydman.[41] Martens himself conceded the transfer of information but stressed that it was nonclassified and was "not party rank and file." All of it came from the Indonesian communist press and consisted of senior cadre names—a few thousand at most out of the 3.5 million members claimed by the party. To Kadane's presumptive charge of complicity in murder, Masters emphatically replied, "At the time names were passed, to my knowledge, we were not aware of the killings."[42] How much this American Embassy data added to or was duplicative of natively generated ABRI data is impossible to know. Most likely it represented a reinforcement of a small fraction of the already known. It was never a sufficient cause, far less a necessary condition, of the killings. But it could not have avoided adding fuel to the fire of mass murder.

A volume of the *Foreign Relations of the United States* which includes Indonesia, compiled from 1964 to 1968, was selectively declassified and carefully edited with an eye toward publication in 1998–99, as Suharto's regime fell, only to be withheld from release when Megawati came to power in 2001. An inadvertent shipment to Government Printing Office bookstores, however, enabled freedom-of-information activists to put it on their website. The Indonesia segments show that on November 13, 1965, the embassy passed on to Washington information from Indonesian police that "from 50 to 100 PKI members were being killed every night in East and Central Java."[43] The statement by Masters that "at the time names were passed, to my knowledge, we were not aware of the killings" may be taken to mean that names were passed on—possibly as early as mid-October—before the embassy's knowledge of the killings was made clear and documented by mid-November. His last words to Kadane were, "I really insist, Kathy, that [if] you're taking the line that we were giving these names . . . to the Indonesians so that they could go out and catch them and kill them, you're absolutely wrong."[44] The statement of an honorable man must be respected. But possible indirect consequences of passing along such information at such a time were not beyond the imagination of diplomatic professionals. Even if the intent of the embassy long under siege is construed as just politically defensive, its impact fed indigenous aggression.

Through November 1965, Ambassador Green's dispatches show huge uncertainties over requests to implement aid to the Indonesian army while Sukarno was still obviously and vocally head of state. The embassy's lack of close connection with Major General Suharto and its faltering resolve both refute the suggestions of former Air Vice-Marshal Dhani and ex-Foreign Minister Soebandrio, on their release from prison in the twenty-first century, that Suharto was a puppet of the CIA.[45]

By December 2, however, Green confirmed an earlier concurrence to provide Adam Malik with 50 million rupiah for Kap-Gestapu, an "army-inspired by civilian-staffed action group . . . still carrying [the] burden of current repressive efforts targeted against PKI, particularly in Central Java." Green and his staff expressly wanted to endorse Malik's role in the army's anti-PKI efforts and promote cooperation between him and the army. "The chances of detection or subsequent revelation of our support in this instance are as minimal as any black bag operation can be."[46]

Malik went on to become Indonesia's senior minister for political affairs, president of the UN General Assembly in 1971, and Suharto's vice president and foreign minister from 1978 to 1983. I interviewed him at his home before his death in 1984: a grave, handsome, heavy-browed, small, and measured man, surrounded by classical Indonesian sculptures and works of art. His image and his eminence are hard to reconcile with his accepting a "black bag" of money from the U.S. Embassy for the purpose of wiping out communists. But he did it.

Ambassador Green's memoirs are laconic on the killings and show no *schadenfreude* or comfort in the disaster of adversaries. "We rather lucked out in Indonesia . . . It was indeed all rather miraculous."[47] Sukarno vigorously repeated his "go to hell" slogan as late as August 17, 1966.[48] Overt help from America to the regime that succeeded him was tentative until 1967. Green's dispatches, however, prove that by November 1965 he preferred covertly to try to help American "luck" along, rather than leave affairs wholly to chance.

Just the same, money and information from the American Embassy were puny and post facto in the larger scheme of things. They do not support North American or other conspiracy theorists in defining the September 30th Movement and Suharto's subsequent rise to power as artifacts of the Central Intelligence Agency. To attribute a half million murders to the CIA as its greatest secret success is a monstrously mistaken compliment.[49] No concrete evidence exists that is in any way proportionate to the charge. To insist on it is to adopt a perverse delusion of American omnipotence.

Indonesia in 1965–66, unlike Rwanda and Bosnia in the 1990s, has had no UN inquiry or International Criminal Tribunal. And, unlike Chile and South Africa—leaders among two dozen nations who adopted truth commissions—there is no serious pursuit of such a form of reconciliation. Victims too many, perpetrators too many, interests too contrary to truth, and times too long gone by.[50] Back then, Cold War scorekeeping was in play. There was no need of a central hate-inflamer as appeared in Rwanda and Serbia. Indonesian society was a tinderbox of deprivation and defensive anxiety. Any of several kinds of provocative action would have ignited a bonfire of fear, retributive anger, and preventive extermination.

Causes and Consequences of the Killings

No mass murders would have taken place without the precipitating actions of G30S. No G30S would have taken shape without a deeply divided and inflamed polity. No such critical inflammations would have erupted without Sukarno's prolonged, contradictory tactics of steer left politically and fuse all rhetorically—which aroused contending interests in contrary ways. Dramatically different groups were tempted, and some became determined, to grab the steering wheel. Maybe General Yani and his intimates on the council of generals would have tried to do so and wrench it to the right. Certainly Colonel Untung and his progressive officers tried to preempt that possibility and to fix the leftward course. They miscalculated and paid for doing so. The PKI leaders in the politiburo, whatever their degree of intuitive or implied commitment, or even secret verbal encouragement to the progressive officers, also paid, with their lives. And so did perhaps a half million other persons.

How could such terrible human cost have been avoided? One could wish that irrational economic policies under guided democracy had not produced scarifying inflation, grotesque enrichment of a few, increasing deaths from hunger, and a dreadful sense that things had veered out of control. In late 1965, in response to this crisis, Sukarno chose to "steer left" and step on the gas, with the result that the nation landed in the ditch. For that extreme state of insecurity, if one must name one name, Sukarno is managerially responsible. For its extreme resolution, if one must name one name, Suharto is managerially responsible.

But naming single names for such enormous events would be simpleminded. In Sukarno's defense, the weak national integration could be traced to the repressive and divisive colonial policy of the Dutch, as well as to geography—the nation's archipelagic fragmentation. And in Suharto's defense, tens or arguably hundreds of thousands of Indonesians willingly participated in the killings.

National nonintegration is common in tropical postcolonial countries. But what shall be said of national frenzy and acceptance of killing? The phenomenon may look strange from the vantage point of a technical culture, more at ease with causing death by bombs and missiles—deaths of persons whose faces one does not see.[51] Distinctive in it are the factors of *nrima* and *amok*. *Nrima*, or passive acceptance, is perhaps easier to understand, especially at levels of society with little education or access to modern information. If Islamic ideas were overriding, the concept of *nasib* prevailed: destiny, one's prescribed lot in life rather than personhood.[52] For those involved in a Hindu-Buddhist sense of time, karmic cycles could not be avoided. In Java and Bali, where the overwhelming proportion of communists lived and were murdered, a strong sense of fate existed. The fact that Islamic righteous jihad and Sivaite destructive purification existed alongside historical passivity is not contradictory. In all-encompassing mortal danger, one man was moved to wield the knife, and the other to yield to it.

Amok, which is invoked by some Indonesians themselves, is a less-than-satisfying explanation for mass events. It has more explanatory power for depressed males who feel a manic urge to murder, in which they may kill many they happen to encounter and then may submit peacefully and guiltily to being summarily killed or finally judged. *Amok* at this individual level is clinically describable. Collective *amok* is conceivable but cannot be contained in clinical description. It suggests the warrior fury with which Muslims of Mindanao hurled themselves against American troops in the Philippine-American war over a century ago, at which time the corrupted term "run amuck" entered the American language. Soldiers, in the face of overwhelming odds, chose suicidal violence as a military tactic. "Both forms of *amok* involve the redemption of honor by frenzied violence resulting in the death of the *amokker,*" according to Robert Cribb. But death lists and clandestine killing grounds do not fit this description.[53] That does not rule out the notion of mob blood lust, fearfully and/or vengefully motivated. While not at all specifically Indonesian, it may be descriptively apt for many of the half-year of killings that occurred.

An Indonesian historian, considering carefully the killings in Jombang and Kediri, allows that individual cases like *amok* may have occurred—as when an executioner had victims lined up, started wielding his blade, and was seized with frenzy—but that the carrying home of penises, ears, and fingers was certainly not done in an eruptive state of consciousness. *Amok* is characterized by suddenness and panic. Enough quantity of slaughter and of grisly order existed here to stand aside from *amok* altogether.[54]

Those who would rely on *amok* with regard to the mass murders in Java, Bali, and elsewhere in 1965–66 may be resorting to an escape from blame: "We couldn't help it." The desire for collective self-exculpation is understandable. But the better part of historical understanding and national reconciliation would be for those involved to acknowledge whatever needs to be acknowledged: that they personally took lives under cover of darkness or group anonymity; that they allowed themselves to be organized by army officers, mullahs, or political leaders to do so; or that as a leader of ABRI, NU, or PNI they organized or allowed to be organized mass murder to simplify their lives. To kill so as to feel less threatened: this was the terrible solution to the civil crisis of Indonesia.

The sequel to the September 30th Movement was Sukarno's extended attempt to protect his allies, rally his supporters, and defend himself. The maneuvers were sustained and his locutions were ingenious, but the facts became plainer with the passing months. NASAKOM as a unifying construct was forever shattered. The KOM part, *Kommunisme,* was discredited, prohibited, or fatally stigmatized. A, for *agama,* prevailed in its diverse Islamic or Muslim-syncretic forms. As for NAS, the army more than anybody now stood for the *nasion.*

For six days at the end of August 1966, the army sponsored a seminar in Bandung that came to be known as the Second Armed Forces Seminar. Its objective was to establish policy and plans for political and economic stability. Its chairman was General Panggabean. According to General Nasution, who attended, technocrats dominated it, particularly economists from the University of Indonesia who taught at the Staff College of the Armed Forces. Thus the names of Professors Wijoyo Nitisastro, Mohammad Sadli, and Emil Salim, among others, entered Indonesian history. These three would remain prominent for more than thirty years. For working clarity, the seminar adopted the terms "Old Order" for pre-G30S. A "New Order" was the goal of those who wanted a political and economic democracy based on the constitution of 1945 and expressed in Pancasila—to eliminate poverty, illiteracy, and backwardness without sacrifice of the principle of anti-imperialism or of belief in God.[55]

General Suharto slowly and steadily consolidated his power and loosened Sukarno's grip upon the nation's consciousness. Sukarno helped undo himself by avowing that communism as an ideology should not be punished for involvement in G30S any more than Islam should be punished for the errors of Darul Islam, or nationalism for the regional rebellions of the late 1950s. On March 10, 1966, Sukarno called a contentious six-hour meeting at the palace to try to persuade political leaders to condemn student demonstrators for focusing on Soebandrio and attacking the Chinese Embassy. The next day, March 11, when he called a cabinet meeting, paratroops surrounded the palace. Sukarno and Soebandrio took off by helicopter for Bogor. Three generals followed by car and confronted Sukarno there later in the day—some say that one of the generals brandished a pistol. In the end Sukarno signed a de facto devolution of his powers to Suharto. A new cabinet followed, led by Suharto, Adam Malik, and Sultan Hamengku Buwono IX.

Sukarno hung on for two full years longer. The MPRS (Majelis Permusyawaratan Rakyat Sementara: provisional people's consultative assembly, 1960–1973) demanded a full accounting from him, then rejected his statement of his handling of national affairs. In March 1968 that delibera-

26. PRESIDENT SUKARNO EXPLAINS HIMSELF. A slow political suffocation of
Sukarno proceeds from October 1, 1965, through formal legislative stripping of all
his powers and titles on March 12, 1967. Here, in December 1966, Sukarno makes
one of his aggressive statements of defense before an apparently unmoved Adam
Malik and Suharto (both seated, left). (Ipphos Photo Archive)

tive body formally transferred the presidency to Suharto. Patience, a virtue
in every culture, is a prime Javanese talent. Suharto exercised it for two and
a half years to be sure that the nation would accept a constitutional deposi-
tion of Sukarno without political backlash.

Things might have proceeded differently. Years later I talked with General
Nasution. "Many Indonesians think, with respect and affection," I told him,
"that this would be a better country now if you had told Sukarno yourself,
in March 1966, that power had to be transferred to you, rather than to
Suharto." Nasution answered by speaking of his grief over the mortal
wounding of his daughter. When he came back over the wall, at daylight
(his hand swirled and swabbed at his chest), "She was all bloodied." A generation later, the bullets were still in their bedroom door.

I pressed my question. He said that one coup begets another, and that if he had taken power, people would have thought he was part of a coup syndrome, as in South America. Indonesia had to avoid this. I rejoined: the counter-coup was established by then, except for formal transfer of power to Suharto. Better that the new government be clean than dirty. "But Suharto is Suharto," he said, laughing, "and I am *myself*."[56] We all laughed. I inferred that in the end he had no genuine appetite for ultimate political power.

Who Learns, and What Changes?

On January 16, 1962, the great revolutionary nationalist Sutan Sjahrir had been arrested. Conspiracy was alleged. No documents were ever produced. No trial was ever conducted. Sjahrir was imprisoned indefinitely, although allowed some family visits. General Nasution claimed that President Sukarno had given him a warrant with no name filled in and asked him to sign it, which he did—a sign of how despotic guided democracy had become. Sjahrir, in his own solitary reading, now saw his nation as less industrialized than Russia in 1914. His criticism of the ever more autocratic Sukarno, however, took less note of social and economic structure than of style: Sukarno's ostentatiousness and flamboyance were overcompensation for his inferiority complex. He perpetuated a system of indifference and ignorance, while receiving loyalty as a deification of the father.

In April 1965 Sukarno let his prisoner fly to Switzerland with his wife and children. Sjahrir had suffered two serious strokes and could not communicate in speech or writing. But he was able to understand German television on March 11, 1966, telling of Sukarno's yielding effective power to General Suharto. Within a month Sjahrir was dead at the age of 57. Sukarno, still formally in office, signed a presidential decree declaring him a national hero and ordering a state funeral with full honors. He was buried adjoining the graves of the six generals killed eight months before. Hatta, who had not spoken in public for ten years, in private had likened Sukarno to Mephistopheles in Goethe's *Faust*. But now he appeared and gave a funeral oration at the grave, observing that "Sutan Sjahrir suffered more within the Republic of Indonesia itself, which is based on the Panca Sila, than in the colonial Dutch Indies, which he opposed." The first prime minister of Indonesia had "died a victim of tyranny."[57]

By mid-1966 new things were happening with regard to cooperative and nonconfrontational foreign policies, economic and foreign investment policies, and social development strategies. Some legacies of 1965–66, however, remain a continuing part of Indonesian inheritance. *Pemuda* defiance, which helped bring down the Dutch and then Sukarno, would one day help bring down Suharto too. Military opportunism, already a prominent and unpredictable feature of Indonesian politics, would become embedded and pronounced. Management by insinuation, intimidation, and punishments would be a feature of Suharto's leadership style. Collective vengeance would remain in the Indonesian mindstream, giving it troubled dreams rather than conciliatory public discourse. In Karoland of North Sumatra, twenty years after the killings, the family of a victim felt it time to call upon a spirit medium to bypass official history and invoke the voice of the dead in an effort partially to heal the incurable. Even so, all those local memories continue to haunt the national consciousness.[58]

Neither Santayana nor Freud, with their injunctions to understand the past at peril of repeating it, have much currency in Indonesia. Given the history of law in Indonesia, Oliver Wendell Holmes is of no consequence at all. But that wounded veteran of the American Civil War, later a justice of the United States Supreme Court, never forgot that all constitutional order is ultimately initiated or restored with a gun. Of this lesson, Indonesia is sadly aware.

SUHARTO

5

THE SMILE OF PROGRESS

I arrived in Jakarta for the first time in August 1967. The mass killings had stopped. The slow rebuilding of state policy had begun. "Development," *pembangunan,* had been adopted as a leitmotif by the technocrats in the army seminar a year before but had not begun to show. The root word, *bangun,* means "to wake up." Ordinary people used the longer noun cautiously. A waking-up? A reconstruction? What would this mean?

I bunked in a decrepit *wisma* (a "house" for tourists) not far from the five-year-old Hotel Indonesia, the first skyscraper in the archipelago, a marvel of fourteen stories. Located at the critical traffic circle between central and south Jakarta, the hotel embodied Sukarno's muscular taste, also shown in Leninesque monuments at other key junctures in the city. I walked the streets of Menteng, once the residential quarter of Dutch officials and businesspeople, now bought or seized by the Indonesian revolutionary elite: thick-walled houses, calm and blocky in white or pastel, with narrow windows to minimize the sun—tropical *haut bourgeois.* Tall trees kept them shaded; sometimes a key room was air-conditioned. In shallow pits near the street, servants burned a mix of trash and garbage, contributing funky wisps of smoke to the urban haze.

Jakarta had only 3 million people in 1961, but in 1967 it was growing rapidly. By the turn of the millennium, it would surpass 10 million. Its paving, sewage, waterworks, electricity, and telephone were early twentieth century; its stagnant, stinking canals were seventeenth century. Large quarters of the city, though rural in appearance and sanitation, swelled with immigrants.[1]

I looked for a place to bring my wife and two small sons, who had remained at our staging base with friends in Manila. All we needed was a small apartment—servants' quarters from imperial days or part of somebody's annex, built for lesser relatives. I quickly got used to rudimentary things in Jakarta and prepared to introduce my family to them. The poor, who lived along the slope-sided canals of Menteng, used the sluggish waters for most of their needs: drinking, bathing, laundering, and bodily excretions. All drinking water in Jakarta had to be boiled.

Shortly after I arrived, Ben Anderson, Irish citizen, Java savant, multilingual genius, and provocative political philosopher, took me to an outdoor Chinese restaurant, where we drank tea, spat chicken bones into pails, and wiped our sticky hands with wet gray rags. I knew Ben's and Ruth McVey's controversial analysis of the "coup" (a study that came to be known as "the Cornell paper") in which communists were seen as innocent victims. I would soon meet Nugroho Notosusanto, a timid young man who had studied at Harvard and who would go on to manufacture official rejoinders in which Sukarno and the PKI were portrayed as perpetrators rather than victims. As apologist, Nugroho would flourish in the ideology business and in the 1980s become Suharto's minister of education. Anderson, for his views, would be expelled in 1971 and banned from Indonesia for nearly three decades.[2]

Later that evening, Ben drove me to the *wisma* on the back of his small motorcycle, through urban stench, smoke, spice, rot, and shit. He dodged potholes, weaved in and out among men pedaling *becaks,* diesel buses farting black particulates, wounded private automobiles, limping taxis, occasional carriages with knobby-kneed horses, and humans of all ages with shoulder yokes or long carry-poles, bearing live things, or once live things, or various things inert. We passed men sleeping on walls, under palms, in their own *becaks,* on communal benches. Men gathered in bunches to vend: their stalls, two wheels and two handles, stood shoulder high, with rows and rows of goods displayed behind fly-specked plexiglass: one with Western cigarettes; another with creamed coffee soda bottles in little slots; a third with fruits. They bought from one another—a cigarette, a snack of satay. They chattered. They slept. A sign on a side street, "Banyak Anak-Anak," warned of "Many Children," who ran up and down in the middle of the passage. More of them poured out of the houses. At the *wisma* I took a cold shower on moldy floorboards and wondered at the pains in my belly.

By the time I was actively negotiating an apartment, I had serious diarrhea and was fast losing weight and appetite. I couldn't face the gritty gray rice, the meager wilted greens, the ratty-looking meatbits of the *wisma* any longer. I said to myself, I had to *eat.* I would go to the famous Sunday evening buffet at the Hotel Indonesia. In the cool of the elegant dining room, I sliced a slab from a bank of poached salmon and scooped a gob from a vat of potato salad, ordered an iced tea, and began to consider which of the crystalline desserts I would choose. Or would it be that startlingly yellow pudding, tapioca perhaps, from Indonesia's own sago?

When the waiters helped me off the floor, I had hardly eaten a bite. Sweat was running down my face. Slender men of tan or mahogany visage, one nearly mauve, were speaking soothingly to me. "Sakit perut," I mumbled, "sakit betul." Sick in my stomach. Really sick. They apologized, seeking forgiveness for whatever of their spread had done this to me. I accepted the apologies as the only medicine in reach. They carried me upstairs, summoned the hotel doctor to worry briefly over me, then had me chauffeured the short hop from plenty famous to empty promise: my *wisma*.

The manager to whom I was paying a few dollars a day summoned his doctor, who heard me out, looked at me carefully, tapped my belly with attentive respect. He proposed an injection in my stomach. I rebelled, reaching for my dictionary. In America we do that only for "mad dog disease." The doctor murmured, shrugging, to the manager, "White men don't like needles in their stomachs."

So I was on my own, and the next morning hired a twenty-minute *becak* ride to the embassy doctor. Stool sample required. Wait days for results. Answer: severe amoebic dysentery. Recommendation: "If you don't want to die, get out of here. Go to Singapore or Manila and get into a hospital, fast." Elizabeth, my wife, had it all arranged for me when I got to Manila. New, private, profit-making hospital. They would poison me for a few weeks with emetine, while giving me compazine so I could tolerate the nausea. In mid-treatment I suddenly developed a severe reaction to the compazine. My hands contracted into claws, my head slumped to my chest, and my lungs could not function. I was sorry that Elizabeth, at my bedside, had to see me die suddenly, in contortions, and—incidentally—so young. She ran for a doctor, who shot me full of reboxin. Things eased up. Over the next few months my fingernails grew out girdled with white bands, testimony to my interlude of oxygen deprivation. I was diagnosed, additionally, as having dengue fever. I don't know whether I got that through faulty mosquito netting in Jakarta or later in Bel Air, a bouncy Manila suburb where one son was now in preschool, the other still in diapers.

Six months later I headed back to a waiting apartment in Menteng for a couple of months of intensified solo research. On the flight in I saw clearly the *padi* and villages of North Java. The billion-seeming tufted green rows of rice shoots, the courses of free water, blue, or white with clay, or muddy; the intricate sluicing connections, the meandering streams. Then as the plane drifted down, profiles of villages, tree clusters that shielded habitation, thatched roofs, occasional tin. And nearer the metropolis, as the villages took on more functions and resources, roofs of rich reddish tile, ochre and russet mixed with black, like Halloween candies to my fresh American eyes—orange and peppermint marzipan, licorice. Ordered and delectable from the air, what would these villages be like on the ground? I could see that they extended into the city itself. Where village became city I could not say.

Within two weeks, dysentery struck again. I knew its pains. Who could help me get some medicine? My best American friends' apartment was in a distant part of the city. At a literary gathering I had met an Indonesian woman—I'll call her Z—who chanced to live nearby. I explained my predicament by telephone. She came, impassive and pleasant, and performed the necessary errands. I got over the amoeba much faster this time. When I was well, she invited me to tea.

On Not Interviewing Sukarno

Z had been a movie actress, appearing in successful films on the revolution at a young age. She had married a Minangkabau businessman, fallen away from him, and then secured a divorce.³ Now she cared for her own children and some nieces and nephews in a household replete with servants. At tea on her balcony we could look out on a small park and lake of sea-green and milk-green and scum-green water, from which gnarled trees rose in loops like acrobatic crocodiles. Black-billed geese, protecting their goslings, honked and snorted at patchy-feathered turkeys, late immigrants, outcasts. We could watch the *krupuk* vendor with his shoulder yoke, carrying big cans of crinkly fried chips of pulverized shrimp. See the miscellany man pushing his barrow, with its bicycle wheels and two long handles made of sawed-off bed legs. Listen to the zither man stationed in a driveway, playing tight strings on faded wood. I knew his big smile, showing metal teeth in his upper jaw all the way back to his molars: a dull silver, like the strings on his instrument. We could hear the cry of "'tay, 'tay" from the satay peddler, and the sounds of the other vendors with their toylike decorated carts: ratchets and hollow blocks, klaxons and drumming chopsticks; the soft rolling gong of the ice cream man.

Z was from Minangkabau. I knew nearly nothing then about that people besides their locus in West Sumatra. For Westerners, they carried the fascination of being the largest matrilineal society in the world. Some called them matriarchal, which they are not. The distinctions should have absorbed me then, but they didn't; only now. I was interested in Z's artistic identification with the revolution, her truncated cinematic career, her business card which carried the title "Siti," meaning "Princess," she said simply. Suharto's daughters would later bear the title "Siti," proving that an armed peasant general who marries a lesser noblewoman of a faded Solonese court can call his daughters anything he wishes. Siti Z had style, intelligence, integrity. She was compact, vigorous, prim. I found her alluring.

She, among several new friends, helped me make appointments with leading political, military, and cultural figures. When I had built up enough such momentum, and the confidence that goes with it, I asked her one day how I should go about seeing Sukarno. He was pivotal to the Japanese occupation and the revolution—the heart of my study—and I thought that even though he had to have military permission to leave his palace at Bogor, I could somehow get permission to interview him there. I did not see it coming, but in a few weeks the Parliament would take away the last of Sukarno's titles, and Suharto would formally become the second president of Indonesia. Z's eyes went wide with alarm. "Don't try to see Sukarno. You'll get yourself in trouble. You'll get us all in trouble."

"All?" She gave me Simone de Beauvoir's novel to read, *The Mandarins*. I understood the message: that Z herself was a feminist sympathizer with Simone de Beauvoir, and her circle of friends were to Jakarta as Simone's Mandarins were to Paris. Mandarins anywhere, I suppose, can be both truly formidable and a bit self-important. I grasped that I was in a high-stakes game in a low-resource society. Z's friends made things occur; but things could happen to Z and her friends if an American researcher, gauche in his innocence, should even propose meeting with Sukarno. General Suharto had publicly absolved his predecessor of complicity in the attempted coup of September 30th, but in their shrewd double game, he and his colleagues were asphyxiating Sukarno with his communist associations and cutting down his power and prerogatives month by month. Two years later Sukarno would die in dishonor. They would bury him far from Jakarta.

I quickly withdrew from the peril I had foolishly proposed. But the imagined mutual danger brought Z and me closer together. We met for tea at her house after dinner. She kept a drowsy little nephew in her arms as chaperone while we talked of mutual interests.

This strange intimacy shot suddenly forward when she asked me to marry her. "Listen," she said. "Don't interrupt. Hear what I have to say. And think about it." She had enough money of her own, she began. I needn't think about that. She wouldn't be a burden to me in America; she could even be of help. She only asked two promises of me: that I would let her travel back to her lands in Minangkabau once a year; and that when she died I would ensure she was buried there, in Minangkabau.

I was consummately astonished. "But I *can't* think about it," I said. "I'm already married. We have two sons. And a third child is coming. It's impossible." I said mollifying things, too, about what an honor and compliment her proposal was. "Anything is possible," she said, and repeated, "Think about it."

I thought I had answered clearly. She thought I had not. Our friendship grew tense. She went silent, seeming to question my courage and sincerity.

I wondered about Minang matrilineality and how powerfully it emboldened their women. I foundered on the question of how much a cosmopolitan feminist might want to get out of the still wretched Indonesia of 1968.

As my remaining days diminished, Z proposed again. I assured her that she was incredibly dear to think of me this way but the terms were indelibly clear. I repeated: I am already married, and we have a third child on the way. On the morning when I was to fly to Bangkok where my wife had traveled to meet me, the plane had mechanical failure. Passengers at the airport were told they could go back home; several hours were required for repairs. I took a taxi to say a further goodbye to Z. When, from her chair, she saw me come in the door, she put her head between her knees. I feared she was fainting with a misapprehended shock of happiness, and I blurted out the mechanical problems and my wish to say a last farewell. We went to a Minang restaurant for lunch, where they pile dishes pyramidally on one another and diners choose parts of several, paying only for what they eat. The spare ribs were like tar, highly spiced and minimal on meat.

Back at Z's house, I picked up my bag and said goodbye again. "No," she said. "I'll see you tonight." "OK," I said, "I'll see you tonight." With that poetic lie I left. In Manila, from the bosom of my cherished family, I wrote her a letter of final parting.

I assume that Z's first marriage had been contracted in the classic Minangkabau way, with arrangements made by her maternal uncle and blessed by the local *adat* (tradition) chief. Her education, years in Java, divorce, and independent thinking made Z a creature of her own convictions, always a Minang. She was engaged to a Canadian journalist when she met me. She must have broken the tie with him. A couple of years later she married an English anthropologist. I don't know who initiated proposals of marriage in her other instances, or how she dealt with her Jakarta Mandarin lover, whom she may have wished to wed but who had chosen someone else. I only know that Z was more than an anthropological shock to me. She was a lasting influence. I wished her happiness in her new Oxbridge life.

The experience moved me later to try to read about and understand the Minang world. Peggy Reeves Sanday, a prominent American anthropologist, finds inspiration for feminism in Minangkabau culture. It surmounts any dialectical contest between female and male. Minang *adat* has prevailed over Muslim patriarchy, Dutch hierarchy, and Suharto's "national culture" of Javanese male dominance. It is "'the genius of Minangkabau' to synthesize contradictions harmoniously." Furthermore, says Sanday, West Sumatra is a rape-free society.[4]

Not really, counters Jeffrey Hadler, who has documented cases of rape in West Sumatra between 1900 and 1940 in the course of his study of Minang men. What does a man there do who wants to make money or a name for himself? He *must* leave Minangkabau, Hadler says. Otherwise, he may some day become a propertyless widower reduced to living in a boy's dormitory.[5]

When I finally traveled to Minang regions, long after knowing Z, it did not feel so different from the rest of Indonesia until Minangs *talked* about how society was constructed. The mother is the "central pillar of the house," whereas "the husband is like ashes on the fireplace" (one puff and he is gone). Being matrifocal in Minang means an emphasis on mother, wife, and sister.[6] Men do *merantau*—make long forays into the outside world to prove themselves worthy of being someone's husband. As more and more men do that now (a side-effect of globalization?), women's hold on the transmission of property, which was determined as their right by the Minang before any era of record, grows ever stronger. *Merantau* tests and strengthens the men; matrilineal property makes for independent women.

I commented on this to Ibu Wahidar, a strong enough exemplar and exponent of the culture for me to think of her, figuratively, as a "matriarch." "Yes, independent women," she answered. "It's a good thing, a social security system. No society is any better than the way it provides for women." "How did it start?" I asked. I knew there are great Minang myths, but I was looking for historical anthropology.[7] "Nobody knows. But it was rather original, don't you think?"

Ibu Wahidar had three married daughters with prominent jobs in Jakarta. When we talked, the best-known of them, Dewi Fortuna Anwar, was a key foreign policy advisor and spokesperson for President Suharto. Wahidar spoke of Dewi, her eldest, as being "100 percent Minang, 100 percent Muslim, and 100 percent Western." From age three and a half, for ten years she lived with Wahidar's uncle, an *adat* leader and Muslim teacher. Then she spent several years in London with her parents; interned in the United States as a congressional fellow on the staffs of Representatives Pat Schroeder and Stephen Solarz; and obtained a doctorate at Monash University, Melbourne. Her English is "international," her mother said: not too roundly British, or too flatly American, or too sharply Australian. Before she was twenty-one, Dewi said to her uncle, "I want to marry someone I can talk to. Either a *bulé* (albino: white person) or one of your sons." "Don't marry a *bulé*," said her uncle, "because *I* can't talk to them." She married one of that uncle's sons.

I remarked on a Dutchwoman's book about the Minang, which talked authoritatively about marriage without ever mentioning love. Wahidar expostulated with force. "What has marriage got to do with love? *Marriage is a business!*" "Well," I observed mildly, "I still think love has a place, certainly in a marriage between equals." Wahidar nodded, understanding an American ideal, and felt obliged to say something less commercial-sounding. "I believe loving comes with caring, don't you think?"[8] I said I think so.

Recently I was surprised and touched to get a letter from Z. We were twice as old as when we had last seen each other. Someone had given her an essay of mine from the Internet. We corresponded and restored a fondness and respect that I believe made both of us happy to express. Her strengths, and what I had learned of the creative confidence of female propertyholders and the constructive careers of men on *merantau,* suggest a counter-factual question. Might it have been more productive for Indonesian society overall if the Minangs had conquered Java, leaving themselves, instead of the Javanese, poised to become the energizing center of a post-colonial nation?

Takeoff, with Technocrats

When General Suharto began his ascent to power in 1965, the life expectancy of Indonesians was low. They earned less and ate less than any people in all of Asia.[9] But already and always, General Suharto had a smile. Suharto's is an engaging smile. Not a toothy Hollywood grin, such as Sukarno displayed in exuberance. But a measured, almost sweet acknowledgment of the beneficence of the gods. A seemingly tolerant Javanese smile, containing an admixture of concession to fate and harmonious address to circumstance. Pak Harto's is a fatherly, controlled, theatrical smile, capable of masking any feeling or desire, including vengeance. Wholly unlike Bung Karno, who radiated personal intimacy, brotherly conspiracy, and a revolutionary generosity that easily flashed into an angry snarl. General Suharto brought his smile to the slow suffocation of President Sukarno's political power; to Sukarno's replacement in office and his house arrest; to his burial next to his mother in East Java in 1970.

Behind the agreeable face, who was this ambitious, aggressive man? He was probably "the illegitimate child of a well-placed villager . . . farmed out to relatives from an early age," according to one of his biographers. His opportunities for education were, by village standards, "extraordinary," even though he never went beyond high school. Like Sukarno, he got a childhood view of lower Javanese officialdom, but as a stepchild rather than a son. Like Sukarno, but for different reasons, he never traveled beyond Indonesia until he was in his forties. He relied on internalized Javanese ethical aphorisms to guide him in the early days, and later he digested staff briefings with extraordinary efficiency. He was guarded, uncurious about the abstract, shrewd about the concrete. Mystical consultations were important to him, but he knew their limits: "If we were in a war and we have to look for a *dukun* [seer, shaman], we would be shot dead first."[10]

27. WOMEN HARVEST-
ING RICE. A harvest in
Java, 1969, before new
seeds and cultivation
techniques have shown
their full impact on crop
yields. (Burt Glinn/Mag-
num Photos)

His practical values were simple and focused: the Indonesian nation; the armed forces guiding it; and its people, who deserve a better life. Suharto had a peasant's commonsense understanding that you must eat to live, that education helps you earn more money, and those with more money eat better and live longer. He showed great appetite for the burdens of state, demonstrated early aptitude, hired good advisors, and listened to them, along with his military. Indonesia's generals had earlier destroyed the Darul Islam and opposed an Islamic state. Now they had destroyed the PKI, while welcoming the anticommunist piety of Muslims. They chose a "third road to modernity: developmentalism."[11] And down that road they drove the Indonesian people.

Back from a decade of exile came Professor Sumitro Djojohadikusumo. He was forgiven for his role in the regional rebellions of the late 1950s. Needed now for his economic expertise, he helped generate the Foreign Investment Law of 1967. Younger Indonesians with doctorates from the United States were swiftly drafted into policy positions: Widjojo Nitisastro, Emil Salim, Mohammad Sadli, and Ali Wardhana. Where Sukarno had at best a Gandhian passivity about conceptual and technological change, and at worst a demonic ignorance of economics, these new leaders were confident that mainstream Western economic thinking could be applied effectively to Indonesia.[12] The technocrats drove down inflation to single digits by 1969 and elevated the confidence of the Inter-Governmental Group on Indonesia (IGGI), a consortium to coordinate aid and credit.[13] As the new government established itself, external grants and loans accounted for nearly a third of state revenues.[14]

Then foreign investment started to flow in. In 1969 Jack Christy, as a young American and new head of "Asia" for ITT, experienced its wild atmosphere. He was met at customs by his mediating agent, Vladimir Gold, a tall Czech emigré with fiery red hair, who nipped at a brandy bottle from waking to sleeping. ITT had the first contract in Indonesia for a satellite receiving center, sited in a beautiful, quiet, mountain-ringed valley east of Bogor. But, Gold told Christy, Indonesian government officials expected $1 million to let it go forward. Christy finally met "General Jo," the minister with responsibility in the case, and told him that the special payment to expedite matters was not legal in the United States. The minister replied, "I'm not sure your project will be successful." With some suspense, however, it did go forward, with no ITT money beyond contract having changed hands.

Christy fired Gold, a flagrant example of the influence-peddler who flourishes in the Indonesian system. Christy enjoyed Gold's panache but wished not to experience such a situation again. Gold then concentrated on his chief enterprise, as a major world trader in human hair and dealer in the long tresses of Indonesian women, which were coveted by wigmakers. He sold it and retired to Geneva, where in half a year, having barely turned forty, he died of a stroke.[15]

The technocrats were united in recognizing the importance of incentives to agricultural producers, in controlling population, and in improving the productivity of Java-based manufacturing and of outer-island exporting. They had no nationalist aversion to foreign aid or foreign investment. They had no prejudice against or for the Chinese but saw them as critical to private-sector growth. Their convergence of views made them appear to be a fraternity, despite distinct differences in personal style and policy preferences. They and those like them became known as "the Berkeley mafia," even though Sumitro was trained in Europe and Sadli looked pained at any mention of Berkeley. "I went to MIT!"[16]

Their presence and influence would last for decades. The Berkeley mafia brushed out stratified Dutch economic thinking and swept away the Marxist leveling of those influenced by the PKI. They replaced Sukarno's economic nonthought with testable concepts—concepts which succeeded. They would work sympathetically or keep their peace until early in 1998, when Sumitro, Salim, and Sadli would split with Suharto. Salim would quit after twenty years in cabinet positions, working most notably on population and environment. He saw Suharto's 1993 choices as a "cabinet of engineers" led by Habibie and Ginandjar—big spenders who pushed the accelerator too hard and brought trouble. When the crisis of 1997 hit deep, Suharto would pull Widjojo out of retirement and publicize him as his special economic advisor, in the hope that past magic would lend present confidence. Economists like Widjojo were needed again to "put on the brakes."[17] But if almost any coherent policy would have worked after Sukarno's madness, in 1997 the solutions would not be so simple. Widjojo, allegedly the wizard of them all and most in the mold of a Javanese power-maven, would survive the sinking of the Suharto ship and go on working with Habibie.

But in 1966–1968 the task was macroeconomic stabilization. The generals and the economists addressed it together. They got a hold on it. Indonesia began an upward economic climb, at first almost invisible, at last seemingly irresistible, that endured for three decades.

Rice

Suharto's childhood background in Kemusu, outside Yogyakarta, with his broken-up and semirural rearing, gave him personal experience of village poverty—a formative influence that surely contributed to his priorities on agriculture and family planning. Retroactive mythologizing by his flacks aside, there is no reason to doubt Suharto's depiction of himself as having a peasant's natural interest in rural projects. On a European trip as president, no photographers present, he gathered his ministers around him to eat rice off of banana leaves with their fingers. He did this to relax himself, but also to educate some of them.

His new government launched an effort to make Indonesia self-sufficient in its key staple. Except in a few eastern provinces, rice dominated, and still dominates, the Indonesian diet. In the Jakarta consumer price index of the late 1960s, it was accorded a weight of 31 percent. During the decade of the 1970s researched varieties of high-yielding rice expanded from 26 to 61 percent of crop plantings. Subsidized fertilizers and pesticides were also intensively distributed until 1987, when government subsidies tapered off. After

28. WET RICE FARMERS. Two men in Central Java, mid-1990s. (Byron Black/author's collection)

the hyper-inflation of the late Sukarno years, price supports had seemed necessary, although excessive protection and taxation were avoided. This effort also insulated the domestic rice market from international fluctuations. Input subsidies and output protection achieved stability in the 1980s, so that world prices were on average 91 percent of Indonesian prices. Producers were satisfied and consumers were fed.

Throughout the period, irrigation networks and other parts of the infrastructure that had decayed in the quarter-century of war, national revolution, and Sukarnoesque convulsions were rebuilt and enhanced. Meanwhile the government advanced research and development, subsidized water rates, and shaped credit policies to the rice sector—offering below-market interest rates, with forgiveness on arrears and even on default.[18]

Altogether, these measures produced an unusual phenomenon for a developing country: an allocation of goods and factors to agriculture in excess of the nonagricultural sector. In 1963 Clifford Geertz had brilliantly described a condition he called "agricultural involution"—increasingly intense

29. RURAL LIFE. Two women at a hot spring by a cold stream. (Byron Black/ author's collection)

cultivation of too little land by too many people. His analysis stiffened expectations that Java had reached its limits of expansion in food production. But from 1969 to 1992 Java increased its yield 98 percent and its total production 156 percent, steadily comparable with Indonesian results in the outer islands.[19]

The Food and Agriculture Organization (FAO), in November 1985, invited President Suharto to address its fortieth anniversary conference. He used the ceremony to announce that Indonesia had achieved self-sufficiency in rice. Suharto deserved this moment of triumph: just twenty years before, in the year Sukarno had projected as one of "living dangerously," the price of rice had soared by more than 900 percent and the president had appealed to his people to eat maize, to conserve dwindling foreign exchange.[20]

Suharto, however, would stay in office long enough to see compound crisis undo his great achievement. By the year 2000, rice had fallen to 5 percent of GDP, from 30 percent in 1970, because of vitalities elsewhere in the economy. Rice was no longer the engine of economic growth, but the politics of rice was again suddenly drawing debate. Rice was the largest single employer in the country, the provider of half the protein caloric intake of the population, a socio-cultural phenomenon. These factors together gave the invocation of "rice" a political magic disproportionate to its economic clout. Spikes in rice prices in 1997–98 and then a collapse to half their level in 2000 put Indonesia on notice that it was facing an old problem in a new form: how to achieve long-term economic growth to lift people out of poverty and how much short-term suffering to ask the poor to endure.[21]

Education and Literacy

Under Suharto, Indonesia got basic teaching and learning under way. In 1965 its primary school enrollment was slightly below the level of India and well below that of China. By 1990 near-universal enrollment had been achieved for children 8 to 11 years old. That progress dropped the illiteracy rate to 18.4 percent, lower than Malaysia yet still much higher than Thailand, the Philippines, and Korea, all of whom enjoyed single digits (and the last only 3.7 percent).[22]

Attendance at lower levels overflowed, as over-age children enrolled in primary schools along with their younger brothers and sisters. Meanwhile, secondary school attendance rates were substantially lower than those of like nations, and tertiary rates were nearly the lowest of all comparable countries. In advanced education and research and development, Indonesia dramatically trailed Korea, an alleged model. The publicity surrounding Minister Habibie's efforts to advance R&D may have reflected an application of resources greater than in the Philippines or Thailand, but without

30. SICKLES ON A TABLE. The rice-sickle or grass knife is a vital agricultural tool and can become a weapon in a mugging or riot. (Byron Black/author's collection)

useful nationwide impact: his focus on domestic aircraft produced far more buzz than boom.

Indonesia quickly realized the tremendous impact of giving a large labor force some schooling, beyond its previous condition of very little or none. But at the secondary level, even though education became and remains a national policy emphasis, labor market bottlenecks since the late 1980s have required firms to go to expensive international sources for many kinds of skilled employees. At the tertiary level, the private sector finally stepped in. By the 1990s, about a thousand private institutions of higher education had achieved total enrollments exceeding the government system and were much more adept at meeting the demand for marketable qualifications.

The Suharto government responded with political apprehension. Its "integralistic" state required a managed ideology of Pancasila. Private universities and colleges, however, were chiefly Christian and Muslim institutions, which appeared to the government as bastions of foreign privilege and breeding grounds for anti-Pancasila thought. The government hindered the recruitment of teachers from abroad, even while badly underpaid government lecturers moonlighted at the private schools to earn more income and enjoy a freer intellectual atmosphere.[23]

With far more humanities students graduating from its public universities than students in science and commerce, and many of them jobless, Indonesian tertiary education may be seen as an unguided system unconsciously prepared to help bring down Suharto. But in the years since his downfall, no element within higher education or outside it has yet adequately shaped a system capable of meeting the nation's rapidly differentiating needs.

Health and Longevity

Two fairly recent case histories in rural Java, from the records of Dr. Januar Achmad, a public health officer, show the dynamics of morbidity and mortality that statistics cannot reveal:

Case 7 (Obstructed labor/Ruptured uterus)
A 19-year-old farm woman, after the membrane was ruptured, still could not deliver the baby. The family asked a traditional birth attendant

31. EDUCATION, 1950. A primary school classroom in Eastern Indonesia shows elementary Indonesian language being taught. (Gift of Niels Douwes Dekker/ author's collection)

32. EDUCATION, 1996. Two girls of Central Java's Dieng Plateau show enough family means to buy school uniforms and sneakers. (Byron Black/author's collection)

to help. On the second day two more traditional birth attendants were consulted. On the third day the family consulted a fourth traditional birth attendant, who used strong massage and pressure on the patient's stomach. The baby and placenta were born spontaneously. But soon after, the mother died.

Case 29 (Puerperal sepsis)

A 23-year-old farm woman gave birth two months prematurely to twins. Placenta was expelled spontaneously and there was normal bleeding. At 6 PM, patient went to the river for defecation but did not return. Villagers immediately launched a search but could not find her until the next day: in the paddy field, unconscious and covered with mud, where they believed she had been taken by spirits. She was carried home on a palanquin. The traditional healer treated her whole body with an application of ginger, fennel, galanga, and *pulau waras*. She regained consciousness.

Nine days later the patient's first child died, causing her depression in addition to a Javanese embarrassment at having had twins. She shivered with fever and weakness. The family called the traditional healer again, who prescribed plain water and *dlingko bengkle,* a plant the local people believe can keep evil spirits away. She died at home the next day. A midwife was never consulted.[24]

The maternal mortality ratio in Indonesia was still high toward the end of the Suharto period, as a consequence of poor medical service infrastructure. From 1985 to 1990 only 44 percent of births were attended by midwives or nurses.[25] The governments of Kerala (which has excellent medical infrastructure despite poverty) and Sri Lanka had assigned midwives at the village level in the 1950s; Malaysia in the 1960s; the Philippines in 1981. But Indonesia began to do so only in 1988. Within a massive primary health care system that was in many ways impressive, Indonesia did not begin to use reduced maternal mortality rates as an indicator of development until March 1997.[26]

Bupatis (regents) control local government agendas (as one of them remarked) "to prevent social unrest and famine . . . As long as everything is in order, he perceives his job is a success." Village leaders do not beseech him to think otherwise, or dare report health problems, for fear of drawing blame instead of aid. In fact, most local governments used revenues generated by health services for other purposes. Nationally, they passed along only 25 percent to health centers themselves, compared with 100 percent in Thailand and Vietnam.[27] Not until 1995 did the Indonesian Ministry of Health introduce a health card for low-income families which entitled them to free government health services. Even then they supplied no additional funding. Often, the new policy became just another local financial burden.

The blind habit of striving to report "no famine, no disorder" is traceable to early Dutch times. Moderate to severe areas of malnutrition were frequent but undocumentable in the New Order.[28] Indifference to health issues can be followed all the way up the line to President Suharto himself, who never once attended a cabinet meeting with these items on the agenda.[29] By treating peasant consciousness politically as a "floating mass," he incidentally ensured that there would be no village-organized health lobbies. Peasants were to be fed and taught, with the implicit assumption that the hardy would endure—like the president himself, a village-raised Darwinian survivor. Nor did it apparently occur to those around him to argue for health expenditures positively, as a strategy of human resource development, rather than negatively, as a budget cost.[30] Suharto's ministers yielded to his prejudices rather than trying to educate him. And international donors played to him while expressing their own priorities—usually by contributing to family planning, to the relative neglect of other programs.[31]

Maternal mortality, of course, is only one of several major indices of health policy. But it helps illustrate the enduring weakness, despite many improvements, in the conditions of Indonesian life. For every disease and cause of death in any nation, one may envision an economic ladder. Its frame is the infrastructure for health promotion and disease prevention. Its rungs are individual income and education. The stronger the framework, the lesser the risk to anyone of unnecessary illness or premature death. But regardless of the framework, the less money and learning one has, the sicker one may become, the earlier one may die. In general, long life tends to correlate with socioeconomic status. Wealthy African Americans are healthier than middle-income or poor whites in the United States.[32]

Indonesia's health ladder was very rickety in 1960, when at birth life expectancy was 41 years. In the chaos of 1965, GNP in Indonesia fell to $30 per capita per year and food supply to 1,800 calories per capita per day—the worst in Asia, including India, China, and what became Bangladesh. But the Suharto years showed tremendous advances in longevity. For the decades beginning 1970, 1980, and 1990, it rose to 49, 56, and 64 years, respectively, a cumulative increase of more than 50 percent. In 1995 life expectancy in Indonesia—at 64 years—was only thirteen years less than in the United States, then at 77 years. The framework of Indonesia's health ladder had been strengthened, and the rungs too. The percentage of totally unschooled Indonesians was cut from 68 in 1961 to 19 in 1990. Increases in income per capita multiplied many times.[33]

World Perspective on Development

In Sukarno's "year of living dangerously," 1965, Indonesian indicators of quantity and quality of life were among the lowest in the world, including Africa. Three decades later Indonesia had surpassed India in life expectancy, income, poverty reduction, low maternal and infant mortality, adult literacy, and sanitation and had surpassed China in most of these categories, while overshadowing its neighbor, the Philippines. Indonesia could imagine catching up with far-away Russia and Brazil and neighboring Thailand and Malaysia. Its data (see Table 3) were comparable to those of a nation that shared both income level and Islam (Egypt); the data far surpassed those of a nation that shared Islam, oil, and a lack of free elections (Nigeria); and they dramatically trailed one that stood as a model among newly industrialized countries but whose own financial weaknesses would soon be revealed (Korea).

The gains from late Sukarno to high Suharto times are remarkable. Yet careful study of *all* less-developed countries across the forty-year span from 1950–55 to 1990–95 shows an increase in average life expectancy from 40.7

Table 3. Indonesia: selective and comparative matrix of quality of life, 1995 (countries ranked in order of purchasing power parity, per capita)

Nation and life expectancy at birth, male/female, 1995	Purchasing power parity, 1995	Poverty (% of population living on less than $1/day) PPP, 1981–95	Maternal mortality per 100,000 births, 1989–95	Infant mortality per 1000 births, 1995	Adult illiteracy as a percent of the male population 15 and above, 1995	Adult illiteracy as a percent of the female population 15 and above, 1995	Access to safe water, as a percent of the population, 1995
S. Korea M68/F76	$11,450	. . . . .	30	10	1	3	89%
Malaysia M69/F74	9,020	5.6%	34	12	11	22	90
Thailand M67/F72	7,540	0.1%	?	35	4	8	81
Brazil	5,400	28.7%	200	44	17	17	92
Russian Federation M59/F72	4,480	1.1%	52	18	?	?	?
Egypt M64/F66	3,820	7.6%	?	56	36	61	84

Indonesia M62/F66	**3,800**	**14.5%**	**390**	**51**	**10**	**22**	**63**
China M67/F73	2,920	29.4%	115	34	10	27	83
Philippines M64/F68	2,850	27.5%	208	39	5	6	84
India M62/F63	1,400	52.5%	437	68	35	62	63
Nigeria M51/F54	1,220	28.9%	?	80	33	53	43

Selected from: World Bank, *World Development Indicators CD-ROM*, February 1997: The Quality of Life, pp. 1–4; Gender Dimensions of Development, pp. 1–4; and *World Development Report* (New York: Oxford University Press, for The World Bank, 1997), tables 1, 6, 7. The data obviously do not show consistent relationships among purchasing power, education, and quality of life. But they are offered to show where Indonesia stood among other nations in 1995, after its surge of improvements.

to 62.4 years. This gain of 53.3 percent is surely extraordinary, with nothing like it recorded in earlier human history. Lesser but significant gain also affected developed nations. Their average longevity increased in the same period from 66 to 74.6 years, or 13 percent. Worldwide, the phenomenon deserves the term "the quiet revolution."[34]

The achievements of the Suharto government are not diminished by saying that Indonesia's gains in life expectancy are embedded in a world revolution. But there is a sobering perspective. No specific global public health measure, such as diphtheria/pertussis/tetanus vaccine, early immunization against measles, or access to sanitation is significantly causative taken by itself. Safe drinking water is modestly significant. By far the most powerful factors in this global convergence are *initial* life expectancy and income.[35] How low you start and how fast your earnings are increasing make the big differences. Indonesia started with low life expectancy and its earnings multiplied fast. It cannot ever have another 50 percent increase in life expectancy in one generation without breakthroughs in genetic engineering. And, of course, still higher income levels will be needed to achieve and sustain any further major gains.

In the "looming Malthusian catastrophe" of the last Sukarno years, the national average per capita in calorie and protein intake was actually lower than the minimum levels supposedly required for subsistence. By early in Suharto's fifth term (1988–1990), however, Indonesian calorie supplies had increased 45 percent and proteins by 50 percent over levels in the years 1961 to 1963.[36] Having significantly trailed the average for all developing countries, it now significantly exceeded their global average, even as that figure itself greatly increased. Indonesians moved on from the survival question "How do I get enough to eat?" to the more alluring question "How much can I earn?"

The Suharto government stayed earnest in pursuit of its broad "Development Trilogy" of growth, stability, and equality. Growth was proven and sustained. Stability was demanded and enforced. Equality, however, is a different kind of question, arresting and elusive. It is at the heart of evaluating Suharto's New Order.

Equality

Fairness is not an easy science. Equity in distribution of income seems to make it definable, but even that does not assure parity in health and nutrition. Economists rely on gray measures like the gini ratio, for which 0 represents perfect equality of income, and 1 represents perfect inequality. Human societies at their extremes by this reckoning were Communist

Czechoslovakia, good at an average gini of .22, and apartheid South Africa, bad at .62. The United States, at an average a little over .35, and Japan, a little under .35, were representative of advanced industrial countries, West and East.

Where stood Indonesia? In seven observations from 1976 to 1990, its gini ratio averaged .34, while Thailand, the Philippines, and Malaysia soared worse: .45, .48, and .50.[37] A strong case exists, implicitly, that Indonesia was being guided by a philosophy akin to Japanese *wa* or harmony, rather than by the gold-rush mentality which appears to prevail in its neighbor nations. But the gini does not sufficiently illuminate the problem, because it compounds too many factors into one number. It certainly cannot measure relative deprivation as subjectively felt. Envy, one of the great driving forces of history, has no thermometer.

Rural researchers reported "immiserization" in Indonesia, especially during the 1970s: increasing landlessness, "exclusionary" labor contracts, human obsolescence in the face of labor-saving technology, unequal access to credit and government services, demise of protective rural institutions. Acknowledging all that, similar studies in the 1990s spoke to living standards that were still rising in the villages—more slowly than in cities but rising nonetheless. The appearance of urban commercial-industrial conglomerates in the 1980s might have tortured and swollen the ginis; they did not.[38] In the Human Development Index, Indonesia in 1975 still stood at the level of sub-Saharan Africa today; a quarter-century afterward, Indonesia was at the level of North Africa, rising above Syria while falling below Tunisia.[39]

For over twenty years after Indonesia's independence, there were no major concentrations of private wealth, either agricultural or industrial. Rundown foreign-owned estates were nationalized between 1958 and 1965. The giant private estancias, latifundias, plantations of Latin America, the Philippines, and Malaysia simply did not exist. And the omnivorous conglomerates of the 1990s had not yet appeared. Both the green revolution (led by rice) and the growth of export-oriented labor-intensive manufactures (cheap athletic shoes, for example) added family purchasing power to the economy and helped peasants and potential urban proletarians see the possibility of becoming micro-capitalists instead.

But more important, Suharto's New Order followed public policies that were pro-poor. We see this in the rice story; in the channeling of windfall oil revenues into rural areas; in nationwide investments in roads, bridges, harbors, airports, and dams, which helped everyone, including farmers, achieve higher returns.[40] And firm macroeconomic management (until 1997) protected the poor from the plague of high inflation.

Poverty is a relative concept, as charts of the early 1990s remind us by making Indonesia's poor appear to be a similar percentage of the population to that of the United States. How far down can one push the official threshold of poverty without defying reason and a sense of proportion? Does it make sense that Indonesia's definition resulted in a proportion of poor people that was only three-quarters as large as Thailand's and only half that of the Philippines?[41] To wield the data in such a way is to pack some really poor people, and many millions of near-poor, into the falsely secure category of the nonpoor. With sharply receding tides, these millions can be beached, bleached, and left bone dry. No longer would they be statistically camouflaged—they would be openly hurting.

A year and a half after the Asian economic crisis began in July 1997, the World Bank's assessment of poverty in Indonesia highlighted the following factors: "a 12 percent decline in GDP could increase the poverty rate by almost 40%" (official Indonesian government figures for 1998 showed that the actual decline of the GDP was even greater: 13.8 percent); "the rural areas will see the greatest absolute increase in poverty numbers" (that is, lack of rainfall, even more than finance, would hurt the poor in most of the country); "in 1996 [before the crisis], it was estimated that 37 percent of the employed were actually underemployed [who] tend to be poor" (therefore reduced GDP plus inflation impoverished this group further, through increasing unemployment, increasing underemployment, and declining real wages). And poverty rates vary enormously by region: in 1990, 1.3 percent in Jakarta, 46 percent in Nusa Tenggara Timur. (When Jakarta, for 1999, was projected a poverty rate of 8.3 percent, how painfully high can one imagine the rates in provinces like Nusa Tenggara Timur?)[42]

"National Resilience"

In the mid-1990s the Suharto government was riding high on thirty years of growth with relative equality. But stability was the third part of its trilogy. Not content to let eclectic Marxism be vanquished in the marketplace of ideas, the New Order exterminated many of Marxism's standard-bearers. Then Sukarno's NASAKOM was supplanted with Pancasila, an earlier Sukarno coinage, which was reminted and established by 1985 as the sole foundation of the state and all sociopolitical organizations. Once in power, Suharto, like many earlier Dutch administrators, promoted a pseudo-scientific, ersatz-neutral, apolitical bearing, while placing dissenters under surveillance and those presumed dangerous in detention.

Pancasila changed often under the manipulation of Suharto's logothetes. But "national resilience," a summary slogan, makes the New Order's main point with brevity and impact. The quilt of national identity was still loosely stitched. The Suharto idea-mongers therefore stressed security as a comprehensive concept for "an integralistic state," while dressing it up in "national resilience." This all-embracing concept included, according to one of its later exponents, Dr. Dewi Fortuna Anwar, "national identity, national economy, and society as well as military capability."[43]

The new Suhartoism immediately pushed aside the antitheses of the Old Sukarnoism. Adventures in foreign areas (*ganyang Malaysia*) were rejected for regional cooperation. Economic autarky *(berdikari)* was supplanted by globalization—the opening of Indonesia to world investment and trade. Domestic political tensions and confrontative polarizations were banished, and a news-Novocaine was injected to dull or quell potentially inflammatory stories. SARA (Suku, Agama, Ras, Antar Golongan) was the operative acronym. It conveyed a policy of suppressing news about ethnicity, religion, race, and intergroup relations.

Economic development became the commanding policy priority. Archipelagic solidarity was the central geostrategic idea. Pancasila was the sociopolitical master glue of state and nation. Political stability, economic growth, and equitable distribution of development benefits were not only interlocking goals but also the foundation of national security doctrine.[44] Together these elements of national resilience were meant to promise a wholly new all-Indonesian destiny.

The low-key development trilogy may appear even more acceptable to the outside viewer who notes Indonesia's extremely low spending for the armed forces, including police: in 1990, 1.5 percent of GDP. Indonesian budget allocations for defense remained roughly constant from 1975 to 1990, while those of the Philippines doubled, Malaysia tripled, and Singapore and Thailand increased seven times.[45] But a viewer who saw Indonesia as a state no more devoted to armament, proportionately, than Costa Rica would be wrong. Off-budget military enterprises, both legal and illegal, generated perhaps three times as much revenue as the formal budget and led to consumerism and rogueries that eroded military professionalism.

While Indonesia was not under any threat of external invasion, it did face, according to Dr. Anwar, internal erosion from "the tendency among the Western governments to link economic concessions with political conditions, such as democratization, protection of human rights, improvement of workers' conditions, and environmental protection." This "threat to . . . national sovereignty" was "disguised economic protectionism as well as a new form of cultural imperialism." The activities of Amnesty International and Human Rights Watch, Asia, are both "dangerously attractive" to Indonesian intellectuals and nongovernmental organizations (NGOs) and therefore "a political challenge to the authoritarian political system."[46]

Suharto's ideologues were not interested in allegedly universal principles. They defined key internal threats to security as coming from the extreme left (communism), the extreme right (Muslim fundamentalism), separatist movements or rebellions (anywhere), and "the ideological threat posed by democratic movements." Those too far out and those who want to break off are dangerous, according to Dr. Anwar. But those who "demand a more open, pluralistic and accountable political system" are *more* dangerous. "In the post-Cold War period the government views these prodemocracy groups and human rights activists as its most immediate threat, for they . . . seek to undermine the basis of power of the New Order government."[47] For free enterprise democrats of the West who enjoyed wide-ranging civil discourse with Dr. Anwar, the adamancy of her views in writing may come as a surprise. But British education and Washington work experience were only additive democratic layers within a woman of Minangkabau origins, Islamic convictions, and a strong taste for order.

Taking her views as representative, we might conclude that the New Order was confident it could snuff out communists and contain religious fundamentalists but feared it could not stifle the democrats. What kind of national development were they getting, however, if education of the ultimate resource, human minds, were not pursued for its own sake, as well as for social creativity? To what degree did national resilience, as formulated by the New Order, contain within itself a recipe for the very opposite: national brittleness?

Development Policy: A Social Visionary

While Suharto's development policies were strongly remedial of Indonesian poverty, they were also top-down in concept and elite-favoring in effect. Soedjatmoko dared to say so, and to fashion an alternative theory of development as a critique of and checkpoint for Indonesian growth in several dimensions.

A child of Solo, center of Javanese high culture, Raden Soedjatmoko Saleh Mangundiningrat would come to be known to the world, with democratic informality, simply as Koko. Standing over six feet tall, he exceeded the height of the average Indonesian male by several inches. Both he and his sister Poppy, who eventually became Sjahrir's wife, stood taller than Sukarno, who was inches beyond Hatta, who in turn stood over Sjahrir himself, the smallest of the group in physique. Slim and supple, Koko was reputed to be a fine classical dancer in the court tradition of his forbears. In his forties, to his chagrin, he balded. Because his eyes were weak and photosensitive, he wore thick tinted lenses. At first meeting, his appearance was austere, commanding, foreign, even other-worldly. But his voice was reassuring. Deep and gentle, it expressed a fair, measured mind and a compassionate heart. As a host he was relaxed and ruminative. Talk and silence were equally comfortable around him. He would cross his legs (very unJavanese) and, with long toes and big bladed toenails, absent-mindedly manipulate the thongs of his sandals. Around his head curled the smoke of his sweet-scented *kretek,* clove cigarettes.

At sixteen he had wanted to become part of the revolutionary underground against the Dutch. His father, a man of medicine, restrained him: "Not until you can do so without hatred." At twenty-one, a medical student himself, Koko, with his friends Soedarpo, Soebadio, and five others, protested against the Japanese who imprisoned, cross-interrogated, and tortured them but still failed to get them to implicate Hatta. Koko endured the torture by summoning passages of Beethoven in his mind. Once freed, with Soedarpo and Soebadio he got an audience with Sukarno, who patronized them with a speech on tactical cooperation with the Japanese. Soedjatmoko broke in to say that the three had come to renounce their allegiance to him.[48]

Koko's closest political affinity for years was with Sjahrir, who as prime minister appointed him, in his twenties, to help present Indonesia's case to the UN (see Figure 13). He continued there for seven years in the service of the republic, then traveled home through Europe and Russia. He found social democracy in Western Europe bourgeoisified; and among the communist nations, only Milovan Djilas, with his critique of Titoism, had honest perceptions.

Upon returning home, Soedjatmoko joined Sjahrir's party and got one of its few seats in parliament. Sjahrir had (earlier) chided himself for being a "dream cobbler" *(tukang mimpi).* The phrase in Indonesian has a wry association with manual labor and lower class work. His protégé, Koko, had been criticized by Anak Agung Gde Agung, a prominent Balinese who became foreign minister, for "daydreaming."[49] But both men of the PSI were analysts as well as visionaries, capable of realistic patience. Koko recognized that the PSI, unlike the four major parties, "had no cultural or religious or class base in which to find support." Parties themselves were less program-oriented vehicles of change than solidarity groups, he said, "tied together by primordial loyalties of great intensity."[50]

Soedjatmoko declined a cabinet appointment from Sukarno in 1957, which so enraged the Great Leader of the Revolution that Koko's publications were closed down. Effectively unemployed, he advanced his studies of mysticism and history. Deep in contemplative practice from an early age, he had had a "shattering mystical experience" while still a student. The outer garb of his thought was the Hindu-Buddhistic Islam of Central Java. The inner mind was conversant with contemporary philosophers like Merleau-Ponty and great figures of Christian tradition, especially Meister Eckhardt. He was at ease in any culture of mysticism, knowing that they were the same.

The only great personal disappointment I ever heard him express was about a conversation never held. Thomas Merton had written him asking for contemplation in Java. Koko wrote back that he could put him in touch with Javanese Jesuits. Merton replied, "No, I want to meditate with *you*." Merton started toward him on his swing through Asia, but days before their planned meeting in 1968 a short circuit killed the monk in a bathtub in Bangkok. The shock to Koko lingered as a profound deprivation. But he quoted Merton to me as writing to him, "Mystics of the world unite! You have nothing to lose but your loneliness."

Soedjatmoko's most systematic book, *An Introduction to Indonesian Historiography*, appeared in 1965.[51] Koko intended to help his countrymen live historically, not dangerously. By knowing the past, they could wisely build the future. He gave Sukarno one footnote reference, a slantwise allusion to the Great Leader's theory of permanent revolution, which was then, in fact, driving Indonesia toward explosive crisis.

Soedjatmoko's concluding essay confronted the destiny of a troubled nation. Its annual per capita earning power in dollars was expressed in two digits: its cultural diversity was enormous; its national identity was tenuous. He addressed Indonesia's challenges with the seriousness appropriate to a country that was both big and old like China and big and new like the United States. He offered his countrymen intuitive understanding of how things do *not* happen (from Sir Lewis Namier, the ultra-specific methodologist); a philosophic resignation to the disjunction between knowledge and living (from Merleau-Ponty as dialectician); and the emancipating force of history (from Reinhold Niebuhr as theologian unafraid of political decisions).

From these and other coauthors, Indonesians as well as Dutch, American, Australian, British, French, and Japanese, he highlighted key conclusions. Indonesian history-writing can fall into any of several traps: the ahistoric acceptance of *derma-nglakoni* (Javanese for fulfilling one's prescribed destiny), nationalist myth-making (Michelet-flavored French history), advocacy of the indefensible (as with certain Afrikaans historians), Eurocentric preoccupations (thrust on Indonesia by Dutch power), and Marxist pseudo-theology (the rabid opposite of *derma-nglakoni*). Lots of stakes upon which one could be impaled: fatalism, patriotism, partisanship, imperialized thin-mindedness, and communist fat-headedness.

He was clear about the discipline required of the Indonesian historian, and by implication the Indonesian citizen: "He must bear as the eternal burden of 'historical man' the realization that he has constantly to work for a new, but still limited understanding . . . In this historical vision of life, it is the task of the historian, with the fruits of his endless efforts, constantly to feed and refresh historical consciousness as a creative impulse in the life of his nation."[52]

Early in his New Order, Suharto made Soedjatmoko ambassador to the United States; he served from 1968 to 1971. Experienced American diplomats say he was the best ever in that job. By the time of Koko's return to Jakarta, however, there was ample evidence of corruption in the new regime and unfairness in its policies. Student demonstrations for reform expanded into riot in 1974 over the visit of Japanese Prime Minister Tanaka. There are stories that Suharto distrusted Soedjatmoko because of the way he ate a mango—with tableware, instead of simply in his hands. Be that as it may, Koko was interrogated and then placed under house arrest for allegedly "masterminding" the anti-Tanaka uproar. Thus the Indonesian national police thrust him in the same role as had been cast upon Hatta by the Dutch, the Japanese, and Sukarno in turn: a disturber of the public mind, a dangerous Socratic presence among susceptible youth.

Soedjatmoko tired of his terms of parole and simply stopped reporting to the police station. The Ford Foundation, which had appointed him to its board, made an international cause out of his detention and got his passport reactivated to attend its trustee meetings. Koko floated upward to wider international recognition and was made rector of the United Nations University, an institute for global learning in Tokyo.

In 1979, shortly before he undertook leadership of the UN University, Soedjatmoko delivered the Ishizaka Lectures in Tokyo. World Bank studies already showed that the UN target date for worldwide eradication of absolute poverty, the year 2000, would not be reached. Living in "a crowded, hungry and competitive world [means] increasing pressures toward greater authoritarianism and oppression, sharper . . . conflicts for scarce resources, and increasing violence . . . between . . . and within nations. Human freedom is certainly the first victim of such a future."[53] Comprehending the statistics, Koko went beyond data to *dharma*: what is required to build a cohesive and just, productive, and creative society. His vision differed in planes, thrusts, and emphases from the other schools of political-economic development—the pragmatic technocrats, the globo-liberals, the statist-nationalists. He put society first. The absolute poor, isolated geographically and psychologically, "in a state of dependency bordering on slavery . . . must have first claim to the total national resources of the country." Therefore, "we will have to turn developmental thinking upside down."

First, eliminate absolute poverty. Second, advance rural development through a basic needs approach. Third, remove other structural imbalances (center/periphery, city/countryside, intraregional disparities), while building an indigenous entrepreneurial class. Fourth, develop the modern sector—which means a new international order in which the North is not exploitative and the South modernizes without authoritarianism.

Specifics? Involve the poor in organizing themselves. Advance functional literacy. Communicate, not just top-down through village headmen but through locally generated information that is culture- and area-specific, and if necessary bilingual. Work with women, through cooperatives and other programs, drawing out their development potential and their hopes for their children, thus democratizing old patriarchal relationships. Modernize both child-rearing and all schooling practices, away from prevailing concepts of social hierarchy. Adopt neo-Gandhian methods of conflict resolution. Village headmen, already arbiters of disputes by failure of soft law in soft states and by decay of traditional law (Indonesia: *adat*), are in danger of being overwhelmed by a clamor for justice. Developmental progress and local justice are not irreconcilable, but it takes wise men to reconcile them.

How—with populations doubling every thirty-five years or sooner, with breakdown of traditional mutual help (Indonesia: *gotong royong*), with excessive migration into cities, with cultivation of marginal mountain slopes, with nomadism and rural banditry—How "will it be possible for people living in such conditions not to be consumed by envy, against their richer neighbors in their village, against the big city dwellers, and on the national scale, towards the other richer countries[?]."

The specter of multimillions of people consumed by envy drove Soedjatmoko to reflections on the need for people to develop their own inner space: "heightened capacity to perceive and contemplate beauty, higher levels of self-awareness, greater sense of humor . . . greater openness for the transcendental dimensions and connectedness of human life, which is the heart of the religious experience."

Not until 1990, the year after Koko's death, was the first Human Development Report issued by the UN. Not until 1995 was a World Summit for Social Development held. Even now the language of such reports, sensitive and sophisticated as they have become, does not venture, as Koko did, into language of the soul. Who, in the inescapably political atmosphere of "development," credibly talks aesthetics as seriously as economics, or speaks of the beauty of an orchid as seriously as he speaks of the discrete slices of a social science piechart? Yet: "The spirit knows no time or number," said Meister Eckhart. "Number does not exist except for the malady of time . . . Time and place are fractions, God is an integer."[54]

Koko drove hard and cleanly beyond statistics to carry the point of development from below: a multi-linked transformation going far beyond what a government could hope to do, requiring every watt of intellectual energy within a society to make it reflective and self-critical. Human growth requires a compassion, a solidarity, a responsibility that transcends "me and them" and requires each person to think and act "only in terms of you and me and in terms of us, the family of humans."[55]

"I like Americans best," Koko sometimes said, "when they are least sure of themselves." He also found that Americans liked his openness and were eager to learn from him. I discovered his impact by listening to Daniel Bell, a great sociologist of American life and prophet of the American experience, explain to me the meaning of *cocok* (the c's are pronounced like ch in choke). Fittingness. Harmony. The emotional aesthetics of the expected. Conformity for the sake of inner peace and social calm. The prime and instinctive Javanese rule of everyday conduct. I knew it by experience but kept silent in fascination while this intellectually combative denizen of New York City repeated the treasured lesson vouchsafed to him by Soedjatmoko.

Clifford Geertz knew Koko steadily after 1951 and sought, unsuccessfully, to bring him to the Institute for Advanced Studies in Princeton, New Jersey, after he completed his leadership at UN University in 1987. But Koko, as Geertz appreciated, was too accessible to needy minds, especially young ones, to accept the shielded study of the Institute. Geertz saw his friend as a "rooted cosmopolitan," the equal in that regard to Adam Michnik of Poland, Desmond Tutu of South Africa, Abba Eban of Israel, and Octavio Paz of Mexico—each of whom could represent his nation with a powerful effect on global conscience and intellect.[56]

Koko was modestly grateful for his laurels—the Magsaysay Award (or "Asian Nobel Peace Prize") and honorary degrees from Yale, Williams, and other institutions. He was attentive to his followers in Indonesia, always available as guru, never withdrawn as mandarin. But contending against a bureaucratic patrimonial state can wear on one's system. An emergency operation yielded, he told me, a prostate much bigger than the average Asian's, more like a Westerner's, he was told; a plum instead of a peanut. He smiled at his own forlorn vanity. Not long after that, completing a seminar in Yogya late in 1989, he was smitten by a massive headache and died quickly of a stroke.

Soedjatmoko never settled for the standard recipe of his times, that raw economic growth will reduce poverty. He set his sights higher: on promoting human rights, fulfilling human needs, and advancing human growth. Focusing on all three, he believed, would further development, order, and justice. Only thus can each society find its own point for optimal balance of freedom and restraint.

6

THE NEW MAJAPAHIT EMPIRE

Cold and reclusive where Sukarno had been hot and expansive, Suharto enjoyed the successes of his personal style in a ruling system which he knotted more tightly with Javanese culture. He anticipated well, inhaled political intelligence to alert himself to the possibilities before him, and acted with ruthless cunning to preserve and enhance his power. Whereas his apparently outgoing predecessor undid himself with autistic fantasies, this "closed" man (Indonesian: *tertutup*) engaged the real world and built up a power momentum that was barely checked and rarely reversed across thirty years.[1]

As a lieutenant colonel in the 1950s and chief supply and financial officer to Central Java's Diponegoro division, which he would later command, Suharto had come under a cloud as a military smuggler. Smuggling was, in feudal language, an appanage: revenue rightly accruing to one's rank in life. If not royally assigned, it might be appropriately seized without moral qualm.[2] In this, Suharto as president would resemble the Javanese rulers of precolonial times. In other ways as well: demonstrating prowess as a warrior, manipulating the interests of subordinates, arranging the appearance of supernatural support, deploying a network of spies, and negotiating political marriages to strengthen his rule and project its future lineage.[3]

Suharto's success as president was not instant or without vulnerabilities. From 1965 to 1974 he was chief among generals in a military government whose bureaucracy was recovering from near-total vitiation. From 1974 to 1983 the bureaucracy grew greatly in effectiveness, and the military remained pivotal, while Suharto steadily built his own power with steely resolve. From 1983 onward a dynastic tendency became evident. The older members of the military aged and paled in influence; the younger men were career-pledged to Suharto's command. The bureaucracy was subject to presidential will. And the president, entwining as many relationships as possible in patronage dependent upon himself, toward the end was clearly disposed and prepared to confer his power upon a genetic successor—his eldest daughter, Tutut.

Sumitro Djojohadikusumo saw the way things were going when he came back from long exile as a failed rebel. In the late 1950s he had left a still post-revolutionary nation in which Bung Karno and Bung Hatta remained key figures—and "Brother" was still a term of respect. He returned to a universal expectation that he would call General—soon President—Suharto "Father." "Why call him 'Bapak'? I'm four years older than he is!"[4] Sumitro was still astonished and amusedly derisive thirty years later. But he accepted the neo-feudal usage, labored in Suharto's cabinet to reconstruct the nation, and reared his own sons for eminence in the military and in business in a manner not undynastic itself.

The occasion of the marriage between Sumitro's son Prabowo Subianto and Suharto's daughter Titiek in 1983 gave the minister insight into Suharto's motivation from the president himself. In the preparatory conversations and family meals together, Suharto told of the deprivations of his youth and his desire to give his family and his country a security he had never known. Sumitro cherished the confession of intimacy. But the massive, ornately ritual wedding (see Figure 46) as a "culmination of [the Suhartos'] ruling cultural vision" wearied him both as an aristocrat and an economist.[5] Years later he shook his head over the social distortions of Indonesia: "Neo-feudal at the apex, defended by a praetorian guard, and supported by patrimonial behavior in business and politics."[6]

Suharto's insecurity as a child is understandable. He had a mentally unstable mother, a largely absent father who made rare, arbitrary, and momentous interventions in his childhood, and an extended family whose nurturance of him was indifferent. His isolation made him consciously work on a calm interior/composed exterior—archetypal values of central Java—and he cultivated that norm to a successful, if nearly obsessional, extreme, as in his wordless receipt of the news of the peremptory shooting of Aidit. Suharto as a young man went on to be first in his training groups in the Royal Netherlands Indies Army, the Japanese Police, and again (in 1959) at the Indonesian Army's Staff and Command College.[7] The gathering of information, its objective analysis, and judgments reached in emotional detachment together describe a rare fusion of the techniques of military intelligence and mystical discipline harmoniously combined in Suharto, aspirant soldier and politician.

This is the man who, before leading a daring six-hour breach of Dutch control of Yogya on March 1, 1949, secreted himself in the caves of Gua Wurung and Gua Selarong to absorb the cosmic powers of Prince Diponegoro, leader of the rebellion against the Dutch from 1825 to 1830. This is the man who, in September 1974, took Australian Prime Minister

Gough Whitlam on a tour of the Dieng Plateau to discuss Timor and concluded the trip in the cave Gua Semar, believed to be a dwelling place of the
clown-god Semar, father of the Javanese and guardian of the island.[8]

The Javanese over centuries had reorganized the classical Indian pan-
theon and tilted it to accentuate Siva and his associates. Suharto, however
unconsciously, replicated the temple tetrad of this Javanese tradition in his
own intimate constellation of political power. Siva (prevailing over Brahma
and Visnu) is the god of gods. His consort, again in a manifestation peculiar
to Java, is Durga, the fearsome goddess of great beauty, many arms, many
weapons. From Hindu mythology, the son of Siva and Parvati is Ganesha,
the elephant-headed god. In Java, he leads the heavenly followers of Siva in
battles against the demons, as *senopati,* or army commander of the kingdom of the gods. Finally, the anthropomorphic deity Agastya is chief intermediary between the gods and humanity, a bearded figure of scholarship
and wisdom.

In Java, the tetrad of Siva-Durga-Ganesa-Agastya fit well with the historic concept of the effective royal set: ruler, queen, military commander,
and priest counselor.[9] Translated into palace practice in the last third of
the twentieth century, the fit continued: at first, Suharto, Ibu Tien, General Ali Murtopo (as head of Opsus, a tentacular organization of military intelligence and other operations), and Lieutenant General Sujono
Humardani, presidential assistant for economic affairs and mystical guru-
at-large to such an extent that some called him Rasputin. The eventual
deaths of Murtopo and Sujono did not disturb the pattern. Into their places
slipped General Benny Moerdani as the new Ganesa and Air Marshal
Budiardjo as the new Agastya.

In time, however, the pattern fractured. Moerdani's ambition led Suharto
to ostracize him after 1993. Budiardjo died in 1997. Most important, Ibu
Tien died in 1996. The inwardly calm, outwardly composed villager king,
like other human beings, needed the understanding and support of intimates. From a psychological view, let alone any mythical tetradic pattern,
without trusted helpers Suharto would not be equal to the crises that
sprang upon Indonesia in 1997. For decades before that, however, his resolve prevailed. Born of youthful deprivation, bred by instruction in Dutch
and Japanese military disciplines, and nourished by immersion in a Javanese
Sivaite cosmology of royal might and magic, Suharto met every challenge
with ruthless patience.

The Malari Uprising

In 1968 Sumitro Djojohadikusumo as minister of trade discovered and revealed that one-third of all foreign exchange applied toward imports was

33. THE SIVAITE TETRAD. Clockwise from upper left: Siva, Durga, Ganesa, Agastya. This pre-Islamic Javanese royal set, roughly equivalent to king, queen-consort, warrior-commander, and priest-counselor, shows some enduring resonance in Javanese political psychology. (Original color drawing by Kathë Chapman Grinstead, author's collection, based on plates in Jan Fontein, *The Sculpture of Indonesia,* and National Museum of Indonesia, *Art of Indonesia: Pusaka*)

being misused. With exchange in extremely short supply for Indonesia, foreign governments were making it available as aid. Of that precious assistance, at that precarious time, perhaps $100 million was being lost in outright fraud. The Jakarta press brought out the facts with mortifying clarity, and repeated student demonstrations forced Suharto to clear the air.

In 1970 he appointed a distinguished Commission of Four, with former vice president Hatta as advisor, to inquire into corruption. Their series of reports was buried in the government, but Aristides Katoppo, editor of the daily *Sinar Harapan,* published leaked copies in a front-page series. The commissioners had told Suharto that corruption was "running unchecked," "a social evil" that was slowing development "in all fields." Using their prestige for pinpoint candor, the commission told President Suharto that reform "must begin at the top." The secret use of extra-budgetary funds in the office of the president must be replaced by "open management . . . no matter what the excuse."[10]

Two corruption cases went to court. Suharto said that the others lacked evidence. As urged, he established a board to oversee the state oil company. He ordered all high-ranking government officials and military officers to prepare statements of their personal wealth. And he announced that he was taking personal command of efforts to eradicate corruption. His tactics may be summarized as nibble, dodge, buck, and posture: let some hard justice be eaten in public; hide most of the sweets of scandal; imply sweeping purification by asking many others to open up; and, by exercising "personal responsibility," ensure that a basically corrupt system remained unchanged.

Arief Budiman, a student who later went into exile, was allowed to see the president in August 1970. He dared to write afterward that the major limit to corruption was social revolution. "Thus, if the corruptors are clever (and in Indonesia they are indeed clever enough) I think they will not violate this 'code of ethics.' Clever corruptors will not destroy the nation; they will keep the nation alive, although very thin."[11] Not as ruthless and desperate a policy as that of the Japanese army, but practices both parasitic and damaging.

By the end of 1973 Japanese investment in Indonesia had risen to $185 million, twice its total in Thailand and nine times that in the Philippines. Forty-five Japanese firms were doing business in Indonesia. If this sudden profile of penetration and expression of new power by Japan were not enough to wake up memories of their "Great Pacific War," the prominence of Chinese Indonesians among their partners—about 70 percent—stimulated ancient resentments. The Indonesian government was trying to promote domestic industry, but Indonesian textile firms were going bankrupt in competition with Japanese producers invested in Southeast Asian synthetic fiber production and with Chinese-Indonesian owners of broad power looms.

These structural realities existed as Japanese Prime Minister Kakuei Tanaka organized a tour of Southeast Asia in January 1974. Pronounced "guilty" in a mock trial in Kuala Lumpur and burned in effigy in Bangkok, he approached Jakarta at a time when inflation and a rice shortage were at their most serious since 1965. A recent anti-Chinese riot had swept through Bandung, and Muslim students had stormed parliament to protest a "secularist" marriage bill. Tanaka met immediate trouble: students on the tarmac at the airport; others attempting to block the roadway into the city. The next morning tens of thousands protested near the state guest house on the palace grounds. Waves of demonstrators hit the President Hotel, operated by Japan Air Lines, smashed showrooms at Astra Toyota, and burned the dealership's entire stock of new cars. The next day, Pasar Senen, a major shopping center with much Chinese ownership, went up in a spectacular blaze. The two-day toll was reported as eleven youths killed and more than a hundred injured. Almost a thousand vehicles were damaged or destroyed, and 144 buildings. In various categories of disruption, looting, or provocation, 820 individuals were arrested. One of the "provocateurs," a leader of Mahasiswa Menggugat (Students Accuse), would always remember his 3 years, 10 months, and 3 days in prison. A grand nephew of the first prime minister, he would go on to get a doctorate at Harvard and emerge in the 1990s as Dr. Sjahrir, economist, businessman, reformer.[12]

Suharto acted on some of the student demands that had garnered public support. He abolished posts held by four senior army officers on his personal staff, removed the head of public security, and dismissed the head of central intelligence. He issued orders to moderate the extravagant lifestyles of senior military officers and civil servants and announced a series of measures to protect indigenous enterprise.

Having retreated four steps tactically, he then advanced several leaps strategically. It was announced that the riots were part of a plot by "radical socialists" to overthrow the government and that trials for subversion would follow. Newspapers and student councils were brought under tight control. Soedjatmoko was arrested as the alleged mastermind of the plot. Student leaders, under interrogation, had readily named him as a prominent source for their ideas. And he had been relaxedly—or determinedly—public with his views, telling Robert Shaplen of *The New Yorker* that Indonesia's ruling elite was "sitting on a time bomb, or maybe, more accurately, a volcano."[13]

To counter the subversive foreign ideas on which Suharto blamed the "disaster," he went back to Sukarno's great Pancasila speech of 1945 and turned it into a fire hose of propaganda. Over the coming years, with secu-

34. THE "MALARI" RIOTS. The arrival of Japan's Prime Minister Tanaka in January 1974 excites violent demonstrations against Japanese penetration of the economy. They were also the first great challenge to the Suharto circle. But military suppression, witch-hunts, and a shuffle of appointments left the president stronger than before. *(Tempo)*

lar theologues reinterpreting it and dogmatic bureaucrats administering it, Pancasila issued forth, drenching the citizenry through schools, army, and government-controlled media. Unlike Falangism in General Franco's Spain, it did not involve a church. Unlike the Iron Guard in General Ion Antonescu's Romania, it was not more fascistic than the dictator himself. Contrary to Peronism in Argentina, it was neither populistic nor prolabor, nor was it attached to the personality of its advocate. Pancasila was intended to be spine-stiffening and nation-shaping. Suharto put a more religious cast on Pancasila than the now-deceased Sukarno ever had, and opened a dialogue between Islam and the state which accommodated the former while further empowering the latter.[14]

In an archipelago not well knit by communication and transportation systems and still wearing a thin fabric of shared history, a major binding factor was surely needed. But no corporatist state adopts ideological zeal without the danger of blinding itself to many realities.

The Oil Boom

When Sukarno named his last cabinet early in 1966—with an absurd 100 members—he made Ibnu Sutowo minister for oil and gas. In the following year Suharto, now the new president, approved creation of a single national oil company, Pertamina, with Ibnu as its president-director. Because his father had been a regent in the radius of the sultan of Yogya, Ibnu had top Dutch schooling, to which he added medical credentials and a history of commanding the Siliwangi division in South Sumatra, including success in talking his troops out of the regional revolt in 1958. When he found himself implicated in a huge smuggling scandal soon after, Ibnu simply shifted over to oil and with Nishijima Shigetada, a prewar Japanese spy and wartime friend of Indonesian nationalists, established himself in the enterprise. Although Shell, Stanvac, and Caltex had long been in operation, war, disorder, and dictatorial squeeze had kept oil an "infant industry."[15]

In the New Order, Lieutenant General Ibnu now had a monopoly of oil exploration, refining, processing, transporting, and marketing, along with free initiative to negotiate with any foreign and domestic parties. He became a more and more prominent figure, described by the Australian journalist Hamish McDonald as "a slim, rakishly handsome man whose dark face often relaxed in a wide dazzling smile, always immaculately tailored . . . He moved in a world of sheikh-like luxury and credit-card extravagance, a fulfillment of the air-conditioned, Mercedes-driven fantasy of Asian escapism."[16]

When the Arab embargo in 1973 drove up oil prices, Pertamina's budget reached half that of the entire national government. Oil was raising Indonesia's national income, enriching its public treasury, and becoming—for a single turbulent decade—the engine of Indonesian development. By early 1975 Caltex, which pumped a million barrels a day in Indonesia without supervision by Pertamina, far overshadowed it as raw producer. But Pertamina's seven refineries had a capacity of 400,000 barrels a day and a network of 2,680 domestic gasoline stations. It also participated in or owned twenty-nine joint ventures and subsidiaries, including oil marketing in Japan, a tanker fleet rivaling the Indonesian navy in tonnage, and a fleet of aircraft that rivaled the national airline. Ibnu Sutowo justified his style, saying that "it is simply not psychologically possible for men who wear threadbare clothing and who ride in old cars or *becaks* to negotiate satisfactorily with men who earn $50,000 a year and fly by company jet aircraft." Lest Pertamina's network of hotels, guest houses, and offices from North Sumatra to the Baliem Valley of Irian Jaya look too imperially presumptuous, the entity entered philanthropy: roads, schools, mosques, and an eye-catching hospital in Jakarta.[17]

But swollen things get noticed. Even investigated. In June 1975 Economics Minister Widjojo put to the parliament an estimate of $120 million owed locally by Pertamina and $2.3 billion of overseas debt. Ibnu did not change his managerial or personal ways. At the first meeting of the heads of government of ASEAN, at a Pertamina resort complex on Bali in February 1976, Ibnu appeared and flew off in a helicopter with Philippine President Marcos to play golf. Too much for Suharto. The issue had become: who was running Indonesia?[18]

The next month Minister Sadli, chairman of the Pertamina Board, called Ibnu to his office for the first time. The public message soon was inescapable: he was "dismissed with honor." Ibnu admitted by sworn statement that he had signed 1,600 promissory notes to a prominent Geneva broker, to provide "collateral" of $1.266 billion—notes signed without reading. His plunge into the supertanker trade—now in the doldrums and earning nothing—had committed Pertamina to the purchase of thirty-four tankers at $3.3 billion. In 1978 the attorney general announced that Ibnu had been found "not involved" in any criminal activity. He was left in retirement tending a private empire of thirty-seven companies.[19] Ibnu Sutowo was not treated as the white-collar criminal his actions may have deserved. Instead, as appropriate to a feudal system, he was reduced in appanage: simply demoted to white-turbaned sheikhdom.

Indonesia had received an oil windfall in 1974 equal to 16.5 percent of its non-mining GDP, which, sustained through 1978, then boomed up to 26 percent by 1980. The end of the second boom in 1981 provides perspective on the oil decade. In total dollars, Indonesia's realization was smaller than that of Nigeria and Venezuela. Its one large oil reservoir, the Minas field of Caltex, was already "old" and increasingly costly to work. Given the diversity of its other resources, Indonesia's windfall as a proportion of its GDP was smaller than Algeria's. The largest share of the good fortune, as elsewhere in the world, accrued to the government.

Unusual in Indonesia's case, however, was the subsequent investment in agriculture and rural development—irrigation, fertilizer subsidies, and rural public works—at many multiples of Nigeria, where agriculture received only 2.5 percent of federal capital outlays. It all could have been worse. Pertamina did help develop the country while developing the oil industry.

Yet, incentives to develop other exports beneficial to the outer islands were inhibited by the oil boom. Developing a broader tax base was also postponed, and along with it the requirement to give more weight to the views of taxpaying citizens. Indonesians were not freed from foreign interests but were more enmeshed with them: debt management was again a major preoccupation, government options were limited, and international lender/donors had to be heeded to some degree.[20] State enterprise assets would still, even in 1995, slightly surpass those of the swelling private conglomerates.[21] And the shadow of Lieutenant General Ibnu's excesses could not be dismissed from modern memory of the public sector. From the 1970s onward, Indonesian cabinets would include a minister for administrative reform, even while an Ibnuesque style of favoritism, and analogous kinds of losses, continued.[22]

East Timor and Henry Kissinger

Twentieth-century Portugal decolonized as clumsily as it had managed its colonies for centuries. A "Revolution of the Roses" disengaged the Portuguese from terrible poverty in Angola, Mozambique, and East Timor after 1974, while generating nasty turmoil in all. East Timor soon had three parties: one favoring integration with Indonesia, another supporting evolution linked to Lisbon, and a third (the Fretilin Party) advocating immediate independence, with an African style of socialist ideology. The foreign spokesman of the Fretilin Party was Jose Ramos Horta, who obtained a letter from Adam Malik, Indonesia's foreign minister, on the right of independence.

But Ali Murtopo displaced Malik as handler of the matter. Apparently confident of international approval of the new Indonesia, he reverted to a Sukarnoesque expansionist mode as in West Irian and Malaysia a dozen years before. Suharto entered the mystical cave with Australia's prime minister in September 1974, and Murtopo emerged in October as his negotiator and project manager. The campaign took shape through Operation Dragon (*Operasi Komodo*), developed by the leading Jakarta think-tank, the Center for Strategic and International Studies (CSIS).[23] Ali Murtopo was the leader of CSIS, and Soedjono Humardhani was prominent in it. The center was effectively Suharto's private information agency, as well as his dirty-tricks group dedicated to sapping political parties that contended with the part of the state, Golkar. An acronym for *GOLongan KARya*—functional groups— Suharto's organization was far less a party in any democratic sense than a quinquennial election machine to serve the regime, using military intelligence and financed by Pertamina.[24]

Harry Tjan Silalahi, Jusuf Wanandi, and his brother Sofyan—all leading young Chinese-Indonesian Catholics—were the administrators of CSIS. These were eminent nationalist youth of the anti-Sukarno generation of 1966. They had adapted to a series of new presidential decrees, concluding in December 1967, which declared that all Indonesian citizens, regardless of descent, enjoyed the same rights and obligations and that discrimination was impermissible. Under this cloak of assimilation, however, the government urged persons with Chinese names to change them, and religious observances "oriented to their ancestral land should be practiced privately." This policy of change-your-name and cloister-your-Confucianism brought about a tripling of Catholic Chinese in all of Indonesia. The greatest impact was in Java, where Chinese Catholics jumped to 28.4 percent of all Catholics.[25]

Name-changing required at least thirteen different documents, including birth, marriage, and divorce certificates, plus the conversion of electricity, water, and telephone accounts. To become certified as new Indonesian in this way was expensive and exhausting. Among those who endured and prevailed were Liem Bian Kie, who became Jusuf Wanandi, director of the CSIS. His brother, Liem Bian Koen, became Sofyan Wanandi, eventually the head of the Gemala Group, a significant conglomerate, and spokesman for Chinese-Indonesian business. Both of them, working closely with President Suharto's aides, were critically compared to the "court Jews" of earlier Europe. Their intelligence and charm notwithstanding, they drew warnings as a "double minority" (both Chinese and Catholic) and were assumed to hold prejudices against Muslim organizations.[26] The Wanandis and Harry Tjan Silalahi collected funds from overseas Chinese sources, notably William Suryadjaya's Astra Group and Liem Sioe Liong's Salim Group. According to the Japanese scholar Shiraishi Takashi, "The biggest secret project that [this] special planning group did was the East Timor annexation plan."[27]

CSIS put out, as it would do for decades, persuasive rationales and analyses to foreign diplomats, journalists, and academics. In mid-1975, however, the situation featured a Portugal that wanted to keep an avuncular clutch on East Timor, an Australia that could be cozened, and a United States, just driven out of Saigon, which was passive. Suharto came back from Washington in July 1975 and, in his first public statement on the matter, ruled out independence for East Timor.[28]

Civil war in East Timor broke out in August and took the initiative away from the secret planners of CSIS. Against hesitancy in his cabinet but with support from Murtopo, Defense Minister Panggabean, and Intelligence Chief Benny Murdani, Suharto lectured his generals, as encouraged by *guru* General Sudjono. The Javanese military-political classics taught the unflinching poise necessary to allow East Timor to "fall" into Indonesia's hands. The gods Ganesa and Agastya were with him, but Fretilin was not. On November 28, 1975, that most irreconcilable party declared the Democratic Republic of East Timor.[29]

The Indonesian government moved quickly to evoke a counter-declaration from pro-Lisbon and pro-Indonesian elements in East Timor that it was "integrated" with Indonesia, and to convoke a biddable parliament to urge "more resolute and positive" action on the Suharto leadership. An attack on the city of Dili was scheduled for December 5: embarrassingly quick, from the perspective of the United States. President Gerald Ford and Secretary of State Henry Kissinger were arriving from China for a day in Jakarta. American intelligence or other embassy personnel successfully got the attack postponed for forty-eight hours, until Ford and Kissinger had left on December 7. Kissinger was said to have simply stipulated that Indonesia execute their plan "quickly, efficiently, and don't use our equipment."

This was patently ridiculous. The Indonesian army had not relied on Russian equipment for over a decade; its major sources were American. What the army did initiate—a clumsy, costly Kostrad paratroop drop—captured Dili, and follow-up attacks secured other towns. On July 17, 1976, Suharto decreed East Timor the twenty-seventh province of Indonesia. The UN never recognized the annexation.[30]

Indonesia maintained the fiction, as in the confrontation with Malaysia a dozen years before, that it had no troops in Timor, only "volunteers." At its height, however, troop strength was 30,000. Even so, it could not find Fretilin forces to steamroll over and had to conduct guerrilla warfare instead: deny an easy environment, destroy food resources, win by attrition. Fretilin replied with calculated raids, ambushes, and sniping. Only late in 1978 did Indonesia have enough control to announce large development projects and allow in foreign diplomats. Four years after civil war commenced, foreign aid workers and Indonesian officials were offering fearful estimates of the number of Timorese who had already died: of factional fighting, then in direct, prolonged Indonesian-Fretilin hostilities, and perhaps mostly by starvation and disease, originating in disruption and advancing through the invaders' malign neglect.[31]

Daniel Patrick Moynihan was at that time the American ambassador to the United Nations. In his autobiography he notes summarily that "China altogether backed Fretilin in Timor, and lost . . . The Department of State desired that the United Nations prove utterly ineffective in whatever measures it undertook. This task was given to me, and I carried it forward with no inconsiderable success."[32]

Moynihan's self-mockery is the more welcome given Secretary of State

35. THE SUHARTOS GREET THE FORDS. President and Mrs. Suharto welcome American President Gerald Ford and Mrs. Betty Ford to Jakarta in December 1975. The brief official visit includes Secretary of State Henry Kissinger. It is followed by the Indonesian invasion of East Timor, uncriticized and undeterred by the United States. (Courtesy of Indonesian Embassy, Washington, DC)

Kissinger's silence on the matter. In 4,000 pages of memoirs he never mentions Timor.[33] Why should he mention it? Would it have mattered to Metternich? As the ultimate American power-realist in his decades of prominence, Kissinger reckoned only with the might and momentum of major powers. He shared a Nobel Peace Prize in 1973 for ending war in Vietnam, while along the way rationalizing the merciless bombing of Cambodia to cover America's strategic withdrawal. Now he was genuinely surprised by and concerned with the massive Soviet intervention in Angola and Soviet support of highly equipped Cuban combat troops that suddenly appeared there. In Cold War calculus, an embarrassment that could echo throughout Africa and engage the U.S. Congress was immeasurably more important than a mere rumble in far-off East Timor. Indonesia had dealt with its own communists. Let them deal now with the Timorese communists (but not until our aircraft leaves Jakarta). Kissinger could not have "saved" East

Timor and never thought of trying to do so. Even Australia, which had a neighborly interest in the outcome, as well as harboring some guilt for having abandoned the Timorese who had helped them against the Japanese, could not have rescued East Timor in 1975.[34]

Kissinger was understandably mum about what State Department personnel called "the Big Wink."[35] Years later, however, a document was leaked detailing a meeting of eight top State Department officials after his return to Washington from the Asian trip with Ford. Kissinger is revealed as enraged by a "disgrace" to himself: a cable sent in his absence that apparently complained to the Indonesian government about use of American equipment in its invasion of East Timor. He feared that fifteen or twenty people in the Department already knew about the cable; that it would leak to Congress; that he, the Department, and American policy would be sharply embarrassed. The give-and-take with his key aides is instructive.

Secretary Kissinger: You all know my views on this . . . It will have a devastating impact on Indonesia. There's this masochism in the extreme here. No one has complained that it was aggression.

Legal Advisor Monroe Leigh: The Indonesians were violating an agreement with us.

Secretary Kissinger: The Israelis when they go into Lebanon—when was the last time we protested that?

Leigh: That's a different situation.

Undersecretary Carlyle Maw: It is self defense.

Secretary Kissinger: And we can't construe a Communist government in the middle of Indonesia as self-defense? . . . On the Timor thing, that will leak in three months and it will come out that Kissinger overruled his pristine bureaucrats and violated the law . . . You have a responsibility to recognize that we are living in a revolutionary situation. Everything on paper will be used against me.

Assistant Secretary Philip Habib: We do not take account of that all the time . . . I think the leaks and dissent are the burden you have to bear . . .

Secretary Kissinger: . . . No one who has worked with me in the last two years could not know what my view would be on Timor . . . I know what the law is but how can it be in the US national interest for us to give up on Angola and kick the Indonesians in the teeth? . . . I don't care if we sell equipment to Indonesia or not. I get nothing from it. I get no rakeoff. But you have an obligation to figure out how to serve your country. The Foreign Service . . . stands for service to the United States and not service to the Foreign Service.

Habib: I understand that that's what this cable would do . . .

36. EAST TIMOR: CHILDREN OF FAMINE. Photographic evidence from Laga, East Timor, February 1981, suggests that the Indonesian government, having annexed East Timor and found it steadily rebellious, used famine as a means of suppression. (Peter Rodgers/John Fairfax Publications, Sydney)

Leigh: There's only one question. What do we say to Congress if we're asked [about military aid to Indonesia?]

Secretary Kissinger: We cut it off while we are studying it. [But secretly] we intend to start again in January.[36]

The military aid to Indonesia did resume after a "modified suspension," largely fictive, was imposed. The eventual costs for Timor continued to increase when unrelieved famine struck the island. Congressional hearings on the disaster show an earnest and largely useless concern of State Department officials and an impotent outrage on the part of human rights activists, in the face of tight Indonesian control of information, movements, and logistics of relief.[37]

A quarter-century later, Henry Kissinger had mellowed. He mildly answered a young Indonesian leader's question about Indonesia/East Timor in December 1975. You have to remember, he said, that the Cold War was

alive and well. We thought it would be over, like Goa, in a week. It was essentially a colonial issue, not a human rights issue; and if you don't know
what to do, stick with your friends.[38]

The dead in Timor from that terrible period of conquest is often said to
have been 200,000. Robert Cribb, however, in the most careful appraisal yet
of population statistics, military capacities and motivations, and all relevant
conditions, concludes that perhaps 50,000 killings (one in thirteen East
Timorese) fits the available evidence. Moreover, there was a roughly equal
"number of deaths from privation as a result of Indonesian re-settlement
policies." The combined figure of 100,000 dead, though half the estimate of
some sources, certainly does not exonerate Indonesia. It only tries to strike
a fair estimate, without either committing blood libel on the accused or
showing mortal indifference to those who died.[39] In any case, Indonesia's invasion of East Timor grievously documents the apothegm of the Russian
philosopher Nikolai Berdyaev: "All history is unrighteous annexation."[40]

Sawito's Moral Challenge

On July 17, 1976, five famous Indonesians and an unemployed bureaucrat
signed a document entitled "Towards Salvation." The distinguished signatures that gave the document credibility were those of Dr. Mohammad
Hatta, former vice president of the Republic, Cardinal Darmoyuwono, the
primate of the Roman Catholic Church in Indonesia, Dr. T. B. Simatupang,
a retired general and chair of the Indonesian Council of Churches, Professor Dr. Hamka, a leading intellectual and Islamic modernist, and R. Said
Sukanto Tjokrodiatmojo, founder of the Indonesian police force and head
of a New Order umbrella body for mystic faiths. The sixth signature was by
Sawito Kartowibowo, a publicly unknown former head of an Agriculture
Department office assisting poor cultivators, who had been fired in 1968 for
his left-wing nationalism and connection to Sukarno.

The modest, apparently insignificant Sawito supplied the dynamite. His
collection of accompanying documents assailed the moral degradation of
the government and nation and included a "Letter of Transfer" modeled on
the Supersemar letter of 1966 by which Sukarno's signature had conveyed
national power to Suharto. Sawito spoke of "mas Harto"—a colloquially respectful term of address, but distinctly less subordinate than Pak Harto—
and his "transgressing of his oath of Presidential office" by enriching his associates, friends, relatives, and himself "in a truly scandalous way." Sawito
proposed that power be legally transferred to the universally respected
Bung Hatta who, made responsible for the upper house of parliament,
would then oversee a general election.[41]

How could this dapper, narrow-shouldered man in his mid-forties, a servant of the state in disrepute, have assembled such talent and dared to shake the establishment? In 1972 Sawito had undertaken with friends the first of three *lelono broto,* rambling pilgrimages in various holy parts of Java which he later described as "metaphysical research expeditions." In a more expressive rendering of the Javanese term, they were wandering freely in a state of deep meditation and suspense of bodily functions, searching for divine inspiration.[42]

What they discovered was recorded in the journal of Sawito's friend, R. Soedjono, a document later seized by the prosecution. A Dutch graduate in law unemployable in the colonial Indies, Soedjono emigrated to prewar Japan and returned to Indonesia with the invaders in 1942 as a colonel, two ranks higher than the Dutch had ever allowed an Indonesian to rise. Soedjono, who eventually held three ambassadorships, most notably to Japan, was matter-of-fact about history when I interviewed him several years before the Sawito affair. But about Subud, the *kebatinan* (literally, "innerness," or mystical) organization of which he was a leader, he was guarded and portentous. He lived in a modernish house in Menteng, Jakarta, but implied that his true home was an infinite mansion of dimensions not describable to a foreign stranger.[43]

Soedjono's journal recorded several years of peregrinations with Sawito. He lugged modern recording equipment along, but things seen and heard and "people" met apparently registered only in deep meditative awareness and not on empirical instruments. At Borobudur, one of the stone Buddhas smiled at Sawito. Supernatural confidence in Sawito was tangibly displayed at midnight near Gunung Saptorenggo. The travelers, their guides, and porters all saw two bright lights shoot down from the eastern sky and enter Sawito's body, knocking him over backward.

More holy places followed, greater profusion of lights, and ever greater spirits submitting to Sawito. A Dutch parapsychologist born in Yogyakarta received telepathic news of the rise of a Ratu Adil (Just King) and took an airplane to Jakarta to invest Sawito appropriately. More kingly spirits were summoned and appeared to confer spiritual legitimacy. The circle of people around Sawito had no doubt that the *wahyu cakraningrat,* or mandate of heaven, was conferred upon him.[44]

In his own writings, Sawito was at pains to merge his thoughts with the Jesuit spiritual evolutionist Pierre Teilhard de Chardin and to supplement his arguments with allusions to Shakespeare, Sun Yat-sen, and Vivekananda.[45] No inconsistency here: among the educated, *kejawen* (Javanese religion) can be cosmopolitan-syncretic as much as cosmically mystical. But a practical defensive tactic may also have been working in Sawito.

The dazzling evidence of his companion, Soedjono, would need modern argument to convince allies as well as critics.

But before Sawito and his co-signatories could go public with their moral assault, government sappers and strategists suppressed the whole collection of documents and neutralized them by pre-emption. First, Suharto, apparently spontaneously, made a speech about how he had never used his position to accumulate wealth for himself or his family. The next day the public were suddenly told that a "dark conspiracy to replace the President" had been foiled. Antisubversion measures were intensified. Selective arrests included Sawito and Soedjono; fifty-two military officers were rounded up for questioning. Suharto, having pre-bleached himself, stood aside from the flurry of besmirchings and recolorings that ensued. Ali Murtopo of Special Operations, followed by State Intelligence, characterized the "affair," itself a dismissive word for political subversion, as "leftist." The "Sawito plot" was an "inflammatory" effort "to set religious groups against one another." Or the whole thing was a ploy to provoke arrest of the five prominent signatories and thereby instigate mass antigovernment demonstrations led by adherents of religion and mysticism.

After befouling Sawito's naive intentions, the government singled out him alone for blame and cast aspersions on his sanity. The prominent co-signers were treated not as traitors but as dupes, so that trial could focus on an unknown.[46] Sawito, however, rapidly became widely known and admired, and support of him generated disturbances that approached the intensity of the Malari riots. When Sawito, on trial, was at last permitted to speak, he testified to the absence of a government of law. In the folk saying, "the fence [was] eating up the crops":

> It is not unusual to hear of police who are thieves, soldiers who pillage and murder the people, watchmen who always sleep, cashiers who embezzle money, customs officers who smuggle, teachers who become prostitutes, leaders who are corrupt; of . . . the poor being asked for donations, the rich being given credit, the destitute being preyed on, bosses doing as they wish while subordinates are half dead, bosses overeating while subordinates go hungry, and of leaders getting fatter while the people grow more afraid . . . The Indonesian nation aspires to build GOD's justice, and all we get is GHOST justice.

The audience, it was reported, exploded in a laughter of relief and recognition.[47]

The defense team could not get the judge to allow any of the five prominent senior co-signatories to testify—all of them presumably seen by Suharto as better diminished by suspicions of senility. Sawito could only ar-

37. TRIAL FOR "SUBVERSION." Sawito Kartowibowo before the clerk of the court on November 14, 1977. The obscure bureaucrat and mystic would become a popular hero and the center of a vortex of political forces, before his conviction and imprisonment. (Ed Zoelverdi/*Tempo*)

gue in defense that he broke no laws by receiving *wahyu* (divine radiance) and being crowned Ratu Adil. Then Sawito went on the attack, with a comprehensive assertion of the necessity of morality in all spheres of government, and "a moral accusation from every Indonesian citizen who has an awareness of freedom."[48]

Sawito by now had millions of fans but no influential defenders. In June 1978 he was convicted of a wide range of charges and sentenced to eight years in prison. His clean record, good behavior, and appeals brought release after five years. By then Suharto had been elected president two more times. Sawito had made the government tremble. In practical effect, some disenchanted New Orderites had banded with marginalized Sukarnoists to test the strength and deepen the unpopularity of Suharto. They aroused the sympathy of much of the still nascent middle class, which tended to benefit by a government based on law and transactions made in trust. But Sawito's prominent co-signatories ducked and rallied no masses. There was no plan to follow, nor was there any clear form of what a Hatta-led administration would be.

Suharto had been exposed, but Sawito was imprisoned. Suharto was battered, and he even let *kebatinan*—the Javanese spiritualism which he then favored and practiced—take a beating. But he prevailed. In the eyes of the Javanese peasantry and the traditional *priyayi*, his own status of divinely accorded kingship was tarnished but it was preserved. Any populist receiver of the *wahyu cakraningrat* could obviously expect to languish in prison. Sawito, child of mystical light, sat in political darkness.

The Petition of Fifty and Pancasila

By jailing two lonely adventurers, Sawito and Soedjono, and embarrassing five prominent religious figures, the Suharto government made it clear that a mystico-moral challenge could be deflected, discredited, and punished. But what might a rational political challenge of fifty do?

In early May 1980 a petition to Parliament, described as a "Statement of Concern," raised serious questions about how the government conceived its power, used Pancasila, and intended to carry out the next elections. The signatories included five military leaders, among them the ever-eminent Nasution, and Ali Sadikin, popular former governor of Jakarta; three prime ministers of the revolution and early republic, Sjafruddin Prawiranegara, Mohammad Natsir, and Burhanuddin Harahap; and an array of prominent civilians. They dared to ask the parliament to consider sensitive issues: Suharto's view of himself as the "personification" of Pancasila and his use of it "as a means to threaten political enemies"; his approval of dishonorable action by the armed forces; and his putting the soldiers' oath above the constitution and urging them "to choose friends and enemies based solely on his own assessment."[49]

A speech by Suharto himself had helped prompt the Petition of Fifty. In an address to the army's paratroopers, the Red Berets, he had denied that his wife received commissions on government contracts and had made their home into "a headquarters for tender awards, commissions, and the like." He also denied, as an old story of students and housewives, that he had a mistress, a well-known movie actress.

Was Suharto faithful to his wife? Was Ibu Tien faithful to the constitution? No court, of course, would decide such questions. But Suharto had the power to direct how parliament would handle the Petition of Fifty. In early August he wrote to the speaker suggesting that any questions about his speeches, which he enclosed, be taken up by the appropriate committee. Given government control of all committees, that ended real public discourse. Orthodoxy was restored: *dwifungsi,* unity of Golkar and ABRI, pre-eminence of Pancasila.[50] In his Independence Day speech for 1980 and afterward, Suharto iterated his best and classic defense: "The one and only way for us to take is to implement development . . . [for which purpose] we must all be able to maintain dynamic national stability."[51]

This language fell upon an especially attuned ear. The prolific proletarian writer Pramoedya Ananta Toer had just spent fourteen years in Suharto's jails. In 1979 the administration of President Jimmy Carter had facilitated his release from hard labor on Buru Island. He noticed immediately the disappearance of the term "nation-building" from the public vocabulary. In its place, to an extent he found loathsome, he heard and continued for years to hear "development."[52] The nation was not yet built, but self-enrichment was on the loose.

The Petition of Fifty had afforded a rare opportunity: students for democracy, Muslim leaders for Islam, and retired generals with the goal of an incorruptible ABRI could come together in a common vision of Indonesia. But the Suharto version of development prevailed through its apparatus of control and repression, buoyed up by the petroleum boom. Following an OPEC meeting in Bali in late 1980, Indonesia's most popular grade, Minas crude, was increased to $35 a barrel—more than twenty times what it had sold for a decade earlier. Suharto's new high-spending cabinet was epitomized by B. J. Habibie as minister of research. His huge "transformative" shopping list of technological and military items ran into sharp World Bank criticism in 1981, and a scaling down of 57 projects valued at $21 billion eventually followed. But that was only announced weeks after Suharto's parliamentary election to a fourth five-year term. The World Bank congratulated the president on his "courageous" response to economic necessity.[53]

Pancasila's five principles were difficult to contradict one by one, or in their binding tensions with one another as a quintet. Their very generality had made them useful ever since Sukarno voiced them in 1945. In 1974, however, Suharto began to turn them into a practical guide for life in Indonesia and to generate a kind of secular *hadith.* In 1978 the MPR obliged Suharto by elevating Pancasila to a status of compulsory moral education of youth and of government officials at all levels. The president and his associates pressed steadily on with what was becoming a corporatist state ideology. In his Independence Day speech of 1982, Suharto advanced again an initiative, previously deflected as draft bills to parliament in 1969 and 1973, to require social organizations and political parties to accept Pancasila as their ideology.[54] Islamic leaders grew increasingly disturbed.

Sjafruddin Prawiranegara, tall, with a full head of white hair, spoke with deliberation and moved in a stately way. He had been president and acting prime minister of the republic's emergency government after the Dutch captured Sukarno and Yogya in 1948. He had become prime minister of the Sumatran rebel government against the republic in 1958. His grace and dignity as a leader included the tragic muted quality of one whose anti-Sukarno revolution had been crushed. Now, additionally, his anti-Suharto initiative and his Islamic concerns over coercive use of Pancasila were being throttled. "What crime . . . has any . . . Muslim organization committed?" he asked in a widely circulated letter to Suharto.[55] His plaintive question went unanswered.

Five months after Sjafruddin's letter, another former prime minister, Mohamad Natsir, cordially untracked me from the series of questions about another era on which I had come to see him. It was *now* that religion was endangered. *Now* free speech is endangered. *Now* "fascism" threatens Indonesia. America must take note. He urged copies of the petition upon me, and follow-up communications, hoping that (improbable as it seemed to me) another American voice could amplify in the United States what was strangulated in Indonesia. Natsir's tone bore the grievous edge of a man wounded simultaneously in his religious faith and his political creed.[56] He railed against Pancasila from every angle, one of which was his perception of the government's effort to raise Javanese mystical beliefs "step by step . . . to the level of a religion," thereby diluting Islam.[57] But it was not *kebatinan* that Suharto was promoting. It was Pancasila. He got his way in 1985, when the government required all associations of any kind to adopt Pancasila as their "sole guiding principle" (*azas tunggal*).

Three younger, less defensive Muslim leaders than the generation of 1945 would try for ways to reconcile Pancasila with Islam and to carry a state political creed in balance with a universal religious faith. They found, moreover, that Suharto's government supported Islamic piety incomparably more than had the Dutch or Sukarno.[58] Abdurraman Wahid, Amien Rais, and Nurcholish Madjid would express their criticisms of the Suharto state for the most part allusively or indirectly. Wahid, for NU, was the most syncretical. He adroitly rendered unto Caesar what was his, while seizing onto all else for NU. Rais, somewhat younger and identified with Muhammadiyah, was the most scriptural at one level and the most opportunistic at another. Madjid, a former general chairman of the Islamic Students Association, developed his own mature, educated constituency by allowing more room than either of the others for modern knowledge and by stressing economic and social justice.

All three of them, doubtless, were surprised when Suharto at the age of seventy went on his first pilgrimage to Mecca in 1991. But that soldier, oriented in succession to Hindu-Buddhist innerness, to Pancasila corporate ideology, and, as a late-awakened Muslim, to world Islamic transformations, was always moved primarily by official duty and the power to get things done on his own terms. He expressed it in calculating command, as a leader determined, whichever way Indonesian society might grow, to bend it to his will.

Prisons, Extrajudicial Killings, and "Security"

There is no mention of the individual in the original Pancasila. And when, in the constitutional debate of 1945, the idea of a bill of rights arose, Bung Karno quashed it. Such guarantees would create "a conflict within the soul of the state."[59] A proper rejoinder, not then rendered, is that the state has no soul in the first place. Only individuals have souls; and they need legal and moral defenses.

The absence of such protections was clear in the arbitrary trials and detentions of communists after 1965. The total of arrests, by Suharto government admission, may have run from 600,000 to as high as 750,000.[60] A Western woman, married to an Indonesian, had offended by translating economic documents for Soebandrio. She testified in writing to conditions she experienced in ordinary prisons. Women abused and tortured; food minimal; medicine absent; rights inconceivable; release apparently arbitrary.[61] Even when those such as she, in the "C" category for least dangerous, were let out, their identity papers were marked "ex-political prisoner," with natural consequences for employability, surveillance, and official shakedowns. Special permits were required of them to change residence or travel outside their cities.

By 1975–76 the Suharto government claimed that 550,000 "C" persons had been released and only 36,000 prisoners remained untried for involvement in the attempted coup. Amnesty International observed that this figure embraced only "A" and "B" prisoners in detention centers near large cities. If all others were counted, the figure might rise to 100,000.

After eighteen months of internal debate over domestic needs vis-à-vis international pressures, and a month after Jimmy Carter was elected president of the United States, the Indonesian security chief announced the intended release of "B" prisoners at 10,000 a year, which would free all by 1979. It appears that this was done; meanwhile, "A" prisoners were managed case by case.[62] One of the last in the "B" category to be released, because he would not sign a statement conceding that he had been justly detained, was Pramoedya Ananta Toer.

Pramoedya had been on Buru Island, from which no prisoner ever escaped—a sweltering piece of the Maluku chain, bigger than Bali but inhospitable to humans. A photograph in 1971 showed him "pitifully shrunk by moral and physical privation." The attorney general joked that "He is allowed to write. But he has no pencil and paper." By 1973 international attention got Pramoedya taken off backbreaking labor and allowed a typewriter. He had survived an early and minimal diet of dirty grain with the meat of anything that could be caught—dogs, cats, snakes, lizards, lizards' eggs. "And beatings kept coming beyond reason."[63]

Pramoedya survived "rehabilitation" and grinding labor among maddened men under ruthless guards. Back in Jakarta, publishing, possessing, or circulating his novels brought terms in jail. But the work survived, ultimately irrepressible: the 1930s, 1940s, and 1950s dramatized in previous novels and short stories; and the first half of the colonial twentieth century in the Buru quartet—novels informed by his destroyed historical researches, first narrated to fellow prisoners and finally written in danger of confiscation, then smuggled out in the hemmed pockets of female relatives. All of Pramoedya's writings, one way or another, say I will survive; I will endure; I will bear witness to the dead, and to the primitive folly of all prisons; I will study the faces of the murderous gods of history. Pramoedya had spent two years in jail under the Dutch and another under Sukarno's generals (1960–61) for writing too sympathetically about the Chinese. Then came fourteen years on Buru. He continued to hear the novelistic voice of Multatuli, the great nineteenth-century Dutch critic of Netherlandish oppression in its Indies: "Human duty is to be human."[64] And now Pramoedya said, with a decent respect for the dead and for a balanced verdict of history, let us search for the mass graves of 1965–66.

He did not write any more. He could not hear anything in his right ear, and only some things in the left, a result of blows from a soldier's gun butt. Those who deafened him also burned his library. But he had produced and he prevailed. His idea of courage was the opposite of Hemingway's, who saw bravery as capital drawn down by expenditure. For Pramoedya, courage was a renewable resource, strengthened by exercise. Which may help explain Hemingway's suicide, Pramoedya's survival.

Pramoedya in 2000 could be found, early most mornings, in an old sarong and a threadbare white undershirt, collecting the debris tossed in the empty lot across from his house; making a pile, lighting it, aerating it with a machete smuggled home from Buru, to keep the flames burning. I saw the trash pile: paper, vegetable matter, plastic, smoking along together in an anti-ecological mass. Pak Pram recalled the destitution of the Japanese period. "At best I ate a bowl of *bubur* [porridge] once a day, and leafy matter from behind the house. That's when my attraction to garbage began." He laughed.[65]

A journalist asked Suharto in 1972 if he really thought Pramoedya knew of the September 30th conspiracy. "'No,' he said with a smile." But, Suharto went on, Pramoedya was a member of PKI's artistic wing, Lekra, and if the coup had succeeded, people like him would have ratified it.[66] On Pramoedya's first trip to the United States in 1999, a graduate student, in earnest public candor, asked, "Were you a communist?" Pramoedya replied that he carried no such card; he was only defined that way by the New Order, which he several times described as "military, fascistic." Who were his favorite American writers? He answered readily: John Steinbeck and William Saroyan.[67] In those names from the 1930s one may seize some of the enduring essence of Pramoedya's spirit: populist, perhaps socialist, certainly individualist, with the gift of listening to ordinary people and understanding extraordinary suffering. In the heady days of revolutionary ideology and socialist realism before G30S, however, Pramoedya had been an uncommonly harsh critic of writers he deemed elite, effete, or trivial.[68]

He does not seek reconciliation in the twenty-first century with independent liberal humanists like Goenawan Mohamad any more than with Suhartoites. He sees a country "divided by murder." A survivor, but daunted and drained, he sees a people who do not understand their history. His books are more accessible to Indonesians now, but they are still on the attorney general's list of those banned as subversive. His inspiration to write any more, he says, is lost to years of imprisonment and persecution.[69]

Across Java, beginning in 1983 for at least two years, between 5,000 and 10,000 extrajudicial killings took place.[70] To the degree that these satisfied a need for public security, they may be dignified with the term "executions." To any degree the armed forces and police may have erred in their choice of targets, the term "murders" more exactly applies. After the elections of 1971 and 1977 robbery and burglary had increased notably. After the election of 1982 these and other crimes appeared to break out in a wave that threatened everyday life in Java, or the serene reinstallation of the president for his fourth term, or both. What to do? Indonesia's police-to-population ratio was only from one-fourth to one-fifth of such ratios in Singapore, Malaysia, Thailand, and Hong Kong. Having only one policeman for every 1,119 citizens, rather than one for every two or three hundred people, was thin security coverage—an old Indonesian problem.

In the context of order/disorder, practitioners of martial arts called *jagos*

had long been enforcers of the ruler's will and protectors of village property. The nineteenth-century Dutch, distrusting their power, marginalized
them but allowed the indigenous administrative elite to continue to use
them as bodyguards, spies, enforcers, and extorters. The more orderly
Dutch civil service of the twentieth century pushed the *jagos* into illegality.
Many of them burst back during the nationalist revolution as local in-
surrectionaries and heroes. But *jagos,* or fighting cocks, not integrated into
the society of the republic, became *gali:* wild ones, on the criminal fringe.[71]

As crime rose in the early 1980s, Suharto's New Order briefly tried legitimizing gangs of *gali* to become guards, in return for the training and guidance required. It did not work. The state then turned to an enormous expansion of neighborhood security systems. That left the operating gangs
criminalized in standard perception, except for Pemuda Pancasila—youth
allegedly in defense of national doctrine but actually muscle for official hire,
and freebooters on the side.

The attempted new system of control divided local security guards, salaried and uniformed, into those responsible for protecting commercial and
public buildings and spaces and those protecting residential neighborhoods.
To these were added night watchmen, a much older and non-uniformed institution. All three were under the training and surveillance of the Guidance of Society division of the police, whose aim was to make all of them a
profession. Their salaries, however, came from the firm, office, or house
employing them. Whereas there had been no *satpam,* or public security
guards, before 1980, they multiplied rapidly in Suharto's fourth, fifth, and
sixth terms. By the end of 1995 they were about 200,000 across Indonesia,
more numerous than police and of course higher in ratio to population:
one for every 900 people. Combining the two ratios, each Indonesian might
consider herself/himself protected by 0.0019 security persons, publicly or
privately paid. In certain markets, malls, bus terminals, office or residential
complexes, the ratio might be much higher, providing more than an illusion
of security. But the raw fact remained that against a determined *preman,* or
thug, in most of Indonesia the best defense was, and is, not to encounter
him alone.

In 1983, however, the security ratio had been more slender still, and crime
was spiking. Violent robbery in 1982 was double its percentage of total crime
two years earlier and triple that of seven years before.[72] The organization of
an administrative answer was the responsibility of General Benny Moerdani,
who now controlled the Armed Forces and the intelligence services as well
as Kopkamtib, the security structure initiated in 1965 suppress communists.
It shifted its focus to "cleansing" the nation's cities of criminal "cancer."[73]

Unless a suspect got off a blacklist, or carried a special card, or reported regularly to a garrison, he might be subject to being hunted down by military squads or sharpshooters, often masked. He might be killed on the spot. Or driven off in the night to a quiet place and shot through head and chest with .45 or .38 caliber pistols. The corpse might be tossed in a river. Or it might be left as display in a public place, frequently with hands bound and often with signs of torture. Multiple bullet or knife wounds—overkills— were often intended to register the punitive power of the New Order. Its defenders might see it as protective and corrective power. Crowds gathered at these displays and talked among themselves. Newspapers took note and were read. They and the public adopted the term "Petrus," an acronym for *penembakan mysterius,* or "mysterious shooting," a euphemism which pointed no finger at the system. But Petrus became the weekend routine, most pronounced on Fridays and Saturdays. It would look like anarchic violence otherwise, a sourceless contagion, frightening to the general population instead of reassuring as intended. Therefore the state perpetrated the killings in signature fashion, leaving no doubt as to authorship.[74]

Even with such a rationale, why naked power, rather than judicial procedures? Why were blacklists treated as sufficient evidence for the killings? Why overkill, literally blowing some targets to pieces? Why the reliance on tattoos in some or many cases as evidence enough of criminality, and not even bother to supply the newspapers with the criminal histories of those killed?

In a calm lunch with Harsja Bachtiar, a subcabinet security bureaucrat at the time, I asked about some of these matters. Negative world attention was rising, but Harsja was undisturbed by it. What else could be done, with crime out of control and the courts slow and understaffed? His justification was the same as in the case of radical surgery for cancer: do something lest it spread. But where does responsibility lie? I asked. He looked at me, almost pitying my innocence. Such an operation, he answered, cannot happen without orders from the top.[75]

Suharto himself, later in his autobiography, wrote proudly about the operation. "Why?—intense fear had gripped the public . . . The criminals had gone beyond any sense of humanity." Procedure?—"we had to take drastic action and give these people treatment commensurate with their conduct . . . But this does not mean that we just shot them, bang, bang, and were finished with it. No! Those who resisted, yes, they were shot. There was no other choice, because they resisted." Public displays?—"some bodies were just left where they had been shot. This was meant as shock therapy so that people would realize that loathsome acts would meet with strong action."

Questions of evidence? Proof of criminal identity? Not addressed. Commensurability of punishment by death with crimes committed? Not considered. Success and social impact of the operation? "And so these despicable crimes came to an end."[76] Thus spoke the ruler. Some of the public were relieved. No one openly disagreed.

Suharto, by 1983, had struck oil, suppressed political riot, stifled legitimate criticism, squelched crime with murder, and smothered anticolonial revolt with guns and famine. His empire was in every real dimension more extensive and, in its venal way, incomparably more vital than ever the fabled Majapahit had been.

THE SOUND OF SILENCE

By the mid 1980s Suharto's number of years as president equalled those of Sukarno, and by 1986 he was confident enough to let his predecessor be officially declared a national hero.[1] Suharto himself meanwhile expanded in character in his own manner. The lean mustachioed young revolutionary officer, cap at a cocky angle, remained somewhere hidden within the ponderous official in the safari suit who read his speeches so monotonously that people turned off the TV.[2] He could not energize loyalty in the way that Sukarno's voice had done every weekend, inspiring owners of radios to put them in a window and turn them on full blast, to share Bung Karno and national pride with the whole neighborhood, blending Chinese and all into "Indonesian identity."[3]

Instead, documents now dressed the nation: constitution and Pancasila. Fear united it—fear of a return to 1965–66. And a new state structure commanded it, in which Suharto at the apex was both president and father. He was Bapak by common consent; he was a model husband and father, as the media repeated; he was the "Father of Development" by parliamentary decree in 1983; and he was also the father of what came to be known grudgingly and apprehensively as "the family," or simply Cendana, after the street in Menteng where his guarded private residence stood, an easy drive from the palace. The Cendana family, Suharto's blood relatives and cronies, would come to dominate the state and the economy.

President and father, political and moral leader: the concept was complete. But the family environment began to swallow up the state environment. As generals aged and retired, as competing politicians faded or were intimidated or bought off, Suharto quietly expanded his power. The acronym KISS took hold: "Ke Istana Sendiri-Sendiri"—to the palace one by one. He dealt with bureaucrats and generals individually and did not let them amalgamate in groups. Meanwhile, after the fall of Pertamina and oil revenues, he increasingly used Chinese conglomerates as supposed drivers of the economy, notably those led by *cukongs*—business "bosses" of Chinese origin, in cahoots with the Indonesian power elite—Liem Sioe Liong, Bob Hasan, Prajogo Pangestu, and Mochtar Riady. Suharto also dealt with each *cukong* one by one.

The methods practiced by Suharto have been recognized by an astute Japanese observer as *kazoku shugi,* a traditional Japanese idea of organization, translatable into English as "family principle."[4] But his deeds are more descriptive than the term. His government more than doubled the number of civil servants between 1975 and 1988, to over 3.5 million in the latter year. But during the same period, the percentage of national expenditure going into public salaries decreased from 42 to 15 percent. The effect was as intended: to increase the number of "servants of the state" on government rolls, while at the same time intensifying their dependency (and, regrettably, their corruptibility).

Even the unfortunate Colonel Untung had shown how deeply rooted the family principle was in Indonesian custom. He had tried to legitimize the September 30th Movement by criticizing General Yani's circle and other leaders for leading luxurious lives. But not with blanket puritanical condemnation. He meant, rather, "Don't let the high-ranking ones monopolize the profits; they must share with the rest of the soldiers."[5] Now Suharto was in charge of a system in which leaders were to care for all the needy and dependent. From the point of view of American business, which could only play into it while fearful of violating the Foreign Corrupt Practices Act, the "whole system was built on undercompensation."[6] That is clinically astute and unchallengeable. It must be added, however, that the whole system was rife with unfairness, imbalance, unproductive motivations, opportunism, and moral rot.

While draining initiative from his civil servants, Suharto also systematically sought to neutralize the peasantry and the urban underclass. All those whom Sukarno might have sought to arouse were defined by Suharto as the "floating mass" and were intended to be herded, negated, silenced politically. Surveillance, police work, and ideology were meant to allay any threats through trepidation or induced torpor. They largely succeeded in doing so.

Pak Harto flourished in this macrocosm of his own creation. In the mid-1980s he began to be shown, microphone in hand, no script, talking to farmers; or, teacup at his side, making a speech to ministers or military officers.[7] This new relaxation suggests that he was not only Father of Development by decree but the successful and confident father of the nation in his own designing mind.[8]

Tanjung Priok and Muslim Rage

The shah, exiled from Iran, had died in 1980, and the Ayatollah Khomeini was in undisputed power there. The Soviets were in Afghanistan but could not get out of the guerrilla war with Muslim resistance groups. Islamic revival in various forms was appearing in Algiers, Cairo, Gaza, Khartoum, Kabul, and elsewhere. Resurgence born of faith and confusion, grievance and resentment, was building into a rage against alien, infidel, and incomprehensible force.[9] Ordinary believers everywhere, including the illiterate, were taking heed, or taking heart.

Whatever might be true on the world stage, Suharto's conceit by now was that Indonesia was his own private proscenium. Muslim leaders had helped establish his New Order. Muslim youth had participated prominently in the killing of communists. Yet he appointed no prominent Muslim to his cabinet in 1968, 1973, 1978, or 1983. After his fourth election, Suharto implicitly rejected a joint statement by Muslim, Protestant, Catholic, Hindu, and Buddhist councils that social organizations "religious in nature remain based on their religion and respective religious beliefs." Instead, he said, it was time for Indonesia to consolidate politically, accepting the national ideology. Pancasila must become the sole basis—*azas tunggal*—of all social and political organizations.

When the government, in 1984, sent to the Assembly five draft bills for that purpose, the port area of Tanjung Priok, in North Jakarta, felt especially challenged. Tanjung Priok was populated mostly by men, many of them young, out of school, and out of work. A disparate set of immigrants from other port towns and islands contributed to an often desperate slurry of men enduring brute labor and low wages. At the urging of lay preachers and street-corner demagogues, this vulnerable group found a noble and uplifting goal in the defense of Islam against the infidels, thieves, and tyrants who ran the nation in defiance of Allah's holy laws.

When security officers removed hostile posters from the As Sa'adah Prayerhouse on September 8, one of the officials was alleged to have entered it without taking off his shoes and the other to have smeared gutter water on the posters. When the officers reappeared later, a shoving match ensued and one of their motorcycles was set afire. Reinforcements arrived and made four arrests, including the head of the prayerhouse. On September 12, Amir Biki, a student activist in 1966, now prominent in Tanjung Priok, built up a crowd of 1,500 and led a march at 11 PM to release the prisoners, chanting "God is great!" They carried both the red and white national flag and a green banner with an Arabic inscription, "There is no God but Allah."

Armed soldiers blocked the roadway. Armored vehicles and military trucks moved in to the rear, preventing retreat. The crowd surged forward. The soldiers fired into the crowd. Amir Biki was shot; when he tried to get up, he was bayoneted. In half an hour, perhaps 63 (officials say 18; some say hundreds) were killed and many more severely wounded. Burning of Chinese shops and homes followed.

"It did not need to happen," Abdurrahman Wahid, chairman of NU, later said, reflecting on the Tanjung Priok tragedy. "They work in the port, and they see Mercedes automobiles being unloaded while they are lacking even clean water in their homes. But they are poor and unorganized, and the government doesn't pay any attention to them . . . They did believe the government was acting to harm Islam, and some of them did have the idea of raising a holy war against the government. But none of this would have happened if there had been communications between the two sides."[10]

A "white paper" appeared in less than a week, signed by twenty-two lead-

38. PROTEST IN TANJUNG PRIOK. From Al-A'rat Mosque in Cakung, Jakarta, the young leader Haji Amir Biki, killed in the Tanjung Priok incident, is buried in 1984. (Bambang Harymurti/*Tempo*)

39. PRAYER AFTER RIOT. Friday prayer outside the Istiqomah Mosque, higher education campus of Dakwah Islam, the day after the Tanjung Priok killings. Note the motorbikes, *becak*, tanks, and newspapers used as prayer rugs. (Bambang Harymurti/*Tempo*)

ers, including retired generals Hartono Rekso Dharsono, former commander of the Siliwangi division, and Ali Sadikin of the Marines, former governor of Jakarta, as well as former Prime Minister Sjafruddin. They invoked the warnings of the late Mohammad Hatta and the late Adam Malik. They attributed the event to a false and suppressive ordering of national life. Tanjung Priok was not an incidental riot but "a consequence of the existing system."[11]

There followed a series of fires and explosions in Jakarta; Sarinah Jaya department store in suburban Kebayoran was burned to the ground. Lim Sioe Liong's Bank Central Asia branches were bombed on October 4, killing two. On October 29 the Marine Corps munitions dump on Jakarta's outskirts began exploding, eventually destroying 1,500 houses, leaving fifteen dead and twenty-six wounded.

Altogether 200 people were said to be arrested, including several "extremist lecturers." The most senior army officer ever arrested, Lieutenant General Dharsono, first secretary general of ASEAN, was eventually found guilty of subversion—trying politically to capitalize on the Tanjung Priok incident—and was sentenced to ten years, reduced to seven. His counsel, Buyung Nasution, a 1966 activist, earlier arrested in connection with "Malari," was found guilty of unethical conduct. Effective disbarment destroyed his law practice and forced his emigration to the Netherlands.

President Suharto pronounced on Tanjung Priok for the first time just before the trials began. "We will wipe out terrorism before it becomes a national disaster. We are all responsible for resolving differences of opinion through democratic and constitutional procedures." He suggested that crises would be avoided by passing the five political bills establishing Pancasila as the "sole basis" for all organizations in Indonesia.[12]

A powerful symbolic reply to Suharto was the bombing of Borobudur. Three weeks after his speech in January 1985, explosives blasted an upper level of the nation's oldest and grandest monument, damaging two statues of the Buddha and nine stupas—bell-shaped, lattice-worked shrines of stone. Beyond those who felt injured in their respect for a national treasure, others might feel personally attacked: Chinese Indonesians who still practiced Buddhism, and *priyayi,* the governing elite, for whom the religion of Java or even Java-as-religion was symbolized in the monument. Perhaps especially Suharto himself. Born in Central Java, an observer of lore and formulas linking the precincts of the temple to the destiny of Indonesia, he had reason to feel that a magical element crucial to his leadership was under attack. Indeed it was. One man arrested and sentenced for bombings of Borobudur and East Java, Abdul Kadir Baraja, represented the tradition of Kartosoewiryo, having headed Darul Islam-Lampung in the 1970s. After release from prison he founded in 1997 an organization dedicated to the restoration of the Islamic caliphate and took part with others, like-minded, in founding the MMI (Holy Warrior Assembly) in August, 2000.

As a continuing consequence of Tanjung Priok, in July 1985 fires in Jakarta destroyed a major shopping complex, a nine-story office building, and the building housing the state radio and television stations. Clashes arose between the armed forces and groups of aroused Muslims, most notably in Lampung, South Sumatra, in 1989. The estimates of the death toll there ran from 41 to over 100—rural Muslims leading marginal lives but just as aroused on behalf of Allah, insulted through Pancasila, as were the stevedores of North Jakarta.[13]

General Benny Moerdani, the commander of ABRI, had launched a Java-wide campaign intended to reassure Muslim leaders and preachers and clarify the government's position. He insisted that religion and houses of worship were being used to promote issues having nothing to do with Islam. He said that his Catholicism was incidental to security measures, as was the fact that those arrested as disturbers of the peace just happened to be Muslim.[14] Moerdani would carry on until relieved as ABRI chief in February 1988 and made minister of defense, from which cabinet post he was dismissed, in the next five-year cycle, 1993. In his first demotion, he would watch the cabinet of 1988 gather around him, a cabinet suddenly containing ten ministers and junior ministers of Islamic prominence. He would see President Suharto, now concerned to lead Islamic forces rather than oppose them, go on *haj* in 1991—the Central Javanese villager at last on a pilgrimage to Mecca.

Moerdani, stolid, bluff, shrewd, was in 1997 defensive about the "de-Bennyization" of ABRI leadership, meaning removal of his personal loyalists—Catholics and others—from key positions. Toward the end of a generously long interview he appeared to answer a question I had not yet asked, about management of the Tanjung Priok incident. "I'm a soldier," he avowed, uncued by me. "If I'm told to shoot, I shoot."[15] I believe he was saying: No one could have ordered me how to handle Tanjung Priok except Suharto.

The incident continued to fester. A brigadier general revealed in 1993 that bodies from Tanjung Priok had been trucked to a hamlet east of Jakarta and buried there. When the Human Rights Commission finally completed a report in June 2000, sixteen years after the event, but did not identify command responsibility, protesters of the Front for Defenders of Islam, dressed in white, attacked the commission's headquarters.[16]

The Rise and Irrelevance of a Middle Class

The language of "class" is useful in describing the changes accelerating in Indonesia during the 1980s only if one is wary of two Western theories about purpose in history. One is academic neo-Marxism. The other is intuitive whiggery, a chipper confidence in the endless potential of an emerging middle class. Neither expectation—radical (even if endlessly delayed) revolution fired by a proletariat or progressive melioration lubricated through a bourgeoisie—corresponds to the events of modern Indonesian history. Neither, indeed, is inevitably anchored in any history anywhere.

A vocabulary of class may be helpful just the same as a way to capture changing phenomena in words. For Indonesia, Java has the largest population and the best-described class dynamics—the *priyayi* of court and bureaucracy, the *santri* of mosque and bazaar, and the *abangan* of field and factory.[17] The period of the 1950s through 1965 was not, in class terms, dramatically different from the 1930s or even from the days before the First World War, except for the absence of an additional layer of Dutch hyper-hierarchism. After 1955, however, notable changes abounded. By the 1980s Indonesia's dusty, clogged, and cranky capital, Jakarta, was booming enough to be a lens for new social analysis, even if it were applicable only to a few other large cities like Surabaya and Medan.

The term "santrification" began to creep into use, suggesting, with a pun, the gentrification of some American cities. At a deeper level, the word summoned the appearance of educated Muslims in the demonstrations against Sukarno in 1966, the reform themes of Nurcholish Madjid in the 1970s, and new levels of Muslim affluence and consciousness, which went far beyond santrification as mere "transformation of the bazaar into a modern economy." According to Aswab Mahasin, an analytical Muslim modernist, rising levels of income and appetite now also meant "the embourgeoisement of their sons and daughters, or the *priyayisasi* of the *santri*."[18]

The Indonesian middle class remained the product of economic change more than its producer. It was the smallest middle class on the western rim of the Pacific. In 1980, 2.1 percent of households owned an automobile, 5.6 percent a TV, and 8.9 percent a motorcycle. Because car ownership was not a prerequisite of middle-class attitudes, and rural needs for a motorcycle did not prove middle-class mentality, one could infer that the middle class constituted something between 5 to 8 percent of the population.[19]

The Chinese still constituted a separate category in Indonesia. If ever the *cukongs* or quasi-*cukongs* among them felt their power, they knew they could be ostracized or shaken down at a moment's notice. Most Chinese Indonesians qualified for distribution through layers of the middle class, but they were rarely allowed to identify with it. They were felt to be—and felt themselves to be—a co-middle class, semi-separate, difficult to assimilate.

Above the middle class was a power elite, small in number but large in its political-business-financial control. Distinctly not an aristocracy, it exhibited the tastes and appetites of the nouveau riche. Even those among it whose style was more refined, and who detested the Cendana family's pseudo-royalty, nevertheless paid it the inglorious tribute of political passivity.

Below the middle class were the teeming millions, the *rakyat*. The people. They, too, could be subdivided, but it is more illuminating to look at their rural representatives. After two decades of economic growth, Indonesia was still 78 percent rural in 1986. That certainly contrasted with at least 93 percent before 1930, but how much had attitudes changed? If urban motorcycle riders carried in their heads some appetite for democracy, that was much less true in the countryside. There, older patronage structures and

40. MIDDLE-CLASS LIVING ROOM, 1982. New levels of living enable some Indonesians, in cities like Bojonegoro, East Java, to watch government TV at home.
(Steve McCurry / Magnum Photos)

routes of advantage persisted, nourished by the state. The only outlet for the rural rebel was a "healthy anarchy" that left him / her free, as an expression of middle-class spirit, to leave the *desa* (rural village) for the city.[20]

In the middle classes of Jakarta itself lay the most rewarding context for differentiated description. In the mid to late 1980s the upper fraction of the city's population *(santri-priyayi)* lived in safe, well-kept residential areas and were employed as expert staff assisting ministers, or as members of parliament, directors general, directors of departments, and heads of state companies. *Santri* group loyalty was a factor in motivating former student activists and alumni groups. Around them clustered business clients seeking the patronage of oil and grain monopolies and the investment coordinating board, or possible ways of advancing their new electronics, auto, or construction businesses, or protection for old forestry, fishery, shrimp concessions. These people were utterly pragmatic. They mixed with Alis and Babas, both. They wanted harmony for the sake of prosperity, and they tended to oppose radicalism in the *Ummat,* the Islamic community.

The next layer of the middle class lived in good houses of the *kampungs* or in select blocks of low-cost brick housing complexes. They were salaried managers, technical experts, consultants, accountants, legal counselors. They were from the independent professions, the media, the NGOs, and third or fourth levels of the bureaucracy. They accepted the nation-state platform of Pancasila and were willing to see the boundary between themselves and the *abangan* below erode, while they themselves sought concerted action with those above them.

The lowest segment of the middle class lived in less-select *kampungs* or new low-cost housing. They consisted of lower-ranking civil servants, petty businessmen, factory and transport workers, employees in urban services. They clung to communal sentiments of solidarity and tradition. Conceiving themselves as courageous new heroes in opposition to the system, some of them even read works of Iranian revolutionaries as protection against an insecure, fragile, and fiercely competitive urban life. That insecurity could be ignited by hot issues or violent repression, as in the Tanjung Priok riot of 1984, when some lower middle class united with some underclass to give voice to an aroused *Ummat*.[21]

After class description, what? Jamie Mackie, an astute Australian analyst, concluded that "however much one might want to believe that the political kingdom will sooner or later be inherited by the good guys in the middle class who have been touched by decent liberal values, the work ethic and a sense of business responsibility, respect for the civil rights of all, and all the other virtues we might like them to develop in society—and that bad guys will then perish as they deserve to—it will not happen soon, and it may not happen at all." The growth of wealth may or may not produce an indigenous bourgeoisie, but to the degree that it might, there was no necessary correlative that democracy would also be produced. In Indonesia, power dominates property.[22] Onghokham, a Chinese Indonesian, pushes the matter further: "The obsession of the Indonesian elite with . . . power, rank and status is as extreme as the supposed Chinese obsession with money."[23]

Would the relative size and affluence of a middle class make a big difference? Juwono Sudarsono has long thought so and, as a former three-time cabinet minister, still thinks so: "All functioning, institutionalized and responsive democracies that have at least US $15,000 annual per capita, [with] 70 percent of the resident population classified as middle class, are liberal democracies." But even then, there are additional requirements: "well-trained, well-equipped and well-paid police, judiciary, and defence forces that underpin democratic government through the professional and accountable provision of public order and security."[24] If Dr. Juwono is right, democracy by Indonesian standards still requires both a huge middle class

41. MULTI-PHASED COMMUTING. One of the signs of a growing urban middle-class life is long trips to places of work. Here motorbike taxi drivers clamor for commuters disembarking from a bus. (Byron Black/author's collection)

and a huge buildup of institutions. This analysis counts both on great economic performance and on "middle-class rage" to make a difference in the end, as in South Korea and Taiwan since the late 1980s. Even were that to occur, the question of how much "Muslim rage" exists in Indonesia would still remain. In some future affluence, would it add to middle-class democratic anger or contradict it—or, in some wholly unanticipated dimension, transform it? Were Indonesia's relative deprivations to deepen instead of alleviate, how would Muslim rage play out then?

Islamic Modernists and the State

Embattled and marginalized Islamic leaders like Natsir and Sjafruddin gave way in the 1980s to younger leaders, not so confrontative of the regime but determined to think and act on a profoundly Islamic basis and willing to accept whatever challenges that might entail. They were Muslim democrats. They were not "Atlantic liberals" in defining individuals as self-contained and solitary beings, but they did understand what might be called a Tocquevillean civics.[25] They denied the need for an Islamic state, but they also denied the concept of autonomous individuals. They focused on a society of participants—a society that would avoid state as idol and markets as fetish. Such a society must be Islamic, but it could also be democratic, giving voice to citizens through voluntary associations and freedom of speech.

Three outstanding representatives of this broad view were Nurcholish Madjid, Abdurrahman Wahid, and Amien Rais. Madjid, the most Tocquevillean in the sense of trusting plural energies, emerged as an Islamic student leader between 1966 and 1971. He consistently formulated fresh positions from the 1970s through the 1990s, combining Qur'anic scholarship with political analysis and social theory. The most steadily eclectic of the trio, he built up a wide following among educated Muslims, and in 1986 established Paramadina, an association for urban proselytization that focused on both the middle class and the elite.

Amien Rais, like Madjid before him, obtained his doctorate from the University of Chicago. But Rais had to work through his thesis subject of Egypt's Muslim Brotherhood before deciding against the ideal of an Islamic state and the violent tactics necessary to achieve it. As head of Muhammadiyah, he led "modernist" Indonesian Muslims, where that word suggested being a Qur'anic scripturalist. Such text-boundedness, from a Western point of view, could readily lead to radical fundamentalism.

Rais and his Muhammadiyah were most clearly modernist in contrast to Abdurrahman Wahid and his Nahdlatul Ulama. The approach of NU to religion was traditional and syncretic, embracing Javanese and other tra-

42. BOYS IN ROTE STUDY OF THE QUR'AN. In 1989 at this *pesantren* in Demak, Central Java, connected to NU, students at early levels receive awards for memorization of the Qur'an. At much higher levels of Arabic study, they receive competitive prizes for understanding. (Abbas/Magnum Photos)

ditions. Wahid's constituency, predominantly rural, was larger than that of Rais—30 million members, versus 20 million for Rais's group before Suharto fell, whereupon, with elections approaching, their claims would bump up to 40 and 30 million respectively. Madjid's organized following was smaller, but he developed uncounted fans from public lectures, newspaper columns, and television interviews, where he presented a ruddy, gently smiling image, with shaggy eyebrows, resonant tone, and balanced reasoning—a kind of Islamic Walter Cronkite, an uncle whose voice one could trust.

Madjid and Wahid were both from the East Javanese town of Jombang. Madjid, known as Cak Nur, traveled from Damascus to Baghdad in 1968 on a crowded trolley dragged by a tractor across the sands by a Bedouin without a map. In Baghdad he met Wahid, known as Gus Dur, for the first time. He felt that Wahid stood out from other Indonesian students in the Middle East because he was so liberal—averse to going to classes but reading widely and thinking for himself. Although both were exploratory thinkers, coming from different *pesantren* would make for different reasoning across the decades.

Gus Dur's grandfather had founded the Nahdlatul Ulama in 1926. His father also enjoyed national respect as NU's leader in the Sukarno years. The boy, Gus Dur, was with his father when the car they were traveling in crashed, and he was by his side waiting for medical help when his father bled away and died. From his later period of cosmopolitan travel, certain tastes emerged; he became a fan of international soccer and a connoisseur of cinema, and he shocked some NU traditionalists by consenting to serve as a juror for Indonesian film awards in the 1980s. He delighted in the brave and poignant voice of the Egyptian singer Om Khalsoum, her swooping and quavering tones, resolutely cherishing the person or accepting the fate of which she sings. Her tremendous range and stamina, her ululating, sobbing way of yielding, her fiery insistence in sudden moments of defiant flair, brought out roars of admiration from crowds such as one usually heard only for a great bullfighter. A man who walked about with these

43. GIRLS EXERCISING WHILE WEARING JILBABS. At a *sekolah* of the Muhammadiyah in Yogyakarta, 1989, the requisite coverings are fully worn even in calisthenics. (Abbas/Magnum Photos)

sounds in his ear likes being in touch with passion. Gus Dur's passion drew others who liked being in touch with him.[26]

Wahid read omnivorously. His favorite modern novel was by Chaim Potok, *My Name Is Asher Lev*.[27] In the book, an orthodox Jewish boy growing up in Brooklyn in the 1940s and 1950s, descendant of Hasidic rabbis and scholars, feels destined, against his father's wish, to be an artist; he succeeds. Asher Lev as an alter ego for Gus Dur reveals him as a man who believed in "the people of the book"—Muslim, Jew, Christian—and in the imperative that they live together in a compacted and cosmopolitan world.

V. S. Naipaul managed to meet Gus Dur at his *pesantren* in Jombang five years before he took over leadership of the NU. Naipaul devoted himself to captivating and condescending descriptions, the mark of his own peculiar mind: endless villages, gateposts intentionally without gates, overpowering vegetation, underpowered learning. Boys smoking clove cigarettes; boys cooking rice-messes; boys "pretending to study"; boys with "the lean flat beautiful Indonesian physique, pectoral and abdominal muscles delicately defined."

Wahid, no boy, was "a short, chunky, middle aged man in a sarong."[28] Naipaul was less interested in Wahid than in the image of a little teacher with bad eyes (worse than Wahid's?) who under a dim light read or chanted in Arabic, never pausing, while the boys followed in their books his class in Islamic law. Naipaul expressed a bemused wonder for this little teacher and his salary of eighty cents a month, "the unlikely successor of the Buddhist monks of bygone times, still living (as the Buddha had prescribed for his order) on the bounty of his fellows, but now paying them back with Arabic lessons for their children." Sixteen years later, in 1995, Naipaul interviewed Wahid again, this time with much more respect but still grotesquely preoccupied with the little teacher's eighty cents a month and his own strenuous disdain for *pesantren* "stupefaction."[29]

Naipaul could not distinguish between the Islamicized Javanism of the *keraton* in Yogya and the Javanized Islam of the *pesantren*. As a Trinidadian-Cantabridgian Indian ever searching for his own identity, he picked up Hindu and Buddhist clues with relish and belittled keys to Islam. But he did begin to fathom appreciatively the sequence beginning with Wahid's grandfather, who in 1896 on returning from Mecca had founded the *pesantren* to bring traditional Muslim learning and piety to the unlearned; continuing with Wahid's father, who believed that struggle against the Dutch and acquiring modern skills and knowledge were both religious obligations; and ending with Wahid himself, a beneficiary of both Islamic and modern education. Naipaul conceded at last that "out of this [NU style of] religious education, whatever its sham scholarship and its piety, and its real pain, there also came a political awakening."[30]

Of the power of that awakening Naipaul had little idea. In 1982, Abdurrahman Wahid, perhaps during the mystical exercises that he practiced, felt the *wahyu cakraningrat* descend upon him.[31] This unpublicized but deeply felt conferral of the mandate of heaven should be understood as not merely desirable but highly dangerous to Wahid, given the fact that Sawito was still in jail for having declared a similar illumination. President Suharto was so confident of his own pragmatically proven mandate that he dropped Adam Malik, former chairman of the UN General Assembly, after five years as his vice president, and chose Umar Wirahadikusumah, a long-time crony general, in his place.

Wahid made news by pulling NU out of party politics early in the New Order campaign for *azas tunggal* (Pancasila as the sole basis for organizations) in 1983–1985, thereby incidentally weakening PPP and strengthening Golkar. Gus Dur then concentrated on building NU strength in spheres of informal political and social activity. An incongruous sequel: Suharto attended the 1989 NU Congress that reelected Wahid as chair. The president beat a mosque drum and pronounced Islamic greetings to help erase the memory of his adherence to Javanese mysticism and the impression that he was anti-Islamic.[32]

But Suharto's ambition outran Wahid's and soon re-estranged the two of them. Suharto beat another gong in December 1990, to open the first national conference of the Association of Indonesian Muslim Intellectuals (ICMI). Then in 1991 Suharto made his first *haj* and had himself well-publicized as in obeisance at Mecca. His new focus was on ICMI as a powerful co-optive device to further a regimist Islam. Suharto installed Habibie to lead it, and Amien Rais of Muhammadiyah, among others, became a compliant member.

Wahid's writings in this period critically distanced him from Muhammadiyah because that organization was composed of "educated people and teacherly circles," whereas NU was drawn from farmers. He was above all angry at ICMI, whose governmental Islam would repress NU's uneasy longings, allowing it only to be heard as "the roaring of a toothless lion."[33] Wahid took the lead of the Democracy Forum, whose very name signaled confrontation with the establishment. Suharto's fury, and his advisors' perception of Wahid as enemy number one, was embodied in the president's military son-in-law, Prabowo Subianto. In March 1992 Prabowo conveyed a warning from Cendana to Wahid of unspecific actions if he continued to oppose the president.[34]

Wahid's defiant counter-suggestibility was almost immeasurable but can be illustrated through confidential conversations. On a trip to the United States in 1992, about fifteen young Indonesian public employees, all tied to government scholarships for advanced study, having been carefully

44. WAHID: OPPOSITIONIST AND ECCENTRIC. Abdurrahman Wahid (glasses, black *pici*) is elected leader of Nahdlatul Ulama, earlier chaired by his father and grandfather, in Situbondo, East Java, December 1984. Gus Dur's charisma and legacy would ensure his continued chairmanship of NU until he is elected president of the republic in October 1999. (Ilham Soenharjo/*Tempo*)

screened through friendship with their host, were recruited to a meeting with a secret guest in the basement of a private home. The secret guest was Wahid—a vigorous, vehement Gus Dur with thick spectacles but still sighted in both eyes. He laid out a conspiratorial plan of destabilization of the Suharto government and revolution against it. How to attack the power grid and water supply; how to take over broadcasting stations; everything.[35] In how many American cities he played out his bad-boy imagination this way, I do not know. Of the likelihood of at least one fink-spy somewhere, Gus Dur should have been ruefully aware. For the Suharto/military reaction he should have been prepared, and perhaps was.

Some of the Wahid entourage are convinced that the auto crash that made Gus Dur's wife a tetraplegic in 1993 was from severed brakes in his car, which she took early from a celebration at which he unexpectedly chose to remain. Others, however, firmly and reasonably deny that and attribute the crash to his sister's chauffeur's driving at 160 kilometers per hour on mountain roads. In any case, Wahid, who had lost his father in a smash-up, now had Nuriyah, his invaluable partner, almost wholly immobilized for life.[36]

Labor

Suharto's government did not care for deliberations outside its reckoning. It wanted no parliament of the streets or the salons or the workshops—only its own lobotomized parliament. Indonesian labor had ridden the country's growth curve upward for thirty years, obtaining real benefits in jobs and wages, which far outweighed the denial of the right to organize that is customary in industrial countries. Such a balanced reckoning was not, however, applicable to other parts of the society—media and the academy—in which free expression is essential, or to democracy itself, for which fair process is definitive.

From a slender base in Sukarno's time, the New Order made huge investments in human capital, chiefly in primary education, leaving employability of the secondary educated as a follow-up problem. Jobs and wages grew across sectors, regions, and rural/urban boundaries. Female participation in the labor force increased dramatically, and at more advanced levels of responsibility than imaginable before. Many women were still domestic servants and many men *becak* drivers, but the economy was transformed. The intelligent use of the green revolution and the application of oil boom revenues to labor-intensive agriculture, rural services, and public works were highly positive; and three devaluations of the rupiah avoided harmful effects on growth and employment, especially in the 1980s.

Net: Indonesia actually became for a while a lesson to countries still lagging behind it in economic development: it showed that targeting help to the poor through education, health care, and infrastructure programs was more effective than trying to manipulate the labor market itself.[37] As a consequence, however, new expectations in labor were clearly rising several years before Suharto resigned. Between 1989 and 1994, total strikes in Indonesia increased from 30 to 885.[38] The top 200 business groups, which had produced 40 percent of a small number of strikes in 1974–1978, produced only 15 percent of a much larger number in 1990–1994.[39] These strikes revealed the birth of a class of smaller entrepreneurs, not necessarily wiser than the far better known national conglomerates. The new "price-takers" as distinct from larger "price-makers" were companies that combined family proprietary characteristics along with struggle in supply and demand, rather than engaging in collusive anti-competitive practices.

Local officials and military officers, however, saw these successes as new opportunities for "rent-seeking behavior": extortion. The arm-twisted entrepreneur could only pass on his higher costs to consumers, or use the apparently safer alternative of exploiting their own labor force. If he violated regulations, however, he might nevertheless find the Department of Labor or the government-organized All-Indonesia Workers Union covertly stimulating labor unrest as a means of extracting special payments. In larger cities, the involvement of the military and police in stifling or stimulating unrest for the purpose of extortion tended to be cautious, because of journalistic attention, but in smaller urban areas there was less restraint.[40]

The then-commander in chief of ABRI, General Feisal Tanjung, defended this military-business collusion which, "as long as collusion is for the good of the people and the state, need not be problematized."[41] Thus he justified coerced "security fees"—specific payments for what should have been salaried duties—and political manipulation of events for the intended professional advancement of officers who were shrewd financial-political activists. Of Faisal Tanjung himself, the story echoed around Jakarta that he played weekly peak-stakes golf with *cukongs*. They contrived generously to lose to him in dimensions appropriate to their own jeopardies, to his status, and to the power at his formal and informal command.[42] Everybody presumably had some sort of a good time, and nobody had to turn in a signed scorecard of any kind, anywhere.

The new wave of strikes in the early 1990s, in any case, occurred in the light-manufacturing sector, export-oriented industries, foreign-owned enterprises, and sectors employing a predominantly female labor force. The new industries, squeezed by bureaucratic-praetorian extortionists, passed on their high operating costs to labor, the factor of production most under immediate control. They cut wages, reduced benefits, extended hours without paying overtime, and refused to meet newly legislated minimum wages.[43]

A case in point was the PT Catur Putra Surya, a watch company that originated in 1980 as part of Indonesia's highly successful move from import-substitution policies to less regulated export markets. There, in Sidoardjo, south of Surabaya, in May 1993, 500 workers went on strike seeking to implement the East Java governor's edict for a 20 percent raise in wages, and because of other concerns. The walkout awoke the local military and administration and produced a swift agreement except on two workers' demands: dissolution of the government trade union and guaranteed non-punishment of strikers. When thirteen co-workers were interrogated at military headquarters and forced to resign, a young female activist, Marsinah, exclaimed to another group of co-workers that she would take the District Military Command to court. That night she was abducted. On May 8, 1993, her body was found, raped and beaten. The murder had taken place at army headquarters.

The frenzy in the press brought out charges by the East Java military command that foreign and NGO agitators bore responsibility. The Java Regional Military Command, angered because the American Embassy's labor attaché had attended a meeting of labor activists, stepped up the rhetorical attack: "If our house is over-run by rats, then the rats must be looked for, the gutters stopped up. Don't leave the house so open that the rats are free to come in." Indonesian bureaucrats spent months spraying foam on this issue. Then after labor riots in Medan in April 1994, a nongovernment union leader, Mochtar Pakpahan, was arrested and the Department of Labor issued a warning to the media to cease reporting industrial conflict.[44] Capital, labor, the military, and the bureaucracy, however, had already exposed the fact that class conflict in Indonesia was by no means dogmatic and dialectical but complex and vertical. Many laborers would thenceforth see their destinies illuminated and lives motivated by Marsinah's death.

Media and Academe

Goenawan Mohamad is a slender, serious man with an occasionally impish smile. His father and mother had known internal exile to a prison camp under the Dutch in the 1920s, and after the Japanese surrender the Dutch again arrested his father and executed him as a radical revolutionary. Goenawan won a fellowship in Antwerp, became editor of a "student" daily after Sukarno's downfall, and read James Baldwin. As a journalist and poet he became dextrous in discerning fact and handling clashes of opinion, and subtle in management of his own blend of poetic solitude and public opposition.

In 1971 Goenawan and his friends founded a new kind of magazine, *Tempo*—a weekly modeled after *Time* magazine, and the first of its kind in Southeast Asia. "We thought nobody was going to buy it, and then . . . we made history." In two dozen years they built its circulation to 200,000, the largest weekly in Indonesia. In 1981 they were banned for a month, then got their license back.[45] The economy still enabled new magazines and newspapers to cater to niche markets of readers.

The government monopoly of television ended in 1990 when Suharto's second son, Bambang Trihatmodjo, levered a license from the Ministry of Information to operate a privately owned network. His older sister followed; so did Suharto's cousin Sudwikatmono, his crony Liem Sioe Liong, and the *pribumi* industrialist Aburizal Bakrie. But the breakthrough was commercial only—and certainly not critical of the power structure. As Goenawan presumed to write in *Tempo*, "The government is naturally pleased to have a frightened press. What is not realised is that from frightened people you hear no sincerity, but distortion. You will not know whether the praise uttered by a frightened man is authentic praise or merely boot-licking." In 1992, *Indonesia Business Weekly* summarized the situation. "Most Indonesians have long resigned [themselves] to the fact that the pen is often mightier than the sword but is absolutely no match for the gun."

After Suharto's election to a sixth five-year term, the authorities, having tried openness in 1990 and regretted it, permitted another experimental round in the second half of 1993. Some Islamic radicals were released from jail; reconciliations were arranged with high-profile dissidents. But when labor, Muslims, human rights leaders, and students generated protests and demonstrations across their range of concerns, Suharto lashed out at them. They were following the "same tactics as those used by the Indonesian Communist Party." Officials vowed to uphold Pancasila against street riot.[46]

The sequence was strangely like that of Mao Zedong letting "a hundred flowers bloom" in 1956 and then close-cropping them all with his power-mower. Indonesians felt a similar shock and ensuing cynical caution. The heresies in the Chinese case had been in a range from liberalism to capitalism; in the Indonesian case, they were called liberalism or communism. In either despotism, a liberal imagination was dangerous to the carrier.

Goenawan's *Tempo* was a standard-bearer. Minister Habibie, early in Suharto's new term, transacted a huge purchase from East Germany of ships with uncertain utility and high adaptation costs. He wrapped it in a $1.1 billion public works package, including upgrading shipyards, acquiring oil tankers, and constructing a new deep-water port. *Tempo* gently ridiculed the acquisition of an outdated navy from a nearly landlocked state, which itself had been bought by its capitalist neighbor. Far sharper critique would have been justified: eight years later, only three of the 39 second-hand warships were still operational.[47] But it was too much for the dignity of the official family. On June 21, 1994, *Tempo* and two other independent magazines were shut down. For the first time in Indonesian history, Indonesian youth, activists, and reporters went to the streets to demonstrate against a specific instance of stifling the press—"arbitrary and despotic in a way affecting many people," according to a later editorial in *Tempo*, and hitting the livelihood and profession of reporters.[48]

The palace reaction was quiet and businesslike. The business manager of *Tempo* was summoned to meet Hashim Djojohadikusumo in the Lagoon Tower of the Hilton Hotel. Hashim was a graduate of Pomona College:

suave, with American idiom and humor, a quick intelligence and gracious laughter, business contacts in Russia and post-Soviet states, and political contacts throughout the Muslim world. No one could present an ultimatum more plausibly than he, the son of former Minister Sumitro and the brother of General Prabowo, one of Suharto's sons-in-law. Hashim said that *Tempo* could open up again if he, Hashim, and the "family" were given the right to hire and fire the editor and if he and the "family" had the first option to buy whenever *Tempo* went on the market.

This offer had to be answered by 8 AM the next day. It was already 10 PM. As the staff later recalled, they gathered at midnight at Goenawan's house. "Decision: The offer of Hashim Djojohadikusumo—even though it gave a chance for *Tempo* to live—was refused. After midnight this decision was delivered in a diplomatic way, because we were certainly afraid. We knew it was Prabowo Subianto himself that deputed Hashim, and we interpreted the word 'family' as 'the Cendana family.'"[49]

So *Tempo* was shut down. But it was too large an institution to disappear. An on-line edition took shape. With the bureaucracy underestimating the impact of that medium, the new version gathered 15,000 subscribers around the world, half of them in Indonesia. And the concept of *Tempo* grew, in its own recollection, like an "intangible . . . fairy-tale creature," nurtured by its very suppression. The turns of fortune would eventually see *Tempo* reopened in a boisterously competitive environment. But for more than four Suharto years it was silenced.

In the academic world, no one could yet see beyond Suharto's political background checks, book censorship, criminalization of dissent, bans on student political activity and expression; the permits required for seminars, the interrogations, cancellations, harassments, and blacklists; the use of military informers as university watchdogs and of ABRI plus police forces to contain, intimidate, or deter demonstrations. Beyond repression there existed a formidable pressure of on-campus ideological indoctrination.[50] Even out of the country, Suharto's agents tracked critics, jailing the university economist Sri Bintang Pamungkas for remarks made in Berlin, under the old Dutch law of *lèse majesté*. They rearrested him in 1997 for founding a political party dedicated to constitutional and legal reform.[51]

Elections

Suharto clearly feared the example of Ferdinand Marcos in the Philippines, a martial law dictator who conceded a "snap election" to defuse democratic pressure in 1986 and then lost power trying to steal it. That April Suharto's government banned Australian journalists from Indonesia after

David Jenkins likened his government to the Marcos kleptocracy.[52] Pak Harto also resented analogies to South Korea. There the former general Ro Tae Woo demilitarized and democratized the government a year before the Seoul Olympics of 1988 but was himself eventually judged and jailed by the forces he let loose.

To make sure he stayed in power, Suharto had required the formation of pseudo-parties and had intensified sham "festival" politics. In the early 1970s, Ali Murtopo took over an army anticommunist group and fashioned it into Golkar, the engine of the establishment: politically organized segments of bureaucracy and society in the service of the state (originally a Sukarnoesque idea) all fired up by the military. After 1976 only two other vehicles besides Golkar and ABRI were allowed under the roof of the parliament.[53] The PPP (Unity and Development Party) consisted of several Islamic parties squeezed together; and the PDI (Indonesian Democracy Party) was a compaction of Catholic, Protestant, and nationalist parties. They amounted to tour buses that had to follow highways parallel to the Golkar railroad tracks. If a crossing somehow appeared, woe to the bus that didn't get out of the way of the locomotive.

District administrators took orders on how their villages should vote. But disappointments accumulated. A newly elected village headman, at the foot of the volcano Merapi, looked back on their political history: "This village voted PPP in 1982. Then we were promised our road would be asphalted if we voted Golkar, so we did, in 1987, 1992, and 1997. But nothing has happened yet. This time I'm neutral. If the people want to choose whoever, let them."[54]

Even from the vantage point of high party power, disillusionment was possible. Sarwono Kusumaatmadja was the new secretary general of Golkar when I met him in 1983: a handsome young man with glossy black hair coming to a V on his forehead, intensely intelligent dark eyes roaming behind his spectacles. He wore then a cadre-gray uniform with short-sleeve shirt, of an almost Chinese militant drabness. He answered my questions with a combination of high Javanese civility and condescension toward one requiring the most basic guidance.[55]

Sarwono grew to become a minister of the environment, outspoken about the fires of 1997 and a Golkar reformist who resigned in 1998 when his faction lost the chairmanship. But a much earlier system shock had already affected his consciousness. "The problem," he told an American audience, "was that Golkar did too well in the 1987 elections." The military and the bureaucracy began to fear that the party would become too independent, turn against them or the president. Thereafter, "Golkar saw itself progressively weakened through the intervention of the military and Suharto

. . . During that time, coinciding with the last five years of Suharto's rule, Golkar became the personal fiefdom of Suharto and lost any semblance to a political organization. They got 74% of the vote [in 1997] . . . outrageous. Vote rigging was totally organized."[56] Sarwono had been too successful as a political organizer, too threatening to Suharto as a proto-democrat. By 1999 he wore a dark business suit and designer spectacles, and with his glowing English he cruised the crowd in Washington's Cosmos Club, looking forward to the first open election in his adult life.

In late 1992 a delegation to the MPR presented a "white book" compiled on the national parliamentary elections concluded some months before. The MPR never discussed or acted upon the white book, but its findings remain a clinical picture of distress and grotesquerie in Indonesian electoral processes.[57]

Military- and government-controlled media favored Golkar. Practical biases appeared through inadequate registration or preventive omission of registrants, such as Drs. Kwik Kian Gie of the PDI Central executive office; through local officials negatively identifying the PDI with the banned PKI; through firing of state employees refusing to vote Golkar; through intentional miscounts; and through mobilization and herding of civil servants, military families, laborers, students, transmigrants, Islamic pilgrims, isolated communities such as the Baduy of West Java, and others, in order to vote for the ruling party. The president by edict prohibited government officials during campaign days from visiting project sites. But he himself officiated at hundreds of projects, including additions to the stock of warehouses, laboratories, and restrooms. His thirty-seven ministers, in imitation, competed "to be the cleverest at utilizing government facilities for the Golkar campaign."[58]

That year in Yogya, forty-three youth carried a bier symbolizing the death of democracy and a white flag indicating their boycott of elections. Arrested without due process, they were forced to eat plywood while in jail. Father Mangunwijaya (Romo Mangun), the great cultural critic and activist of that city, supported a movement to lower the Indonesian flag as a nonviolent action in protest. Silence and symbolic action were to remind the authorities that the people are "not clay to be shaped at another's whim." Romo Mangun went further to say that the voice, including the silence, of a suffering people reflects the voice of God.[59]

Blank balloting, introduced as a protest by Arief Budiman as early as the 1971 election, had become a prominent factor between 1987 and 1992. Its acronym, Golput (for *golongan putih*), signified "white group" and conveyed abstention, protest, purity, and comical play on the oppressive acronym Golkar. Such genuinely expressed noncooperation in 1992 was estimated at

10 million.[60] Members of Golput carried its ubiquitous white banner and wore quiet smiles, non-discernible as angry, humorous, fearful, distressed, or all at once. They were a loosely organized fourth major force in the election.

The white book on that election seems composed in dissociative despair but does break through, from moment to distracted moment, in respectfully irate prose:

> The bureaucracy is supposed to serve society. It is salaried with the people's money, so that in almost all states bureaucrats are called civil servants. Only in Indonesia are civil servants called servants of the state . . . Equipment, buildings, employee salaries—all are supported by the people's taxes. So Golkar ought to come to its senses . . . [And] if PDI and PPP are unable to stop this fraud, they had best stop being parties. Change their names and become associations of comedians or rotating credit associations.[61]

The white book distinguished between "real fraud"—the thousands of instances of deterred, herded, or manipulated votes—and "inherent fraud" arising from the basic faults of the political system itself. Real fraud should be actionable. Inherent fraud invoked the Golput revolt. Mentioning recent democratic upthrusts in Thailand, Myanmar, Taiwan, and Korea, the report concluded that "the safest change comes through general elections, but if these elections are manipulated, defrauded, beaten and raped, then the . . . people's aspirations can explode through channels outside the system." They conceded that the election of 1992 was "secure, orderly and peaceful." But they recommended that, because of its fundamental inherent fraud, "it must be cancelled for the sake of the law."[62]

They were ignored. The Suharto establishment repeated its election practices in 1997. Golkar even overshot its target and won with 74 percent of the popular vote. PPP, the establishment Islamic party, won 22 percent. PDI, the party stolen from Megawati Sukarnoputri, was cut to 3 percent. Suharto as politician never tried to require complete silence. He preferred rehearsed approval or predictable choruses and, in his critics, either inaudible soliloquies or denatured squeaks.

Manhattan Yankee at the Sultan's Court

Gordon Bishop of New York City—poet, businessman, and journalist, descended on his father's side from Russian Jews—probably engaged with the life of Central Java more deeply than any American has ever done. He bears the scars of fifty surgeries and still deeper emotional wounds, yet his passion is intact, running a healthy range from love to hate.

"I'm a kid of the Sixties," he says. He had published poems in *The New Yorker* and *Poetry*. He had accompanied Andrei Voznesensky on his first tour of America. Hating the war in Vietnam, he traveled around the world in 1969–70, liked Bali best of what he saw; returned there, to Ubud, to document dance dramas and trance rituals; then lectured in American universities and at the Asia Society in New York.

Yogyakarta snagged his imagination. He wanted to live there, alone, "no buffer zone barrier, which is what a Western friend means." So he explored Yogya by *becak* and with his blazing charm talked himself into living inside the village precincts of the sultan's palace, as its only foreign resident.

He struggled with language. Then his life was upended. On August 17, 1974: Independence Day. The parades and promenades and flirting were as Bishop imagined nineteenth-century America on the Fourth of July. "Then, I saw this woman . . . It stopped me in my tracks . . . I was almost afraid to look at her . . . I was melting, tongue-tied." She was clearly with her sister, who wore a polka-dot dress with miniskirt, "too modern" for Bishop. But she, the one he fixed on, was in Yogya classical dress. "We're talking ravishingly, shockingly beautiful."

He went to buy a cigarette and collect his mind, 'Jono, his young language teacher, reported she had followed him with her eyes, but now they could not find her. Gordon kicked the tire of his motorcycle. "What a schmuck!" "What smuk?" 'Jono asked. "*Schmuck* . . . total jerk, asshole. Someone who messes up a once-in-a-lifetime opportunity." 'Jono promised to help him look for her. A long search. Bishop took Javanese dance lessons five times a week from a great master. "I was handsome and athletic then." One dusk, coming back on his bike from a lesson, he saw her "in the liquid golden light from the sunset, over the old bathing grounds of the Sultan, his pleasure garden, site of orgies, a ruin now." She was in a *becak* with a guy. He followed but lost them. By Christmas he was depressed and broke. To renew his one-year visa he had to go to Singapore. On a walk 'Jono pointed out two other women to him. Bishop impatiently quoted D. H. Lawrence to him: "Those who look for love don't find it. Only the loving find love, and they don't have to look for it." At that point, a door opened, and *she* walked out, with the same sister as before. "I *knew* I wanted to marry her."

From inquiries about the address he learned that she was the preeminent female palace dancer of the time, and a princess. But who was he? He was so broke after he returned from Singapore that he slept under a tree in the rain in Jakarta. He had just enough money for a bus to Yogya; nothing to drink on the way or to pay the *becak* driver at the end; 'Jono's father covered.

He wanted to marry Raden A. Siti Achidia Nanies Sunardi Suryodiprodjo: a direct descendant of Panembahan Senapati, who launched Mataram's imperial expansion in the late sixteenth century, and of Prince Diponegoro, who vainly fought the Dutch in the early nineteenth. Her father was a master in *pencak silat,* Javanese martial arts, and her mother a renowned artist in *batik.* All this he learned later. He found the sister ("We thought you were a tourist with your guide"), who told him where to find Nanies. This time it was she in a miniskirt—"a strange image."

Bishop and Nanies sat down with her father and mother. He had been told never to ask her out alone until a fifth or sixth meeting. So he broke through the *cocok* reserve by proposing they *all* go to Borobudur the next day. Which they did, every ten days in the rainy season, Gordon getting soaked each time, never seeing the mother again, talking to the father every time. In April 1975 he told 'Jono he wanted to propose to her. 'Jono told him the proper way: "I will go propose *for* you. I will take *batik* as a present and speak to her parents."

'Jono came back shaking. He had proposed as intended. Her mother broke all the dishes in the kitchen. "A foreigner marry my daughter? *Over my dead body!*" Across the previous three or four years Nanies's parents had already received and declined 86 formal marriage proposals for her.

An older relative intervened helpfully. "We are in a modern age now." He arranged that they meet at his house. Gordon proposed to Nanies there, directly. "I was talking and talking. She was super-Javanese. Shy. Saying *nothing.*"

Three weeks passed. "One morning her two brothers come. I was running my cassette, playing jazz on a car battery. That's all. We just listened [no conversation, just taking in the jazz] . . . They went away . . ." 'Jono said, '*That's* the answer. She's going to marry you!'"

Gordon "sent a giant thing of flowers to her mother" and went to pay respect to her. He and Nanies waited eighteen hours at the central telephone office in Yogya to get a line to the United States to tell his own parents. His mother was delighted. His father only reminded him it was time to come home, because he wanted to buy him a seat on the New York Stock Exchange.

They set their date by mystic horology: July 22, 1975. A letter arrived from his father, telling him to "come home alone and immediately" or be disinherited. They ignored it. Shortly after their civil ceremony Nanies's father coughed violently, spat a pint of blood and collapsed. In the hospital he was diagnosed as having tuberculosis. With the discipline of a martial artist he had been containing his pain until his daughter was married.

Java insists that transitions of all kinds be seemly and stately. Tradition requires that a new bride live at home with her parents for a week after the wedding. Because of Nanies's father's illness, it was two months before they could release themselves from her home for a honeymoon.

Bishop had sold nearly everything in his small house to pay for the traditional ceremony of the wedding. By then he owned only a few clothes, a small motorcycle, and a toothbrush. Javanese neighbors and friends, now disabused of the notion that Nanies was marrying a rich man (because all Americans are wealthy), gave generously, as wedding gifts, household articles to fill up the places emptied by sales.

When Bishop finally brought Nanies to Palm Beach, not only his mother but his fiercely skeptical father loved her. The mother was shocked to learn only then about her husband's disowning letter, and she subsequently learned other things about his behavior that made her divorce him. He re-

45. CIVIL WEDDING. The civil marriage of Gordon Bishop and Raden A. Siti Achidia Nanies Sunardi Suryodiprodjo in Yogyakarta in 1975 is attended by her immediate family. (Gift of Gordon Bishop/author's collection)

46. ROYAL WEDDING. The ritual marriage in 1983 of Major Prabowo Subianto to Siti Hediati "Titiek" Suharto takes place in the Audience Hall of Taman Mini Indonesia Indah, the giant theme park launched by the president's wife a decade before. Three thousand dignitaries and guests attend, equipped with a 52-page manual, "The Wedding Ritual," issued by the First Family. (Ilham Soenharjo/*Tempo*)

married. She, in Bishop's grinning remembrance, "married a Palm Beach gigolo." But after several years both of them divorced. They re-wed each other and lived contentedly until he died, accumulating a total of forty-three years together in their two marriages.

Bishop's father-in-law, in his prime, could disarm eight beweaponed men in simultaneous attack. His mother could apply up to a thousand *batik* decorations in a single bolt of cloth. Within easy reach of them, he and Nanies bought a house in Kota Gede (known for its silversmiths) owned by princes of Mataram. Bishop studied *kebatinan*. But even living the *keraton* life completely, he was still the son of a businessman. He eventually turned to business himself, and with Nanies launched a frontier sales company for Javanese fabrics, pottery, furnishings, and artifacts. They aimed to hit top-level Western outlets. Their Javana Collection, both antique originals and reproductions, trod some of the ground already opened up by Inger McCabe

Elliot of China Seas but ranged far wider. They moved from a trade-only store on Third Avenue in New York City to a complex gallery-shop (called Tropics) in Soho, and to Palm Beach too, and gathered momentum.

They needed a big partner to expand, and therefore took in Hashim Djojohadikusumo's Semen Cibinong: the second largest cement company in Indonesia. It was the flagship of Hashim's own conglomerate, flourishing under the royal umbrella of the Cendana family, into which Hashim's brother, Prabowo, had married. Bishop retained 25 percent of the company and worked into the incorporation—Article 18—a requirement that 80 percent of the shares must vote for any reorganization. It was effectively a minority veto. "I knew Hashim when he was a nice guy," Bishop recalls. "But he got bigger and bigger and bigger . . . [Earlier,] others had taken advantage of him . . . There's nothing worse than a nice guy who decides to never be nice again, who decides to be a *tough* guy."

Hashim put $5 million behind their plan of a "national identity collection" of furniture, toys, garments, jewelry, with a showroom in Bali like Bloomingdale's: a one-stop full-service center for foreign buyers, "where they could get a million dollars of stuff at the end of their trip and then take two days on the beach." Bishop himself got another $8 million to assist "small enterprise" from a cabinet minister who lined up eight fertilizer executives to do as he asked, a million each.

Bishop and Nanies believed themselves ready to enter the world of superfashion. Not even open yet, they already had their first order: Nieman Marcus for $4 million. Hashim, however, was running into trouble in the cement business. He began to say, "Every day my brother asks me for money for generals in East Timor and North Sumatra." There were also "business culture" problems in his cement-led conglomerate. "I won't give another penny to this handicraft shit," he said. The Gulf War was about to break, but Bishop hardly noticed it. Hashim called to inform him of a conglomerate-driven reorganization plan at an impending meeting. He obviously wanted the $8 million Bishop had raised for his project. Gordon reminded him of Article 18, which Hashim had forgotten. He looked it up while they were talking.

What followed soon after was "one of those calls." Gordon had heard of them. Now he received "one of those calls from the First Family." Not directly, of course. The wife of a friend of Hashim conveyed ever so indirectly that if he and Nanies did not go along with the reorganization, Bishop, for his own security, had 72 hours to pack his bags and leave the country. He consulted a Harvard-trained Indonesian lawyer, who told him you can't fight an airplane with a pea-shooter. They went along. For six months "I watched him destroy the company. It was like watching an abortion."

Stripped of any authority, Bishop was drawing a salary, and within the shell of the still-existing joint corporation he owned a blue-ribbon health insurance policy. But he had not yet felt Hashim's full malevolence.

On March 30, 1993, Bishop, Nanies, and their only child, seven-year-old daughter Naomi, were being driven from home to Jakarta after the Idul Fitri holidays. Indonesia has left-side drive, and businessmen, especially foreign ones, use chauffeurs. Around a curve on a mountain hill, with a deep drop to the left and only rock to the right, Nanies behind him, Bishop in the front left seat suddenly saw a bus and a truck opposite, racing each other to pass. His driver had time only to avoid the ravine by swerving across the road against the mountain. The bus at high speed smashed the left side of their Toyota van.

In and out of consciousness, aware only of pain, blood, emergency, Bishop asked for a phone, croaked out the number of the U.S. Embassy to activate his name on their list of residents. Need helicopters. "Who will give the guarantee, at $25,000 each?" Bishop named an American and a former Indonesian cabinet minister. Both obliged. But the copters couldn't fly until first light of morning. At a community health center overnight, his only medicine was bottled water, for which they sent to the next village. Nine generals accompanied the 'copters to the site, where it took half an hour to clear a landing area among thousands of peasants who had never seen such things before. Bishop, strapped down on a flatbed truck, was aware only of endless pairs of peasant eyes peering at him.

In the Jakarta hospital they found he had broken nine ribs and his left leg, in many places. His pelvis was split three inches wide. His once-handsome face would undergo a Frankensteinian reconstruction into an assemblage of arbitrary scarfields. For three weeks in intensive care he gasped out and scribbled messages to Nanies. Then his sister, who had flown out from the United States, felt he was strong enough to be told she was dead. Their daughter had survived, cradled by a maid at the cost to herself of a major concussion and back injuries. Naomi last saw her mother with blood coming out of a hole in her forehead. She wondered what it meant when later she saw them pull a sheet over her face.

As Bishop recovered his grip on life, weeping with Naomi over the loss of Nanies, he learned of a business action taken while he was in a coma. Hashim's associates had cancelled his medical insurance.[63]

THE LAST YEARS
OF LIVING SECURELY

The Suharto regime was a predatory state.[1] Other regimes with different standards of living were also consumers for their own benefit: the Philippines under the martial law of Marcos, Mexico under PRI and Carlos Salinas Gotari, Nigeria under most generals, and Russia under Yeltsin. In the crunch between the common weal and the hungers of the powerful, appetites at the apex win. "Pre-capitalist" or "post-communist"—it doesn't much matter. Where critical institutions are missing and countervailing forces are weak, the state devours markets, and the powerful consume wealth as they wish.

At the theoretical extremes of political economy are roving anarchic banditry and all-embracing majorities that treat minorities as if they might be among future majorities.[2] Between these extremes the Indonesian regimes of both Sukarno and Suharto fall into place. The former tried to bring a quasi-communist central direction to an ill-ordered structure and failed. Suharto then imposed a successful quasi-fascistic central command, under which nearly everybody fared better, or much better, than before. His family and associates fared well indeed.

Suharto proved that a stationary bandit is preferable to roving banditries. He did not eliminate all of the latter. But his leadership demonstrated that providing more and more public goods also allows incremental maximization of the presidential rate of theft. What he did not demonstrate, or even attempt to show, because he did not understand it, was that providing secure markets generates self-compounding and self-insuring success. With well-defined individual rights protected by law, with absence of predation of any kind, and with constructive social programs addressed to advancing education, health, and technology, no modern society can fail.[3] But Suharto's society did, in the end, fail. It crashed because it strangulated law and went light on education, hollow on health, and bizarre on technology. Above all, instead of augmenting markets, it swallowed them with gluttonous regularity.[4] The late Suharto period is a story of an ogreish power-center that did not merely devour markets but chewed down or starved other major institutions as well.

Some moments in Suharto's individual career may be considered transformative. In 1965–66 the soldier became a mass murderer, assuring power through fear. In 1978 the president became an ideological obscurantist, promoting a mindless Pancasila program that suppressed people's real problems.[5] In 1992 the autocrat became a dynast, reneging on the promise in his 1988 autobiography to seek no more terms in office. Finding his reversal unchallenged, he began to consider his will unopposable.

Somewhere in that first quarter-century of rule, in addition, the parasite became a predator. In the 1970s his wife, Ibu Tien, had earned a reputation for opening doors and being paid back in commissions. By the late 1980s and early 1990s her children went from market-nibbling to market-swallowing, as the Cendana family evolved into omnivorous consumers of monies

47. PEMUDA PANCASILA, 1986. Yorrys Raweyai, leader of paramilitary thugs operating as patriotic youth. Note anti-drug posters. (Manang Baso/*Tempo*)

and goods, resources and opportunities.⏋At its center, the president still desired to be recognized as a villager who had made good and had not forgotten his roots: the just patriarch of a model clan with modest family values. The picture was dizzyingly, criminally, contradictory. But for citizens to challenge it as pompous, hypocritical, and immoral was deeply dangerous.

Bolstering Suharto was his success in the eyes of the world, as well as in Indonesia's own.[6] All the indices of longevity and standards of living were up and continuing upward. What then is the argument for casting the leader down? In the outside world, Suharto's evils went largely unnoticed, while his achievements were rewarded with accelerating foreign investment. But nothing is forever. That larger world, from which Suharto believed he was safe, was already being transformed by financial transactions moving at a speed and across spans previously unknown. Politico-economic weather systems could hit whole regions or travel inter-regionally.

Suharto's sixth full term, from 1993 to 1998, may be seen as the last years of living securely—at least for Cendana. But a measure of Suharto's power even during this portentous time is this: despite the serious disturbances of the last twenty-one months of that period, he would obtain his seventh term of office in March 1998.

Taming the Military

After Suharto's consolidation of power as defense minister in 1966, a "Brigade of the Sick at Heart" came into being, as even Nasution was maneuvered into a backwater in 1968. By the mid-1970s it was clear that whatever the original purposes of "dual function"—the doctrine that the armed forces had both a defense and a sociopolitical role—its consequence was three kinds of generals: professional, political, and financial.[7] By 1977, after twenty years of *dwifungsi,* ABRI personnel serving outside the Defense Ministry had risen to 21,118.[8]

By the late 1970s and early 1980s a group of retired generals were concerned about the military in three overlapping areas: excessive entrepreneurship, which diluted professionalism; an enormous spike in corruption; and undue anti-Islamism.[9] But the time was late for concerting forces against the president, and the cases were not well joined; the concept of a loyal opposition was missing and an adequate leader for it was lacking. Always, a slash-or-stash mode of loyalty was at play. Slash the critic: "Most of these people [the retired generals] are just as corrupt as anyone else," said Jusuf Wanandi in 1980, as one of Ali Murtopo's executive colleagues. "We have a laundry list. We can hit back if they want that." That surely overstates the extent of corruption among retired officers, but it certainly ex-

presses the modus vivendi of the palace tetrad—including Ibu Tien, who
tried to cut off funds to a prominent Jakarta charity founded and chaired by
Mrs. Nasution.[10]

An accomplished group of retired generals, with sympathy from the
minister of defense and the army chief of staff, began to advocate a "Turk-
ish model" under which the military would withdraw to the mountaintop
(or at least stay on horseback), keep clean, and intervene politically only in a
national crisis. President Suharto's camp made clear he had no sympathy at
all for this model. Brigadier General (Hon.) Notosusanto, later rector of the
University of Indonesia and minister of education, said "that ABRI, going
down in the mud, will get spattered also by the mud . . . [And] if the nation
goes down the drain—to use an extreme example—ABRI is responsible."[11]
Suharto met his military critics with a series of blacklists and ostracisms
that kept them from public appearance or expression and from receiving
bank loans, permission to leave the country, or even invitations to palace
functions. The insult was deeply felt by people like Lieutenant General Ali
Sadikin: "There were many in our group who fought for this country before, during, and after the revolution. And they are treated like this. But others are Chinese who did nothing, nothing, and they share in everything."[12]

Suharto also helped the loyal to help themselves: the "stash" mode of
loyalty-building. At this he set a personal example, and for this he punished
nobody. His example infected the whole military. Questioning the entrepreneurship of officers was not in order. Even excellent military analysts from
Australia do not have the word "corruption" in their indexes; they address
the problem through the prism of dual function.[13] The journalist David
Jenkins, who explored the subject as part of a monograph, dared to liken
Suharto to Marcos only days after the flight of the Philippine president into
ignoble exile in 1986. He did so on the front page of the *Sydney Morning
Herald*. The Indonesian government promptly banned all Australian jour-
nalists from Indonesia.[14]

Corruption fed upon entrepreneurial opportunity and was connected to
a sense of military indispensability, apartness, and superiority over civilians.
Indonesia, in short, had not solved either end of the double problem of
peace and order: (1) subordination of the military to civilian political government; (2) control of government by popular consent and rule of law.[15]
The cohesion of the military as managers of constitutional violence was
potentially a danger to Indonesia. The *dwifungi* model that the legalistic
Nasution had initiated in 1957 flourished indifferent to his later critique of
it. It contained within itself the looming tragedy of a sub-professional and
unaccountable military, collectors of personal wealth and political power.

Their "two functions" were essentially blended into one, primitive and diffuse.[16]

The military, even in the 1990s, still proudly thought of itself as "the backbone" of Indonesia. Rather than a spinal column, however, ABRI functioned like a notochord, far too soft and uncoordinated for an infant nation. Its proud record of winning hearts and minds in prevailing over Darul Islam was forgotten. They were chiefly losing hearts and minds in East Timor and Aceh. And too many officers were lining their own pockets in the process.

Suharto had once been dependent on his armed forces, but no longer. His own children, emerging as serious business players, displaced the military in oil trading, airlines, and timber, which had previously contributed to ABRI's budget and to the bank accounts of political generals. It was unwise for any business person—military, *pribumi,* or Chinese—to complain about these new partakers of the national pie.

Guy Pauker, a renowned American military analyst, supported Suharto and ABRI through all this. He had been in Southeast Asia, especially Indonesia, frequently since 1955. He trusted an army that had regained, in that decade, one-sixth of its national territory. Later, he also trusted a government that had "ruthlessly succeeded" against communism—unlike the effort in Vietnam—with international aid totaling only 1 percent of the an-

48. SUHARTO AT HIS PEAK. The president smiles at the height of his achievement and power in 1989, as his fifth term in office commences unchallenged. He indicates in his autobiography that this will be his last term, but his refusal to let go would create a long crisis of succession. (Ali Said/ *Tempo*)

nual cost of Vietnam and with no American lives lost. As late as 1991 Pauker judged Suharto to fit the model of autocratic but successful modernizers like Ataturk and Park Chung-hee. Not until 1996, shortly before his death, did Pauker concede the "rapacious personal enrichment" of civil and military elites under Suharto's regime.[17] Suharto was speeding down the path of failed modernizers like the shah of Iran and repressors like Ferdinand Marcos.

In 1988 Suharto appointed a non-combat general, Sudharmono, as vice president. In 1993 ABRI, angered over the previous appointment, reclaimed some public initiative by pre-emptive nomination of General Try Sutrisno for the post. But Suharto defused that move by uncomplainingly adopting Sutrisno as a reliable former personal adjutant who was far less likely to oppose than to echo him. That proved to be the case. Suharto defanged the military still further by dropping General Moerdani, after two terms as minister of defense and security, from the government altogether.[18] At the time of his ouster the experienced field commander and former chief of staff, blunt and charismatic, was still influential. But marooned in an office at the Center for Strategic and International Studies, he was reduced to gnashing his teeth, protecting his reputation in history, and cultivating his dwindling core of supporters.

When I interviewed him in October 1997, General Moerdani made much of five instances in which Pak Harto was out of order—it had climaxed just over two weeks before, on October 6, when Suharto had himself decorated as a five-star general. Only General Sudirman (the commander of the revolutionary army, who died young of tuberculosis) and General Nasution (who was accorded it as an honor long after retirement) had ever held that rank. And only the parliament could confer the rank legally. Ignoring the law entirely, Suharto's sycophantic entourage had had someone else sign the paper, so that they might flatter the president with the suggestion—an "honor" that he readily accepted. Suharto with five stars on his shoulders provoked intense disgust in Moerdani. Presidential indifference to legal procedure would further weaken morale in the armed forces.

I observed that whenever Suharto left office it would be necessary to reinvent everything. General Moerdani corrected me: "We will have to wait until Suharto *dies*. He will go on influencing people and events."[19]

Coercing the Politicians

In addition to lobotomizing the military, Suharto caponized his cabinet. Ibnu Sutowo, long before dismissed as superminister of oil, offered himself and Moerdani as evidence that speaking up to Suharto got one pushed out.

"Suharto has no interest in creative or independent actions. Look at the people around him now. They're all like this [smiling and bowing with hands folded over the pubic area]. Even when they know big mistakes are being made, they remain silent and agree. No one has any guts."[20]

Where would new energy and fresh assertiveness come from? From social developments beyond Suharto's control? By the mid-1990s the American embassy estimated the Indonesian middle class—households with annual income over $5,000—at between 14 and 18 million people.[21] But would they petition? A group of scholars even explored the subject of an "emerging proletariat," which they found diverse beyond any European connotation of the term: a working class of 20 to 33 million at a minimum, with many uncounted women and children and many workers at uncategorized functions.[22] But would they protest?

Sarwono Kusumaatmadja, former Golkar secretary-general, then minister of the environment, had seen new energies arising in Indonesia's society—business lobbies, urban professionals, and middle-class organizations. He did not cherish the proletariat as an endangered species or see the middle class as a guarantor of democracy. He simply asked who was going to express and protect new interests? Sarwono had participated in the politics of ideology (pounding home the importance of Pancasila), but now he saw the politics of interests as inescapable. In a more restless, creative social environment, Golkar should become a "true political party"—not manipulating amorphous functional groups but mediating among significant *interest* groups and expressing their needs, coherently and proportionately, on the national political stage.[23]

Suharto throttled such hopes. In October 1993, as head of Golkar's board of patrons, he installed B. J. Habibie, as minister of research and technology, to manage the party's congress, and he inserted his long-serving minister of information, Harmoko, as party chairman. What was billed as the "civilian-ization" of Golkar accomplished other Suharto goals. He had asked Harmoko to sound out the country in 1992 to see if the people still needed and wanted him. His minister assured Pak Harto that the people had responded overwhelmingly with their desire for his continuing as president. Now Harmoko announced a new 45-member executive board of Golkar which included Suharto's daughter Siti Hardijanti Rukmana (Tutut) as a vice-chairman and his son Bambang Trihatmodjo as treasurer, along with sons and daughters of friends, peers, and cronies. Marzuki Darusman, a former member of parliament who would return to try to fashion a new Golkar in 1999, summed it up as "nepotism on a grand scale . . . for the sole purpose of re-electing Suharto again in 1998."[24] Suharto proved him correct by sending Harmoko out into the nation again in 1997 to ask "the people" if he should continue or not. The answer of course was: "The people *want* you, Bapak. They *need* you."

The past is inescapable and will return. But Suharto even tried to banish history. In 1987 he prohibited the display of any images of former President Sukarno. A few underclass partisans dared display decals or tattoos in defiance. In the same year Megawati Sukarnoputri, one of Sukarno's eight children and his oldest daughter, was elected a member of parliament. In 1992 the Partai Demokrasi Indonesia (PDI), the artificial box into which the New Order had packaged old nationalists, Sukarnoites, and Christians of various flavors, performed surprisingly well. In the next year the PDI chose Megawati as their leader.[25]

What was to follow for Mega may be seen as consistent with the suppressing of her father's picture—also, perhaps, as a sign of a less confident and restrained Suharto, ill-served by the style of his intelligence system. Its habits of baroque hypothesis and auto-suggestion easily led to distorted conclusions. In 1993 a former head of Indonesia's State Intelligence Coordinating Body said in a published interview:

> As intelligence officers, we make up issues, and we disseminate them in the press, radio or television. We treat them as if they were real. When they are already widespread, usually people will talk about them and they tend to add and exaggerate the issues. Finally the issues will come back in reports. What is so funny is that these reports incline us to believe that these issues are real. In fact, we get terrified and begin to think "What if these issues are real?" The general then laughed.[26]

When the self-delusion of the establishment meets the untested ambition of its opponents, discord can easily turn into disorder. One year before the election of 1997, a splinter group of the PDI launched a factional Congress in Medan, North Aceh. They claimed to have letters of support from two-thirds of PDI's 300 nationwide branches but were actually able to produce signed and procedurally thorough documents from only one-quarter of them. It was, in fact, a government-manipulated rump proceeding to remove Mega from the party chairmanship.

One member of her PDI executive board, Laksamana Sukardi, had resigned as a CitiBank executive to help her. He warned the government that the PDI could bring "tens of millions of people into the streets" in support of democratic principles. Mega herself spoke much more dramatically than her matronly attire of blue polka-dot dress and comfortable shoes would suggest. She declared that "we want to consolidate ourselves as an independent party and not to be a stooge of the political framework." On June 20, 1996, the PDI brought not millions but 5,000 marchers into the streets of Jakarta wearing red shirts and carrying "Megawati for President" signs. Police and soldiers with riot shields clashed with rock-hurling demonstrators. Those who preferred managed conformity were upset at this "immature" and "un-Asian" confrontation with the government.[27]

Submerged emotions were breaking out. A new pro-Megawati coalition of thirty NGOs, called the Indonesian People's Council, took shape, anchored by the Indonesian Legal Aid Foundation. Some Muslim groups for democracy declared that Mega had been "unfairly robbed," and elements of the Toba Batak Protestant Church, annoyed at military intrusion into its mission, seemed to join the upsurge. Student groups with national connections, long dormant, awoke. Muchtar Pakpahan, after release from prison over a workers' uprising in Medan in 1994, brought his Indonesian Workers Welfare Union, abhorred by the government, into the pro-Mega camp. More was ahead.

Behind the scenes was Gordon Bishop—volunteer American instigator, cheerleader, motivator, and co-conspirator. In 1995, two years after he had lost his beloved Javanese wife and nearly his own life, in a terrible car accident—he left Indonesia on one day's notice when he woke up blind in one eye. Tests and operations in New York City revealed a rare brain tumor, which only 50 percent of patients survive five years. "Live life to the fullest, Gordon," his doctor counseled him. How the hell do you do that? he asked himself. With a quarter-century of residence in Indonesia as grounding, he determined as his remaining mission in life to help bring down Suharto, along with the family that had extorted the business that he and his beloved Nanies had built.

Ibu should go down with him. She was a key part of the fearful mix. Madame Tien Suharto had patronized Bishop's wife and daughter, while quietly terrorizing many others. He recalled an intimate social occasion years before when his hatred had welled up and he realized he could reach out and strangle her. "Do it, Gordon," a voice told him. "Just do it." But he didn't do it. He went into a bathroom, looked into a mirror, breathed deeply. In April 1996, shortly after Gordon returned to Jakarta, Mrs. Suharto suddenly died. Bishop saw a nation in respect but not in mourning. His own calculation was that President Suharto would now be easier to address, foil, even vanquish. He did not realize that Ibu Tien herself had become so sick of power that she declared to a personally trusted minister, "I just want to lie down and die." Three months later she did.[28]

Bishop got in touch with Gus Dur (Wahid), who brought him into his confidence and later into planning conversations with Megawati, Wahid's friend since childhood and an ally now. Alone with Gus—the two of them "just four eyes" in the Indonesian idiom—Bishop jested that there was actually only one eye. Wahid, who was slowly going blind with diabetes, enjoyed the bizarre humor. Bishop looked around for bugs. "I don't care if they listen," Wahid said. Bishop would later strike an immediate note of intimacy with Megawati, identifying and admiring her earrings of *emas budi,* gold from the Majapahit era. She was impressed with his expertise. She talked calmly about when she would be president. "Aren't you worried about security?" he asked her. She touched her earrings; they were her guardians. They talked as practitioners about *kebatinan,* Javanese contemplative discipline. She tested him by asking him her birthday. He immediately declared, correctly, January 23. "I was really in the zone, then," Bishop recalls.

Megawati's first speech in English, written by Gordon Bishop, was at the Foreign Correspondents Club on June 10, 1996. She said that if her opposition party wished to do so, they could close down schools, factories, and offices and bring the country to a halt. But they were not going to do this now, even though the regime had embittered countless people. It was the most confrontational speech ever directed at Suharto.

Bishop intensified his friendships with the two key oppositionists through gifts. For Gus Dur, who had said "You are a brother to me," he brought *dodot:* a double-size healing *batik,* embedded with profiles of the powerful clown-god Semar. This early nineteenth-century artifact had cured ailing sultans and a semiparalyzed Dutch governor general, who willed it back to the *keraton* on his death in 1910. For Mega: a pair of ancient Javanese masks, one of which, worn in a dance of unrequited love at the *keraton* in the 1840s, had enough bothered the then-governor general that he had ordered its nose cut off. Bishop sent them in a box to Mega, through Laksamana Sukardi, who entrusted the box to his daughter, driven by a friend in a Mercedes. Then: "Laksa calls up: 'Gordon! . . . The box started flying around the car!'" They had to stop driving, catch it, calm down, proceed. At Mega's house they placed it on a table "and it starts flying all over her reception room."[29]

Meeting with Gus Dur for several hours on June 18, Bishop proposed that they follow through on her threat. Shut it down now. Wahid said he agreed. But (aside to Bishop), "Mega is on a pedestal, and she's a prima donna . . . I'll either have to guide her, or go for the number one position myself." They planned. Yes, Martin Luther King, Jr. and Gandhi were borne in mind. Still, airports would have to be shut down, and other public facilities. *Agents provocateurs* would be used against them. They would need medical teams. If things went wrong, there might be a bloodbath, and maybe 5,000 dead.

Bishop, who had "never even killed a deer," stayed awake a whole night asking if, 5,000 dead, he could live with himself. Yes, in this cause. They tried the plan gently on Mega, talking around the edges of it. Even so, she was hesitant. Wahid said to Bishop afterward, "Forget Mega. Let's give her a fait accompli." They would have a secret meeting: Laksamana, Muchtar Pakpahan, Marsillam Simanjuntak (previously burned, once jailed), and a student leader of choice.

"Then," as Bishop remembers, "they came after me." Suspecting bugging, he changed his suite. A woman in the hotel's business office, a fan of Megawati, warned him that there were nonetheless officials of military intelligence in rooms to the left and right, as well as above and below his new room. His planning was also running into two kinds of wild suspicion: contacts of Muchtar told them that Bishop had been sent by the Clinton administration to destroy Suharto (and who on the far left wanted to abet imperialism?). Several in Megawati's own circle were saying, "He was sent to destroy *us*" (paranoia of the marginalized).

Bishop prepared a follow-up speech for Megawati. He read it, just to her and Gus Dur, in late June. At 45 minutes long, it evoked dead Indonesian heroes and heroines, summoned principles of human rights, and called upon Suharto to resign. Four or five times during the recital and after, Gus Dur said, "That's the *wahyu*"—an obscure remark to most foreigners, but clear enough to Bishop and to Mega. In Wahid's perception, Bishop was the voice of the mandate of heaven. Wahid had told him he had seen in a dream help from a foreigner, coming like a helicopter, with an overview of Indonesia's problems and needs. But this speech was *heavy*. "Mega has to make the decision herself," said Wahid. Just as he had faced down Suharto's attempt to take over NU in 1987, so she could face down the threat to PDI now, if she chose. Megawati decided not to give the speech.

Bishop, under surveillance, feeling in danger, sought embassy help, which was refused as inappropriate. He got his passport stamped out to Singapore. He knew he was being trailed by two military intelligence agents. But he also knew he was in the clandestine protection of two presidential guards hired by Gus Dur for night work and special influence and paid by a sympathetic businessman. They helped him get back from Singapore without a stamp and without interrogation by military intelligence. Gus Dur was "cool as a cucumber" about all the subterfuge, not to mention the immense portent of their subversion. He tried to persuade Bishop to stay on. But Bishop decided, after Mega's unwillingness to give his second speech, that it was time to go. Again, spirited through by suborned presidential guards, he left without interrogation or an exit stamp and returned to the United States on July 4, 1996.[30]

Around Megawati Sukarnoputri was a loose assortment of disparate

grievants, concerned with underemployment, economic disparity, rural dis-
placement, censorship, and corruption. Some major NGOs stayed aloof.
Mega herself vented pique over the Suharto-inspired rump PDI but offered
no strategy for amalgamating and motivating the forces swirling about her.
The NU established no formal bond with the movement, but its chairman,
Wahid, now openly declared his sympathies for Megawati.[31]

Here, foreshadowed, were some dynamics of the unexpected national
election three years later: inchoate elements of a civil society, a shy Megawati, a coy Gus Dur. But the focal activists nurtured aggrieved memories
of injuries to over seventy of them during their march of June 20. They
held the Jakarta headquarters of Mega's PDI, a white office building of
the colonial era, and refused to relinquish it. They played guitars. They
hosted "free-speech forums" where speakers railed at government corruption. They danced into the night to music from West Irian. They assured
themselves of outside sympathies with heated cell phone conversations.
But, *The Economist* reported, "more brandished bamboo staves or metal
pipes . . . Some are prepared, even eager, for a fight."[32]

To the government, the speechifiers and guitar players were defiant
squatters. When an ASEAN conference concluded and the last foreign ministers left, ABRI proceeded with forceful eviction. Not that they didn't
weigh consequences. A military officer called the head of an Indonesian
brokerage house to ask what would happen to the Jakarta stock market if
they proceeded with the assault. He was answered: it will drop. The attack
was launched at 6:30 on a Saturday morning, July 27, 1996, to minimize
financial consequences.

The human consequences were 5 dead, 149 injured, and 23 listed as missing. Gus Dur at the time was asked how many were killed. He said, "One
hundred." Someone observed there was no count anywhere near that. "It's
all right," he answered, "the army tells such big lies, it's OK if we tell little
ones." Years later a reporter early on the scene mentioned to Goenawan
Mohamad that he had seen no signs of blood. Goenawan exclaimed, "Why
didn't you tell me that earlier?!"[33] The banned editor, now informal "chief
of propaganda" for the opposition, wanted to maintain his reputation for
accuracy.

A combination of soldiers, hired thugs of Pemuda Pancasila, and riot police took the PDI headquarters, but they failed to prevent youths from
torching at least a dozen buildings, including car showrooms and the six-
story Ministry of Agriculture. The military were later reported as proud
that so few had died, and they attributed the low fatality figure to their having equipped themselves with rattan batons from local furniture makers,
rather than relying on gunpoint or bayonet.[34]

In Jakarta's worst riot since Tanjung Priok in 1984, and previously Malari in 1974, the military could claim some sort of success in having left fewer dead than before. The stock market went down only 5 percent in its next two days of trading, while the rupiah also sank. Financial sensibilities were both optimistic and jittery. The head of research at Nomura Securities in Jakarta said corporate profits could grow 18 percent in 1996, the highest rate in Asia. But the new nervepoint was political risk. "What better image to present to foreign investors than to torch the import-export bank," a commentator remarked with irony, watching as glass and burned rubber fell from its charred remains. Even when the riots settled down, the central question would come up—Suharto and succession.

Despite their nonviolent speeches, the PDI and the NGOs had shown terrible crowd control. The army, which had had most students as its allies in 1965–66, was now clearly pitted against them, and clumsily so. They had overreacted and had made a martyr of Megawati. But prompt promotions went to key planners and players. Brigadier General Zacky Anwar Makarim was made head of the Strategic Intelligence Agency. Bambang Yudhoyono was advanced to major general. Yorrys Raweyai, thug leader, was appointed to the MPR.[35]

Where was Suharto's once deft touch? All that seemed to matter now was mop up, stop up, shut up. Muchtar Pakpahan was rearrested at home one night at 11 PM. The student head of a coffee shop socialist group, the People's Democratic Party, was also arrested. The old rhetoric of "communist threat" was trotted out.[36] Youth were taking blood oaths, "prepared to die" for Megawati.[37] She herself met a *New York Times* reporter in a pink flowered housedress and through an advisor-interpreter "spoke slowly and cautiously, as if avoiding puddles in the rain." "You are asking me to be candid and say what is the truth . . . But that is difficult. I am a woman. I am not so rude as to say harsh words." She was willing, however, to take credit for going beyond the legacy of her father. "I encourage people to speak up because I have discovered they are living in a culture of fear, like ghosts. I have worked hard to teach them about the rights and responsibilities of being good citizens, and it has been an eye opener for them."[38]

But aside from opening the people's eyes, she had pulled up far short of Gordon Bishop's second draft speech. She was distinctly nonconfrontational about President Suharto. Her limited party agenda focused on greater opportunity for jobs in government. Rather than advocating fundamental changes, she wanted to see the system followed more faithfully. What system? According to *The New York Times,* when she heard the crowds chanting her name, she said, "I have mixed feelings of sadness because after 50 years of independence it is still like this. They have lost their dignity and when they say 'Mega, Mega,' they want their dignity back."[39]

Russia had tried *glasnost*—more open expression—while failing in *peres-*

troika—restructuring the system. China was succeeding in economic re-structuring, while suppressing free speech. But Indonesia's prime personal symbol of opposition did not dare for great change in either direction. Megawati in 1996 wanted more than tea and sympathy. But not much more: a slice of patronage and a taste of openness. Three years later she would agree with me that Suharto's overreaction against the PDI was a sign of his terminal weakness.[40] But at the time she behaved as if he had enduring strength.

Cukongs and Old Chinese

How did Indonesia become an "emerging tiger," or "emerging giant," when it had low tax collection (12 percent of GDP) compared even with Thailand and South Korea and when its codes of business law were often hangovers from colonial times "ill-defined, antiquated, and opaque," in the words of one commentator."[41] What little law there was had been jack-hammered to pieces in the Japanese and revolutionary years. Then, in the Sukarno period, revolutionary officers and politicians were given companies and concessions left by the Dutch. The last concessions were confiscated and Dutch citizens expelled in 1957–58. Well-positioned Indonesians without business training took over and carried on without critique by the press or correction by the judiciary, their opportunism setting a tone which New Order rapacity would exceed.[42]

The Jakarta Stock Exchange was born in 1977 with one company. Only in 1989 when it was revitalized did it begin to require that listed companies (of which there were 174 by 1993) disclose financial statements. Compliance was uncertain, and the quality of information questionable. When I asked a top official of the exchange, in 1998, for an estimate of the collective debt-to-asset ratio of the listed companies, the only answer was a rolling of the eyes.[43]

The net social entropy of the system and its economic vulnerability cannot be quantified. But it may be illustrated by the fact that banks had little recourse if borrowers failed to repay. Adam Schwarz, whose courageous research eventually led to denial of a visa, summed it all up: "If a bad debtor is brought to court . . . more often than not the judge is paid off and the case gets thrown out. Unable to pursue bad debtors through the courts, or to foreclose on collateralized assets, banks simply charge higher rates to Indonesian borrowers, costs which are then paid by consumers or tacked on to the price of Indonesian products sold abroad."[44] These interlinked conditions were depriving the government and the people of development momentum and meant danger in the long run.

A leading business consultant and connoisseur of Indonesian conditions, James Castle, put together a "Road Map to Indonesian Business Groups" at the height of supposed tigerishness in 1997. The intricate and tersely descriptive poster shows 140 of the most significant groups, of which about half have "listed interests." That half of them were not listed companies suggests how strongly the idea of family business was and remains. "Privately held," a prim Western phrase, does not begin to describe the situation. We are looking at family holdings that expand in all directions— through a wide range of businesses and blood or marriage connections, so that the branches of the family tree sag with commercial-industrial entities.[45]

Only about 40 of the top 140 were the property of persons of all-Indonesian ancestry. Of those 40, sixteen were "First Family." The other 100, by inference, were chiefly owned by Indonesians of Chinese ancestry—whether from many generations back, or few, or none. The latter, successful immigrants, included Liem Sioe Liong, who left Fujian at age twenty-one and arrived in Central Java in 1937 with nothing but ingenuity. He peddled peanuts, cloves, bicycle parts, and miscellaneous else, much acquired on credit. During the revolution he sold clothes, medicine, soap, food, and military supplies to nationalist forces. In the 1950s he became an important supplier to the army's key Diponegoro division in Central Java, whose chief supply and financial officer was then Lieutenant Colonel Suharto, later its commander.

Suharto trusted Liem. They later ascended to power together. By 1990 Liem's Salim Group had revenues (including 40 percent overseas) of $8–9 billion. Their domestic sales were equivalent to about 5 percent of Indonesia's GDP. The conglomerate held the country's largest market share in private banking, cement, and several commodities, with major stakes in auto manufacturing, processed foods, chemicals, and real estate, while continuing to grow in other enterprises and other locales: China, Asia, Europe, and the United States. The group by then comprised over 300 separate companies employing 135,000 Indonesians. Their assets were two or three times larger than any other Indonesian privately owned enterprise.[46]

In December 1993, Minister for Research and Technology Habibie told a parliamentary hearing, without evident anxiety, that the country's ten top conglomerates controlled nearly a third of the Indonesian economy. Such overdevelopment at the top was complicated by the fact that most of those businessmen were Chinese Indonesians. *Pribumi* complaints arose. They were partly assuaged by the project called Team 10, which had provided special handouts in the 1980s to "indigenous businesses" until it was shut down for excesses. When Liem Sioe Liong and Prajogo Pangestu bailed out a bank owned by Suharto's *yayasans* (for-profit "foundations") which had lost nearly half a billion dollars speculating in foreign exchange, the president insisted on rewarding them by cutting them in on major *pribumi* projects—thereby damaging both *pribumi* morale and inter-ethnic relations by putting patrimonial payoff above all other considerations.[47]

Suharto often demonstrated that he had not only a soldier's answer to power questions and a patriarch's answer to social questions but a peasant's view of questions of economic scale. Having solved big problems by coercion and collusion, he would address other—also large—socioeconomic problems in sentimental and superficial ways. An example is the Jimbaran Declaration of August 27, 1995. Suharto called about fifty major business executives together for a conference in Bali. He got them to sign up behind two commitments: (1) as a "voluntary duty," to help the government "lift up" the poor by giving 2 percent of their business profits annually to that cause through a government-connected foundation directed by the president; and (2) as a commitment of business friendship, to extend business opportunities to small and middle-sized corporations and to cooperate with them to better their development.[48] Laudable, no doubt. But dubious as well. The goals should have been addressed by social policy long before and enabled by better government revenue collection. Or furthered by objective tax incentives and other programs pursued in a reliable legal atmosphere.

The Jimbaran Sekretariat's final report came less than three years later. It concluded its activity under the rubric of the early *reformasi* era, Suharto having resigned a month before it appeared. Business disruption, not to mention devastation, is not mentioned in the text but may be inferred from the figures. Notable among those who had responded to Suharto's invitation, in order of largest pledges, were Astra International, Bank Danamon, the Salim Group, the Lippo Group, and Bakrie Group—four Chinese-Indonesian groups and one *pribumi*.

In its first year, June 1996–June 1997, Jimbaran raised nearly $1.5 billion, 123 percent of its goal. Astra and Bakrie generously surpassed their targets. Salim nearly reached theirs. Bank Danamon did not make two-thirds of its goal. Lippo, in a year they were later revealed to be contributing to Bill Clinton's presidential campaign, gave less than 1 percent of its pledge. In its second year, Jimbaran ran smack into the Asian financial crisis. Performance plummeted. Astra, savaged in sales, produced nearly nothing; Bakrie, nothing at all. Danamon fell to one-third of its goal, and Salim managed one-half. Lippo achieved the only 100 percent record besides Sinar Mas (appearing for the first time), but only did so by cutting its unmet commitment of the previous year by three-quarters.[49] Commitments for 1998 were nugatory. An early Kabinet Reformasi announcement on June 3, 1998, swept the scheme into a wider family prosperity program.

Aside from this report on collection of revenues, I know of no record of expenditures or projects advanced, although I have seen public relations photographs in the newspapers of awards under its name. Genuine program assessment would require, as a start, full public accounting of the records of this and other presidential *yayasans,* which may be a long time coming. Or never.

Two misunderstandings attend Chinese Indonesians. One is a standard journalistic formula that with only 3.5 percent of the population, the "Chinese" control 70 percent of the Indonesian economy. That formula traces back to an excellent study by Michael Backman in 1995. But the journalistic cliché exaggerates the picture unless other factors are noted: (1) state-owned enterprises, like the giant oil firm Pertamina, were excluded from Backman's calculations; (2) foreign-owned businesses like Freeport

49. *BECAK* AND PASSENGERS. An unhurryable mode of transportation, the trishaw, pictured against a subtly shadowed wall in Solo, Central Java in 1989. (Abbas/Magnum Photos)

McMoRan, the largest taxpayer in Indonesia, are also excluded; (3) if ownership of the largest "Chinese" private sector groups is carefully studied, it reveals heavy interlacing with the Suharto family and other *pribumi* ownership. The Salim Group, identified with Liem Sioe Liong, actually also involved two *pribumi* relatives of President Suharto and an Acehnese associate of his cousin Sudwikatmono. The Sinar Mas group, identified with Eka Tjipta Widjaja, maintains ties with a real estate firm owned by Suharto's half-brother Probosutejo and does joint ventures with a conglomerate owned by Habibie's brother Timmy.[50] Taking all these factors into account, a sounder generalization for the late twentieth century might be: Chinese Indonesians managed perhaps two-thirds of Indonesia's private market capitalization and owned a large share of it in concert with President Suharto's extended family and *pribumi* oligarchs.

The second, and grosser, misunderstanding would be to characterize all Chinese Indonesians in the image of the most gluttonous *cukongs*. The rural retail store owner has nothing to do with them; he rises and falls on his own in a turbulent economy and may or may not be a good neighbor. Immigrant *cukongs* of unrestrained greed, however, arouse an especial ire in the general population and also in long-established families with a Chinese heritage. Norma Zecha traces her own family back five generations in Indonesia, and her late husband Kwie's family back more than five hundred years to the Majapahit era. Her Chinese-Indonesian great-grandmother eloped at age sixteen with a Czech artist-adventurer and lived to the age of 91, marrying two Chinese after two widowhoods. But she kept the Zecha name, which conferred Eurasian status under the Indies government, thereby allowing "assimilation up" in the Dutch system. When the grand dame was dying, she had a gramophone put on the table next to her bed and ordered, "You don't cry, you play me my favorite Viennese waltzes." Her family kept her body in state over ice for weeks, until friends from all over the world could come to final services. Servants spent a month producing a tower of figurines representing her life, which was then consigned to funerary flames.

I asked Norma the meaning of the inscriptions above the Confucian altar in their front hall. "I can't tell you, can't read Chinese. My father-in-law could have told you . . . But for me, that altar means respect for your forefathers. You do not forget where you came from. You don't pray to your ancestors, or to their pictures, you just remember them. By the soul tablets, inside the altar, you can check how many generations it has existed . . . Now we observe All Souls Day; serve tea and food at the right phase of the moon."

As an American-trained sociologist, Norma spoke objectively about the ethnic impact of the Dutch system. But her emotion surged about some of those born in China and recently arrived in Indonesia: "Those *singke'h,* they are so Chinese we can't understand them. Liem Sioe Liong speaks Bahasa badly, with a Chinese lilt. His first wife is still in China. He's interested only in making money . . . unscrupulous . . . Prajoga Pangestu is maybe second generation . . . Eka Widjaya another first generation. Their grasping behavior feeds the prejudice."

Norma sighed. Established Chinese who have principles lose out to these Chinese who have none. "Really, we get along better with *pribumi.*" She returned to matters of family heritage and different accommodations to the present: a brother with a cosmopolitan chain of elegant hotels; a daughter in international finance; a son in the same field, who is nonetheless deeply Javanese in culture and a performing expert in gamelan. Suddenly Norma laughed: "Old money was once new money!"[51]

Corruption and Proto-Capitalism

In the late 1970s Lucian Pye and Karl Jackson tut-tutted those Westerners who "often mistake for corruption [what] is a culturally legitimate way of initiating a dependence relationship."[52] But experience accumulates and is shared. Now those who argue for greasing the wheel of growth must consider whether or not corruption will break the axle of total development—social, economic, institutional.

As a Muslim pluralist, Nurcholish Madjid takes the view that the Qur'an showed the way for a "vice-regency of man" under God to "reform the earth," safeguarding it from destruction and corruption. He even finds Qur'anic authority for the law of "checks and balances" in the "struggle for the betterment of life ('*jihad*' in its generic meaning)."[53] His bringing the Qur'an and James Madison into spiritual convergence is a fertile feat. But such conviction must face the daily fusion of foreign willingness to bribe and the pronounced Indonesian bribability.

Japan is a historic example.[54] The forced resignation of Suharto brought forth revelations in Tokyo newspapers on corruption in Japan's Official Development Assistance to Indonesia. That aid program, the largest in the world, climbed to $960 million in 1996, a year when Japanese private investment in Indonesia was $76 billion dollars—also the "number one amount in the world." Within such transactions, including construction of university buildings in Indonesia, a dark "rebate culture" flourished, with rewards, donations, entertainment expenses, mediation fees, agent fees, and order fees. Dimensions of the problem may be felt in the fact that one Japanese construction firm, Taisei Kensetsu, had been involved in 66 contracts in Indonesia and had paid irregular "construction fees" of $600 million. A Japanese agent, interviewed anonymously, described the "open secret" of misuse of another country's aid money: "When we finished our work, we delivered cash (contained in a bag) to the director of the Minister's Secretariat, Ministry of Transport, and to other government branches . . . To protect their status, [they] usually give money to the 'upper' people. So I'm sure Suharto received the money."

The elaboration of the rebate culture included paying to avoid arbitrary penalties. Japanese companies called this "the second tax." Among Indonesian public officials, in turn, the justification for these practices was "a second wage." "The government made the public servants wages very low in exchange for their various opportunistic rights. Indonesian officials were told to make use of that privilege to earn their living." Minister of Investment Hamzah Haz, lecturing in Tokyo, justified rewards to ministers and "cooperative organizations" in every office "which support the life of public servants and officials."[55] At the same time, Haz promised to lead any investigation of alleged corruption or fraud—a rote reassurance of the Suharto era and an empty one, given that his premises would make malpractice almost impossible to define. Suharto's downfall, however, did give courage to Japanese critics of the nexus of corruption between their nation and Indonesia, with its especially negative impacts on the cost of food and transportation in household economics and on land use.[56]

How did American companies play into this culture? Large ones with convictions could apparently brave their way through, while smaller ones struggled to make contacts while saving their consciences. A modest company with a capacity to mount extensive cable communications systems was run by a former U.S. Navy fighter pilot called Top Gun, aided by a former Seal with lots of action in Vietnam, who called himself Snake. Top Gun and Snake arrived in Java in the 1990s at an apparently propitious time. A Hong Kong friend started them off with Sinar Mas, then an $8 billion company, with executives they found intelligent and careful. Sinar Mas guided them to see Tutut Suharto. Then to see Habibie. "I'd love to be the first foreigner to fly your plane, Minister Habibie," said Top Gun. But the minister seemed bored. He preferred sales calls to courtesy calls.

Back at Sinar Mas, when push came to shove at board level, its matriarch and chairperson decided no: if they moved with these Americans, it might compromise their cell phone business—already established with presidential favor—because the Lippo Group was going after cable. And Lippo's Riady family was in tighter than themselves with the Suharto family. "Don't step on toes" prevailed, Javanese style, rather than "Slug it out, toe to toe," American style.

Snake then used his personal network to contact the assistant minister of communications, who received Top Gun and Snake swiftly and advised them to see an entrepreneurial eminence who could make things happen. This was a gambling casino owner. In their meeting the casino owner brought forth "twenty henchmen," as Top Gun recalls. Everything went smoothly, and they were ready to put the deal in contractual form when the visitors were told that there would be some "undocumented expenses."

Snake exploded. "What do you mean, undocumented expenses? How dare you suggest that to the Chief Executive Officer of our corporation? Don't you know that in America he could be put in *jail* for that?!" He kicked Top Gun under the table. The casino maestro and henchmen were soothing. No offense was meant. Just local procedures. Everything could be worked out. Outside, Top Gun turned to Snake and began, "What the hell . . ?" Snake cut him off. "Don't worry. They want the deal. They'll work it out to squeeze somebody else for the bribe."

Thus relaxed, Top Gun made sure the contract squared with American law and business ethics. For the arbitration clause, he chose Singapore as a rule-of-law site. When the contract came back for their confirming signatures, all twenty pages were clean and agreeable but for one word. "Singapore" was crossed out. "Jakarta" was written in. Rule-of-law would not apply.

What to do now? They had great technology to offer and could still make a lot of money for their shareholders if they partnered with the opposition—linked up with Lippo. They were advised that the best way to join the action was in Little Rock, Arkansas. There a lawyer had opened his own firm to represent Lippo and James Riady, a friend of former governor Clinton, who was now president. Top Gun began commuting to Little Rock, a city less mysterious than Jakarta but still not perfectly transparent. Then campaign finance charges appeared against Riady, who eventually received, in 2001, the largest fine for such a crime in American history. The prominent author of a management consultancy paper praising Lippo's network-building had overlooked some transcultural and ethical problems that had already reached the Oval Office in the White House.[57] Samuel Huntington's way of seeing "a certain amount of corruption a welcome lubricant easing the path to modernization" was meant, in 1968, to apply to traditional and relatively uncorrupt societies.[58] The second filter excludes Indonesia, and the first excludes the United States.

As Top Gun and Snake reviewed their project, the Indonesian crash of 1997 ended their labors. Despite successful businesses in other parts of the world, their board was forced by the Asian undertow to sell the corporation.[59]

Being there early and growing large was the best insurance of prosperity. Freeport-McMoRan Copper and Gold Inc., based in New Orleans, arrived in 1967 as the Suharto regime's first foreign investor, a midsize miner of sulfur, and obtained what exploration later revealed to be the world's largest known copper and gold deposit. Proven ore reserves in the open-pit mine at Grasberg are worth about $60 billion (see Figures 104 and 105). Indonesia in 1973 lacked expertise in drafting mining contracts, and the one concluded then had no safeguards for the environment or indigenous tribes. Looking back, Mohammed Sadli, then minister in charge of foreign investment, admits that "Freeport got away with murder."

The company's forceful CEO, Jim Bob Moffet, is a former University of Texas football player, known for his impersonations of Elvis Presley. He deserves better to be known for visionary explorations and massively successful investment gambles. The changing environment of his company's success, however, drove him toward programs for assuaging environmental damage and compensating surrounding tribes, neither of which could satisfy escalating demands on those fronts. His sharp political instincts have moved him to put on his board such unlike men as Henry Kissinger and the Aumungme leader Tom Beanal. They also led him into extensive dealings with Ginandjar Kartasasmita, Suharto's minister of mines (1988–1993); to guaranteeing loans and profits to a purchaser of Freeport infrastructure assets who later became minister of manpower; and to guaranteeing a loan to Bob Hasan when Suharto pushed his crony into the picture, with Freeport pledging to cover shortfalls in Hasan's interest payments. These arrangements, notably irregular by American standards, needless to say passed the test of Indonesian law.[60] Freeport McMoRan continues to be highly profitable. When besieged by critics of corporate neocolonialism, Moffet's stock answer is that his company is Indonesia's largest taxpayer. That is true.

Even while Suharto remained in office, the former top government auditor, Gandhi, dared to declare that "our management supervision system is too weak to fight collusion and corruption." High officials proceeded with unnecessary projects; allocated inflated budgets to well-connected contractors; forced state-owned companies to buy shares in poorly performing private companies close to the power-elite; invested state money in banks in return for commissions; sold state assets at reduced prices in return for cuts of the proceeds; and evaded taxes through collusion. Investigations could take three years and have no deterrent effect because a procedure for full public disclosure was lacking.[61] These were not problems caused by Chinese immigrants. They were lodged deep in Indonesian history and habit.

Even while Indonesia lagged Taiwan and Korea in the 1960s and Thailand in the 1970s, the government eventually allowed a constructive influence of domestic capitalists on state policy. Once it moved, realistically, toward an export-oriented economy instead of an over-protective one, the state lost leverage on its patronage network and on the ability to bully business dependents within a benefice system. The government had to attract international capital—now the tone-setting element—including Indonesian and Chinese-Indonesian firms with international identity and operations. Certain business conditions had to be assured: low wages, a skilled workforce, efficient infrastructure, predictable taxation, acceptable terms of investment and repatriation of profits, and political stability. The government clearly worked on those factors.[62] The economy by the late 1980s, while certainly not democratic in the sense of organized coalitions of oppositionist civilians, showed early signs of entrepreneurial pluralism. Organized business lobbies, while careful not to confront the state executive or the armed forces, were wielding some power, especially in insurance, textiles, and pharmaceuticals.[63]

Twenty years after Sukarno's last rant against Western imperialism, Indonesia was clearly part of an international capitalist system. Yet Indonesia's capitalism looked relatively weak even in relation to other Southeast Asian countries.

First, there was an extraordinarily high percentage of Chinese Indonesians in that level of the economy, against whom discrimination was rife, generating concealed ill-feeling in return. By contrast, in Singapore there was "no problem" by demographic definition, in Thailand there was largely effective assimilation, and in the Philippines there were relatively flexible citizenship laws. Indonesia's laws and attitudes, however, motivated the Chinese toward quick returns obtained by speculation and parasitism, followed by salting profits abroad.

Second, government intervention in the economy, which had proven effective in accelerating development in Japan, South Korea, and Taiwan, notably bogged it down in Indonesia. Despite the ability of the technocrats to keep macroeconomic policy usually sane and stable, micro-distortions by Cendana intervention were building long-term vulnerabilities.[64]

Third, technological deficiencies were extreme. Continued reliance on foreign companies in that regard—with Indonesia again the most pronounced example—would mean, a Japanese analyst said, that such "capitalism will never become an autonomous propelling force of economic development."[65] Indonesian capitalism was structurally flimsy and derivative.

Habibie, Technology, and Strategic Development

For its Independence Day celebration in 1976, Indonesia became the world's third country after Canada (1972) and the United States (1974) to use a satellite for domestic communications. The system of forty earth stations had cost a billion dollars, equivalent to a quarter of the entire national budget for that year. It proved again that Suharto did not lack vision from his own peculiar point of view: he named the satellite Palapa after the oath taken by Gajah Mada, the chief minister of fourteenth-century Majapahit, who had vowed not to eat the mystical fruit Palapa until all regions of the archipelago were unified under his realm. Suharto aimed at having an archipelagic worldview of national unity and harmony delivered at ordered times to all places and to all layers of society.

Palapa did tremendously improve domestic long-distance telephoning, and through government-subsidized village television sets it spread the national language and the New Order's ideology to remote places. That included the regime's version of history constructed for mass consumption as TV movies. Eventually, however, Suharto's dynastic capitalism undercut his own soporific propaganda. Between 1987 and 1994, five private television stations were licensed, all to Suharto's children or friends. Even such restricted ownership led to competitive diversity in what flowed from Jakarta, including factual and, finally, critical reporting. The uncontrolled culmination was live broadcasting of the Semanggi incident in November 1998, in which government troops fired upon a mass of unarmed demonstrators (see Figures 71–73). A medium intended to instruct citizens in national harmony wound up illustrating the state's violence.[66]

Suharto had hired Habibie as a major technical advisor to himself and to Ibnu Sutowo of Pertamina in 1974, before he made Habibie state minister for research and technology in 1978, where he would remain for twenty years. When Suharto was stationed in Makassar, he had known Habibie, half a generation younger, as a Muslim teenager from Sulawesi, whose mother came from Yogya *priyayi*. Preternaturally bright and frenetically articulate, Habibie had gone on to study in Aachen, West Germany (where the activist Romo Mangun, studying architecture, knew him), and obtained his doctorate in aeronautical engineering. He spent more than twenty years in Germany and rose to become a vice president of Messerschmitt before returning to Jakarta. Suharto summoned him home from foreign eminence with the idea of starting aircraft production and establishing an agency to control all science and technology in Indonesia.[67]

Together, through two oil booms and two oil slumps, they achieved their institutional goals. The larger national strategic goal, however, was a shortcut to industrialization. That was ill-starred from the start. Habibie's favorite thing was building airplanes. With a billion dollars by 1990, his flagship of the strategic industries, IPTN, had produced a turboprop 35-seater under license from Spain, various helicopters under license from Germany, France, and Bell-Textron (U.S.), components of the Boeing 737 airframe, and so on, all geared to both military and civilian use. Also, underwater torpedoes (German) and rockets (Swiss and Belgian).

The shipbuilding divisions in his strategic grasp built tankers, cargo carriers, utility vessels, tugboats, and inter-island coasters under license from Mitsui, and fast patrol boats under a German license. And by cooperation chiefly with Siemens but also with some Japanese companies, he produced a great array of telephone equipment, from standard desk phones to small satellite earth stations. Arms and explosives were produced in a similar way. A research institute worked on strategic electronics, components, and materials.

Where Sukarno had believed that making Indonesia great lay in summoning the revolutionary will of the masses, Suharto believed it lay in producing "planes, ships, communications equipment and weapons," even to the point of rescuing Krakatau Steel, a rusting remnant of Soviet aid to Sukarno, and funding it through Ibnu Sutowo's near bankruptcy of Indonesia and the second oil recession of the early 1980s.[68] No one doubted Suharto's willpower. But the true precondition for sustained development was more of what Suharto had begun so well—education, which now required strengthening through the secondary and tertiary levels.

Two obsessives do not make one genius. Suharto and Habibie convinced and motivated and supported each other with the zeal of a loving uncle and nephew. Habibie, not a military officer, not a U.S.-trained economist, not supported by the World Bank or the International Monetary Fund, nonetheless had what it took to command tremendous resources and influences. The Japanese political scientist Shiraishi Takashi summed it up: "He enjoyed Suharto's patronage."[69]

But all of these achievements for a strategic neo-Majapahit flew in the face of two sound and resolute sources of advice: General Moerdani and the technocrats. Moerdani, in 1984, went on record with his mission of reorganizing the armed forces, since he expected no conventional war "in island Southeast Asia for the indefinite future." He stressed internal security problems of social disorder and subversion. Assault rifles for infantry long in the field; military transport capable of take-off and landing on short airstrips; highly maneuverable helicopters; radio phones and telephones—that would do it.[70]

The Berkeley mafia, for their part, wanted attention focused not on technology but on labor-intensive or resource-based industries. Instead of turning the Agency for Technological Assessment and Application "into a small Indonesian version of [Japan's] MITI," they would presumably have directed attention to the fact that 90 percent of forty-seven state universities had no research budget. And the National Research Council budget was be-

50. AIRPLANE, 1946. General Sudirman, on top of an engine, wearing a dark cap, examines with aides a captured Japanese fighter plane. As a symbol of revolt, they named it "Diponegoro," after the nineteenth-century Javanese prince who fought the Dutch. (Ipphos Photo Archive)

ing swiftly cut, from already negligible to insultingly small: $140,000 by 1988–89.[71] A corollary to these fatal deficiencies in research, including medical research, was the relatively weak protection of Indonesians through health insurance—less than 14 percent of the population in 1994 had it, and the distribution was dramatically skewed by income, with corollary impacts on availability and use of health services.[72]

The poster girl and the tragedienne, both, of this misdirected development was Pratiwi Sudarmono. Her grandfather was a regent in the system of the sultan of Solo. "I am Javanese, aristocratic background," she told me.[73] "Even now in my own family, feudalism is felt in everyday life. If you come from blue blood, you can sit in front at a marriage ceremony, while ordinary [people] sit in back only . . . Even in Yogya-Solo [the titles] Raden and Raden Mas are still used at the universities . . . You have to bow to higher rank and you cannot fire him." At the University of Indonesia, "We cannot *see* it, but we can still *feel* it . . . I cannot become professor even though I have Ph.D.; cannot, because older person doesn't have it yet. Even without scientific achievement, he gets it first . . . These things have been practiced since the Dutch era . . . For woman, even worse. We must fight double or triple to get acknowledgment of our achievement."

Pratiwi researched and wrote in Japanese, getting her doctorate in molecular biology and biotechnology at Osaka University. She returned to Indonesia in 1984, after Indonesia's second purchase of a satellite from the United States, when that country had extended an invitation to Indonesia to choose an astronaut for training in America. She was among 4 of 207 applicants chosen to go to the Johnson Space Center in Houston for testing, where she emerged as the top candidate.

Dr. Sudarmono trained and was scheduled to fly with the *Challenger* in

51. AIRPLANE, 1991. Minister Habibie shows visiting Arabs an airplane manufactured and assembled in Indonesia. Habibie's preoccupation with symbols of national power leads him, unsuccessfully, to seek a nuclear reactor from the United States. (Courtesy of the Habibie Center)

June 1986. But it met catastrophe in January. Christa McAuliffe, the school-teacher astronaut from New Hampshire who died in that explosion, was Pratiwi's roommate. Afterward, because of their identical helmet and uniform size, Pratiwi trained in Christa's surviving equipment. Remembering, Pratiwi's impassive countenance does not change, but she blinks an extra time or two. She kept on refining her microbiological research protocol and retrained a month every year from 1987 to 1992. Houston and Washington kept assuring her she would fly. But NASA, fighting legal suits over *Challenger*, for ten years allowed only military personnel to go up.

Needing a role model of its own, Indonesia reclaimed Pratiwi. "I brought the hope of a new vision of science for the young." Habibie gave her a small office for tropical agricultural biotechnology. "He had no vision how to manage our resources in biodiversity and agricultural lands." Indonesia's experts do not understand pathogenesis, she said. Engineers cannot build quake-resistant buildings. Heart surgeons with a crisis in mid-operation do not know what to do. "When our rice is attacked by virus or insects, we don't know how to develop resistant strains . . . We buy seeds and plant them. But if they don't grow, we don't know our soil, climate, microbes, to cope with it . . . So when the crisis comes, we realize all industry [manufacturing] is just *assembly* with ingredients from abroad . . . This is the worst part of Suharto's 'development'—no science proper to our state of development."

Pratiwi worked on Habibie, and in 1992 he reopened the Eykman Institute, named after the Dutch scientist who, in the 1920s, won a Nobel Prize for his Indonesia-based work on beri-beri. "In my life, up to now, this is my greatest achievement. I'm an astronaut . . . I have an image . . . So I can propose biomedical projects . . . A lot of Indonesian scientists abroad came back to work here . . . We've joined the human genome project." Her own work now is with the genomes of bacteria, how they evolve in transmitting diseases to humans. Pratiwi was the first molecular biologist in Indonesia. Now there are over 2000 biological specialists advancing work in medicine, forestry, veterinary, and environmental studies. "On a world map we are not blank anymore." The United States has a trial malaria vaccine, "but they are already behind, because the spirochete is evolving faster *here* in Indonesia."

She has been back to the States several times. "You have what we are lacking, equal opportunity . . . Before we thought only of U.S. in business, but [now] we see it as community development model . . . for common people to have right to have aspiration, speak out freely."

Working with Suharto and Habibie? Suharto was undereducated and overimpressed by Habibie's degrees. Together, they put money in the wrong places, downstream projects instead of upstream processes. Pratiwi did research on dengue hemorrhagic fever and on typhoid, but the government did not apply it; she was told to buy somebody else's product, not to develop her own. Meanwhile, Indonesia trailed all her ASEAN neighbors. "We need to run 10 times, 50 times faster to catch up."

After 1992 Pratiwi had no more talks with her sponsor in the system. From 1992 to 1997 Habibie did not come to his ministry at all, not one day. He was "in the political struggle" with ICMI, aiming to become vice president. So Pratiwi and her colleagues created a framework in the National Research Council to try to push neglected areas—biotechnology, medical technology, chemical, agricultural, other, even social sciences. "But it didn't work. Nobody empowered the process." Obviously poverty alleviation was a top priority. But why cut science first? Obviously big investments went to oil exploration; but why did basic scientific/technological development get nothing? "The Minister of Education this year [2000] declared there are zero money for research." Pratiwi repeated the allocation with baffled patience: "*Zero.*" Her facial expression had not changed throughout the conversation, except for moments of lifting her eyes to entreat the sure attention of the listener. Her tone barely varied throughout her recital of scientific distortions and abortions from on high. Her voice was even, uninflected, dispassionate, letting the data do the damage. She was a model *priyayi* Javanese woman, but also part of a service group that had broken off from Golkar, founding a forum for women of all religions and backgrounds.

A talented and ambitious scientist, Pratiwi long ago gave up her youthful dream of the Nobel Prize in Physiology or Medicine. Qualified, fit, and trained as an astronaut, she will never leave the earth. A Javanese fatalist, she is the opposite of a defeatist. She will pursue basic microbiological research and, having drawn others around her, will keep alive in her country the idea that an Indonesian woman can do original, life-saving medical study, whatever the surrounding atmosphere.

Suharto Unlimited

How rich was Suharto, and how did he get that way? In 1997 *Fortune* magazine put him at $16 billion. He was then the world's sixth richest man on a list of 160 people with personal wealth estimated at $2 billion or more.[74] After the crash in 1998, *Fortune* put him at $4 billion, which tied him for eightieth on their list.[75] They had apparently divided their estimate by four, which was roughly what the crash had done to most Indonesian wealth in that year's time. A dozen years before, an American embassy official in Jakarta had snarled to me that Suharto was "the world's richest man."[76] Profes-

52. "LIPSTICK FOR MOTHER." Dede Eri Supria's 1981 painting is based
on the features of a justly famous heroine of education, Princess Kartini
(1879–1905), who died in childbirth. She was used by the Suharto regime
as a mother figure in service of its ideology of state-as-family. This painting captures that imprisonment (hair dryer), false beautification (lipstick),
and fundamental betrayal (an almost bloody tear of suffering). Will the re-
volver that Mother lays alongside her cheek be used in suicidal rage or in
murderous revenge? (Sidup Damiri/Collection of John McGlynn)

53. PRATIWI AS ASTRONAUT. A NASA photograph captures the leading Indonesian microbiologist, Dr. Pratiwi Sudarmono, in training for space flight
before the *Challenger* disaster. Despite years of frustration, as Habibie distorted science budgets to procure aircraft and military hardware, Dr. Pratiwi
would raise the level of Indonesia's standards of research in microbiology and
immunobiology. Although the Suharto state cast her as a "Durga" by making
her its technological poster-girl, her real character as an "Umayi" or nurturer
shines through nonetheless. (Gift of Dr. Pratiwi/author's collection)

sor Jeffrey Winters later put his wealth at $30 billion. Wealth fluctuates. Methods of estimating it differ. But precision hardly matters when one has reached the condition of a Suharto. He was possessed by what Nikolai Berdyaev, the anti-Soviet philosopher of history, long ago called "the bourgeois' most fantastic creation . . . the most uncanny and horrible in its unreality . . . the kingdom of money . . . [which is] not only an outrage upon the poor and destitute, [but] the plunging of human existence into the fantastic and the visionary."[77]

Suharto began with kickbacks in the 1950s from Liem Sioe Liong and Bob Hasan (The Kian Seng), to whom he awarded contracts in rice, uniforms, and medicine. When Suharto became chief of the Army Strategic Reserve Command (Kostrad) in Jakarta in the early 1960s, he set up an army *yayasan*, the Dharma Putera Kostrad Foundation, as a money channel.[78] As president he would elaborate and perfect this kind of instrument in grotesque ways contradictory to the understanding of foundations in the West, which are not for profit but for philanthropy.

Some of Suharto's *yayasans* built mosques and schools and hospitals. But the main purpose of his foundations was to amass wealth. In 1969 he granted what became a total monopoly over the import, milling, and distribution of wheat and flour of PT Bogosari Flour Mills, owned by Liem's Salim Group. After he handed control over Kostrad's foundation to his successor as its commander in the mid-1970s, he and his wife then began to proliferate their own family-based foundations, which took control over the flour mills, milling wheat acquired through foreign aid (U.S. PL-480). They went on to create a total of 97 *yayasans,* controlled by themselves, their six children, the children's spouses and the spouses' parents, Suharto's cousin, his half-brother, Ibu Tien's relatives, trusted military men, and intimate associates such as Habibie, Hasan, and Liem. They bought stocks, built companies, lent monies to businessmen.[79]

The *yayasans* accepted "donations." Suharto extended his Jimbaran agreement among business leaders of 1995 into a national policy in 1996, aimed at poverty alleviation. By the terms of this decree, each taxpayer and company making more than $40,000 a year had to donate 2 percent of income to a special *yayasan.* From a Western tax perspective, this was redistributory fiat. There is no reason to believe that monies received were administered with special scrupulousness. Reformasi rescinded this particular measure. But civil servants and military personnel were still required to donate a portion of their monthly salaries to the Amal Bakti Muslim Pancasila Foundation, used by Suharto to win Muslim support—still another power objective abetted by his *yayasan* structure.

Soon after Suharto's resignation in May 1998, the attorney general examined the books of the four largest *yayasans*. One of them, Supersemar, had disbursed 81 percent of its funds to unauthorized pursuits. "These foundations," Attorney General Soedjono said, "were set up to deliver social services, but Suharto has distributed the money to his children and friends." When the cabinet officer delivered his preliminary report to President Habibie, he was fired five hours later, allegedly for stepping outside the line of command on another matter.[80] It was within Habibie's power to order all Suharto assets frozen and to accelerate investigations, but he did neither. Perhaps nowhere in the world had the purpose of "foundations" been more corrosively traduced for personal political and profit-making purposes than in Suharto's Indonesia.[81]

The Suharto children were introduced to dynastic plutocracy through Pertamina and the petroleum trade. After Ibnu Sutowo was fired in 1976, Pertamina was forced to export oil through two unnecessary companies, in which sons Bambang and Tommy acquired large stakes in the 1980s. Suharto-family companies received a total of 170 contracts from Pertamina in insurance, security, and other services. Commissions for the unnecessary companies, even with low oil prices in 1997–98, yielded $50 million a year. Canceling the service contracts in 1998 saved the government $99 million a year, according to one announcement.

The World Bank estimates that between 1988 and 1996 Indonesia received more than $130 billion in foreign investment. This was also the period of the most intense politico-entrepreneurial activity by the six Suharto children, most of whom had entered business before then. Three of them built or were major holders in large conglomerates, and any one of them could become a major player in an international deal, unless a sibling was there first. In order of estimated wealth (by *Time* magazine), the children's personal net worths were Bambang, $3 billion; Sigit, $800 million; Tommy, $800 million; Tutut, $700 million; Titiek, $75 million; Mamiek, $30 million.[82] At least four of them had highly expensive personal properties overseas. Two of them loved to gamble with stakes in the millions—Sigit (a notoriously and comically large loser) and Tommy, who was also an accomplished stock car racer, once sponsored by Marlboro. Tommy was responsible for one of the greatest incongruities in modern business life: a heavily protected "national car," manufactured in Korea, called the Timor, after the province Indonesia had taken in a bloody annexation.

The Suharto family owned several hotels on Bali and in Jakarta, as well as 100,000 square meters of prime office space in the capital; 40 percent of the entire province of East Timor; and real estate in Indonesia approaching the size of the Netherlands, its once imperial ruler. *Time* estimated that between 1966 and 1998 more than $73 billion passed "through the family's hands." How much clung to their fingers is not known. *The Wall Street Journal,* however, reported heavy investment losses through misjudgments over the years, including their greedy involvement in the Busang gold mining project in Kalimantan, which turned out to be one of the greatest scams in mining history.[83]

Then came the family's losses in the crash of 1997–1999. At the end of that, *Time* still estimated their current holdings at $15 billion—about what *Forbes* had estimated Suharto personally to be worth in 1997, or half of what Jeffrey Winters said Suharto was worth years before. If *Time* is correct (and Suharto lost his libel suit of 1999 against them for $27 billion), in thirty years of power the Suhartos amassed, accrued, and to a great degree lost the pre-crash equivalent of one-third of the annual GNP of a nation of over 200 million people. In the United States, where such a feat would be obviously impossible, that would be equivalent to one family generation playing around with $2.5 *trillion* dollars.

More striking even than the magnitude of the Suharto family's wealth is its tentacular presence in everything: oil, gas, forestry, plantations, petrochemicals, mining, banking, property management, real estate, food imports, standard media, telecommunications, hotels and tourism, toll roads, airlines, clove production, automobile production, power generation, and miscellaneous manufacturing. Such omnipresent control and influence has not been wiped clean or restored to the people by nationalization. It continues in fact through sidekicks, sycophants, shadow-holders. Opportunistic successors are all too ready to be mini-Suhartos in style.

Can one reach back for an explanation of these levels of corruption to the eighteenth-century merger of mercantilism and feudalism? Yes, the Dutch East India Company was so far away from home that arrant self-enrichment became a norm. The indigenous kingdom of Mataram itself was largely defined by appanage, benefice, and arbitrary power. The Netherlands' *ethici* eventually, from 1875 onward, brought in law and policy to temper Dutch colonial greed. Indonesian nationalists, from 1908 onward, briefly grew up in a climate that expected indigenous morality to expel foreign reformers and then to surpass them. But the raw parasitism of the Japanese empire and crass opportunism from the revolution onward wiped out these noble aims.

Far-gone history does not excuse Suharto any more than near-past history. Not that history mattered much to him, any more than the standards of modern nation states mattered to him, unless focused in the power of multilateral lenders when Indonesia was short on revenue. Suharto lived in his own dimension of time, that of a patriarchal villager become ingenious patrimonialist.

After the mid-1980s, in apparent proportion to his unchallengeability, Suharto increasingly used the Javanese maxim *tut wuri andayani,* suggesting that he was the all-seeing parent guiding children in learning how to walk.[84] Perhaps he truly meant it as an expression of love and did not intend to insult his whole nation by infantilizing it. He did care to be thought of as a loving father; and he had truly led Indonesia out of its developmental crawl.

One may, however, summarize what Suharto had achieved with regard to power by the middle of his sixth term in a less respectful way. He had nullified ABRI as a counterforce, while making it both dependent on his lead and suppliers of his security. He had turned Golkar into a personal political vehicle as distinct from a national political party. He had expanded attention to the business interests of the nation, while introducing his own children as a financially commanding element whose commercial gorge required satisfaction. His concept of "strategic development" with Habibie, and its grotesque emphasis on heavy technology, left Indonesia with terrible weaknesses in education, health policy, and research in the life sciences. Instead of taking advantage of its unthreatened regional security to accelerate advances in these fields, Indonesia remained an intellectual backwater.

In addition, Suharto nearly silenced, and certainly intimidated, almost all ordinary elements of constructive and corrective criticism upon which a polity may rely. Instead of advancing a pluralistic society—seen as a good in Latin America since the mid-1980s and in Eastern Central Europe since 1989—Suharto supported Pemuda Pancasila and other groups of rogues and thugs, thereby furthering what may be called an anti-civil society. From these institutional deficits and misdevelopments there was no procedural way out. A prominent member of Forum Demokrasi saw no available remedy but "crisis-hitchhiking."[85] The dreadful prospect was that any exit sign was false and led back into the maze.

BEHIND, BEYOND, BENEATH
THE POWER STRUCTURE

In constructing a state to control a national society, Suharto used his own island, Java, as its cultural center and model. Even as he fashioned a shell of
military-economic power like other tropical despotisms, he nourished a be-
hind-the-scenes antique power structure, often unrecognizable to Western
business people and journalists, that was at its cultural core royally Javanese. There were other realms, however, beneath his attention and beyond
his control, where Indonesian life was also lived. Beneath attention: tens of
millions of those whose levels of living, as in much of West Timor, were
not significantly helped by macro-policies—poor people even by Indonesian
standards. Beyond control: those of Aceh and Irian Jaya who were striving
for independence, and notably the East Timorese, recently conquered but
still fiercely resistant.

The extremes of Suharto's Javanism were perhaps felt by educated Indonesian women more than any other group. He ordered the creation of
Dharma Wanita (literally "Duty of Women"), an organization that subjugated all women to a hierarchical structure which duplicated those of the
government, civil service, and the military where their husbands worked.
All were treated as women of Java, wherever they were from, and as wives
of their husbands, whatever their independent career or talent; and all,
of course, were in the service of the New Order.[1] An openly rebellious
woman, or even an impassively noncompliant one, could endanger her
standing in the eyes of the regime, jeopardizing her husband's career and
her family's future. Women as prominent as the wife of General Nasution
felt the palace freeze.

Suharto's regime was more mercantile-opportunistic than the Netherlands East Indies Company and more culturally repressive than the kings of
Mataram. If Suharto Inc. exceeded the Marcos regime in the Philippines
as a kleptocracy, then Suharto Rex surpassed any other recent Southeast
Asian regime in native traditionalism. All of these governments, including

Suharto's own, were "modernizing." Suharto's recipe, however, included a massive feudalism which ensured that modernization would be chiefly statistical.

At one point Suharto, as president and general, required the military to accept a classical Javanese saying as a strategic philosophic guide for the armed forces:

> Ing ngarso sung tulodo;
> Ing medya mbangun karso;
> Tut wuri andayani.

A three-star general from Minangkabau went to a Javanese friend privately and said, "I've learned to repeat this, but what on earth does it mean?" The Javanese sympathetically translated it for him:

> Lead from the front;
> Motivate from the middle;
> Animate from the rear.[2]

As a politico-military maxim it has the epigrammatic terseness of classical Chinese exhortations and the glib plausibility of a modern management guru. The befuddlement of the Minang general, however, shows the obtuseness of Suharto regarding the impact of leading an ultra-diverse Indonesia by using Javanese tradition as a resource to reinforce his power.

Not until his last decade in power, when he went on a pilgrimage, did Suharto feel the need to connect with Islam's universal religious authority to bolster his Javanist charisma. He did not fear an Islamic messiah, or Mahdi, arising in Indonesia. Whatever the force of various Muslim separatisms, only twice in the last century had anyone styled himself that kind of Islamic redeemer. Those who made the *haj* from Indonesia did not spread the idea of a Mahdi but brought back the *tarekat* instead, the specially devoted religious orders or brotherhoods.

The native idea of the Ratu Adil, or Just King, nonetheless remained extremely powerful in Java. At a cyclically occurring propitious time, there would appear a divinely inspired figure to set the world right. Sukarno had recognized how these attributes clustered around his earliest mentor, H. O. S. Tjokroaminoto. He focused the idea in his own career on the Joyoboyo Prophecy, which he manipulated during the Japanese occupation to promote the idea of his having received the *wahyu cakraningrat,* or divine summons to lead.

Even though mass organizations tended to evaporate such inherited ideas, Sawito came along, in 1976, as the self-convinced recipient of a new ordinance from above. Suharto's overreaction showed his fear of any an-

54. WAYANG KULIT, c. 1950. This *dalang* (puppetmaster) and his flat shadow puppets made of leather use contemporary figures (Sukarno foremost) to suggest current political themes. The much more common mythical narratives deal with grand wars, court intrigue, great loves, magic, and comedy. Destinies of gods and humans are intermixed. (Gift of Niels Douwes Dekker/author's collection)

nounced bearer of the *wahyu* and claimant of the title Ratu Adil. But the cultural environment could no longer support a claim such as Sawito's. The villages were emptying as people went to the city. Urban communications, especially TV, were reaching the villages, and, without ending popular credence in magic, dried up belief in a mandate of heaven. When the crisis of 1997 arrived, divine appointment was not an item anyone would think of putting on his public résumé.[3]

Even so, Abdurrahman Wahid would cherish the aura of *wahyu* in his heart and among an inner circle of friends. Megawati Sukarnoputri's private behavior would also make clear her belief in immaterial causes and happenings. Indeed, among most Indonesians, any knowledge of scientific reasoning was overcome by raw considerations of survival. In that quest, propitiatory or ritualistic behavior might help. In Java especially, endless layers of magical and mystical thought were available, and anyone from the most primitive animist to the most sophisticated contemplative could turn to them. Suharto himself, even after publicly embracing Islam, continued his private preoccupation with the royal coordinates of Javanism.

I met Romo Mangun (Y. B. Mangunwijaya) in 1997, after he had retired as a Roman Catholic priest and architectural planner for the poor but was still a social activist and a prolific writer. I knew his reputation in all these areas and especially admired his eighth novel, *Durga Umayi*.[4] Mangunwijaya was a classical outsider, and his simple style of living helped radiate to others the courage of his convictions. His own story was intriguing. He had been recruited into revolutionary forces at age sixteen by a compelling young officer named Suharto, and he rose to be a section commander in the Students' Army. At a reception for nationalist troops after victory over the Dutch, he felt an affliction of conscience through the speech of an officer who declared: "Please don't welcome us like this! We are not pure youth, not the flower of the nation. We have killed, burned down houses, our hands are covered with blood. What we need is: Help us to return to being normal human beings."[5]

A Catholic, Mangunwijaya was inspired to become a priest and to follow a spiritual path instead of a road to money and power. Ultimately, in the 1980s, he used a hunger strike as the peak of nonviolent resistance to Yogya authorities. They were aiming to relocate a group of the homeless for whom he had raised money and designed a community center that gave them shelter, study, and voice. Romo Mangun was not only a defender of the poor—those who shined shoes, peddled newspapers, scavenged, and begged—but a voice for a new generation he described as "possessing radar in their hearts which can easily pick up the ripples of universal values."[6]

Mangunwijaya believed that the wartime Japanese had been deeply, damnably formative of modern Indonesia. Sukarno's guided democracy had turned into an autocracy that "kills the exploring mind and the creative energies of the people" while it stimulates "indigenous feudalism, fascistic and colonial behavior . . . like weeds in the rainy monsoon." Mangun ridiculed the Greater Indonesia, Inc. of his times with its ultimate acronym: IPOLEKSOSBUDHANKAMLING—a ludicrous compression of syllables meaning ideological-political-economic-social-cultural-defense-security environment. He publicly wondered if the republic had really done more for the little men and women than a continuing Netherlands Indies would have done.[7]

I wanted to meet the man fearless enough to say such things at the height of New Order power. His house on a noisy *gang*, or alley, in Yogyakarta was simply constructed, and the room for eating became the room for conferring by pushing back the small chairs from the table. A bowl of white rice, a dish with cuts of chicken and boiled green vegetables in broth, and a pot of Indonesian tea with little cups were filled again and again. Cats sneaked among human legs and table legs. The cook/housemaid gently and respectfully cleared. On the wall of an alcove-like room adjoining appeared the only visible religious object: a small, locally crafted and simply stylized Virgin Mary. I was disappointed that it contained no mystery or aesthetic appeal for me. But we did not talk religion; I had come to Romo Mangun in his role as social critic.

I saw a slight, compact, white-haired, white-goateed man, hair artistically long, eyes bright and skeptical behind thick glasses, voice low, sonorous, measured. His first look at me seemed reserved, suspicious—what sort of charlatan or spy have we here? But a mutual friend intermediated easily. Over three hours much was said. The distillate was simple. The financial crisis of 1997 had just begun, but in Romo Mangun's view, although Suharto's corruption of power was dangerously far advanced, his command of the army, the people, and the system still seemed unshakeable.

Romo Mangun told his students and followers to keep themselves patient and clean—*bersih*—until opportunity should come, perhaps in 2003 (the next general election), 2008 (the centennial of the founding of the first nationalist organization), 2028 (the centennial of the Indonesian Nationalist Party's founding), or even 2045 (a hundred years after the Sukarno-Hatta Proclamation of Independence). I could hardly imagine such extended patience. But when I later repeated Romo Mangun's instructions to young activist friends, angry, agitated, unled, the words seemed to have a remarkable effect of steadying and strengthening them.

As the night wore on, Romo Mangun grew less guarded, more eloquent. For greedy brutality, he said, "Suharto combines in himself the attributes of a King of Mataram, a Japanese military commander, and a Dutch plantation lord." He owns the state, he guards the state, he *is* the state. The novelist waxed to his theme. Suharto uses silence powerfully. He intimidates. He is capable of the acts of Panembahan Senopati, founder of the Mataram dynasty and initiator of its expansion in the late sixteenth century. Senopati used his daughter to lure the freehold area leader, Ki Ageng Mangir, to his court. As he embraced him closely on arrival, he impaled him on a *kris* concealed beneath his flowing robes and projected from his belt. Romo Mangun stood and acted it out, arms grasping round an invisible visitor. "Ah, welcome, my friend, welcome to my *court!*"[8]

Even five months later, when the rupiah had weakened Suharto as nothing else could and Romo Mangun could foresee that in as little as three months, or within one year at most, Suharto would be forced out of office, he still could not become an optimist. I wondered if the problems of Suharto's children, his state corporations, and the *yayasans,* which would continue after Suharto's regime collapsed, were the reason behind Mangun's pessimism. "Yes. And will still leave the problem of Javanese culture. It has not internalized modern values. It needs a 'renaissance' to cope with global life. If we remove the oppressor—and remember that Suharto, as bad as we know him, is ultimately an *example* only—we still have *Javanese culture* to deal with." He chose his words carefully, a writer who had given the problem full metaphoric thought.

> Javanese culture is like a tapeworm. It is very unlike the tooth and claw of the Russian bear, or the Chinese dragon, or the lion of the Netherlands and the UK, or the beak and talon of the American eagle. It is "aesthetic" and silent; it is polite (no commotion); it is insinuating. It weakens without turmoil and it is ultimately deadly. Javanese culture, like the tapeworm, cannot be yanked out or cut out. It will require strong and repeated doses of medicine to "free it out."[9]

Attack and Defense in the Mystical Realm

I first met Soebadio Sastrosatomo in 1968. Brother of the businessman Soedarpo, Soebadio had been a member of the PSI (Socialist Party), which Sukarno banned in 1960. Aggressive in style, magnetic, a trifle bombastic, he enjoyed the role of guru, drawing to himself young followers. He had at first welcomed the New Order but, like his friend Soedjatmoko, grew disenchanted.

As Suharto's tenure lengthened, Soebadio turned simultaneously critical and mystical. He tried to salvage the meaning of Sukarno's message for Indonesia and by 1991 expressed it as "sovereignty in politics, self-sufficiency in economics, integrity in culture."[10] By January 1997 a few hundred youth in an orderly demonstration at his house in the Menteng section of Jakarta offered him the leadership of the Council for Indonesian Sovereignty, and he accepted. He published a short, forceful attack on the Suharto regime as unconstitutional—as violating the essential wisdom of the founding fathers (among whom Soebadio counted himself).

The government banned the pamphlet. Suharto was quoted in a meeting of twenty-seven provincial governors as slamming Soebadio's book, saying that PSI persons were "misbehaving." "Be serious if you want to fight me . . . Don't play games . . . [The] PRI [People's Party] are in jail now—that is what happens if you play with me." Soebadio was formally charged with "intentionally insulting the good name of the President."[11] But he was not imprisoned. When I met Soebadio again, thirty years after our first conversation, he was proud of having been arrested a total of five times by the Dutch, by the Japanese, by the Sukarno regime, and by the Suharto regime. But now even prouder that Suharto did not dare to keep him in jail. "Why didn't he dare?" I asked. "Because he knows that I am more holy than he is."[12]

As Suharto approached his seventh term, Soebadio, emboldened by a mystical revelation, loosed another blast, likening Suharto in this new pamphlet to Dosomuko, "Ten Faces," a demonic king in the *wayang* puppet tradition who is "notoriously evil." He declared Suharto's regime to be "rotten," "bankrupt" and "infected with gore."[13] He signed his attack on February 10, 1998, from Mount Lawu, where in legend the last king of Majapahit, Brawijaya IV, had died (and where, in fact, Suharto's late wife was now buried). Soebadio's utterances from the sanctums of Central Java defied Suharto's own cultivated associations with its history, legend, and magic. Soebadio's offenses at this point could have been considered beyond those of Sawito, who had been scathingly tried and jailed twenty years before. Had Suharto lost his will to oppress?

By his actions more than his words, Suharto showed how deeply immersed he was in Javanese mythology. When Sukarno had evoked this realm in the 1950s, the Batak journalist Mochtar Lubis had derided it as "magico-mysticism" and earned himself years of house arrest. Javanism remained, however, a world with its own assumptions about cause and effect. A world of legendary kings, of *wayang* figures in a continuous Indonesianized story derived from the Indian epics *Mahabharata* and *Ramayana*. It featured figures with Javanized names, evolved local characteristics, and innovated characters who acted in a world of arcane allusions and tantalizing prophecies.[14] Predictions were capable of being denied as never meant, or as misunderstood if they fail to come to pass, and equally capable, in retrospect, of being averred as clearly foreseen, had one only heard aright and remembered the metaphorical bounty offered by whatever prophet or guru was speaking.

What happens in Java is embedded in sacred geography and liturgical theater and accordingly requires interpreters. They are *dukuns*—readers of the signs, tellers of the way through dangers, propitiators against malignant forces, summoners of appropriate sacrifices. In dated language from King Arthur's court we might understand them as soothsayers. Or we could call them seers—meaning those who see farther and deeper than others. But, more exactly, *dukuns:* persons recognized in practice at a village level on a range from shaman to sorcerer, at a national level as wizards.

Air Marshal (retired) Budiardjo was a *dukun.* Highly ranked and long trusted by Suharto, and former minister of information, he was also consid-

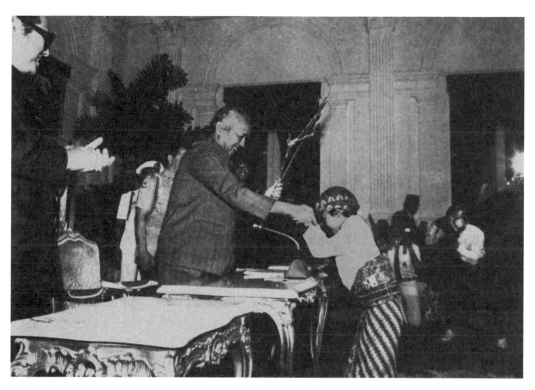

55. SUHARTO, *DALANG*, AND LORD BIMA. In connection with a *wayang* festival on July 17, 1978, the president receives a gesture of fealty from a dwarf *dalang*. Suharto holds a puppet of Lord Bima, one of the heroic Pendawa brothers in the classic Javanese myth about the wars of the Bharata dynasty. (Ipphos Photo Archive)

ered by the president as one of the most authoritative of the various *dukuns* from whom he sought counsel. Budiardjo had in later years fallen away from Suharto in political leaning but maintained a friendship and what may be called a consultantship. Early in 1997 Suharto appears to have been told by another *dukun* that "the nail of Java has come loose." "The nail of Java" is Mount Tidar, an insignificant-looking hill in Central Java, only a hundred meters high. Too small to be seen from the top of the great 1200-year-old temple of Borobudur, twenty kilometers away, it has nonetheless acquired symbolic magnitude, perhaps because it looks like a pounded nail head, perhaps because of its key location. Being told by a *dukun* that "the nail of Java has come loose" was akin to having a trusted member of the Chinese court warning an emperor that "the Mantle of Heaven is in danger of slipping from your shoulders." Unless, Suharto concluded, he put the ailing Budiardjo to work.

Budiardjo, severely ill, connected to tubes and attended by Western doctors, was summoned by Suharto to Central Java. Against his doctors' advice, Budiardjo collected himself and arrived within twenty-four hours. He agreed to be the impresario of a special *wayang ruwaten*, or cleansing ceremony through shadow puppetry. He selected the *dalang* (puppeteer) and the elements of the performance to be held, dispatched invitations to certain significant people—none of them in Suharto's cabinet—and returned to his room. The Western doctors gave up trying to tell him what to do.[15]

From the breadth and potency of what Budiardjo arranged, and given the seriousness of his final illness, it is clear that he would never have initiated this ceremony on his own, for it would have looked hugely presumptuous, even grossly ridiculous. But this was an order from the ruler of Java (and of all Indonesia, of course, but the "outer islands" tended to be forgotten at such moments or were thought to follow the magical magnet of Central Java). This command, according to Father Franz Magnis-Suseno, was equivalent to delegation from the *wahyu cakraningrat,* and with it Budiardjo "could open up the whole metaphysical realm of Java . . . which he did, in his own way."[16]

Franz Magnis-Suseno is a German-born Jesuit sociologist and expert on the culture of Java who had taken a Javanese addition to his family name. He, along with others, including Aristides Katoppo—a distinguished editor and publisher, then largely suppressed like other critics—received an invitation in February 1997 to a Ruat Dunia, to be held at the house of Budiardjo in Central Java. "Ruat Dunia" can be translated "Cleansing of the World" or, more portentously, "Exorcism of the Cosmos." Neither Magnis-Suseno nor Katoppo had ever seen anything so styled in his whole life. My American reaction, on hearing about it, oscillated between "Gee whiz" and "Holy shit!"

The two invitees each flew from Jakarta to Yogyakarta. Taking a taxi to a medium-sized stone building about five hundred meters from Borobudur, Magnis-Suseno was surprised on arrival to see that the majority of the attendees were prominent critics of Suharto. Even Soebadio, soon to be charged with the equivalent of sedition, was present. The first act of the *wayang,* which would go late into the night, was a *Murbakhala*—an exorcism for houses, children, curses of whatever kind. It contains an obligatory forty-minute mantra, during which the curtain is raised and no shadow puppetry takes place. The extended verbal incantation that follows is the heart of the exorcism.[17]

In the middle of this act, Magnis-Suseno was surprised to be invited into the private quarters of Budiardjo. There he saw Katoppo, likewise honorably summoned to the bedroom of the host, who was unable to rise.[18] Katoppo found Budiardjo with *dukuns* holding each foot and one his right arm. These attentions were bringing back focus in his eyes and resonance in his voice. Katoppo took hold of his left arm to help.

The Western doctors had counseled Budiardjo: when you're on your deathbed, don't go traveling. Let go in peace. But Budiardjo overruled his physicians for the sake of his president and was attempting his last act for the security and welfare of Indonesia, as understood by the New Order. He talked with Katoppo and Magnis-Suseno and the few others present about his own death and burial. A *kyai* from Ponogoro, a city of mystical traditions in East Java, entered carrying incense.[19] Budiardjo then spoke with vigorous purpose. A stick from the wood of which *kris* handles are made should be fashioned as a spike and planted under a mojo tree at the foot of Borobudur, a few hundred yards away. All of this was done, within the hour.

That was the key act which Suharto, nearby, was awaiting. Immediately strengthened by having Java nailed together again, he commanded his aides to find him a place to make a speech. They located a new *haj* hospital, still not yet dedicated, and arranged it at once. Suharto that night spoke *ex tempore* and was quoted in national papers the next day, to the great puzzlement of his ministers, who were not invited to the *ruaten* and did not know what it was all about. The speech included a remark that he would *gebuk* (clobber) his enemies, a verb of choice on other occasions when he was expressing public feistiness.

Budiardjo asked Katoppo that night if he had done the right thing. Katoppo answered, "If you feel sincere about it, of course it's the right thing." Air Marshal Budiardjo died two weeks later. Katoppo, seeing Suseno afterward, wondered if a better answer to Budiardjo might have been, "If Java is nailed together, all Indonesia will hold fast."[20]

Magnis-Suseno had been released from personal attendance upon Budiardjo to mix with others during the intermission. The tall, ascetic, white-haired Jesuit and Javanist had encountered and talked with Sultan Hamengkubuwono X, who was present not as a critic but as the ruler of the special district of Yogyakarta. Himself the presumed bearer of paranormal or supernatural powers, the sultan gave further validity to the unique ceremonies. Suseno had not been privy to the symbolic spiking down of Java, but I reminded him of it later. As a testing observation, I said, "Whichever *dukun* told Suharto that 'the nail of Java has come loose' gave him information as important as anything that Bakin (Indonesian military intelligence) or the World Bank could supply." "MORE SO!" said Suseno.

But his own greater interest was in the next act of the *wayang*.[21] The second act, or *lakon*, in the night-long series was *Semar Kuning*, the story of the Pendawas, usually the heroes in the raging mythos of Java. But here they conspire in a rare and unnatural way against the god Semar. (Javanese gods, like Greek gods, have human characteristics and frailties as well as supernatural powers.) Semar is fat and jolly and he farts a lot. The populace sees this Pendawa plot as a "dirty act . . . for personal greed! . . . and badly destined!!" because they like Semar. And when, in the end, after lengthy twists and turns, the Pendawas repent, the audience is greatly relieved because they also like the Pendawas.

Magnis-Suseno explained to me that *Semar Kuning* was staged in order to give Suharto a chance to repent. All the invited audience knew he *should* repent, and Budiardjo invited them, as his last political act, to use their sympathetic energies—enlisted with the powers of *wayang*—to persuade him to repent. The Pendawas are sincerely remorseful; Suharto should likewise be contrite. Because of the Pendawa remorse, Semar comes back to them. Everything which in the meantime had come loose, as always happens when Semar leaves us, all now settles back in the right way with his return.[22]

So Air Marshal Budiardjo, required by Suharto at great risk to his life to intervene with the cosmic forces, did so in a way that was loyal to his own understanding of how things work in Java. First he arranged for a symbolically powerful "renailing of Java together" to take place. This was overtly reassuring to the president, who acted on it at once. But Budiardjo was also true to his own perception that Suharto himself had become loose and needed to be nailed down again. The decision to stage *Semar Kuning* before an audience of distinguished oppositionists was an act of physical and moral courage on the part of Budiardjo. He used an empowering order from the president as a massive and sublime evocation of the Javanese metaphysic in an attempt to get Suharto himself back in place.

As we now know, all such efforts failed. But when Katoppo and Magnis-Suseno sought each other out in Jakarta ten days later, they did not discuss whether it would work. Rather, they asked, "Why were *we* invited into the dying Budiardjo's bedroom during the vital mantra?" Katoppo's view was that he represented non-Javanese Indonesia, while Magnis-Suseno was invited as a Western social scientist (or, as Suseno's own recollection has it, "for the rest of mankind"). In any case, they believed they were chosen by Budiardjo and given an inside view of all proceedings so as to serve as outside validators.

The years since certainly do not point to this moment as the beginning of a self-reformation by Suharto. Only 1,200 dead in Jakarta in May 1998 would bring him to a reluctant apology. But Katoppo and Magnis-Suseno witnessed what may be the most potent of all attempted invocations of the gods in modern Javanese affairs. Depending on the nature of future presidents of Indonesia, it may have been the last great effort to bring the purify-

56. SEMAR. A *dalang* with wooden puppets *(wayang golek).* The fat, white-faced clown god, Semar, to the left, is believed to be "protector of the island of Java." *Wayang* figures had lifelike proportions before the fifteenth century, when they became highly stylized in response to Islamic aversion to representing the human form. (Tara Sosrowardoyo/INDOPIX)

ing powers of Javanese mythology, metaphysics, and morality into play against Lord Acton's maxim: "Power tends to corrupt and absolute power corrupts absolutely." Because Javanese public life demonstrates that truth so vividly, it was reasonable to think that only Javanese gods could do anything about it.

Erosion of Social Equity

Jan Pronk was once a Dutch cabinet member and a longstanding force in the Inter-Governmental Group on Indonesia (IGGI), which had served since 1967 as the chief funnel of foreign aid to Indonesia. The East Timor massacre in Dili's Santa Cruz cemetery in 1991 moved him to introduce a human rights condition to future aid awards. That, in turn, triggered Suharto to re-

Three Ways of Living

57. COURT TRADITION. Nanies Bishop, at home, a few years before her death in a bus/car crash. Outside Yogyakarta, this former house of a prince of Mataram contains elements of high Central Javanese style: floor tiles, pressed tin ceiling, chandelier, cut-glass mirrors with ornate wood frames, stained glass windows, and symmetry in all décor. (Gift of Gordon Bishop/author's collection)

58. PROVINCIAL TRADITION. In Sumba (halfway between Bali and Timor), a girl and three dogs are at leisure amid several tombs in front of a traditional *(adat)* house with "high-hat" shape and roof of thatched grass. (Marla Kosec)

59. URBAN POVERTY. Stilt houses over stagnant water in Penjaringan, North Jakarta, 1998. This area was ravaged by fire in October 2002. (Byron Black/author's collection)

fuse assistance. IGGI's contribution at first had been nearly 30 percent of government revenues, but was now a much smaller slice.[23] Suharto did not declare, as Sukarno had over a quarter century before, "To hell with your aid!" But his implied and implacable message was "To hell with your human rights."

In a world that binds aid to trade and investment—directly in the case of Japan, more indirectly with the North Atlantic powers—the several donor nations found a way to keep financial assistance flowing to Indonesia. They changed the name of the group, met in France instead of the Netherlands, left out Pronk, and dropped the human rights clause. Suharto and Indonesia went back to accepting the handouts.

But Pronk's mind and heart were too involved with Indonesia to let go. He chaired a colloquium on poverty, with numerous participants—Dutch, Indonesian, World Bank, Australian, and other. Their published product, *Development and Social Welfare: Indonesia's Experiences under the New Order,* never mentions Suharto by name.[24] It does recognize the accomplishments of a quarter-century. Whereas many countries had achieved structural adjustments and quite a few had reduced poverty, very few had succeeded, as Indonesia had, in both. Whether or not Indonesia should be considered a "model," as some wished, a careful survey of facts regarding food, water, electricity, declining child mortality, and rising access to basic education showed it had earned its move, in the early 1990s, into the UN ranks of countries with "medium" levels of human development, well above the Indian subcontinent, much of the Middle East, and Africa.[25]

But the poor, even by strict definitions, still numbered 30 million, in a 1990 population of 180 million: 10 million in the hills, 10 million in the plains, and 10 million in the cities. They were, and remain, heterogeneous: the landless in the plains; farmers tilling less than half an acre; most of those scraping by in a village with one-crop agriculture. Dwellers in remote areas; elderly rural folk; youthful urban nomads—some would even include "all women" as a category, because they were officially considered instruments of policy rather than participants in a process or beneficiaries of results.

Setting the poverty line just 10 percent higher would add another 10 million people to the number of the poor. Other higher-reaching concepts of impoverishment would exclude only the upper bourgeoisie, in business and the military. According to Warda Hafidz, a brave young activist who had begun her career in women's issues and was moving, as Suharto's sixth term approached, toward a defense of the urban poor, poverty was the result of land-grabbing and evictions and would require a "multiple, qualitative, humanistic definition."[26]

Opening up the Indonesian economy to foreign private enterprise had created more employment but, given the composition of the 30 million poor, could not further reduce that number. Already, more inequality had resulted; still greater inequality could be expected. Pronk, who had watched the process for two decades, asked why Indonesia should automatically assume its ever-increasing amount of "official concessional foreign assistance," when other, poorer countries received much less? He asserted that the Indonesian government should prepare for the second half of the 1990s with new options for ensuring economic growth and reducing poverty, in case lessening foreign capital inflow, both official and private, dramatically curbed development momentum. Nobody forecast the domestic crash and foreign investment plunge of 1997 and after, but many feared, from any cause, a possible surge in jeopardy for Indonesia's poor.

Pronk articulated a clear consensus: "Economic poverty has decreased while inequality has increased . . . Much remains to be improved in terms of participation . . . because its lack is a form of poverty . . . [and] because it is a condition sine qua non to further improve other kinds of poverty."[27] The poor, in short, were outside the consciousness of the power structure. Those who saw it could implore to get them noticed, but no one could prescribe a way to get them included.

Secessionists in Aceh

If many of Indonesia's poor were horizontally obscured from government notice, there were also those who felt laterally excluded from the Indonesian nation. Many Acehnese, farthest west in the archipelago, cherished an Islamic culture far closer to Mecca than Jakarta. And some Irianese, farthest east, felt themselves to be, culturally, just the opposite—their ethnicity, traditional folkways, or Christianity made them hunger for independence from rule by Muslims of Malay heritage.

The Acehnese, by the mid-1990s, numbered nearly 4 million people, making them as numerous as the Minangkabau and somewhat moreso than the Bataks. The province was producing nearly one-third of the liquefied natural gas of Indonesia. It was temporarily quiet but structurally unhappy. Ninety-five percent of its revenues from natural gas extraction went to the central government. To a rebellious Islamic history was now added growing economic grievance.

Political turnover since the Indonesian revolution had produced three different leadership classes in Aceh. The traditional aristocrats, the *uleebalang*, had given way, in 1946 and after, to the *ulama*, religious leaders who generated a social revolution to accompany the national one, unlike what happened in most parts of the archipelago. They pledged allegiance to the new republic but defended local interests zealously enough to win limited autonomy as a "special region." The first twenty years of Suharto's New Order, however, generated enough economic and social change that a third leadership group, a development elite, scrambled to the top.

If Suharto's success was "the emasculation of the *ulama* as a social group capable of challenging the ideology and authority of the regime," as one expert has claimed, there were accompanying social grotesqueries.[28] Despite extractive wealth and industrial development, 40 percent of Aceh's villages were classified as poor in 1993—putting the province in the nation's bottom quartile and worst among the eight provinces of Sumatra. Impoverishment in contrast with enrichment undermined the authority of the development elite. Those Acehnese alienated from the bureaucrats and adrift from the *ulama* were presented with another means of political expression: the Free Aceh Movement (GAM). Its leader, Hasan di Tiro, was an expatriate descendant of a hero of the struggle against the Dutch, a man alleging a

60. THE GREAT MOSQUE, ACEH. The architecture of the Mesjid Raya in Banda Aceh was inspired by Persia and Mughal India. It demonstrates the orientation of Acehnese westward toward Mecca, rather than eastward toward Jakarta. (Abbas/Magnum Photos)

lineage back to Sultan Iskandar Muda of the early seventeenth century, greatest of Aceh's rulers. He claimed liberation authority for all Sumatra.[29]

As an unlikely modern capitalist leader, an *uleebalang* imperialist, di Tiro had little success with GAM in 1976. But when his movement re-emerged in 1989, it had more centralist rot and local resentment to work with. Their guerrilla force consisted largely of unemployed young men, mostly from peasant families. But now support also came from other strata of society: not just veterans of Darul Islam and disaffected, retired, or deserted ABRI soldiers but some village officials, civil servants, PPP and Golkar politicians, businessmen, traders, teachers, and students. Most seemed to want an "Islamic Indonesia" or a "federalist solution" but were willing to support GAM's independence-seeking, Libyan-trained core of hundreds of fighters to see what they could get.[30]

The reply of the Suharto government was not "partnering" in the spirit of Nasution's work on guerrillas. It was counter-insurgency in the Benny Moerdani mode: crush them. His euphemistically named "security approach" meant arbitrary arrests and detentions, systematic home-burning, "disappearances," rape, and the dumping of unidentified corpses at roadsides. Between mid-1989 and mid-1991 deaths probably totaled 2,000, mostly unarmed civilians killed by Indonesian military forces.[31] There was certainly savagery on GAM's side as well. But as in East Timor, a brutal strategy of counter-insurgency that featured recruitment of local militias produced the same results: social trauma, sullen alienation, the search for a way out. Any purgatory by definition contains more promise than hell.

Struggle in Irian

The first modern event to dent the Stone Age areas of western Papua occurred during the Second World War. Sightseeing American soldiers in a DC-3 crashed at the northern end of the Baliem Valley, high in the central mountains of then Dutch West Irian. The survivors were reached by a rescue flight before they could feel the hospitality or hostility of the Dani warrior-farmers of that region. The wreckage remains. Robert Gardner, an American anthropologist, spent six months there in 1961 and returned in 1989. He found an "elaborate network of warring confederacies," with "perfectly straight and exquisitely balanced" twelve-foot spears and sturdy four-foot bows with barbed but unfeathered arrows. The object of their ritual fighting was "to take only the life necessary to adjust the alternating balance of deaths between conflicting groups." Then they celebrated with tribal victory dances, before returning from deadly sport and pageant to "lives of quiet industry and calm purpose."[32]

Gardner's accounts of both his visits are eloquent in their melancholy.

He early realized that "our efforts to be either transparent or objective were doomed from the start, and the largest truth was that our very presence could not help but create an inescapable burden of hope and dreams."[33] When he came back he found a boy swineherd, Pua, grown to a man, who had built a "lodgement" for tourists, "a sort of full-scale and utterly faithful diorama [of Dani material culture] waiting for people to use it like some back-lot movie set . . . the Dani equivalent of our own Pilgrim or colonial reconstructions."[34]

Soon after Gardner's first visit, the Dutch yielded to the political pressure of President Kennedy and military forays by General Suharto's Mandala Command, as ordered by President Sukarno. They gave over the giant province, with a total land area greater than California, to a brief UN trusteeship, followed by transfer to the Indonesians. The Indonesian government was to conduct an "Act of Free Choice" in July 1969. A photograph of that event shows a large hall full of unsmiling seated appointees, men in unfa-

61. STONE AGE MEN WATCH FIRST CINEMA. In 1989, Dani tribesmen of Irian Jaya watch themselves in the film *Dead Birds* (1961) by the anthropologist Robert Gardner (right). Behind them, Indonesian policemen watch everything. (Susan Meiselas/Magnum Photos)

miliar khaki uniforms, who were recorded as unanimously choosing to remain with Indonesia.[35]

A Free Papua Movement (OPM) nonetheless simmered away in low-level conflict with the Indonesian military. A human rights advocate alleges documentation of 921 deaths in Irian Jaya from military operations in the period 1965–1999. In 1996 for four months OPM held hostage thirteen scientists and others who were conducting highland forestry research. They wanted money and international recognition. After negotiations by the International Committee of the Red Cross failed, an army operation led by Suharto's son-in-law, Prabowo, cracked through to rescue the hostages, with numerous deaths.[36] Embarrassing as the incident was for the regime, it felt unshaken. East Timor, after all, far more restless, was under effective control.

Misery in East Timor

The divergent colonial histories of the halves of Timor help explain their differences. The western part of the island was Dutch and the eastern part Portuguese. Three centuries of lazy dispute were settled with a boundary line by treaty in 1869. The Dutch were rising in their phase of systematic exploitation at that time, and the Portuguese were falling further into slumbering neglect. The Dutch had West Timor torn from them, like most of the rest of Indonesia, in 1949. But the little they had done for it was more than the Portuguese had done for East Timor, which was next to nothing. Portugal held on to East Timor out of nostalgic pride, and then suddenly let it go in 1975; people at home wore post-Salazar carnations while their government jettisoned plantations abroad.

An American couple in an amphibious jeep had made a splash appearance in Dili in 1962 and were attentively feasted by the Portuguese governor general. He boasted that they "put into" East Timor $1.5 million a year, or something then above two dollars a person.[37] Where did that munificent sum go, besides to colonial salaries? When the Portuguese pulled out, they left only twelve kilometers of paved roads.

The Indonesians laid down plenty of roads—so they could move their troops in against the guerrillas who fought them so strenuously. Their military presence with the infrastructure it required and their trading corporation, which took over exchange of commercial goods, became the most prominent features of the new East Timorese economy. Jakarta prevailed, without true victory. Guerrilla and anti-guerrilla war carried on, at a lower level, while the Indonesian government in the 1980s poured in cash to build schools, purvey culture, win hearts and minds.

These Indonesian infusions raised East Timor statistically above West

Timor. But numerical data are one thing, and emotions are quite another. For the West Timorese, to be swept into Indonesia in 1949, along with other Dutch provinces, was a natural event, one even worth celebrating. Granted, one form of inattention was traded for another, but patriotic identity was a net gain. For the East Timorese, on the other hand, the post-mature collapse of the Portuguese empire brought no independence, as it had in Angola and Mozambique, but merely a new imperial master. Receiving more financial attention from the Indonesian government than their brothers and sisters on the other half of the island did not compensate the East Timorese for being deprived of an identity. Not to mention the cost in lives: as many as 100,000, half of whom were killed in the takeover and half who died of illness or starvation.[38] Bombardment of rural areas and the forced reconcentration of people had disrupted the normal cycle for growing and harvesting food. Whatever numbers are ascribed to death by famine and disease caused by the invasion, killings by ABRI, and killings by Fretilin (in probable descending order), the dimensions of loss rise toward comparison with Cambodia, where 1.5 million out of 8 million people were exterminated by the Pol Pot regime between 1975 and 1979. But the East Timorese case had its own characteristics: an ethnically and religiously different people were subjected to famine, murder, torture, and rape. Also to symbolic violence, demonization, and demographic dilution.[39]

Poverty is measurable; misery is not. By world standards both West and East Timor were poverty-stricken. But the East Timorese were soul-stricken as well. Every family had lost a member, and most families felt they had lost a future, too. Embattled on a half-island, as a non-nation, as a dislocated culture, as a savagely diminished population, the East Timorese were collectively and categorically miserable.

The government in Jakarta, however, thought they had done enough to quash rebellion and spread instruction in Indonesian that they might yield to foreign clamor and show the fruits of their labors. Having kept foreigners and their own nationals out of the province except for closely managed official tours, they "opened" East Timor in 1989. A month later, Carlos Felipe Ximenes Belo, recently made a bishop, sent a letter to the secretary general of the United Nations, declaring that "we are dying as a people and a nation." He dared to ask that the UN, by its charter, promote a "REFERENDUM" to learn "the supreme wishes of the Timorese people." Nobody at the UN acknowledged receiving the letter for five years.[40]

Belo felt again the lesson of political numbers that the Vatican bureaucracy had already taught him. The Catholic proportion of East Timorese had leaped from 30 percent to 85 percent in roughly the same years as the resistance of Solidarity and the KIK (Catholic Intellectual Club) to Jaruszelski's Communist regime in Poland, and for some of the same reasons. The church was a politico-cultural rallying point.[41] "The church, the priests and the religious are the three factors which threaten East Timor's integration with Indonesia." So said Suharto's son-in-law, Prabowo, stationed there as a major in 1989. "The people must turn against them."[42] But in the eyes of Vatican diplomats, the hundreds of thousands of Catholics in East Timor were a much less valuable constituency than the several millions of Catholics in the rest of Indonesia, whom they preferred not to offend. If Rome was paralyzed by political numbers, why should the UN be expected to act more holy than they? The East Timorese represented perhaps four-tenths of 1 percent of all Indonesia.

The Santa Cruz massacre, however, raised the stakes. At a climax of demonstrations in late October 1991, a pro-independence youth was shot and a Timorese working with the Indonesians was knifed to death in the San Motael Church. The family of the first youth held a mourning mass and commemoration march, announced as nonpolitical, on November 12. But between the solemnities at San Motael and the laying of flowers on the grave about a mile and a half away, banners appeared for independence and for the Fretilin guerrilla leader: "Viva Xanana!" Military array also made the moment ultra-political. ABRI was there with troops, police, plainclothes infiltrators, and provacateurs. What started the blaze of gunfire at the cemetery? In the Timorese view, intentional counter-subversive provocation. In the Indonesian government's view, an unacceptable infraction of public order. The initial cause, whatever it was, is less important than the fact of the troops' sustained fire at pointblank range into an unarmed crowd, without a call to disperse. Unarmed people cowering behind gravestones were beaten and shot. By the time a furious Bishop Belo got to the cemetery to intercede, dozens of people lay on the ground, ripped by bullets, and inside the chapel six youth, beaten or shot, were praying and singing hymns of mercy. Visiting the military hospital later, the bishop found more than a hundred there, some of whom he had taken home safely the day before, now "injured so severely that they were beyond recognition."[43]

What was the death toll from Santa Cruz? Jakarta at first said it was 19 and later raised the figure to 50. Kohen's biography of Belo used an early estimate of 271, plus "disappearances." I take as reasonable the figure offered by a Timorese-born human rights lawyer, who puts the immediate dead, the subsequent dead, and the inexplicably missing at around 200.[44]

What mattered more than any exact number was the camera as witness. Five journalists—two Australian, two British, one New Zealander—had died in November 1975 trying to film the Indonesian invasion. Sixteen years later, documentation of the Santa Cruz massacre survived. Max Stahl's videotapes, buried in the cemetery, were retrieved and smuggled out by a Dutch freelancer. Aired on European and American television, they made globally and irreversibly clear the nature of governance in East Timor.[45] Suharto established a National Human Rights Commission and installed a Council of Military Honor to investigate. Its findings and sanctions were modest by outside expectations: three officers dismissed from the army, three more removed from their positions, nine soldiers and a policeman court-martialed. But as an action unprecedented in Suharto's rule, it was spectacularly distressing to his officer corps. He later invited all 121 battalion commanders to his ranch in West Java and distributed $3.5 million to improve morale and conditions for the troops.[46]

Late in 1992, ABRI captured Xanana. Lieutenant Colonel Prabowo himself was in charge of the operation, which acted on information from a tapped phone line of Jose Ramos-Horta, the Fretilin publicist in exile. Some allege volunteered information, as distinct from intercepted. In any case, the army had the focal leader in hand and swiftly convicted him, with the judge cutting off his defense plea. Why, a daring journalist asked, interviewing Prabowo, didn't you just blow him away when you had him, in the usual ABRI style? Prabowo's confused inability to answer convinced the journalist that Xanana's own courageous and stoic dignity saved him.[47]

Attitudes in the field did not change. "East Timor is like hell," Belo told Reuters in 1994. Indonesian soldiers had trampled on Communion wafers; army intelligence agents made obscene comments to Timorese nuns; young activists in jail were forced to swallow rosary beads.[48] Belo himself was subjected to eavesdroppings, obstructions, intrusions, and threats of death, while his parishioners endured jailings, beatings, rapes, and killings. Throughout he maintained an intercessory role, capable of admonishing either side for excess or unwisdom, rising to high anger when necessary and returning to sublime, tough-minded patience. He did not theorize. He did not descend to platform politics. He spoke simply as a churchman, a priest, a courageous human being. "Reconciliation is a message from the Church which has a moral value. It is eternal . . . [and] also contains the value of justice."[49]

Secret meetings in 1986 and 1991 with the guerrilla Xanana did not make Belo a revolutionary. His routine meetings with the Pope did not reduce him to a functionary. His message, and the meaning of East Timor's situation, were reaching the larger world. In October 1996, the Nobel committee in Oslo named Bishop Belo recipient of the Nobel Prize for Peace. It was shared, after a tied committee struggle, with the international publicist Ramos-Horta. Horta's costumes, over time, ranged from Che Guevara fatigues in the 1970s, to discotheque sophisticate at the Council on Foreign Relations in New York, where he spoke with open-necked shirt and sports jacket, to pseudo-ecclesiastical white in an appearance on American television at millennium-time.

Days after the Nobel announcement, President Suharto flew into Dili, according to a long-prearranged schedule, to dedicate the second largest statue of Christ in the world—surpassed only by the mountaintop Jesus over Rio de Janeiro. Funded chiefly by Garuda, the state airline, the monument stands on a promontory at the eastern end of the curving embrace of Dili's harbor. The features of the Christ are strong: a Melanesian archetype. His arms are outstretched but not oriented inland to the Timorese. Westward rather—to Jakarta, it is said, or, taking a direr view, for the geographic line does run that way, to Mecca.

Suhartoesque numerology further compromised the gift. The statue was 27 meters high, symbolizing the 27 provinces of Indonesia. Its dedication was to celebrate the twentieth anniversary of the annexation of East Timor as the latest of those provinces. Belo received this giant symbol of good intentions shamefully mixed with power motives in stoical style. He was invited for a helicopter ride with Suharto—a swoop around the Cristo Re (Christ the King) in the company of the crypto-godking of Indonesia. He accepted without astonishment the fact that Suharto never once mentioned to him the Nobel Prize.[50]

But the Pope saw the value of the award. After Stockholm, Belo stopped over in Rome. At the Vatican, he received coldly polite reminders from bureaucrats of the primacy of pastoral care—as if Belo did not know his people. But Pope John Paul II understood. He knew how the prize in 1983 had helped Lech Walesa in Poland. He radiated good will and spoke of the Nobel as a "shield" for Belo's further work.[51]

Poverty in West Timor

How poor can an Indonesian be? Arguably the worst off are the homeless and jobless of Jakarta, who cadge and cower for a living, hanging out at stop lights and knocking on the windows of dark Mercedes that slink around the city. They point to their open mouths. They press their lips to the windows and breathe on the glass of the locked car doors.

At a higher level are those large families, a few of them semiemployed, who dwell in congested parts of the port areas of North Jakarta. They cram into ramshackle huts on stilts above the stinking canals, gross with garbage, rubbish, and fecal sludge. In such *kampungs,* where "the poor sell cigarettes to the poor," inhabitants puzzle over the headlines of the tabloids and wonder where the street of opportunity lies. Relative deprivation is real. Its

deepest reality is unquantifiable. The name of Allah may be evoked in passive acceptance or in anger. Steady illicit labor may be better than no work
at all. Sudden looting and rioting may feel, to participants, like a mere rage
of reasonability.

The poor of both West and East Timor are of a different kind from the
poor in Jakarta. The towns of the island, small and modest, contain their
proportion of poverty, but they make up a tiny part of Indonesia's "urban"
poor. As for the poor of the plains, Timor has its fair share of that as well;
and the poor of the hills, more than enough. The whole island is notably
mountainous and meager in rainfall. Technically, East Timor is mostly
forest woodland (76 percent) and grassland/fallow land (13 percent). But today the former is mainly barren limestone mountain slopes and the latter
mainly barren limestone flats.[52]

Government statistics show West Timor (as part of Nusa Tenggara
Timur) to be in the poorest province of all in per capita income—$388 in
1996. East Timor, sharing the same modest bequest from nature, grows one
premium product for the international market, Dili coffee. But coffee did
not account for its higher regional GDP per capita near the end of the
Suharto era ($421 in 1996). The rise came about through government-
financed education, health care, and infrastructure.[53]

In any case, other provinces have mountain and forest populations, rugged terrain, and little infrastructure—Kalimantan, Irian Jaya—but those, by
contrast, have valuable exportable resources: logging, copper, gold. Some
wealth trickles around in such places. But not among the Timorese, who
call themselves "the dry people." Whatever the crash of 1997 and the calamity of 1999 may have done to per capita income figures is not yet clear.
Before these events, both provinces exceeded Haiti (whose per capita income was $330 in 1997); today, both the province to the west and the new
nation to the east hope they have not sunk to the level of conflict-riven
Cambodia or mountainous, destitute Nepal ($300 and $210 respectively in
1997).[54]

It was early November 1997 when I arrived in Kupang, West Timor's capital. Moderate rains should have begun by then, heralding the monsoon season. But there was no rain at all. Deep drought sucked Indonesia dry. Heavy
smoke from fires in Kalimantan and Sumatra, blown westward, had blackened the skies of Sabah and Sarawak, dropping soot in the swimming
pools of Singapore and even reaching Thailand. Malaysian officialdom has
banned the use of the word "smog," so a polite regional euphemism had
been adopted everywhere: "haze."[55]

Galuh is the youngest daughter of Soedjatmoko. Like her then-partner
in NGO work, she coughed quietly and often. They did not notice it, and

they dismissed my concerned remarks. If particulants were inflaming their lungs, it was best ignored. Galuh had been working in West Timor for several years on indigenous peoples' rights, women's issues, and a broad spectrum of specific human rights. She was then just past thirty years of age, tall, like her father, but much sunnier and less contemplative than he. Like her two older sisters, she inherited his idealism and was putting bottom-up development into practice. After her education at Swarthmore College in Pennsylvania, she had spent two years in Philadelphia working for Choice on its hotline in sex education; then several years for an Indonesian branch of Oxfam. She had answers for her alumni questionnaire on point of view since college—not "less liberal" or "the same," but "*more* liberal." She underlined the word conversationally. *Much* more. She didn't speak of being "angry" or "radical," but her adamant opposition to New Order mega-development and theft was clear. Her small office was trying to protect tribal lands in the mountains against a marble-quarrying corporation about to descend there with government help. We would head up there and stay with Petrus Alamet (Om Pe'u) and his clan in Lelobatan, a four-hour trip.

The office's dark green Japanese Land Rover was missing its four-wheel drive. The gear had been stolen. We took off anyway, with no more traction than a commuter sedan. Along the asphalted flatland road we passed miles of low walls of reddish gray stone, built of volcanic spittle small as fists, big as melons. "Velcro rocks," Galuh called them. Their molecular qualities make them stick to one another other like adhesive coral. Natural good fortune, because mortar requires water. Dwellings beside the road were of dusty slats and lattices made of the long spiky fronds that gyrate up the trunks of the *lontar.* From parts of this ubiquitous local palm, houses are built and roofs thatched, pigs are penned and chickens cooped. Or edible things are left to run companionably with the red dogs and the brown cats. This *Star Wars* landscape of black and white, gray and russet was redeemed by minimal green: government-funded *sawah,* irrigated rice fields. The rare flame tree or bougainvillea stood out like a jewel.

In the few leafy uncut lontar palms, a barefoot boy would soon ascend with his machete, toes clasping the limbs, until he could hack away overhead the wood needed for a building in disrepair. The fate of trees on Timor is to become amputees. Whole rows of trunks stood denuded of limbs, lopped off at the top or down as far as light tools can go, their abbreviated torsos testimony to low tech, little rain, many needs.

We wound and bumped upward over gutted roads, some axle-bending-deep with cavities, others cut along cliff edges, blasted arbitrarily through unfriendly rock and weathered to one-track passage. We forded streams so dry they barely licked the two hubcaps on our vehicle that had not been stolen. I stared at perilous ditches and precipitous canyons, growing mile by mile more aware of the pitch of the sun and the terrible implications of El Niño for the sustenance of slash-and-burn farmers. Six months later Oxfam would report that the West Timorese were reduced to eating *putak,* a tree bark normally used for cattle feed.

"My mother came here years before she was married," said Galuh. "She was a teacher . . . a special literacy project. She crossed this river in full formal working dress." The river now was a trickle among rocks. We were in T-shirts. It was hot. Dust swept into our nostrils and settled on our sweat.

The cool of the highlands assuaged some of the dangers of the road, the dizzy veering to avoid obstacles and an occasional vehicle, the constant gear-shifting and crater-dodging. As respite from the hundred white-knuckle mini-incidents of the ride, we made one stop to buy vegetables and cookies and kerosene to present our hosts.

Across a highland valley Galuh pointed: "There it is! See!" She meant the tree planted in memory of her fiancé, with whom she had worked here and who had contracted malaria too often and died of its complications, two years before. She had been shocked at his waning energy. He was young; he was strong; he was dedicated to the poor; she loved him. How could he die? At the Muslim funeral in Jakarta she felt like throwing herself in the casket with him. She wailed with grief when an old woman said they were really married. When I saw her afterward she was looking haggard and smoking cigarettes. In the way of a surrogate father, I cautioned her against this new habit. Now she no longer smoked and was able to pass by the thigh-high banyan tree in Lelobatan, a healthy green marker, with a casual salute. We entered the domain of Om Pe'u.

"Om" means uncle. Pe'u was not married but was the undisputed boss of the extended family that lived with him—sisters, nieces, nephews, others—ten or twelve members of a shifting population inhabiting three sturdy shacks lined end to end. The third and lowest-lying one was mainly the cook house. The middle one had a big space for eating and talking. Our guest beds were slightly uphill in what reminded me of the troop train I slept in as a gandy dancer on the Alaska Railroad in 1950. You can't easily get from beginning to end without going through the middle. There were good mosquito nets and a light blanket to wrap myself in if the mountain night proved cool. The privy was a lean-to over a large creased stone, tilted downhill. When I squatted over it, slapping at insects, I thought of Baruch Blumberg telling me, "The major sources of infectious disease are mosquitoes and other people's feces." An odd place for internal dialogue with a Nobel Prize winner for medicine.

Om Pe'u's lands are the topographic equivalent of a badly written waltz.

They are all hills and dips and swerves and turns. Unless you take the briefest perspective, no straight furrow is possible. But that's not a problem, because no straight furrow is intended. Cultivation is a matter of digging a series of holes and planting the desired seeds: dry rice, corn, cassava. The farmer turns all the earth over by hand, not finely, but in chunks with a long-handled heavy tool: an implement whose blade is at a hoe's angle to the shaft but whose shape is spadelike. Well-adapted to dealing with an agricultural sea of hummocks, tussocks, rocks, and mini-ravines. Some of the tillable soil in this irregular landscape is at a walk distant enough and rugged enough for Pe'u to have built a lean-to, where he sleeps at night when working his outer lands. There he breakfasts on betel, lunches on whatever is munchable, and waits to dine until the night he comes home.

Om Pe'u owns a couple of cows. His semi-wild horses—only a handful—are small, nervous, nimble in the hills. At least one of them has to be kept tame enough to mount and ride bareback, so that Om Pe'u can run down and rope one of the others and lead it to market. Such means beyond subsistence—such "surplus"—make Petrus Alamet a relatively well-to-do Indonesian peasant. The glaucous-looking eyes of one of his young nephews, the infected cut toe of another, the blackened rash on a female cousin's foot testified to lack of medical care here. But whatever the index of poverty, his shrewd gaze and his short laugh told me his wealth by other measures: independence and contentment.

Pe'u's family, Galuh, her comrade, and I ate dinner after the sun went down. Om Pe'u proudly cranked the generator and got two naked low wattage bulbs going in the dining area. Sitting in a wide rough rhomboid of benches and stools, we ate rice and white cabbage and bits of chicken in home-butchered shapes from plates in our laps. Cups of water, like everything else, tasted not unpleasantly of woodsmoke. The center of the inner circle was Om Pe'u. Galuh does not speak much Tetum, but she translated his Bahasa Indonesia, which was too fast and provincially idiomatic for me.

Yes, there were more fires in the forests than last year. Yes, they were feeling the drought. But still, as you could see, they had enough to eat. He lingered a bit on the price of staples: rice, salt, flour, sugar, cooking oil, kerosene, and so forth, which had gone up 70 percent since June. Om Pe'u made no connection between those prices and what was already called, in the West, "the Asian financial crisis." Nor did he make any angry linkage between his vote for Golkar in May and economic phenomena since then. A vote is a vote. West Timor gave 97 percent to Golkar, and his area gave 100 percent. So what? The only known behavior was to vote yellow, vote the banyan tree symbol, Golkar, for everything, all the time.

He used the Indonesian term *pasar bebas* and even the mixed-language term *market bebas*. But "free market" did not represent Hayek or von Mises or any cause-effect phenomena to Pe'u. It meant a phase of history that began when the first Westerner came to reside in this area, an Australian missionary in 1972. Now other people, such as me, occasionally appeared. Free market means social connectedness. He gestured to a sister, who wrapped a *selendang ikat* around my neck, a Timorese decorative scarf. As part of the ceremony, and climax of his rhetoric, he wove a series of poetic assurances that Galuh had trouble translating. "Now we are bound together, no roads will have to be cleared, no bridges are washed out, the path is open . . . We are free to breathe together, and for our hearts to beat together."

Another ritual sped up the action and conversation just before bedtime. "Chewing betel" is actually making a micro-sandwich of areca nut and powdered lime in a betel leaf. The lime interacts with other ingredients to give the chaw its famous red color. The vegetable ingredients contain a fast-acting chemical "upper." As the buzz hits you, your eyes may roll in their sockets. Galuh was practiced. I was chicken. I apologized for my sensitive stomach. She characterized me to Om Pe'u, anthropologically, as an observer. I rolled an areca nut foolishly between my fingertips while the others gnashed and spat. Galuh cast her long serene Javanese face into aggressive jaw-work and hawked hearty gobs of vermilion on the packed-earth floor. One of the lesser ladies tidied up after the others with a bamboo brush, whisking blobs of dirty quid out the open door. It's not as if you could stain the carpet.

I slept well until the first roosters crowed, about half past four. We breakfasted by six on rice gruel. Before the hot workday began, two neighboring male relatives came by, an older one healing from a broken leg, to share post-breakfast betel. They untied the drawstrings on their purses of ingredients, liturgically sharing the elements, rattling their brains and rolling their eyes with *pinang sirih*. In the far fields the lift you get may carry you past the need to eat lunch.

Galuh says that in the time of her grandparents, who were of the court society in Solo, betel chewing was still common among the aristocracy. The verb "to marry" was *meminang sirih,* meaning, roughly, to share betel. I was reminded of meeting the grandmother of a young Vietnamese woman in 1958 whose father was a key Swiss-educated minister in the ill-fated cabinet of Ngo Dien Diem. Grandma descended the stairs before dinner, shook my hand in limp semblance of Western style, and smiled demurely. I cannot forget her blackened teeth, file-sharpened to points, which were a mark of beauty in her Vietnamese generation and those before her.

Om Pe'u paid us an honor prior to our departure. The *rumah adat,* or traditional house, was built aside from the main train of dwellings. A snapshot by Galuh reminds me that I was almost as tall as this semi-conical house, which, completely thatched, looked a bit like a beehive. Om Pe'u's head came barely to my shoulder. His round dark eyes looked august to the camera, his slightly frizzy hair was black streaked with white, like his grizzled brief beard. Obviously he was much younger than I, and I much taller than he; but I remember him as "older," a giant and wizard in his own realm—former local secretary of Golkar, for which he showed relaxed disdain, and an interpreter of *adat,* for which his respect was deep and earnest.

He took us inside his beehive through its single bee-sized door, which I had to enter on hands and knees. When my eyes grew accustomed to the dark, I could see bundles of corn and bunches of onions hanging from ceiling rafters above, smoking to every Halloween shade, sub-orange to near-black. Om Pe'u, squatting with us, pointed out the fertility sculptures he had commissioned. They stood out from the dark door lintel and key beams: chicken, cow, goat, pig, horse, dog; man and woman on either side of the door. Thus was fertility guaranteed and tradition maintained. Nowadays people cut costs, he said, because *rumah adat* cost more to build than common houses. But he scoffed at those who carved figures into the wood. Not he. Not effective. Not *adat,* unless they are fully sculpted, three-dimensional and separate.

When I exited the hive, magically rich with its aroma of smoke, I blinked in the sunlight. One more gift before we parted. Pe'u pressed into my hands a sawn chunk of sweet-smelling sandalwood, the size of a big man's fist. I thanked him and we laughed about getting this controlled export past the road police. I told him I would give it a place of honor in my study. Galuh translated; Pe'u objected. It must not just sit. "You must pick it up, clasp it, roll it in your hands"—he demonstrated—"and *smell it often.*" I promised him I would behave as he instructed me. The little fist of sandalwood has kept its perfume. I dream of taking back to Pe'u a chunk of Pennsylvania cedar.

I heard a couple of years later, in the *reformasi* period, that Petrus Alamet was invited by Jakarta for the first nationwide conference of indigenous peoples. When he came back home, he told tales of his hotel—a huge building with palm trees inside on its marble floors. His room, high in the sky, had its own latrine, which sucked away your wastes with a loud noise of water. Om Pe'u still felt there was no place like home. But he was now part of a nationwide manifesto, and of Indonesians organizing themselves in still another new way.

A memory of Galuh, hiking in the weird, stark moonscape hills of West Timor. She imitated the sounds of goat, lorek (bird), and totek (lizard) as we came across them. We saw a passel of Om Pe'u's wild livestock in the upper badlands. They frisked away from us. Now she neighed. Galuh said, "If I were a horse, I'd be happy here." I said, "You *are* a horse." I felt the rare gratification of making an intimate jest with an Indonesian and having it understood as the compliment I intended: you, Galuh, are a free-spirited filly of great energy and grace.

The road from West Timor to East Timor is rugged, slow, and bumpy. Stops are welcome to allay fatigue and thirst. In August 1997, Sabam Siagian was traveling it by auto. A Batak raised in the Dutch Reformed tradition, former editor of the Jakarta *Post* and former ambassador to Australia, he knew his own country well. His group came upon a town west of the border at a TV-watching hour and were invited in to share it, village style. Sabam understood the rural meaning of TV, whatever its content. But this was a spellbound communal moment. What foreign programming could invoke romantic reverence? It was a special relay from the UK— the funeral of Princess Diana. The last rites for the princess to the sick, the stricken, and the maimed. Marching, liturgy, prayer, and bells for the fairy-tale beauty, radiant, vulnerable, dead far too young.

"Dorie," Sabam said to me, in his muscular English, flavored with Dutch R's and L's and vowel values, "Suharto and his family, they think they are royalty. But nobody cares. They think, Suharto's children, they are a dynasty, that the people revere them. But they don't. Suharto should see this, should experience this, on the border of West Timor and East Timor, people watching, little children included, almost worshipful. Princess Diana is their royalty. This *English* girl. Because of *television*. Suharto can do what he wants. But there's a real . . . " Sabam used the word as a sage does, carefully, "*revolution* going on. In the minds of Indonesian people. Because of television. He can't control that. He can't command their loyalty. Now they give it where they want to."[56]

INDONESIA BURNING

I was back in Jakarta for the first time in four years. My wife, by the grace of God, good doctors and nurses, and sheer guts, had survived a serious cancer. Now, October 1997, free to travel, I was asked for my impressions by a senior Indonesian employee of the World Bank. I replied with the obvious: "I observe Indonesia's forests burning, and at the same time its currency and stock market melting down." "Don't you see," the woman interrupted fiercely, "that the people are also on fire?" This chapter is about all three fires.

Asia was already polluted and environmentally degraded beyond any other great region of the world when the El Niño of 1997–98 arrived. In the previous thirty years Asia had lost half its forest cover and fish stocks and depleted a third of its agricultural land.[1] Then in June 1997, the trade winds shifted direction across the Pacific, in their first major reversal since 1982. By early July sea-surface temperatures off the coast of South America were four degrees centigrade above normal. Oceanographers and meteorologists had for months predicted this El Niño, an interaction between warm sea water and global atmosphere recently occurring in irregular phases. When severe, an El Niño in the west Pacific causes agricultural shortfalls, scarcity of surface water, lowered forest productivity, and diminished flowering and fruiting. Rainfall in parts of Kalimantan would decline to 10 percent of normal volume. The drought of 1982–83 and subsequent fires, attributable largely to human mismanagement, had been the greatest of the century. Now they would be surpassed. Meteorologists' warnings proved unable to prevent disaster.

Islands on Fire

The forests of Sumatra and Borneo exceed even the Amazon and Congo basins (more easily imagined by peoples of most NATO nations) in the richness of their ecosystems.[2] There, Indonesian trees, plants, animals, and insects have evolved over giant spans of time, surviving drought-induced fires for at least 17,500 years. In 1924 a map of what is now Central, East, and South Kalimantan showed 94 percent of the area covered by forest. Human action, however, has cut into it with vast man-made plains of coarse grass.

The chainsaw, along with modern road-building and harvesting equipment, has made profitable the logging of tropical rain forests. Suharto's New Order advanced on Sumatra and Kalimantan with a legal framework supportive of special harvesting concessions. By the 1980s this attack on the rain forest made Indonesia the world's largest plywood producer.[3] Infrastructure development, job production, and generation of capital may be considered benefits, but against them must be weighed Indonesia's rates of deforestation, estimated between 1.5 and 3.0 million acres a year. When logging, mining, and transmigration open up virgin forest, illegal loggers and spontaneous settlement follow, as well as more systematic degradation from timber plantations and permanent estate agriculture. These attract still more migrants. Forestlands thus stripped and degraded regrow slowly, if at all, while their agricultural potential may tend rapidly to drop.[4] Top-down consumption of the forests contributed to Suharto's thirty-year statistical growth record. But there was no parallel data publicized, top-down as it deserved to be, regarding silted-up dams and irrigation facilities, increased flooding and drought, high financial burdens, and social conflicts escalating at least proportionately with felt ecological disturbances and resource scarcities.

With serious drought in Java, Sulawesi, and Irian Jaya, and catastrophic phenomena in both Kalimantan and Sumatra, the Ministers of Forestry, Agriculture and Environment combined publicly to announce that a majority of the fires were purposely set by commercial plantation firms to clear forests and vegetation.[5] Too late. The firestorms of agribusiness were impossible to control.

Peasant practitioners of slash-and-burn agriculture obviously set fires too. But analysis of 1982–83 showed that corporate-disturbed forest areas burned six times as large as those affected by shifting cultivators. The logging industry was "clearly implicated" by its system of leaving much combustible material on the forest floor, creating canopy openings that promoted understory vegetation, cutting "highways" to extract logs which in turn became avenues for fire penetration, and illegally returning to logging blocks sooner than the thirty-five years permitted by regulation.[6]

While these practices persisted, a major new factor by 1997–98 was the rapid growth of palm oil plantations. Their developers achieved rapid land clearing by large-scale imitation of slash-and-burn farmers. Ironically, areas already damaged by fire in 1982–83 were targeted by the government for a second burning in the 1990s in the name of "sustainable development." In tons of production the palm oil industry had multiplied almost eleven times between 1978 and 1997, with private estates and small holders rising from one-third to two-thirds of the production, compared with public estates.[7]

As Indonesia's ecological-financial crisis deepened, the Internationl Monetary Fund inserted itself into the 1998 agreements with the Indonesian government to open palm oil production to foreign investors. Bob Hasan, a Chinese Indonesian with a scraggly moustache and under-eye pouches the size of tablespoons, was then Suharto's closest crony. He uttered nationalistic complaints about the IMF interfering in the development of Indonesia. But such nationalism was disingenuous, coming from the Cendana coterie that had already profited from plywood and timber plantations and had moved on to palm oil.[8] The same spirit of calculated naiveté appeared in Hasan's answer to inquiries about plantation fires. "Why should we burn the forests? We need the raw materials. It doesn't make sense."[9] He continued to shift blame to small cultivators and "communist" NGOs.

But the minister of the environment, Sarwono Kusumaatmadja, directly blamed "irresponsible plantation operators." The minister of forestry suspended 176 cutting licenses. The companies of Liem Sioe Liong, Prajogo Pangestu, and Hasan, tycoons tight with Pak Harto, were all implicated. They filled in their report forms by blaming dropped cigarettes and malpractice by other companies. Within two months most of the 176 licenses were reinstated, and after six months perhaps only five companies were being prosecuted.[10] In March 1998, as he formed his seventh cabinet, Suharto made Bob Hasan his minister of industry and trade, thus expanding Hasan's de facto power over forestry into de jure control over all industries. Figuratively speaking, the modern Bhairava Buddha as fiery godking was readily morphed into the modern Siva, god of destructive consumption.

The seasonal rains had failed. The fires swept on. As reported by the *Los Angeles Times,* around and along the road to Balikpapan were "flames no bigger than those from the coals of a barbecue grill . . . [giving the] land an eerie reddish glow . . . whipped to and fro by hot heavy winds, [they] . . . crept to the very doorstep of Omar Kamorusun's one-room wooden home, an hour's walk from the nearest water. For generations Omar's family had fire-cleared the land for rice and peppercorn, controlling it with ditches and firebreaks. 'If we do not burn, we do not eat.'"[11] But now they themselves were in danger of being cooked alive.

The so-called haze had reached Malaysia and Singapore in July. By September the air pollution index, in which a level of 100 is unhealthy and 300 is hazardous, hit 849 in Sarawak. Prime Minister Mahathir donned a face

62. MAN AND UNCONTROLLABLE FIRE. After drought, dense blazes in Kalimantan are part of Indonesia's massive losses to fire in 1997–98. (Paul Lowe/ Magnum Photos)

mask and declared a state of emergency there. In Kuala Lumpur the upper stories of the twin towers of Petronas, tallest buildings in the world and Mahathir's own mega-symbol of development, were invisible from the ground. Southern Thailand was hit, completing a region-wide rout of the tourist industry. Airplane flights were cancelled. Two ships collided in the Straits of Malacca. An airliner crashed in North Sumatra. Schools and businesses closed. Hospitals filled.

The haze got international media attention. President Suharto took the extraordinary step—for him—of issuing two public apologies to neighboring countries. Indonesian fire-fighting efforts, assisted by Malaysia, Australia, and the United States, were largely ineffective because of "poor coordination, lack of equipment, and insufficient training."[12] An American C47 dropped water bombs near Surabaya, making the front page of *The Jakarta Post*. But no significant fraction of the money and manpower necessary for the job was available. Only nature could extinguish what plantation man had ignited. The monsoon season, which normally lasts six months in Western Indonesia, tapered off in less than two months.

By January 1998 satellite images picked up hundreds of hot spots again in East Kalimantan and Southern Sumatra: newly set fires, smoldering peat that had burst into flames, and continued burning of underground coal seams ignited by the fires of 1982–83. Vegetation was drier; water was scarcer. The army had agreed to a more active role in fighting the fires than in 1997. But it then had to reduce the troops so assigned because of civil unrest arising from the economic crisis. In mid-April a UN Disaster Assessment and Coordination team said that 10,000 firefighters and extensive water bombing were necessary. The United States government pledged $2 million to help, and the United Nations approved a $10 million package a week later. The new minister of the environment, Juwono Sudarsono, estimated, however, that extinguishing the fires in East Kalimantan alone would require $2 billion.[13]

In late November 1997 the Indonesian government declared that the rains had arrived and the fires were over. But the fires ignored the government's pronouncement. They burned into May of 1998. One day the computer sensor picked up 4,000 fires in a mapping area where Doug Fuller, an avid, athletic American geographer, worked on an international team sent over to help. An Indonesian operator was worried: "The Ministry won't like that"; he changed the threshold to show 800 fires instead.[14]

Although normal rainfall returned to Sumatra in 1998, it did not return to Kalimantan. There, insuppressible fires raged from January until El Niño relaxed in mid-June. Minister Juwono gravely acknowledged that handling the fire disaster ranked fifth on the government's agenda for handling crises: above it were alleviation of poverty, generation of employment, public health care, and stabilizing the rupiah.[15]

The 1982–83 fires in East Kalimantan had burned an area larger than the states of New Jersey and Connecticut combined, for which German forestry experts estimated total fire-related losses of commercial timber, peat-swamp timber, non-timber forest products, and future timber production at $9 billion.[16] Fifteen years later, what did the still wider fires mean? Sorting among international data, one may reasonably accept an estimate that 5 million hectares of Indonesia were affected, of which 20 percent was forest, 50 percent was agriculture/plantation, and 30 percent was unproductive.[17] This would equal 12,355 square miles: an area nearly half the size of Maine. Costs of fire and haze to Indonesia and other countries in 1997 alone exceeded $4.5 billion, more than the legal damages assessed in the Exxon Valdez oil spill in Alaska and the chemical disaster in Bhopal, India, combined.[18] Negative consequences for investor confidence: not included. That amount alone, if socially invested for Indonesia, could have distributed basic sanitation, water, and health infrastructure to over 100,000 rural villages.[19]

But in fact the final mean estimate of costs for 1997–98 was $9.3 billion, more than double the initial estimate.[20]

Adding areas burned in 1982–83, 1994, and 1997–98 but excluding the fires of 1987 and 1991 and the as-yet incomplete results of research on losses in Irian Jaya in 1997–98, the total area burned comes to 17.4 million hectares.[21] That is over 65,000 square miles, or roughly the size of Taiwan, the Netherlands, Belgium, Vermont, and two Hawaiis combined. That's still less than half the size of California, and yes, some of it burned twice. Much of the area was unpopulated, and some of the fires resulted from unavoidable acts of nature. But the frequency and unmanageable ferocity of fires in Indonesia are attributable to the visible hand of man and the allegedly invisible hand of a free market system. That system, actually out of control, was justified within the Suharto cabinet as part of the "dirty phase" of capitalism. Ah, so then. When does the clean phase begin?

The fires might have roared on, ignored by the rest of the world, had it not been for the catastrophic smoke. Having a few years earlier banned the word "smog," the Malaysian minister of information on April 20, 1998, warned his nation's broadcast media, at risk of having their operating licenses revoked, also not to use the word "haze." The media had already called global attention to the haze as a visible disaster spreading over a region inhabited by hundreds of millions of people. Invisible, however, were alterations to the global atmosphere and damages to the health of humans, animals, and plants from sooty particulates and from toxic gases: carbon monoxide, nitrogen dioxide, formaldehyde, and benzene. Not to mention the contributions to global warming of fires smoldering in peat bogs sixty feet thick.

What are the ecological impacts of fires like these? The species composition of recovering forests (many do not recover) are changed for decades. In Tanjung Putung National Park, tree species declined from 60 per unburnt hectare to 15 after burning. Areas that burned twice or more were generally devoid of trees. Soil erosion in Kutai National Park accelerated tenfold after the 1982–83 fires.

Fires can move at 7–8 kilometers per hour. They kill most small slow-moving animals and put creatures with specific requirements in food, habitat, shelter, or climate at risk. Leaf-eating monkeys and fruit-eating birds die. Insect-eating birds increase explosively in response to a population explosion among insects, who live on and in the enormous supply of dead wood. A few years after 1982–83 wild pigs returned to abundance in Kutai. So did wild water-buffalo. Many deer perished initially, but their populations recovered. The Malayan sun bear, however, is thought to have declined beyond recovery. Most land reptiles die in such fires but may repopulate, except for large species like pythons. Crocodiles and water turtles—deep-water creatures—can escape as the fire goes by.[22]

Orangutans, adaptable and omnivorous, switched post-1983 to eating bark and young stems until fruit reappeared in the forest. The 1997–98 fires and their aftermath seems to have stressed them beyond their ability to survive. Many were killed by flames; many others by humans. Orphaned juveniles were sold into the illegal pet trade. In 2002 a new colony of orangutans was discovered, but not likely of a mass great enough easily to survive publicity and poaching.

Burnt soils lose their water retention. Rain becomes runoff, carrying heavy sediment and biological pollution from dead plants and animals into rivers and streams. As waterways become smothered in mud, fish life—hit by new diseases—declines, while algae bloom. When rivers discharge their heavy sediment into the oceans, reducing the salinity of sea water, corals die.

What happens to human forest dwellers, both traditional tribes and more recent transmigrants to Sumatra and Kalimantan?[23] While they are a minor cause of fires, they suffer major effects. Depletion of agricultural land in Kalimantan cannot have improved relations between indigenous Dyaks and transmigrant Madurese, and almost surely worsened them.

Juwono Sudarsono—tall, handsome, talented, eloquent in English, and a modern Javanese archetype of courtly gravity—was minister of the environment in Suharto's last cabinet before becoming minister of education and culture in Habibie's successor cabinet and civilian minister of defense after Habibie. He had been on his first cabinet job only weeks when he publicly regretted his inability to create a sense of urgency among government officials concerning the continuing fires. He compared lack of government control in this critical instance to the "lawlessness of the American Wild West in the nineteenth century."[24] There, of course, he touched an American nerve, given the near extinction of the buffalo and the aggressive marginalization of Native American cultures in that period. But the ecological analogy is inexact. More appropriate was the history of Vermont, once almost wholly forested. By the late nineteenth century, uncontrolled slash-and-burn agriculture combined with rapacious logging had turned much of the state into barren hills and seasonal mud. George Perkins Marsh, observing these phenomena, early spurred the modern science of ecology. His *Man and Nature*, published in 1864, articulated many of the remedies that make Vermont and other places livable today.

Between 1982 and 1998 Indonesia probably burned down seven or eight Vermonts. Doug Fuller was struck by the earnest hard work of many Indonesians who wanted to rescue and restore their own environment. They, and he, were distressed by satellite images of Borneo which showed few hot spots on the Malaysian side and almost nothing in peninsular Malaysia. Fires don't respect borders. Aerial maps, therefore, are revealing differences in policy and management.

I asked him how severe was the total impact of the Indonesian fires of 1997–98? Those in the Amazon were getting a lot more attention from the State Department, a hemispherically oriented press, and amateur ecologists. Even fires in Florida, which burned "only" half a million acres, got American television coverage, evoking sympathy for the destruction of trailer parks and the evacuation of whole counties.[25] In prima facie gravity, however, taking into account human density and the loss of forest cover, the Indonesian fires were certainly worse than those in the Amazon and the most severe ever in Indonesia. Indeed, the Indonesian fires of 1997–98 were "probably the most destructive in the modern world."[26]

Financial and Economic Meltdown

"Tulipmania" in Holland in 1636–37 has become the archetype of over-trading, discredit, and financial catastrophes among North Atlantic nations in the last four centuries.[27] Euphoric speculation and massive crash may have been latent in Indonesian behavior, but nothing earlier resembled the horrific hemorrhage that began in July 1997. Westerners have wry axioms— "Men go mad in herds, and recover their senses one by one"—but Indonesians have not yet fused such images into wisdom. A newspaper headline, "Seperti antelop lihat singa," catches fright scattering: "Like antelopes sighting a lion."

The Indonesian poverty line was, and is, defined so low as to be unlivable and almost unimaginable by Western standards. The middle class, by any strict definition, made up probably less than 8 percent of the population when crisis hit in 1997. The state, under Suharto, was largely unthreatened by middle-class criticism and wholly unconcerned about social security policies, which Bismarck, a century before, had introduced into the German Empire to keep workers loyal to the state. The power of the Indonesian state was ensured by repression and threat, tactical deployment of the military, and opportunistic payment of underclass demonstrators to intimidate the middle class. Life insurance was and is a rarity and health insurance a luxury; pensions are pittances.

Indonesia entered the third quarter of 1997 with some mildly expressed alerts from indigenous economists concerning reversals in the alleviation of both poverty and inequality.[28] The World Bank clung to its then crystallized 1993 view of the "East Asian miracle." Sustaining high growth with equity became the theme of its midyear major report on Indonesia.[29] "Improved government and institutions" were—incredibly—added to a litany of compliments and reinforcements. Paul Krugman's essay entitled "The Myth of Asia's Miracle" was faintly acknowledged, however; it had warned that East Asian growth, based largely on physical and capital accumulation, would slow down.[30]

In the boom years from 1990 to 1995 Indonesia was one of the world's ten fastest growing economies, at 7.6 percent. Of what were then called the "High Performing East Asian Economies," Indonesia recorded (from a lower base) the largest improvements of all in life expectancy, infant mortality, adult literacy, and reduction of percentage of population below the poverty line.[31] Brazil, of course, had also lived through a so-called economic miracle from 1957 to 1977, until oil price shocks and debt crisis exposed its unsustainable policies.[32] But who in Indonesia had a policy memory for Brazil, its airplane industry, and other uncompetitive protected sectors? Indonesia would make its own mark on history with evaporation of finance and erosion of human development.

The shocks began in Bangkok. Since 1996 Thailand had been experiencing slumps in the stock and property markets, a slowdown in export growth, and an outflow of capital. When its central bank floated the baht in July 1997, values collapsed. Monetary authorities were overwhelmed. Meanwhile, Indonesia's stock market index had been rising and actually continued to rise until a few days after the Thai crisis began. Then the crisis diffused swiftly to much of East Asia, with differing effects according to the differing characters of the national economies. Four nations felt the most immediate financial shocks: Indonesia, South Korea, Thailand, and Malaysia.[33] Of these, Indonesia's problems accelerated and compounded in the most humbling and even horrifying ways. The IMF came far more swiftly and magnificently to the rescue than it had done for Thailand. But the $43 billion total package for Indonesia did not arrest the downslide.

In 1998 the "Asian contagion" began to look like global pneumonia. According to market analysts, South Africa, Brazil, and Russia were in great danger. Although the state prosecutor estimated that criminals controlled about half of Russia's GNP, the Clinton administration pushed a $17.1 billion bailout through the IMF. The oligarchy sneaked the first installment out the back door and overseas. On August 17 the bailout collapsed. Russia stopped propping up the ruble and defaulted on domestic bonds. The massive failure in Japan of the Long-Term Credit Bank, followed in the United States by the catastrophic condition and over-zealous rescue of the giant hedge fund Long-Term Capital Management, proved that prosperous and allegedly advanced countries had their vulnerabilities too.[34]

Late in the summer of 1998 the fever over emerging markets had chilled to icy fear, exposing naive assumptions that currencies do not devalue and countries do not default. A financial analyst admitted to *The New York Times* that "everybody agrees that if the Hong Kong peg were to go, the attack on Brazil would be relentless, until there were no international reserves left . . . It's not because there's a real connection between the economies . . . It has everything to do with perceptions, and the psychosis of the market."[35]

Only those Americans who lived through the Great Depression and its 25 percent unemployment have any concept of what a true bottom, as distinct from disconcerting dips or even painful dives, can be. In fact, Hong Kong held its peg. Brazil received a $41.3 billion bailout from the IMF, after intervention encouraged by President Clinton and Treasury Secretary Robert Rubin, and so escaped until its next cycle of improvidence and 35 percent devaluation in January 1999.

Indonesia, however, fell unrestrainedly and almost unbelievably. Combining its equity market losses and currency drops against the U.S. dollar meant a slashing of 91 percent in the value of its assets in little more than a year (see Table 4). For comparison, it took three years for the Standard and Poor's Index to decrease 87 percent at the beginning (1929–1932) of the Great Depression in the United States. As a "fundamental underlying explanation" of the Asian crisis, one economist concluded that the "Japanese model," which had been agglomerated proudly into an alleged "Asian model," was, despite its enormous successes, realizing "cumulative negative effects."[36] The causes? Enormous waste of resources in political decision-making (Japan's steel, Korea's shipbuilding, Indonesia's "national" car); neglect of the domestic economy; excess capacity in export industries and deteriorating terms of trade, leading to currency depreciations; and social and political corrosion from personal favoritism.[37]

Why was Indonesia hurt so badly? If over-borrowing and under-regulation were common throughout the region, Indonesia's behavior was dangerously lax. For years the government had successfully avoided a decline in export competitiveness by purchasing foreign exchange to maintain a steady nominal depreciation of the rupiah. It then borrowed from the private sector to prevent any expansion of the money supply. This policy not only stimulated foreign borrowing by the private sector but led to a general underestimation of a large exchange rate risk. Because capital inflows were unhedged, the economy was vulnerable to sudden large-scale outflows. The Indonesian government, seeing how the Thai central bank had used up reserves trying to defend its exchange rate against the dollar, almost immediately allowed its exchange rate to float.

Those who held unhedged risk went into panic. Rapid outflow ensued.

Table 4. A capital misery index: value on September 15, 1998, of US $100 invested July 1, 1997[a]

Nation	Value of investment
Japan	61
Taiwan	61
Hong Kong	51
Singapore	38
Korea	26
Philippines	25
Malaysia	24
Thailand	23
Indonesia	9
Average	35

a. Derived from Kevin Evans, "Economic Update," in Geoff Forester, ed., *Post-Soeharto Indonesia: Renewal or Chaos* (Singapore: Institute of Southeast Asian Studies, 1999), pp. 105–128; table 6.4, p. 120.

Devaluation followed. Economic and political meltdown were under way. Corporate foreign currency debt could not be repaid because its cost soon quadrupled. The banking system was quickly beyond immediate rescue.[38]

In March 1998 I had lunch with Hashim Djojohadikusumo, the still-charming, boyish-looking graduate of Pomona College and son of Sumitro. A major young conglomerate owner, his close Suharto connections defined him as part of the Cendana family. He sat down and introduced himself with debonair candor: "I am insolvent." He prided himself on having ignored his American business school's advice to integrate. He had diversified into cement, banks, mortgage companies, and other activities, of which only one, palm oil plantations, was bringing in money. Later, one of his employees told me his debts exceeded $2 billion. Others told me he was now living grandly in Switzerland. Not until 2002 did his transactions bring him into temporary detention. Few imagined that his glamor, connections, and cash would yield to binding judgment and jail.

When the Indonesian government at last requested help from the IMF, the fund responded with a bailout program publicized at $43 billion. That impressive number broke down into $10 billion from the IMF, $8 billion from the World Bank and Asian Development Bank combined, $20 billion in stand-by loans from several governments, and $5 billion of Indonesia's own funds tacked on for impressive effect. In practice the amounts were released by the IMF in political driblets: a $3 billion tranche in November 1997 was for short-term defense of the besieged rupiah, which was hurt further by President Suharto's disappearance from public in late 1997—

63. SCAVENGER. This man migrated to North Jakarta from Eastern Indonesia many years before. In the late 1990s he is living on scraps and refuse in the Sunda Kelapa area of the harbor. (Jody Dharmawan/author's collection)

64. SECURITIES TRADERS. Two traders, two computers, four telephones: Jakarta in the late 1990s. (Jody Dharmawan/author's collection)

much later revealed as occasioned by a mild stroke. A wholly unrealistic new budget for 1998 brought down the rupiah again. And Suharto's announcement of B. J. Habibie as his choice for vice president shot it briefly to its bottom: 16,500 rupiah to the dollar, from a pre-crisis level of 2,400.

Worsening conditions and noncompliance by the Suharto government brought about further unobserved agreements with the IMF and unresolved disagreements. A fourth compact was reached in April 1998, and eventually there would be eight versions within the first year of IMF involvement.[39] In all versions, "structural reform" played a large role, themes upon which Suharto's own economic technocrats and IMF officials tended to agree, to the great discomfort of the family.

Jeffrey Sachs and his colleague of the Harvard Institute of International Development Stephen Radelet saw the troubles as a crisis of success (not felt in the more laggard economy of the Philippines), one that could be described in terms of contagion, panic, and mishandling. Indonesia's financial plummeting resulted purely from a shift in investor confidence. The IMF just made things worse.[40] Ross McLeod, a leading Australian expert, also felt banks were closed too precipitately, which contributed to panic. McLeod acknowledges that "the existence of anti-competitive policies designed to enrich the favoured few was deplorable," but those policies, he insists, had been compatible with generally beneficial high growth. In an emergency room full of train crash victims, "the doctor will have better things to do than haranguing those present about smoking and drinking to excess."[41] (I would argue differently: locomotive engineers driving on marijuana should be fired and subject to trial.) In fact, moral hazard in Indonesian banking had been steadily accelerating since the deregulations of 1983 and 1988.[42] "Family," crony, and many other banks could no longer be kept going on a pretense of solvency.

IMF director Michael Camdessus made matters worse by looming with folded arms over a seated Suharto while the president was signing the very first IMF agreement. The position of the head is critical in Javanese culture, especially in deference to the head of the sovereign. Suharto cared so much about such posture that in ordinary receiving lines he extended his arm far out and low, palm in and fingers down, so that handshakers were forced to dip their knees and lower their heads in relation to him, even if they hadn't already enough cultural sense to bow. Now the front pages carried a photo of what appeared to be a French schoolmaster diminishing the president of Indonesia by his minatory bearing—widely felt to be a national insult. Camdessus later tried to pass the matter off as a "photo-op" pursued on the advice of Paul Volcker.[43] The diplomatic damage was done. But it was nothing compared with the socioeconomic crumbling underway.

Did the IMF's stress on structural reforms merely worsen the crisis? I
don't think so. The international business community had largely played
the local game, without pressing for reform. Most domestic voices for
change had been forced into exile, jailed, intimidated, or ignored. In a critical situation, only a body of world standing could get a hearing for politico-
economic defeudalization.

Japan was the obvious external candidate to restart regional growth. But
the Japanese stock market bubble had broken in 1990, from a point where it
was worth 151 percent of Japan's GNP. Its real estate bubble, valued in 1990
at five times Japan's GNP, also exploded.[44] The combined loss in monetary
and land value by 1998 was $12 trillion: the equivalent, inflation adjusted,
of all Japan's financial and material losses (excluding human losses) in the
Second World War.[45] Indonesia, therefore, had no economic locomotive to
hitch up to. Nor, for the first ten months of crisis, could it unseat its own
engineer.

Social Flammability

A post-Christmas riot in 1996 in Tasikmalaya, west central Java, threatened
a fundamentalist Christian family, which went to international email for
help. It was seven months before the krismon (krisis moneter: financial crisis)
began. But social firestorms were breaking out in Indonesian cities.

The wife spoke: "We long for your prayers in this situation, not for ourselves but for kingdom-related reasons [Thirteen prayer concerns follow]. . .
Many reports are continuing to stress that it was not Santri—Isl[amic] students who were involved in the rioting. Yes, [it is said] they would demonstrate, but they would never get involved in destroying the property of others. Pray for the truth to come out and for people to face it." The husband
continued, after careful walks around the city: "There was a bit of carnival
feel . . . A lot of people aren't so sure they're so sorry that all of this has
happened. Some of this comes out of a feeling of hopelessness / disillusionment, but some of it is outright deception by the Deceiver."[46] Later reports
noted the destruction as focused on police because of the origins of the riot
in "police headquarters beating and insult of a pesantren master." The mob,
estimated at 1,500, destroyed "8 churches, 14 police stations, 89 shops, four
companies, six banks, three hotels, 107 cars and 22 motorcycles."[47]

Tasikmalaya, which had recently won an award as "the cleanest city in Indonesia," lay in wreckage, dismay, and shame. Gus Dur attributed the riot
to forces trying to discredit NU, while Amien Rais saw it as an explosion
against economic disparity, corruption, and government arrogance. Even as
inquiries and trials proceeded, other cities were hit by violence—notably

Pekalongan, Banjarmasin (130 dead), and Ujung Pandang. By the end of 1997, according to a count by Christian sources, the number of church burnings in Indonesia since 1992 was reaching 500—an ugly new phenomenon of unprecedented intensity.[48] Many of the churches were Chinese but some were not, as in Tasikmalaya. There, a Batak and a multiethnic Protestant church were burned. Whatever the causes—racial, socioeconomic, or mixed—the result was Christian sanctuaries damaged or destroyed by Muslims.

The seriously increasing number of such events moved the Department of Religion of the Republic to commission a study by a leading academic center on village and regional affairs, P3PK at Gadjah Mada University in Yogya.[49] The director of the survey was Loekman Soetrisno, a bulky, brusque rural sociologist trained at Cornell, pragmatic and totally free of deconstructionism, neo-Marxism, and fancier academic fashions. The senior member of his team of twenty was his old, distinguished teacher of history, Sartono Kartodirdjo. Their findings are the most searching analysis available of the troubled social dynamics of Indonesia in the end-state Suharto years, at a time when there was no sign yet of his departure.

Professor Loekman's team went to seven cities or areas in sudden uproar or sustained unrest between 1995 and 1997, where collectively there had been perhaps a thousand deaths and certainly hundreds of millions of dollars of damage. With extensive field interviews they proceeded to analyze the causes in each case and to extract a schema of happenings in them all.[50]

In West Kalimantan and in East Timor, large numbers of internal migrants sponsored by the state were pivotal. Muslim Madurese transported from their overcrowded island to live near pagan or Christian Dayaks bred every kind of cultural tension between those groups. The state did not mediate ill will, but actually intensified it through bureaucratic expansion which lacked local participation. Corruption, manipulation, and the absence of justice produced corresponding decline of the authority of the state. In East Timor the introduction of large numbers of Javanese Muslims among Catholic Melanesians led to political and economic insecurity for the latter. "Restless youth" entered into violent clashes with "the state," represented by ABRI. The military were intent on forcing integration by operations of their own, regardless of clogged channels of law and political expression or the absence of any such channels.

Back on the poor and crowded island of Madura, structural poverty was leading to weakness in ethnic identity, to fear, and thence to external migration. There, in Sampang, clashes with state authorities flared in the elections of 1992 and 1997. Authorities, lacking credibility, further weakened it by use of naked force.

In Pekalongan, on the north coast of Central Java, there was a clear and unwelcome shift of the reins of the economy from *pribumi* to non-*pribumi*. (The word "Chinese" appears on no charts of the P3PK study.) Negative perceptions were worsened by a discriminatory state apparatus. Classical race riots broke out, with non-*pribumi* as targets.

In Banjarmasin and Situbondo the presence of external agitators is clearly suggested, but "not enough evidence" was available for a definitive conclusion. In Banjarmasin in South Kalimantan, on the last day of the 1997 elections, 13 churches were wrecked or burned and 123 died in the burning and looting of a department store. Local bureaucrats were seen as corrupt and ineffective in a discriminatory economy where big business was overly influential. Situbondo, in East Java, was marked by segregation and noncommunication among Chinese, Madurese, and bureaucrats. "Stagnation of social will" led to collapse of the local social structure into violence against itself. The presence of external agitators was again remarked, but neither their motive nor their motivators could be identified.

The seventh locale was Tasikmalaya, where the analyzed markers of danger and the vectors of tension were the most numerous of all. That city displayed an industrial labor society inside a santri Muslim atmosphere. Class, race, and religion were all involved in the ascent of Chinese Indonesians to the top of the heap and, at the same time, descent of *pribumi* to the bottom of the pile. In an authoritarian and feudalistic atmosphere, state officials were believed to be in paid collusion with the non-*pribumi*. The targets of anger were various: police, government offices, banks and shops, churches and schools.[51]

Many churches destroyed in Situbondo in October 1996 were rebuilt by cooperation between Christian and Muslim communities. Stimulated by events there and elsewhere, a Nationality Forum for Indonesian Youth was founded in February 1998, representing Nahdlatul Ulama, Protestant, Catholic, and Hindu youth, to provide grassroots and intercommunal communication.[52] But such healing as might be taking place could not keep up with the rupturing that continued, silently or noisily.

With so many of the nerves of the society inflamed and sinews of the government strained, what could be suggested to minimize repetition and aggravation of these conditions? Loekman and his colleagues brought forward a diverse menu of recommendations:

(1) Respond to the demands of ethnic minorities (a distinctly multi-cultural, "Bhinneka Tunggal Ika" answer);
(2) Share power (devolution, local autonomy, and revenue sharing were clearly indicated in many regional and local situations);

(3) Re-evaluate transmigration policy (which was creating as many as or more problems than it solved);

(4) "Socialize" religious missions and institutions (develop tolerance and diminish militancy in religious curricula and teaching methods);

(5) Redefine the meaning of religion and add to the five recognized ones—Muslim, Catholic, Protestant, Hindu, and Buddhist—Confucianism as a sixth (the Chinese for decades had been arbitrarily pushed toward what appear to be exclusively Chinese Christian churches, where they became double targets of riot, because they had no recognized option to pursue the Confucian tradition of their ancestors);

(6) Open up SARA and consider "affirmative action" (the regime rule of nondiscussion of ethnicity, religion, race, and intergroup relations simply worsens situations where ventilation of difficulties and grievances are required; therefore, test the applicability of policies adopted by Malaysia after its race riots of 1969, to tackle problems of economic, social, and political imbalance).

The findings were clear. The recommendations were comprehensive and solid, even if controversial in the case of SARA and affirmative action and theoretical in the case of Confucianism.[53] As a law of bureaucracy, of course, the chief reward for a good report was disregard.

I met Loekman and Sartono when they were finishing the report. I tested various details of conspiracy I had heard in Jakarta of the riots they had studied. They had heard similar things and more, but they concluded that absence of conspiracy must be assumed when sheer military-official incompetence is adequate to explain what happened.

Sartono stressed that the attacks in Tasikmalaya included automobile showrooms and "rich hotels." For him, that proved motivation not only against the Chinese, and certainly not just Christians, but a lashing out against the wealthy. I asked him why there were no church burnings in the nineteenth century. I accepted, on his authority, that nineteenth-century peasant revolts had been strictly against the Dutch as oppressors and as *kaffirs*.[54] Now, in the Indonesian nation, the oppressors were more various and the targets more diffuse. But rage can get focused if Chinese Indonesians are rich and disdainful and if they build an ostentatious Christian church. Why not burn it and thus relieve one's feelings against the alien, the unbeliever, the plutocrat, and the bureaucratic housepet all at once?

Sartono later conceded that the report had never adequately analyzed the peculiar intensity with which Chinese were targeted. "Maybe it has something to do with Islam," he said.[55] Maybe. Despite its universalistic aims, Islam has not received Indonesian Chinese the way Buddhism has embraced

Thai Chinese and Catholicism has embraced Filipino Chinese. Maybe Islam is, in that way, partly causative. In such a general way so is the hierarchy of the Dutch period, with its suffocating colonial sociology. Former Minister Mohammad Sadli, however, had been caustic and concrete in reply to my query on riots in several cities: "Are there basic *economic* causes?" "Yes," he replied. "But the rioters don't throw stones through the windows of rich *hajis*."[56] A delicate way of redirecting my focus to fact that the social targets of these economic grievances are likely to be Chinese, Christian, or both.

Loekman, eyes bulging with diagnostic impatience, stressed the overarching findings of the P3PK report. The people are *"fed up"* with government indifference, corruption, and repression and their message is bursting out in aimless frustration. His published report invoked a powerful string of causes: a sense of powerlessness, confusion, and cynicism; lack of faith in institutions; and resentment of a bureaucracy that appeared to be "partial, unjust, exploitative, marginalizing and impoverishing." All of these were connected to "various other structural illnesses which emerge as consequences of the management of capital with the support of the state."[57]

Our conversation was more direct. When I pointed out some achievements of the state in the last thirty years, Loekman bristled. Too many foreign writers have spent too many compliments on that for too long. "Indonesia doesn't need another Pak Harto ass-licker. His body is already covered with saliva."[58]

The Critics: Half-Paralyzed

No clergy of any faith had gone to jail in Indonesia as Dietrich Bonhoffer had against the Nazis, to his eventual execution. Arguably, this was a police state only about six hours a day, and a Pancasila state only two hours a day. Suharto was never as fanatic, as paranoid, as systematically vengeful as Hitler. Thuggish intimidation and corruptive cooptation got done what he wanted. He had used both on the PDI in 1996, to subdue the only political party that directly challenged him. Megawati, at best a silent secular icon, was now nearly invisible as a leader.

Romo Mangun was not anybody's party man but was a classic civil society activist. In his retirement he was looking for an opening in the power structure to exploit, but he could not find one.[59] Mangun noted that Amien Rais, the leader of Muhammadiyah, based in nearby Solo, had called for national repentance *(tobat)* and clean-up *(bersih)*. Such a statement was influential, coming from the head of a Muslim organization claiming 22 million members, but it was offensive to two significant categories of Indonesians at large: those who genuinely believe they have nothing publicly to repent or clean up; and those with guilty consciences.[60] Shortly before that, Amien Rais had publicly declared that while Indonesia could not have a free election under its present system, it should at least have a poll—a direct challenge to Suharto, who loathed confrontation.

The Nahdlatul Ulama, the only organization bigger than Muhammadiyah, was alleged to have 30 million members—the largest single Muslim organization in the world. Its leader, Abdurrahman Wahid, had been for the longest time a critic of Suharto, but his was not an unwavering path. At our first meeting, when he was kind enough to come to my hotel room, I asked myself how did he inspire 30 million believers? Not with the broad shoulders, deep voice, and cinematic profile of a Billy Graham. Gus Dur was slight, blind, chubby, soft. He rested one hand on the arm of a wife of a mutual friend, the other on a walking stick. He was wearing loose off-white robes, a black *pici* cap, and sandals. He looked humble, comfortable, faintly Middle Eastern. He settled into a chair to talk. He accepted questions easily and answered unpredictably in a voice of soft surmise, latent with quips and quiddities—laughingly deflective, earnestly direct, or simply, "ia, ia, ia," yes, I realize that.

I asked, "What is the aim of your public association with Tutut, President Suharto's eldest daughter?" Gus Dur answered that he was concerned, after Suharto destroyed the PDI, that too many of its members might shift to the PPP, a state vehicle containing Muslim zealot leaders and radical conservatives. So, as a vote-tilting proposition in the election of 1997, he leaned toward Tutut and was seen with her in Golkar environments.

I asked about his public remark that if the vice president was nominated in an unconstitutional way, he would mobilize two million people in the streets against it. What did he mean? He answered, "That was actually a message to the 'Gang of Six' who are conspiring . . . to ensure the nomination of Habibie as Vice President. They are Habibie himself, Feisal Tanjung, Prabowo, Hartono, Harmoko [and one other whose name I missed] . . . I chose that statement as a way of projecting my influence against such a possibility."

"If Al Ghazali [the great reconciler of Sufism and Islamic orthodoxy, 1058–1111] were alive today, I imagine he would say all nationalisms are false religions; and Pancasila, because dogmatic, is an especially false religion. What is your comment?" Gus Dur replied without allusion to broader Islamic history but plunged into modern Indonesian politics, in 1983, when President Suharto declared Pancasila as *azas tunggal,* the sole basis of Indonesia.

After Pancasila was subsequently declared an "ideological and constitutional base" and not a faith, NU cast its own definitive articles to state that

65. BATHERS AT SULFUR SPRINGS. Forgetting any *krisis*, bathers at Gunung
Rajabasa in Lampung rub themselves with sulfur as skin medicine and general
tonic. (Byron Black/author's collection)

its *creed (aqidah)* is Sunnid doctrine and that the *azas* of the Indonesian state
is Pancasila. That took *azas* out of the field of religion altogether, and, simultaneously freed the meaning of their Muslim *creed* from state context. "I
need to tell people this in a very simple way . . . wearing *pici* (pointing to his

66. SUHARTO BECOMES FIVE-STAR GENERAL. Attended by chiefs of staff of the armed forces and police, Suharto accepts a fifth star in 1997, arranged by sycophants and authorized by his own signature. Previously, such an honor was bestowed only by action of parliament on Generals Sudirman and Nasution. (Hidayat Surya Gautama / *Tempo*)

cap) . . . Pancasila has to do with earthly life, while *aqidah* has to do with this *and* the hereafter world."

I concluded by complimenting Gus Dur in Indonesian on speaking his conscience. "The forests burn, and you speak." He nodded. "The rupiah burns, and you speak." At Jusuf Wanandi's invitation, he told me, he had addressed a corporate gathering against the flight of capital. "The people are aflame," I said. He interrupted in English, laughing, "And the presidency goes up in smoke!"[61]

Voiceless and Endangered

I've lost the letter now, but I'll never forget it. The first letter, early in 1998, from a name I did not know in a *desa* I'd never heard of. Elizabeth Ary Krisnawati. She wrote from the southernmost part of the Special District of Yogyakarta, about three-quarters of an hour, I later learned, from the city, in a fairly well developed rice-growing village of Central Java.

In a straight-up-and-down lower case handwriting, she apologized for writing me. Her brother, who worked for Romo Mangun, had taken my address from the business card I'd left with the priest (and which he'd apparently left on an innocent surface). Nobody there could help her. Maybe I would know someone in America who could. She apologized for being sick. She couldn't do anything about it. She was twenty-one when her kidneys began failing. She had been a medical student but dropped out for surgery. A year before, her father had saved her life by giving her a kidney. But they had to keep the new kidney going with immunosuppressive medicine, which is expensive. Before the *krisis moneter* they could just manage to do it. But now this *krismon* was so much worse, they had sold nearly everything. She felt she was taking away life from her family. But she also felt still young and did not wish to die.

My first reactions were strong and conflicted. *One:* Why should I respond to a supplication from a stranger using stolen information? All the American and world causes in the mail, asking for money, were enough. *Two:* "You are not my poor." From somewhere in memory, Emerson's brush-off to a beggar in Boston: Leave me alone. I have enough commitments already in Concord. Let your own city and its people look after you. *Three:* This girl is sincere. And she is endangered. You looked like a rich American to her brother—someone who could help. And you *are,* by *their* standards, rich. So why don't you help?

I gave the letter to my wife, who said, net: "Why don't you help?" I undertook inquiries through friends on kidney disease. There were no international foundations in the business of helping the stricken, as distinct from research support. I wrote what seemed to me a letter of genuine sympathy, with assurance of prayer (the first name, Elizabeth, indicated she was Catholic), and advice to try local government and *yayasans* and her own former medical school.

Of course, she explained gently in response—an exchange of letters took four to six weeks—the Special District of Yogyakarta had no program. There were no local foundations. And her medical school did not have any information to help her, let alone means to help. I arrived in Indonesia for my next visit unresolved on what further, if anything, to say or do. I raised the problem to Romo Mangun over the phone. He was obliquely embarrassed that his houseboy, the girl's brother, had gotten my address because of his own carelessness with my card. "She's better," he said. "Her father sold some rice land to pay for the treatments. Now she is off treatment. But she's better." His tone indicated that it was all an Indonesian matter, ascribable in its punitive unfairness to Suharto, his children, and his cronies. Their mismanagement of the nation. I need not be involved. Perhaps, I inferred, I should stay out of it so as not to offend Javanese dignity. Maybe, however, it was just Romo Mangun's dignity.

I asked my friend, Sobary. I told him the whole story from the beginning. He nodded with understanding. "I can see you feel the burden." "Yes, I feel a burden. I don't know what to do about it." "Drop it," he said pleasantly, with a shrug as if loosening a backpack, letting it slide to the floor. "It's not your problem. I get lots of letters like that. Because I'm a writer, people think I'm rich." He grinned at the absurdity of a freelance columnist becoming wealthy. "I can't help them. And you can't help her. So don't feel the burden. It's not your burden." "OK," I said. I tried to let it slide away. "OK. Thanks." Christian and Muslim advisers agreed. Let it drop.

But I couldn't get it out of my mind. Within a week the MPR was going to acclaim Suharto for a seventh term. Would this girl, born under his regime, survive his misrule? On my second and last afternoon in Yogya, I arranged for a taxi to get me to Bantul. It might be tight making my plane back to Jakarta. But that was my excuse for escape, if I needed one. The hardest part was finding her *kampung* house address, a letter-number coordinate. We had gone down a long, weaving road through *sawah*—no more becaks, bikes, scooters, four-wheel drive vehicles, just an occasional individual on foot. My driver asked four times. He was using narrative now. The girl with *sakit ginjal*—kidney sickness. Everybody knew about her. But the directions were hard to follow to the house of her father, Pak Sudiro. Finally, in the rain, my inquiring driver motioned to me from a porch.

The family was home, and surprised. They assembled fast in polite Javanese attention, without exclamation. But the faces were open and hopeful.

"Pak Sudiro!" I addressed the father, a tall white-haired man wearing sarong and turban, in bare feet. He snapped his body to attention in a way that made me think he'd known military service. He introduced his wife, a son, and then Ary. Ah, so she was called "Ary." She came forth simply: round-faced, with an appealing, uncomplaining countenance and yet with an intelligent mortal sadness rare in youth anyplace. In one economy she had lived, and in another she faced death.

She did not speak much English. Maybe I inhibited it. Or maybe she had labored even longer than I thought over that letter. So I carried the conversation—in attempted felicities that spiraled down to the subject of her health. I apologized for my Indonesian—*rusak*—"busted." That got a laugh from Pak Sudiro.

I showed Ary an article from the front page of the previous day's *Jakarta Post*. One hospital alone was seeing 2,000 outpatients with terminal kidney disease. They might have to give up dialysis because its cost had quadrupled. But, I could see, statistical company does not relieve individual misery.

We sat in the semidark of the unlit front room on this rainy afternoon while I looked for a better approach to the subject. I said that I had gone to St. Agustus Church in Kota Baru, Yogya, that morning; and I had prayed. But I felt that more important than prayer was bringing my feelings to them this afternoon, which was all I could bring. "I haven't the power to change the system." Pak Sudiro nodded with understanding.

What was left to do but rely on your own immune system and hope your body grows stronger? I was appealing to Ary now. I couldn't understand much of her reply, which was about a friend trying an alternative treatment through the peritoneal membrane.

I addressed Pak Sudiro instead. We must trust in Ary's own body and in God, *Tuhan Yang Maha Esa*. I apparently pronounced the T-word with insufficient aspiration of the "h." That leaves the word for "the Lord" sounding like *tuan,* or a mere "mister." "*Tu'-han,*" said Pak Sudiro in an emphatic friendly way, as if agreeing with me, that's indeed where trust must repose. "*Tu'-han,*" I repeated.

I drank the sweet tea offered by his wife (why was I the only one served? short supplies?) and sighed with pleasure. "I enjoy tea with lots of sugar." She smiled. I explained about getting back in time for the airplane to Jakarta. We rose and orchestrated steps that brought us outdoors together under the eaves. We shook all around once, saying farewells. And then again, before I stepped through the puddles to the car.

Ary looked at me modestly and earnestly, and she uttered in English her only entreaty of the day. "I hope we can be friends." I regarded her with reassurance. "We *are* friends." And then I left, responding to their waves, and waving at last to her brother, who guided us backing out of the narrows onto the asphalt—the brother who had stayed in the background for the whole meeting and never sat down, the one who had started the whole thing by lifting the address off my card on Romo Mangun's table. His theft of information illuminated to me the condition of tens of millions of Indonesians. Their slim security was threatened with poverty. For some of them, like Ary, it was a matter of life or death.[62]

Indonesia was burning.

SUCCESSION

FORCING OUT SUHARTO

"Do you want to see him?" I wasn't sure. "I don't want to intrude," I said. Sobary, a Muslim journalist with wide-ranging friendships, smiled. "Don't worry. He wants to see you. Everybody intrudes." So we drove to the hospital on March 4, 1998, and spent twenty minutes maneuvering in the parking lot, where a woman in a blue blouse handed out aquamarine tickets of entry and four male traffic managers waved their arms before we could grab a suddenly open slot.

We walked down semi-outdoor corridors with fronds drooping in our faces. My nostrils registered both "heavy" and "sharp"—tropical vegetation and Lysol. Number 6, with "VIP" posted above it, was Gus Dur's room. Two young male personal assistants led us to an exterior porch, where we sat facing barbed wire and huge air-cooling tanks, waiting until other visitors departed. Yesterday Assistant Secretary of State Stan Roth was here, during his visit to Indonesia with former Vice President Walter Mondale to see President Suharto and to push for a reform cabinet, at President Clinton's request. Roth had stolen away from that futile charade to come here, to the hospital, to see Abdurrahman Wahid. The leader of the world's largest Muslim organization had been smitten with a stroke. The assistant secretary was a faithful payer of visits, including one to Xanana, leader of East Timor's guerrillas, serving a twenty-year term.

Earnest conversation in Javanese flowed around me. Sobary explained. Some *dukuns* came in last night when nobody was present, with special medicines for Gus Dur and gave them to him. "Really? What kind?" I asked; "Obat normal, inyeksi, apa?" There was headshaking at my pharmaceutical notions. "Just food. Special food." Sobary smiled in a certain way. "Magical food?" I ventured. "Magical food," he smiled again.

"Who were they?" "Nobody knows." "Gus Dur doesn't know?" "No. Gus Dur says maybe they came in a dream." "So," I puzzled, "maybe they walked into the room and gave him special food. Or maybe they walked into his dream and gave him magical food?" "Yes. *Jin.*" "*Djinns?* Not real people? Even if they came into his room in real space and real time, they were not real people?" "Right. That is correct," Sobary said.

I took a deep sigh and a cultural leap. "Roch istimewa?" "Yes." Everyone smiled appreciatively. I had stabbed out a phrase meaning "special spirits." In linguistic bliss, I forgot to ask how effective their magical food was proving to be. We were motioned into the room and gestured into chairs at the bedside. Abdurrahman Wahid was lying in fetal position, wearing unmatched pajama top and bottom, both too short even for his small frame. He had fallen asleep, using his folded hands as a pillow.

Sobary moved in to massage Gus Dur's arms. I flinched at the thought. In the middle of a long day, Sobary had offered me a "Korean massage" in my hotel room, which had felt like intense *shiatsu*—pinchings and thumb diggings into hands and feet that made me grunt and convulse. But with Gus Dur, Sobary was gentle. Wahid raised his one openable eyelid and recognized his self-appointed nurse. Sobary reintroduced me and began talking. Gus Dur replied in Bahasa Indonesia. An assistant, waiting for the moment to feed him, spooned a micro-pea soup into his mouth. Gus, his head not even raised, let it flow down his gullet. Sobary and the assistant gently daubed the spill with napkins and offered a sip of water. Head still flat on a pillow, Gus Dur clamped firmly down on a bent plastic straw and sucked in the water fast and loud.

The television was playing the current MPR session that would in days adopt the steamroller ticket of Suharto-Habibie. "I'm glad you came," said Wahid in English. He turned and curled again to let Sobary's hands proceed with massage. "Suharto, I know him. You have to be patient. He will use Habibie up. I know him." His voice grew agitated. "Heart by-pass, half a liver, Habibie can't last. He will use him up. Then put in his daughter, Chairman of Golkar, as vice president, to succeed him. The five people who will matter . . . [he trailed off] I know him . . . "

I felt alarmed at his agitation. "Gus Dur, you must get your strength back. Grace of God to you, and renewed health." "Thank you. That *circus* at Senayan!"—he nodded at the TV—"I'm glad I'm here, not there. I know how he thinks. He thinks he's worn me out. But I'm watching him. I don't need to be in government to criticize him." "No," I said; "Government would tie strings around you, cut off your circulation." "That's right. He will do half a term. Then throw away Habibie and put in his daughter in '79." Sobary interjected. "You mean '99?" "Yes, '99."

Wahid started to theorize about the *aliran,* religious and cultural channels of faith and behavior. "Indonesian wisdom recognizes them all—Christian, Hindu, Buddhist, Confucian. Islam is universal. Indonesia doesn't put them in opposition. Or to Western science, either." A hospital masseur relieved Sobary, sat Gus Dur up, worked on his back. "No," I said: "They are in dialectic, Eastern and Western thought. A balance, a complimentarity, not an opposition." "But Rushdie, Naipaul. They are too Western." "Right. They are dark hyper-rationalists," I said, expressing my own doubt about these great deracinated talents.

"Yes. I'm glad you came," Gus Dur said; "What is your name?" "Dorie." "Dorie," he says. "Sukarno understood all religions, but not Suharto. He is too rationalist. Too much money. Power-corrupt, too dark." "It will all be made known, Gus Dur. It is known already. As Emerson said, 'The world is made of glass.' Everything is clear in the end. Already we see what we need to know." "I like that," Gus Dur said. Sobary, who had resumed massage when the orderly left off, repeated, as a question, "The world is made of glass? Emerson?" "Ralph Waldo Emerson," Wahid said firmly, as if to embed it in Sobary's mind. "I'm glad you're here," he said to me, "an American who understands Asia."

In came doctors, talking in Javanese, laughing. We were excused.[1] I wondered how Gus Dur would pull through. Nothing in that hospital room cued me to visualize this stricken, *djinn*-visited man, nineteen months hence, as president of the republic.

Suharto and the Rupiah, Sliding

In August 1997, on the occasion of the annual Independence Day speech, Suharto had taken his usual posture of imperturbable fixedness, reminding his people what they owed his New Order for gains over three decades. History was in his hands: the teleology of material development and the theology of Pancasila. Everyone had heard it before. That's why it was true. Therefore it was still true.

But in December, Suharto disappeared from public view, failing for the first time to attend a conference of ASEAN presidents. Much later the story circulated that he too had suffered a mild stroke. In any case, the rupiah was dropping fast, and Suharto knew he had to get back on his feet. He appeared before the press in mid-December and weakly joked that those who proclaimed him dead were obviously deluded.

The rare press conference was an ordeal. Capital flight from Indonesia? One estimate given from the audience was $150 billion, equivalent to two-thirds of the pre-crisis annual GNP. How could this capital investment be wooed back? The people must trust the government and the rupiah, Suharto replied. But *how*, when the government itself doesn't have faith in the rupiah? Kwik Kian Gie, an economist, one of Megawati's most intimate advisors and author of *I Dream of Becoming a Tycoon* (1993), pressed hard.

Sofyan Wanandi, an independent spokesman for Chinese-Indonesian big business, pressed hard. Sofyan proffered names more internationally trusted than those Suharto mentioned as his financial crisis managers. In an even more daring effrontery, Sofyan declared the desirability of Chinese members in the president's next cabinet. Having assured his public that he was alive and in charge, Suharto withdrew from the podium.[2]

In the health war, Suharto, fifteen years older than Wahid, would only decline. Gus Dur would snap back from a second life-threatening hemorrhagic stroke in the same year, following a minor ischemic stroke earlier in the decade. In an astounding turnabout, he would succeed Habibie as president and try to tease billions of dollars back from a "retired" Suharto.

But in early 1998 these events were unthinkable. Shoppers had panicked in January and swept supermarket shelves nearly bare of staples. Rumors exaggerated scarcities and prices. President Suharto ordered distribution of food supplies in Jakarta to avoid more panic and sent generals to supermarkets telling housewives to be calm. Suharto's daughter Tutut publicly exchanged $50,000 as part of an "I Love the Rupiah" campaign. A modestly educated cocoa trader from Sulawesi, thriving in exports and wishing to follow her patriotic example, naively exchanged a million dollars.[3] When Suharto's highly unrealistic budget was publicly announced, the rupiah plunged below 10,000 to the dollar. When he next indicated his preference for Habibie as vice president, national and international aversion hammered the rupiah down to an utter low of 16,500 to the dollar, one-seventh of its pre-crisis value.

The president's children brought in Stephen Hanke, a professor who ran an applied economics program at The Johns Hopkins University, to advise them. Hanke, styling himself an expert on currency boards, counseled the family to peg the exchange rate at 5,000. In what countries was such a solution used? In Bulgaria, where hungry pensioners massed in silent marches to protest their deprivations; in Argentina, where all depended (before utter crash a few years later) on the discipline of the widely respected finance minister, Domingo Cavallo; and in Hong Kong, where high standards of transparency prevailed. Without either a Cavallo or transparency, without even the tattered Communist safety net of Bulgaria, Indonesia could ill afford a currency board. It was too clearly a device for Suharto's family and cronies to buy dollars for 5,000 rupiah each, instead of being savaged at 10,000 by their own borrowings and speculations.[4]

Suharto struggled with the International Monetary Fund over this scheme and over their structural reforms, thus delaying implementation of the IMF letter of intent of January 15, 1998. Meanwhile, social disorder grew. Human Rights Watch Asia found in the first five weeks of 1998 more than two dozen incidents of demonstrations, price riots, bomb threats, and bombings on Java alone, and the unrest was spreading to other islands. They admonished Suharto and his senior officials that "if they continue to fan the flames of anti-Chinese fervor, they may well destroy the country they purport to cherish." In a mass meeting at Sunda Kelapa mosque in late January, a general lashed out at rats leaving a sinking ship, a clear reference to Chinese Indonesians. But Amien Rais, leader of Muhammadiyah, at the same meeting said the worst offender was a "giant sewer rat"—a clear and daring reference to Suharto himself.[5]

Sofyan Wanandi's earlier press-conference retorts to Suharto about the cabinet and vice presidency had brought a visit from Liem Sioe Liong, who told Sofyan that he was being fired from his positions in the *yayasans*. Thus the inner circle of Suhartoites extruded any outer-circle business leader who dared to express independent thoughts. Soon afterward, Sofyan had direct conversation with General Prabowo, the president's son-in-law, who had recently, in public, implored Muslims to join him in fighting "traitors to the nation" and privately had made his bias even clearer by his expressed willingness "to drive all the Chinese out of the country even if that sets back the economy twenty or thirty years."[6] "You Chinese Catholics are trying to topple Suharto," Prabowo said to Sofyan, who replied, "Only Muslims or the Army are strong enough to do that. It's ridiculous to think groups as small as Christians and Chinese here could do it."

Sofyan asked about the vice presidency: why Habibie, of all people? Prabowo's answer: because he is Muslim, with ICMI support; he is internationally recognized and linguistically fluent, he has developed strategic industries, and Suharto owes him for taking him to Germany for important medical attention. Sofyan dismissed the first three reasons as insufficient nationally and the fourth one as purely personal.

This vehement disagreement further soured the relationship between the two men. An investigation of Sofyan for alleged culpability in bombings then followed. He went briefly to Australia for his personal security. Much later a member of the intelligence unit who questioned him, feeling guilty, admitted privately to Sofyan that they had manufactured the email about the bomb plot in which he was allegedly involved. Given the manner in which he was accused and accosted, Sofyan came to believe that Prabowo was the mastermind of malevolence against Chinese Indonesians in the climactic month yet to arrive: May 1998.[7]

A Case of "Javanese Defiance"

Dr. Soedradjad Djiwandono served Suharto for ten years—five as a junior minister of trade, then five as governor of the Central Bank (1993–1998). His father had been a musician at the court of the sultan of Yogyakarta.

Soedradjad said that his rearing in court culture made him a classical Central Javanese: nonconfrontational, never a nay-sayer, always a yea-sayer; adept at dressing things up for the dignity of all concerned, especially for superiors. One of eight children, all of whom became Catholic by choice, he had married Sumitro's daughter, which made him Prabowo's brother-in-law. Family life grew complicated when Sumitro began to publicly criticize Suharto, his elder son's father-in-law, and when Prabowo, whose angling for power included anti-Chinese tactics, began to alienate his Christian sisters, one of whom was Soedradjad's wife.

Soedradjad revealed to me that the Central Bank maintained an internal distinction between "official reserves," which were publicly declared and in July 1997 stood at $21 billion, and gross reserves, which were not publicly declared in order to prevent raids upon them by the government itself. Gross reserves stood at $29 billion when the contagion from Bangkok and elsewhere hit Jakarta in July 1997. The bank repeated the defensive techniques it had earlier used, as against the $800 million drains of 1994 (in the wake of the Mexican crash) and 1996 (after the crushing of PDI). It widened its intervention band. But this time the rupiah kept plummeting. "Everybody kept buying dollars . . . This external shock could be endured if internal structures were sound. But there were significant weaknesses in the financial and real sectors," Soedradjad recalls, "which bred contagion of panic."[8] Soedradjad traced political weakness back to the constitutional debate of 1945, where the Javanese Supomo prevailed over the Minangkabau Yamin, and "integralistic kingship" thus won over "democracy." The sociological changes of the 1990s required a shift in the "Yamin direction," but from Suharto "resistance was supreme."

Bank closings? Soedradjad proposed some from late 1996 through April 1997, because technical journals had identified thirty banks that needed to be shut down. Suharto asked him to wait until after the elections in May. In July the crisis hit. When Indonesia sought IMF help in October 1997, they received it, with macroeconomic stress on restructuring, transparency, and a legal/supervisory base. Along with, at last, a selection of sixteen banks that should be closed.

The key October discussion, with Suharto present to hear recommendations by a high official of the IMF, had occurred at a 9–10 PM meeting. Soedradjad as governor of the Central Bank left the list with the president at the end of the meeting, having mentioned Probosutedjo's bank but not Bambang's. It was the Javanese way. "I didn't want to embarrass him twice in one meeting. So I mentioned his half brother's bank, and let him read about his son's bank."

Suharto had three days to change his mind, but he did not call Soedradjad. "His children got mad at him over this at a family gathering." Suharto did not renege on the signed agreement with the IMF to close the banks. But he yielded to anger from his relatives and allowed his half brother and his son to *sue* Soedradjad and Mar'ie Muhammad, the Central Bank governor and the minister of finance, charging, among other things, "conspiracy to defame President Suharto so he would not be reelected" by the upcoming MPR.[9] It was Suharto's Javanese way. But the lawsuits further debased the rupiah, already weakened by the public's having (correctly) viewed the closing of some first-family banks as proof of severe financial illness.

It bothered Soedradjad not to have spoken directly of Bambang's bank to Suharto. Rumors of his own firing reached him on February 12 through Wijoyo, the most Javanese in style of all the technocrats, now re-embraced as an advisor by Suharto. While Soedradjad went to Bali to host a meeting of fourteen Asian governors of central banks, they left him alone. Then President Suharto summoned him on February 17 and thanked him for long service. Soedradjad expressed gratitude for the opportunity. And also, "I showed him my Javanese defiance." In the course of a fifteen-minute report on recent events, including the bank closings, he brought up Bambang's bank. "That was your proposal," Suharto said. "If I had made a different decision, people would say it was for my brother or son. But as *citizens,* I agreed they had a right to sue you in court."

Soedradjad, on a senior fellowship at Harvard, later reflected on the whole strange episode. "I was trained as a Javanese to be happy but not too happy, be sad but not too sad. Don't feel any extreme, and certainly don't show it." Family complicated the matter. "Because my wife's brother, Prabowo, is married to Suharto's daughter, it made it harder for him to fire me earlier . . . We are a lazy, greedy people, and we take short cuts [or avoid the hard task] . . . Prabowo had his own troubles with Suharto and believes he was finally betrayed by him . . . As for me, working with Suharto was like a scarlet letter . . . I suffered guilt by association . . . But I was not corrupt. That's what pushes me to talk and write."[10]

Middle-Class Protest

Through the newspapers, many weeks in advance of the MPR session, three of Suharto's former ministers had, independent of one another, advocated a change of leadership: Emil Salim, Mohammad Sadli, and Sumitro Djojohadikusumo.[11] They had neither suasion with Suharto nor much to fear from him. Sadli later wondered if they had stuck with him too long. Yes, I would say. A break five years earlier might have helped generate more energy for reform.

Being a minister in office, face to face with Suharto, was a different matter. Soedradjad Djiwandono's "Javanese defiance" was humble, muted, and indirect, even as he was being fired. Frustration, humiliation, and inner fury all manifested themselves in oblique and mannerly ways—in composed face, controlled voice, and seemly deference. The "tapeworm of Javanese culture" emptied him of confrontational energy.

"But when housewives organize, as in Argentina in the '80s and in South Korea, let the regime beware."[12] Sadli, who said so, had in mind the networks of his own wife, who was an NGO powerhouse. A younger woman, Karlina Leksono, also proved the point. An astronomer on the faculty of the University of Indonesia, with a highly developed interest in history of science, she was fed up. Javanese culture had been applied by Suharto's regime with bureaucratic rigidity to women, reducing them to dutiful subservience. But for Karlina, scientific method did not coexist easily with gender oppression and official obscurantism. She gathered a group of her friends to talk about social conditions. Early in 1998 the grotesque rush on supermarket shelves had included middle-class Mercedes owners behaving like food scavengers. But what about the poor? Many earned no more than 2,000 rupiah per day, which now bought only one order of *bakmi,* street noodles, or one meal a day. The price of condensed milk had gone from 8,000 to 21,000 rupiahs per can, a price impossible for many mothers to afford. How could the lower middle class and the working poor, not to mention the rapidly growing underclass, feed their infants?[13]

Karlina and her group chose their name carefully: Suara Ibu Peduli: the Voice of Concerned Mothers. Voice, because women had been told too long to shut up. Mothers, because who can be against them? Concern, not protest, because they were keenly aware of the repression they could face. On February 23 the group arranged to gather to pray at the great focal site of Jakarta, the main roundabout outside the Hotel Indonesia, near the Grand Hyatt, Bambang Suharto's hotel. Police challenged what they were doing. "We are praying for hungry Indonesian babies." They were arrested for gathering without a permit, thrust into police trucks, and rushed to headquarters. Across a period of sixteen hours they were interrogated by officers and low-ranking police, including those of the vice squad, and were detained in cells. But they were celebrated by the newspapers, including the international press.[14]

To all such criticism and negative publicity, Suharto reacted in a way unsurprising to those who knew him: he dug in deeper. The classically educated German Jesuit Franz Magnis-Suseno, who was deeply versed in Javanese culture, in early March expressed his private assessment of the president in tragic Greek terms. Suharto was suffering from *ate.* He was blinded with passion—an indiscriminate lust that embraced money, weapons, all forms of power. At one time he had consulted widely, at least until 1978, but thereafter more and more narrowly, until now, in the things that truly mattered, he consulted nobody but himself. He was as isolated as King Lear. He was moved only by hubris and the momentum of age. He accepted advice being tendered him by other international leaders only as homage. He was as sightless as a man who stares at the sun, while believing himself filled with divine illumination. Such a situation, Suseno concluded simply, could be changed only by the army or by the people: by an upstaging or an uprising.[15]

Emil Salim, a Minangkabau, a straight thinker and clear speaker, wanted to give democracy a push. He let himself be thrown in the parliamentary fray as a vice presidential candidate, the only one running against the Golkar nominee and Suharto's choice, Habibie. Salim's aim was to try to close the gap between official politics and social reality. Golkar told him to lay off. He refused. After a list of 180 distinguished independent thinkers who supported him was published, "my fax machine melted," he said, as 10,000 more signatures came in. I waited to see him at his home in mid-March, drinking tea, staring at Chinese porcelain flowers in a pagoda-shaped cabinet, sitting on frumpy fat easy chairs, grandmotherly and Dutch. Modest, genial, with twinkling eyes, Salim told me of speaking to 3,000 students at the University of Indonesia in late February. They said, "Lead us, we will gather twenty or thirty thousand, we'll carry banners up to the MPR." But he warned them: the *preman*—opportunistic thugs—would follow, looting behind and around you. This will be unlike 1966: the army will not be with you, but against you.

"Bullshit!" some cried. "Transvestite!"—a stinging Indonesian insult, conveying both the treachery of "turncoat" and accusations of cowardice far beyond "wimp." Salim faced down the radicals of immediacy. "We must know what we want, in detail. Ideas have legs, yes. But this is not a dash, it's a marathon. We must aim for 2003." More emphatic protest followed. "You force my conscience? You want me to stand before the MPR without a concept? And with some among you dead, satisfying only the press and television? No! If I die, let my tombstone read, 'Here lies the conscience of Indonesia.'"[16]

Salim prevailed in applause, but he lost, overwhelmingly, in the supine MPR. Suharto was now president for the seventh time, with Habibie as his vice president, chore boy, and sycophant, brilliant, manic, erratic. I asked Emil, "What are you going to do next?" He spun me a vision of enhanced civil society. He had formed Gema Madani—later translated into English as The Resonance of Civil Society—an organization to realize the civil tolerance and social universalism of the Prophet Muhammad. Gema Madani would generate systematic ideas on parties, on elections, on discourse with the army about its functions. It would start to build an internal safety net of NGOs, where private contributions could be put to work guaranteeing food and medicine, cash for work, infrastructure at basic levels. The organization would initiate a corruption watch, so that voluntary private eyes could be matched with new daring in private voices and reshape an effective public conscience.[17] I enthusiastically wished him well. The development of a civil society, however, does not guarantee a democratic polity. Germany in the 1920s and 1930s was rich in civic associations and rife with voluntary movements. That did not prevent, but sometimes converged with, racism and hypernationalism.

The development of an active and nonfanatic popular political consciousness was nonetheless vital. That had been the theme of my early March meeting with Amien Rais. Perhaps slightly under average height for an Indonesian male, he was an intense man, despite the informal short-sleeved shirt he wore. His most striking features were curled graying dark hair and intensely alert, surprisingly warm brown eyes. Surprising because his reputation for brusqueness and sharp speech had me defensively prepared. But he turned out to be a good listener, quick in appreciative repartee. I saw no sign of the man who had made anti-Christian and anti-Jewish statements in years past, and for a while I accepted his own view—one that had been temporarily adopted by international journalists—that he had grown beyond such prejudice.[18]

Mas Amien engaged me swiftly with an attack on intolerable corruption in the Suharto regime and the need for national repentance and renewal. He took pains to assure me he was *not* for an Islamic state; that modern Islam can coexist with Pancasila; that a humanized capitalism would be far better for Indonesia's development than the totalitarian money-ism in place now. He responded most strongly to my adjectives *terang, bersih, jernih:* the need for governing practices that are clear, clean, pure.

Rais inquired with great interest into scenarios of opposition in other countries, of which I had some knowledge. In Chile, democratic leaders had spent a weekend at the beach in 1987 to select one among them, lest General Pinochet defeat divided critics in the referendum of 1988.[19] In Manila, "people power" rose up against Marcos's attempt to steal the snap election of 1986; Cory Aquino, widow of the murdered Ninoy Aquino, received the dextrous support of the United States government at a time of high crisis.[20]

Mas Amien smiled engagingly. "You should be my consultant on people power." That would be my last spontaneous smile from him. When we later met in crowded circumstances, his countenance was of a public man and his eyes were cool with calculation. But in this meeting he pressed to make clear, with a trace of embarrassed frustration, his efforts to get together with Megawati and Gus Dur. The three critics of Suharto with the largest national followings had not met. And it was not for lack of trying on the part of Amien Rais.[21]

Where Is the Wahyu?

Sarwono Kusumaatmadja, the former Golkar leader and cabinet minister, said of March's MPR meeting: "It's a perfectly coordinated catastrophe. Corruption, a succession dilemma, forest fires, air crashes, drought, Wahid's stroke—we got it all."[22] One could add, from the point of view of Western institutional inventory, legislative paralysis, economic nosedive, and poverty upsurge. But Sarwono's list is telling insofar as the popular imagination in Java still conjured with the *wahyu cakraningrat,* or mandate of heaven. Whether Suharto early believed or self-protectively assumed or theatrically pretended he had it doesn't matter. The awesome coincidence of natural disasters with human misfortunes would look to many Indonesians, Javanese especially, as celestially ordained. To hungry peasants, to riderless *becak* drivers, even to the keepers of oral tradition in the Solo River Valley who, three decades before, began to manufacture lineages to augment Suharto's legitimacy, it would appear as though the *wahyu* were being withdrawn from him.

Any well-trained businessman would have expected some kind of prepared succession. Suryo Bambang Sulisto had an MBA from the University of Wisconsin and had developed a miniconglomerate, including Lyrik Petroleum, by the time he was in his forties. He accepted an invitation in the early 1990s to attend a series of courses at Lemhanas, the National Defense Institute, where extremely few civilians were allowed among the military officers in attendance. After several weeks, Suryo could not hold back his natural question: what planning was in place regarding the future of corporations and *yayasans* currently under ownership or management by the president and his family? When his question finally sank in, one of the less stupefied generals said, "You're asking about what happens *after* Suharto? We can't even talk about what's going on *now!*" A general privately remarked to him, "If demonstrators number 5,000, we oppose them. If 500,000, we join them."[23]

Student demonstrations in 1998 swelled to great proportions on the symbolic New Order day, March 11. By late March they were clearly a national phenomenon. Gadjah Mada University in Yogya had been calm in

1966, so subdued that anti-Sukarno student activists in West Java sent them lipstick and powder as a rebuke.[24] Now Gadjah Mada put forward 25,000 demonstrators on the day Suharto was reelected, and the students persisted with their protests week after week. University wives set up soup kitchens to feed them and the poor suffering from the *krismon*—monetary crisis. Surabaya in East Java joined in; Lampung in South Sumatra; Ujung Pandung in South Sulawesi; Medan in North Sumatra; and Bali. Students were constrained by riot police formations, often backed by troops. But they longed for confrontation. They were a national movement, not closely coordinated but mutually inspirited by email and cell phone. They felt their potency.[25]

Insurgent consciousness caught on with artistic groups. A movement arose under the banner of Ruwatan Bumi 1998 (Earth Exorcism 1998). It resembled the "cultural fever" that accompanied the democracy movement in Beijing in the late 1980s. It carried an environmentalism corollary to its calls for political action, on the model of Eastern Central Europe at the same time, where at moments environmentalism led the movement, as in Slovakia's Eco-Glasnost.[26] Yet Ruwatan Bumi 1998 included special Javanese qualities of ritual cleansing and cultural purification. Between early April and early May there were at least 170 performances, Internet-linked, in major cities: music, dance, drama, video, pantomime, installation art, poetry, prayer, and *wayang* shadow puppetry. Can we really do the Chinese dragon dance? Dare we ridicule Suharto with a *wayang* story? Yes, said the eager artists; and yes, said the hungry audiences, a mix of peasants, merchants, and aristocrats. A group of prostitutes put on their own show in Yogya, humorously bemoaning the lack of business since the crisis began.[27]

Nothing seemed to arrest economic decline—not even the third IMF agreement within six months. That was the parlous state of affairs in late April when Amien Rais journeyed to Washington for a panel on religion held by USINDO (the United States-Indonesia Society). Retired ambassadors, active bureaucrats, journalists, and academic swimmers in think tanks, including myself, were in his audience as Mas Amien proceeded through reasonable remarks on religions to a description of Indonesia's descent from "Asian tiger to Asian beggar." People below the poverty line were down to one or two meals a day and unrest was rising. According to nature and the Qur'an, for every group there is a limit. Suharto cannot stop the clock.

I feared that much being said in Jakarta among key players was at cross purposes. So I asked, "Is there a genuine *basis* for dialogue between the students and ABRI?" Rais answered that he was happy with the students' challenge to the regime. Sooner or later they would electrify the whole society. If the army gave a green light, that would be the end. He himself, Amien said, had put the question to ABRI in March: "*Either* protect Suharto and his family or protect the nation." Their original answer was "We protect both." But just a week ago, he had been cheered by their change of answer: "We must protect the nation." And a new arithmetic: "1,000, we will crush; 10,000, we will be silent; 100 million, we will go with the people."[28] He had gone recently to seek guidance from General Wiranto, who, in what Amien felt was honest dialogue, had opened the conversation by saying, "Please give *me* some advice . . . "[29] A buzz ran around the room—the peculiar faintly impolite hum that professionals and expert amateurs can generate in the Cosmos Club. Heads turned toward one another. 1966 again? Students and army together, mediated by others? A sign that these really are the last days of the ancien regime?

Prabowo Subianto was not likely to think in terms of *wahyu cakraningrat*. Recently promoted to lieutenant general at the age of forty-six, he was now in command of Kostrad's 27,000 men, the strategic reserve and key Jakarta area garrison that his father-in-law, Suharto, had held in 1965. Earlier he had led Kopassus, ABRI's special forces command. Still earlier, he had spent several years in East Timor, the battle laboratory of ABRI. Prabowo's very name expressed a military-revolutionary heritage. His father, Sumitro Djojohadikusumo, had named the child after his own younger brother, a martyr hero of battle against the Dutch in Yogya, and had encouraged him to go to the military academy. Raised to such a calling, with such expecta tions, Prabowo looked for historical exemplars. He found a supreme model in Ataturk, who had driven the Greek and Armenian Christians from Tur key, unified it, and modernized its culture out of its Ottoman lassitude. As a military leader Ataturk had arguably achieved the most with the fewest re sources of any general in the twentieth century. Whoever was his model, Prabowo, in the judgment of some peers and observers, complicated his talent with his passion for military stratagems and his raw appetite for political power.

Prabowo's exceeding ambition, abundant charm, and fluent English was belied by his record of accident, error, anger, and cruelty.[30] Early in his career, training in Germany, he broke both legs in a parachute jump. In 1983, as a major, he married Suharto's daughter Titiek at Taman Mini-Indonesia audience hall before 3,000 dignitaries, in a three-hour "traditional Javanese wedding ceremony" (see Figure 46). The summoning of past ritual and legendary associations to assure the public of present order was a 'Harto-Tien command performance. Only *Tempo* magazine dared to comment that "the event, performed by the bride's family in accordance with Solonese ceremonial etiquette, appeared to be ordered with the exactness and precision of a commander of war."[31]

Fortified by the palace connection, both Prabowo and his brother Hashim Djojohadikusumo, a businessman with his own *pribumi* conglomerate, became messengers of the regime in shutting down journalistic and political critics. Hasyim tried to pressure Goenawan Mohamad to sell his banned *Tempo* to him. Prabowo, as lieutenant colonel, invited Gus Dur to his battalion headquarters in 1992 and warned him to stay out of politics and stick to religion. Later, he warned Cak Nur to resign from KIPP, the election-monitoring unit that Goenawan Mohamad had set up, which was denounced by the then armed forces commander Feisal Tanjung as "obviously unconstitutional."[32]

Prabowo, some said, became driven by a desire to "solve" the East Timor question and thus ensure his place in short-term history and his future position at the highest levels of power. But his methods in the field alienated his boss, General Benny Moerdani, armed forces commander at that time. "I sent Prabowo to East Timor to set up long-range patrols," he told Adam Schwarz. "He became obsessed with catching Xanana. He had gone out of control. I heard reports that Prabowo was beating patrol leaders when they came back empty-handed. I had no choice but to bring him back to Java." Prabowo went from protégé to subversive regarding Moerdani. Such daring endangered his relationship with Suharto.[33] Having Benny cast out, even having Xanana finally brought to Jakarta in manacles, did not resolve the resistance in East Timor.

Prabowo, by several private accounts, finally chose to go to his father-in-law, review the costs of continued hard-line repression, and propose instead autonomy for the twenty-seventh province. No luck. Suharto, adamantly opposed, intentionally deaf, heard no brief, gave no relief.[34] Relations between father- and son-in-law, already delicate, possibly began then to sour into mutual mistrust.

American military and diplomatic observers on site, pre-1998, credited Prabowo for vision in national affairs and for instances of cracking down on human rights offenders in East Timor. Watchers of human rights, however, saw him as far more responsible for offenses than for any attempt to clean them up. Independent-minded Indonesians looked at him askance: Sarwono in March 1998 privately called him a "nut case"; Amien Rais labeled him a "criminal."[35] An American colonel could not reconcile Prabowo's hard image with his "soft handshake." The problem was less one of flaccidity than of unpredictability. He could not trust such a limp hand in a military man, now a lieutenant general.[36]

Prabowo had by now not only his military confreres and allies but a strong network of radical Indonesian Muslim supporters. His brother Hashim was friendly on business travel with Hasan Turabi, the brilliant Islamist-Leninist responsible for the radical cast of domestic and foreign policy in Sudan of the 1990s. Hashim was giving money to help feed and outfit his brother's fighting units—to ensure their loyalty in an army short on resources everywhere and sometimes even short on rations. He was also, in 1997–98, his brother's mouthpiece and increasingly his intercessor with the press. Indonesians who remembered that their father, Sumitro, had been a diplomatist, foreign agent, and attempted coordinator of the rebellions against Sukarno in 1957, before returning to aid Suharto ten years later, were concerned what the brotherly grand design for the republic might be. *Wahyu* or no *wahyu,* a seizure of power appeared as a possibility.

Suharto, in his latest new government, had put Prabowo in charge of Kostrad, the strategic reserve, presumably ABRI's most effective large unit. He left his loyal former adjutant, Wiranto, as commander of the armed forces, while additionally giving him the portfolio of minister of defense. The military was thus balanced off between "family" and "cadre": a son-in-law whom Suharto did not fully trust and a professional soldier who did not trust Suharto's son-in-law.

As for the rest of the cabinet, balance was forgotten. It was crony and family to a bizarre extreme. The archetypes were Bob Hasan as minister of trade and industry and Suharto's daughter Tutut as minister for social welfare. Hasan, who headed a plywood cartel that was supposed to be broken up under the IMF reform package, made his initial statement a defense of monopolies. He was the first Chinese Indonesian in a Suharto cabinet, but his voice was for opportunism rather than equal opportunity. Tutut had apparently advised her father on all his cabinet appointments. It was thought that Suharto was grooming her as his successor. The Australian journalist David Jenkins summed it up nicely: "At a time when Indonesia faces Herculean challenges, it finds itself with what might be called a Caligulean cabinet."[37]

Internet and Cell Phone Resistance

Pius Lustrilanang is a modest, pleasant, intelligent man. Also courageous. He was thirty years old and the secretary of SIAGA (Indonesian Solidarity for Amien and Megawati) when, on February 4, 1998, he was kidnapped at a bus stop in Jakarta, blindfolded, driven outside the city, and placed in a cell, naked. Accumulating evidence persuaded him that his abductors were members of Kopassus, special forces. They tortured him and about ten others at their base in Cigantung. Electric shocks to the genitalia were mixed with threats and interrogations. "They wanted to know the constellation of the opposition, the alliances between different leaders." After two months he was released from detention, given an airplane ticket to his hometown, and told that if he ever spoke openly of his experiences he would be killed.

On April 24 he chose to testify before the National Human Rights Commission, one of the oases of courage in Suharto's desert of repression. He had a Dutch visa in his pocket. After he detailed his experiences in detention, friendly escorts took him to the airport and put him on a plane for the Netherlands. On May 7 he testified in Washington before the House Subcommittee on International Operations and Human Rights. Afterward, at a study group of the Council on Foreign Relations, he spoke of the need for "people power" in Indonesia. I observed that "people power" in the Philippines, where the phrase arose from the movement in 1986 against Marcos, had elements that Indonesia presently lacked: strong democratic tradition, a martyr (Ninoy Aquino), and an agreed-upon opposition leader (Corazon Aquino). Pius's gently smiling answer was, in essence, that Indonesia would manufacture its own mix.[38]

Months later, eleven members of Kopassus were arrested for alleged involvement in the kidnappings, and in August their former commander, Lieutenant General Prabowo, was "honorably discharged" by Wiranto from ABRI for the abduction and torture of political activists. It does not absolve Prabowo to observe that ABRI as an institution should also bear responsibility and that Wiranto, in consolidating his command, found in the charges a highly convenient way to remove his chief opponent.[39]

Indonesia's turbulence produced the first martyrs of the crisis just five days after Pius talked with us. Students at Trisakti University in Jakarta, affluent by Indonesian standards, gathered in the thousands on May 12 to demonstrate for an end to Suharto's regime. In the by-then common slogan—attributed to Christianto Wibisono, a middle-aged Chinese-Indonesian democrat and business analyst—they protested against KKN: *korupsi, kolusi, nepotisme*. The cognates for corruption and nepotism do not enter my Indonesian dictionaries until the 1970s; for collusion, not even in the 1980s. Obviously there were no satisfactory root words in Arabic, Sanskrit, Javanese, or proto-Malay. But Latin, Italian, Middle English, or Middle French roots will do in a pinch. Modern Indonesians needed the terms and used them with triumphant delight, as describing massive misdeeds that were undermining the society they wished to invent. I had heard a young priest employ them in a stirring sermon in St. Augustine Church in Yogya in March. Now Trisakti students and many others all over the archipelago were displaying them on placards held defiantly aloft.

That morning Suharto was out of the country, trying to manifest his confidence by attending a conference in Cairo. The protesters at Trisakti, encouraged by the soldiers' relative leniency thus far, had begun to push rallies beyond the campus gates, despite clear warnings from the military. They now planned to take their rally down the highway a few miles to the national parliament building. They assembled at 11 AM. A lengthy standoff ensued against two rows of riot police, backed by truckloads of reinforcements. The students sang, made speeches, sat on the pavement in protest, endured a heavy downpour of rain. Late in the afternoon, university administrators brokered a face-saving deal: students would retreat to campus and police would move back their line.

At that moment a Trisakti dropout, later suspected of being a paid informer and provocateur, began shouting obscenities at female demonstrators. Male students chased him toward police lines. Their running action ignited a police charge about 5 PM. Tear gas, batons, and rubber bullets rained down on the demonstrators. Then the cracking sounds of lead bullets. Two students were injured; four more were killed, all by shots to the head, neck, chest, or back at an angle of entry suggesting that the shots were directed from an overpass. Forensic experts said the bullets had come from Steyr rifles, issued only to a handful of special police units. Two police officers, a first and a second lieutenant of the anti-riot brigade, were charged with disobeying orders and not controlling their troops.

Suspicion turned to rogue elements—sharpshooters of Kopassus masquerading as police—and to the former commander of Kopassus, Lieutenant General Prabowo. He went to the home of one of the slain and before the father, a retired army second lieutenant, held a Qur'an above his head, performing a *sumpah,* or holy oath. He swore before God he did not order the Trisakti killings.[40]

A commemorative ceremony at the campus on the next morning, May 13, was the last of the persistently peaceful demonstrations that had gone on for two months. After many injuries of students in Solo on March 17 and violent clashes in Yogya on April 2–4, student protests had sustained an astonishing level of nonviolence in the interest of democracy and the new overriding slogan *reformasi.* They relied on cell phones and email, which allowed a loose and spontaneous national coalition of energies to arise, with no structure that the government could spotlight nor any strategic plan it could deflect.

Enthusiasts would call this the "first Internet revolution."[41] More accurately it would appear to be an Internet resistance, successful in achieving a transfer of power. Against the handful of computer experts in the Indonesian military, there were thousands on campuses whose ingenuity would prevail. In Jakarta, times and dates and meeting places were encrypted to prevent disinformative alteration by any possible military interception.

In 1986 in Manila the key rallying technology for citizens had been radio. By 1989, in Tiananmen Square, Chinese demonstrations had been organized by cell phones and world-publicized by faxes, before being crushed by the cold steel of tanks and lead bullets of soldiers. The high point of the fax machine was perhaps the 1992 uprising in Thailand, where students faced down soldiers so effectively that the king dissolved the military government in favor of civilian leadership. The Internet became prominent in the international meetings of the mid-1990s held to support the Zapatistas in Mexico. Likewise in Belgrade: when the government shut down independent media, "B-92," and other stations in 1996, dissidents against the Milosevic government resorted to the new capability of Real Audio and the kinds of Internet image resolution that far surpassed fax.[42] But there was insufficient outside response, and the Serb dissidents, after about sixty days, subsided.

What, in Indonesia, was different enough to accelerate a conclusion? Answer: nationwide riot. The students turned against the power structure by using the satellite communications that the government itself had advanced since the early 1970s to connect and control its archipelagic population. Maybe, if sustained across many more months, their palm-held weapons and Internet assault would have brought about the world's first electronic, hygienic, and irenic resolution of a government crisis. But that is to attribute more patience to youth, more forbearance to the hungry, and more rationality to the military than is natural. Suharto's rule would end in chaos.

Jakarta in Riot

On the morning of May 13, during and after the memorial service for slain students at Trisakti and speeches by many of the government's critics, a nonuniversity crowd gathered outside and began marching. Email no longer prevailed. Car smashing and mall-mayhem were the order of the day. The violence spread, as the rioters—mainly young urban poor—hit automobile showrooms, shops, and hotels, all symbols of a wealth they could not share; churches whose faith was alien; a hospital whose services they could not afford; any edifice proud-looking enough to attract their hunger for destruction.

From the university area in the Tomang district, a few miles westward and slightly north of Monas (the National Monument), rioting first flowed mostly westward to Tangerang, an industrial belt signifying cheap labor, quick investment return, and all the anger gathered into the term "urban proletariat." Then it leaked eastward toward the center of the city and headed toward Glodok, the Chinatown of old north Jakarta, with looting of electronics shops and other sources of goods. Businesses all over the city closed. Traffic scuttled toward the safety of garages. Toll-takers abandoned their booths. Cars were stopped and checked for Chinese occupants. An angry demonstration erupted on Jalan Sudirman, in the heart of the modern business district, giving special shivers to the elite. Four and five star hotels, several owned by the Cendana family and still enjoying significant foreign patronage, were troop-protected, as were the presidential palace and residence and key government buildings. Many wealthy Indonesians fled their homes for luxury hotels or airport hotels; others—particularly Chinese Indonesians—caught flights overseas. The American Embassy orchestrated a massive evacuation of all but key personnel and of all American citizens who chose to heed the official warning to leave the state.

Rioting went on through the night and spread on Thursday, May 14. It hit Bekasi, the East Jakarta industrial equivalent of Tangerang to the west. "Ordinary small shops nearby, *pribumi*-owned, were hit by roving mobs. It was very scary," Dewi Fortuna Anwar remembered. "Menfolks in our neighborhood slept outside the house; my house, my husband included."[43] The violence streamed northward to Tanjung Priok and the harbor and even trickled southward into modern suburban areas.

It was mall time now all over the city. Not just televisions and computers but banks, automatic teller machines, and other money targets were hit. Large malls, menageries of consumerism, with their big shiny durables and their little gee-gaws and everything one always wanted but couldn't have, were looted and sometimes torched. The results were disastrous for the greedy or careless who got trapped inside; from Yogya Plaza in East Jakarta, recovery workers eventually turned up 174 charred bodies.[44]

Ginandjar Kartasasmita, coordinating minister for finance and economy, put out a count of 2,479 shop-houses (Chinese family retail businesses) damaged or destroyed; 1,026 ordinary houses, 1,604 shops, 383 private offices, 65 bank offices, 45 workshops, 24 restaurants, 12 hotels, 40 shopping malls. Plus 1,119 cars and 821 motorcycles. A serious body count had been quickly initiated by Karlina Leksono and her Tim Relawan Kemanusiaan (Volunteer Team for Humanity) to counter army and police minimizations. In addition to summoning paramedics for help whenever possible, she organized and dispatched citizens with cameras to hospitals and morgues all over the city. They came back with 1,193 separate photographs of corpses.[45]

It was, by any measure, the worst riot in Indonesian history. In its anarchy it resembled the so-called *bersiap* (watch-out) period, the months after the Japanese surrendered in 1945 and before the Dutch returned. But now there was more to lose. And much more *was* lost. The horror dawned slowly on global newspaper readers at breakfast tables, on TV watchers home after a day's work. Not until June did the rape stories appear. Partly because victims were too traumatized to talk about them; partly because rape brought lasting shame upon its victims. But the Kalyanamitra, an NGO devoted to helping women and led by chairwoman Ita Nadia, was allied in this cause with the Volunteer Team for Humanity and the Jesuit Romo Sandyawan. They helped assaulted women who came for help or to whom they were directed. Incidental to medical assistance, understanding, and comfort, they gathered data. They originally claimed 168 rapes, one-third of the count of total assaults on women reported by human rights activists. An official fact-finding team later confirmed 52 rapes, without denying higher possibilities. But the government ignored and tried to suppress the implication of even that lowered count.[46]

Pretending that rapes had not happened was not only obtuse but obscene. The *Jakarta Post* opened the subject up. A group of men had stopped a city bus and forced out all non-Chinese women; inside the bus, the men raped those among the Chinese women they considered beautiful. In another instance, arsonists broke into the lower floors of an apartment building and set fire to it. They ran upstairs and found three sisters hiding. They pushed the oldest into a corner, saying "We don't want you because you're too old and ugly," and raped the other two in front of her. Then they pushed the two younger sisters into the fire, where they burned to death. The mother, when she heard the news, died of a heart attack. The survivor went to a psychiatric hospital.[47]

Gus Dur, who had spoken early in defense of and sympathy for Chinese Indonesians, spoke again on behalf of women and against those who violated them. Anonymous phone calls told him to shut up or his daughters would be next. Gus Dur did not shut up. He was accustomed to threats.[48]

Soedjati Djiwandono, elder brother of the dismissed governor of the Central Bank, distinguished newspaper columnist, and Catholic lay leader, was sickened at heart by these discoveries. He began to review what *keIndonesiaan*—Indonesianess—meant to him. It could not mean, it must not mean, he told me, what he was made to feel when he visited San Francisco—that Indonesians are rapists of Chinese women.[49]

On the first day of rioting, May 13, between 4 and 5 PM, Wiranto ordered the Jakarta military commander, Major General Syafrie Syamsuddin, an ally of Prabowo, to send troops to control the violence. But according to a high-ranking military officer, Syafrie shuffled troops rather than effectively deploying them, and Wiranto was displeased with his response. Prabowo urged Wiranto to allow him to bring his special reserve units from outside the capital into the city. Wiranto refused. Instead, he phoned his commander in Central Java to send troops to Jakarta. That journey, he knew, would take at least a full day. Indonesia's key commanders, it appeared, were concentrating personally loyal forces rather than trying to control rioters.

In the week previous, hundreds of young men trained by Kopassus—under Prabowo's command from 1995 until February 1998—had been flown from Dili to Yogya in chartered planes and then to Jakarta by train. And just after dawn on the 14th, Kopassus troops escorted young thugs from Lampung in south Sumatra into the capital.[50] If these accounts are correct, Prabowo, through his allies and recent command, had imported minions to create more trouble even if Wiranto did not give Prabowo's present command, Kostrad, permission to put down the existing trouble. His motivation may puzzle a Westerner who is unaware that classic Javanese tactics include stirring chaos to discredit a rival or to seize power.[51]

With Jakarta in fiery, blood uproar, Wiranto nevertheless left the city to go to Malang for an "installation," taking commanders of battle-ready troops near Jakarta, including Prabowo, with him. He was apparently spurred by word from the commander of the Brawijaya division in East Java that he had a request from Prabowo to move his troops to Jakarta.[52] Prabowo, having made this request without Wiranto's knowledge, motivated his superior to fly across Java to countermand this insubordination and to keep eye and ear not only upon Prabowo but upon other commanders who might use their cell phones to give other unwelcome orders. Meanwhile, Wiranto summoned to Jakarta troops loyal to himself from Central Java. That strengthened his own presumptive power in the capital, while leaving the hometown of Amien Rais ungarrisoned. It exploded in severe riots. Wiranto felt confident in leaving his commander for social and political affairs in Jakarta. General Bambang Yudhoyono was discussing with civic leaders plans to ask Suharto to resign.[53]

Jakarta burned, partly as a consequence of Prabowo's attempt to enhance his power there and Wiranto's refusal to let that happen. As commander, he was unwilling to leave Jakarta in the hands of Kostrad and Kopassus, "assisted" by thugs and irregulars from east and west, let alone have Prabowo units enhanced by Brawijaya. The capital raged, during inaction of the regular Jakarta division under the command of a Prabowo ally and while its police were given confusing and restraining orders. A community military liaison, in regular communication with the local military command post for two days, was told, "If you are stoned by the rioters, respond with a smile. I order you only to smile, that is all."[54]

Let Jakarta burn; order the military, the police, the paramilitary, the semipro security to smile. The alternative to self-preserving poise, to motionless observation of a spasm of civil suicide, Wiranto may have thought, was an attempted intramilitary power coup by Prabowo, even escalating to a civil war on key parts of the Java land mass to determine whose guns control Indonesia. Meanwhile, through General Yudhoyono, who had international experience and the confidence of civilians, prepare an atmosphere of exit for Commander-in-Chief Suharto when he returned from Cairo.

I still find it hard to accept this military freeze-up as an explanation for the deaths of nearly 1,200 civilians and the rapes of scores of women in a capital city containing many tens of thousands of troops, with more standing by immediately outside. I later had an opportunity to inquire of Lieutenant General Yudhoyono himself how this could happen. Yudhoyono, who had trained in the United States and served in Bosnia, was accompanied by two major generals. On the question of instigation by Prabowo, their answer was firm: "Tidak ada bukti [There is no evidence]." And that answer, hauntingly, was repeated as far away as Medan, where a civil rights lawyer, active in ethnic reconciliation, commented on the similarities to Jakarta in the method of initiating riots that he observed in Medan: dark-clad men in trucks arrive, incite, move on, repeat. But who provoked the provocateurs? "Tidak ada bukti." There is no evidence.[55] On the matter of paralysis because of internal conflict between Prabowo and Wiranto, my army interlocutors were discreetly uncommunicative. The removal of Prabowo from active service would have to continue to speak for itself. On his discussions with civilians, Yudhoyono would only say that Muslim leaders, university rectors, and others were involved.[56]

I returned to the question of chaos and carnage in a capital city, as a matter of professional performance. Why were no troops or tanks in evidence for two whole days? All three generals broke readily into speech here. On the size of Jakarta; on its massive underclass; on its capacity to overwhelm troops by sheer numbers; on the volatile flow of unrest, unpredictable and uncontrollable, from sector to sector of the city; on the wisdom of husbanding force until the fury died down; on the principled aversion of the army to shooting civilians. I heard all this as uttered in sincerity and as spilled out in troubled profusion. I accepted it as their defensive rationale. But when the generals specifically referred to police in Los Angeles likewise keeping off the streets until the worst of the riots was over, I thought that was not a good model of police or army behavior.[57]

The answers of the three generals, sincere and friendly men, completed my convictions. On May 13–15, 1998, the Indonesian army and police had demonstrated a paralysis of will at the top as a result of contention for power. Also revealed were severe deficiencies of communication through the chain of command, want of clarity and confidence in mission, and lack of competence in crisis. Why? An American military expert offered in retrospect a laconic summary: "Yeah, they were protecting their asses."[58]

Much of what we can credibly think about the May 1998 violence in Jakarta and elsewhere is owed to the appointment, by the Habibie government that July, of a Joint Fact-Finding Team (TGPF, *Tim Gabuan Pencari Fakta*). Although its membership was conflicted and its schedule overpressed, it represented a valuable breakthrough in Indonesian public procedures—an effort at objective assessment of a violent trauma relatively soon after its occurrence. Serious deficiencies of the report arose from its tolerance of vague testimony from military leaders Prabowo Subianto and Syafrie Syamsuddin, from Zacky Anwar Makarim, commander of ABRI intelligence, and from Sutiyoso, governor of Jakarta. A crippling omission was TGPF's failure even to include ABRI commander-in-chief Wiranto on its list of interviewees. These men, closely questioned, might have had to give up knowledge about the elite and the street—about manipulation of gangs of thugs and even military out of uniform by the highest levels of power. Or they might have lied. They were not merely "protecting their asses." They were maneuvering for power. TGPF remains an important precedent in Indonesian history. But its limitations are evident in that Wiranto, Makarim, and Syafrie, uncorrected, would proceed to lay secret plans for East Timor. These would result in another thousand deaths less than a year after the final "fact-finding" report was issued on the violence of May 1998.[59]

On May 15 at 10 PM, a general called Sofyan Wanandi and warned him, as Sofyan recalls it: "You're on Prabowo's hit list." He took a plane to Singapore. Five months later, he was still distraught that 60 percent of Indonesia's entire military force had been in Jakarta, but against the rioting they had used no stun guns, no water cannon, no tear gas, no motorcycles, nothing. And now Prabowo, self-exiled in Jordan, was out of reach of further inquiry. The military, he said, all of them, were too much in debt to Suharto to push investigations in which Prabowo might say too much and further undermine the military in a time of crisis. I protested that to cut off inquiry was terrible. It was vital to get at the truth. Sofyan looked at me as at an educable naif, with a pitying smile: "This is *Indonesia*."[60]

Sofyan's brother, Jusuf Wanandi, was moved by the May riots to summarize three decades of privileged observation of Prabowo's father-in-law, President Suharto: he was not interested in bringing the Chinese Indonesians into politics, the civil service, or public life. He treated them like concubines to be enjoyed but not recognized.[61]

Glodok, Jakarta's Chinatown, is in the north of the city, the center of an area of about four square miles containing between 2 and 3 million people, a packed part of an urban agglomeration of over 10 million. Budi Lim knows it intimately, having grown up there as the son of an immigrant who became a textile merchant. Budi internalized the romance and beauty and history of the city in his heart, became an architect, aimed to make Jakarta again what old Batavia was once called, "the pearl of the Orient." He had built his firm up to dozens of architects; their practice included scores of projects. He dreamed and planned to make a long stretch of the city's aorta, Jalan Thamrin, as walkable as Copenhagen. The financial crisis forced him to cut his office to the barest core. Now the riots were an ugly reminder of the enduring under-belly of the city's history. "I don't talk politics. I'm Chinese." Budi, normally gentle and measured in expression, said it curtly.

But he generously offered to walk me around Glodok. Two weeks after the riots, he said, "the smell was still there . . . but not like overcooked hamburger, you know? Like *dead* meat. Not a nice flavor."[62] The large white City Hotel stood in reminder, not a high-rise seared by one sky-seeking rim of flame but a largely horizontal structure whose black scars offered evidence of many fires ignited at the same time. The electronics distribution area was completely, savagely hit, knocking Jakarta business off its feet as well, leaving "broken men" and exiles. Across Indonesia, tens of thousands of Chinese exiles? In one estimate, 150,000.

The scene began with "instigators" coming in convoys, with chanting groups. They stripped tires off cars and began burning them. Others on motorcycles went into nearby *kampung* areas crying "free food, free TV, electronics!" People came. One Chinese saved his store by phoning the police. He had been steady in his protection payments, but now he added an extra $25,000. The buildings on either side of him, I saw, were sacked.

All kinds of targets were hit, including a mortuary—empty now, cleaned up, looking vaguely like a small indoor parking lot. A custom among Chinese who are non-Christians is to put small pearls in the eyes and nostrils and under the tongue of the dead. For that loot, three bodies in the mortuary had been stripped and robbed, including a niece of Budi's friend, just twenty years old. The corpses were then hanged naked and burned with the building.

From what could one take heart? In one area *pribumi* street stalls were mixed with Chinese. The *pribumi* set up barricades and used themselves to stop the flow of vandalism and save the stands of both groups of vendors. Two kilometers away, a relative of Budi's had led a Chinese community in arming itself with big kitchen cleavers, small knives, even lightning rods off the roofs. Wearing motorcycle helmets for defense, they withstood up to six hours of stoning and threw the stones back.

Budi's major project was restoration of the National Archives building, an eighteenth-century Dutch plantation and government house with grounds extending to the river. High ceilinged, with beautifully proportioned assembly and dining rooms—and tight slave quarters—its wood was rotting and plaster was flaking when Budi took on the project of transforming it into a multipurpose museum and cultural center; his team provided supportive architectural and archaeological studies. The site bordered a major asphalt artery along which came rioting marchers in May. Budi's craftsmen and laborers protected their work by arranging themselves as a polite human shield at the gates. The mob flowed madly by.[63]

Budi finished the project with a Dutch foundation grant whose value was suddenly enhanced by the appreciation of the guilden over the rupiah. The restored Arsip Negara opened in November, rebuilt, relit, beckoning, a thing of beauty in special bright white "breathing" plaster, with new beams and doors and repavilioned with new pillars and girders, all painted in soft gilt and rich oxblood. Danger made Budi move his young family to Singapore for safety, and his business shifted toward building residences in Bali. But the son of the immigrant Lim could at least bequeath one triumph to the beloved city of his birth and hope.

To a *pribumi* and *pegawai negeri,* the riots were deeply disturbing in other ways. Dewi Fortuna Anwar, Minangkabau par excellence, had just finished three months of advanced training in state service—using, among other things, Al Gore's ten principles of reinventing government. She was a leader of a major think-tank study on the military, and at the time of riot she was serving Vice President Habibie as special assistant for foreign affairs.[64] On the night of May 13 at 9 PM she could not get a military escort home and was told by a soldier she was better off *without* a military escort. She saw the rioting as "well-mapped and instigated," whipped up not only by men on trucks and motorcycling agitators but by scenes on television itself. The looters were local. Bank Niaga, owned by *pribumi,* was left alone. Chinese-Indonesian banks were hit hard. Standard Chartered Bank, not alone among international banks and other concerns, paid many millions of rupiah per day to have tanks parked in front of their edifice. "As seen by the military," Dewi commented, "another business opportunity."

She reinforced the LIPI study already published about military dual function: "Dwifungsi is not working . . . When you need green they're not to be seen. And they appear when you don't need them." What Indonesia requires, she said, is more and better-trained police who are not subordinate to the military and who will not "fall back" in a crisis because they do not feel that it is their responsibility. And Indonesia should have separate and highly mobile military units. They should not be trained in riot control but trained instead against military insurgence. We cannot have real democracy

67. ARSON IN OLD JAKARTA. The riots of mid-May 1998 hit hardest in
Glodok (Chinatown). (Budi Lim/author's collection)

in the future, she added, without a civil bureaucracy: bureaucrats who really run things, indifferent to politics, subordinate to the policy determined
by whatever government was in power. In Thailand, the bureaucracy functions, as does the legal system—not just the king.[65]

Some Indonesian observers evoked terms like "state-sponsored terrorism" and "ethnic cleansing" to describe actions against Chinese Indonesians
allegedly initiated by Prabowo and his radical Muslim supporters. But these
terms appear to me to be too rational, control-focused, and incongruously
borrowed to describe the Jakarta madness.

Central to another theory is a meeting on the afternoon of May 14 among senior generals and influential civilians, allegedly to revive Kopkamtib, the security apparatus invented in October 1965 against the communists, and to grant its emergency powers to Prabowo.[66] This explanation seems to me too suppositious to be compelling. Linking abductions, Trisakti killings, and riots in one grandly engineered emergency, these theorists attribute more Satanic imagination and power to one man than my understanding of the shrewd, hungry, but fallible Prabowo can contain.

Still other conspiracy theorists, seeing similarities in the rioting of Jakarta, Medan, Solo, and elsewhere, looked for a single mastermind: Suharto initiating them in order to invoke the special powers he had recently extracted from the MPR; or Prabowo initiating them to discredit Wiranto and advance himself.[67] But a mega-mess has more explanatory power than a mastermind. The study group chaired by Loetman Soetrisno much earlier

68. RESTORATION IN OLD JAKARTA. At the same time that Chinatown burned, the National Archives building nearby, originally a seventeenth-century Dutch plantation, was undergoing restoration for use as a cultural center. Workers on the site quietly ranged themselves at the gate, with tools for defense, as rioters marched past. (Budi Lim, architect/author's collection)

had shown deterioration of urban social and economic conditions, politicization of ethnic and religious differences, and opportunism by thugs and gangs, as well as occasions of "instigation" either by rogue military or elements of ABRI behaving like mafia in gang wars. A central national conspiracy was not in play. National confusion was taking the form of deadly disorder.

Yes, there were too few soldiers for too many cities in eruption. And yes, one of the standard, although deplorable, options of the Indonesian military in the face of crowd violence was "let it burn." The actions and inactions of Wiranto and Prabowo on the critical days, however, suggest that a "tired military" was not an important factor compared with paralysis of leadership at its apex. How many soldiers died for Pak 'Harto's vision of Indonesia? Nearly none. Nor would they, as long as Wiranto saw a prolonged crisis as strengthening ABRI over the president and Prabowo sought an opportunity to tilt history or his father-in-law in his favor.[68]

Net: anti-Chinese sentiment was an historical given; civilian frustration with Suharto's repressive government had grown across three decades; sudden deprivations had been deepening across the previous ten months; and internal warfare had classic Javanese precedents in which two competing commands, jurisdictions, or individuals let a matter be decided, whatever the cost in native lives, by bloody local contest. The struggle between Wiranto and Prabowo, intensified by Suharto's brief absence, was such a contest, in which ordinary people were treated as dispensable.

The contest could be changed, and take on a deeper shape, only when the ruler came home to calm his subjects. By now, however, the dictator had to face a populace both exhausted by riot and aroused to ask the meaning of their lives. From his conference in Cairo, President Suharto landed at Halim air force base at 4:40 AM on May 15. One hundred armored vehicles escorted him to Cendana, his home in central Jakarta.[69] Only then, at last, did tanks and battalions manifest themselves collectively in the city center, as firemen continued to extinguish blazes and families looked for missing loved ones.

Pressures for Succession

The residence of the speaker of the DPR and MPR, Harmoko, had been burned, as had Suharto's own house in Solo, Central Java. The home of the billionaire Liem Sioe Liong was ransacked, the outer walls painted "Anjing 'Harto" ("Suharto's dog"); his art collection was piled in the street and torched.[70] These castle-compounds were among thousands of destroyed houses and shop-houses. But whatever was happening was not over. A slower, collective emotion was still unfulfilled.

"There is no national explanation for the fact that at certain moments, one million people can gather in a square, spontaneously, without having been called there. Why? It is a metaphysical phenomenon," wrote Ryszard Kapuscinski, a journalist who had seen it happen in several countries. "Societies are heavy bodies. They are enormously patient. They are stable and can wait. Societies tend to conserve their status quo without revealing any desire for change. They move slowly and with great difficulty. Only after a long period of accepting suffering and humiliation does the decisive, highly irrational moment arrive when this society says: 'Enough! We cannot wait anymore. Not one day. Not one hour.' This is the overwhelming sensation of the moment of revolt."[71]

Suharto continued to behave as if he had endless days. He canceled the fuel price increases announced at the beginning of the month. After meeting with him, Hartono, former army commander and now minister for home affairs, told the press, "I have warned you all that behind this was the Communist Party's remnants."[72] But no Marxist voice or figure could be heard in the din or seen in the haze.

Amien Rais was working with student groups and his own Muhammadiyah to sustain street protests and the clamor for Suharto's resignation. For National Awakening Day, Wednesday, May 20, he pledged to bring a million people onto the streets of Jakarta, where the destination would be the National Monument, near the presidential palace and government buildings. Kapuscinski's theoretical million were there, somewhere; but in Indonesia they would not magically appear. Someone needed to summon them, at some place, at some time. Gus Dur was still recovering from his stroke. Megawati had spoken with others at the Trisakti funeral service but was otherwise not evident in the citywide blur of plots, petitions, phone conferences, television appearances. Mega had timidly considered "millions in the streets," and Gus had threatened them in recent years; but now, in the crunch, no such words escaped the lips of either leader. Rais was the one to utter the words. Tension built.

Nurcholish Madjid, meanwhile, had been meeting with generals since March, notably Bambang Yudhoyono, about his plan for a peaceful, graceful resignation process. Suharto, he said, must admit mistakes, apologize for economic crisis, create a social safety net, relinquish gains from "wrong policies," and give up power after new elections in January 2000. The secret conversations led to an invitation for Cak Nur and like thinkers to come to ABRI's campus at Cilangkap, south of Jakarta, where, to their surprise, a lecture hall was filled with attentive generals. Cak Nur gave voice to his plan and sensed collective relief among the generals, assent. Then, from one officer, the frustrated cry: "But who is going to *tell* him?!?"[73]

Now Cak Nur felt free to publicize the plan. The press gave the idea fa-

69. PROTESTERS ATOP PARLIAMENT. Demonstrators were also inside Indonesia's halls of legislation. Student penetration of the grounds on May 18, 1998, shown here, could not have occurred without the tacit consent of General Wiranto. After Suharto's resignation at 9 AM ON May 21, many would stay to protest Habibie, and militant Muslims would arrive as counter-demonstrators. On the evening of May 22, marines would easily escort both groups away. (Rully Uesuma/ Tempo)

vorable coverage but found its election schedule too far away, while most generals still thought it too pressing. Suharto's press secretary nonetheless found it of high interest and asked Madjid to come see him. He arrived on May 18, accompanied by a businessman, Fahmi Idris. Into their meeting, as a surprise, walked Lieutenant General Prabowo.

Prabowo: You're crazy to demand that the First Family return their wealth, because they don't have any.
Cak Nur: Is that so?
Prabowo: You should suggest to Suharto that he make Habibie president.
Cak Nur: The problem is that the military doesn't support Habibie.

Prabowo: Don't worry about that. I will protect Habibie. Why don't you ask Suharto to make me armed forces commander so that I will have more power to protect Habibie?
Fahmi Idris: Why don't you just ask Suharto yourself?
Prabowo: Because Suharto doesn't like me.

Whereupon Prabowo left.[74] A meeting of Cak Nur and others with Suharto himself ensued that night. The president promised an announcement the next day that he would resign, but he did not specify an effective date. He asked to meet leaders of the Muslim community at once. Nine were chosen. Cak Nur tried to include Amien Rais as vital to the changes afoot, but Suharto refused him, probably as too frontally critical and "street-threatening." Cak Nur tried to spare Gus Dur because of his delicate health, but Suharto insisted on getting him there, presumably because he wanted the broadest possible band of Muslim support and because Wahid had recently befriended his daughter Tutut.[75]

When the meeting came, Wahid's behavior, on others' accounts, struck Rais as "sycophantic." Gus Dur's public appeal for the students to get off the streets in order to give Suharto a chance to make good on his promises angered Rais, who saw this as a slowing of hard-won momentum. Accounts of the meeting also infuriated Habibie, when they reached him; Suharto had been dismissive of his capacities as a potential successor. Habibie then confronted the president, presenting himself as Suharto's best chance for a dignified retirement.[76]

If Suharto were attempting to drape a protective Muslim cloak about himself, other layers of his imperial raiment were falling away fast. Speaker Harmoko, previously the obsequious reassurer of his president's popular support, astounded journalists at a press conference on Monday the 18th when he called for Suharto's resignation. Harmoko had delivered the election goods for Golkar in 1997 but was then dumped as information minister and passed over for the vice presidency. Student protesters were sauntering through his parliament halls. His residence was still smoking. The fire of his loyalty had gone out. He gave Suharto until Friday to step down or face hearings on impeachment.

The armed forces inserted themselves. General Wiranto said that Harmoko's was only an "opinion" and of questionable constitutionality at that. Wiranto, as former personal adjutant to Suharto, maintained an apparent loyalty to him. He was unwilling to see street mood depose him or mob rule replace him, which could only threaten the already discredited army.[77] Loyalty to ABRI was by now probably paramount in his mind, along with loyalty to the future of its commanding officer, himself.

Students had begun entering the parliament grounds on Monday the 18th. They camped there and grew in numbers. They chatted with patrols from the marines, the branch of the armed forces long considered most understanding of the demonstrators, and, if not sympathetic, at least not implicated in killings. The Wiranto wing of ABRI was stressing that they did not want a Tienanmen massacre in Jakarta.[78] The Prabowo wing, through Prabowo's ally, the chief of staff of Kostrad, warned Amien Rais that the military was not afraid of "another Tienanmen" and a "sea of blood" if his rally of a million went ahead.[79] I phoned Jakarta on the night (there) of May 19 and talked with Suryo Sulisto. I said I would pray for Indonesia. Suryo, in a dozen years of friendship, had always been a calm, smiling, secular entrepreneur, Javanese in demeanor. But that night he was a Muslim. He said he was praying, too.

Early on the morning of May 20, Mas Amien went on the radio and called off the rally, a decision supported by Cak Nur on television.[80] Rais would have had his million men, but they would have faced barbed-wire barricades on major arteries, tanks and armored personnel carriers protecting key locations, and tense troops, whose orders were unknown but whose posture was resistant and their behavior unpredictable. A leader is known by his restraint as well as his forceful initiative. Amien Rais, in this instance, proved himself capable of statesmanship.

The students, as the core of "people power," never achieved the primacy of the marchers chanting "Wir sind das Volk" in Leipzig and Dresden in 1989, who brought down Honnecker's East German communist regime. Nor, with Habibie in the presidency for months to come, could "people power" be said to have done in Jakarta what it did in Manila in 1986: replace Marcos with a democratic Cory Aquino.[81] The youthful populists and their semi-establishment advocate, Amien Rais, however, were a major part of the seachange in Indonesia.

The mills of the gods were slowly grinding, and Suharto would eventually be ground down. Yusril Mahendra, Muslim activist and speechwriter for Suharto, with Cabinet Secretary Mursjid, had assembled a list of forty-five candidates for the reform committee with which Suharto had agreed to work. Yusril would serve as secretary. But they couldn't reach many of them, and others refused. Cak Nur himself declined repeated calls and emissaries. "In that case," Suharto said, "if such a fellow as Nurcholish Madjid won't help, then I can't do this job anymore."[82]

At about 11 PM on Wednesday, May 20, Cabinet Secretary Mursjid delivered to Suharto a letter drafted earlier that day by Ginandjar Kartasasmita, his long-time protégé, a nationalist close to *pribumi* businessmen, a Golkar eminence, and coordinating minister of the economy. Thirteen fellow min-

70. INAUGURATION OF HABIBIE. Indonesia's third president, B. J. Habibie, is sworn in. His predecessor looks on, concluding thirty-one years in office. (Courtesy of the Habibie Center)

isters joined him in signing and in asserting that they would not enter a new cabinet. Ginandjar had, on the side, agreed with Habibie on his taking over the presidency. Wiranto had, among many meetings, likewise apparently had concluded that Habibie, even if undesirable, was "constitutional." Without ever using the word "resignation," he probably voiced his concern to the president over keeping the city secure much longer without such a change.[83]

The legislators had quit Suharto. Most of the key cabinet had seceded from him. He was unable to wrap a reform council around himself. Students and other protesters inhabited the parliament and were camping on its roof. The army had used one big mobilization in Central Jakarta to give him time to think but was unwilling to go further. Suharto decided to resign and let Habibie succeed him—to rid himself, as he had earlier said to

Demonstrators of November 1998

A new parliament session brings renewed protests against President Habibie, General Wiranto, and ex-President Suharto. On its last day, November 13, "Black Friday," at least fifteen persons are killed by live bullets and hundreds are injured. During the days of action, some counter-demonstrators are also killed. Numerous soldiers, police, and others are also injured.

71. STUDENTS GATHER TO PROTEST. (Gift of Yenny Wahid/author's collection)

72. DEMONSTRATORS HUDDLE AGAINST TEAR GAS. (Gift of Yenny Wahid/ author's collection)

73. PAM SWAKARSA COUNTER-DEMONSTRATORS. "Volunteers" called Pam Swakarsa carry sharpened bamboo staves and other weapons to "defend the MPR." Most, but not all, are members of militant Muslim groups. Paid a dollar a day during the legislative session by Wiranto's army, these counter-demonstrators signify the army's use of the underclass to defend the regime against the middle class. (Gift of Yenny Wahid/author's collection)

Cak Nur, of this presidency, so that "this curse of a skin rash and itching will end."[84] He still did not realize, maybe he never would, how many and how deeply Indonesians itched to have him gone.

Madeleine Albright had used a graduation ceremony at the United States Coast Guard Academy to urge Suharto to "seize an historical opportunity." He probably never heard her and wouldn't have cared. Her real audience was American and domestic—a select group of congressional liberals. Suharto, as Donald Emmerson observed, like Sukarno before him in 1965, "had overestimated his indispensability within a field of forces grown fatally unstable."[85] The IMF as the voice of international bankers, the students as the pulse of middle-class and national conscience, the mob as the raised fist of the suppressed, his own collaborators as greedy-handed opportunists: all opposed him. To avoid Sukarno's fate, Suharto resigned his presidency to Habibie in a short, stiff ceremony at 9 AM on May 21. Then he was chauffeured a brief ride home to his well-guarded personal residence in Cendana.

This would have been the end of an era in Indonesia were there indigenous traditions that losers retire quietly and that a loyal opposition is vital to constitutional strength. But such traditions will be long in nurturing. Suharto soon said to family and friends that he would take aggressive revenge on those who had brought him down. Did he mean Ginandjar and the cabinet that deserted him? Or Wiranto and the ABRI generals who subtly undermined him toward the end? No. Almost certainly he meant the reformers who had longest dared to oppose him and had somehow won: the improbable clown Wahid and the unbudgeable matron Mega. On them and their kind he would demonstrate *tiwikrama:* the power to transform himself into a huge giant.[86] Suharto's choice of Javanese vocabulary for his feelings promised Indonesia something very different from an era of *reformasi.* It projected a classic *wayang* war of vengeance. Having ruled for two decades with Pancasila as ideology and for most of another decade as a reborn Muslim, he must now retreat behind the scenes. There, in a psychic and political realm always basic to him, Suharto would aim to reign through a Javanistic mytho-chaos of money, guns, and momentous hidden influence.

STROKE

Of the three East Asian nations aided by the IMF during the end-of-century financial crisis, two had helped themselves by swiftly changing governments. In 1998 South Korea and Thailand were on the way back. But Indonesia's GDP would drop almost 14 percent that year—a gouge that suggests problems of opacity, oppression, and institutional vacuum deeper than economic policy could fix.

Habibie, whose designation as vice president had driven the rupiah to its all-time low, was inaugurated president on May 21. That afternoon Lieutenant General Prabowo jumped the chain of command to demand of Habibie that he be put in charge of the army. Instead, Habibie and Wiranto, now in league, demoted Prabowo and the next morning announced Wiranto's promotion as both minister of defense and armed forces commander. Prabowo, in furious disbelief, arrived at the palace packing a sidearm and accompanied by trucks of Kostrad troopers. Denied entry to Habibie's office, he visited Suharto and got only rebuke.[1] Later, after an ABRI investigation, he acknowledged responsibility for abducting activists in Jakarta (several of whom are still "missing") and was removed from active service. He exiled himself for two years to Jordan, whose new young King Abdullah he had known as a fellow commander of special forces.

Habibie, out of scientific realism and a quirky populism, befriended democracy and reform in an attempt to win a new presidential election. With only seventeen months to establish his record, he had no choice but to try to deal with the forces of globalization that had helped destroy the power of Om 'Harto, his "uncle" and patron. These "faceless ghosts" of market forces—to use the words of Goh Chok Tong, the harassed prime minister of Singapore—sat down with him now, wearing the business suits of the IMF.[2]

Five Hundred Years of Globalization

A five-syllable word that means different things to every user asks to be clarified. It surely means an immense change in the proportion of things, peoples, and ideas crossing borders, in relation to those remaining stationary, to epitomize Anthony Appiah's essay on the matter. And, clearly, the acceleration of science and the "active embrace of financial and entrepreneurial risk" are at the heart of the matter, as Anthony Giddens suggests.[3]

It may also help to insist that Western-led globalization has been accelerating since its breakthroughs over five centuries ago. When Zheng He led giant Ming armadas all the way through the Indian Ocean to Africa in the early fifteenth century, he brought back "auspicious giraffes" to the Ming court. But a satisfied appetite for tribute and Confucian disdain for commerce ended such Chinese impulses of exploration in 1430. Did part of Zhang He's fleet actually reach the Caribbean in 1421, as recently imposed on cartographic evidence? If that were proven by marine archealogy, it would only emphasize the point of Confucian indifference to enormous maritime prowess.

Commanding much smaller ships and flotillas as the fifteenth century gave way to the next, European navigators rounded Africa, passed India, and reached China, where the Chinese had long-since forgotten the adventures of Zheng He. Not only were Westerners outflanking Chinese seapower, which had earlier been their superior, they were in the same era beginning to outpace Islamic science, which they had previously trailed. As critical dates in Western schoolbooks suggest—1452, 1453, 1492, 1498—several compacted forces were bursting forth. Gutenberg's printing press allowed a rapid growth of popular learning and exchange of Western scientific progress. The fall of Constantinople to the Ottoman Empire forced Europeans to abandon overland trade routes in favor of sea routes to the East. Cristoforo Colombo was looking for the East Indies when he bumped into North America. Vasco da Gama, sailing around Africa's southern tip, actually reached India and was followed by successors through the Straits of Malacca into Chinese tributary territory and the archipelagoes to the east. The mandala state of Majapahit was by then dead or dying. At its very strongest, it could not have withstood the concentrated forces of Western commercial appetite, capitalistic adventure, navigational science, and military technology.

The global wars of 1756–1763, 1796–1815, 1914–1918, and 1939–1945 repeatedly illustrated that competing systems of mercantile imperialism would duke it out in corners of the world remote from their central conflict, until they finally realized that the cost in blood and money could be avoided and that colonies, once nationalistically aroused, were not boosters to metropolitan economies but drag anchors instead.[4]

Meanwhile, the analytic logic of time, space, cause, and effect applied in technology, industry, and warfare gave North Atlantic countries a new and lengthening lead in science and power over Chinese and Islamic cultures. Private competitive enterprise, minimally regulated and of increasing transparency, combined three major forms of intense social acceleration—invention, information, and investment. The Chinese water clock lost out to Western mechanical oscillators because it was both a functional failure (clogging with sediment that corrupted its long-term operations) and an elite secret (knowledge of time was, according to David Landes, "a confidential aspect of sovereignty, not to be shared with the people").[5] The Chinese water clock could never generate or regulate an industry; it could not be a precursor of a digital transformation in technology; it could not energize a people to become more aware of their productivity measured in time, or sensitize them to the rights of rewarded productivity.

By the third quarter of the twentieth century, acceleration of electronic inventions, spreading access to information, and expansion of investment to the middle classes had irreversibly prevailed.[6] By the last quarter of the century, two major forms of social organization were in the final stages of a competition, and in that contest free-market rationalism would prevail over Marxism-Leninism. As John Gray says, the failure of central planning in the Soviet Union and China "marked the end of an experiment in forced-march modernization in which the model of modernity was the nineteenth-century capitalist factory."[7]

Indonesia, Brazil, Nigeria, and scores of smaller countries were left with variants of "democratic capitalism" as models. Most such nations expressed their systems in ways either weak on democracy, thin on capitalism, or both at once. All, including the most advanced industrial nations, manifested Promethean bravado in their disregard for nature and Faustian hubris in their expectations of technology; and, in their quest for wealth, all were subject to the disappointments of Midas, whose touch of gold turned his own daughter to cold metal. Not long into the new millennium, the alleged model of models, the United States, generated two bankruptcies, WorldCom and Enron, whose combined corporate debts exceeded the entire gross national product of Indonesia. The auditor for both corporations, Arthur Anderson Co., fell into disrepute. Between March 2000 and July 2002, the American stock market contracted in value by $7 trillion—more than 40 percent. Executive hubris and greed were everywhere apparent, as were opaque conspiracy among some corporate officers, securities analysts, auditors, lawyers, and politicians. It was left to better leaders and true exemplars to restore trust in the system—as had been done in the past.

Under frail presumptions, Indonesia had been Southeast Asia's "emerging giant" until it was smitten by financial forces beyond its control and by its own combination of government and private-sector indiscipline.[8] Paul Krugman had seen well in advance some of the limits of the so-called Asian miracle. The astounding rates of growth of the early 1990s were attributable in part to taking off from relatively low base points and to using up labor-intensive potentials for gain.[9] A widely experienced development economist and investment executive would tell us that stock market "fair values" were actually predictors of trouble even after their re-evaluated highs of 1993.[10] As usual, however, nobody deciphered the utterances of the equity markets until after disaster.

Other causes contributed as well to the wider Asian debacle. China's devaluation of the *renminbi,* a stealthy process that continued for a few years before its formal announcement on January 1, 1994, amounted to 50 percent. This huge devaluation, coupled with China's aggressive trade policy, was clearly mercantilist and restrictive of trade growth in ASEAN. Managed exchange rates in major ASEAN economies nevertheless continued to attract foreign capital. Fiscal surpluses drew in still more foreign investment, and the cycle turned vicious in the form of overvalued exchange rates.[11] On Wall Street and in other financial centers, lemming behavior followed. Orders were placed without careful analysis. According to the Indian president of Orus Research and Investments, "It is a moot question whether senior managers know more or less than yuppie traders about what the determinants of growth are in an emerging country. What is clear is that both are heavily influenced by the latest fashion (literally) on Wall Street."[12]

Macro-commentators on the Asian financial crisis could not account for the extreme consequences in Indonesia or the timidity of its recovery, so they glided by with the phrase "except Indonesia."[13] But Karl Jackson, who knows the country and the region, noted the microeconomic messes there and elsewhere. He went back to Edward Banfield's study of Sicily in the 1950s, *The Moral Basis of a Backward Society,* and invoked from it the phrase "amoral familism" to describe the behavior of Suharto's kin, cronies, and imitators.[14] Such greedy short-sightedness, set amid weak banks, wild real estate speculation, managed exchange rates with overvalued currencies, and political uncertainty (most notably in the succession question regarding Suharto himself) created the scene for a colossal financial implosion.

There were no corrective energies to reverse the damage. Government supervisory and regulatory forces were weak, inexperienced, easily traduced. Corporations, with few exceptions, were dreadfully lacking in modern planning and control mechanisms. There was no ability, let alone a will, to reform, because special interests constituted the regime itself.[15] "The family" was sovereign in a market-swallowing state. It fed itself and its clingers-on as a *nusantara* mafia, eating the economy alive, from the inside out.

Toraja: Local Texture and Integrity

Still, one did not have to go deep into Papua and back to the Stone Age to find Indonesians little affected by the Asian financial crisis. On the great four-fingered island of Sulawesi, as large as the United Kingdom, price swings for coffee, chocolate, vanilla, lumber, and tapioca—the major products of this island—were largely positive in the late 1990s. The northernmost mountains of Southern Sulawesi contained a people who lived largely apart. In the town of Rantepao, a nine-hour drive up from Ujung Pandang, there were some television sets, and before the *krismon* (monetary crisis) small commercial passenger planes flew in and out of its little airport. As for the valley of Sesean, an hour more remote to the north, the only flying things there were birds and insects, spirits and occasional curses.

The highlanders of the region, called Toraja, raised wet rice on beautifully terraced hills. Unlike the lowlanders of South Sulawesi, the Bugis and Makassarese, they had no tradition of a sacred king whose potency had been expressed in a centralized court and written script. In the hills, some of which range over 9,000 feet above sea level, there were only the *tondok* (settlements), whose local dimensions and ritual relations rose and fell with the strength of *to kapua*—"big men."

The ritual medium was, and still is, meat. The big men held no titles, offices, or regalia that suggested continuity.[16] They established their places, or lost them, in feasts of honor, distributing quantities of sacrificial water buffalo and pigs. Early "globalization" touched them without changing them. When Malacca fell to the Portuguese in 1511, much of the spice trade reorganized itself around Makassar (now Ujung Pandang), which connected shipping routes in four directions. The Dutch East India Company wanted and got a monopoly of that trade in 1609 after having allied with the local Bugis prince. The Bugis expanded their conquests, piracy, and smuggling in other parts of the archipelago, consolidated other Bugis statelets, and even marched north into Toraja to compound their empire and bring the "True Religion," Islam, to the pagans of the hills. Torajans, however, united to repel them—all but one village, an outcast ever since—after which they fell back into the greater comfort of their mountain religion and the shifting minicantonments of the "big men."

Toraja society had three or four categories of persons, depending on locale, with nobles at the top and slaves at the bottom. In the mid-nineteenth century, when the price of coffee beans shot up in Europe, the excellent arabica coffee of the highlands became more in demand ("globalization" plodding onward). And during decades when coffee prices dropped, the slave trade increased. Torajan highland nobles sold off live bodies of the bottom caste to the royalty of the labor-short lowland coasts, perhaps to a total of 12,000 persons.[17] No surprise: globalization even today has not extinguished slavery in parts of North and West Africa and the Arabian peninsula.

In 1905–06 the Dutch grabbed the four major lowland kingdoms of South Sulawesi to satisfy their last pangs of imperial hunger. They managed to digest Bali only in 1906–1908; after decades of war, they barely swallowed Aceh in 1910–1912. When the colonial troops came north, most of the "big men" in Toraja gave in to them. But Pong Tiku, with his natural raw courage and military experience from local struggles, went into the most rugged mountains to sustain guerrilla warfare. Against him, the Dutch used Javanese, Batak, Timorese, and Ambonese troops. They complained about the cold. The governor general ordered an all-out assault with heavy artillery. The Torajans resisted, legend has it, by filling bamboo blow guns with chili powder and blowing them in the faces of the Dutch, then killing the blinded enemy with knives. In Volkman's account, they fought with "everything from hot pepper juice sprayers and spears to cannonballs."[18]

Pong Tiku's men finally surrendered. He himself, rather than being exiled like other resistance leaders, was executed by the Dutch.[19] Not until 1964, when the Tanah Toraja legislature nominated him as a national hero, was his bravery and vision recognized.[20] Pong Tiku was the perfect Sukarnoesque expression of revolutionary valor without capital or technology. He was one of the last holdouts against a now systematic Dutch amalgamation of empire organized to control oil newly discovered in Sumatra and Borneo, to administer the "ethical policy" of the Dutch (how can we improve the natives unless we conquer them?), and, in the Torajan instance, to convert an enclave of paganism to Christianity as another focus of resistance to the spread of Islam.

Oral history is chiefly a memory of trauma. The Japanese occupation was, for the Torajans, "our most bitter time," making them nostalgic even for the Dutch.[21] The full-scale rebellion of Kahar Mudzakkar in South Sulawesi in 1950–1965, which was linked with Darul Islam, made most Torajans fight off Muslims to avoid forced conversion, pillage, and slaughter of their pigs. They converted to Christianity faster than through Dutch missionaries. Early in 1965 Kahar Mudzakkar was killed, ending Darul Islam there at last. The mass murder of communists months later affected only a few Torajans but left villagers fearful of being labeled communist or atheist. Suharto's development era then opened the way for Torajans to move up in wealth, move out for modern work, or relive the ancient rituals.

Torajan society in Sesean is not serene. It goes "meat-mad" with the ritual politics of slaughtering water buffalo and pigs. One's sense of self, of place in relation to others, is defined and redefined in funerals at which old debts are paid and new ones initiated by the division of meat. To the eye of a sharp anthropologist: freshly slaughtered, barely bled, the butchered chunks are flung from the center with a shouting of meat-receivers' names, and intense observation of "calling order, the cut of meat, and its size . . . In the meat-flinging and animated conversation, everyone attunes himself to the subtleties of what is being tossed, when, and to whom." Explosions of shame and offended throwing of bones or water buffalo excrement may follow.[22] Affluence can be achieved apart from the meat culture, but decisions about human value are still publicly made in cuts of buffalo flesh.

The gears of society, economy, politics, and religion mesh in this ritual. The "big man" uses the politics of meat to expand his power by feeding others. He folds village and clan into a *rombongan* or "temporary cone of power" focused upon himself, his good fortune, and his costly generosity, all displayed to his politically magnetic or religiously magical advantage. "When Torajans disclose their genealogies they often include some references to what was cut for whom."[23]

All of this is part of the *aluk,* or traditional religion. Buffalo carry the dead into the world beyond. The size of funerary slaughter in this life is both testimony to worldly status and guarantee of security in the next world, just one membrane beyond the present one. This life of conspicuous consumption is more focused, potent, and ritually furious than anything Western ever described by Thorstein Veblen. The repetition or change or omission of ancestral acts enshrine and redefine ancestral religion. The carnal display of consumption kicks the economy into temporary overdrive, or into an unseen depletion through excess.[24]

When a wealthy Protestant was celebrated and interred near Rantepao in 1978, the reported cost of $225,000 drew local criticism from Christians for its irreligious focus on foreign guests and Jakarta dignitaries, and criticism from the national press for its gross extravagance. But a "big man" defended maintaining these differences of caste: there would be no tourists coming to see Toraja if it were not feudal. Others take silent satisfaction in a few pale-faces with their cameras, for even if they do not know what it is all about, prestigious visitors from afar honor Torajan ancestors, expand the ritual field, and intensify the center of the social universe.[25]

Sesean, for me, is the most beautiful mountain valley in the world—steep and green in far more dramatic ways than Bali or Italy. Intricately terraced with wet ricelands like the mountains of the northern Philippines but, unlike that Ifugao region, crazily dappled with huge megaliths and other volcanic spew. The air is clear and silent. In 1998 Dennis Heffernan, Bernie

Scher, and I went there because it is friendly, calm, and far from the capital city. Two and a half days after leaving Jakarta, we awoke to rooster-crowing in Batutomongo, 9,000 feet up. Our feet thudded on the plywood floors, as last night's roaches skittered to the corners. Four dollars a night for me, but no cost for Bernie. His wife, Marla Kosec, had got emergency attention and transportation for the father of our host during his heart attack two years before.

Aras Parura was not only our guide but the owner of a tiny hostel noted in adventure travel guides for its big breakfasts. Lithe and graceful, with wavy black hair, glowing brown eyes, and a dazzling smile, he proudly told us that in a Balinese bar his sharp-edged profile got him mistaken for an Egyptian. His four siblings worked in Jakarta. He had tried the big city once, where Dennis had landed him a modest office job. But he soon came back to Toraja, where he had his own *adat* (traditional) house and granary and simple guest lodge high in the hills, a long drive from his parents in Rantepao. He lived among the 400,000 Torajans in the highlands, rather than among the equal number now scattered through the rest of the archipelago or overseas.

His father, like his mother, was *bula'an*, of the nobility, from a word meaning gold. The descending caste descriptions mean iron, palmcore, and little fruit. Caste functions are not sharply delineated in either his father's or his mother's area, but everyone is aware of them. In his father's part of Toraja there is no king, but in his mother's there is one. Before retirement his father was chief of Protestant education for all South Sulawesi, a position which, arguably, gave him more real policy power than any traditional Torajan king had ever had.

Dennis and I hiked south, Aras in the lead, down to Tikala. Bernie had to be careful of his cardiovascular system after having bypass and pacemaker operations in his early seventies. "Someday," his wife Marla had said, with the cheerful objectivity of one thirty years younger and a medical professional, "his little heart is going to stop beating. Already there's an arrythmia, big gaps between beats sometimes. So you guys go easy on him." She remained in Jakarta, organizing a foundation for rehabilitation of heart, stroke, and trauma patients—pure volunteerism for a smitten society.

The year before, the great El Niño drought was felt even in Pong Tiku's region. But this year water was plentiful. Terraced rice was a month or six weeks short of the second harvest. We plunged downward for miles through the terraced padi—rice plots tightly engineered by hand, embedded with monoliths and megaboulders, beautifully bounded by narrow mud-stone retainers just wide enough to walk on. Water played slowly over the greatest boulders, between the smaller ones, leaving metallic traces of verdigris, russet, and lavender glowing in the sun: copper, iron, manganese. But the triumphant color everywhere was the green of springing grain. My eyes swam in it; my brain swarmed with it. I grew drunk on chlorophyll.

One misstep on a slippery ledge of packed earth and I might fall thirty feet. I watched where Aras set his boots. I had only my sneakers and an unpredictable left knee, reconstructed after a blindside clip in a soccer game severed two ligaments. The knee was forty-three years old when that happened. Now it was sixty-seven, hard at work, and joining in praise of God. I forgot about my Medicare card and my pensioner's angst at what Russia or Brazil was doing to Wall Street. I descended ledges of padi, in knife-edge awareness that I might never again know such dizzy natural happiness.

Dennis, behind me, fifteen years younger, favored his right knee and shared giddy manhood, the two of us acceptable trespassers on the work of thousands of rice farmers across scores of generations. This day, burial sites were our punctuation points. The joke was to find a place for Bernie. The most serious stop was at the great rockface where Aras's grandfather's tomb was chiseled in, topmost, long green fern fronds growing out from it, promises of abundance in the next life. One hundred and fifty buffaloes were sacrificed when he died. At ground level were two new tombs, each accommodating a cross with the horns of the *kerbau*. They looked like great wall safes, with doors outlined in white or black and red. On the ledge of one vault were gift offerings to ensure the comfort of the transient beyond: an empty plastic water bottle, a clump of blackened bananas, two full packs of cigarettes, "Kansas" brand on one side, "Nikki" on the other.

We told Bernie, on our return, about that and about Pana', a hundred-foot slab of whitish stone beside a creek and shaded by huge bamboo. Dennis showed photos of Pana'. I pointed to a large unchiseled space three-fifths of the way up on the right side. "Nah," Bernie said, "not high enough." "Higher you want?" I asked. "Higher and bigger. I need plenty of room. What if I got visitors? Can't send them to a motel. They travel all that way? One or two guest bedrooms I gotta have." We laughed.

Bernie took pleasure—we all did—in calculating the value of 150 buffaloes. Aras figured a pre-*krismon* average of $700 each, and much more for pie-bald or albino ones, heavily muscled and long-horned ones. So his grandfather's funeral cost well over $100,000, even before counting pigs and horses slaughtered; clothing, food, and drink; reservation of burial grounds; and the price of gifts from the guests. "It's the engine of this economy," said Bernie. "There are always people out there who haven't died yet."

We asked Aras how the recession affected Toraja. *Krismon?* Yes, but coffee, chocolate, tapioca all sold at good export prices. Tourism? Different. Aras's face fell a little. Stories of drought and fire. Stories of riot, rape, murder slowed travelers to a trickle. Those were Borneo, Sumatra, Java stories. It was unfair. Toraja was green, calm, and beautiful, but after us Aras had only one group of six coming for one day in the last two months of the year. He brightened and dismissed the *krismon*. "It makes no difference. We are always preparing. We are always raising buffaloes. We are ready in advance. And then we celebrate."

I watched him one day, grooming a big buffalo in his father's garden in Rantepao, with some house servants. They brushed and picked it clean and rubbed unguents into it. Barefooted, I sat on the grass while the *kerbau* munched away, inches from my toes. When they were done, Aras took two fast steps from behind the beast and vaulted onto its back. He sat on the untroubled, unmoving buffalo and smiled radiantly at us. I imagined he was raising this one specially for his father. When the father's heart did fail a year or two later, I heard that they could not generate a funeral on the scale of the grandfather's but had to wait and plan a merged feast with two other families.

Between hiking days we went to a funeral of Aras's "friend's Mom"—the second and most public of two funeral days, to be followed by two more family days of slaughter and ritual, and then a fifth day, actual burial. As we approached the funeral grounds we heard the sounds of shrieking animals. An arc of bamboo led into a field perhaps a hundred yards long by thirty wide, surrounded by dozens of crimson bedecked spectator boxes with upswept Torajan roofs. The atmosphere was rodeo-like, but instead of bucking broncos, it featured crumpling buffaloes.

On the right from the entrance, a podium and microphone. This open news booth gave periodic updated broadcasts of givers attending and their gifts. Somewhere in there, I trusted, was the large box containing packs of Kansas cigarettes costing 200,000 rupiah, or about $9 from each of us three Americans. We had presented it, wrapped in newspaper, to a family member at the gate, who thanked us with dignity.

The sun was intense. I was wearing my long-sleeved dark blue Java batik shirt and the dark green sarong that Aras insisted I wrap around my gray cotton trousers. Stuck and wrapped in my own sweat, I thought, and then I saw a whole campground of hogs trussed, downside up, to bamboo frames. Several were squealing, some frothing at the mouth, and one, inert, oozed blood from his flank where a knife had suggested he shut up.

The altar was decorated with a simple white cross on maroon cloth. The only other sign of Christianity was a Torajan parson in black tunic making his rounds among the family boxes. Women sat in black with gold jewelry; men stood apart, smoking. Other than parish schmoozing, I did not see where Christian ritual entered. I did not hear "Amazing Grace" or "Ave Maria." I saw a circle of men perform the *Ma'bodong*. Fifty of them, arms around each other, some smoking, revolved counterclockwise in a slow shuffle step to the steady beat of their own chant, a great reverse chime-clock of human voices, moving from phrase to phrase of mythic recital upon signal of their "choirmaster." While they revolved, boys darted in and out through the legs of their elders to play in the middle of man-noise, myth-sound, tribe-song, in which they would someday sing, and for which each too would one day be the solemn cause.[26]

We sat on bamboo mats in a big section reserved for Aras's relatives and made small talk. Where from? Family members? Bernie was in elegant dark colors with a black *pici* lightly capping his head. When I said he looked like Suharto, others laughed, but Bernie shuddered. "Don't do that again." He looked around. *"Zug auf mir nisht.* Don't say that about me!" I obeyed his sudden Yiddish command. "Really you look more like a youthful Jack Benny." He smiled.

A buffalo's throat had just been slit. The knackers were on him, six or seven of them, slitting away the hide to be saved and stretched. One sawed off the head to get the horns, which would adorn a *tongkonan,* or *adat* house, of the giver. The swarm of men tugged and rolled the headless, skinless heap belly up, a glistening white mound of fat and fascia in the noonday sun. One man hacked off the upthrust legs. Another straddled and with a large ax cracked open the chest cavity. Others pulled back the ribs with splitting sounds until they stuck up, fencelike, in the air. Then, with another series of split-cracks, they stripped away the two rows of upright ribs.

Bernie winced, but he couldn't tear his eyes away. He had twice had open heart surgery. They slashed off breast-cuts, then flank and loin steaks. For that they eased the way by gutting open belly and bowels. Two men reached in and grabbed big scoops of dark green grass, the creature's last meal. A near bushel, it looked like. Then on to micro-butchery, tossing parts onto palm leaves for roasting; passing guts to a specialist—slave class, I suspect—who would carefully squeeze intestines free of detritus. Guest families were given packets of meat in heavy tan waxed paper. This was a decorous crowd. No complaints, no hurling of feces, as seen by Volkman on Sesean. Status was either assured or silently reevaluated. Cooking began.

Bernie was looking impassive, sad under his *pici,* like (I do not say) a deposed Suharto. "I remember," he remarked, "this beautiful little white horse . . . Three years ago. *Beautiful.* And right here they slit his throat." Bernie, adopted into the Parura clan, had shown them his chest scars. But he was unable to follow their sacral reasoning. He remonstrated with me,

Toraja: Funerary Images

Black and white photos of the 1940s and color shots of the 1990s convey different feeling. But the practices remain essentially the same.

74. MOURNERS gather around a casket carved in the shape of an *adat* house. (Niels Douwes Dekker Collection/Kroch Library, Cornell University)

75. FUNERAL march proceeds from village to gravesite. (Niels Douwes Dekker Collection/Kroch Library, Cornell University)

76. RITUAL SLAUGHTER. Buffalo and pigs are conducted inside for their role in the festival of mourning. (Marla Kosec)

77. TAU-TAU. Effigies of the dead are carved in rock galleries. (Marla Kosec)

out of their hearing. "No good reason to kill that horse so young." Three years before, Bernie himself had been able to navigate the mountain like a pack pony.

On our last day Dennis and I continued our mock search for Bernie's resting place, hiking to Palawa. This was an eastern destination, whereas before we had trod south. Down-stepping slippery stones in sluice beds carried us eventually to the great upper torso of the Sesean terraces, with its hundreds of unfoldings toward its belly line, over which we could not yet see. We stopped, drank water, marveled. After hours of further walking we are suddenly aware of having entered lower terraces, hundreds more, narrowing and then folding out again into low extended flatlands, almost imperceptibly terraced.

In this moist earth it is strange to speak of oases, but we spotted a few: naturally elevated miniplateaus, ten or twenty feet above the level of the rice fields. On them grew palms, bamboos, and flowers, amid small clusters of *adat* houses and rice barns. Extended families of twenty to forty people lived there in nearly complete self-sufficiency with their buffalo and small, passive dogs. One place in particular was rich in megaliths—oblong dishes, hunkering frogshapes, and vertical plinths, each carved by man and weathered by nature from the time some priest long ago blessed this as a holy place and initiated a settlement for the rounds of toil, fertility, and ritual sacrifice that are distinctly Torajan.

The only Bahasa Toraja we knew was "Apa kareba?"—"What's new?" or "How's it going?" On the other side of the mountain the replies had been smiling but formal: "Kareba melo"—the news is good. But this side of the mountain was more empirical. "Kareba makan," replied a girl on a balcony, a bowl in her hand. "Eating time." "Kareba kerja petani," said a middle-aged woman with a sickle in her hand. "Kerja keras biasa" (thin, wry, genuine smile): "Farmer's work; hard work, as usual." "Kareba atap baru," from two men on wooden crossbeams, tugging corrugated metal into place. "Time for a new roof." They were humorously conscious of being espied from beneath.

In a *padi* with no seedlings visible, a weathered man looked up at our greeting. "Kareba tidak," he said emphatically. "No news." He wrinkled his brow, reached down for a handful of muck and threw it at a boulder. He grinned at me. "Kareba lumpur!" "Mud time!" Aras howled, kicked his foot in the air, and hopped forward several times, hooting. Spontaneous laughter on his part, and a tribal identification cry, maybe once a war cry. We jounced along down, calling "Kareba lumpur!" to each other, three happy tramps in mudtime.

We found a grand unscarred megalith for Bernie, with a big wet wallow of a *padi* pool in front of it. How much is it worth? we asked Aras. Well, the land itself, two young buffalo, short horns—he tapped above his wrist watch—or one big longhorn, he tapped near his elbow, "Four million." For the stonework to carve out the crypt? "Four million again." We reported to Bernie those prices, plus four million megalithic surcharge. He laughed. "Megalithic surcharge! So you're *brokering* this deal?" "Sure," Dennis grinned. "Cheap at the price. Current bucks, maybe one thousand six hundred total. You can't get that in the States."

Bernie looked relaxed. But the problem—Aras apologized for it—was collective ownership of the land. It would take forever to negotiate a sale, which, even then, for a non-Torajan would never be secure. Don't worry about it, Bernie told us. He recounted the story of the man from Queens dying in the hospital: in a coma on his deathbed with relatives around him arguing over where he should be buried. Bensonhurst, says a brother, the Masons have a great cemetery there. No, North Jersey, said a niece; it's more beautiful in North Jersey. The wife shook her head. Why not Queens? All our life we live in Queens. But the argument only worsened. Suddenly she turned and shook her husband. "Where do you wanna be buried?" He opened one eye. "Surprise me."

Aras's queenly mother wanted him to get married. He was thirty-two years old and handsome. "I will arrange something excellent for you with one of the family, a second cousin maybe." Aras was shocked at the idea of an intra-clan marriage. He raised horrified genetic objections, new to his mother's understanding. He thanked her but promised to find a bride for himself.

For variety in his life he took a trip to Bali. He carried with him an emblem of the *kerbau,* stylized as on houses and graves with horns meeting overhead, whereas in fact they swing out and forward like great dull blades. He showed it to a tattoo artist and the result was visible on his left bicep. His mother inevitably saw it. "What have you done with your body?!!" His father did not remonstrate but gave him serious doubtful looks and mild head-shaking. Aras told his mother not to worry, he would have it erased. As we walked under the midday sun, Aras stripped to the waist, and I saw a second tattoo, same size and design, on his right shoulder blade. I asked when he got it. "Same time as the first."

Aras imagined that when the *krismon* was over and the tourists returned, his business would pick up. He would tell them about the *alukta,* the traditional religion, which now his own body symbolized. He would teach the mountain children not to beg money or candy from tourists but to respect the old ways. Religion was not segregated from politics, economics, or other Western categories of society. Toraja was *tondo lepongan bulan, tana matarik allo:* round as the sun and the moon in governance, religion, and culture. In proof stood the mortuary climaxes in which the identity, status, and wealth of the passer-on are established along with those of the lingers-here, the latter happy in the conviction that the departing soul, rightly crossing the thousand bridges beyond by *kerbau,* would have the power to strengthen his descendants in things that matter: children, rice, buffaloes.

Of course the old ways were wearing thin. In 1995 the regional Bureau of Statistics divided religious denominations into 69 percent Protestant (up from 53 percent in 1970) and only 6 percent Alukta (down from 38 percent before). Catholics at 17 percent and Muslims at 8 percent filled out the new picture, both now exceeding Alukta.[27] But traditional architecture was managing to persist. Only 5 percent of Torajans actually dwelled in a *tongkonan* house, because a Bugis or Makassarese style lowland semi-urban home was cheaper to build. But a family compound without the giant upsweeping roof of a *tongkonan* and a traditionally designed rice barn might be considered without character.

Aras Parura wished to exemplify and preserve such traditions. But the financial crisis was deepening. No tourists. He went back to Jakarta, got odd jobs, fell in love with a Javanese girl who sold automotive parts. Her parents refused him as her husband. But she loved him—who could not love Aras, at least a little? She loved him a lot. They married.

Was Aras, too, a loser to globalization? Had CNN, the bad news channel, dried up his tourist trade? No. He sickened of the big city and persuaded his wife to return with him to Toraja. I hope she is endeared to his *kerbau* tattoos. She must understand what they mean for the year far ahead when she may have to bury Aras Parura.

Financial Implosion

Torajan culture illustrates life remote from financial centers, where urban commentators were preoccupied with various views of globalization. In April 1998 the Harvard Institute for International Development, the secular temple of globalization discourse, wrote that "the collapse of the Indonesian economy is one of the most stunning and shocking events to hit the developing world in the past several decades." But they did not see the President Suharto, or the presidency, as causal. After a knowledgeable litany of past successes came an invocation of sudden failures: "Millions of Indonesians, many surviving just over the poverty line during the good times, have lost their jobs." Food production has been disrupted by drought and crisis. Export commodity prices, especially oil, are falling. Investors, foreign and domestic, fleeing. Banking system, moribund. With thousands of firms facing bankruptcy and closure, contraction for 1998 is projected at 15 percent. (It eventually came in at 13.8 percent.) "This single year collapse in growth is among the largest recorded anywhere . . . in the post-World War II period."[28]

What caused the Indonesian collapse? Stephen Radelet and his renowned colleague Jeffrey Sachs, both at Harvard, blamed the IMF's having closed sixteen Indonesian banks in October 1997, thus producing a frenzy of withdrawals elsewhere, and overseas capital flight. The IMF may deserve criticism for its overdrawn mission, underinventive policies, and bad timing. But didn't Radelet and Sachs know that *thirty* banks had been tagged, in Indonesian technical journals more than a year before, as closable? A panic was waiting to happen. Metaphorically speaking, the Indonesian political economy was supersaturated with poisons. Overconcentration, underregulation, and arbitrary repression bred adventurous folly and its sister, hyperanxiety. Any of several large catalysts would have precipitated panic.

Suharto's government produced the conditions that would define the crisis, by suppressing information and distorting the institutions that might have softened its impact and speeded recovery. Paul Wolfowitz, former ambassador to Indonesia and assistant secretary of state for East Asia/Pacific, contrasted the states newly in crisis with the grotesquely negative artifacts of the Marxist social laboratory: the ideologically strangled productivity that held China back for thirty years after its revolution and which continued to stunt North Korea after fifty years. The real "marvel" in other Asian nations, therefore, had been sustained growth rates of 5 percent or above *despite* their high transaction-cost economies. Until now, such growth had succeeded in obscuring the inefficiencies caused by corruption.[29]

The global financial environment hit its low-point in September 1998. Russia's approaching default on $200 billion of foreign debt was looming as the largest such government failure in history. Brazil's stock market lost 40 percent of its value in seven weeks, while the government lost $20 billion of its reserves.[30] Japan was staggering, unable to shake out of a decade-long recession. Its prime minister, Keizo Obuchi, sized up part of his nation's plight by saying publicly that the total liabilities of the virtually insolvent Long Term Credit Bank of Japan are "worth 1.2 or 1.3 times the total economy of Indonesia."[31] There was little cheer in this fact for Indonesians, Japanese, or the pushers of the "Washington consensus" who were insisting that Japanese growth would be the locomotive to pull Asian economies out of their depression. That engine could only chuff in its roundhouse.

An overheated President Clinton, addressing a private audience at the Council on Foreign Relations in Manhattan, spoke of the radiating Asian financial crisis as "the biggest financial challenge facing the world in half a

century." The world balance of risk, he said, had shifted from controlling inflation to stimulating growth. The United States, therefore, must work with
Japan, Europe, and other nations to do that. He had asked the World Bank
to double its support for the social safety net in Asia. He would urge use
of $15 billion in IMF emergency funds to stop financial contagion from
spreading to Latin America. Congress must meet U.S. obligations to the
IMF. Having quoted the Federal Reserve Chairman as saying, "We cannot
forever be an oasis of prosperity," Clinton said he had asked Greenspan and
other financial magi "to recommend ways to adapt the international financial architecture to the twenty-first century." If we do the right things,
Clinton concluded, we can "lift billions and billions of people around the
world into a global middle class and into participation in global democracy
and genuine efforts toward peace and reconciliation."[32]

Despite Clinton's visionary resolve, some things got worse at home.
Within nine days, the Federal Reserve Bank of New York chose to organize a cash infusion of $3.5 billion from commercial banks and invest-
ment firms to bail out Long Term Capital Management, an American
hedge fund (actually a firm engaged in high-risk speculation) based in
Greenwich, Connecticut. The fund was led by a former vice chairman of
Salomon Brothers, along with other Salomon alumni, and it had two Nobel
laureates in economics on its board. In an almost wholly unregulated field
of investment, this fund had borrowed money to points where its commitments exceeded its capital by 50 or 100 times. Liquidating its huge positions
now might drive faltering markets lower or even generate panic selling. Despite LTCM's being, in the words of a prominent New York financier, "off-
shore, opaque, and just as arrogant going down as coming up," the Fed
organized a highly unusual rescue for it, equal to one-fifth of all IMF emergency loans to Thailand.[33] The American example (criticized as "crony capitalism, Wall Street style") showed that overborrowing, underregulation,
and dangerous speculation were not limited to developing economies and
that Nobel laureate brains do not insulate greedy dealmakers against disastrous hubris.

Indonesia had already succumbed to default on its debt on January 27,
1998, by announcing a temporary freeze on debt servicing. Its government's gentle international decorum in such matters silenced most critics.
One exception was the economist Jeffrey Winters, who within ten days of
the Thai crisis had accused the World Bank of letting "roughly a third" of
its program funds in Indonesia be wasted through corrupt leakage into local government bureaucracy.[34] Dennis de Tray, the World Bank's representative in Jakarta, much later acknowledged that 20 percent, as "the roughest
of rough guesses," had indeed been lost in such ways. He couched this un-

comfortable public confession in an appeal for cooperation in combating "the cancer of corruption."[35] Crisis, however, had apparently so accelerated the cancer's growth rate as to make it inoperable. The Indonesian state Audit Agency reported in 1999 that 48 banks had misused 95 *percent* of the rp. 144.5 trillion injected by the Central Bank in 1997–98 as emergency liquidity support credits.[36]

Early in 1999, in a restricted document, the World Bank completed a ten-year reappraisal of Indonesian country assistance, within a thirty-year overview. The development success story was graciously restated: "From one of the poorest in the world to lower middle-income status by 1996, when per capita GNP reached $1080." Yet the bank acknowledged that the timing and severity of the crisis surprised it, and "overconfidence" had left it underprepared. The halo effect of success felt by all Indonesia's donors had generated over-optimism, and customary praise seemed to dull the impact of their accompanying "strongly worded policy notes": "On balance, the outcome of the Bank's strategy over the past decade, the Bank's performance as well as the Government's performance, are all rated as marginally satisfactory." Were bureaucratese translated into ordinary speech, the impact of the key words would have been "sharply disappointing."

The reply from Boediono, minister of state for national development planning, courteously protected past gains, queried some conclusions as premature, and disavowed belief that "our policies and institutions were as seriously flawed as described in the Report." It challenged as confrontational the idea of leveraging aid to bring about social and political change; such arm-twisting would probably damage both investor confidence and economic growth. The minister wondered rhetorically if the authors would "favor making assistance to China conditional on the establishment of a democratic political system, a free press, electoral reform, and broad-based participation of the civil society?" In short, "marginally satisfactory" was too harsh. Pressing earlier for changes highlighted now might have led to a severed relationship, making Indonesia an international pariah. Continuing on the reform program we were building together would "deliver exactly what has been missing" and in "even two or three years" would restore a "very impressive record of delivering growth, poverty reduction, and social welfare."[37]

As an exit interview de Tray gave a "long unprepared speech" to the Indonesian Forum of Economists. He stressed "weak institutions . . . the legal system, the financial system, the civil service, and an underdeveloped democratic process"; and he pointed out "one very strong and unsustainable institution," Suharto the individual, who did not deliver on institutions as bridges among people and could not keep up with change. "Globalization

operates at light speed along fiber optic cables, while institutional development takes decades." How now, then? Indonesians must understand the
concept of conflict of interest. Americans must learn patience to operate
across cultural gaps. How then, now? "What should I have done when I arrived in July 1994 that would have provided a softer landing for the Indonesian people and its economy?" De Tray promised to reflect more on it.[38]

An area of even more dramatic growth reversal was revealed in a World
Bank report from James Wolfensohn and Joseph Stiglitz released to the
Washington press. In Eastern Europe and the Soviet Union the number of
people living under the poverty line (there, $4 a day) had grown from 14
million when the Berlin Wall fell to 147 million a decade later.[39] No economist or journalist was recorded as asking the questions a historian must put:
What price democracy? What cost civil society? Where basic connective political and social tissues are lacking, to what degree and for how long are
economic reversals acceptable in reaching for them?

Social Apoplexy

By late 1998 Indonesia resembled a victim of severe cerebral hemorrhage: it
suffered from aphasia, amnesia, and paralysis. It couldn't speak. It had lost
its memory. It couldn't move. Not until a new election law was devised by
the old MPR and an open popular election held at last in June 1999 was Indonesia able to draw a deep breath and attempt to reoxygenate its systems.
Then a new MPR could meet and at last elect, as it did in October of that
year, a president to succeed Habibie. Meanwhile, for seventeen months the
Suharto surrogate did his best to protect his boss, himself, and the Cendana
cronies. In a mood of reconciliation, however, he released many political
prisoners and promoted democracy by advancing free media and open elections.

Ginandjar Kartasasmita, Suharto's finance minister, who continued in office under Habibie, gave his summary of the situation on September 1,
1998. The nation had a burden of $140 billion in debt ($60 billion public;
$80 billion private). It could not service the debt. The rupiah, at 10,700 to
the dollar, held less than a quarter of its pre-crisis value. Inflation was running at 80 percent. One-fifth of Indonesia's labor force was unemployed.
But Indonesia, at last abiding by the terms of its IMF agreement, was beginning to merge state-owned banks and shut down others. Through IBRA (Indonesia Bank Restructuring Agency) it would attempt to restructure the
$80 billion in private debt, rather than threatening a moratorium on losses,
as Russia had done. As the rupiah strengthened, subsidies on food, fuel, and
electricity could be cut and a positive growth rate could be foreseen in two
years.

A sage commentator in Hong Kong compared Indonesia with Russia in that both had collapsed currencies, suffocation by debt, and political crisis. He could have added observations on rip-offs in high places, criminality and anarchy in public affairs, and provincial separatisms in both countries.[40]

Poverty lines differ vastly from nation to nation. In 1998 in the United States the line stood at $16,600 annually for a family of four, which meant (a year later, in September 1999) that only 12.7 percent of the population was officially below the line, the lowest level in nearly a decade. But data based on a minimal food budget defined in 1965 and adjusted upward for inflation was no longer representative of America's eating habits or spending needs. The Census Bureau's studies suggested raising the line to $19,500, which would suddenly define 17 percent of the population as being in poverty. Meanwhile, American opinion polls put the line definitely above $20,000 to "live decently" or "get along in the community"; and the National Academy of Sciences, including extra cash for emergencies (fix a car, repair a roof, buy health insurance), put the threshold between $21,000 and $28,000. Defining a new American "poverty line" is subjective, not scientific. And clearly political. The Clinton administration, declaring that more work was needed, passed the decision on to the next administration.[41]

Indonesia's poverty line was meager and much more elusive, even when an apparently simple standard, "a dollar a day," was evoked. Accurate information is hard to gather when interviewees fear both the tax collector and pressures to share any surplus with friends and neighbors. But while Americans were reading statistics on their obesity, Indonesians could have learned that their caloric and protein intakes between 1961 and 1990 increased from an average below minimum subsistence to levels exceeding Developing Asia for calories, and approaching it for proteins.[42] Once unimaginable luxuries—a small refrigerator, a moped, a TV—were within the reach of millions of households. A postmortem critique of the communist leader D. N. Aidit, after his summary execution in 1965, was that he had secretly owned a refrigerator. For Pramoedya Ananta Toer, after release from labor prison on Buru in 1979, "development" sounded like a savage word. But most Indonesians were grateful for the policies that brought them *more:* agricultural productivity, rural development, economic diversification, facilitation of the private sector, and stimulation of manufacturing and trade.

Whereas in 1970 60 percent of Indonesians were classified as below the poverty line, by 1996 it was only 11 percent. Both overdefinition at the beginning of the New Order and underdefinition toward its end helped to exaggerate its achievement in alleviating poverty. But in the main, major progress had been made.[43]

Now what? Defining poverty in rupiah per day as the currency gyrated was not feasible. Analysts such as those in a World Bank study group could only hang onto the pre-crisis baseline of 11 percent in poverty in 1996 and pursue their studies: "The poverty rate will be higher in 1998 no matter what poverty line is chosen." In rural areas income declined more for those at the lower end than for those at the upper end, while in urban areas the greater drops were at the higher end of the distribution. Fishermen benefited greatly from devaluation of the rupiah, but other dwellers in coastal areas were negatively affected.[44]

Those classified as poor in 1997 were poorer still in 1998. Some households moved out of that category, but more moved in. The greatest negative effect, because of very large falls in real wages, was among rural laborers without land of their own. Some producers in rural areas were, nevertheless, benefiting from price shifts favoring food and export crops. The relatively well off, however, especially in urban areas on Java, were notably hit by the "shock."

To maintain themselves, most households were clearly cutting down on nonfood items and were reallocating a share of consumption away from meat and fruits to rice, tubers, and less welcome vegetables. Clear as this situation might be to any housewife, how would social scientists characterize it to one another? Using an initial 11 percent base rate, they determined that poverty went up to 12.4 percent in 1997 and to 24.3 percent in 1998. It therefore rose 100 percent. Does that overstate the impact? Let's just say "poverty doubled."[45]

A RAND study on investment in human capital minced no words. "Among poor households in urban areas, 15–19 year old males have been largely protected from the crisis at the expense of their younger brothers and sisters. In the rural sector, poor households have substantially cut back on education expenditures and the axe has fallen on 15–19 year old males as well as 10–14 year old males and females . . . For these households the impact of the crisis is likely to be felt for many years to come."[46]

Marla Kosec, Bernie Sher's wife and an expert in physical therapy, was called on for help in a great variety of cases during this period. Two were especially indicative. An expatriate executive who lost his major contract was pulled back from a roof ledge in October 1997, only to try suicide again in February 1998 by drinking a quart and a half of mosquito repellent. His employees found him "twitching like a cockroach under bug spray." He died a month later, a victim of a hyper-stressed society. The number of patients admitted to neuropathy units increased 25 percent per month from July 1997 through February 1998, nine out of ten of them suffering from broken blood vessels. One of them was Abdurrahman Wahid, who suffered two hemorrhagic strokes in half a year. Wahid's family reached out to Kosec, who aided with advanced rehab techniques until she was blocked by

Javanese doctors; they thought that walking a patient in a swimming pool was dangerous overexertion. When Gus Dur held a press interview to prove his leaderly resilience, bandages from a cerebral shunt operation projected from his head like symbolic horns on a statue of Moses.[47]

A Sewing Machine for Ary

Ary's father, Pak Sudiro, was a mosquito control officer before he retired on a pension of about 250,000 rupiah per month ($100 before the crisis; $25–$35 after). The fifth of six children, Ary was unable to continue medical studies after getting a kidney transplant from her father. As she approached age 24, she saw most of her friends already married. But "I think it's impossible to find a man who can accept me. I can never have a boy friend. I am afraid people give me a call *perawan tua* ['old maid']. I feel I have no future sometimes. I only believe God have make a good plan for me."[48]

In the middle of the *krismon,* she worried about helping her parents pay for her medicine, but it was impossible to find a job. I wrote in sympathy, wished them a Happy Easter, and sent a photo of my wife and myself with our three children, as Ary requested, because "you are," she said, "my first friend from another country." I also dared to send four prayers that I translated into Indonesian. The one I loved best was by Mechtild of Magdeburg, a German woman of the thirteenth century:

> Lord, since you have taken from me all that I had of you, yet of your grace leave me the gift which every dog has by nature—that of being true to you in my distress, when I am deprived of all consolation. This I desire more fervently than your heavenly kingdom.

I don't know what Ary thought of the prayers. She never expressly acknowledged them. Were they too far from the spirit of a Central Javanese Catholic to be helpful? Or was she, understandably, preoccupied with the pressures on her family, on herself? She wrote about computer courses, too expensive to enroll. Medicine, too costly but necessary. "I don't know how long my family can hold out in situation like this. I don't afraid to die but I just afraid to be sick again."

She asked me for some stamps to give a friend for her collection. She asked what is the difference in English between "only" and "just." She wrote about the demonstration of a million people in Yogya in the northern squares of the palace grounds, peaceful without the presence of ABRI, as the sultan of Yogyakarta spoke supporting *reformasi,* national reform. She mentioned almost casually in May that Suharto had resigned.

I sent Ary some beautiful commemorative stamps. She had entered a dressmaking course less than two kilometers from her house and had decided on becoming a *modiste*. She had been asking, "Why not I die right now," but she was thinking, "I will try to [get] through this life what ever it is."

She had thought more about KKN. "Just because one family (Suharto's family) all Indonesian in suffering." In Bantul and villages around it, there were large demonstrations against the regent, Sri Roso Sudarmo, because he had given a billion rupiah to one of Suharto's foundations in order to get a second term. The reporter who revealed it, Udin, had been murdered. The people wanted the *bupati* "down and be judged."

Ary was thinking about "political krisis and krisis of leadership." Her main feelings were expressly local: the people of Yogya still consider Sultan Hamengku Buwono X as their king, to *mengayomi* them. I translated *mengayomi* from my Javanese-English dictionary as meaning to shelter or protect, as a great tree provides refuge from sun and rain.

Updated *krismon* news (mid-August): Her father's pension now only bought their family rice. For soup, side dishes, soap, electricity, they had to rely on others' earnings. They had their own well and cooked with their own wood. Maybe they must sell the house of her father's birth, but her grandmother still lived there with her aunt. Then Ary outright asked for a "personal donation" and gave me her bank account number. I wrote back asking the cost of a sewing machine.

With one of her brothers, Ary researched prices and sent me pictures. The basic Singer looked like the family machine I remembered from my boyhood in the 1930s. I sent an international wire transfer for $150, which I thought would buy a much better Singer than that and also pay for lessons.

I got back to Yogya in October of 1998. There was a note at the hotel saying she hoped I wasn't disappointed she hadn't bought a machine yet. She really needed one that could "zigzag"—do more designs (20) than a straight-line machine (6). I went to her house by taxi, again needing several sets of directions on the way. When we reached winding alleys in wet rice land, three middle-aged men smoking cigarettes knew the family, the case, and even the fact of the foreign benefactor. They gestured eagerly, smiled broadly at me, and I smiled back with shared roadside pleasure.

The commotion of our arrival brought all the family out of the house, thirty yards from the road, under darkening palms. Ary first, dressed in red and smiling. She had gained at least fifteen pounds. Her cheeks were chubby and flushed when she smiled. She said she was still taking immunosuppressive medicines. I did not ask her how they afforded them. Her father was dressed in semi-Western style this time, for they had all come home from part of a three-day wedding celebration. We talked, drank tea. He absented himself.

Ary and I talked about our sewing machine project. I said I was most interested in her growth (*perkembangan,* flowering). She smiled modestly and prettily and again I noticed her apple-bright cheeks. I did calculations on the back of an envelope and ponied up. Monies sent to her bank account: 1,584,000 rupiah; all the big bills in my wallet: 500,000 rupiah. Still not enough for Singer model 970. So I emptied my wallet of small bills: 18,500; and threw in an American tenner: 70,000. That should buy her the Singer zigzag model, with 11,500 rupiah left over.

Ary's mother watched the pieces of paper currency mount on one another. Then she gave a small but genuine-seeming smile to me and to the pile. So that's it, I said, using rehearsed language which I hoped was not offensive: we have reached the limits of my gift. Since I had gone beyond my promise (to about $290 at current exchange), I felt happy and said so. Ary said she was happy too.

A crashing downpour made the light in the front room dim. We were almost unable to hear one another. But I got out my last remark in Indonesian, "I hope there are no more free-market surprises." Ary listened with fatalistic calm and without reply. We shook hands, exchanging *selamats* all around, including with the older sister, who wore a motorcycle helmet and apologized for not speaking English. I scudded out into the new mud with Ary. Another round of shakes and thanks.

Schoolchildren had pushed the stalled taxi up parallel to the house. It still wouldn't start. Two brothers pushed us down the alley toward the rice fields until the ignition kicked in. As the driver raced the motor, coaxing it toward steady rhythm, I reached out the window for a last touching of hands and farewells.

Ary wrote me about the state being like a family (but *not* the Suharto family) in that there are many *sukubangsa* (tribes or ethnic groups) within it, which should get along by themselves. I agreed that local autonomy, as in Yogya, was a valuable principle but not an absolute one. The state could rip apart, I wrote, like badly stitched clothing.

Her next letter said it was her happiest Christmas in four years. That was from the time she became ill.

Why the Grinding Down of Indonesia?

A Southeast Asia that had been playing a leading role in global commerce before 1630 went into more than three centuries of decline, not only in trade but in urbanism and cosmopolitanism.[49] For Indonesia, independence from the Netherlands may have implied at last a new embrace of creativity. But in the late 1960s, a prominent economist regarded it as "the number one economic failure among the major underdeveloped countries."[50] By

1993 the World Bank saw it as a contender for number one success. By 1998 it was the world's most dramatic disaster. Centuries of funk, decades of surge, and sudden friability require historical perspective for understanding.

A century and a half after Vasco da Gama rounded the Cape of Good Hope, Europe's military and industrial technology was going into overdrive, together with commercial innovations, organizational logic, and supporting legal framework, while all of the same factors in the archipelago were shriveling, stagnating, or subordinating themselves. Without a native center of scientific inquiry and political coherence, the islands later called Indonesia could offer only outgunned peripheral battles against the Dutch, rather than fronts of politico-cultural resistance. As Han China, far more powerful, crumbled in dynastic ineptitudes, it was small wonder that a Java-centered Indonesia should fragment and involute.

The Indonesians were unfortunate in having the Dutch as their masters, for Netherlanders themselves sank in acumen and achievement among European imperial powers. Other European nations, notably England and France, were passing it by. Only Portugal grew softer faster than Holland, and the history of East Timor as a colony is testament to its flabby indifference. The whole period 1750–1870, according to David Landes, was a "long pause" in which Holland was "going nowhere." Only with the "second industrial revolution" of electricity, diesel motors, chemicals, and scientific agriculture did it kick back into action.[51]

An imperial speech from the throne in 1901 made Javanese poverty an ethical preoccupation of Dutch colonial economic policy. But while Dutch GDP per capita continued to grow at a rate of 1 percent a year over the course of 130 years, Indonesia's grew at rates one-third to one-fifth as fast. By hugging Indonesia to its bosom, the Netherlands did little to improve native breathing capacity.

Having expelled world war-exhausted colonizers, with the aid of the UN and the United States, Indonesia took up a brand of nationalism in the Sukarno period that wracked the nation and daunted foreign investors with retributive rhetoric and expropriation for the state, without compensation. Cumulative net private inflow of foreign funds for the whole period 1950–1965 is estimated at only $50 million.[52]

Modern economic history in Indonesia appears to begin with the Sumitro-advised Foreign Investment Law of 1967. A table of cumulative foreign investment over thirty years shows proportions of the billions that flowed in. The role of the United States is obviously modest: slightly above the Netherlands, less than half that of the UK, a third that of Japan. If Hong Kong, Singapore, and Taiwan are combined and considered as "Sinica Oceania," they have an investment impact larger than Japan. Collectively

containing fewer people than the island of Sumatra, these regionally involved Chinese, with their similarities of business culture, have been the
largest recent force in foreign investment. Nonetheless, all things considered, total foreign capital inflow during the Suharto period has been less in
relation to Indonesian GDP than in the 1910s and 1920s.[53] When Indonesia's
boom years of the twentieth century are objectively reviewed, they appear
to have occurred half a century before Suharto.

Psychologically, however, one cannot get far making that point with educated Indonesian professionals, let alone lesser-educated voters. Foreign nations and the multilateral consulters and lenders (IGGI, WB, IMF, ADB)
have come to be seen in the last generation, even when objectionable, as in-
separable from the Indonesian economy. This unexamined psychology of
dependence in acceleration of change underlies much ordinary discussion
of "globalization." But how important, really, is recent foreign direct investment to Indonesian growth? Careful study has shown it to be marginal and
even distracting.[54]

Bill Clinton had said in September 1997 that the world faced its greatest
economic crisis in half a century. A year after the Asian crisis began, however, the IMF World Economic Outlook remarked only that there had been
the "mildest of the four slowdowns in the world economy in the past three
decades." Yes, several Asian countries had felt reversals. Brazil had devalued.
Russia had defaulted. But there was little impact on China, India, or Africa.
Growth in the Euro-zone accelerated in 1998. Who had gotten hurt? A Japanese expert on Indonesia rather sullenly remarked that Japan had driven

Table 5. Top ten investors in Indonesia, 1967–July 1997[a]

Nation	$US millions	Number of projects
Japan	38,712.5	965
United Kingdom	27,819.2	226
Hong Kong	17,805.8	360
Singapore	17,553.5	659
USA	13,220.8	270
Taiwan	12,558.5	552
Netherlands	11,339.6	169
South Korea	9,556.9	449
Australia	6,390.4	269
Germany	5,299.7	109

a. "Castle's Insight Indonesia," 1, no. 6, 31 Aug. 98, p. 14, based on *Kompas,* 11 Aug.
98. Compare Booth, table 6.4, p. 263, for breakdown of foreign inflows by type of
investment.

Asian growth while America rode. Worse hit than Japan were "emerging market economies unlucky enough to have become dependent on imports of private, debt-creating capital and foolish enough to defend pegged exchange rates."[55]

Between 1993 and 1997, international investors had poured more than $500 billion into "Opacia," *The Economist*'s amusing term for emerging economies whose banks and companies borrow dollars short-term to finance long-term local projects; where firms lend each other money off the balance sheet; where there is no effective bankruptcy law and "corruption is rife."[56] Hot money in; hot money out. Now hot money back in again. Little had been learned, Paul Krugman said of Asia more than once.[57] *Nothing* had been learned in Indonesia, said a savvy international investor representing a world-class venture fund. Wining, dining, private helicoptering; shell games, routine duping, including self-deception; savage political finance—all were as before, with no net forward motion.[58]

Applying a perspective of centuries rather than several quarters to these phenomena, a British observer saw both Marxism-Leninism and free market economic rationalism as "variants of the Enlightenment project of supplanting the historic diversity of human cultures with a single universal civilization." Both are reckless toward the environment and unsympathetic to human casualties of economic progress. But the United States lacks hegemonic power to make universal free markets even a brief reality; it acts to stall or veto reforms and cannot prevent fractures into blocs, regional hegemonies, local military adventurism, and resource wars, all of which amount to deepening international anarchy.[59] A little humility may be in order. If one takes "cultural pluralism" seriously, then "market pluralism" might be conceived and understood with equal seriousness, as long as transparency is a prevailing value in each, coordinate to both.[60]

Indonesia was still suffering, worst of all, from a financial crisis that was lifting in other countries. In the *kampungs* no one cares what George Soros might say. By February 1998, the combination of drought and economic crisis produced acute "food insecurity" for at least 7.5 million people in 53 districts within 15 provinces of Indonesia. The UN's World Food Program, which had closed its regular work in Indonesia two years before, returned at the government's request. They had worked together on hunger and poverty from 1963 to 1996, beginning when Mount Agung erupted in Bali. Over the next thirty-three years the new agency expanded worldwide to handle about one-fourth of global food aid, with an annual turnover of $15 billion. The WFP combined emergency aid with long-term agricultural support programs, public health centers, and education in nutrition, health, and child care. Indonesia bettered its standing so effectively that the WFP could exit.

Now the WFP was needed again, in every dimension of its capacity. Workers resumed emergency operations in May 1998 in the midst of what was now called *kristal* (a contraction of *krisis total,* which means total crisis). Their actions illustrate what was being felt by ordinary Indonesians: food-for-work programs were set up for urban parents to enable them to eat and to meet school fees for their children; emergency staples and bottom-up development projects were begun for drought-stricken rural areas like East Kalimantan; emergency aid went to soaring numbers of internally displaced persons as a result of Christian-Muslim clashes in Maluku, Dayak-Madurese fighting in West Kalimantan, and violence in East Timor (in 1999) which drove people toward refugee camps in West Timor.[61]

Opacia, Rapacia, and Absentia

Granting that Indonesia had been only thinly built up by the Dutch and was then dismantled and beshambled by Sukarno, and acknowledging that foreign investment under Suharto was exaggerated in quantity and illusory in durability, still, the unusual debilities felt by Indonesia in the mega-crisis following 1997 needed some further explanation. Three major dimensions of Indonesia's national deficiency have powerful explanatory value: its lack of transparency in business and government, its hyper-exploited environment, and the weakness or absence of institutions conducive to democracy and civil society. These three unlovely sisters may be named Opacia, Rapacia, and Absentia.

Rounding up the usual suspects as causes of the Asian financial crisis—excessive short-term capital borrowing, panic psychology, and so forth—is insufficient for long-term explanation. Iwan Jaya Azis emphasizes instead high transaction costs, or the cost of negotiation, information, and enforcement in business arrangements. If all business and government dynamics are personalized, if objective information is negligible, if enforcement of law is arbitrary (or auctionable), and regulation is miniscule (or again, up for subornation), then in bidding for projects, only a few have (or even only one has) a significant likelihood of winning the job, because of the required close link to powerful politicians. When incestuous transactions prevail among a presidential-corporate-foundation complex, true entrepreneurs are hobbled in trying to compete. Adjudicability of property rights and well-defined rules are both necessary but absent. Smoothly functioning markets must aim for the efficiency that prevails only at zero transaction costs. Instead, Suharto's Indonesia made those costs "essentially infinite."[62]

Despite having open-capital accounts (a "good thing") early in the Suharto period, Indonesia increasingly found itself with only one effective institution—the presidency, expressed by Suharto himself, with his family and cronies hanging on. The other strong institution, the army, was loyal to the president by policy and to Suharto personally by its deepening dependence on presidential appointments and booty. According to Azis, "When the economy was booming, the military gradually transformed itself from a repressive force into a mechanism to share some of the national wealth." Once the communists were no longer a danger, the army went from suppression to exploitation.

Azis has pointed out resistance by Dow Chemical to the high transaction costs asked by one of Suharto's sons for Chandra Asri, a failing petrochemical combine of crony Prajogo Pangestu. He sees IBM as "another company known to be strict in repulsing improper deals with the Indonesian partner." On the other hand, Bimantara, under Suharto's son Bambang, managed to attract among its foreign partners Ford Motors, Union Carbide, Waste Management, Hughes Communication, Nippon Electric, and Tokyo Marine and Fire Insurance. The distorting and obscuring impact of such monopolies and cartels as Bimantara put Indonesia at the bottom of the list for Asian countries in 1999, as ranked for transparency by the Hong Kong-based Political and Economic Risk Consultancy, Ltd. Worse than China.

A surge of development halved Indonesia's agricultural sector (from 30.2 percent in 1975 to 15.4 percent in 1996) while boosting the industrial and service sectors. The same surge produced population growth, urbanization, and poverty which interacted upon environmental degradation.[63] Two years into total crisis, urban poverty either increased two and a half times or tripled, and total, including rural, poverty in Indonesia either more than doubled or increased more than three and a half times.[64] As in Bangkok, Manila, and other cities, the mega-urbanization of Jakarta, especially in the 1980s and 1990s, brought the emergence of new townships on the outskirts at an alarming rate. Not only did they have overwhelming environmental impacts on water, soil, and air but they encroached on environmentally sensitive areas like northern Bandung, the Puncak corridors, and Jakarta Waterfront City.

Although potential deterioration in health and education seems to have

Table 6. Increases of numbers in poverty (millions): alternative calculations

Year	Central Bureau of Statistics (CGS)			National Socioeconomic Survey (SUSENAS)		
	Urban	Rural	Total	Urban	Rural	Total
1996	7.2	15.3	22.5	7.2	15.3	22.5
1998	17.6	31.9	49.5	22.6	56.8	79.4

78. URBAN DEVELOPMENT: RANDOM, ARRESTED. The architectural signature of Jakarta, the Bank Negara Indonesia, looms blue and beautiful behind a "see-through skyscraper," one of many projects on which construction was suspended after 1997. Ordinary *kampung* settlements are also visible, and a small mosque is just out of sight in this photograph taken in November 2000. (Sidup Damiri/ author's collection)

been "fairly successfully" arrested through social safety net programs, environmental factors steadily worsened.[65] Osaka and Tokyo by 1990 had reduced air pollution (measured in suspended particulates) below New York and Chicago, but Jakarta's level, five times that of Japanese cities, was much higher than Kuala Lumpur and even Bangkok.[66] Remedies were available, but unused. A policy mix analysis shows that health costs could have been reduced and GDP growth not seriously affected if combined policies had been adopted: unleaded gasoline required, vehicle fuels taxed, two-stroke engines phased out, and emission standards imposed.[67] In agriculture, had the integrated Food-Crop Pest Management Program introduced in 1989 been intensified with a "strategic" program, both a higher GDP growth rate and lesser health costs could have followed. With a less poisoned habitat, people would have become less sick and more productive.[68]

When all the dynamics are arrayed, what did the most damage during

the end years of the Suharto boom was resource depletion followed by degradation of the natural environment. Azis has acknowledged that many resources were left out of his depletion calculation. I would, for instance, observe that his calculations of damage to the ecosystem were far too low,
because forest fires were not included, for which governmental inattention and macro-plantation mismanagement were two major, documentable
causes. All that omitted, Azis still found that during 1990–1995, consumption of fixed assets ran from 7.3 percent to 8.0 percent of GDP. Imputed
environmental costs, without even reckoning fires, subtracted another 1.5
percent to 2 percent from net national product.[69] Ordinary GDP figures,
therefore, were overstated by as much as 10 percent, and growth rates (the
kind published in newspapers and financial newsletters), in consequence,
were seriously inflated.

Azis concluded the obvious: that "growth may entail excessive liquida-
tion of [the] natural resource base," not to mention debilitation of the human resource base. For the strategic future, the logical policy direction
should be toward "more emphasis on less resource-intensive exports and
raising the productivity of resource-oriented export industries." These findings have a simple implication: that Indonesia must rebuild its economy and
the potential of its citizens while at the same time leaving behind destructive environmental habits.

How had Indonesia ever flourished in the first place? (1) Through the revolution toward self-sufficiency in food, stimulated by enormous subsidies
and credits from the government. (2) Through liberalization and privatization in manufacturing, which generated higher output growth despite
KKN. (3) Through widespread investor optimism, domestic and foreign,
which led to relatively low-rate, certainly high-risk loans with expansionary
impact. Such a robust growth story, in a land of rip-offs, could only end
in massive bust. Technological lag was significant, and disruptive capital
flows were serious; but weakness in institutional structures was the factor
that overwhelmingly tipped Indonesia, when rocked, into hypercrisis. That
which is absent cannot absorb shock or restore trust.

Indonesia's protection of property rights was among the best in East
Asia, and better than anything in Latin America—comforting to foreign investors, as little as that mattered.[70] Even with improvements, however, by
1997 Indonesia's market liberalizations compared it favorably in that regard
only with Venezuela, Mexico, Colombia, and Brazil. Its weak position on
corruption was comparable only to Argentina, Colombia, and Mexico (I
would add Nigeria and Russia). Its sorry judiciary was comparable only to
Colombia. Its bureaucracy was among the worst in East Asia, with only the
Philippines (which was actually improving) as a "counterpart."[71]

The comparisons were unpropitious, because they were with so many nations with caudillo/cacique historics, of military leaders or systems run by business bosses with private armies. When the caudillo goes down, his caciques go with him, and the illusion of security for ordinary people is shattered. Through the institutional void howl the winds of hunger and rage.

NEW LEADERS, NEW ISLAM

Most of Indonesia, in 1998–99, wished to become a democracy. Several strains of Islamic thought contended to capture—or transform—that idea. Of the leaders aspiring to the presidency, some wore fabrics of Islam variously interwoven with Indonesian history and tradition. Others were more notable for a basic dress of Pancasila. All had a new population to deal with, in contrast with the 1950s and 1960s. Suharto had wanted to make sure that young people were not educated to be atheists—thus the New Order requirement that "all elementary students [receive] the same mandatory religious instruction from state certified teachers." Such regulations increased the number of Muslims far beyond Suharto's original intentions. Indonesians completing senior high school increased from 3 or 4 percent in 1970 to more than 30 percent in the mid-1990s.[1] Instead of the slender education, religiously lax, of Sukarno times, Indonesia now had many more literate citizens, and far more religiously conscious ones.

The main currents of new (and old) Islamic thinking may be sorted out in rough order of their accord with *reformasi*. From greatest to least sympathy with it, they are: pluralist, syncretist, scripturalist, opportunist, Islamist, and jihadist. Nurcholish Madjid represented the first kind. As a university student and Islamic leader before the crisis of 1965–66. he had been threatened with death by the communist PKI. As a still young man, he called for rethinking Islam. In striking public presentations in 1970–71, he asserted that the idea of Muslim parties and an Islamic state were serious errors. They sacralized things that are actually profane. The Qur'an, he pointed out, does not require an Islamic state. Devotion to the uncompromised oneness of God, however, is wholly consistent with reason and science, because the creator's majesty is found in nature and nature's laws. "Thus modernity resides in . . . discovery of which truths are relative, leading to the discovery of that Truth Which is Absolute, that is Allah."[2]

In pursuing a doctorate at the University of Chicago, which he com-

79. AT WORSHIP IN JAKARTA. In 1993 Muslims gather for prayer in Istiqlal—commissioned by Sukarno as the largest mosque in Southeast Asia. (Bruno Barbey / Magnum Photos)

pleted in 1984, Madjid widened his examination of social scientific and religious thinking from outside Islam; and as an Eisenhower Fellow in the United States in 1990, he strengthened, from intuition to conviction, his view that democracy is an open experiment.[3] While never departing from a core of classical Qur'anic learning, Madjid's pluralism stood in distinct contrast to the oversimplifications required of political leadership. He stood for humane discourse and an open society—one that could develop through contending institutions with checks and balances. Consequently, Cak Nur was everyone's democrat and no one's candidate. So cast, he felt temperamentally fulfilled as an independent moral force, founder of a modern Islamic university, and a frequent media commentator on public affairs.

Madjid's "twin" in the eyes of some was Gus Dur. Also born in Jombang, East Java, Wahid was not, however, a true intellectual sibling. He came out of a different Muslim boarding school with a different tradition. While universalizing his learning in ways not dissimilar to Cak Nur, he adhered closely to his rural constituency of Nahdlatul Ulama (NU), with its syncretic embrace of Sufism and Javanese ritual traditions, including Hindu-Buddhist atavisms.

Different from both of these men was Amien Rais, with his taste for the activism of the Muslim Brotherhood, an organization that originated in Egypt in 1928 but had been banned there since 1954. Even though he himself pulled away from the idea of a Islamic state, his scripturalism kept him at the head of Muhammadiyah, the oldest major Muslim organization in Indonesia, and second largest after NU. His ferocity of views, spontaneity of expression, and nationalism awoke pride among Muslims wearied with the West's dominance and superiority. He was middle-class, urban, rational, and prone to demagogic impulse. He was "modernist" in relation to Gus Dur (meaning, the Qur'an without Javanese culture) and "fundamentalist" in relation to Cak Nur (the Qur'an without western social science). But like Cak Nur he had a Ph.D. from the University of Chicago, and like Gus

80. MUSLIM DEMOCRATIC PLURALIST. As a moderate national leader of Muslims, Dr. Nurcholish Madjid is well informed in modern natural and social sciences. Here, he is at home with his wife, Omi Komaria. Between them is a calligraphic and decorative rendering of the opening of the Qur'an. These verses, "Al-Fatihah," are said to serve many of the same functions as the Lord's Prayer in Christianity. (Sidup Damiri/author's collection)

Dur he enjoyed the challenge of rallying millions by spoken and written word.

While those three leaders were recognizably democratic reformers, two of them with parties behind them, there remained two other major Muslim forces, one a political party, one not, in both of which Muslim law overshadowed democratic principles, or swallowed them up altogether. PPP (Partai Persatuan Pembangunan or Development Unity Party) had been constructed by order of Suharto as a Muslim catchall party, and it continued to function, like Golkar, with old momentum in the new environment. It was "opportunistic" in ways that the Republican and Democrat parties in the United States are also opportunistic. Its leader, Hamzah Haz, was an establishment political operator, less distinct for his individual views on Islam than for exploiting the democratic environment to allow his party to avail itself of sentiment against Golkar's repression and against any secularism detected in the other candidates.

At an extreme of Islamic thinking was the nonparty organization Dewan Dakwah Islamiyah Indonesia, as intolerant as Cak Nur was inclusive and as scripturally rigid as he was pluralistic. The late Muhammad Natsir founded it in 1967 as a "propagation council" to counter the inroads of Christian missionary projects. As propagators of Islam, the Dewan Dakwah responded to being shut out from political power by "moving down market, directing their appeals at the urban poor and the lower middle class," according to Robert Hefner's summary. As a panacea for society's ills they offered Islamic law *(shari'ah)* and ritual observance and "denounced conspicuous consumption, governmental corruption, Javanese mysticism, Muslim liberalism, and the economic dominance of the Chinese." Since one enemy is simpler to attack than many targets, they identified all these forces as part of a larger conspiracy to "Christianize" Indonesia.[4] While Indonesia's central Islamic tension was between those who believed Muhammadiyah was right in religion and those who felt NU was right in culture, the Dewan Dakwah nipped at the heels of both with "correct" dogmatic teeth of law and piety.

Dewan Dakwah followers were Islamist but not necessarily jihadist. Only later would ethno-religious tensions reveal those few, from differing backgrounds, who believed in the use of violence to achieve Islamic objectives. Indonesia had always contained potential jihadists, who saw an uncompromising Islamic state as the supreme end and violence as a justifiable means. In the early years of the republic, Kartosoewiryo's followers had killed many thousands and died for their aims in the Darul Islam rebellion.

In the mid-Suharto years a self-styled branch of the Muslim Brotherhood

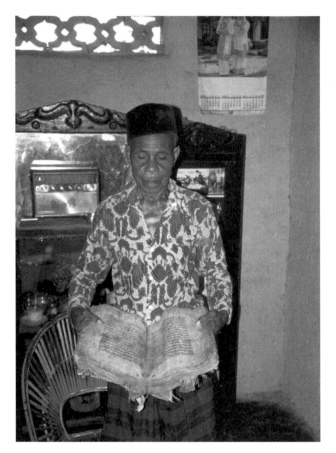

81. PROVINCIAL ULAMA. A teacher of Islam on the island of Alor displays a copy of the Qur'an that is six hundred years old. (Cathy Forgey)

operated as an underground movement and brought off the bombing of Borobudur in 1985. Jail and exiles then kept it quiet, but it would declare itself in public just before the parliamentary elections of 1999. In this *reformasi* atmosphere of openness, the first national congress of *mujahadin* gathered in Yogya the next year. It concluded on August 7, 2000, with the establishment of the Indonesian Holy Warrior Assembly (Majelis Mujahadin Indonesia, or MMI). On that date, fifty-one years before, Kartosoewirjo had proclaimed his Islamic State of Indonesia, followed by a dozen years of heavy bloodshed. The precedent and its portents were ominous for a peaceful, pluralistic Indonesia.

For a while the most charismatic figure among the jihadists was Ja'far Umar Thalib, partly educated in Pakistan and Yemen and experienced in Afghanistan. A Wahhabi revivalist and a Salafi puritan, he organized the Laskar Jihad in 1998. Two years later he exported them eastward as a paramilitary front of 10,000 members against Christians in Maluku, Central Sulawesi, and Papua. Nationalistic, and critical of Osama bin Laden's worldview, Ja'far directed his forces with martial zeal and effect until he was jailed in 2002 for slandering President Megawati.

The supreme advisory council of the MMI, meanwhile, was led by Abu Bakar Ba'syir, and included several prominent personalities such as Deliar Noer. Noer's links back to the Masyumi party of the Sukarno era, and its "modernism," dignified the presence on the council of anti-modern hyper-textualists, of whom Ba'syir was one. Ba'syir had been arrrested in 1978 for promoting an Islamic caliphate throughout Southeast Asia. His organization became the Jemaah Islamiyah (JI: Islamic Community) which seeks a merged state for all Muslims in Southeast Asia—Indonesia, Malaysia, the southern Philippines, and southern Thailand. He had emigrated to Malaysia in the early 1990s with disciples, but *reformasi* allowed him back, and he established a network of reactionary boarding schools, centered upon his Ngruki *pesantren* in Central Java. To the MMI he declared the necessity of *shariah*. The rejection of Islamic holy law must be countered by *jihad*.[5]

Some French intellectuals diagnosed neo-fundamentalists such as these jihadists as part of an ebbing tide of global Islamic revolution, and therefore of minimal strategic consequence. Were they right? Some Indonesian Muslim pluralists saw them as sure to lose momentum when Indonesia regained its social equilibrium.[6] When would that be?

In the late New Order environment, power struggles continued on shaky pre-*reformasi* premises. Gus Dur had disappointed many reformists when, in the first half of 1997, he befriended Tutut Suharto, traveling with her on the Golkar campaign trail. Always mercurial, he repositioned himself yet again for reform after the Asian financial crisis broke in late 1997. In December Wahid joined with Megawati and Amien Rais in a move that looked sassy and futile at the time but was proven brave and fertile later: they demanded that President Suharto step down.

That step energized the frenetic General Prabowo in behalf of his father-in-law's regime. After a public ceremony on January 23, 1998, to break the fast of Ramadan—a ceremony where ultra-conservative Muslim activists tied to Dewan Dakwah were present—Prabowo was said to have privately provided them with documents detailing the "Jewish-Jesuit-American-Chinese" effort to topple Suharto: a giant conspiracy of the IMF, the United States, Israel, CIA-Mossad, and Indonesia's pro-democracy movement.[7] This incongruous, indeed impossible, assemblage of elements would continue to fester in hyper-Islamic thinking in many parts of Indonesia.

By May 1998, however, Suharto had left the palace, and by August Prabowo had left the country, which made Indonesia safer for reformers. But the three oppositionists who had gotten together to denounce the regime could not agree to announce a coalition and thus assure that *reformasi* would prevail.

Gus Dur and the PKB

As the senior and most world-traveled of the three reform leaders, Gus Dur seemed the most likely to initiate and host meetings for unity among them. But he tended to estrange himself at key moments from his "sister," Megawati. Personal clashes left him unable to think of Mas Amien as a "brother" in the cause of reform. Trying to bridge differences in the religious and social views of their respective Islamic organizations, Gus Dur generously initiated a visit in mid-1998 to Amien, the younger leader. But after it was reported back to him (truly or falsely) that Amien had described the gesture to associates as a "surrender" of Gus Dur, all the good the visit may have achieved instantly vanished.[8] Amien, perhaps sincerely, professed puzzlement at why Gus Dur did not seem to like him. He formulated an amusing apothegm: "There are three things about which one cannot be sure: (1) the course of a marriage; (2) when you will die; and (3) what Gus Dur will do next."[9]

Those who tried to find an anchor for Wahid's beliefs in the writings of Muslim theologians came up with different answers. An American expert cited the mysticism of the tenth-century orthodox Sufi, al-Junayd. An NU and Madurese intimate of Gus Dur said his behavior was more akin to that of al-Farabi, another tenth-century Sufi, more heterodox and extravagant, heavily influenced by Plato and the ideal of a philosopher king.[10] Whichever may be the case, Wahid's behavior reminded me of the Sufi concept of "Wisdom of the Idiots" and of Taoist depictions of Lao-tzu riding his ox backwards, as a sacred fool attempting to awaken a dulled world.

Not even Alwi Shihab, dutiful Sancho Panza to Wahid's Quixote, could predict his boss's behavior. Sulawesi born, Alwi had been with him in Cairo—going to the movies, attending the soccer games. Getting a Ph.D. there and another one in the United States, Alwi was two doctorates up on his boss, but he readily acknowledged that Gus Dur was leagues ahead of him in political savvy and energy. Alwi told me a story that seemed to encapsulate the strange confluence of Indonesian politics and religion at the highest levels. In mid-1998, he said, ex-president Suharto was attending Friday religious services at various local military stations, at each of which he conferred with General Wiranto, who was also attending. Habibie, now president, started showing up too, so that he could make the two-way conversations triangular. Alwi's brother, Qureshi Shihab, was also present, having been Suharto's minister of religion, still on call to him for religious counsel and for annual services in memory of Suharto's wife, Ibu Tien. Habibie was trying to press Qureshi into service for *his* government, but Qureshi, out of loyalty to his brother, was hanging loose to see what Gus

Dur would do. Alwi, reflecting on turbulent ambitions at the pinnacle during transitions of power, commented with a mild smile, "You see how easily your friend becomes your enemy."[11]

In July Gus Dur formally announced the long-planned founding of the Partai Kebangkitan Bangsa (PKB), the Party of the People's Awakening, with an open membership recruitment system and without ethnic or religious prejudice. He cited a key NU edict of its 1935 Congress, "that it is not obligatory for Indonesian Muslims to establish an Islamic state." Wahid maintained that Indonesia comprises three major races: Malay, Austro-Melanesian, and Chinese. He declared himself as having some Chinese and Arab ancestry. Matori Abdul Djalil, chosen as chairman of the new party, announced, in turn, that "if necessary [it] would be ready to form a coalition with other political forces."[12]

Alwi, now a vice chairman of the PKB, tried to separate religious sentiments from recent riots. "The Muslims . . . would never say 'God is great' while raping women. This is because believers in God never remember their God when they commit sinful deeds . . . Also Muslims would never condemn Jesus while setting ablaze a church, because honoring Jesus (and the other messengers of God) is one of the six principles of belief in God."[13] In late September 1998 Alwi felt that a reform coalition would get 55 percent of the vote. "And then," said Alwi, with a modest, innocent, vulnerable smile, "we will run the country."[14] Ah, I thought with a sigh, God help you.

To realize his political ambitions, Wahid needed a modern physiotherapist. He found one in Marla Kosec, wife of my friend Bernie Scher, with whom I traveled in Toraja. An American who became Gus Dur's confidante and critic as well, Marla was born O'Duffie and grew up in Florida. Having survived ovarian cancer at age twenty-three and now not yet forty, she was a big, strong, broad-shouldered woman, with gray hair in a military buzz-cut, lipstick in a thin purple line. Her green-gray eyes were often smiling, but when they were not, she radiated the pale, powerful allure of the Angel of Death.

Marla was a hospicer and New Age philosopher repelled by the materialism and bureaucracy of American medicine. As a superb physiotherapist specializing in victims of heart attack and stroke, she eventually drew Indonesians behind her to fund a rehabilitation clinic. She trained the staff herself, and in no time they were managing sixty patients—an astounding feat of philanthropic entrepreneurship, teaching, hands-on management, and therapy in a nation convulsed with unrest.

Gus Dur heard about Marla and asked her for help. His stroke had taken away most of the eyesight in his one good eye. His wife, Nuriyah, was a tetraplegic from her car accident. He was depressed. He invited Marla out to stay at his place, "chickens and all." She went, with Bernie. Under her healing hands, a friendship flourished. Compassion from Gus Dur and Nuriyah in turn touched Marla. "He asked me to be his sister." Wahid offered generously to help with her clinic. When Marla had to go to America to be with Bernie during his third heart operation, they kept in touch by phone. Marla exploded on the rapes of Chinese women during the May riots. "The people who did this are *Muslims* . . . In the name of God, the sight of God, Gus Dur, *say something!* This is not a political issue. It's moral, *religious*. I can't deal with the politics of your hospital. I don't want to be involved in it!"[15]

On August 11 Wahid called her. He wanted her to know that he was going on national TV to expand his position critical of those doing violence to Chinese. He had received letters threatening that "if you continue to support the Chinese, we will do to your daughters what we have done to them." He wanted Marla's appreciation of his courage. But now she said, "Have you talked it over with your daughters?" (No.) "You can't sacrifice your children! You've got to talk it over with your daughters first!" Gus Dur: "You are my best friend." Marla: "No. I'm your worst enemy. I'll sit on one shoulder and hop to the other until you get your balance."[16]

Amien Rais and PAN

Despite advice from Alwi and others, Gus Dur became even more dismissive of Amien Rais. He criticized Amien's extreme Islamic views, his support of affirmative action policies, his frequent changes of view (he took an Indonesian breakfast of fermented soybean cake and for dinner ate Western sweetcakes). "I'll not work with Amien Rais regardless of the cost," Gus Dur vented.[17]

The cost, pragmatic friends worried, could be the election. The depth of Golkar's unpopularity was unproven, and the extent of its hidden purses untested. This was no time to alienate other Muslims. Deliar Noer, general chairman of the recently founded Islamic People's Party (Partai Ummat Islam), commented: "Gus Dur is tolerant of others, but why isn't he tolerant of Islam?"[18] He argued that Islamic morals incorporated in law could reform a society torn and corrupted by Suharto's regime.

The Islamic organization which claimed to have the most members after NU was Muhammadiyah, at 28 million and growing. Founded in Yogya in 1912 and still based there, it was now led by Amien Rais. Drawing on that base, in 1998 Amien decided to start a political party (PAN) to compete on a modernist secular plane against Gus Dur's PKB. Both parties could be likened to political automobiles with reformist chassis and a Pancasila body. But their engines ran on different fuel: Amien's PAN on Muhammadiyah textualism and Wahid's PKB on NU cultural syncretism. Neither would receive as many popular votes as the Muslim political vehicle PPP, engineered on a Suharto chassis with an Islamic body and fueled by inherited patronage. But the support behind any one party was irrelevant to the question bedeviling Indonesia and puzzling the world: could Muslim reformers unite to defeat Golkar and its potential allies?

Amien tried hard. His simplicity in style of life, like Gus Dur's, was at that time unchallengeable. Almost 60 percent of the premises of his pink stucco home, about 600 yards in perimeter, were given over to an Islamic kindergarten with 200 students. The car he drove to his lectureship at Gadjah Mada University was an '88 Suzuki. In front of his house was a Chinese food shop managed by his wife, who also managed the kindergarten in a building made of bamboo.[19]

His leading role in getting rid of Suharto put him in the forefront, he knew, of an even harder task: rebuilding Indonesia. He drew large and vocal crowds and sat cross-legged until he rose to the microphone. An enchanted reporter for *The New York Review of Books* wrote, "At fifty-five he has a boyish quality and a lilting way of speaking."[20]

Amien had grown up in Solo, another Javanese court town. His mother and father were both devout ("pure,") urban Muslims, who worked for the Sukarno government's department of religious affairs. On scholarships in the United States, he studied at Notre Dame and received his doctorate in political science at the University of Chicago. His doctoral program included a year at Al-Azhar in Cairo, where his research focused on the Muslim Brotherhood, which had resisted both Nasser and Sadat. Rais concluded by rejecting the Brotherhood's religious justification for violence, as well as its idea of religious fundamentalism as a guide for modern Muslims. "Where [he asked] is the source of legitimacy in an Islamic state? The Koran or the people? Who is the sovereign? The people or God?"[21] Like Gus Dur's PKB, Amien Rais's PAN would adopt the Pancasila as their party "basis," conceding that a modern state serving the people should treat them as politically sovereign. As for the moral sovereignty of God and the cultural dynamics of Islam, they must be acknowledged and acted on, not in a context of an Islamic state but within the hearts and minds of individuals in a Muslim-majority society.

Both reform leaders needed to gather at least two kinds of possibly discomfited support. One was Muslims more Qur'anic and comprehensively orthodox than themselves. There Amien had an advantage. The other was non-Muslims, especially members of the Christian church, including

Chinese Indonesians who found themselves, either by conviction or by political refuge, under its church bells. There Gus Dur had the advantage, not
only because of his own universalism but because of Rais's anti-Christian,
anti-Chinese record.

When Amien returned to Indonesia in 1982, he was rankled that
"Suharto had left Muslims behind, they were left out and had no political
voice. I looked around and it seemed that Chinese and Christians had all the
power."[22] When Suharto did his pro-Muslim *volte face* and created ICMI in
1990, Amien accepted prominence in it: he wrote a column in its newspaper
Republika; chaired the council of experts who selected research projects for
government support; seized the opportunity to utter national warnings
against "Christianization of Indonesia"; and finally assumed leadership of
Muhammadiyah, where he was not only true to its strict religious mission
but also able now to "offer jobs for the faithful, while always pledging loyalty to the regime."[23]

By 1998–99, however, under free-press interrogation into his past, Amien
claimed that he had turned against the president when Suharto became the
greatest threat to Indonesia. South Korea had set a good example for treating malfeasant former leaders, he said: give them severe sentences, death or
life. Or try Suharto and then pardon him, "provided he returns everything
he has plundered during his presidency." Rais now spoke positively on the
"wonderful aspects of democracy as practiced in the U.S." and the affirmative action plan for Malays in Malaysia's New Economic Policy. Rais
was highly negative about Islamic extremists in Iran, Afghanistan, and the
Sudan.[24]

Habibie, ABRI, the bureaucracy, and Golkar, he told an American audience, were still *there,* an enormous Suharto structure to be overcome. Foreign investment would understandably remain on the sidelines until it saw
election results and a credible government. Certain political groups were
promoting bloody crimes as a provocation of the masses and as an invitation to ABRI to take power. He reported a recent conversation with
Wiranto, ABRI's commander. Amien: "You are chief of ABRI. You *must*
know who are the provocateurs of these inhumane killings." Wiranto: "Security and defense are also in the hands of the people." Amien: "Your intelligence system goes from Sabang to Merauke. It must *know* . . . who is responsible for the crimes." But he remained unanswered.

Questioned on the three main reform parties, Rais described all as having
Pancasila as their ideological base. As constituent base, however, his own
consisted of orthodox Muslims *(santris),* mostly urban, plus others; Gus
Dur's base was also practicing Muslims, but mostly rural; and Megawati's
base was mostly nonpracticing Muslims *(abangans).* After the election, the

optimal scenario was a coalition of all three. "The political parties that believe in a *shari'ah* state will not get more than 25 percent of the vote," Rais projected. He overestimated. In the end, all parties based on Islam together got less than 18 percent, only two-fifths of their achievement in 1955. But the behavior of Rais would suggest more affinity with Moon and Star, the Justice Party, and Hamzah's PPP, all of which openly declared for an Islamic order, than with Gus Dur's syncretist PKB or Megawati's secular PDI.

I asked Rais privately why the Pancasila and reform parties did not build a coalition *before* the election? Were the differences in the *aliran* too deep? He answered, "We need to see the results of the election in *numbers*."[25]

Megawati and PDI-P

Megawati Sukarnoputri spent her first twenty years in the shade of a loving and indulgent father and her next thirty years in the shadow of his ever-threatening successor. Both experiences may have served to stifle initiative and expression, while she cultivated other characteristics—maternal and stoical—that were becoming to an eldest Javanese sister. Sukarno in 1963 raised the prospect of her marriage to a young parachutist hero whom he had recently decorated in the West Irian campaign. But then Major Benny Moerdani was already betrothed. Mega eventually married an air force lieutenant, by whom she had two sons and was pregnant with a daughter when his plane crashed in Irian Jaya in 1971, only half a year after her father's death.[26] In mid 1972 she eloped with an Egyptian of whom her family disapproved. One and a half hours after their marriage in a Religious Affairs Office, her family reclaimed her and two weeks later steered her through the Special Islamic Court of Jakarta, which dissolved the bond. "She said she was hypnotized," says a family friend, who did not press further.[27]

In 1973 Mega married a South Sumatran named Taufik Kiemas and raised her children while he built a chain of six gas stations in Jakarta's Chinatown. She opened a flower shop with four friends in 1979, supplying several of the city's fanciest hotels, though she "didn't know anything about the business part" of the enterprise. Sukarno had claimed that his daughter desired to become an agro-engineer, but his overthrow had led her to discontinue courses at her father's alma mater, the Bandung Institute of Technology.[28] Her dream of being part of laboratory-based solutions to the nation's food shortage, so that the crisis of 1963–1965 would not recur, would be fulfilled by scientists of other nations. Mega settled for loving flowers and arranging them.

Suharto had made sure that Mega's father was buried far from Jakarta—near his mother in East Java—but he allowed a partial rehabilitation of

Sukarno in 1979. Perhaps, at a deep layer of motivation, Mega entered politics with the PDI in 1986 in order to ensure his full restoration in the minds of the people. But if she would become the heroine of many young women and the beneficiary of modern views emphasizing the equality of all human beings before God, the fact remained that every one of 56 Indonesian Islamic books on women analyzed as late as 1991 supported "conventional discourses." Not only male preachers with wide audiences but many female preachers held patriarchal views about the proper role of women.[29] The Megawati who sought power to rescue her father from Suharto's purgatory would ultimately, as she approached the presidency, encounter an invisible but emotionally tangible *purdah*—a sexist curtain between herself and the realization of her ambitions. She was not only secular—the daughter of the formulator of Pancasila—but she was female. These facts kept many Muslims at a distance from her.

Nonetheless, many other people were drawn to Megawati's enigmatic majesty, which combined, in curious ways, courage, patience, and passivity. In 1998–99 she puzzled would-be followers and dismayed loyalists with her inaction after Suharto's fall—a behavior that was hard to reconcile with her years of resistance to his regime. After all, daughters of heads of government in India, Pakistan, Bangladesh, and Sri Lanka had been elected to top office on their fathers' heritages and then reelected on their own first-term record. Megawati's prospects of joining that group seemed excellent: she had the longest experience in national politics of all the Indonesian reformists—going back to 1986. She motivated herself with photographs of her father at home and with other echoes of her father on campaign trails.

Perhaps her heritage explains why she rejected comparison with Corazon Aquino of the Philippines, who entered politics in the same year as she with an upset electoral victory over the dictator Ferdinand Marcos. Cory was the widow of a political martyr, assassinated because he was Marcos's most formidable opponent and critic. But Megawati was a daughter of a man who died a slow unnatural death, never touched by harsh hands but politically asphyxiated in his home arrest, so that in the end, often tearful, he hardly spoke to his family. A more apt comparison to Mega's sorrowful patience was Aung San Suu Kyi, daughter of the revolutionary father of modern Burma. Even after her democratic election victory was taken away by the military in 1988, she carried on her campaign against the thugs who tried to restrict her and her followers, and on behalf of a people she described as "wearied of a precarious state of passive apprehension where they were 'as water in the cupped hands' of the powers that be."[30]

With her entry into politics, Megawati helped to build her party's share of the popular vote from 8 percent in 1982 to 11 percent in 1987 to 15 percent in 1992. That was enough to prompt Suharto to crush the PDI a year before the election of 1997. She knew fear and spoke consolingly to her people of it. She knew brutality and withstood it. She was nurturing and stoical in ways that endeared her to the masses. She was the daughter of a president who did not use his office to enrich his children. She was long-suffering, patient, practical—all virtues anywhere but almost worshipably so in the Indonesian opposition of the 1980s and 1990s. But she lent herself perhaps too easily to becoming an icon for her party, instead of seeking to find and express an independent political character for herself.

After years of making mild public statements and evading interviews, at last, in 1998, she began independently to insist that Suharto should step aside. Early in that year she received a reporter from *Vogue,* a woman who had waited days for the interview and had been warned (against military wire taps) not to mention Megawati's name on the phone. She asked Megawati if she feared that her life was in danger. Mega nodded but smiled. "I believe I have people who love me and they are watching very closely over me." The visitor studied her carefully:

> It's the brow, the high forehead, and the heavy eyelids that give her face nobility. She is short, broad-hipped and full-breasted, with a handsomeness framed in elegance . . . a loose, dark, below-the-knee skirt with a soft scooped-neck blouse, and low-heeled black leather pumps. Her legs, which she keeps crossed at the ankles, are bare and unshaven. Only the outsize pink-tinted eyeglasses and the jade and gold jewelry on her fingers and wrists reveal the slightest taste for luxury . . . She is not Benazir Bhutto . . . champion debater, a wily girl, one of the world's sexiest politicians. She is certainly not Aung San Suu Kyi . . . [lacking her] orchid beauty, her brilliance of intellect, her hardness of spirit.

So unchic, what vaulted Mega into the pages of *Vogue?* According to Gus Dur, "She's not a politician, but that's precisely what attracts people to her. In a way she's the consternation of almost every group. Even groups like ourselves, because we don't know what she will do." "I am no Indonesian lady," Mega said for herself. "I am different from them. You know our culture . . . that it is still a tradition that the woman has the duty to stay in the background. That is why I think I am rather unique." "If you were a man, and not a Sukarno, would the government have handled you differently?" the reporter from *Vogue* asked. "This is not because of gender . . . This is politics. It's the power I have . . . I can hypnotize people."[31]

Months later, Suharto was out of power and Mega's campaign began to

82. MEGAWATI, GUS DUR, AND AMIEN RAIS. The three most prominent reform politicians infrequently conferred in private and rarely appeared jointly in public. Here, in 1999, they are caught on a dais together. (Kemal Jufri/IMAJI)

come into focus. She had a rousing opening rally in Bali in October 1998, hitting hard at thirty years of mushrooming corruption: "Now we must destroy the fungus." When she spoke of lack of food for the children of peanut farmers (some now as badly off as in 1964, when she delighted her father with plans to be an agricultural scientist), "her voice wavered emotionally."[32]

One of Mega's key advisors, Laksamana Sukardi, formerly with City Bank, spoke at the Harvard Club in New York in January 1999. His description of the Suharto system was terse and powerful: power-franchising had provided about 30 percent of the increase in GDP; it was a mode of economic growth driven by corruption and fueled by foreigners, "like driving a car at 250 miles per hour without a seat belt."[33] Laksamana's kind of advice was behind Megawati's nicely structured speech in Singapore the following March, in which she defined seven causes of crisis and laid out the principles of competitive politics, an open society, and a transparent economy.[34] A week before the election Mega was asked if she was ready to compete ("tusk it out with") Habibie. She laughed. Not just she but all her party. They were ready, win or lose.[35]

Habibie and Golkar

B. J. Habibie grew up in Parepare on the southwest coast of Sulawesi. He habitually wore a black velvet cap, traditional to Indonesian nationalism since the 1920s but associated in his case more with the Muslim intellectuals of ICMI, in charge of whose adventures Suharto had placed him in 1990. His eyes flashed with intelligence, but he twisted his legs when he talked, rolled his head, exploded in manic gestures. A high-pitched voice and defensive style belied whatever gravity there might be in his opinions. Physically slight, he frequently twitched like a comic *wayang* puppet. He became president of Indonesia on a few hours notice.

Suharto had named Habibie his vice president in March 1998 because as a surrogate son, or at least a spiritual nephew, he posed no threat to himself. But when Suharto toppled out of office two months later, the question became real: what would B. J. Habibie mean to the Indonesian nation? His two major associations had been with Suharto, from the time Habibie was a teenager, and with Germany. There, many years of education and employment, up to the level of vice president of Messerschmitt, had made him, he acknowledged, three times faster reading German than reading Bahasa Indonesia. The German way of doing international business, like the Japanese way, involved noncontractual transfers of money to make things happen, or to reward smooth happenings, or simply to enrich propitious contacts. Such payments were notoriously hard to document, but *Der Spiegel* produced a photocopy just before Indonesia's parliamentary election of October 1999 showing a remittance of 200,000 marks in 1991 from Ferrostaal to Habibie's private account with the Deutsche Bank. In 1999, "according to our arithmetic," the CEO of Ferrostaal said, "Habibie will be president again."[36]

Other stories became credible in this light. Leaving a meeting of major international electrical concerns at the conclusion of negotiations, Habibie was said to remark, "Don't forget my million dollar commission." A former chairman of Siemens gave this evaluation: "We brought him along, we built him up, then he turned and put the bite on us. Now he's got a castle in Germany that makes mine look like a garage."[37]

In 1999 a German business magazine complained about Habibie that "what we've experienced is a Germanized form of Indonesian management."[38] But some Germans were not complaining. Interatom, a subsidiary of Siemens AG, won the bid to construct Indonesia's first full-sized nuclear reactor in 1981, even though American, Canadian, and French contenders underbid it. In 1994 Habibie got Suharto's approval to buy thirty-nine used ships from the East German Navy against the wishes of the Indonesian Navy and ABRI commanders, and at a price three times that agreed to by the minister of finance.[39] Having learned such games from Suharto and then having replaced him, Habibie was unlikely to prosecute his predecessor. Indeed, he conferred on Suharto the dignity of political protection for service to his country, while Wiranto provided military protection. Seventeen months later, when Habibie was gone from office and reformists were freer to look for pilfered national assets and prosecute officials for squandering national resources, the trail had gone cold and the cash had been sequestered.

Newsweek, early in 1999, queried Habibie on his chief connection and asked him why he didn't change the system. He answered: "I'm [Suharto's] close friend. He treated me like his own brother, sometimes like his own son. Once he asked me what I thought about the economy. I told him: 'Don't be mad, Mr. President. In my eyes the economy today is an early, dirty, primitive, capitalistic economy.' 'Yes,' he said, 'but any society must go through that tunnel.' I told him, 'But don't stay too long in that tunnel.' That's all I could do. I was just a small minister."[40]

But Habibie was not satisfied with being a "transitional president," as the reformers for a while convinced themselves he intended to be. He wanted to be elected in his own right. He got the endorsement of Golkar, led by Akbar Tandjung. And he would take every step, or through Golkar permit every step, to make it happen, including allegedly diverting World Bank Society Safety Net funds in the amount of $800 million to Golkar and other establishment candidates; distributing monies through cooperatives, 30 percent of which was lost in corruption, according to an Asia Foundation study; and at one point directing allocations of approximately $18,000 to all MPR members as rewards for service.[41] An indirect electoral system looked beneficial to Habibie. Even Daniel Lev, an expert on Indonesian law and an eloquent critic of its abuses, said that as incumbent, with all that meant in money, machinery, and momentum, "It's likely that Habibie [will be] elected."[42]

That might not be such a terrible thing, some educated Jakartans began to say. Habibie had liberated political prisoners. He had opened up a free press—dramatically, unrestrictedly free—upon the proposal of Lieutenant General (retired) Yunus Yosfiah as minister of information. He was keeping to a schedule for free elections. He had even offered East Timor a referendum on its future. Habibie was a democrat at heart. And if not, he had reconstructed himself that way as a political artifact, because only as a democrat could he get elected. Even Gus Dur, by July 1999, said that Pak Habibie "may even meet all the requirements to be called a reformist."[43] But Wahid was almost never without a good word, under the right circumstances, for a questionable personage. And by that moment, the votes had been counted. Golkar had done well, and serious coalition-groping was at last beginning.

Reformists at Ciganjur, Chaos in Semanggi

The MPR had opened its first post-Suharto meeting on November 10, 1998. Political reform was at stake, and the reformists were in continued disarray. General Wiranto had freshly hired an alleged 125,000 "volunteers" as a civilian militia called the Pam Swakarsa, especially to guard the MPR and President Habibie. Protesting students were out in huge numbers, demanding an investigation of Suharto's corruption and an end to the military's role in politics. Against this middle-class swell was arrayed the dollar-a-day underclass, organized under the banner of Pam Swakarsa, carrying sharpened bamboo staves (see Figure 73). Some withdrew after several were killed in clashes with citizens resenting the group's presence in their neighborhoods. But other elements, recruited and harangued to "defend Islam," wore headbands in Arabic: "There is no God but God." They did not withdraw but became part of a rising ferment and violence that threatened a repetition of the disaster in May.

Among students, a naturally broad range of opinion and tactical style existed, including the anarchistic bloc of them called FORKOT.[44] But constructive elements, using Karlina and Ninok Leksono's house as a base, were persuasive enough to force Gus Dur, Amien Rais, and Mega, together with each other and with Sultan Hamengku Buwono X, who belonged to no party but had independent credibility. They met at Wahid's simple residence. A student commando deputation "practically kidnapped" the sultan from transit in the Jakarta airport to bring him in.[45] The Ciganjur Four, named after Wahid's neighborhood, issued a statement on November 10 declaring Habibie's government "transitional," urging acceleration of the date of elections, and demanding an end to the military's role in politics within six years.

Most students found this "mainstream opposition" statement too sluggish. They intensified their protests, with 50,000 thronging the assembly building and area. At Semanggi, on November 13, the final day of the MPR, last restraints dissolved. Provocations by Pam Swakarsa triggered chaos, to which students, angry citizens, and undisciplined solders contributed. Troops opened fire with live ammunition. At least 15 people were killed and 500 were injured.[46] As late as March 2002, the DPR reiterated its stand that three waves of sniper killings—here at Semanggi, previously at Trisakti (May 12, 1998) and again at "Semanggi II" (September 18, 1999)—must not be classified as gross violations of human rights. This stance allowed generals Wiranto, Djadja Suparman, and Syafrie Syamsuddin, among others, to ignore summonses from a special Commission of Investigation on those incidents.

The Habibie government instead arrested retired army generals, critics of Suharto, on grounds of treason. Rumors flew that Gus Dur would be arrested. NU followers promised "to defend our leader to our last drop of blood." Wahid called Generals Wiranto and Bambang Yudhoyono to test their intentions and then assured his followers that no blood sacrifice would be necessary.[47] Most groups likewise talked themselves out of the spirals of suspicion, frustration, fear, and revenge that had wrecked Jakarta just six months before. Those who took time to assess the new decrees of the MPR could at least see that Pancasilaism was softened, the president was limited to two terms, and both regional autonomy and human rights were now strongly stipulated in print, if not in practice.[48]

Many more died at Semanggi than at Trisakti, but the Habibie government did not fall. Even though there was now a timetable for elections—in June 1999—students were further radicalized. The Ciganjur Four, the hope of the reformists, appeared capable only of a suspicious quadrille, a competitive card game, the antithesis of charismatic partnership. How would Indonesia go forward?

In late November a back alley brawl over a parking lot franchise for a gaming house led to escalated fighting between a group of migrant Ambonese and some local Jakartans. Thirteen of the heavily outnumbered Ambonese were hacked to death. The media focused on religion, but that was just one facet of the conflict. The Jakarta spark ignited social tinder far eastward in Kupang and Maluku, and world media soon carried scenes of spreading communal violence, including decapitated heads held triumphantly by the hair. Wahid lamented that "the government is losing control. We may not make it to the election."[49] He was said to be working seventeen hours a day and writing fifteen articles a month, for seven Jakarta publications, including his own new NU daily.[50]

"Hidden Kiai" and the Pharaoh

As NU leader, Gus Dur was only one *ulama* among the body of such men learned in Islam. Sometimes he must heed; must even heel, as in this story I heard and tracked down in the second quarter of 1999. Three *kiai mastur* ("hidden kiai") went in late 1998 to the chairman of NU in East Java, the distinguished Hasyim Muzadi. They asked him to take them to Gus Dur. Surprised, he agreed. At the meeting with Gus Dur, they announced that he should "go see the tyrant [Suharto] seven times" in order to bring peace to the land, just as Moses had gone to see the Pharaoh, as told in the Qur'an.

Gus Dur, off balance and perplexed, said he could not do that. He was an opponent of the ex-president. The *kiais* replied, are you the religious leader of NU, our Moses, or not? Gus Dur, still recovering, balked by querying, what good would it do? The *kiais* answered that it was revealed and mandated in the Qu'ran, and, they repeated, it would bring peace. Gus Dur asked, but what if it failed? What would the people think of him then? The *kiais* replied that this answer revealed him as just another popular politician. His attitude was not consistent with his being religious leader of the NU.

Gus Dur agonized over the matter. After several weeks—and now that the violence in Maluku gave him popular cover to do a repellent thing—he went to see Suharto. "Seven times?" I asked Alwi Shihab incredulously. "Seven times, as in the Qur'an," he affirmed. "And Suharto received him seven times?" "Yes. But the violence continued, and Gus Dur said publicly it was no good. Suharto was of no help, and he wouldn't see him again."[51] In this way, it appeared to me, Gus Dur had managed to support a popular impression (also his personal conviction) that the deposed Suharto, through henchmen, was still behind much destabilizing mischief in Indonesia, in order to keep New Order forces as strong as possible irrespective of any election. In addition to verifying this belief, Wahid also had succeeded in performing his felt obligation to his *kiais* after humiliating effort, thus satisfying his "deep constituency" in the NU.

In East Java I pursued the story to Hasyim Muzadi himself. He generously drove two hours on a Sunday to meet me at NU headquarters in Surabaya. Barefoot young men dozing on benches snapped to attention. Muzadi ordered tea and cakes in a huge meeting room for the two of us. He confirmed the outline of the events as I knew them, while adding layers of religious convictions and motivations.

There were actually four *kiai*. "Special *kiai*," Muzadi called them, not "hidden *kiai*," who are even more holy. The special *kiai* pray and fast, uninfluenced by the society of this world. They only venture advice to leaders in very special situations, "matters of *force majeure* . . . They know the future, they know the past, they know many dimensions of cases," Muzadi said. "They can explain the problems of Indonesia in real and metaphysical terms . . . how it all happened because of the morality of the leader . . . but this is secret knowledge, interdimensional knowledge, which is opened only in a very dangerous situation of the society or the state."

"These four have a special community . . . not by email or fax," Muzadi smiled. "They are part of a brotherhood"—here he burped agreeably over the tea and cake we were sharing—"without *surat* (letters). But they know the future." I could not bring forth an answering burp, but I expressed grateful understanding: simultaneous inspiration had guided four men to have Gus Dur call on Suharto and to tell him, as "Pharaoh," that (1) the people dislike his opposition to reformers; (2) the people believe he can give money to the government to build up Indonesia again; (3) the violence in Ambon, Banyuwangi, Sambas, and other places is connected to Suharto's control, and he should now stop it.

Muzadi explained. A Qur'anic injunction requires that before you attack

your enemy, you must give him a warning first. "And this is Gus Dur's purpose," Muzadi explained. "To warn him, not to accompany him or befriend
him. He is a rival." All of this mission sprang, furthermore, from a specific
Qur'anic verse. Muzadi wrote it out for me in Arabic and in English. Holy
Qur'an, Sura Anazi'at, verse 17: "Go to Pharaoh, because his is not the true
way."[52] Provided so freely with the text, the ethic, the inspiration, the motivation, the aim, what else was there for me to question? I asked: "When
will all this have an effect? Or was it, as Gus Dur had feared beforehand, a
wasted effort?"[53] "When was Moses successful?" was the countering question. Not in his immediate task, was my answer.

After intense conversation, we were looking at each other amiably.
Muzadi said, his eyes smiling, "Maybe you are a *kiai*." I said I thought not.
But I was moved to add, "In Christianity, all time is one." Muzadi thought it
over. "In Islam, all cases are one."[54] There we left it.

Two comments of Pak Muzadi hummed in my mind. One was that "Gus
Dur is the father of the nation." The expression sounded odd to me, although it was earnest and twice repeated. Americans speak of only one
man, George Washington, as "father of his country," and we mean it historically. Muzadi's statement was meant to capture Gus Dur's daily duty: father to a national family, shepherd to a flock of millions. The other remark
vibrated with cultural, religious, and political implications: Gus Dur benefits by the "interdimensional knowledge" given him by his *kiai*. NU believes
this differentiates it from Muhammadiyah and Amien Rais, who have only a
rational and formal approach. Because they tend to fundamentalism, they
cannot see the interdimensional. I understood Muzadi to be telling me that
NU is mischaracterized when it is called "traditional"; it is actually more
advanced in spirituality than Muhammadiyah. As he talked, the distinctions between party and religious base dissolved in both cases (PKB and
Nahdlatul Ulama; PAN and Muhammadiyah). And Gus Dur's alleged "eccentricity" or "irrationality" was pictured as the natural consequence of
his having special knowledge. His public statements, when misunderstood, are often "shock therapy" and "can be understood only in the future
tense."[55]

Grateful as I was for these insights, I remained in a state of Presbyterian
wonderment about their grounding. The next time I was back in East Java I
sent messages by mail, fax, and phone to Hasyim Muzadi asking to meet
the four special *kiai* and promising to respect their anonymity. I received no
reply. Now and then on a corner busy with *becaks,* in a marketplace buzzing
with flies and shoppers, or in wet rice fields watching farmers sweat, I
would imagine that among those men might be one of the special *kiai* of
Javanized Islam, or even one of the hidden supermasters of that religious
culture, a *kiai mastur.*

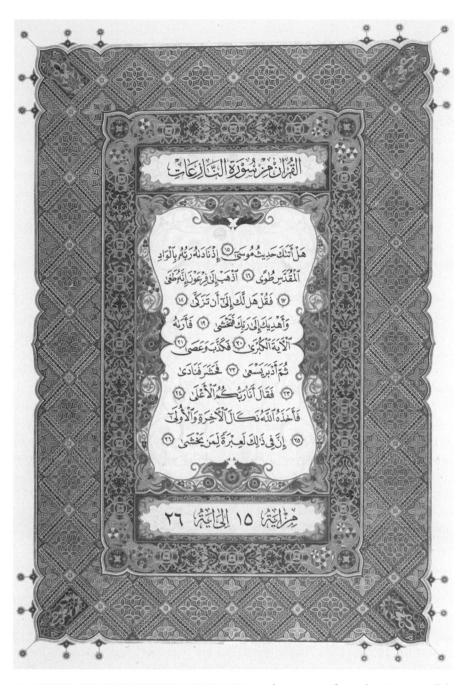

83. MOSES CONFRONTS THE PHARAOH. In this passage from the Qur'an, Allah calls upon Moses to offer grace to the ruler of Egypt, a blasphemer and rebel against Divine Law. Pharaoh's rejection brings his downfall in this world and everlasting punishment in the hereafter. This original illuminated calligraphy (September 2001) of Surah 79: 15–26, uses rose, coconut, lotus and jasmine flowers, and designs from batik and traditional bridal dresses, among other elements. (Achmad Haldani D, Aries Kurniawan, Ahmad Zawawi, and Baiquni Yasin / author's collection)

Alwi Shihab bore the lessons of the hidden *kiai* on me further. Many of the *ulama* in NU react negatively to Muhammadiyah because of its roots in the nineteenth-century Wahhabi sect of Saudi Arabia: too fundamentalist, puritan, or "modernist," or all three at once. But NU, Gus Dur, and Alwi believe that Qur'anic text is not alone divine. There are signs of God all around us, in other people, nature, and history. Religion should reach out to culture, rather than dictating what culture should be.

Alwi said that Gus Dur "may even have acted himself by mystical inspiration . . . He lives very simply. He spends many hours alone in mystical exercises." When nothing changed in the world of riot and murder, Gus Dur washed his hands of Suharto. To his followers he declared that peace will come to Indonesia in one month: "Just believe me." This was both a prediction and a summons coming out of his own contemplative ecstasy. Alwi: "When Gus Dur says, 'Just believe me,' it isn't merely conversational. It's a command."[56]

Gus Dur and Alwi often spoke with each other in the Arabic they shared in Cairo, and they did so over these matters of the *kiai mastur* and Suharto. "Al-siasa chida," Wahid quoted a classical Arab sage: "Politics is deception." Alwi laughed in admiring appreciation of his old friend Gus Dur. "Always be aware of his mystical speculation *and* his political calculation."[57]

To explain these events to his larger public, Gus Dur used a panel discussion in March 1999 at Jakarta's Hotel Grand Melia on "Quo Vadis Indonesia: Where Is Our Nation and Country Going?" "Don't underestimate Suharto," Wahid warned. "Although he has no position, he still has power. He can [even] reshuffle the military structure while in retirement."[58] Gus Dur cast himself and NU as national peacemakers: incendiary incidents could be attributed to Suharto, either as the power-mad mastermind or as the *dalang* unwilling to control his puppets when they became unstrung.

Marla the Healer

Marla, by phone as political commentator: "I saw this lady called Megawati for a couple of hours—and she *doesn't have a clue.*" Moved by Indonesia's crisis, Marla had persuaded sixty corporations to contribute to her wellness center, located inside a major hotel, but she was sickened that hotel management did not take care of the staff, firing "little people" who were only earning fifty dollars a month. The clinic's clientele contained too many of the political elite and their children, who came back because they were bored. She found more "magic in the ICU unit" of a major hospital. "I buried forty people this year . . . after making forty friends." It was then she had decided to open her own *yayasan.* General Benny Moerdani had given her a house for it, and Gus Dur made a start-up contribution.

Marla was also embraced in Wahid's household, where Gus Dur was still recovering from his second stroke of 1998 and hurling himself into political travel. From Europe, to consult on an operation to restore his sight, he "returned a saddened man . . . no operation, no possibility for him to see himself as the saviour." He opened up to Marla, who sat on the bed with him.

Gus Dur: I am an angry man.
Marla: Why?
Gus Dur: More murders in Ambon and the outer islands. And it's because of Suharto.
Marla: Why bother being angry with *him*? Why do you let that man live in your mind rent-free?

Gus Dur laughed with delight.

Wahid still did not give up on restoration of his sight. He accepted an invitation to get a medical consultation in Salt Lake City and also expected there a contribution of $5 million for social programs of the NU.

Marla: You got some Mormon in a private plane meeting you in LA? Flying you to Salt Lake? You're really kissing ass!
Gus Dur: What do you mean?
Marla (laughing): Just an American colloquialism.

A bomb went off in the great Istiqlal mosque near the presidential palace. Twenty people were reported decapitated in Ambon. But Marla was more distressed by the storm currents in Wahid's household. Gus was "being seen everywhere" with a woman named Yola, actually in the Golkar minister Ginandjar's employ, with whom he had a relationship of several years. He wanted to take her, together with his wife, as companions to Salt Lake City. This deeply disturbed his wife and daughters. The press much later brought out a previous affair with another woman, named Aryanti. For the present, however, Gus Dur's family and friends protected him as candidate from the consequences of his own bad judgment. These matters were far less inflammatory in Indonesia than the Clinton-Lewinsky tangle, which had brought the United States to the edge of constitutional crisis.[59]

A press conference, meanwhile, probed for Mormon motives in giving Wahid money, implying advancement of their missionary endeavor through a Muslim leader who needed political funds. Daughter Yenny rebuked a reporter saying, "My father can't be bought by anyone." Marla counseled her to stay cool and "keep your sacred relation with your father."

Marla herself was furious over the behavior of a Mormon industrial developer, whom she phoned for logistical help at Wahid's suggestion. By phone that personage from California boasted of paying all Wahid's transportation, meals, and services; of assembling a famous team of surgeons;

of organizing members of the Mormon Church to fast and pray for Wahid. "You know he's got an aneurysm pressing on his occipital nerve. He could die at any moment." Marla thought, "Who the fuck are you to share that confidential information about him with a stranger? I already know it, but you don't know me."[60]

Marla got me worried enough about Gus Dur's associations, decisions, and expectations that I phoned him in Salt Lake City. They had operated on a vertical nerve to pull up his eyelid and let in more light, and would do a horizontal nerve in six months. Wahid, as usual, was in a roomful of people. One of them was former Ambassador Paul Wolfowitz, who later told me he had told Gus Dur, "You've got to get over this thing with Amien . . . If reformists will lock arms, Golkar will have no place to sit when the music stops."[61] Gus Dur told me he was "reading" (being read to from) Paul Theroux's book on his friendship with V. S. Naipaul across thirty years and five continents. Afterward, I took another look at Theroux and was struck by Naipaul's comment on a character in *The Secret Agent:* "Of Winnie, Conrad says, 'She felt profoundly that things do not stand much looking into.'"[62]

I felt I had learned a shade too much about Gus. Marla's account of her words to him stayed with me. "You're on the throne of life. You're king of life, but you're not being honest with yourself. That other throne you want to be on, you couldn't endure it . . . Whatever it's gonna take, you gotta look in the mirror . . . Why should [others] seek someone who isn't living the truth?"[63]

Keeping Marla as a friend, despite her ruthlessly direct appraisal of him, was a tribute to Wahid's ultimate honesty and strength of soul. A few months later, Marla received an offer that might have tested that friendship from her side. Her expertise in rehabilitation of stroke victims was now so widely known that a female doctor, prominent in the care of ex-President Suharto, approached Marla for help. He himself was weakened by a series of small strokes. Finding herself in a quandary, Marla wanted out of it fast. "He's already dead spiritually. There's nothing for me to work with."

"How do you know?" I asked. I wasn't tempting her to accept the work, but I insisted that she must allow for some resonance in Suharto of *kejawenan*. Some mythological attachment to Semar, perhaps. Something to work with. But she didn't want to see him or evaluate him.

I said, "You don't want to be the *bulé* [white person] they blame if he dies." Marla said, "I don't care about that."[64] I believe that—as a statement of her courage. I suppose she really did consider that Suharto, spiritually, had died long ago.

ELECTION 1999:
REDS, GREENS, BLUES, YELLOWS

To make life in a modern country stable, fair, and hopeful takes more than democracy. The total weave optimally includes rule of law, accountable business, and civil society networks. But democracy is a primary and natural hunger in ordinary men and women: Let us be heard about who leads us, and how they do it.

Since 1988, fifty countries have made a transition to democracy. Some seem secure, like Taiwan and Poland. Some fragile, like Nigeria. Some illusory, like Cambodia. There, in July 1998, with large international monitoring teams present, 97 percent of voters turned out to cast their ballots, and the press hailed a "miracle on the Mekong." But a majority in the assembly soon proved less weighty than dictatorial control of security forces.[1]

Indonesia approached its first open national election in fifty-five years with great hope, and with enormous attention from the international "democracy industry"—valuable money from organizations and precious time from people of many countries. By early 1999 the United Nations Development Program and Habibie's interim government had launched an effort to raise $90 million (one-third of it from the United States) for voter education, election administration, and poll-watching. Eventually, more than $60 million was raised, $34 million of it from Japan, almost wholly earmarked for the Indonesian government. The United States gave only $193,000 for the UNDP Electoral Program but conveyed an amount equivalent to two-thirds of Japan's total through USAID and NGOs in an aggressive attempt to foster civil society. The Dutch gave about half the American amount, to the same ends.[2] Sudden injections of foreign money, however, produced infighting among Indonesian distribution organizations, which "sprang up like American dot-com companies."[3] Japanese money did not reform the state. American and Dutch aid did not transform society in support of democratic procedures. Earlier and more sustained attention, less money and more stamina, might have better helped dedicated Indonesians sink deeper foundations for democracy.

The accreditation team, chaired by Nurcholish Madjid, recognized forty-eight parties among the vastly greater number seeking official status. They hoped to use eight colors to differentiate ballot symbols, but no printer in Indonesia could handle more than four colors plus black. Distinctive party emblems were therefore vital; yet confusion abounded among animal, agricultural, astronomical, and religious symbols.[4]

Most voters would simply remember their own party by its color: red for PDI-P, green for PKB and PPP, blue for PAN, yellow for Golkar. Foreigners could pick a single word out of a long party name to fix them in their minds (struggle, awakening, unity, mandate, service). Fruit jokes revealed the mixed character of some parties: PKB was a watermelon—green on the outside but reddish on the inside. PPP was a lime—green on the outside but yellowish (Golkar-like) on the inside, even though PPP took some staunchly non-establishmentarian and pro-Islamic stands.

To follow personalities made matters dramatically simpler. Mega, red. Gus Dur, green. Hamzah Has, also green (his party used the Ka'aba as its symbol, but on the PPP's flag it looked less like a shrine at Mecca than a modest corner delicatessen). Amien Rais, blue. Habibie, yellow. Golkar's symbol of a banyan tree on a yellow background suggested the ultimate in shady protection and the dropping of fruits into the skirts and pockets of those who were patient. Those five parties would eventually produce a little less than seven-eighths of all popular votes. But in a mixed presidential/parliamentary system, there would be neither an electoral college nor a run-off to determine the winner. The president for a five-year term would be determined by parliamentary vote in October, hence by coalition politics, however transient the teamwork of the parties.

The great first moment in this sequence would be June 7, 1999: the *pemilu,* a contraction of *pemilihan umum,* or general election. Fearing a possible recurrence of the murderous ruckuses of the year before, international schools closed early and sent their students home to their parents, and businesses cleared their offices. The U.S. State Department had issued a travel warning as early as February, and bottom-fishing business scouts went home to make investment cases to their principals. Chinese Indonesians with overseas lodgings went, or remained, abroad. *Pribumi* business people took vacations. The rich and advantaged, protecting themselves, missed the fun: a phenomenal outpouring of ordinary voters, determined to exercise an orderly choice.

For them, this was *it:* the first opportunity for a free national election in forty-five years. It was a time to do what matters in a democracy. Valid bal-

84. BALLOT AS ELECTION EDUCATION POSTER. For voters' understanding of what they will see in the polling booth on June 7, 1999, the numbers, colors, and symbols of the 48 parties contending in the general election are widely publicized. Eventually the five leading vote winners would be no. 11, PDI-P; no. 33, Golkar; no. 35, PKB; no. 9, PPP; and no. 15, PAN. (Author's collection)

lots were cast by 105.8 million voters—an absolute number greater than the record U.S. popular vote of 105.4 million in the Bush-Gore contest of 2000. The Indonesian turnout was 93.5 percent of registered voters, greatly exceeding the American high of 63 percent for the Kennedy-Nixon contest in 1960.[5]

I arrived in Sumatra shortly after the two-week period of formal campaigning had begun. Rallies and cheerleading and demonstrative gatherings had started long before, of course, but now we were in the campaign itself. The greatest good of reform thus far, Cak Nur felt, was the freedom to associate and to speak as one chose. The year since Suharto was forced to resign had vented a lot of pressures, which accounted for the relative lack of violence in the campaign. Still, he warned, the last PDI-P rally day, June 3, could get a little dangerous.[6]

TV offered strangely stilted presentations by all the forty-eight recognized parties, several each day for several minutes, solitary spokespersons laying out credos, principles, or manifestos from behind giant desks or slender podiums, reading their words, rarely looking up. The chance to gaze the tiger in the eye—the television lens—was largely lost. Sri Bintang Pamungkas, less than a year out of jail, wavy-haired, darkly handsome, fashionably dressed, and professorial, contrasted sharply with the many older, obese men in powder-blue suits and dark *picis*. But style didn't help much in the end. Sri Bintang's party did not win a single national legislative seat, a fate shared by 29 of the 48 contending parties.

The heart of the battle was in rallies, which made the blood pound faster. Night after night, TV was impeccably fair in covering these events party by party, region by region. One could tell something of a party's prospects by the thickness or thinness of the crowds and by the animation or automation of the speakers. Occasionally the camera dwelled on a memorable spectator. For Massa Marhaen party, which was neo-Sukarnoist with a farmer-labor, lower-class thrust, the camera picked up a woman of early middle age in a red jacket. Glossy brown hair surrounded her fair, squarish face. Her eyes gleamed with the patient intelligence of a mother presiding over a toddler's birthday party. Deep, sweet humor in her eyes, happy that the political children were having a good time.[7]

On the screen were cascades of trucks and motorcycles pouring down an alley or an avenue, unified in their green, blue, yellow, or red. Bikers carried buddies on their shoulders. Youths danced on shuddering bus-tops, gaping at the camera, eager for face-time; they grimaced with purpose, raised hands in party signals. A telejournalist stopped to interview two nervously smiling pre-teen boys, their faces and hair sprayed green and gray and black. What will they say to the world? "Allahu Akbar!" God is great! To my Amer-

85. GAMELAN PLAYERS. Hands of musicians play the *reyong*, in a gamelan orchestra (*gong kebyar*), Kerambitan, Bali, 2001. (Linda McKnight/author's collection)

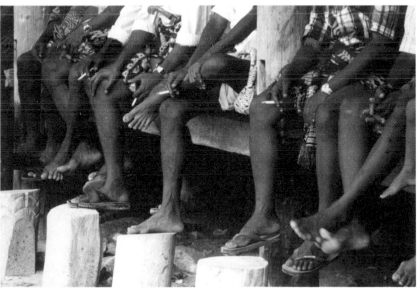

86. MEN ATTENDING RAJA'S FUNERAL. Feet of men attending the funeral of the raja of Sumba in the mid-1990s. A horse is being slaughtered as they watch. (Marla Kosec)

ican eyes, they could be painted up for Halloween, impishly declaring "Trick or treat!"

Frequently a party leader demonstrated how to vote, with a sample ballot larger than a page of the London *Times Atlas of the World,* showing which of the six rows down, which of the eight symbols across, is theirs. Look, he repeats, here is our number. Here is our beloved symbol, our constellation or faunal/floral emblem, our prevailing color, our unique expression of our mission to meet the country's need. Do not confuse it with the mauve-alligator-asteroid party just one row below it, which, if you were not careful, you might punch instead. Don't weaken us, don't strengthen them by even one wrong vote. Get it right, *like this.* And with his long baton he pierces through his true party symbol, as the voter must do on election day.

A dazed contentment settled over me. People crowded around television sets, which were functioning as public utilities—seeing themselves as voters instead of subjects, as part of the sovereign will of the people, expressing at last an unrigged representative democracy. For the second time, among aged Indonesians; for the first time ever for most. I hoped that the colors that would matter in the short-term were brown (the fatigue shirts of the KPU—Election Commission—officers) and white (the color eventually decided upon, after unseemly acrimony, as the uniform of the observer teams).

Most important: how was the KPU going to prevent coercion, tampering, mistransmission of results? On election day there would be more than 500,000 Indonesians in observer capacities, as party poll-watchers, as functionaries attached to the Rectors Forum, as members of the independent UMFREL, as volunteers of the student-organized KIPP. They would in turn be supported by nearly 600 foreign observers from 30 countries, monitors welcomed by the Indonesian government. The joint National Democratic Institute/Jimmy Carter Center group was one of these.

What of village chiefs chosen under Suharto? What of the local religious authorities with tremendous influence? Nurcholish Madjid had assured questioners in Washington that the village chiefs were now afraid of the people, instead of vice versa. Nur, himself a kind of pan-national *imam* with a reputation for being above the fray, observed that they were sensitive to the national changes taking place and could be expected to answer voters who sought their counsel in such a spirit. Still, it bothered me that in the far rural areas, where radio and television were scarce, some people didn't yet know that Suharto had resigned. Many of these people had never voted for any party other than, as bidden, Golkar.

Paul Wolfowitz, as assistant secretary of state for East Asia and the Pacific, had helped to ease Ferdinand Marcos out of power in the Philippines and, as ambassador to Indonesia, had irritated Suharto by encouraging more "openness." Now he was worried that the reformists would blow it, as the two Kims had done in Korea's presidential election of 1989, leaving victory to President Roh Tae Woo. As an independent citizen, Wolfowitz was trying, just as many prominent Indonesians were, to get the reform parties to work together. He privately asked Cak Nur why he did not do the same, or take a leadership role himself? Nur, as usual, politely demurred. He came back to his conviction that the task at which he was most effective was trying to guarantee good process.

Now I was on a 2,500-mile trip through nine cities from North Sumatra to East Timor, a month's solo travel with the general election in the middle. Television took me everywhere else. PAN in East Java, a shot from above: Amien Rais, with bodyguards surrounding him, shook and nodded his way through a pack, then paused before a set of stairs leading to a mike. Snatching a comb from his pocket, he swiped it through his hair before emerging to speak to a sea of faces.

Yusril Mahendra rocked from heel to toe, speaking with youthful force to a Bulan Bintang (Moon and Star) crowd. The camera profiled the paunch gathering under his white robe. The Islamist audiences were marked by the white *jilbabs* of the women—flower beds of round white buds with face-designs inside, radiating both mystery and social engagement. The Moon and Star purists were tearing what votes they could away from Amien's rationalist and semi-secular PAN and from Gus Dur's avowedly universalist PKB. They would eventually win thirteen seats, best among the Islamists.

PDI-Perjuangan, red for Mega, could not get Islamist votes and did not try. In Surabaya, a caravan of their longboats paddled on the river, so heavy with enthusiasts as to be barely above water. Red and black banners displaying the white-mouthed black buffalo were mounted on long poles and swung slowly, daringly, side to side in long arcs. The crafts rocked down the river, somehow not tipping, not swamping, demonstrating elegant balance in dangerous waters. Often white smoke curled in front of the camera, cigarette exhaust puffed steadily up by nicotinists old and young—many very young—sitting, listening, and dragging as they engaged, trancelike, in the new public game.

A rock barrage had struck Golkar trucks and cars in Jakarta. The police investigated, rather than the Election Commission, for the miscreants were not of an opposing party. Underclass youth had been promised hire as cheerleaders for Golkar but were given less money than expected. Some of them unsuccessfully demanded 50,000 rupiah (about $7). In disdain, they used Golkar T-shirts as wipe rags, then proceeded to rain rocks on the party's parade.

Campaign rules prevented the largest parties from rallying on the same day in the same city. I arrived in Jakarta in time to be swarmed around by a PPP parade, surprising in its vigor and in its show of green. PAN's blue on the next day could not surpass it. All the Jakarta parades, wherever their main speech was given, concluded at the traffic circle and fountain in front of the Hotel Indonesia. Acrobatic enthusiasts climbed the welcome monument there and draped banners upon it—against regulations which no police presumed to enforce.

Would 1999 be as democratic as 1955? Difficult to predict, said the distinguished Australian scholar Herbert Feith, because of "violence, the presence of hoodlums, as well as a continued influence of bureaucrats." Golkar was expanding its network through the bureaucracy, just as Sukarno's PNI had done. Feith drew attention to the absence of the Communist Party (which had won 16 percent of the vote in 1955), to the possibility of all Islamic parties of all kinds again winning 45 percent of the vote (not nearly, in fact), and to the inevitability of power-sharing, or coalition government (he was foreseeing Megawati-Amien as likely to remind the people of Sukarno-Hatta, but that alliance did not happen).[8]

The biggest parade of all came on Thursday, June 3. Megawati's "Struggle" party produced the largest procession of human beings I have ever seen. Mega had by April become a more public woman. Her efforts at unity were reminiscent of her father's style:

> At the polls there will be only one name and one symbol . . . You must remember only one name, Ibu Megawati, and only one symbol, the wild ox of Java with the white mouth. Of the forty-eight political parties, only our symbol has a white mouth.
>
> Some have said I shouldn't become president because I'm a woman. I should take care of the home, take care of the children and cook. How many women are here? Raise your hands! Only about one-tenth of the crowd. Women have been intimidated to not take an active role in politics . . . All of you mothers should bring your children to the rallies. They are the future leaders of our nation . . . There is no reason you cannot compete at the polls . . .
>
> Finally we are becoming aware that we are wounding our own body, the people of Indonesia. Do you really want this? Since the time of Prince Diponegoro, we have tried to forge a strong nation, a respected part of the international community . . .
>
> So please, children, do not just cause a stir without really understanding the history of our nation. I don't want to be called a Balinese, Javanese, Sumateran, Irianese, Sundanese, whatever—I want to be called an Indonesian.[9]

The high probability that red "struggle" would lead the popular vote by far moved Habibie and Haz to try to form a yellow-green alliance with blue-green, that is, with Amien (PAN) and Gus Dur (PKB). Elements among the reformers moved in counter-fear in May to try to consolidate all that had fallen apart since the meeting between Amien, Megawati, and Gus Dur in November 1998. The result was known as the "Paso Communique," after the street address of Alwi Shihab, who as vice chairman of PKB hosted and promoted the discussions. Despite their having Golkar as a common opponent, drafting the document proved difficult for the three reformers and highlighted their aversion to meeting together and to including the sultan as a widely popular and trusted independent. Their linkages were clearly not a coalition, far less an alliance. Then, abruptly, within a week, Amien, on behalf of PAN, signed a totally separate blue-green accord with PPP and Partai Keadilan, angering Gus Dur and making Megawati unappeasable.

When early vote totals appeared, Gus Dur criticized Amien again as untrustworthy. Alwi went to Amien to make amends. From that meeting Amien came out saying that Gus Dur was qualified to be president if strong enough and able to perform.[10] The common front of reform was obviously broken. Megawati's gender, Gus Dur's health, and Amien's paucity of votes were all being touted openly by the others as handicaps. Far too keenly felt now was the jest I had heard in Yogyakarta: that the leading personalities of reform were blind, deaf, and mute (Gus, Amien, Mega). Reformist weakness enhanced the chances for Golkar and any coalition it might fashion.

Selo Soemardjan was a member of the national committee supervising observation of new election regulations. He remembered clearly the election of 1955. Some aspects of voter awareness had changed little. At a school in Central Java he had very recently seen a displayed photograph of the deposed Suharto:

Selo: Whose photograph is that?
Answer: That's the President.
Selo: But where is the Vice President?
Answer: We have no vice president.

Golkar, said Selo, was using its power in the MPR, the DPR, and state institutions to maintain and defend itself, because it was aware that its name was mud in Jakarta. There, party loyalists kept their yellow jackets in bags unless police were present to support them. But in the provinces their symbol and system were still strong, even in West Sumatra and Central Java. The flow of instructions ("Push the banyan tree symbol") and money was descending from national to provincial to regency levels and had already reached the villages. Some ordinary villagers were traveling to Jakarta to make voluntary reports to the KPU on money given by Golkar.

Question: On what conditions?
Villager: If Golkar wins, keep it. If Golkar loses, pay back with interest.

A village student from Selo's class reported Golkar giving 20,000 per household.

Question: What do you do?
Student: I take it. Then I do what I want.[11]

The student's spirit was in line with the theme of some reform parties: "Take Golkar's money, and vote for *us.*"

The closing rush of the campaign was publicly buoyant and exciting. Mega and "Struggle" were the most vibrant of all. I had been part of the crowd at the Lincoln Memorial in 1963 for Martin Luther King, Jr.'s "I Have a Dream" speech. And again, in Philadelphia in 1979 for John Paul II's first visit to the United States as Pope. But in sheer size and sustained activity this was incomparable, whatever it lacked in gravity.

As I returned to my hotel at 10:30 from an early appointment in South Jakarta, the red traffic was already shaping up. I went out in front on the south side of the giant field in which stands the national monument. The procession was there already, thick and boisterous and young, drum-pounding, bottle-tapping, gong-slapping. Mufflers off, the motorcycles gunned themselves in rhythmic bursts: rat-tat-tat, tat-tat. Every size and kind of vehicle—bicycles, mopeds, *becaks,* autos, vans, buses, flatbed trucks. I received the PDI-P three-finger salute and punched it back, followed by two thumbs up. Grins, blown kisses.

A political exile from Sri Lanka was on the hotel wall with me, snapping pictures. He was an Amnesty International officer who had arrived to join the Carter Center's observation team. "Yesterday I saw the blue ones, that parade. This one is ten, twenty times! . . . This energy! Most I ever see in Asia! This is more than India politics. Never did I see in India!" It was a college pep rally. No, high school, with much grade school. At least a third were below voting age.

After my lunch, the tide had not abated. Costumes, painted faces, beribboned trucks and bannered buses, red, black and white, came on and on. Youth on the bus-tops were stretched out, sun-fired and metal-baked but not too weak for salutes. *Reformasi!* Megawati! Victory! My Indonesian guests at dinner, who had mingled in it, said it was a "happy crowd," unlike the hard-edged PDI-P rallies of 1997 resulting from the Suharto attack of '96. I checked with a doorman how long the march had gone past our hotel: 11 AM to 5:15 PM. Six and a quarter hours. Who could defeat such a joyous mass, celebrating its freedom, its hope?

Election Day

The American expert cited poll figures: whatever advantage PDI-P rolled up in Java and Bali, Golkar would still do significantly well there and would take as much as 75 percent of the vote in some of the outer islands. The general election was "Rent a mob." "Buy a legislator" would follow. So the massive red carnival I had enjoyed, the old hand said, was the equivalent of "soccer fans celebrating *before* a victory."

Election day, just the same, was elevating. The streets were almost totally clear of traffic. Jakarta on June 7 was a walking city, full of people strolling and polling: free, enfranchised, expressed, and satisfied. That night I stayed with friends who were official monitors. They drank Tiger beer and waved their fingers, test-dipped in the indelible ink which for all actual voters was a sacred and mandatory immersion. For days afterward people preserved their mark-of-the-voter as a memento. Those who wished to be tidy again found it difficult—pumice stone, nail polish remover, whatever one tried had little impact. Only the generals I later interviewed waggled uninked digits. "Neutral!" they declared, with almost comic insistence.

The mood was not the same everywhere. A friend posted to observe in Ambon asked an early voter how conditions were in his region. That weathered and composed man broke into tears and told of the recent attack on his Christian village by Muslims coming from two directions. *Pemilu* there brought no special cheer.

But in Jakarta, election officials, at counting time, held up each ballot, one by one, before appreciative crowds who hailed any choice, cheered any party except Golkar. Like other capitals in Southeast Asia, Jakarta is usually an opposition city. Taxi drivers laughed, "Golkar takut"—scared and in hiding. The upper-end drivers, Silver Bird and Blue Bird, alleged themselves to be 90 percent for Mega. These were not polls, or samples, but boasts.

An Indonesian executive who held two passports had managed to get himself certified as an observer by using the foreign one. With his wife he sat with us eating and drinking in amazed euphoria. "I think I know what a great day is. We have four children, and each of the days they were born was a great day . . . This election," he searched for the words, "this election feels like my fifth child."[12]

Jimmy Carter

Jimmy Carter at 75: bouncy step, bright eye, balanced mind. His center, jointly with the National Democratic Institute, had put together a delegation of 100 observers and support staff from 23 countries, welcomed by the

Indonesian government. Carter praised the massive national effort of domestic monitoring and all the Indonesians working for a democratic election, toward a more democratic system, an economic recovery, and "a position of respect in the world." His own teams, a small addition to that, were being deployed across 26 provinces. East Timor, he gently reminded his listeners, was not recognized by the UN as the twenty-seventh province of Indonesia.

Questions from the press brought out savory additions from Carter: "Out of 25 or 30 elections we have monitored around the world, this is the most fully committed. This participation is *overwhelming.*"

Press: What can you contribute?

Carter: We can show that the rest of the world is really interested . . . Our presence, and others with access to the international media . . . will attest to an open, honest, fair and accurate election by the Indonesian people.

Press: But doesn't Golkar have all the advantages?

Carter: Around the world, inevitably the incumbents are the strongest and richest and have an advantage . . . But there's such a serious commitment from the Indonesian people that I expect their will to choose their own parliament and president will not be affected . . . Irregularities may occur and mistakes will be made, as in every nation . . . Have they been deliberate, or part of a pattern subverting the will of the people? If so, we will not hesitate to make that statement.

Press: But is monitoring really effective? And do elections make a difference anyway? I think maybe they don't.

Carter: I don't agree with you on that. I think . . . [the] observers from Indonesia supplemented by a few international ones is important . . . And elections *do* make a difference. Nigeria is the latest, and a dramatic example, [of a democrat replacing an autocrat] . . . Likewise, the African National Congress in South Africa is much more responsive to the people than the predecessor government.[13]

I slipped into the Carter assembly room a few times on the day after the elections to hear monitors who had returned from the regions give sample reports. Prostitutes, garbage collectors, and the military mingled with other citizens, equally interested. There were inconsistencies in voter lists and lack of checking for indelible ink noted by the large number of domestic observers. The party monitors, however, seemed less concerned and behaved much more like NGOs than political parties. Despite some violence and anomalies in Aceh, a majority of districts held reasonable balloting there. Overall (one observer said), "This is the seventh Asian election I have monitored. And this is the smoothest and the best in participation."[14]

Two days after the election, Carter's team issued a twelve-page summary of findings. "More than three million Indonesians worked diligently and for very long hours as polling officials, political party agents and domestic non-partisan election monitors. The delegation was impressed that so many of these people were young, which is an important indication of hope for the future."

Deficiencies were noted in transparency and logistics of election administration. There were allegations of money inappropriately used, especially Social Safety Net funds for campaign activities. In East Timor, Aceh, and Irian Jaya, issues of separatism and clashes between the military and the populace "reached beyond" the conduct of the elections. Delays in tabulation and release of results by the Election Commission must be expected. But all these "shortcomings do not at this time appear to have affected substantially the processes on polling day itself."[15]

Carter, before he departed, took hold of the issue of slow returns to say they "do not indicate improprieties, but they do arouse concern." He added concerns about how the nonelected members of parliament (238 out of 700) would be allocated and designated and about the "unpredictable process" by which the president will be chosen. Before the attack of press questions, Paul Wolfowitz accented the enthusiasm of the Indonesian people and the potential for this becoming the world's "third largest democracy."

Press: Tass, the Voice of America, and a German paper all jumped on slow returns and serious discrepancies.

Carter: The KPU is itself disappointed by mechanical failures. Beyond that, signing off on the process from polling place to village to subdistrict, all the way to central counting may be overmeticulous, as officials seek to honor and assure the process, rather than to subvert it. We assume the process is orderly, unless there is an allegation to the contrary.

Press: When will we know? When will we *know?!*

Carter: We won't know until November whether democracy has come to Indonesia in its fullest form . . . I would be glad to come back if necessary . . . I've never been involved in an election so profoundly important . . . because of its signal for peace, democracy, human rights, and freedom . . . So we're not leaving until the process is completed.

Ending the hot session, Radio Free Asia asked, "Is there a message here for China, Vietnam, and Burma? Carter said, "Yes, to all those countries and to others as well. It's especially important that this nation, with more Muslim believers than in Africa or Russia or China or the entire Middle East, is interested in democracy . . . So it's especially important if they *do* achieve success in these elections."[16]

87. PROTEST AGAINST GOLKAR. A slow count after the general election arouses a demonstration in July 1999 organized by PRD, a radical splinter party, at Election Commission headquarters. Some police, perhaps jittery because of rumors that demonstrators carried bottles of acid, fired rubber bullets into the crowd. One clipped the extra camera at the waist of the photographer of this shot. (Kemal Jufri/IMAJI)

The Sultan of Yogya as Sheltering Tree

I had been working for months on helping Ary before I headed to Yogyakarta once more. The price of her immunosuppressive medicine was rising beyond her family's capacity. A monk had been helping to pay the costs. But then he died. Now what?

I found the retired CEO of a major pharmaceutical firm to be sympathetic. So was their "manager of community partnership," but they didn't make the medicine she needed. For Ary to inquire of other firms, she had to supply full information. I was glad it was the late twentieth century and Ary was alive. I was sad about the huge financial costs for her family, as she tried to titrate her system between excess toxicity and insufficient absorption of what was keeping her alive. I wondered about Indonesia in systematic economic crash, trying to administer democracy as a cure. Would an overdose be lethal? Would a cultural equivalent of organ-transplant rejection occur?

My contact found the multinational company in Indonesia that made Ary's medicine and put in the request. We waited. Two and a half months seemed like a long time to me, and I made repeated inquiries, motivated by Ary's writing, "I am very happy you so care about me. Even my uncles and aunts never give attention as big as you do."[17] Then the wretched news arrived, by relayed handwritten fax. The cyclosporin-making multinational had checked with its general manager in Indonesia. "I am sorry to say we cannot provide the drug free. The financial hardships in Indonesia go far and deep. It would be difficult to make exceptions."

I put all this in Indonesian to Ary just as I left for Jakarta and received there a long understanding letter from her with a few facts and feelings. Her latest doctor's bill indicated she needed almost 60,000 rupiah (about $8) for medicine every day for her life. She wished not to depend on others. She only wished to be useful, to feel proud of herself, to be able to "step forth prettily" *(tampil cantik),* to have experience as a woman, and not always to be a problem to her family, to her brothers and sisters, and to herself. She was making shirts and school uniforms for her extended family, even a purse, on her sewing machine. Would I like to come see the machine myself?[18]

Yes, I would. The night before I saw Ary, I met with the sultan of Yogyakarta, Hamengku Buwono X (HBX). His father (HBIX), vice president in Suharto's first two terms, had refused reappointment, allegedly in disgust over the growing greed of the president. His son, now in his forties, showed up in a poll by *Tempo* as the leading candidate for vice president, associated with any one of the three major reformists.[19]

I had expected a friend to accompany me and to help with a session that would be almost entirely in Bahasa Indonesia. But he couldn't make it. And by the hour of the appointment, 7:30 PM, the sultan's interpreter was off duty. So as I walked with a guard from the outer public limits of the palace toward the Keraton Kilèn, or western palace, where I would be received, I worried about not speaking Javanese. I considered apologizing for not addressing the sultan in high Javanese—*ngkramainggilaké*—but that would get us off on the wrong foot, implying that I could manage some humble Krama, or even some ordinary low Ngoko; or that I had the faintest idea how to manage any of the variants of Javanese, a subtle and hierarchical tongue. Which I didn't. I would just apologize for my weak Indonesian.

We padded along in the moist darkness, past the open-porched homes of attendants and artisans. The gathered, humid quiet calmed me down. We passed through the numerous ungated thigh-high walls, a puzzling zigzag. This is an architectural requirement, I later learned, not for some Napoleonic reason of security but to confound Satan, who travels in a straight line. That confused me, because I think of the Devil as the ultimate zigzagger.

I was turned over to two barefoot teenage boy attendants, who ushered me into the reception room; they lit lamps, fired tea, provided a cold egg roll, kept their eyes below mine. I would have twenty-five minutes, it turned out, to study the place. Four tables in the room, loaded with china, crystal, pewter vases, sculptures, and display plates. Chinese, Japanese, Javanese, and other, with demigods, mythical beasts, flowering birds, contending colors. On and under a big round glass central coffee table were bowls of matchboxes from all over the globe: restaurants, hotels, KLM, the presidency of Indonesia. High-bourgeois appetite for world tourism; low-bourgeois taste for eclectic display.

The sultan entered softly. He was nearly as tall as I, which automatically induced me to winch my knees and neck in a microbow, as a show of respect. He shook my hand, sat swiftly opposite, lit a cigarette. He apologized in English for his English and switched into Bahasa Indonesia. There we remained, except as I tried occasionally for clarifications. He asked into my travel plans and dwelt on the local high spots—Borobodur, the Prambanan, and some new archaeological discoveries. I remembered that an Australian scholar had dismissed him as "just a mediocre businessman." I thought, however, he was probably rather good as the supreme tourist spokesman for an area of great cultural riches. If English royal labels can tout marmalades and tweeds, why can't the sultan of Yogya rhapsodize about his heritage of Hindu-Buddhism, compelling to international travelers?

The sultan dwelt on the character of Yogya. How it had been a center of the revolution and earned its autonomy as a "special district" for that reason. How its universities, especially Gadjah Mada, founded as the Dutch were being defeated, drew students from all over Indonesia. It was a university town, polyglot, polycultural, and yet somehow united by serious investment in study. Not as crime-rife as other major Indonesian cities, Yogya was a kind of blast furnace of Indonesia-ness, melting down provincial talent from all over, leading them to intermarriage, blending them into responsible citizenship. He spoke earnestly, with conviction, repeating his sense of inherited duty to maintain these standards. I thought: where political ethics are low, noblesse oblige stands high.

What about the crisis of May 1998? He told with modest satisfaction the story of a million people gathering in the *alun-alun,* the esplanades outside the palace. One of the sultan's advisors told me that a dream of the sultan's wife about the appearance of his father had persuaded her that he must go public, even though she was quivering with fear about the circumstances.[20] They had insisted that the military and police keep out of sight, so that a picnic atmosphere could be maintained, with the selling of water and fruits and ices under the sun to slake the thirst of the crowd and to enable his speaking the truths that might cool their fever. He had said that Suharto had lost his legitimacy and that Indonesia needed reform. The people had come to hear that and were satisfied. No riot in Yogya, a city that kept its head. "Of course we took a chance."[21] Nearby Solo had burned and would burn again. It lacked a charismatic sultan to hold it together. Authority there had rotted, the Chinese were burnt out, and there were more dead than even in Jakarta.[22]

The sultan proceeded, with a shade of contempt, to speak of how Suharto had once approached him to discuss the marriage of one of his daughters to a Suharto son. No chance. The president's greed for power had tarnished him, lost him the *wahyu*. He came from the peasantry, had forgotten the people, tried to found a dynasty and failed. A cock crowed, loud and near, at almost ten at night.

I said that a *Tempo* poll showed him, the sultan, as everybody's preferred vice president. He said that was up to the people and the parliament. Among presidential candidates he clearly preferred Gus Dur, whose blend of Hindu Buddhism with Islam gave the ritual comforts and certainties that Javanese needed from birth to death. Of what value, compared to that, was the textual clarity offered by Muhammadiyah? Thus he disposed of the candidacy of his close regional neighbor, Amien Rais.[23]

I had been silently assessing the sultan as a national figure. His nobility was more than genealogical. But this elegant, resonant man sat straight-backed, elbows on chair arms, forearms elevated, wrists limp, or hands suddenly expressive in dancerly gestures, a cigarette always alight and trailing smoke in the fingers of one of them. The posture, I felt, might project too much of the cafe aesthete for democratically elected national office.

I told him the story of Ary, her difficulties, and how in the national peril she needed the feeling of *diayomi,* being protected by the sultan. He seemed gratified, and in the course of clarification took and corrected in his own hand the spelling of a key word on my notepad.[24]

The twelve members of Ary's family who lived within easy distance of one another had among them one motorbike, which seated two, and only one telephone. I reached the brother-in-law, the owner of the vehicle on which they shift-rode, Sundays, to masses at churches three or five kilometers away. He hiked over my message that I was coming. Twenty minutes before my taxi got beyond Yogya's city limits, the size of buildings scaled down to one-story strings of apothecaries and modistes and photo shops;

88. TANAH LOT. The most famous of the Balinese Hindu sea temples, on the southern coast of the island, accessible only at low tide. (Jody Dharmawan/author's collection)

of eating places and boutiques for car parts; specialists in tires, or oil cans, built up in pyramid display; in wheels for motorbikes. I passed the O'Brien School of English Conversations and the Jogja School of Manager. Then rows of specialty booths *(afdruks)* of painted wood the width of a Western man's shoulders, where, seated, the owner sells from his micro-inventory.

Within another twenty minutes I was passing through brick and sawn-tree country, monuments and pediments, recently manufactured antiques. A whole village for pottery, where the earth yields up good clay. Then a huge orange-on-pink cement gateway with a bas relief monster face, serving as proscenium arch to fields of wet rice. Acres of green now, and fewer houses. We stopped for directions five times. Hadn't I been there before? Yes, I answered the driver, but I have no idea how to return.

Pak Sudiro's is one of four or five Christian families in a village of many hundreds of families. Close by was a mosque, whose amplified summons to 6:00 PM prayer fell on our ears. In previous elections, Golkar officials had come to the house to coerce his vote; this time they left him alone. He gleefully brandished a church notice that listed five parties for which a Catholic

89. BALINESE MEN AFTER PRAYER. This snapshot suggests the aesthetic languor and liturgical ease of Bali. But riot overtook the island when Megawati, whose grandmother was Balinese, was not elected president by parliament despite her electoral plurality. She had initiated her campaign with a mass meeting in Bali. (Jody Dharmawan/author's collection)

might reasonably vote. Number one was Megawati's PDI-P. Gus Dur's PKB was third. The rest were expressly Christian. Pak Sudiro was thrilled to be part of Mega's apparent success in an election that was "free and honest."[25]

"Do you want to see my machine?" Ary asked. Indeed I did. She took me to her workspace in the adjoining central room of the house. "Everybody's room." Perhaps five paces by three, it opened to an exit space on its south wall and to two dark adjoining rooms north and east. To the left of the opening a clean white plastic object, smaller and narrower than an old-fashioned typewriter, sat on a little work table. My gift, her Singer zigzag. Above it, on a pegged wall shelf, were a couple of dozen spools of different colored threads. She showed me the cams, black plastic wafers of different shapes to drive different stitch patterns. "Much more modern and complex than my wife's machine," I enthused. Above it on the wall was a multicolor print of Christ as a handsome *bulé* ("albino") with light brown hair and beard, gazing earnestly upward. Not my kind of art; but supplication and approval-seeking were vital to Ary's life, and I entered my prayer for her.

We went back to tea. I noticed a bowl hardly bigger than a quart of gin, in which swam seven or eight pastel-colored fish, small as fingertips. A recent gift to the family from an employed brother. So, I thought, they were at least that many grains of food ahead of hunger.

I thanked Ary for understanding that although I had been unsuccessful in getting her medicine donated by a corporation, I had made every effort I could. She nodded sweetly. I said she need not feel obliged to write me any more, given lack of money for postage. But she should feel, whenever she thought of me, that her wishes are my hopes. She nodded gently again. "Thank you."

Her father returned, and I repeated to him how the negative decision was reached at the highest executive level by the drug manufacturing firm in Indonesia. There were too many cases. I begged to apologize for my failure. He smiled and burst out a declaration: "I forgive you." I told of my conversation with the sultan, in which I had mentioned Ary and her wish to be "sheltered" by him. I showed them the sultan's handwriting on my notes, with his parallel and guiding motivations: *mengayomi* = to protect (the people); *mengayemi* = to give hope (to the people).

My driver was back from prayer at the mosque. Warm handshaking farewells all around. And then, before I got into the taxi, "Permisi," I said, looking at her mother. "A Christian American gesture," I said to Ary. I kissed two fingertips of my right hand and touched her forehead near the hairline. I got in the taxi. It backed in anticlimactic little arcs until it could lurch forward over a stone step. Then it growled goodbye. My hand was out the window, waving.[26]

Looking Back from Balearjo

The votes took several weeks to count. The people waited for the Election Commission. Then they waited for the meeting of parliament in October that would reveal the climax of coalition politics—choosing a president. PDI-P received 34 percent of the votes and PKB 13 percent, which meant that allied with minor parties they would have a majority of the 462 elected representatives. Gus Dur finally arranged to say that Mega could be president, with himself as chair of the MPR (which would now meet once a year as a superparliament) and Amien as chair of the DPR (the standing national legislature). But what would the provincial and functional representatives do, who made up the rest of the MPR's 700? Golkar money could change the outcome. The armed forces' delegation of 38 was itself large enough to tilt the balance and to be either a king-maker or a queen-maker.

With these questions in the balance, I took time to look into village life in Java, to understand where it had come from and where it was now. In 1953 an American sociologist, Nathan Keyfitz, formed part of a group studying the East Javanese village of Balearjo under the guidance of the distinguished Professor Widjojo Nitisastro. Keyfitz returned in 1985, on a restudy supported by Economics Minister Dr. Ali Wardhana. The two studies establish a matrix of data and impressions for a village carefully chosen as "representative" of Java in size, agro-geography, and access to a major city without close proximity to it. Now I went there myself, in October 1999. I intended to understand economic development from a point beginning in the early Sukarno era, through gathering hurrahs in the middle of the Suharto period, right up to the economic quake and after-shocks of 1997–1999. What had Balearjo become, and how had it fared?

I had companions: Ali as driver and Ratno as interpreter (not their real names). It was their first sociological exploration. Ali and Ratno argued over the turns out of the big city, Malang, and the meaning of the directions I gave them from Keyfitz's article. Cement, asphalt, dirt; giant belching diesel buses, crowded blue vans *(bemos),* and motor scooters carrying commuters and grocery shoppers. Then bikes and walkers; workers with carry-pole loads of produce. Ali, a shaky young tobacco addict, chain-smoked cigarettes. I was reliant on Ratno for rapport and information and worried that his manner as a retired army sergeant major would interfere with the clear communication I sought. I needn't have been concerned. In conversations his brilliant buck teeth and bulbous nose gave him a comical honesty of demeanor. We were an unlikely, defenseless trio. But we got answers, despite the strangeness of my questions, because we were genuinely interested in Balearjo.

One villager of whom we asked directions seemed a throwback to the Sukarno era. In his hand he bore a rice sickle. His turban was a thin and meager wrap against the sun, even more faded than the thread-specific, rock-laundered shirt that hung on his narrow torso. His face was lean and carved with work; his voice, gaunt with deference, evoked a time when children wore tatters or went naked; when there were no schools or mosques or health facilities in the village; when dwellings were made of vegetation. But the place had changed since Keyfitz described it forty-six years before. Now we saw simple uniforms on schoolchildren and white T-shirts on toddlers. Molded cement blocks at corners and on gateplaces carried the great pastel-colored revolutionary dates, "19" and "45."

The village chief was napping. His wife woke him. He was muscular,

90. CLIMBING THE GREASY POLE. Independence Day, August 17, has become a time for local games and celebrations. Here a contestant vies for prizes atop a slippery climb. (Jody Dharmawan/author's collection)

confident, reserved. He stroked his glossy black hair into place, and his rugged black moustache, and his underarm hair. Yawning apologetically, he pulled a long chain that turned on the high overhead naked bulb so I could take notes. He got seriously engaged with what Balearjo had been before his chieftainship and what it was now. His wife brought out tea and sugar for us all and then produced their teenage daughters to ask me questions about America: mainly, how do you get there? Meanwhile, their father asked, how do you live there, and how many hours do you work?

Arraying my data with that of Nathan Keyfitz is like placing a plucked lime alongside two cultivated pineapples. But here is the result, for the purpose of swift general impressions. The villagers of Balearjo are clearly better fed, better clothed, and much better housed than forty-six years before. They are healthier, better educated, and, for good or ill, TV-informed. They are more mobile in several senses. A significant number travel by *bemo* into Malang to work in a cigarette factory. A significant proportion of the increasing number of high school graduates move to Surabaya or Jakarta. A surprising number go overseas for higher pay in laboring opportunities and send significant remittances back to their village families. And an astonishing explosion has occurred in Islamic building, schooling, and observance. What are the interplay and relative effects of increased religiousness and greater doses of television? I don't know. But it appears that in Balearjo, as in small-town America, the call of worship exists in some crude correlation with the density of material/commercial images on the tube. To sense which is winning in Balearjo would take careful definition and resident study.

Four questions to the chief gave me some summary evaluations:

Question: What is the biggest event or project of the last fifteen years?
Answer: Roads, schooling, houses, mosques. Many kinds of development, little
    by little.
Question: What is the most desired aspect of further development?
Answer: Asphalt and telecommunications.
Question: What is the effect of the *krismon* [financial crisis]?
Answer: There is none. [*Tidak ada apa-apa:* the only non-credible reply I re-
    ceived.]
Question: What will be the main hope of Balcarjo from the new government?
Answer: As long as everything is cheap and good, everybody is happy.

Back in Jakarta, with gratitude to Balearjo and to Keyfitz, I shared the data with Dr. Pramoedja Rahardjo, executive director of the Community Recovery Program, an NGO with national scope. He was less sanguine than the chief and much more disturbed. Yes, they have television, but can they pay its electricity costs now? Yes, they have a health center, but can they buy medicine? And health services? A diet *(nasih campur)* can be described, but is it there to be eaten? He had seen recent high incidence of malnutrition in parts of rice-growing West Sumatra. "Figures on *mesjids* are not about morality. The right indicators are crime rates, rapes, etc. Figures on *langgars* (a sort of micro-mosque) are evidence of different sects; they are an index of lack of community cooperation."

Dr. Pram opened up a big cooperative study of the nationwide impact of the financial crisis, and we searched for the subdistrict Gondanglegi, of which Balearjo is a unit. Impact was assessed at four levels (small, medium, large, very large) in five categories.[27] "The reality," said Dr. Pram, looking at me insistently, "is that people don't know what to do. They are really suffering. Very, very great suffering."

I was chastened by this lesson. Dr. Pram, a Ph.D. from Florida State University, strove to supply a larger perspective. Yes, they were in a terrible cri-

Table 7. Balearjo: notes on 46 years of village development[a]

Item	1953	1985	1999
Population	+/−2400	3894	+/−4100
Income per capita, annual	$100	$250	Not available
Housing and lighting	Bamboo/thatch; some kerosene	90% brick/stucco; some electricity	Brick, cement, tile; 100% electrified
Schools	None in the village	2 primary schools	2 primary schools 1 madrasa (Islamic)
Mosques	None in the village	3 mesjid	4 mesjid 24 langgar (small prayer houses)
Hospital/doctor/ visiting nurse	0/0/0	0/0/1	1 puskesmas (community health center)
Diet	Rice, 4 months corn, 2–4 months cassava, 4–6 months	Rice all year	Nasih campur, 3x/day (50% rice, 50% corn)
(a) Daily wage	Rp. 4.00	Rp. 1,000	Rp. 8,000 (farmer) Rp. 8,000 (worker in city cigarette factory)

(b) Price of rice	Rp. 1.80/kilo	Rp. 280/kilo	Rice 2,200/kilo; Corn 750/kilo
a/b: Buying power of daily wage in rice	+/−2.25 kilos	+/−3.5 kilos	+/−3.6 kilos
Planting of sugarcane	2% of land	33% of land	1% of land (farmers felt sugar factory buyers were cheating them, and stopped planting ten years ago)
Television	0	60 sets in village	+/−650 sets (or about half of the households)
Emigration	Nearly 0	Most high school graduates to cities	25% of h.s. graduates go as far as Surabaya and Jakarta; 600 relatives of residents work overseas (Hong Kong, Taiwan, Saudi Arabia)

a. Nathan Keyfitz, "An East Javanese Village in 1953 and 1985: Observations on Development," *Population and Development Review*, 2, no. 4 (Dec. 85), pp. 695–719; author's field notes, Oct. 26, 1999.

Table 8. Effect of the crisis on Balearjo's subdistrict[a]

Context	Impact of crisis, 1997–98
Unemployment and social issues	Medium
Education	Large
Availability of food and goods	Large
Economic resilience	Large
Health and family planning	Very large

a. Badan Pusat Statistik, Ford Foundation, and World Bank, *Laporan Survei* [Survey Report of the Impact of the Crisis by Levels and by Districts Throughout Indonesia] (Jakarta: February 1999), table C13.7, pp. 269–270.

sis. The figures for Balearjo might have been a lot better in 1996. Maybe now, as the data suggest, village Indonesia's buying power has been beaten back only fifteen years, rather than twenty-five years, as some journalists were saying. But that's still a long retreat. "The people are in panic. They are squabbling with each other. The new government means we are breathing fresh air in the tunnel. But we are still in the dark . . . we cannot see the light . . . The people do not feel *led* . . . do not feel *trust*. They are in social hysteria."

All this might have been avoided had they stopped Suharto sooner. But it was not his fault alone. "All of us were at fault for letting him go on, letting Harmoko lie to him. 'The people still love you.' Suharto was really thinking about the country." But his wife and children did him in, brought him down with their own excesses. Dr. Pram accepted the view of Suharto's own food taster, who had collapsed at the Manila summit of ASEAN hosted by Cory Aquino ten years before. He was willing to swallow hidden poison for Suharto. But not for Ibu Tien and their kids.

Dr. Pramoedja would not let me go without his own statement of gratitude to his government and the larger world. On scholarship money from the Suharto regime, he had been trained in the United States and had come back, indebted to his own society and devoted to it. He might not even be here, might be just a tour guide, might be dead of malnutrition or shot in the head. How, as a child, had he survived the 1950s? "I got a UNICEF immunization, and one cup of milk every morning. I thank Sukarno; and I thank USAID for showing that the American people care about our survival."[28]

EAST TIMOR

In 1990 Saddam Hussein asked why, if Indonesia could make East Timor its twenty seventh province in 1975, he couldn't add Kuwait as a nineteenth province for Iraq.[1] Answer: the Cold War had ended; new presumptions of national, civil, and human rights prevailed. Opposition to communism, Suharto's rationale for invading East Timor in 1975, did not apply to Saddam's invasion of Kuwait, a naked oil-grab. After the massacre in Dili in 1991, however, Cold War logic began to vanish for Suharto's annexation of East Timor as well. By the end of the century it was clear that for two dozen years East Timor had been a critical drain on Indonesian resources that could have been used for economic development. Instead of fostering the emergence of a middle class, funds for the campaign to integrate East Timor had guaranteed dominance by the military sector throughout Indonesia. East Timor had become a training ground for an officer corps practiced in unchecked tactics of suppression for Aceh, Irian Jaya, or any niche of restlessness.

In Indonesia's twenty-seventh province, the second-largest statue of Christ in the world turns its back to the miseries of East Timor. But the presence of Indonesian arms and soldiers had caused a surge of Catholicism in the region. After dawn on a Sunday in late June 1999, I walked to Bishop Belo's compound on the waterfront at the eastern end of the city of Dili. I sat on a folding chair four rows from the outdoor altar—a raised platform of white stone with four giant tree trunks as pillars, their bark still on them, and a thatched roof overhead. At the back was a brightly colored mural of the Last Supper: no languorous Renaissance composition, but the antic action of men busy eating, drinking, and arguing. Seagulls loitered on the ridge line of the roof. From behind the bishop's residence the crow of roosters welcomed worshippers to the service. Chairs filled, and standees jammed the entire garden beyond its courtyard gates.

For the Eucharist we filed forward through all aisles, a priest at the head of each. The bishop commanded the central aisle, carrying in the crook of his left arm a giant silver cup with stacks of white wafers the size of American quarters. The very old let him place the host inside their mouths. The very young extended their tongues far out for it. When I reached him I adopted a middle-aged compromise and swooped the wafer in with a lizard-like suck. It dissolved fast.

Treetops shielded us from the stunning morning sun. I felt almost cool, happy to be there, watching queues move silently by, serious faces, gleaming eyes, countenances dull with pain, all part of a mystical and practical community. Very few heads of white hair. Many children with parents. The very young joined in confession of things we ought not to have done, and things we ought to have but had not done.

Assurance of forgiveness and grace. We filed out, perhaps two thousand people. Several silently reached for my hand, slipping their palms against mine, not to shake it but as if tendering a sign of the self. I clenched each

91. FERRY, THIRD CLASS. The journey between Kupang, West Timor, and the island of Roti is representative of inter-island travel throughout the archipelago. (Cathy Forgey)

gift lightly and swiftly released it, smiling. The hesitant-radiant Timorese smile came back in return.[2]

Signs of the Disconnect

A limited opening of East Timor by the Indonesian government in 1989–1991 had ended with the Santa Cruz massacre. Xanana, leader of the Fretilin guerrillas, had been captured in 1992 and was serving a prison term of twenty years. Major General Prabowo, commander of Kopassus (Special Forces) Group 3, attempted to crush what survived of the independence movement by using irregular troops—hooded "ninja" gangs dressed in black and operating at night—and, in main towns and villages, militias trained and directed by Kopassus commanders. Human rights abuses rose. The army's determination was captured in the name of its 1997 campaign, Operation Eradicate.[3]

Then Indonesia's monetary crisis *(krismon)* hit and quickly worsened into a total financial, political, and social catastrophe *(kristal)*. Military operations in East Timor were costing the government a million dollars a day. When the unrest climaxed in Jakarta with Suharto's resignation in May 1998, Prabowo, by then lieutenant general in command of the Strategic Reserve, was demoted and chose exile in Jordan. Thug and militia activity ebbed in East Timor. Throughout the middle of 1998 huge discussion forums took place in Dili, aiming at a referendum. Foreign Minister Ali Alatas dismissed plans for differing periods of graduated autonomy as "all pain, no gain" for Indonesia.[4] Habibie's government continued to look for an exit strategy, needing to picture itself as democratic to its own public (headed toward a general election in June 1999) and as reasonable to the international community (both private investors and bureaucratic lenders).

But the Indonesian military had suffered many casualties over nearly a quarter century, and some soldiers thought of that blood as an investment whose interest was the integration of East Timor into Indonesia. Others, leading generals who had served in East Timor, had made investments there of a literal kind: in timber, marble, coffee, sandalwood, and oil. At the apex of such shareholders were Suharto and his family. The military's intolerance of a new era of openness registered during the last quarter of 1998 in a massive influx of ABRI personnel and new recruits across the border from West Timor. A still more flagrant symbol was the arrival of 400 Kopassus Special Forces from Java by ship on November 4, 1998.[5]

By this time President Habibie was becoming ripe for inspiration. Dewi Fortuna Anwar had "led him into understanding" of the East Timor situation—backed by papers from ICMI that dismissed any strategic and economic importance of the region to Indonesia and stressed its cultural unassimilability.[6] As he wrestled with the matter in late December 1998, Habibie received a cable from John Howard, prime minister of Australia, declaring cooperative concern about East Timor and suggesting a multiyear resolution of the problem. A signed letter from Howard followed on January 17. Habibie took it home with him one day and laid it on his night table when he went to bed. In the middle of the night, he awoke, turned on his light, scribbled his solution to the East Timor problem on Howard's letter, and went back to sleep. When Habibie rose on the morning of January 21, 1999, he reviewed his sudden illumination and found it good.

Habibie had a meeting with the American ambassador, Stapleton Roy, that morning and gave him the handwritten "policy paper," which Habibie said he would be announcing to the press soon. Roy, who had observed Habibie in office becoming steadily "more presidential," could not help thinking that this action on East Timor was impulsive and indiscreet. The foreign ministry called the ambassador's office later that day, politely requesting a copy of the policy statement, which apparently only Roy possessed.[7]

Habibie remained proud of his initiative, which would put the future of the province to its people themselves. If the East Timorese did not accept the wide-ranging autonomy offered, then the government would ask the parliament in October/November to "let East Timor go." Making autonomy a take-it-or-leave-us proposition had a peremptory and dismissive tone, which Habibie only intensified by implying on TV that the East Timorese were noncontributors to Indonesia—Catholics inhabiting barren rocks. His foreign policy advisor stated it more palatably: "Why do we have to hang on to East Timor if it is hurting us so much [internationally] and the East Timorese feel so unhappy about it?"[8] Further Indonesian negotiations with the Portuguese and the UN produced the idea of a "popular consultation" that at last met the request for a referendum that Bishop Belo had made ten years before. There would be a UN supervised ballot in early August. Habibie hoped to win it, but that whichever way it went, he thought, it would relieve Indonesia of this burden and improve his chances for the presidency, which he avidly sought.

Much of the army was unhappy or furious over Habibie's inspiration. They had not been consulted. Neither had most of the cabinet, except post facto. Wiranto and Ali Alatas were notably stunned.[9] Civilian officeholders lined up dutifully with the president, whose political fate, in most instances, was their own. The military shut up, sullen. But its command for Eastern Indonesia had under way a covert project named Operation Clean-Sweep. Its rationale was that East Timor was a territory wracked by civil war and incapable of self-government. It aimed to sabotage the referendum and eliminate leaders of the independence movement. In March 1999, Kopassus released $2 million to finance paramilitary operations. Groups of trained militia included Besi Merah Putah (Red and White Steel) and Aitarak (Thorn). On April 6 a large group of Red and White Steel, supported by soldiers and mobile police, attacked a church in Liquiça sheltering 2,000 pro-independence supporters who had fled earlier violence. They killed 57 and wounded 35; 14 others disappeared.

The operation moved on to Dili. There, in mid-April, a militia group attacked the home of Manuel Carrascalao, a pro-independence leader who was sheltering people in his garden. His seventeen-year-old son was killed trying to dissuade the militia from entering. So were many in the garden.[10]

As militia operations spread eastward, 54,000 people were displaced by the end of May, according to human rights groups. By early August church sources raised the figure to 80,000. Many of the displaced were herded into camps controlled by the militias. This was the situation on June 4 when the unarmed United Nations Assistance Mission in East Timor (UNAMET) raised the UN flag in the capital. They were received by the senior military adviser from the Indonesian government's referendum team, Major General Zacky Anwar Makarim—the same man who was in charge of the covert Operation Clean-Sweep.[11]

High Tensions

I arrived two weeks later in Dili. With UN personnel flowing in, no hotel rooms were available, but Galuh Soedjatmoko found me a bed in a peripheral building owned by the Salesian Brothers outside the city.

Galuh had left her flourishing Oxfam center in West Timor, as well as a new NGO specializing in human rights, women's rights, and victims' rights that she had launched there, to move to Dili. Her natural sympathy had dissolved the suspicion East Timorese might have felt for a Javanese woman. She built up a vibrant women's NGO, FOKUPERS, whose acronym meant Communications Forum for Women of Loro Sa'e (using a national name instead of the provincial "East Timor"). She led a five-day women's workshop on rape and torture. Galuh described the work as taking place "where there is no distance between the victim and the . . . helper, counselor, who might be the *next* victim. Outside of Dili, which is relatively safe, first the military and then the militia, all boys with guns, can just take what they want."[12]

Two weeks before, five militia had entered the house of one of the women in the workshop and had threatened her husband. In order to avoid violence or dragooning, he had fled into the forest. The militia, humiliated by his escape, decided to "humiliate him in return" by raping his wife. They did so, one by one, on the bed under which her children had hidden themselves, quietly paralyzed with fear.

Another woman, raped when very young, had had five miscarriages. She had recently adopted a child. At the workshop each person was invited to choose an object that symbolized herself. This one chose a flower with several buds. "One of them was forced open," she said, "but I am saving the others for my family."

Still another, Felismina, with grave, sad eyes and clots of gray in her curly hair, was held a political prisoner for five years. She was "tortured with guns and with snakes." Galuh calmly anticipated and answered the question I was ashamed to ask. "I don't know how intrusive they were." They had prevented Felismina from bathing when she had her menses. Years later, among her recurring nightmares was one in which she and her clothes were covered with blood. Since helping Galuh to found this new network, her nightmares were diminishing. She had recently dreamed that her clothes were washed clean out of her hands by a clear brook and carried away downstream. Galuh taught me a basic reaction to torture and rape: you go out-of-body to escape it, and you return only with self-loathing. The military know that—that's why they do it. It takes a long time to heal.

Two of her women escorted me back to the Dom Bosco Training Center in the oldest, smallest taxi in the world. They pointed to two young men in khaki, jogging before us faster than the motion of the taxi. "Militari." They directed my attention to different centers, notably a large one at the intersection where the airport road leads to the city. Scores of youth performed ragged exercises there. "Milisi." Militari, milisi, militari, milisi—the army and its paramilitaries. The sight and the refrain provided the raw themes of my visit.

Patrick Burgess was chief of staff of the UN Humanitarian Office in East Timor. He was also, for the present, its entire staff—a tall, gray-haired Australian in his early forties, muscular, practical, skeptical. He and Galuh were in love. He was preparing an evaluation of the security environment as a precondition to registration, campaigning, and referendum. In one town he saw approximately 400 young men loosely marching in a field and carrying sickles, machetes, knives of all kinds. He stopped to ask, "What's going on here?" The Indonesian officer in charge gave an order and all the young men bent down to work with their instruments. Then the officer answered the Australian, "Grass-cutting." Men thus dragooned were crudely trained as militia. Others were roving with pro-independence guerrillas. Or in flight from both sides. It was difficult to find men over seventeen who were not either enlisted or displaced. Opposing the militia was dangerous. In his travels Patrick was told of a woman who was decapitated and whose head was presented to the local militia chief as a trophy. Her family, not daring to reclaim it, had to bury her body headless.

I was feeling bourgeois, confused, torn with helpless anger. I had come from serious conversations in Jakarta about Habibie's inspiration and its implementation. "How," I asked, "can a useful popular ballot take place under conditions like these?" "It can't," said Patrick simply. It sounded to me as if it would take not six more weeks but many months or a year to achieve secure and sufficiently objective conditions. Nobody disagreed.

Several of us were eating *ikan bakar* for dinner again. Following the convention, a connoisseur from our group had opened the restaurant's ice chest and picked a big fish for outdoor grilling. Silver mackerel tonight. Beers for the UN folk and the foreign correspondents and for Galuh; any kind of cola for me, hugely dehydrated as I was in this humid town, and no air-conditioning.

"It astounds me," I said. "This direct contravention of Indonesian government policy." "It's always that way here with central command and field operations," said Geoff Robinson, an American scholar. "The same way in Aceh, but there one local commander was also into smuggling and drugs." "It astounds me," I repeated. "Join the club," Patrick said.[13]

Aniceto Guterres-Lopez had founded and was executive director of HAK (an acronym that also spells the word for truth or right in Indonesian, as opposed to wrong). He ran his Timorese human rights agency next to Galuh's office. "History writers have been those in power, serving their own purposes," he said. "History is looking into a mirror, seeing yourself. But the East Timor mirror is fogged and broken. People don't know what really happened." The Portuguese, in his view, left little behind but a feudal structure, unequal gender relations, and the need to build a civil society.[14] The Japanese were a vicious occupying force. "But *this* is the worst of all, the most bastard regime in the world." When the Indonesians came, they said, "We are taking you back to the lap of the mother." Their rationale was Majapahit. Aniceto dismissed that. "You can prove with ancient pottery that the Chinese were here, but nothing proves the presence of Majapahit. The Indonesians talked of Gajah Mada, and a wish to unite all of 'Nusantara,' and for East Timor, a lost child, to come home. We don't know what all that means. That's *their* history. All we know is that if the father is mean [Portugal, Japan] that's OK, that's the way fathers are. But if the *mother* is mean [Indonesia], that's *worse.*"

Aniceto was eight years old, a student, when East Timor was annexed in 1976. In his area, near the border with West Timor, he saw the war in the way people died in camps; how other people suddenly disappeared, never came back. In 1982 he traveled to the only high school in Dili. There, for the first time, he learned from other students that the same things had happened in other areas. "Understanding the killing of powerless people really changed me." He went to university in Bali on an Indonesian government scholarship; there, he studied human rights and law in order to express his thoughts—"the way my father learned to express himself with Dutch ideas," Galuh chimed in. After the Santa Cruz massacre got world attention, Aniceto and others founded HAK as a human rights organization in 1996, to work as a legal instrument for the oppressed.[15]

The war had already come close. Some weeks before, neighbors had telephoned Galuh and Aniceto one night to report that armed militia had entered their offices. Galuh called up Mark Dodd, a stringer for leading Australian newspapers. Dodd arrived on the scene with them, carrying his only weapon, a video camera. He pointed it at the intruders. After an ugly standoff they left, pounding their weapons on nearby parked cars and shooting their guns in the air.

How Important Is the Retina to One's Vision?

When the retina detaches from the inner surface of the eyeball, there is no pain, no appalling sound of ripping, not even a ping. It just peels away and folds inward, like wallpaper in a steamy room. This happened to me as I was getting ready for bed in my solitary cell at the Dom Bosco Training Center. I just noticed a muddy tan film across the lower inside quadrant of my left eye. I hoped it would go away. When I woke in the morning, it was still there. I remembered a friend who had suffered a detached retina in the Amazon. By the time he got back to the United States the damage was irreversible, and he wore an eye patch for the rest of his life.

It was almost as hard to get out of East Timor as to get in. No seats on the planes. But Galuh landed me a room at the Hotel Turismo, where I could phone the airport from the front desk. I went ahead with my interviews. I had a final talk with her, at teatime in the Turismo's bar. Outside in the garden courtyard were giant green plants with leaves like elephant ears and faded pink plastic chairs and tables. Two European men sat there, nervous middle-aged companions who had discovered a huge mistake in their vacation itinerary. Inside, seeking a faint tinge of air-conditioning, sat the news junkies, the history rats, and the UN peace dogs after a day of trying to shepherd scattered flocks of population. Time for beer and television. As Galuh and I talked, we were astonished to see Wiranto and Xanana (who had been upgraded to house arrest) appear on the screen together, at a news conference about negotiations toward disarmament. Two handsome commanders: a four-star crooner and a guerrilla-poet.

Galuh told me of the documents leaked to her that she had spread in Dili to the UN and the world press. The first showed that the local regent had appointed Eurico Guterres as coordinator of the Pam Swakarsa, or official volunteers for public order who were defenders of the autonomy campaign. This was "ironic," Galuh said, because Eurico was the head of Aitarak, the militia that had invaded the Carrascalao household and killed Manuel Jr., along with many more. All costs of Pam Swakarsa, the document said, will be paid with government money.

Then she received another document, signed by a different regent, proposing that social safety net funds—World Bank monies—be used for the autonomy campaign and for the Pam Swakarsa defending it, to the extent of three billion rupiah per regency. Attached was a copy of a reply from the governor general agreeing to the proposal for four regencies. Galuh fed it to Warda Hafidz in Jakarta, whose critique of massive diversion of social safety net funds was under heavy attack in the capital.[16] A nocturnal cabinet meeting ensued, after which Dewi Fortuna Anwar announced that the government would not allow misuse of World Bank funds for such purposes.

Galuh, in retrospect, wished she had run the story harder in Jakarta. The international NGOs and the "solidarity groups" did not see the alliance between progressive Indonesians and the East Timorese. Nor, she believed, did they see the malevolence of the militias, who were East Timorese working against their own people. Galuh said, "I feel like a white person working for Nelson Mandela . . . But I've got years of work to prove my track record." While she was working for Oxfam in West Timor in 1991, the Santa Cruz massacre drew her attention to East Timor. "For a long time I wanted to come in here." She traveled to Dili in 1996, met Felismina, earned her trust, began to think of a new phase of work in this ravaged area.

"Why," I asked, "are you drawn to suffering?" Galuh was a little taken aback by the question. But she had thought a lot about it; she had talked it over with Patrick. "I am attracted to injustice, because that darkness helps you to see the light. The darkness shows the potential for human nature; the opposite, the goodness, the hope is there too."[17]

Galuh's is not an isolated view. A UN special rapporteur documented systematic use of rape by the Indonesian military in East Timor, Aceh, and Irian Jaya. Thirteen women from seven countries visited East Timor as a delegation shortly after I was there and reported systematic abuse of women. The victims dared not go to the only option for most, the Indonesian military hospital, where further abuse and humiliation would await them; or to police or the courts, which were Indonesian; or indeed anywhere at all, because women who have sex before marriage were considered unclean and shunnable. Sympathy was found only in nunneries.[18]

Galuh quickly sketched a whole architecture of human rights as she understood it: civil and political in one dimension, social, economic, and cultural in another, which included the right to health care and integrity of the body. Her two main fields of concentration, women's rights and indigenous rights, ran through the whole structure.

Patrick joined us, and we ate simple fare. I thought about darkness and light. Patrick had been with the UN in Rwanda. He had seen corpses with eyes gouged out. Pregnant women with babies carved out of their bellies. "The horror," he said. He had read Conrad. "The horror," he repeated. It sounded like a prediction.[19]

I gave up my cherished room at the Turismo, with its cold shower, hot air-conditioning, high-speed roaches, and surveilled faxes. I gambled on standby and won a seat on the plane to Bali—the first hop toward surgery in Philadelphia, a week after my semi-blinding. On board I met Luis Varese, a Peruvian, vice-chief of the local UN Refugees Commission, who was on his way to report to his boss in Jakarta. Driving alone through the mountain roads of the province for twelve days, he was convinced that what he had seen were not "refugees" (an international term) or even "internally displaced persons." They are hostages, he'd said. "They are in *situacion coercitiva.*" There were 40,000 to 60,000 people in camps where the army forced them to listen to propaganda broadcasts at 6 or 7 every morning which urged them to vote for integration with Indonesia. They were not going to be released until after the "popular consultation," presumably to ensure correct voting.

Luis had with him (but did not show me) photographs he had taken of ABRI and militia headquarters side by side in numerous settings. There was no question of long-distance handling or behind the scenes puppeteering. The militias were the creatures of the army and did as bid—allowing, of course, for their own idiosyncratic excesses. The situation reminded Varese of Guatemala, where militias were likewise army-related and employed, with brutal results in that case for more than forty years, until a genuine popular election changed the situation. Even then, when the bishop of Guatemala City submitted a "Report of the Mute" which listed numerous killings and disappearances, he was murdered two days later.

We parted at the airport in Bali. Luis gave me a surprise. "Pray for me," he asked. He was not anxious about reporting in Jakarta. He was talking about his return to East Timor. "I will," I said.[20]

Registration and Referendum

Eighteen years of neo-Majapahit presence had done what three years of the Japan's Greater East Asia Co-Prosperity sphere had done—killed, one way or another, as much as 12 percent of the population. East Timorese linked the two periods of foreign occupation in the same breath as *Japoneses* (Japanese) and *Javaneses* (Javanese).[21]

Now, in August 1999, the question was how many Timorese were alive, adult, locatable for registration to vote on their own future? The answer, UNAMET discovered, was more than 445,000. Balloting conditions, however, remained a key question. Reports from UNAMET personnel on site were able to achieve a three-week postponement of actual voting, until August 30. Longer would have been better, for neutering the militias and ensuring voter security. But topmost UN officials wanted a clear and concrete result for Indonesia's meeting of parliament in October. And so the balloting went forward at the end of August. An astonishing 98.6 percent of those registered made the effort to vote, which often entailed many miles of walking to a polling station and back. Then the UN counted the ballots, with Carter Center and international observers again present, as they had been for the general elections in June.

The Indonesian government had insisted that whatever the outcome, its own responsibility would cease no earlier than January 1, 2000. This meant that ABRI units were in place as the main enforcers of order, while unarmed UN personnel were present to guarantee a fair voting process. How many ABRI were there? Official government figures had earlier indicated withdrawals down to 6,000 men. But figures leaked or sneaked out of Cilangkap, the Indonesian Pentagon, some months before indicated double that number of soldiers, plus another 9,000 "spontaneous youth groups" (militias or paramilitary) and public officials with ties to the army, suggesting a total Indonesian military presence of about 21,000. Portugal had been able to keep order in its sometimes fractious colony with a garrison of only 1,500 men. But keeping order now was incomparably more difficult.

Portugal had signed onto the referendum agreement, while trying to avoid any responsibility for the colony it had abandoned. The United States had increased arms supplies to Indonesia to a peak in 1982–1984 of over a billion dollars (by the terms of the Mutual Defense Agreement of 1958, the arms were to be used "solely for legitimate national self-defense").[22] But the 1992 election of Bill Clinton led, the following year, to the first American vote in the UN to censure Indonesia for human rights violations. Australia, drilling for oil in the Timor Gap and having negotiated a treaty with Indo-

nesia, was subject to the most strenuous turnaround. As early as 1962 the
Menzies government secretly believed that there was no practical alternative to eventual Indonesian sovereignty over East Timor but did not wish
to see it happen by force of arms. When it did happen that way in 1975,
the Whitlam government turned a blind eye. Its prime minister disliked
ministates and considered East Timor unviable, so Australia became the
only Western country formally to recognize Indonesian sovereignty in East
Timor.

By early 1999, however, Prime Minister John Howard was urging Indonesia to grant self-determination, up to and including independence. Neighboring events had raised Australia's consciousness of the need for action,
even though its entire national army was only one-tenth the size of Indonesia's.[23] A posture of "honor" by Portugal, sales of weapons for "self-defense"
by the United States, and a "blind eye" from Australia may have been realistic as part of a Cold War strategy, but they appeared hypocritical by standards of self-determination and international morality ten years into a Hot
Peace.

On September 3, Kofi Annan in New York and, on September 4,
UNAMET in Dili simultaneously announced that 94,388 persons had voted
for Habibie's proposal, 344,580 against it. Nearly four out of five East
Timorese voters (78.5 percent) rejected the Habibie government's option
for continuing ties with Indonesia.[24] For those who had expected otherwise,
the decisiveness of the result was stunning.

Explosion

The voting day itself was as calm as, or calmer than, the all-Indonesia
general election just twelve weeks before. Given East Timor's preceding
months of intimidation and localized mayhem, this new behavior was astonishing. It proved the capacity of a high-level regional military order—in
this case led by Major General Zacky Anwar Makarim—to control the behavior of the militias. In expectation of a close vote, a calculating order
could have said stay cool to win or formally to contest a tight loss; if we
lose, go hot and wrest by force as much territory as possible for annexation
to West Timor.[25]

But four to one was not a close vote, and immediately after its announcement the behavior was hot. Was it a fixed vote? There was no question
which outcome most UN personnel favored. But no basis in fact for allegations of collective UN cheating on procedures or results was shown.[26]
What to do then, if you are Zacky Anwar Makarim and Eurico Guterres?
Scorched-earth policy: burn the evidence of two dozen years of occupa-

tion; burn the city that is the center of independence activism and of international presence. On September 3, as intimations of the results seeped out, Aniceto Guterres-Lopez, the lawyer and human rights activist, watched, aghast, as smoke rose from bonfires consuming decades of documents at intelligence and interrogation centers. Two days later his own home was destroyed by arson. Then his offices for HAK and Galuh's neighboring offices for FOKUPERS were riddled with bullets and razed.[27]

The tabulated result of the vote was announced on September 4. Generalized violence began at nightfall. Guterres left Dili that day. In 1991, at twenty-seven years of age, he had been a courier for an independence group until turned by Kopassus torture, some said, or with promises of fortune. He emerged later as an integrationist and in 1999 as the leader of the street-cruising, gun-waving Aitarak. Photos show him as sensual-looking with a sullen hauteur. Impassioned, given to wearing a black Kopassus baseball hat and threatening journalists, he now argued that two-thirds of East Timor should remain with Indonesia. "I'm an East Timorese and an Indonesian citizen. That's my human right."[28] Perhaps he left the city to attend to that larger strategy. His own underlings went on a destructive rampage. General Wiranto flew from Jakarta to the Dili airport and back on September 5. By never going into town, he gave the impression that he did not care to see what was happening, or knew what was meant to happen, or feared for his own safety.

Bishop Belo had said, "East Timor is like hell," as early as 1994. Now he said it again, discovering how deep the levels of hell may plunge. On September 6 armed militia stormed into his home and grounds and drove out 6,000 refugees at gunpoint, killing some and abducting others before they shot up or burned down the bishopric—offices, sanctuary, statuary.[29] Belo survived and was evacuated to Australia. Many priests and nuns who stood their ground elsewhere were killed.

On September 7, after a long night's dispute in cabinet, Habibie's government announced martial law for East Timor. The purposes were not clear. Was it to control the militias? Was it to deter international intervention? Both or other? The UN Security Council had condemned the violence "in the strongest terms" and decided to send a mission of five ambassadors to see for themselves what was happening.

With regard to military psychology and behavior, many things were happening at once. In ABRI's detachment of soldiers there were 6,000 East Timorese, many of whom were now deserting, along with up to 1,000 police. But Kopassus was infiltrating regular ground units and taking over de facto command as a guard against undermotivation. Kopassus also had influence in the paramilitaries going back to 1978, which it had organized

92. ATTACK BY AITARAK. Aitarak militia members attack unarmed pro-independence supporters in the Becora district of Dili on August 26, 1999, a few days before the East Timorese referendum. Indonesian armed forces, deployed to create a secure environment for the balloting, stood by and in some cases participated directly in killing supporters of independence that day. (Anastasia Vrachnos/Sipa Press)

to search and destroy Fretilin guerrillas. Kopassus was seen commanding Aitarak in Dili. The rationale, from the local chief of military intelligence, was simple: "We had to help them counterbalance Fretilin. I don't want to leave behind the people I've worked with unprotected."[30]

The descent into chaos was chronicled by Alan Nairn, a writer for *The Nation,* who had received a concussion at Santa Cruz cemetery in 1991. He was banned from Indonesia and East Timor but had made it back despite military intelligence and had remained despite the militia. His inside accounts by cell phone roughly substantiate outside assessments that the first week of violence was against individuals, along with forced evacuations en masse. The second week's agenda was to wreck the infrastructure, with messages of hate in defeat and spite in retreat. When asked by cell phone why the Catholic clergy were a target of militia violence, he summed up the worst: "Well, I think the military is sending a message to the Timorese that all taboos can now be broken, there are no more limits . . . They're just sending the Timorese the message: You have no place left to hide. Our terror is total."[31]

Meanwhile, Xanana Gusmão's relayed orders were keeping Falantil, the armed wing of Fretilin, out of military engagement and in reserve to protect refugees fleeing into the hills. Xanana was released from house arrest in Jakarta on September 7, but he refrained from returning home immediately. As an aide said, "He understands that committing suicide doesn't serve the interests of his people."[32]

When Secretary General Kofi Annan said Indonesia had 48 hours to get the situation under control, Foreign Minister Ali Alatas replied in combative huffiness, "Why should we be the subject of so much abuse, so much accusations, so much pressuring? Don't hector us." He added: "Don't talk about peacekeeping when we know and you know you won't be able to get peacekeepers on the ground within a week unless you want to shoot your way into East Timor, God forbid." Alatas and President Habibie cancelled their scheduled presence at a meeting of APEC (Asia Pacific Economic Cooperation) in Auckland, New Zealand, in order to avoid pressure for deployment of foreign troops. On September 9 President Clinton described the Indonesian government's response as a "big blank" and called for an end to "this madness."[33]

National Security Advisor Sandy Berger had remarked, days before, that if the United States had to clean up every mess in the world, then his daughter's room needed attention. From this gaucherie he sank to obtuseness: "Because we bombed in Kosovo doesn't mean we should bomb Dili."[34] But some American officials were having serious conversations about what, if anything, to do. Admiral Dennis C. Blair, commander-in-chief of the Pacific, was dispatched to Jakarta and spent a pointed half hour with General Wiranto, asking him "to belly up to his responsibility." American Army Chief of Staff General Harry Shelton had three or four telephone conversations over several days with Wiranto, based on friendship established years before at Fort Bragg; and Wiranto, after traveling again to Dili with the Security Council's mission of five ambassadors, eventually answered Shelton cooperatively.[35]

In a vital act of foresight that may have saved many lives, Prime Minister Howard's government had been readying a peacekeeping force of several thousand men for the moment when they might be invited in. When indeed, given the required preconditions of official Indonesian invitation and Security Council resolution? Jose Ramos-Horta was everywhere in print and on the air asking where was the morality that had led the United Nations and the United States into Kosovo to end ethnic cleansing? What would be the credibility of the UN and its secretary general if their sponsorship of a peaceful and unmistakably clear ballot were violently frustrated? Far-flung editorial opinions agreed with him: East Timor was in danger of a scuttle-and-run disaster after a peaceful ballot, as had happened earlier in Cambodia; and the UN, accordingly, was in danger of collapsing like the League of Nations.[36] But the UN, at all levels, did not wish new shame, in addition to that heaped on it for letting massacres occur in Rwanda and at Srebrenica with its peacekeeping troops present.[37] Indonesian negotiators had kept UN troops out, but now killings were in progress that were not justifiable to the world at large.

What finally persuaded Habibie's government to admit foreign peacekeepers? A hearing in the U.S. House of Representatives yielded a balanced statement from Congressman Tom Lantos: nobody should get in the position of waging war against Indonesia, nor should the innocent and destitute of Java and Sumatra be punished for a national military out of control. President Clinton delivered the necessary clincher, by suggesting the withholding of financial aid. President Habibie, on September 13, finally invited the UN to send in a peacekeeping detachment.

Eventually a force of 9,900, called InterFET, was assembled around an Australian core of 5,500 and an Australian commander. Thailand, Philippines, Singapore, and Malaysia, in descending numbers, joined in, with several nonregional states. Only a handful of Americans were to be engaged in logistics and transportation. In the end, without blocking aid but hinting at IMF curbs on it, Clinton tilted the game. Indonesia had not needed aid or wanted it in the different ways of Egypt and North Korea. But now it was in economic crisis. An American expert said, a bit grandly, "It is as though an industry of peace is our greatest export."[38] If so, this export shipment arrived late.

Despite the Indonesian government's admission of peacekeepers to implement the results of the ballot, ABRI was obstinate and grudging. General Wiranto, to cheers from retired military officers at a party, dedicated a song to foreign journalists. He sang the soupy American ballad "Feelings," but instead of bemoaning a lost love, he sang of East Timor. Wiranto performed *dangdut* (modern Jakarta crooner-pop) well. I had heard a CD he made when he wore fewer stars; in the cover photo he wore a leather jacket and dark glasses and rode toward the camera on a motorcycle. Since that time, he had learned to make policy statements. But "Feelings" was a strange, mawkish, and hypocritical substitute for straight talk.[39] Only subsequently did documents emerge showing repression, coercion, and destruction as among carefully prepared options of military planning against, and in retribution for, a pro-independence vote.[40]

Smoke Slowly Clearing

The United Nations Human Rights Commission in Geneva decided by a narrow margin to debate the East Timor situation; it was "a close call" won over strong Asian opposition. At the same time, Indonesia agreed to set up an inquiry under the aegis of its own national human rights commission, to look into breaches of humanitarian law.

As for a transition toward a new status for East Timor. "Start now," Robin Cook, the foreign minister of the United Kingdom reported himself as saying to Alatas, because East Timor is "a territory with no government, no civil service, no police force, none of the apparatus of a state to provide for the welfare and safety of the people."[41] A month later a USAID official came back from a trip to East Timor fuming at the UN "boy bureaucracy": the $150 million that the UN had asked for, if pledged, budgeted, and provided, was far more than East Timor could right now rapidly absorb. It could create lasting dependency. An austere NGO veteran sighed in exaggeration over the Australians dropping by parachute gleaming cappuccino parlors into Dili's smoking ruins.[42]

Galuh, over whom I had worried for weeks, emailed some friends on September 30 from Sydney. The security and communications arrangements made among her women's network had been swiftly overwhelmed. The house in Dili that she had bought and renovated with Patrick had been destroyed, along with their young puppy. On the night of September 5 her office was attacked and burned, with thirty people inside the building. Galuh was crouched, against wild gunfire, on the floor of Patrick's office in the UN compound, "crying, praying, holding on to the mobile phone which was my only connection to what was taking place at the HAK/FOKUPERS office across town." UNAMET persuaded the Indonesian police to bring the thirty people to the police station, among thousands of others. Then she organized an airlift for them out of Dili and got out by luck herself on a small plane hopping to Kupang.

In West Timor Galuh found the madness newly located, with innumerable East Timorese in danger from integrationist militia with looted goods. Some of them were kept as hostages, and 80,000 still languished in militia-controlled camps in early 2002. She and others organized a small effort to hide and smuggle to safety those who were especially threatened. Her former neighbor, "old Oom Abraham, the local swindler and conman," as she called him in a email, who had spent a few years in jail, there befriended, before release, "two sophisticated high-ranking political activists thrown into the Kupang jail for organizing the Santa Cruz march." Now they needed him. He took more than twenty people into his shack for refuge.

"Oom Abraham can barely feed his [own] family, has no connections to the outside world, no real political understanding of what is happening to his friends, but there he was taking that risk . . . That is where I am at this point—trying to reconcile small acts of love and great exploits of hate. In the small acts of love department, I am madly in love with Patrick." They were safe. They would go back. "I don't know where Felismina is and worry about her all the time."[43]

One of the first to return was Sander Thoenes, Jakarta correspondent of London's *Financial Times*. He rode a motorcycle-taxi into the Becora district of Dili, where his driver encountered six Indonesian soldiers. Thoenes was shot dead off the back of the vehicle. A young Indonesian photojournalist and friend of his, on the scene next day, saw blond hair but did not recognize Sander. The face of the corpse had been flayed back to the skull.[44]

The Media and "Joyo"

For a quarter of a century East Timor had been under various degrees of internal news blockade, most of them nearly complete. The smuggled videotape of the Santa Cruz massacre in 1991 did not play on Indonesian TV. Five journalists—two Australian, two British, one New Zealander—had been murdered while covering the original Indonesian invasion of East Timor, without an official protest from their governments.[45]

Now was different. At one time there were 400 foreign correspondents in Dili, a city the size of Santa Ana, California. Perhaps they got the story all wrong. How many spoke Indonesian, to learn what was really going on? (None, surely, spoke Tetum.) Some, nonetheless, took a close look at the militia instead of confining themselves to stories that would provoke predictable sympathies (independentistas hacked to death) or angers (military-militia collusion in violence) in faraway readers. One journalist told of a pro-integrationist recently stabbed to death by a man taking revenge for a relative killed in 1991. Another described memorial rites for "Placido Ximenes . . . buried in Dili this week with the finest pomp and ceremonial the Aitarak militia could muster. The cortege began in front of Aitarak headquarters, a run-down hotel in the town centre. An honour guard of 50 spluttering motorbikes rode on the vanguard, followed by four-wheel drives, pickup trucks and charabancs. Driving them, crammed inside, squatting on the running boards and sitting on their roofs, were the Aitarak men—a cross between the Hell's Angels, Dad's Army and the kind of small-time gangsters to be found in Third World cities everywhere."[46]

The East Timor story was having a galvanizing effect among some in

America, especially through the efforts of an independent webmeister using the name "Joyo." Since 1996 he had been sorting out thirty or forty stories a day on Indonesia from among the four or five hundred he read at night. He put them on line as a public service to 2,000 people, globally, who sought to receive them. The intensity of the work, his discriminating selections, and his steady reliability made "Joyo" a legend and an addiction among those who needed to know or cared to know about Indonesia.

Now, after three years of anonymous objectivity, "Joyo" was incensed about East Timor. For the first time, he allowed himself to editorialize to his web addressees. Privately, without restraint, he addressed his old friend Megawati, through her close advisor, Laksamana Sukardi: "Where are the so-called reformers now—and why are they utterly silent—in the face of much worse atrocities committed against Timorese by the same military and thugs who attacked the students [in 1998] and PDI headquarters [in 1996]? When will good, decent Indonesians wake to the fact that the Indonesian military and their hired thugs have killed and brutalized more of their own citizens than the hated Dutch and Japanese colonists ever did? . . . If the horror in E.T. continues for several more weeks, in conjunction with the backdrop of Baligate [the Bank Bali scandal], it's likely that sanctions will start to be imposed, international funding and investment will be suspended; the Rp. will hit 12,000+ again; social upheavals will ensue."

Joyo proposed that Mega ask for an emergency session of the MPR to declare East Timor independent (highly unlikely, given her policy stance for national unity). Pages of plea poured from him to Laksamana, some of it slipping into whole uncorrected paragraphs in capital letters. "DO NOT REPEAT DO NOT SQUANDER THIS OPPORTUNITY TO WIPE THE SLATE CLEAN, GET RID OF THE REAL DISEASE WHICH IS THE REAL CAUSE OF NEARLY ALL OF INDONESIA'S PROBLEMS. AND MAKE MEGA PRESIDENT WITHOUT BEING CONTROLLED BY SOME DUMB KILLER GENERALS WHO ARE RESPONSIBLE FOR FUCKING EVERYTHING UP!!!!!!!!" He finally quit, "trembling with rage," sending a message to Laksamana entitled "THANKS FOR YOUR TOTAL SILENCE!"[47]

The dispatch of multinational peacekeepers to East Timor cooled Joyo off. His media blitz, combined with the work of many others, had helped make intervention possible. *Time*'s technology editor for Asia wrote a feature piece subtitled "We won't tell you who 'Joyo' is, but he's someone you should know." The editor complimented expert use of the internet by the East Timorese Action Network and by Jose Ramos-Horta, who had vowed a campaign of cyber-terrorism if Indonesia tried to sabotage the ballot—

"More than 100 computer wizards" were ready to launch specially designed computer viruses to cripple the Indonesian government, military, banking, and financial institutions. Whether any such actions were launched is not clear. Arguing for UN intervention was more effective than pushing anarchy.

Time observed that "when it gets its nationhood, as it surely will, East Timor will be the first country to have been created in the Internet age, in part *by* the Internet age."[48] To Indonesians and others who depended on him, Joyo himself revealed his identity on a trip to Jakarta eight months later. Having survived the terrible automobile crash that killed his wife, and the subsequent deadly melanoma that made him blind in his right eye, having anonymously poured out from New York for four years the best of the world's free press on Indonesia, Gordon Bishop returned to Jakarta to try to help independent journalists there organize a free investigative news publication.

The Jakarta-based, Indonesia-led foundation AKSARA undertook a study of press responses, international and domestic, in the month before and the month after the East Timor referendum.[49] The data showed a huge skew of attitudes, best summarized in short statements. A Jakarta-based writer for the *Far Eastern Economic Review* said negative foreign tone arose from Indonesian authorities frequently hiding the truth and appearing to "deny . . . the existence of the corpse at their feet." The Indonesian ambassador to Australia took a more historic and philosophic view: that when Indonesians were fighting for independence in the 1940s, they got sympathies for self-determination against the Dutch, and therefore might understand why East Timor now did against themselves. He could have added, but did not, how uncomplaining Indonesia had been over the perfunctory way the UN gave over West Irian to Indonesia in 1969. An editor of *Media Indonesia* put starkly the attitudes prevailing among Indonesian journalists: international confrontations strengthen nationalism. The Australian attitude, especially, seemed a betrayal of long-cultivated friendship and triggered a reaction against "large white foreigners carrying weapons on what had shortly before been Indonesian territory."[50]

As Aksara's chairman wrote, East Timor was more painful to Indonesia than foreign observers cared to believe, and would remain so for many years, a "hurt . . . hidden in the 'closets' of our most radical minds."[51] In the openness and sustained balance of the report, one can feel Chairman Nono Anwar Makarim, brother of General Zacky Anwar Makarim, quivering with a successful effort at objectivity, and admirably succeeding.

The Indonesian Military Revealed

Desi Anwar, previously an anchor on a major evening television news program, expressed herself freely in mid-crisis on the Indonesian problems that East Timor dramatized for the world to see:

> The Indonesian military, with its peculiar dual-function (holding both the sword and the ploughshare) evolved from being the saviour to becoming the scourge of the nation . . . For many in the military, losing East Timor, a place they considered their own where many of them have died to save it . . . is the biggest form of humiliation, and proof that a civilian-led government with democratic ideals is not in the country's best interests . . . Once again ordinary Indonesians have to witness the military become firefighters for fires of their own making. It is a game of spitefulness, violence and contempt that Indonesians know only too well but are too impotent and the leaders too disorganized and divisive to prevent.[52]

Where Desi Anwar saw the military as a dire threat to incipient democracy, foreign experts saw ABRI as an enemy to its own professional reputation. Colonel (Retired) John Haseman, a former American military attaché in Southeast Asian nations, wrote an article for *Jane's,* the international periodical on military affairs, evoking an earlier failure of military intelligence, in Burma, when a national election had been finally allowed in 1990. The Burmese military told the foreign diplomatic community that the government party would win as much as 60 percent of the vote. At the polls, however, the Burmese people gave a huge mandate of 85 percent to the National League for Democracy and its associated regional parties. Haseman saw Indonesia's well-financed covert operation in East Timor, using intelligence apparatus from Kopassus, police, and an expanded militia base to attempt comprehensive intimidation, as a stupid strategy followed by a disastrous fiasco, utterly lacking what any covert operation must have, which is "plausible deniability."

Most important was the failure of military leadership: "Any military commander, including the armed forces commander-in-chief, is responsible for what his men do or fail to do. By this standard, General Wiranto must bear responsibility . . . [for the fact that] men in the pay of his army . . . conducted reprehensible acts in East Timor, failed to perform their mission to provide security and order in the province, and failed to fulfill the commitment of their nation given to the United Nations to guarantee security in East Timor prior to, during, and after the balloting." Despite "violent thuggery at its worst," Haseman concludes that the international community should not isolate the entire army because of a "vengeful cabal of hard liners" but should help reform the Indonesian defense establishment to prevent recurrence of such events anytime, anywhere, ever again.[53]

Cooperation at last began to appear between InterFET forces in East Timor and Indonesian forces, which had pulled back to West Timor. The MPR on October 20, 1999, formally released East Timor from Indonesia and was glad to get on to other business. Two Americans highly experienced in evaluating the Indonesian military (whom I have designated K and L) reviewed together the now diminishing crisis in the light of years gone by.

K: The registration and turnout were indicators. But the TNI thought they could keep the independence vote under 60 percent, get the MPR to drag the question out, and win a compromise. The 80 percent result knocked them silly. Wiranto was . . . slow to act. He's not stupid, but he is Javanese—thinking "we'll get past this somehow," as did many senior military. But when Admiral Blair came in, and in a gentlemanly way, one on one, severed military relations, this did the trick. After that? Economic sanctions and an international tribunal, they completed the case . . . The real principals in East Timor, however, were Zacky Anwar, Syafrie Syamsuddin, Adam Damiri, and Tono Suratman. They followed Benny Moerdani's security approach: "You have to be more ruthless than the other side. Make sure you do it to them first."

L: The TNI is in crisis, with a big rift between officers and men. The one-stars have lifestyle problems, and the economic crisis is hitting all others [of lesser rank]. Morale is low. There are rivalries between the services so bad that they've nearly come to blows near Jakarta. Wiranto, except some scapegoating of kids, hasn't punished anyone for anything. No adequate investigation yet of Trisakti and Semanggi [firing into crowds of demonstrators, May and November 1998], or even a conclusion to the inquiry on student abduction. Until 1990 the army had a special place in the minds of the people. But Suharto corrupted the officer corps to protect his own and family interests, and then it began to fall apart. No civilized army should behave that way [as in East Timor]. You just don't shoot unarmed people, period . . . The army somehow lost the coherence it had against Darul Islam, in its approach to East Timor in 1975–1979. It went right into hard-core military operations without the preparatory phases of psychological warfare and civic action . . . Then the army lost its integrity [when Suharto corrupted it] . . . Now there's an old general in the MPR who says, "The next president has got to ask for the retirement of all three star generals, and many two stars. Corruption even surfaces at the colonel level."[54]

Were such lessons learned among Indonesian civilian leaders, let alone military ones? Juwono Sudarsono had said in 1984 that the army was the only institution capable of governing Indonesia. But as a humane man, he ventured the thought to me in mid-1999 that Javanese and other Indonesians had not treated the East Timorese as human beings *(diwongke)*. When he was appointed the first civilian minister of defense in over forty years, he found that Wiranto had hand-picked the minister's staff. But his position for a while apparently reinforced his old convictions about the military as Indonesia's backbone. In an interview with *Time*, he criticized the UN as "now a virtual arm of American diplomacy" and "not a neutral partner on the ground [in East Timor]. There was a systematic attempt to bamboozle us. We were had by the U.N., had by Australians, had by the Americans." I challenged Juwono on every aspect of that by email but got no reply.[55]

A few months later, however, Juwono broke ranks. In July 2000 he publicly declared that riots were being timed to connect to and deflect court cases involving Suharto or past high officials. "Those financing the unrest have more money than the security forces themselves . . . I can confirm that there is a deliberate and systematic effort to overburden the security forces, in order to create the impression that the government is ineffective." Days later a bomb went off in the attorney general's office an hour after a visit by Tommy Suharto. Juwono declared what preliminary investigations clearly indicated, that Tommy's bodyguards had planted the bomb. In August he was supplanted in his cabinet position. When I next saw him, in December, he reflected on having served successively as minister of environment, of education, and of defense. He smiled. "*All* my positions were 'defense.'"[56]

David Jenkins, an experienced Australian reporter, caught up with a newly mustachioed Habibie in Paris on a summer day in 2001. The whole Timor explosion in September 1999 would have been slighter, or even completely avoidable, Habibie said, if Kofi Annan had kept an agreement to deliver to him the voting results three days before any official public announcement. But Annan broke his word, gave him only thirty minutes notice, and should bear some responsibility for what happened. An informed Western source confirmed that the results were indeed unilaterally advanced by the UN, a "stupid" and "disastrous" decision. Jenkins's own analysis—astute, I believe—minimized the timing and faulted both Habibie and the international community for "never imagining . . . that the Indonesian generals could be so mendacious, so callous, so obtuse and so incompetent, despite warnings that they could be all those things and more."[57]

The behavior of top generals in the New Order was consistent within the luxury of their strategic isolation. Feisal Tanjung, who had risen to become Habibie's coordinating minister on politics and security, was the compre-

hensive example. In his authorized biography he described his secret operations in 1969, hidden from UN observers, to ply West Irian representatives
with food, drink, and cigarettes and "manage" them up to the day of their
votes on the Act of Free Choice. Perhaps he imagined that thirty years later
a similar trick could be pulled off. Army attitudes in documents salvaged by
HAK show frequent use of the term "floating mass," suggesting a belief
in the manipulability of the Timorese and a failure to understand their
twenty-four years of resistance. Even when General Tanjung's first projection of a pro-integration vote of 75 percent was revised downward, they
believed that doling out food and medicine in the final weeks could bring
the pro-Indonesia vote to 56 percent. When on voting day they got less than
half of that, Tanjung and many others resorted to accusing the UN of rigging the vote. The army apparently learned nothing by its own intelligence
failures—its overestimation of the tactics of buy, dupe, and terrorize and its
gross underestimation of Timorese adaptive resilience. In conducting counter-insurgency wars in Aceh and Papua, the military seems to have learned
only that they should never again allow a referendum.[58]

The Full Report of the Investigative Commission into Human Rights Violations in East Timor (KPP-HAM) declared after careful work that between announcement of the ballot and the formal handing over of East
Timor to the UN, the crimes that occurred "are so systematic, planned, collective, massive and widespread as to constitute gross violations of the
Geneva Convention, as well as of national law." Mass killings, torture and
maltreatment, enforced disappearances and evacuation, violence based on
gender, scorched earth and destruction, terror and intimidation all demand
legal accounting, "and the official status of an individual provides no special immunity." The cross-hatching of evidence found by the Indonesian
Commission required—but has not yet received—investigation of General
Wiranto, Lieutenant General Johnny Lumintang, Major General Zacky
Anwar Makarim, Major General Adam Damiri, and Major General (ret.)
H. R. Garnadi, to cite only those with stars on the shoulders among all
named.[59]

Careful Western scholars, reviewing TNI planning documents of various
sorts that became public, find them inauthentic or inconclusive. Also irrelevant: because the strongest evidence was not in documents but in behavior—notably, the ability of the TNI to turn violence on and off (off for the
day Wiranto visited with the UN Security Council delegation) and on again.
The repertoire of acts was consistent with the range of counter-insurgency
violence committed by the military over the last thirty years—so consistent,
in fact, as to constitute in itself a "culture of violence," indicative of serious

"institutional pathologies" going far beyond named individuals and requiring thorough reform.[60]

East Timor, Infant Micro-State

Before ABRI fully revealed its covert policy of fiery and bloody defiance of the UN-sponsored referendum, a Washington, DC, think tank asked me to give a presentation on Indonesia and East Timor. Surgery to repair my left retina by binding my left eyeball with a silicone buckle had produced temporary uncoordinated vision. I was wearing a black eye patch. The audience responded freely to the subject, and afterward the director of the institute, a retired general, took me aside to offer his comments on East Timor. He was partly of Native American blood, he declared. He had served in Vietnam, and he spoke Chinese fluently. In his view, Native Americans, Vietnamese, Montagnards, Tibetans, and East Timorese shared the same affliction: an unwillingness or inability to accept the benefits of the larger culture around them and to let themselves be constructively assimilated. Resistance, he im-

93. CHILDREN OF TIMOR LORO SA'E. In the relative security that followed the arrival of international forces, a number of neighborhood boys in Liquiça "adopt" Galuh Soedjatmoko, an NGO leader, and Patrick Burgess, chief of the UN Humanitarian Office. Later, in February 2001, Galuh and Patrick marry, with ceremonies in both Australia and Jakarta. (Gift of Galuh Soedjatmoko/author's collection)

94. WAITING FOR XANANA. A crowd of 5,000 in Ermera, East Timor, awaits the arrival of the guerrilla hero, former schoolteacher, and poet Jose Alexandre Gusmão, in December 1999. With the Sergio Vieira De Mello, the UN Transitional Administrator, Xanana speaks on themes of reconciliation. (Gift of Simone Duarte, GLOBO, Brazil/author's collection)

plied, only troubled the world and weakened themselves. "Think about it!" he urged me.

I have thought a great deal about it. Father Rolando prevails in my mind over the well-traveled general. A Filipino priest and leader of the Salesian Brothers outside Dili, Father Rolando would eventually take 10,000 refugees into his compound and surrounding lands and in the perilous days of September arrange to fly them to West Timor, where they would find food, beds, and shelter in a sports stadium in Kupang. One early morning in June he had stayed after breakfast to talk with me about the looming situation (which took my mind off my partial blindness). Of Indonesian attitudes, he concluded mildly, "Their *unity* thing . . . I don't understand it. The Holy Roman Empire didn't last *forever*. It broke up in many states."[61]

No empire is sacred. None is eternal. Certainly not some neo-Majapahit as manifested in East Timor, where the ancient specter of the Siva-Buddha god-king, knife and blood-bowl in his hands, once again stood on a mound

of skulls. And whatever its intentions, the Indonesian military, which is not a myth, was becoming understood worldwide not as preserving the Indonesian nation-state but as dividing and defaming it.

A writer in *Foreign Affairs* described East Timor in 2000 as lacking "not just doctors, dentists, accountants, lawyers and police, but also tables, chairs, pots, and pans . . . stop signs, traffic signals, and street lights." It was near a state of "no economy." Projected revenue for that year was $16 million, chiefly from duties on commodities consumed by foreign UN officials, journalists, and NGO employees.[62] But never fear: UN peace-builders, after Kosovo and East Timor, "now bring not only police, but laws and courts; not only administrators, but administrative structure and tribunals; indeed, almost all the requisites of a modern state except modern citizens."[63]

Citizens are, of course, nourished slowly, and sometimes in great adversity. Felismina, who was separated from Galuh for many weeks, had run to the mountains in September and had survived. Joyously reunited in Dili late in 1999, they resumed work. The first installment of their report, with its documentation of rape, sexual violence, and sexual slavery, hit *The New York Times* front page on March 1, 2001. Felismina, herself a torture victim, was the key investigator, coordinating the efforts of FOKUPERS "to collect testimonies of women who were raped, tortured, or who witnessed the killing of a family member . . . Now, women are coming out of the woodwork saying this happened to me in 1980, you have to record this too . . . Other people go to the field in search of survivors and many are reluctant to speak. But when [Felismina] goes, she is able to convince them to speak."[64] One road to citizenship is the courage to prevail over horror with truth.

On May 20, 2002, East Timor officially became the independent nation of Timor Loro Sa'e. President Megawati of Indonesia was there, with in excess of 100 security guards, concerned more for international support at the moment than for hypernationalist votes in her parliament. Former President Bill Clinton was there on behalf of the United States. Kofi Annan was there to represent the UN, presumably having learned from East Timor the lesson that his Algerian advisor in peacekeeping, Lakhdar Brahimi (later prominent in Afghanistan), formulated so neatly: "The Secretariat must not apply best-case planning assumptions to situations where the actors have historically exhibited worst-case behavior."[65]

The elected president of the new nation, José Alexandre Gusmão—Xanana—looked out upon a people with a per capita income of $168 but with the hope of royalties in 2004–2005 from the Timor Gap oil fields. Life expectancy was 57 years and literacy only 37 percent among rural people over age fifteen. Xanana had chosen Portuguese as an official language (spoken by only 5 percent of the people) and the American dollar as the official currency. The phone system was run by Telstra, an Australian company. The UN peacekeeping force would be phased out within two years to allow the indigenous defense force, currently 600 ex-Falantil guerrillas, to grow. "I remind everyone," said Xanana, "especially the leaders: discipline to affirm our power, tolerance to affirm democracy, reconciliation to affirm unity." If Timor Loro Sa'e is to embed the lessons of Kosovo, he might have added the rule of law as a precondition for all else, as learned in Bosnia.[66]

Timor Loro Sa'e was quick to adopt a truth commission, which many nations emerging from dictatorship or war in the last twenty years (but not Indonesia) have set up as an emotional purgative and corollary to democracy. The UN estimated 1,000 deaths (and KPP-HAM as high as 2,000) in the transitional violence. Two of them, murders in the town of Viqueque, resulted in the arrests of opposing gang leaders. For the lesser participants in the murders there was an all-day ritual, with an *adat* judge presiding and several hundred people watching. Barefoot, costumed, cross-legged on the floor, "the judge delivered a long, chanted song detailing the crimes and asking for reconciliation." He slaughtered a cow and sprinkled the central figures with its blood, to cleanse them. The local Catholic bishop celebrated Mass, and the men signed a 21-point agreement on their future behavior. Feast, concert, and soccer match followed.[67]

But who shall get Generals Feisal Tanjung, Yunus Yosfiah, Hendropriyono, and Syafrie Syamsuddin to join in this ritually cleansing atmosphere? Transcripts leaked by Australia's Defence Signals Directorate indicate that they, among others, set up an anti-independence intimidation project early in 1999 and, when that failed, followed through with orders to their militias to wreak havoc and force flight. Indonesia will not allow an international tribunal to investigate. In its own trials for human rights violations, the prosecutors appear to subvert their case and abet the defense. All ten Indonesian security officials thus far tried have been acquitted.[68] If criminal responsibility can never be assigned, when will it be possible at least to have an *adat* ceremony on television, watched by millions of Indonesians, culminating in General Wiranto's singing his confession—in *dangdut* rhythms if he wishes—and asking national forgiveness for his unsoldierly behaviors of 1999: insubordination to his president, dereliction of duty with respect to Indonesia's agreement with the UN, and gross violations of human rights as detailed by Indonesia's own KPP-HAM?

16

ANARCHO-DEMOCRACY

The last step of the first open election of a president in Indonesian history, the parliamentary conclusion, was unpredictable. Megawati's party had a third of the seats in the MPR, and Golkar somewhat more than a fifth. Gus Dur's party had an eighth, and Amien Rais, by pooling his PAN votes with Islamist splinters, may have controlled a tenth. If Mega, Gus Dur, and Amien had behaved as a reform coalition, they could have entered with assurance of about 55 percent of the seats, as some political scientists intuitively predicted over a year earlier. But the three had rarely met and failed to cohere throughout.

Mega had shown neither taste nor talent for the required negotiations, and Wahid and Rais had displayed their mutual dislike. Wahid, in addition, deprecated his "sister" Mega's competence. On one occasion he said, "Mega is stupid, but she loves people"; on another, "Mega is stupid, but she is teachable." Sukarno's daughter kept her peace. Meanwhile, with calculated hypocrisy, Gus Dur shook his head over those *ulamas* of NU who would not accept a woman as president. Rais was more Qur'anically adamant about the point, despite there having been female prime ministers over Muslims in Pakistan and Bangladesh, over Hindus and Muslims in India, and over Buddhists in Sri Lanka.

Akbar Tandjung, Golkar's prime tactician, hoped to profit by the reformists' disarray, winning by money politics and power deals enough loose or disaffected votes to preserve Habibie in office. But in late July, following steady evidence of other Golkar party corruption since February, the Bank Bali scandal disclosed $78 million of kickbacks to a company run by the treasurer of Golkar and a circle of men tied to Habibie's informal election team.[1] Akbar himself would later come under investigation for receiving (with many others) off-budget personal loans from Suharto's Presidential Aid Fund and for massive diversion of Bulog administrative funds to Golkar purposes.

Next, the East Timor vote and violence deeply embarrassed Habibie personally, because he had initiated the referendum in the first place. His late-blooming democratic instincts and free-press policies, nevertheless, enabled him to make a comprehensive and intelligent appeal to the MPR. That, with Golkar money, gave him a good chance to win. Acceptance or rejection of his accountability speech would determine the fate of his government.

The MPR had installed state-of-the-art electronic voting machines, but, fearing a fix, its members demanded to see representatives parading across the stage, one by one. On national television I watched with Indonesian friends as votes were recorded with black markers on a white tally board, like a grade school arithmetic lesson: four vertical lines with a diagonal slash equals five. The process went on until 1:30 in the morning. Only near the end was it clear that reform ("white") Golkar votes, added to reform military votes, would enable "reject" to prevail over "accept." The result was 355 to 322.[2]

If Habibie could not be elected, then who would be? Politicking, from hotel suite to hotel suite, was mercurial into the morning. Appeals to party, to *aliran*, to personal interest, to regional solidarity, to prejudice, through every conceivable power of suasion, went on until the moment of voting for the president. In a contest that now pitted "sister" against "brother," the previous popular vote was forgotten. Cabinet positions were now the major political currency. Akbar for the establishment, Amien for Islamic textual values over feminism, and Wiranto for the interests of ABRI were the most dextrous players.

On October 20, I lunched with Marla Kosec. She said, "Gus is getting money from all over—Western sources, Indonesian sources, Chinese sources . . . It comes in plastic bags. And you know what? He just hands them to the *dukuns!*" She laughed. "What is this, post-stroke syndrome?" More gravely, she remarked on Wahid's being forty pounds overweight, with an occipital aneurysm and uncontrolled blood pressure. "You're my sister," Gus had told her, "you know me very well." She'd replied, "But you don't know who you are anymore, or who you want to be." She shrugged. "He wants to be president."[3]

Afterward I tried to reach a friend's business office but got stuck in a traffic jam outside the Australian Embassy—in one of the paid demonstrations against intervention in East Timor that went on for exactly fifty days. When I reached the office I was greeted, *"Alhamdulillah!"* and was stunned to learn that Gus Dur had been elected to the presidency. One of Wahid's own staff exulted in astonishment with an American friend, *"Can* you fucking *believe* it?"[4]

In their head-on collision, Gus Dur had beaten Mega by 373 votes to 313. Significant parts of his victory came from "black" Golkar and from "central axis" Muslim votes committed in the crunch to Gus Dur by Amien Rais.[5] As soon as the result became national, some regions went irrational. Riots broke out in Megawati's strongholds in Central Java, where Amien Rais's home compound in Solo was burned to the ground. Rampages in Bali included a fleet of taxicabs bashed to pieces by hired thugs yelling, "No blind man as president!"

Meanwhile, I sat down to chat with Cak Nur, in a hotel hideaway that his friends had arranged to shield him from pressures about the vice presidency. During the weeks, days, critical hours of the presidency, he had felt that "I should not intrude." Now, with the vice presidency, the whole process was repeating itself at super-speed. Cak Nur's advice to Akbar Tandjung was to let Mega have the office and accept for himself the role of chair of the DPR, awaiting better chances for Golkar in 2004. As for Nur himself: "Wiranto is seeking the vice presidency for shelter [from war crimes inquiries]—the worst of motives—which would be a *perfect loss* for reform and the economy . . . [If I were to run and win] this is the kind of person I must deal with and defend." I argued that only someone like himself could show the people how domestic reform and international inquiries on war crimes converge in human rights. The argument appealed to Nur, but he said with a smile, "I am a solitary man."[6]

Fires were rising in Den Pasar as I flew toward that city, but by the time I landed it was calm. Megawati had gone on TV and declared to the rioters, "I am your mother. Listen to me. I want you to go home." Gus Dur had nominated her for vice president. After Akbar Tandjung and Wiranto withdrew, she beat Hamzah Haz by 396 to 284 votes. By dinnertime on October 21, Indonesia's ticket was fixed: Gus and Mega. Wahid stood triumphant, but his political supporters were at cross-purposes: the alliance of convenience between PDI-P and PKB; the anti-Habibie votes of white Golkar and military reformists; the anti-Mega votes of black Golkar and Rais's central axis.[7]

The "miraculous victory" put into Indonesia's supreme office a man of great will and guile, who had been guilty of nothing but wily about everything. He was suffering from years of progressive and poorly treated glaucoma, myopic degeneration, and diabetic retinopathy, all further complicated by two strokes that destroyed some visual pathways in his brain.[8] Indonesia's new president could not see beyond his dinner plate. He would have to guide the nation by ear, as a great soul and a grand seer.

Hydroponic Government

Days after he took office, President Abdurrahman Wahid received five of us for leisurely conversation: a journalist, a novelist, and a priest, all Javanese;

an Australian journalist; and me. The Javanese journalist fell asleep, having been up all night at a showing of *Parakesit* (The Coming of the New King) at the TVRI auditorium—a *wayang* performance symbolizing the return to power of the forces of good. The palace and cabinet forces who had attended it were notably drowsy today, but the president was chipper. I asked him, "Gus Dur, when did you decide to become president?"

He answered cheerfully: "The day *before* . . . Because of the situation. Only then did I throw my hat in the ring." Four of us talked it over afterward in a coffee shop. None of us believed him, but all of us accepted the answer. We knew of his conviction of having, in some sense, received the *wahyu* many years before. He had answered a journalist who asked him earlier that year, in the midst of operations on his eye, if he were going to run: "I don't know, but if I do, I'll win." He had ignored two Javanese among us who had begged him, for the sake of his own health, to take the role of Cardinal Sin of the Philippines, who had bucked the powers of the dictator Marcos with his own moral and quasi-political leadership. Now he was enjoying his triumph. Mega did not know how to lead. The PDI-P, Wahid said, was full of money politics and "that was the bullshit of it." But PDI-P and PKB together were able to shoot down Habibie and Akbar and back off Wiranto: "That was the beauty of it." He exulted in his opportunity and jested of his hope. "I would like to take all the corrupt bureaucrats and corrupt conglomerates and the *preman* [thugs] and send them all to Buru." Laughing. "I will not let them leave until they promise to change."[9]

But how, I wondered, was Gus Dur going to sweep away established forces and entrenched habits and work as a lone and central moral force? He had won in part by belittling Mega and by criticizing Amien. While consistent in his opposition to Golkar's long record, he was opportunistic in accepting the help and support of its reformist branch. His staff saw plastic sacks of money coming into his office steadily and just as swiftly being dispatched by him to party leaders, *ulamas,* and civil organizers. None of the money was accounted for, none remained in the office. "Campaign finance reform" was not on the table in Indonesia. The nation was in the grip of a patronage blizzard. The first freely elected president in Indonesian history was now in office, having received only one-eighth of the popular vote, having no firm coalition, but owing numerous political debts. The claimants for cabinet positions came on him fast and furious.

Power-sharing was logical enough at the top: Gus Dur and Mega, president and vice president; Amien Rais, speaker of the MPR; Akbar Tandjung, speaker of the DPR. Some notables made the cabinet: Laksamana Sukardi as minister for investment and state enterprises development (but how was he going to attract foreign investment?); Marzuki Darusman as attorney general (a bright and ambitious Golkar reformist whose major task would be prosecutions of Suharto and corrupt Golkarites); Juwono Sudarsono as the first civilian minister of defense in half a century (but without a military habituated to reporting to a civilian). Wahid voiced a sound instinct—to reduce the large Suharto-era cabinet to about sixteen members, less than half its previous size. But when the cabinet was finally announced, it consisted of thirty-five members, described as "establishment figures who sympathize with reform—not . . . reform figures who are hostile to the establishment."[10] Even that description could not comfortably include General Wiranto, enraged at being offered and then denied the vice-presidency. He demanded and obtained the position of coordinating minister for politics and security for himself; chose his own defense minister and staffed that office; and forced Lieutenant Generals Yudhoyono and Agum Gumelar into the cabinet, which required their retirement from the army, thus stifling their influence for military reform.[11]

The ministers consisted of seven each from Muhammadiyah and NU; six military officers (the same number as in Habibie's cabinet); twelve non-Javanese, including four from South Sulawesi, where a Habibie faction had switched to Gus Dur; one each from Aceh and Irian Jaya; a Hindu from Bali; and the first Chinese Buddhist in decades, Kwik Kian Gie, part of Mega's brain, as coordinating minister of the economy.[12] This "unity" cabinet lost no time in starting to squabble, and the storms generated by his "rainbow" of advisers hovered over Gus Dur's head like a thundercloud. Despondent, he called a revered religious leader from Pekalongan, Kiai Ma'sud, to come see him in the palace. When the *kiai* asked "What's the matter?" Wahid replied, "This cabinet . . . it's not my cabinet . . . It's the cabinet of Amien Rais. Of Wiranto. Of everybody. Not mine." When asked what he was going to do about it, Wahid's responded, "I don't know. What should I do?" As one *ulama* to another, the visitor delivered the right, the safe, the ultimate advice: "Contemplate."[13]

By the time Gus Dur gave a speech to an international business audience in Bali the weekend after his election, he was in good spirits. He seemed freshly stirred by the NU interpreters of the skies who found signs there of *sasmita kelangitan,* "heavenly revelation."[14] Westerners were instructed by his protocol staff to wear business suits. Wahid came in batik and sandals. He reminded us charmingly, "I don't like to wear shoe," and cheerfully said he would continue to refer to Vice President Megawati Sukarnoputri as "Mbak [Sister] Mega." His informality was welcome. So was a sincere restatement of his convictions on democracy, rule of law, equal opportunity, and regional autonomy. But the incoherence of his strategy concerned me. He spoke of immediate travel plans, of imagined Asian alliances, of strengthened commercial ties with Israel. How wonderful for Indonesia to have an accessible leader, I thought. But I wanted to remind him of what

95. PRESIDENT WAHID WITH SUHARTOS. The new president visits the Cendana residence of former President Suharto on March 8, 2000. "Tutut" (Siti Hardijanti Rukmana), Suharto's eldest daughter, is on the right, peeking over his shoulder. Wahid's frequent publicized discussions with the Suhartos would give him the unfortunate appearance of a "fixer" and weaken the public's esteem for him. (Rully Uesuma/*Tempo*)

President Clinton's advisors banged home in 1992: "It's the economy, stupid!" I wanted but had no opportunity to say, "Stay home, Gus Dur, and concentrate on the economy. Get your team focused on what to do!"[15]

Instead, he traveled to fifty countries in his first eighteen months in office, exceeding his office's budgeted travel funds. He added level upon level of economic advisory councils until a savvy Western diplomat privately likened it to a "triple-dip ice cream cone—and it's melting!" Extending a hand to Israel was superficially courageous, but it inflamed Islamists, whose support he needed in other matters. Worse, as I knew from an intimate presidential advisor who shared his myopia on the matter, he thought that by leaning toward Israel he could encourage support from "Wall Street Jews." An ignorant notion. Wall Street has no creed, only calculations.

In another example of intellectual bravado, Wahid recommended lifting the ban and ending sanctions on communists, and he expressed personal regret for the role that NU forces had played in the killings of 1965–66. His integrity as a religious leader shone through, but his timing as a political leader was terrible. His job, now that the Pharaoh was gone, required him to be a Moses: to be single-minded, to point the way, to lead on with infinite patience in the wilderness. He couldn't manage.

Abdurrahman Wahid paid three world-class advisors to tell him what to do. What Henry Kissinger said is not known. Lee Kuan Yew, apparently, told him to fix the economy. Paul Volcker, as Gus Dur himself acknowledged to Westerners, told him he could not give any advice because the president had no structure beneath him to carry it out.

Around this time, a high official of the American embassy, speaking to

The New York Times, described Indonesia, run from Jakarta, as a "hydroponic government"—an airplant, not rooted in the soil. Where was it getting its nutrients? Gus Dur did not believe in his own cabinet and was not fully supported by it. Those elected to parliament owed their seats not to voters in districts but to party bosses, who received them by electoral formula and apportioned them by favoritism. Now a president with only 13 percent of the popular vote, unrooted in his cabinet, badly needing to cooperate with a parliament similarly unrooted in the people of its districts, instead faced off against it.

A major precipitant of his clash with parliament was Wahid's own behavior. Early in his administration he had asked for and received a large gift from the sultan of Brunei to address humanitarian problems in Aceh, but apparently he had deposited the money in a personal account. He had also sought some means of siphoning government monies from the administrative pension fund of Bulog for peace projects in Aceh. He backed off when told a letter would be necessary, but his masseur Sapuan (who had also massaged Suharto and had a *dukun*esque reputation) acted as intermediary apparently to extract the funds from Suondo, an administrator expecting advancement for his assistance. Many of the critics who brought this to light were hypocrites, guilty of worse. But Wahid was reprehensibly sloppy, and his behavior clouded the *reformasi* atmosphere. Direct address to the facts, with apology, might have blown it all away, leaving Gus Dur to be understood as a *pesantren* master unaccustomed to accounting and audit procedures, a newly elected official who was learning that part of his job in an embarrassing way. Instead he stonewalled, argued with inquiring legislators, and intensified public suspicion of KKN on his own part by his very denials.

I saw Gus Dur briefly in June of 2000, following a short visit with Alwi Shihab, now foreign minister. I had been sitting in the foreign minister's waiting room, surrounded with portraits, so I asked Alwi which of his predecessors, which included Hatta, Haji Agus Salim, Adam Malik, and Ali Alatas, was his model. He referred to none of them. "I am part of this *presidency,*" he said, "and this presidency is *part of me.*" His sudden ear-to-ear smile was not gluttonous but giddy. I thought, "God help Indonesia."[16]

was given a few minutes with President Wahid himself. I sensed that he
s trying to sort out persona, mystical illumination, *wahyu cakraningrat,*
d responsibilities of office.[17] Wahid's astute minister, Sarwono, warned
m that his wildly impulsive behavior and remarks were being used to un-
ermine him and his government. "There is an importance to protocol in
our job. You must distinguish among person, president, and head of state
. . like father, son, and holy ghost. Don't mix them up!"[18] Before appointment to the cabinet, Sarwono had warned that if Gus Dur continued to in-

sist on being "a very interesting person . . . the sense of crisis will be lost."[19] Now it was happening. Wahid prevaricated about a revealed affair with a woman named Aryanti a few years before. Criticism did not appear to move him to self-examination on any subject but rather drove him to naked evasions—to eccentricity, irascibility, effrontery, and, in the deliciously exact word of Soedjati Djiwandono, "pettifoggery."

Wahid battled the legislature as if he possessed the *wahyu* and the legislators were illegitimate, until late in August when such behavior accelerated talk of his impeachment. He dampened the crisis with humor and semi-apology and a promise to revise the cabinet with the advice of Megawati and her party. He did reshuffle the cabinet, but without satisfactory consultation with Mega. He relieved Juwono (hampered by a stroke in office) but replaced him with a lesser entity. He kept Marzuki, who was plodding on with prosecutions. To a group of surprised foreign visitors Wahid proclaimed he was going to indict Ginandjar. To me in the United States, in September, he declared he had sixty more indictments to unleash. There would be no impunity for the Suharto family, he added.[20] But it was well known that a bomb had gone off in Marzuki's office toilet, and he could not trust his own legal staff in pursuit of key cases.

Worse yet: Wahid fired Laksamana Sukardi on undemonstrated grounds of corruption, thereby losing a talent, alienating the PDI-P, and making a ferocious enemy of Laksa himself, generally regarded as one of the cleanest men in government. Sukardi's mistake, apparently, had been to oppose the bailout of Texmaco, whose CEO, Marimutu Sinivasan, had recently contributed $250,000 to Wahid's NU and employed thousands of his NU followers. President Wahid then assisted Sinivasan in wangling a $2.7 billion deal through IBRA, a restructuring questioned by the IMF and World Bank as well as Minister Sukardi. To defame and dislodge his key critic, Sinivasan provided Wahid with allegedly incriminating evidence. The president, of course, could not read it, but Sinivasan accompanied the document with spoken advice. Wahid, without availing himself of the eyes or judgment of his personal staff, secreted the document in a private drawer and proceeded to fire one of his best ministers.[21] At a subsequent cabinet meeting the president went so far as to designate three conglomerate leaders, now his political supporters, who should be above prosecution. One was Sinivasan.[22] At that moment, if not before, Wahid reduced his credibility to that of a duped factional leader, with chiefly regional support.

On November 8, 2000, I was privileged to watch the American presidential election returns with Wahid in his study. While Dennis Heffernan managed the TV volume by wand, I interpreted the Cable News Network figures on the screen. We saw the United States enter a five-week crisis to determine its president, but with procedures that would produce a result

96. CHINESE LUNAR NEW
YEAR, 2000. A Chinese Indonesian burns joss sticks in celebration of the new year. President
Wahid lifted restraints against
Chinese religious observations
in public, which had been imposed by the Suharto government in 1967. (Kemal Jufri/
IMAJI)

without one bayonet's being unsheathed. Meanwhile, I had the sorry sense
of an Indonesian presidency that was concentrating on the wrong things—
such as replacing the giant red carpet in the Istana by a giant blue carpet, on
the advice of a *dukun*. Gus Dur himself, a sad, isolated figure, sat in shorts
and a Hawaiian shirt and shivered in his own air-conditioning until we
wrapped a blanket around him.[23]

By February 2001 Wahid's errancy and irascibility had engendered an
overwhelming vote of censure in the MPR. By the end of April, a second
such vote seemed (to all but himself) to mean that the third and final constitutional step would be taken no later than August. In the meantime, who
was tending the store? Combined public and private debt exceeded the
Gross Domestic Product by nearly two-thirds. In the 2001 budget, 52 percent of state spending was designated for debt service, compared with less
than 7 percent for health and education combined. But many questioned
whether even those targets could be met. Talks with the IMF were at their
worst since the crisis began. If other private donors deserted Indonesia, the
economy would be in danger of collapse.[24]

IBRA and Indonesian Business Competitiveness

The Indonesian Bank Restructuring Authority was supposed to be at the center of a fiscal solution. But IBRA, created in 1998, while holding nearly $60 billion of troubled assets, was having political difficulty following the course of its alleged model, the Resolution Trust Corporation, whose restructurings during the American savings-and-loan crisis had minimized those losses a decade before. IBRA named six different chairman in three years, during which time the authority recovered only a tiny fraction of the $70 billion spent by the government to rescue its banks. The situation they inherited was comprehensively sick. The State Audit Agency in 1999 found that 48 banks together misused 95 percent of the central bank's emergency liquidity support credits, injected during the financial crisis of 1997–98.[25]

The most luminous asset in IBRA's hands was 40 percent of publicly traded stock of Astra, which had for a decade been at the top of Indonesia's overall business rankings. More than two years after IBRA was formed, President Wahid himself finally supervised the sale of Astra to prove his government's viability to the World Bank, the IMF, and international investors. Singapore's Cycle and Carriage paid $506 million for a controlling 23 percent stake in it. The Singapore government backed it up with direct ownership of 7 percent, and 10 percent was split between Lazard Freres and a vehicle of George Soros's Quantum Fund. Because this deal was "stage-managed," an IBRA staffer said, it was "useless as a model for future sales."[26] After a two-year battle over Astra, Indonesia had lost native control, and Astra itself fell in ranking behind Gudang Garam, maker of the clove cigarette preferred by Indonesia's 90 million smokers.[27] At a meeting in which she was removed as Astra's CEO, Rini Soewandi "broke into tears more than once defending her record."[28]

But there was anguish of a professional kind for an investment banker managing a boutique house called Widari Securities. Its acronym represented its three principal investors: General Wiranto, Fuad Bawazier, and Rini Soewandi herself. She apparently pried Astra Securities loose from her conglomerate, and with supporting knowledge of IBRA (as its ex-chairman) and commanding information on Astra (as its CEO), manipulated Astra stock transactions as the major holding of Widari. (After Widari's president left this tangle for a fresh start, Fuad Bawazier carried on the company under the name Madani Securities.) Putting Widari in high speculative play in a diseased market probably did not earn its three principals great profits. But their activity itself led a high official of the American Embassy to complain to Attorney General Marzuki about "insider trading" by Soewandi. The minister chuckled at the quaint American technical term. That completed the diplomat's conviction that there existed

Table 9. Asset recovery by IBRA, 1998–2001, compared with other Asian nations[a]

Nation	Value of assets taken over (billions)	Asset value as a percent of GDP	Percent of assets sold
Indonesia	$57.8	57	7
Korea	84.0	11	48
Malaysia	10.3	12	61
Thailand	13.0	11	70

a. *New York Times,* April 10, 2001, p. C1.

an "extraordinarily explicit conspiracy among elites in Jakarta" not to rock each other's boats. For archetypal elite figures, the three serve well: an impressively wealthy political general with presidential ambitions, who would involve himself with Islamist groups to create instabilities favoring a leader-on-horseback; a Yemeni-descended financier-politician, 'Hartoite and Islamist, lover of intrigue and backer of Amien Rais, eager to serve as kingmaker to any probable king; and an industrial-financial leader (Wellesley graduate with an American MBA), highly attuned to patrimonial government, whose trading was an unhappy epitome of financial behavior in Jakarta.[29]

I was shocked to hear the story. But I remembered that Tanri Abeng had once talked to me at length of Lee Iacocca and Bill Gates and then had come under indictment for anomalies over privatization efforts which fell under his cabinet authority.[30] Mochtar Riady would talk to me of Alvin Toffler and Peter Drucker, although his son, James, would have to plea-bargain his way to paying a fine of record size, $8.6 million, for illegal campaign contributions to Clinton—funds designed to expand the Riady family's Lippo business network.[31] So why should I have believed that Rini Soewandi, by citing Jack Welch of General Electric and Jacques Nasser of Ford, could herself rise above the dangerous suctions of the business culture around her?

A McKinsey global study of corporate organization released in mid-2000 evaluated Indonesia (along with Venezuela) as so rare in good corporate governance as to warrant paying a 27 percent premium to buy shares of a well-managed company: the bottom of its charts.[32] Indonesia's business culture also fared poorly in a global competitiveness survey of 53 industrialized and major developing nations. It not only placed 52nd in corruption and 51st in judicial independence but was absolute last, at 53rd, in both state funding of scientific research (where Taiwan was 24th) and private sector spending on research and development (where Malaysia was 31st).[33] Being at the bottom in both of these last two categories was not promising in an era when continual upgrading of export products was vital in the face of competition from China, India, Latin America, and Eastern Europe. In the following year the International Institute for Management Development, a top Swiss business school, ranked 49 major countries in business competitiveness, using 286 criteria in four categories: economic performance, government efficiency, business efficiency, and infrastructure. Indonesia, at 49th, came in dead last.[34]

Business competitiveness, of course, is only one aspect of national productivity, comprehensively considered. But Indonesia's condition had a special dimension, lamented by the post-Suharto senior economics minister Kwik Kian Gie. If there were a full legal crackdown on those guilty of corruption, "economic activity will grind to a halt as most business people will be in jail."[35]

Corruption

A practical fable of modern times: The great Garuda, mythical eagle and national symbol of Indonesia, was laboring in flight because leeches had covered his body, sucking his blood and making him too weak to fly. Finally he crashed into a swamp and lay in the mud, not moving. Kancil, the brave and sympathetic mouse-deer, said to him, "Would you like me to get rid of those leeches for you, so you can fly again?" But Garuda declined. "If you nip off these parasites, the swamp is full of others waiting to take their place. I prefer leeches I already know."[36]

The end of the Cold War blew away the hypocrisy that had induced donor nations to ignore political corruption in anti-Communist countries. Newly active media overcame taboos against discussing corruption.[37] Transparency International, founded in 1993, began publishing its index. After the mid-1990s, the World Bank and IMF, for whom corruption had been a hushed topic, began to ventilate it. In "perceptions of corruption," Indonesia was ranked infamously low, with only Nigeria beneath it among the world's major nations. The World Bank itself, stung by political-economist Jeffrey Winters' estimate that a third of its funds in Indonesia had been lost to corruption, finally issued a local statement. "The central issue is not whether 20 percent of development funds were or were not misappropriated, because figures such as these are the roughest of rough estimates. What really matters is that corruption is widespread in Indonesia and it poses a major obstacle to economic growth and fairness." The statement summoned Indonesians, especially civil society leaders, to help battle the "cancer of corruption," together with the government and international donors, who had reached "consensus . . . on the need for good governance, openness and transparency."[38] Two and a half years later, the Indonesian government preempted an IMF announcement that a second tranche of $300 million for social programs was being withheld, because the first award of $300 million, part of the recovery package of 1997, had "disappeared."[39]

One of the saddest announcements of the *reformasi* era was one of the least noticed. The new chairman of the Supreme Audit Agency reported to the DPR in a plenary meeting that the 1999–2000 state budget was affected by "irregularities" to the extent of 45.6 percent of its value. The amount of funds thus compromised was more than eleven times what Indonesia was to receive in loans that year from the IMF. A senior UN-related official said there was "nothing terribly romantic" about all this, obviously a consequence of insufficient pay, ineffective supervision, and absence of punishment for infractions.[40]

International officials, as the example shows, were numbed. International businesses were coopted into silence—a kind of commercial equivalent of the Stockholm Syndrome, in which they start to identify with the culture that holds them captive. National ministers, if not corruptors themselves, were thwarted or threatened if they oppose. The scene toward the end of the Suharto era through the Habibie period, and Wahid's as well, was very like the last trembling years of the Sukarno era. An absence of central stability accelerated corruption, on the unspoken premise of "get rich before you get replaced."

A half century after Indonesia became a nation state, its social system remains ultra-hospitable to corruption because of enduring feudal and colonial characteristics, a commanding role of the state in economic life, and, like Russia, a sudden enfeeblement of that state.[41] Corruption can be readily inventoried, from "service payments" at the lowest levels, up through grand corruption in the judicial and legal system, the police and the military, to presidential money politics. How can it be reduced? One expert says that the steady pressure of donor agencies over the course of a generation will prevail. Simply avoid donor fatigue, and it will happen.[42]

A brave spirit in action, Teten Masduki of Indonesia Corruption Watch, expressed his belief that civil society is growing vigorously, bringing them 2,500 corruption cases to be investigated in one year. A small staff could only investigate "big fish," but people such as Djoko Chandra and The Ning King had engineered mega-scams exceeding the size of the Bank Bali mess. Keep hooking big fish; keep them dangling before the public. Teten, a slender flat-bellied man in his thirties with dancing eyes and a crew-cut moustache, smiles readily, showing a front incisor chipped at a sharp angle. Despite death threats, he enjoys his sporting life on behalf of the people.[43]

Such optimism must be weighed against the answer of Nurcholish Madjid when I asked him for the origins of corruption in Indonesian history. He gravely replied: when the first official accepted *zakat* (religious tax) as *hadiah* (a gift). His answer means that the problem is centuries deep in the entire culture.[44]

Military Roguery and Disrepute

The Indonesian military was slow to give up adherence to its doctrines of 1962 and after. Throughout the Suharto period it used them to defend often delinquent behavior. Civilians, however, at the end of the century, began energetic reviews. Immediately after Suharto fell, the National Institute of Science (LIPI) published a secret study commissioned by the government in 1996: it was critical of the dual-function concept that inserted ABRI deep into the nation's socioeconomic development.[45] The institute followed it with another volume, critical of the business functions of the military.[46] Two more studies followed: one criticized the military's role in party politics, and one brainstormed about the military's possible roles in the reform movement. Advancing toward a goal of civil supremacy could only thus far be considered "half-baked or in fact half-hearted."[47]

These studies collectively asked for a professional military by world standards—one removed from socioeconomic development, out of party politics and parliament, out of business, responsive to civilian leadership. ABRI's comprehensive territorial and development doctrines and practices, by contrast, made it resemble an army of occupation. It needed to be totally reconceived.

Intelligent military men made shrewd efforts to get with it. General Wiranto, as minister of defense and commanding general, published a pamphlet attempting to reposition ABRI in October 1998.[48] Lieutenant General Susilo Bambang Yudhoyono, chief of staff for sociopolitical affairs, delivered a thoughtful speech in Singapore, setting Indonesia in its regional and global context and adverting to universal values. He put forward his own "dream" of "10 pillars of the national life," which in effect fused several values of the *reformasi* movement with military concerns for unity, social order, and security / stability.[49]

How far would he dare to dream? The test came months later when Major General Agus Wirahadikusumah, with sixteen classmates of 1973 from the military academy, advanced a comprehensive volume on military reform for an ABRI which now was called, as it had been in the Revolution, TNI. Their ambitious, intellectualized effort cast aside dual function and embraced globalization, democracy, and the supremacy of law.[50] But Yudhoyono, who had promised to provide an introduction to it all, in the end withheld his name. That symbolic restraint was played out in practical matters in the months that followed.[51]

President Wahid himself held little real concept of military reform except to get rid of bad guys. When General Wiranto was named among those responsible for human rights violations in East Timor in 1999, Wahid used the excuse to sack his commanding general early in 2000. But it was a prolonged, inept, and unconvincing exercise—initiated publicly in Davos, continued noisily on the way home through Asian capitals, delegated to his civilian minister of defense, Juwono Sudarsono, who failed him; reversed on arrival in Jakarta, and conclusively counter-reversed the same evening by agonized advisors. They persuaded their president to follow through for the sake of *reformasi* and personal credibility. A nonentity bowed in as Wiranto stepped down.

The man who had only months before been a powerbroker maneuvering for the vice presidency now became the darling of Jakarta's disc jockeys and talk shows. In a deep and mellow professional voice, Wiranto sang *dangdut* in Bahasa, with Middle Eastern, Indian, and Western features mixed in the genre. A music originally popular with Muslim youth of the lower and lower-middle classes but risen to general middle-class acceptability, a careful protest music of the early and middle Suharto period, it was now sung for pop sympathy by a top general who had lost his job.[52]

Wahid, looking for a "good guy" to run Kostrad, rammed through his choice of Lieutenant General Agus Wirahadikusumah. But the new man overestimated reform momentum just as grossly as his president had. His outspoken populist style was received among colleagues as nonmilitary or even antimilitary. When he exposed the disappearance of $20 million from Kostrad Yayasan enterprises under his predecessor, the military set up an honor court to try the accuser. In effect, Wirahadikusumah's honesty received the same treatment by the new TNI as Prabowo's abduction, torture, and complicity in the murder of political activists had received from the old ABRI. His denunciation of the military's territorial system as derived from Dutch colonial force structure and his attack on military racketeering (discotheques, brothels, gambling dens, narcotics) were popular with the public but left him ostracized by the army.

President Wahid, meanwhile, was in such trouble with parliament that he gave up trying to influence military appointments and made no effort to prevent the dismissal of his new Kostrad commander after only four months in office. Agus Wira's home, once a salon of reform and journalistic hubbub, suddenly went quiet. He faced six years of isolation before retirement but died of a sudden heart attack at the age of fifty. One of the nation's prime needs, and one of Wahid's priorities, had required careful preparation and steady attention, but real overhaul of the military had been lost in vacillation and haste. A possibly reluctant contributor to Agus Wira's book was Ryamizard Ryacudu. His essay is highly defensive against "slanders" of TNI and shifts responsibility onto police mishandling of murders and exaggerated publicity over events like Prabowo's kidnappings. All defects could be resolved by return to the revolutionary army's "paradigm of 1947."[53] Ryamizard became commanding general of the army in 2002.

The TNI did give up the doctrine of dual function and yielded internal security to the police. In its Leadership Meeting of April 20, 2000, however, TNI did not give up territorial administration, domestic intelligence, or its many unaudited enterprises. These made TNI—in admittedly very different American terms—a combination of Pentagon, activated National Guard, FBI, Department of Commerce, and Small Business Administration, entirely unresponsive to the attorney general or to the General Accounting Office. One assessment put the military budget at rp 20 billion, offline income at 80 billion, and real needs at about 50 billion. Therefore the other 50 billion available, instead of making a more secure Indonesia, was being used for non-necessities, improper purposes, and personal enrichment.

The military drew back from parliament but then let politicians urge them to stay in and on. It withdrew from internal security and thrust an unready and ill-trained police forward to do it all. Then, facing no external threat, it concentrated its attention on combating separatists in provinces where rich rake-offs were available to territorial commanders. Determined to retain prerogatives and influence, as well as to avoid prosecution for violations of human rights, elements in TNI were willing to bleed the reform government dry, all the while professing no intention, ever, of instigating a coup.[54]

One of Wahid's ministers identified to me four former Suharto cabinet members as having private armies generating or abetting unrest. By their very existence they inhibited effective action by regular security forces. Another Wahid minister, hearing the names I supplied (without the source), confirmed them and described their motivations: General Feisal Tanjung, "Suharto's guard dog"; Ginandjar Kartasasmita, "self-enriching by nature . . . with a naked power-need"; Harmoko, "disappointed not to have been made Suharto's vice president and ready to demonstrate his Madura power-base"; Fuad Bawazier, "galled not to be chosen for a coalition cabinet . . . an elitist intellectual compelled to test his own ideas . . . doesn't believe in democracy . . . Organized Laskar Jihad to show how smart he is . . . to prove his orthodoxy and probe the weaknesses of Wahid's government."[55] Why is there no concerted investigation, I asked, of a group which included an international consultant and a Harvard-trained Indonesian lawyer? Of the first name, for instance, of the four above? There was a new whistle-blowing law, wasn't there? Yes, "But dead men don't blow whistles."[56]

The size, nature, and precise disposition of private armies and hired thuggeries was beyond any individual's investigative capacity. But their very existence, combined with a "tightly controlled cabal" in the TNI itself, made for a highly fragile situation.[57] President Wahid should have asked for public support to deny Suharto cronies and military rogues their anti-government guerrilla warfare. Instead, he wasted key months in tactics that only multiplied the number of his own adversaries.[58]

In 2000 during Ramadan, disorder advanced into mayhem; thirty-eight different churches and other locations across Indonesia were bombed on Christmas Eve. Muslim and Christian leaders, NGOs, and other public figures united in the Indonesian Peace Forum (FID) to prevent religious overreaction. But a concerted destabilization plan was clearly at work. FID sent an investigating team out for two months, questioned seventy witnesses of bomb attacks on churches, and concluded that the perpetrators in the field, particularly those with special relations to the military, had been given a chance to escape. The bombings, FID announced at a press conference, were to create such disorder as to make the people "support the return of authoritarianism . . . the return of the New Order regime." The leaders of the group went to see Minister Bambang Yudhoyono and President Wahid. Yudhoyono had already seen the president. He said, to the astonishment of the FID delegation, that the facts implicated some "former colleagues and superiors" of his own. As the deputation silently wondered who that might include besides Wiranto, Minister Yudhoyono encouraged them to draft a presidential decree to investigate the matter. Led by Bara Hasibuan, they negotiated with Yudhoyono's office a joint panel involving themselves with personnel from the military, the attorney general's office, police, and intelligence. They submitted the draft decree and pursued it. "But it vanished . . . there was no response whatsoever."[59] Bara wonders who got to Wahid and/or Yudhoyono and warned them not to pursue an investigation.

In fact, the *tiwikrâmâ* threatened by Suharto two and half years before—the period of wayang wars initiated by displaced New Orderites—was already giving way to other dynamics. The FID investigators could not know what Indonesian police would later piece together: that the 38 Christmas Eve bombings were planned and executed by Jemaah Islamiyah toward its aim for a caliphate throughout Muslim Southeast Asia.[60] *Jihad* now overshadowed *tiwikrâmâ* and would do so at least until extremism was discredited by the Bali bombings of October 2002.

Yudhoyono later diagnosed continuing danger from anonymous sufferers of "post-power syndrome" (notably, perhaps, in Wiranto and Fuad Bawazier).[61] Some ambitious men were brazenly willing to help some Islamist militants in order to generate instabilities containing opportunity for themselves. Their own ends bore no resemblance to hopes for Indonesian democracy and civil society. They behaved like mandala masters of centuries past, experimenting to see how much power they could accrue to themselves. In modern terms they were generating tests of anarcho-democracy by their own anarcho-fascism.

Separatisms: Aceh and Papua

The East Timor denouement of 1999 expanded the problem that Aceh represented to Indonesia. The situations differed fundamentally in that the UN was not sponsoring a ballot on integration into Indonesia or self-determination. Surrounding powers—Singapore, Malaysia, Thailand, the Philippines—had far more to fear from a nearby Muslim separatism than from a faraway Christian one. When he first traveled in Aceh as a candidate, however, Wahid blurted out support of a referendum.[62] His reaffirmations and redefinitions of that as president were not accompanied by any consistent social or military policy. A "humanitarian pause" in fighting during 2000 made no headway toward resolution of the crisis.

Four interconnected Acehnese agendas—political, religious, economic, and human rights—were contending for Jakarta's attention.[63] Leadership in the capital did not clarify them so that the nation could move on, and leadership in the province could not galvanize them for secession. Hasan di

97. ACEH: GAM FLAG. A follower of the Movement for Free Aceh waves the flag of their independence movement, which regathered momentum after the fall of Suharto. (Kemal Jufri/IMAJI)

Tiro was ill and GAM (the Free Aceh Movement) was split.[64] Complicating the political agenda were the actions of SCAM-GAM, a local group of opportunist parasites, and SHAM-GAM, army rogues masquerading as rebels and creating trouble to ensure their own job security.

The MPR had tried to help. Law 25 of 1999 redressed the issue of how rent on natural resources should be divided between Jakarta and the provinces, with fast-track effect for Aceh in 2002; but experts already saw that the Arun gas fields would dry up a few years later. Law 45 increased the local authority of Acehnese in their religious affairs, short of full codification of shari'ah law. Meanwhile, the attorney general promised full investigation into abuses of military power, but army cooperation was minimal, transparency absent, psychological closure for victims not apparent. Violations went on.[65] GAM nationalists labored to leave behind an argument for restitution of the historic sovereignty of Aceh and to find a new and reasonable case for national self-determination.[66]

The military's way of improving things remained embedded in its unique sense of what was effective. A reformist brigadier general acknowledged to a national moral leader that when renegades were identified in SHAM-GAM, they were not tried by regular army channels, for that would generate unfortunate publicity. Instead, they were silently shipped to Merauke and "made to disappear" in Irian.[67] Presumably killed.

By late 2002, the efforts of a dedicated international NGO in Geneva to broker an accord was backed by potential international donors gathering in Tokyo. But whether the introductory terms, a cease-fire and disarmament, would work well enough to proceed to elections was in doubt. Sydney Jones of the International Crisis Group gave it a 15 percent chance. Neither side wished to give up arms. Meanwhile, there were steadily more Acehnese deaths per day than deaths in Palestine, and cumulatively a total of 12,000 since 1976; maybe the world did not take notice because many Acehnese themselves dated the war back to 1870, versus the Dutch. International recognition for GAM was improbable, considering the proximity of the Malacca Straits and the suspicions of Southeast Asian neighbors. But the rebels still strove to be considered pro-Western and democratic. GAM had sharply rebuffed Jafar Umar Thalib's effort to open a branch of Laskar Jihad in Aceh, lest itself be considered Islamist-terroristic.[68]

In the brief Habibie presidency, the desultory and occasionally deadly stalemate in Irian Jaya had risen once to high diplomatic drama. In February 1999, a month after his proposed referendum on East Timor, Habibie promoted a "National Dialogue" in Jakarta, with a delegation of 100 Papuans selected and brought for the purpose. They chose as their leader Thom Beanal, an Amungme tribal leader from near the center of Freeport McMoRan's mining operations. Beanal was well known for being the plaintiff in a lawsuit against the company brought in the Louisiana courts (which failed) and for wearing Savile Row suits. Differently famous in the delegation was Yorrys Raweyai, born in Papua of a Chinese father, but largely resident in Jakarta and a leader of the pro-Suharto youth group Pemuda Pancasila.

Thom Beanal startled Habibie and the twenty-one ministers with him by declaring, in the group's statement, the aim to remove Papua from Indonesia eventually and to form a transitional government under the UN immediately. Habibie waved away a booklet handed him by Akbar Tandjung; then, speaking without notes, he congratulated the Papuans on their dignified aspirations but advised them to "contemplate . . . again." Dialogue ended at that point.[69]

Numerous flag-raisings followed in Papua, with corresponding violence. Papua's "Morning Star" banner was at one point welcomed by President Wahid but at no point by the military. Five key figures of a subsequent thirty-one-member Papua presidium were jailed on subversion charges for advocating secession from Indonesia. Their chairman, Theys Eluai, was a physically formidable man, a traditional leader from Sentani, and a signer of the contrived Act of Free Choice of 1969. But having a Golkaresque past in Irian Jaya did not stifle his or others' aims for independence; and relaxations of attitude in Jakarta during *reformasi* allowed many hearts to nourish them. Wahid twice said he wanted the prisoners released, and police began to consider letting them go in time for Christmas 2000. But Eluai and the other prisoners declined to accept either humanitarian release or "release as a political motive by Gus Dur."[70] Indonesia's president was revealed again as impotent, both with his own army and with dissident separatists.

Indonesian security forces were able to get the Papua flag pulled down, but they paid a price in violence, particularly in Wamena in October 2000.[71] OPM-like guerrilla assaults accordingly resumed. The best hope for a non-murderous resolution of the crisis was in plans for regional autonomy. The Indonesian special package that parliament conveyed in November 2001, however, was—in framework and emphases—unsatisfactory to many Papuans. Because special autonomy had long been an elusive, disappointing, and contested condition in Aceh, it was hard to imagine what would make it more easily digestible in Papua. Some, like John Rumbiak, an NGO leader, focused on dignity and modest goals: "I want to be recognized for my Papuan identity within Indonesia."[72] Civilian leaders of Papua were not well coordinated among themselves nor with the OPM guerrillas, who suffered their own disarray. Papuan moods of anger about the past and millenarian hopes for the future were not nearly as focused as the TNI, grimly determined to hold on to this province.[73]

What if every province in Indonesia that mentioned or threatened inde-

Table 10. Economic implications of secession movements after independence of East Timor

Province	Principal industry	American corporate presence	Provincial contribution to Indonesia's GDP (%)
East Kalimantan	Oil and gas	Mobil, Unocal	5.0
Riau	Oil and gas	Caltex, Conoco	4.7
Aceh	Gas	Mobil	2.9
South Sulawesi	Agricultural commodities	—	2.3
Irian Jaya (Papua)	Copper, gold, gas	Freeport, Arco	1.6
Maluku	Timber, agricultural commodities gold	Newcrest	0.7
Total:			17.2[a]

a. *Far East Economic Review,* December 2, 1999, p. 20. I cast this data in wider perspective in testimony before Congress: *Indonesia: Confronting the Political and Economic Crises,* Hearing before the Subcommittee on Asia and the Pacific of the Committee on International Relations, House of Representatives, 106th Congress, First Session, Feb. 16, 2000, pp. 26–28, 75–80.

pendence actually got it? The *Far East Economic Review* calculated that the total subtraction would be about one-sixth of Indonesian GDP. In a wilder reckoning of fragmentation, the present nation could become a Bangladesh (Java) encircled by a couple of Congos, some Arab sheikhdoms, and some Caribbean republics. So fluid had the situation become in 2000 that a provocative Australian historian challenged a conference to consider why Java, with its cheap labor and its massive potential as a market, should not instead secede from the rest of Indonesia?

Ethno-Religious Violence: Maluku and Kalimantan

Separatism was strongest at Indonesia's geographic extremes, west and east. But ethnoreligious conflicts were becoming rampant in between. George Aditjondro, a Christian anthropologist from Eastern Indonesia, saw cultural oppression as a major underlying cause, arising from centralized policies of transmigration. His view: mainstream Javanese and Sumatrans hold a bias against darker skin color—a bias found in the Javanized Indian epics *Ramayana* and *Mahabharata* and intensified by centuries of European domination. That disfavor is most pronounced against Melanesians of Irian Papua, who have dark skin and frizzy hair, and persists to some degree against the less dark, curly haired inhabitants of the Moluccas (Maluku) and of the island string of which Timor is the largest element, whose peoples long ago intermarried with Malays. Prejudice exists not only against melanoderms of any kind but also against those who live close to nature, such as the Dyaks of Kalimantan. According to Aditjondro, "The term 'ndyak' in the popular Javanese language practically means 'barbarian.'"[74] The Jakarta government's policy of encouraging migration of Javanese and Madurese outward to relieve population pressures tended to intensify these prejudices and to inflame counter-reactions.

When race was not a problem, religion was. Often both were at issue. Should the East Timorese have been expected to be indifferent to oppression against them? The Papuans unexcited by alien exploration and settlement of their lands? The Dyaks untroubled by massive intrusions of Muslim Madurese? In Maluku, where there had once been pockets of rough parity between the Christian and Islamic population, the Suharto government not only helped relocate Muslims there to outweigh Christians but withdrew development projects from the region and siphoned off wealth through corrupt military governors and civil service.[75]

A flammable point was the island of Ambon, affected by an influx of non-Ambonese Muslims, erosion of traditional village government, land scarcity through urbanization, and the emergence of Western-style gangs among Ambonese youth. All of these washed away what had once been a proud inter-village, inter-religious alliance through the *pela* system, which probably arose through resistance to the Portuguese and Dutch. Until the 1980s the system still worked in various localities for diplomatic and genealogical reasons. It provided mutual assistance in times of crisis, in building major projects, or in sharing food, and symbolized both Ambonese identity and Muslim-Christian unity. Cooperation and syncretism went so far as to locate both Muslim and Christian paradise at sacred Mt. Nunusaku, on the island of Seram; and this "Nunusaku religion" was occasionally reaffirmed when a Christian village built a mosque for a Muslim one, or vice versa.

But religious education by the 1970s was elevating both Islam and Christianity above such expressions of *adat*. In 1979 Suharto's regime changed all village governmental structure with a new *kepala desa* (village chief, Javanese style), replacing genealogical rajas and *adat* guardians. Transmigration altered the Christian-Muslim ratio from 55–45 to an even split. McDonald's, the Internet, and cell phones quickly followed; so did overpopulation, feuding, and fission, until a new atmosphere could be characterized as, "Your God is no longer mine."[76]

Violence between Ambonese Christians and local Muslims erupted in Ketapang, North Jakarta, in December 1998. It started with a turf war over parking lots and other concessions in a gambling and red-light district. Flight, fright, and television transmitted the violence to Ambon itself and then throughout Maluku. The death toll in the next two years was estimated as high as 10,000 in a population of 2.1 million, with a tremendous

98. CHURCH IN AMBON. A riot in 1999, in the capital of
Maluku province, leaves this church in ruins. Three years of
inter-religious violence leaves 5,000 to 10,000 dead by 2002.
Nearly a third of the provincial population of 2.1 million become refugees. (Rully Uesuma/*Tempo*)

displacement of peoples. The magnitude of the mortality may be measured
against the average death rate from political violence in Northern Ireland in
modern times, which had been 100 a year in a population of 1.5 million.[77]

The first phase of fighting, ending in April 2000, was with homemade
weapons and bombs, in roughly equal strength. President Wahid wrung his
hands and appointed Vice President Megawati to lead reconciliation efforts,
but she interlaced her fingers and took a vacation to Hong Kong. Hearing
only passive good intent from the central government, fiercer Muslims
tilted the fight by sending forces from Java, Sulawesi, and Sumatra that had
trained near Bogor as Laskar Jihad, or Forces of Holy War. Although Christian militias had initiated atrocities, Laskar Jihad now became the primary

violent force, as well as the greatest symbol of the government's impotence.

Wahid ordered Laskar Jihad not to transport its troops to Maluku, but they took a commercial ferry from Surabaya anyway and picked up arms that had been separately shipped for them. Presidential interdiction proved meaningless against military-bureaucratic collusion. One of Wahid's aides conceded in September that the president had retreated to a tacit agreement with Laskar Jihad that the government would leave them alone in Maluku if they would not burn churches in Java. Presidential power in such matters was clearly diluted by the activities of Islamist generals like Djadja Suparman, who as head of Kostrad had diverted $20 million from its foundation to support Laskar Jihad; by whomever allowed the military to pass arms directly to Laskar Jihad in Maluku (videotaped by CNN); and by Zen Maulani, who when he took over BAKIN staffed its intelligence offices with ultra-green or Islamist officers. Two years later he would stand outside the

99. LASKAR JIHAD. Militant Muslims with samurai swords demonstrate at the parliament building on April 10, 2000. Trained by an army faction, and allegedly financed by an Islamist former member of Suharto's cabinet, they defy interdiction by President Wahid. After traveling to Maluku, with modern arms they tilt the balance of battle there. (Bernard Chaniago/ *Tempo*)

home of Abu Bakar Ba'syir and rail to the press against arrest of the leader of JI. Amien Rais momentarily took a green extreme position when he whipped up a crowd by alleging that agents of "international Zionism" were causing the troubles in Maluku and elsewhere. In Washington in April 2000, when I quoted him from the daily *Detik* and publicly asked him please to substantiate or retract his comment, he replied with evasions and with a waving of his hand under his nose. "I could smell it," he said.[78]

A foreign military expert, locally experienced, described the army as "thinned beyond trainability or coordination" to handle such a crisis. Because troops were sent to Maluku "unsupported in supplies, they forage and steal; levy everything and defend nothing . . . hire out trucks, sell ammo, even join one side . . . Soldiers in the field capture exotic birds for overseas sale . . . Everyone [in the military] in Maluku is sending money home [so there are] . . . disincentives to solve the problem."[79] "Rogue elements at work" is Jakarta's description of what transpired. "Green clique connivance" was clearly involved. "Systems dysfunction" is a more comprehensive term but too clinical. So how does one explain the prolonged killing when intervention clearly could have availed against it?

The anthropologist Aditjondro saw in the chaos a central and comprehensive military agenda. His projection can be summarized in five points:

(1) Increase administrative strength through expansion. Defend the "territorial structure" of TNI by showing the need to reawaken dormant military commands; whereas Benny Moerdani had reduced them to ten, Wiranto's plan enlarged them to seventeen. To justify a need for more firefighters, set more fires. The territorial structure flourished as a parallel government, a "state within a state," where orders flowed down from the top (the national capital) to the bottom (subdistrict), while bribes to facilitate promotions flowed from the bottom to the top.

(2) Increase political strength by dividing the opposition. Although dual function was theoretically renounced, it was in practice being enhanced by driving a religious wedge between students and reformists in Maluku and throughout Indonesia.

(3) Repair broken archipelagic links. The loss of Christian East Timor had weakened Indonesia's chain of defense. In the future, Christians in Maluku might prove as troublesome as those in East Timor. Therefore, deploy Javanese Muslim militants into the Spice Islands to strengthen the southeastern flank of the republic against further separatism or intrusive Australo-Western sympathies.

(4) Advance the business interests of the military. Do not just pump assets into unaudited *yayasans* and conglomerates that benefit officers but make petty entrepreneurships available to enlisted men as well.

(5) Use distraction to defend against investigation. Let fighting in Maluku

flare whenever President Suharto is interrogated regarding corruption or General Wiranto is interrogated for responsibility in human rights abuses in East Timor.[80]

Does this list overdetermine the motives of the military? In Indonesia, comprehensive fear is often a much healthier stance than unexamined innocence.

A New Zealand journalist, daughter of a progressive Presbyterian minister who was motivated by her own skepticism that religion could be at the core of so much chaos, undertook a hazardous solo trip in January 2000 to four disturbed eastern provinces. Over the course of six days, she saw the results of violence against Christians in Lombok, was turned back twice from North Maluku, and "lost track of the fantasy that any government body was dedicated to extinguishing the ever-widening circle of fire." Religion was indeed an inescapable cause, along with fear, ignorance, jealousy, and deprivation. Murder in the name of religion, she found, was a two-way street. A Muslim woman on an escape flight to Bali, with tears in her eyes, said the whole thing was wrong: "We are all brothers and sisters, Muslim and Christian, we are all born of the body of Abraham."[81]

The terrible virus of communal warfare then jumped to Poso in North Sulawesi, soon killing 250, destroying 3,500 homes, and driving 70,000 people to become refugees—numbers which continued to rise. A reporter experienced in Bosnia quizzed inhabitants for causes and concluded that "the town's social structure had rotted away at its core . . . Police, courts, local government, houses of worship, the media—had all failed in Poso." Worse still was the discovery, as he pressed on, that "longer work schedules . . . undermined an Indonesian tradition of neighbors playing a large role in raising children." The social void had been filled by satellite television and alcohol. Now by murder. Refugees could not help but take the "disease" of emptiness and revenge to other islands.[82] The professional self-respect of the Indonesian military, stirred in part by international criticism, did not begin effectively to control and calm the situations in Ambon and Poso until 2001–02.[83]

In Kalimantan, as in other parts of the world, moments of mass irrationality were fed by relative deprivation, flagrantly exaggerated rumor, and cunning elite manipulation. Historical wrongs seemed to be repeated in yet other acts of injustice. The result was an eruption of satisfying violence (indeed, "hatred is the longest pleasure") aimed at destruction or banishment of the enemy—acts understood as unifying and necessary, part of an extended sequence of transactions.[84]

Classic Indonesian examples of this unhappy global habit occurred in West Kalimantan in 1967, when Dyaks turned against the Chinese, and in 1997 and 1999, when they turned against Madurese transmigrants.[85] In 2001

100. MADURESE FLEE DYAKS. During the Sambas riots of 1999, this burnt-out house serves as a temporary place of refuge for Muslim transmigrants in West Kalimantan. (Rully Uesuma/*Tempo*)

the violence spread to East Kalimantan. Cultural dissimilarities were basic to the confrontation: Dyaks hunt and eat pig; Madurese loathe and abjure these practices. Dyaks treasure their knives but conceal them; Madurese honor their curved sickles and display them. Jagged misfits of habit produce suspicion, misunderstandings, mayhem. Dyaks, with their far greater numbers, are the natives. Madurese, with their aggressive business skills, are the "intruders." The government's transmigration policies enable the violence; relief of crowding on Madura incubates murder on Kalimantan.

A neutral resident estimated that in 1997 "fewer than two hundred Dyak eople were killed, and roughly four thousand Madurese."[86] In 1999 Malays oined Dyaks in killing Madurese.[87] When the violence leaped over to East Kalimantan in 2001, aid workers estimated at least two thousand dead. A hundred thousand Madurese tried to flee the area, raising the total of internally displaced persons in Indonesia to well beyond a million.[88]

With accumulated hatred and suspicion a kind of working capital, the dividends were mimetic violence. And again President Wahid was ineffectual. He brought dates and holy water back from Mecca for dislocated Madurese and then irresponsibly mentioned possible independence for Madura. Vice President Megawati made a sympathy trip to Kalimantan in his absence, urged on her by aides for the political gain she might make in the eyes of the public. While the political leaders dithered, the military dallied. The real question, said Colonel George Benson, who remembered a once-responsible ABRI, is "When is the Army going to *show up?*"[89] The answer proved to be: only when it appeared safe.

Every modern society equips soldiers and police to engage in lawful violence in order to prevent illegal excesses that can spread to comprehensive disorder. The Indonesian military was not performing that vital function. Separation of army and police soon produced 90 instances of turf wars between the two, over protection rackets.[90] The Indonesian concept of the heroic soldier, expressed by Nasution half a century before as a guerrilla in partnership with the people, was completely lost. Too often the Indonesian soldier was now a bystander, a provocateur, or a parasite.

The police were no better. Their numbers were only one quarter the ratio recommended by criminologists, and their support from the military was withdrawn. In the closing years of the millennium, after Indonesia's first fifty years as an independent state, a failure of law and order in Jakarta led to vigilante killings of petty thieves; elsewhere, those who stole goats, ducks, shoes, and TV sets were executed. When mega-thieves live in luxury,

101. LITTLE ONE, NOT SWIFT ENOUGH. Dyak attacks on Madurese spread from West Kalimantan to Central Kalimantan. From near Sampit, in February 2001, a European priest, appealing for international help to prevent the murder of refugees, put this and other images on the web.

102. VIGILANTE JUSTICE. The alleged culprit and the alleged crime (perhaps sorcery) are not identifiable, nor is the Javanese town where this occurred in the late 1990s. But the handshake of the policeman and the vigilante suggests the breakdown of formal law and order in the *reformasi* period. (Web photo relayed by Byron Black)

why not murder pickpockets? Against injustice and frustration, the result was inverse amok: many going crazy against one, instead of one against many.

Government officials do not keep records of this nature, but one Jakarta hospital morgue recorded 205 violent deaths in fifteen months, and human rights organizations estimated over 1,000 in the year 2000. An example: Astani Raisin, 37-year-old unemployed laborer, was apprehended at 4:00 AM as he was stealing a bird's nest and its eggs from a distant relative, in order to feed his wife and three children. Cries of "Thief! Thief!" brought scores of villagers with sticks and rocks, with which they beat him for an hour. At daybreak they stripped him, doused him with kerosene, and burned him to death.[91] Against vigilante killings of suspected witches and sorcerers, police were equally passive.

Quality of Life: A Review

Indonesia had been suffering frequent critical setbacks when the UN Development Program published its Human Development Report in 2002, presenting data collected in 2000. A comparison of Indonesia's per capita income near its peak in 1995 with that in 2000 shows the nation losing ground in relation to nearly everyone. Where it had been on a par with Egypt in 1995, it slipped backward. Where it had been ahead of China and the Philippines, it fell sharply behind. It appeared in danger of joining nations like Russia and Nigeria, whose best per capita incomes had been achieved many years earlier—so-called failed-growth nations.

Was this economic manner of reckoning the only one, or indeed the best one, for assessing the progress and relative rankings of nations? Perhaps not. Indonesia's measures of income inequality were among the least distorted in the group (Brazil's being the most grotesque). Indonesian poverty may have doubled, but its data on literacy and improved water resources, the result of decades of attention, were holding firm. UNDP tables showed Indonesia as making great measured gains in human development since 1975, and extraordinary gains from a very low base in 1965.

When dynamics of globalization moved Arab social and intellectual leaders to challenge per capita income as a commanding measure and to consider several other factors as more compelling, a new index was designed. By the different standards of the Alternative Human Development Index (AHDI) 2002, Indonesia does better in relation to its neighbors and to other large nations. Table 11 takes primary notice of the AHDI, as well as older standards. Such a perspective allows Indonesia to be seen more hopefully and perhaps more accurately than newspaper narratives, which tend to dramatize short-term entropies and unravelings rather than long-term gains.

Happiness, Social Capital, and Culture

How happy can a nation be? How unhappy? The United States doubled its per capita income between 1958 and 1986 without increasing its "happiness."[92] Similarly, Japan's felt felicity remained essentially unchanged during this period as its per capita income increased more than five-fold. Once we escape abject poverty, it would seem, living standards do not have as much of an impact on our happiness as before, because of our species' extraordinarily swift powers of adaptation—to bioallergens, to boorishness, to creature comforts, to different speeds.[93] Those inquiring into happiness as a guide to social policy note that within given countries the highest status groups are happier on average than the lowest status groups. But over time if economic conditions advance, the social norms of expectation rise also.[94] There is no ultimate state of plenty at which whole peoples will believe (in a nineteenth-century delirium of expectation) that they need only to study, make love, and be happy. An early student of the subject, George C. Homans, concluded that "any satisfied desire creates an unsatisfied one."[95]

Table 11. Indonesia: selective and comparative matrix of quality of life, 2000 (countries in order of Alternative Human Development Index, AHDI)[a]

Nation and life expectancy	AHDI among 111 countries: rank	Probability at birth of not surviving to age 40 (%)	Adult illiteracy % age 15 and above, 1999	Population % not using improved water resources
Philippines 69.3	33	8.9	4.7	13
South Korea 74.9	38	4.0	2.2	8.0
Thailand 70.2	52	9.0	4.5	20
Brazil 67.7	53	11.3	14.8	13
Malaysia 72.5	59	5.0	12.5	5.0
Indonesia 66.2	**69**	**12.8**	**13.1**	**24**
China 70.5	72	7.9	15.9	25
India 63.3	80	16.7	42.8	12
Egypt 67.3	92	10.3	44.7	5
Nigeria 51.7	107	33.7	36.1	43
Russian Federation 66.1	NA	30.1 (to age 60)	—	—

a. For the purposes of breakthrough in the *Arab Human Development Report 2002* (New York: United Nations Development Programme and Arab Fund for Economic and Social Development, 2002), pp. 166–167, its authors and editors use six indicators they believe valid for an age of globalization: life expectancy at birth, educational attainment, freedom score (civil and political liberties), women's access to power in society, internet hosts per capita, and carbon dioxide emissions per capita. The lead author, Nader Fergany, sums up their philosophy thus: "Beyond the two fundamental human capabilities of health and knowledge acquisition, a human being needs to be empowered by freedom for all. It is time that average income be dethroned as the primary means of empowerment in human societies" (p. 21). Among the global impacts of such evaluation (by AHDI) are to lower the rankings of

My intuition would strongly add that retreats from previously satisfied desires stimulate unhappiness.

There exists a comprehensive world database on studies of happiness but no general survey of Indonesia's population on those questions. Obviously, among large nations, the United States as effectively federated and Japan as

Environmental Sustainability Index of 122 countries: rank	Population below national poverty line (most recent year available)	Income inequality: richest 10% ratio to poorest 10%	Year of highest value $PPP (1975–2000)	Purchasing power parity, per capita $PPP 2000
111	36.8	16.1	1982 ($4072)	$3,971
95	—	8.4	2000	$17,380
74	13.1	11.6	1996 ($6896)	$6,402
28	17.4	65.8	2000	$7,625
52	15.5	22.1	1997 ($9151)	$9,068
86	**27.1**	**6.6**	**1997 ($3481)**	**$3,043**
108	4.6	12.7	2000	$3,976
93	35.0	9.5	2000	$2,358
67	22.9	5.7	2000	$3,635
116	34.1	24.9	1977 ($1160)	$896
33	53.0 (below $4 a day)	23.3	1989 ($12,947)	$8,377

the U.S. (because of carbon dioxide emissions) and a number of Arab states (because of deficits in knowledge and freedom and because of disempowerment of women). Indonesia, instead of being ninth among eleven selected societies ranked by per capita income, rises to sixth among ten societies evaluated by factors in the AHDI. Other data chiefly selected from: United Nations Development Program, *Human Development Report, 2002* (New York: Oxford University Press, 2002), pp. 149–151, 157–159, 190–192, 194–196; information footnoted within tables. Column 6 is derived from the Center for International Earth Science Information Network (CIESIN), 2001, using assorted data, 1990–2000. See partly analogous Table 1, Chapter 5 of this volume, for comparisons, 1995, near height of Indonesia's economic momentum.

ethno-culturally homogeneous are more suited to such studies than Indonesia.[96] But speculation is allowable.

The psychological spaces that constitute "livability" of course have many dimensions beyond income. Non-coercive governments and freedom of the press seem to correlate positively with national happiness in various parts of the world. Political violence and the necessity of political protest correlate with relative unhappiness.[97] So imagine the state of mind of a people who must contend with simultaneous failures of the military and police, ineffectual executive and legislative branches of government, with judicial nullity and financial necrosis? Some unhappiness is surely likely. When all of that is accompanied by inflationary erosion of personal earnings and threat of a permanent debt trap which minimizes the government's already puny efforts in education and welfare, the average Indonesian might justifiably feel a certain level of misery.

The only Nobel prize Indonesia can claim was awarded to the Netherlander Eykman early in the twentieth century. He turned research on beriberi away from attempts to discover what was poisonous in various forms and varieties of rice and asked instead what, in an overwhelmingly rice-dominated diet, is critically *missing* for nutritive health? In a similar way one might ask, at least of the Jakarta scene at the outset of the twenty-first century, what is *missing*? Speaking comprehensively, I miss a sense of commonweal, or public interest. The dictionary equivalents, *kesejahteran bersama* and *kepentingan umum,* are limp phrases rarely used. And when I asked a distinguished Javanese senior columnist with a British Ph.D. what the historical reasons for this condition might be, he responded with an immediate smile: "Provocative question." I gave him my email address, hoping for a considered reply, but he never answered further.

Indonesian society in some layered sense goes on "developing." But civil society in the sense of a network still grows in a fragile way. And common identity—Indonesia-ness—has been tattering for some time. Meanwhile, the game of class analysis in Southeast Asia has been advancing since the mid-1980s, trying to understand surges forward in differentiated wealth and behavior. The Singaporean government was attentive to the implications of change and took measures to ensure that their city state did not divide along ethnic lines (Chinese, Indian, Malay) but instead nurtured a commonly successful and relatively homogeneous capitalist culture. By 1995 thirty years of growth had "obliterated any overt poverty" in Singapore and made it "a matter of contextual relative deprivation." In a four-class system, all classes were new and mutually mobile. The poor were those who could not own but could only rent a public housing flat; the working class were "blue-collar" workers struggling toward the median; the middle class those who could conceive of owning (though only half of them were able to do so) "the premier cultural icon of the middle class in Singapore"—a car. The rich—top civil servants, capitalists, multinational executives, and prominent professionals—were a thin 3 percent among whom "the privilege of wealth . . . includes escaping the clutches of the nation-state" (but never altogether). The ruling party suppressed "display" and insisted on "humility" for its ministers and members, in order to lower pressures on the middle class for competitive acquisition. The government denounced any "politics of envy" and promoted a mixed ideology of meritocracy and "communitarianism."[98]

In Thailand the two main streams of the "middle class" have not yet fused—the consumer middle class, newly rich, which favored the military in the conflicts of the 1970s, and the occupational middle class, many of academe, media, and NGOs, who favored the uprisings of 1973, 1976, and 1992. They had some success in drawing the rich along with them in the third instance. Both segments share a prejudice that the lower classes can be bought and are not worthy of democracy. Each believes that democracy belongs to "us"—a middle class still fragmented, unfused, becoming something.[99]

The Thai case is partly suggestive of Indonesian dynamics which are not yet that far advanced. Jakarta's middle class, especially, can be divided into consumer and occupational, but their combined numbers are far smaller and their cleavages greater than in Bangkok. Identity behavior, both Muslim and Chinese, has become consumerist to hedonistic. Jakartans, too, are prone to lip service toward the lower classes, or to hypocritical indifference toward them, and they manifest palpable fear of the underclass at moments of unrest. There is no culture of modesty or suppression of flagrancy in wealth, such as one finds in Singapore.[100]

In smaller cities and even in Yogya, the newly rich cling to local security and identity and certainly to state protection; and they still express community solidarity in traditional ways, especially at times of death.[101] In Jakarta, however, behavior of many nouveau riche is a travesty of Western television: it consists of high living and fleeting repentance.[102] If the Philippines had long ago settled into an "anarchy of families," there were at least traceable lineages and definable culprits.[103] But Indonesia's capital city early in the new millennium was an anarchy of arrivistes and a cacophony of cliques. Back when all were gathered under the fictive but well-armed fatherhood of Suharto, political and financial "family" was relatively stable. After his departure from office, lord/liege relationships broke down and have undergone continuous renegotiation since. The voices and felt influence of a Weberian capitalist middle class, with saving graces of stewardship and broadly conceived political conviction, have been faintly detectable at best in a din of self-interest.

"This history suggests that *both* states *and* markets operate more effectively in civic settings," Robert D. Putnam said, speaking of the social pact in the last ten centuries of Italian history. The differences there tween South and North have elaborated, and, despite regional reform in the South since 1970, reversal is not yet clear regarding "the vicious uncivic circles that have trapped the Mezzogiorno in backwardness for a millennium." Local transformation of local structures take a long time. "Building social capital will not be easy, but it is the key to making democracy work."[104]

How does personal trust become social trust and thereby usable social capital? Putnam summarizes the actions by networks of civic engagement that make it happen: (1) increase connection and penalize defection; (2) "foster robust norms of reciprocity"; (3) facilitate trust-building information; (4) provide continuities in collaboration. The accents are long-term and horizontal. Vertical patron-client relationships, by contrast, invite exploitation from the top and shirking beneath. They leave dilemmas of collective action unsolved. In horizontal North Atlantic solutions, feudalism yielded to capitalism in the eighteenth century and autocracy to democracy in the twentieth.

Through such dynamics, and corollary qualities in individuals, there may be some usable wisdom for Indonesia.[105] But it is hard to avail of far-off lessons when right at home popular representation is oblique, markets are opaque, and civil society is oppressed. Indonesians have reason to feel that often investigations will be aborted and justice will be thwarted. They do not expect to be the beneficiaries of intelligent programs of research and development. They properly fear the presence of hit men, officially and unofficially hired, as hidden persuaders in matters of dispute. And they dread the manipulation of religions into politically motivated bloodlettings.

Forward-looking actions, in small steps, had best accompany sweeping historical scans. There is no "all" of Indonesian history, as we have seen, that lends itself to ready analysis. But the centrality of Java, and its population mass, allows some things to be said. There is no Asoka in its history, nor any Akbar—no Indian combination of the imperial and the benign, the soldier and the compassionate universalist. Two able rulers, Sultan Agung of Mataram (1613–1646) and Sultan Hamengkubuwono I (1749–1792), stand out, the first obtaining general but porous control of East and Central Java and the second achieving a restoration of sorts but with sharp focus only in Yogyakarta.[106] Regrettably, more typical are the examples of Panembahan Senopati, a cunning brutal localist, who, if set in Japanese history, would have been a losing feudal *daimyo;* and Pakubuwana II, who at a time of crisis yielded to "squalid tergiversation" and lost everything.[107] The styles of the latter two rulers evoke, in turn, Suharto and Wahid in the late twentieth century. Too many of Java's kings are fools; and always the commoners are the kings' footstools.

Were one arbitrarily to isolate a preeminent trait that remains both a beauty of Java and an occasional curse to Indonesia, it might be *rukun:* the principle of solidarity through social harmony, achieved by individual concealment of dissonance in all relationships—a model type that tends to persist even in mobile and national "modern" personalities. But every Javanese will see the dynamics differently.[108]

Mochtar Buchori finds Java robbed of energy by "cultural involution" after Europeans prevailed in the mid-eighteenth century. His educational, linguistic, and artistic examples of such involution are richly interesting. But in a context of seeking sources of social capital, they only illustrate passive aesthetic retreat.[109] Pramoedya Ananta Toer rails against Javanese culture, from a Marxo-populist stance, as "feudalistic"; which re-embeds us in the vertical, begging the question of why there were so few anti-feudalists until the mid-twentieth century. Pak Pram, seeking to explain murderous tendencies in Indonesia, summons a charge against "Sivaite tradition"; but this, he acknowledges, cannot begin to explain horizontal murders in Maluku and decapitations in Kalimantan.[110] Romo Mangun until his death was sharply critical of the "tapeworm" of Javanese culture——all that is devious, insinuating, parasitic. In the uncandid, Romo Mangun suggests, lies the corrupt. In the over-refined commences the decadent.[111] Java, I conclude, has as great a cultural problem to confront and correct as Kang Youwei saw in late nineteenth-century China; but over a century later the Javanese have barely begun to address it.

Goenawan Muhammad smiles slightly—not ironically: to open, instead, the way for a redefinition. "There is no 'Java.' There are *many* Javas." Goenawan modestly pictures himself as from ordinary circumstances in a small town in North Java; his father was executed by the Dutch. In a few sentences he distinguishes his views from any court traditions of Central Java or any syncretic Islam of East Java.[112] Many Javas, he insists; and which ones should be assailed?

Franz Magnis-Suseno has forty years experience of living in Java. A native German who added a hyphen and adopted a Javanese particle to complete his name, he is an Indonesian citizen. I asked him, "What are the best and the worst in Javanese culture?" He enjoyed the question, which nobody had ever put to him before. "Javanese accept others in a positive way; they don't try to change them. If you have their internal idea—*manungaling kawula gusti,* the unity of servant and master—it enables a quiet positive acceptance of things, which brings you [many Javanese] to a deeper level of being."

On the other hand? "Power tends to corrupt, and the closer to power a Javanese is, the worst of his culture comes out . . . The Javanese way of communication is broaching things always from the edge of, from the view of power. There is no concept of conflict management . . . Even agreements imply power relations. And if you are really strong, you are free to do what you wish to do. You don't *need* agreements. [So much, I thought, for contract, cohesion, and cooperation as preconditions for building social capital.] Javanese cannot distinguish between communication and manipulation." [So prepare to be lied to: to be charmingly used; or to be charmlessly, even harmfully overrun.] Franz regarded me, regretfully, from a calm center of contemplation.[113]

A Sundanese, experienced in power near the apex for twenty years, went further. Sarwono Kusumaatmadja insisted, smiling agreeably, that he was raised in *West* Java. But in Yogya and Solo especially he has seen what others call cultural involution. "Teachers must give their pupils *less* knowledge than they have in order to keep them in line." Educational involution is thereby inevitably systematic, minimalizing, anti-serendipitous, counter-developmental. When behavior so trained rises to the top, with feudal ideas going back to Javanese agrarian kingdoms, you inevitably get the "Mataram syndrome." "Synergy does not occur to such people. Sharing is not done. Life is not even a zero sum game, but always threatens to be a *minus* game."[114]

To live with intelligence and compassion, we must entertain alternatives to the silly putty of Western modernism and to the styrofoam of hyper-marketism. A Confucian reminds us also that we must "appreciate how primordial ties rooted in concrete living communities have helped to shape different configurations of the modern experience."[115]

In Indonesia, there's the rub. "Primordialism," a word commonly used there but rarely in America, means deep and unthinking commitment to the *aliran,* to keeping to one's own channel of belief, averse to compromise, suspicious of other streams of life. The word suggests carrying a blade to shed blood rather than a life-jacket to keep oneself, and perhaps someone else, buoyant. More and more Indonesians, nonetheless, are rising above primordialism and, selectively, adopting objective values in public life, at least as suggested by two key terms—transparency and due process.

In the first enthusiasm of the general election of 1999, I saw the future rather as Nurcholish Madjid did: four more such open and fair elections, and Indonesia would be safely democratic. But my focus now seeks far beyond 2019, because I have understood that Indonesia needs much more than "democracy." It needs all that is required to anticipate, reflect, and reinforce democratic values: fair markets, honest courts, incorruptible police, a not-for-profit military. It needs not only "civil society" but every instinct that constrains against "amoral familism" and broadens one's instincts and vision beyond self and blood relations, beyond the primordially-bonded into activities that build social capital.[116] Indonesians, if they want democracy, need far more than a capacity to recite new civics lessons and to voice advanced models of capitalism. Many must practice them, as some already do, without split-level values—a bicultural rift that denies them in the inner heart while articulating them in a foreign tongue.

To do primordial banking is a contradiction in terms. Worsened by internal robbery and errant speculation, that was the story of Bank Summa. A grotesque alliance of Abdurrahman Wahid and "Family" conglomerates, it failed the NU constituency for which it was designed and then failed altogether. There are better ways to bank, and young Indonesians are learning them; better ways to build business, organize NGOs, conduct independent journalism; better ways to lawyer, doctor, politick; do agronomy, forestry, microbiology, immunology. All are being learned now, and hold out the promise of an incremental triumph of professionalism that may eventually put primordialism in its place. At the same time, concepts of a professional police and national defense force must continue to struggle and eventually prevail over the mixed parasitism and pusillanimity that mars much legal arms-bearing now and gives what should be the noble face of the warrior-protector a leer of the Mafioso, who lives on and breeds mistrust.

On simpler, deeper levels still more can be said. Edward Luttwak, after some gyration in his political views, has said it well of the United States: "I believe that we ought to have only as much market efficiency as one needs, because everything that we value in human life is within the realm of inefficiency—love, family, attachment, community, culture, old habits, comfortable old shoes."[117] That, and much more, Simone Weil evoked with her expanded use of the classical Greek term *metaxu:* those things "which warm and nourish the soul, and without which . . . a human life is impossible."[118] A dreadful aspect of the killings of 1965–66, and of the anarcho-barbarisms into which parts of Indonesia descended beginning in 1996, is not only that some die but that so many survivors are robbed of *metaxu:* the ordinary comforts of life. These are not consumer durables but what is humanely enduring: security of home, family, friendship, community; the chance to do justice in small things; walking humbly with God or Allah, or Tuhan Yang Maha Esa; smiling upon one's neighbor, who though he may practice different rituals, can still smile back, exchanging the conviction and reassurance that "Your god is still my god too."

Many in advanced industrial societies are becoming aware that the diseases of overdevelopment—weapons of mass destruction, ecological devastation, consumer glut, spiritual poverty—pose dangers to themselves and others. These are in part the magnifying and distorting mirrors of underdevelopment—poverty and hunger unaddressed, justice obstructed, blindness to strategic planning, manic indifference to social compact. A continuing and accelerated dialogue on many levels is necessary to temper the hubris of the mighty as well as to spark the vision of the meek. Trying to build a proud and willful nation-state, as Sukarno did, led to helpless brittleness. Trying instead to build a powerful state-nation, as Suharto did, led to inexcusable brutalities. Indonesia since independence may be said to have been torn between anarcho-democracy and anarcho-fascism.[119] As it experiments in the twenty-first century with ways of becoming a more stable, just, and productive country, one may see hope in many ordinary people organizing in new ways. And one may hope for some extraordinary people capable of thinking "one nation/several systems," and building a community of communities.

Among the plentitude of international indexes now available (usually measurements for entrepreneurial purposes), another is needed, perhaps, to illustrate comparative effectiveness in reducing poverty. But all of these are preoccupied with material standard of living. I dare ask whether there are not appropriate questions to be raised, individually, socially, even internationally, about existing standards of loving. How well is human sympathy revealed and compassion demonstrated in action? Not that such things should be calibrated for comparison and competition. They ought not. The ultimate game is immaterial and the final scorecard is invisible.

Acknowledging that, however, puts us squarely in the realm of spiritual calculus, at a time in world history when parts of the House of Islam are venting rage against the West and seeking to rebalance accounts that are decades or centuries old. In that global reckoning, the peripatetic V. S. Naipaul has seen a universal civilization emerging, in which he reckons with the "immense human idea" and the mighty beauty of the pursuit of happiness.[120] He obviously does not speak for Arab or other terrorists. They will articulate in their own way. But happiness in the measured sense he means is both individual and mutual; it is contractual, noncoercive, synergistic.

It is clear that the angriest Muslims are from the least democratic societies, and that massive parts of the Muslim world, those whose peoples have at least a share of democracy, such as Indonesia, are much less likely to export suicidal terror. That does not relieve a larger, more stable democracy such as the United States from the responsibility of understanding complex societies unlike itself and of trying to relieve poverties far deeper than its own. Insofar as we fail to help assure for our neighbors those things "which warm and nourish the soul," the social environment of our own souls will to that degree remain in jeopardy.

EPILOGUE:
SUKARNO'S DAUGHTER IN THE PALACE

I first met Megawati Sukarnoputri on a day when President Wahid had left for Singapore. I remarked, in Indonesian, on her being *presiden sementara*, "provisional president." She corrected me in English: *"acting* president." She finished our hour of interview as she had begun it, on a stern note of protocol: "You haven't finished your tea and cookies!" I put away my notepad and returned, standing, to my place at her huge cut-glass coffee table under enormous chandeliers. I munched down the last cookie, gulped the tea, and raised cup and saucer over my head in an improvised royal salute to her, before bowing my way out.

She had handled my questions, pre-submitted in Indonesian as required, with what were largely campaign answers. Except for the one on which I had hoped for a novel reply—her father's interest in *kebatinan* (inner spirituality) as found in some of his speeches. She denied that such an interest existed in him. "That was *Suharto*," she said, forcefully derailing the question. Because her party has Christians and secularists in it, and because her grandmother was a Balinese Hindu, I suppose she did not want to allow any more angles of attack by Islamists on Sukarno religiosity.[1]

Megawati is noncharismatic but possesses a heavy presence and a certain grit. A leading female member of her party exclaimed in exasperation, as might be uttered of a minor but sacred monument, "We have to support her, because she is *there*." She must not be despised or ignored; what would obedience bring? A rising star in the American Department of State—proud of having gotten to know her well—when asked to describe her attributes, answered in a reverent hush, "She is *limited*."[2]

But there seemed to be few limits to Megawati's patience. She endured Wahid's personal slights and political undercuttings. During his long exercise of a self-undermining presidency, she pressed no advantage, chanced no critique. In February 2001 the parliament, by a vote of 394–4, with Wahid's party walking out, censured the president. Everything was in correct procedural order for a vote of impeachment no later than August. The grounds for removing him now had shifted from KKN—as natural to Indonesian politics as grease to the floor of a garage—to the sad, solid charge of incompetence. Some of his own senior *ulama* were privately referring to him as "Pak Dur," dropping the honorific "Gus" for just plain "Mister."[3]

103. TV WITH GUS DUR. I emerge from Istana Merdeka, Indonesia's "White House," on November 8, 2000. President Wahid invited Dennis Heffernan and me to watch TV returns of the U.S. presidential election. We had the strange privilege of interpreting the Bush-Gore deadlock for him as it unfolded. (Dennis Heffernan / author's collection)

As time approached for the next session of parliament, Megawati remained magnetically taciturn, while Wahid appeared to suggest that millions of his supporters would march on Jakarta. A key aide, and honest man, Wimar Witoelar, insisted that he had heard his president on the telephone until early in the morning, counseling nonviolence.[4] That is entirely credible. But the beleaguered president, reduced to regional and religious support, all but invited raging forces—with intimidating intent but unpredictable consequences—to the capital and then tried to make the unruly beast behave. His actions may be understandable because political operators opposed to Wahid were organizing students en masse and paying them.[5] As it turned out, the numbers responding to Wahid were many fewer than he imagined, and casualties far fewer than others feared. In last-ditch street politics, NU behaved in a manner to which Gus Dur years before had complained that Suharto and ICMI were trying to reduce it: the roaring of a toothless lion.[6]

Cornered, Wahid now took the frequently discussed and extraordinary step of trying to get his cabinet to declare a state of national emergency and dissolve the parliament. But the army, notably Lieutenant General (ret.) Susilo Bambang Yudhoyono, coordinating minister for political and security affairs, declined to support him. The president's last initiative was to fire Yudhoyono, Marzuki, and Sarwono, three independent, intelligent ministers, among others, for disloyalty. When the parliament in late July voted overwhelmingly for his impeachment, he had only the shell of a government left. He went out at night on a balcony of the palace in his shorts to address assembled followers. He refused to leave the premises. Constitutionally, he asserted, he was still the president.

Megawati, who had been assembling allies, waited him out as she might a dotty sibling. Having now been elected 592–0, she conducted presidential duties from the vice-presidential office. After four days Wahid evacuated the palace, completing a democractic transition in which his successor and the parliament had been uncoercive and forbearing.[7] Now all eyes and ears were turned to the cabinet that the new president announced after lengthy consultation and negotiation. The list was reassuring in experience and education. Nine ministers had served in previous cabinets, and eleven had advanced graduate degrees from American universities.[8] Susilo Bambang Yudhoyono returned as a top coordinating minister, in the same post he had held until Wahid fired him. For economic affairs the appointee was Dorodjatun Kuntjoro-Jakti, respected economist and former ambassador to the United States. Laksamana Sukardi, state minister for revenues and state companies, was back, as was Kwik Kian Gie, head of the National Development Planning Board. Rini Soewandi found her way up from the wreck-age of Astra and its purchase by Singapore, to become minister for trade and industry.

Much hinged, economically, on Laksamana's responsibilities. He knew well that massive asset sales by IBRA and privatization of state companies were necessary, even though "for most Indonesians it looks like selling the country." In a consolidated strategy, "We need to separate the principle of commerce and the principle of subsidies. Subsidies should come from the tax dividend, from profit of SOEs [State-Owned Enterprises], and we will give it through the budget transparently."[9] Such a vision had a capacity, jour-nalistic covers said, to "save Indonesia." But in time experienced Indonesian observers saw "retired generals brokering IBRA assets" and SOE revenues feeding the biggest parties—PDI-P and Golkar. Laks was perceived as im-potent against nationalism, cronyism, and former-ownerism; against anarchistic bribe takers and the democratization of corruption. "Com-batting corruption from inside the government is like asking the Gambinos to clean up the mafia," said one of Laks's friends, who asked that he be un-derstood in the light of the American military-industrial complex, massive corporate welfare, sweetheart partronage, and effectual public funding of lobbyists who wrangle huge legislative concessions.[10]

Hamzah Haz of Kalimantan, having now won (over Akbar Tanjung, 340–237) the vice presidency which he had previously lost to Megawati, es-tablished his Islamic party (PPP) at a new level of prominence. Yusril Izra Mahendra, a more pronouncedly textualist Muslim (Moon and Star Party), became justice and human rights Minister. Gus Dur's former PKB party chief, Matori Abdul Djalil, became defense minister, continuing the refor-masi protocol of civilian leadership but still without military clout. Among the problems to be faced by Matori, totally lacking in such experience, were not only genuine professionalization of the military but oversight of opera-tions to cope with separatist forces, of which GAM, with 3,000 guerrillas in Aceh, was the best organized and equipped group. Also, piracy had quintu-pled worldwide between 1995 and 2000, with Southeast Asia, and mainly In-donesian waters, accounting for the majority of attacks reported each year.[11]

A significant position was omitted from Megawati's first list: who would be the new attorney general? After Marzuki Darusman left that position, he commented on the delusionary behavior of his president and on his own office's failures to build and sustain certain cases. Against Ginandjar Kartasasmita: "You can't pin him down on ordinary misdeeds, such as com-missions and markups. We're talking here about sophisticated methods of benefiting from projects that are not readily apparent."[12] Against Fuad Bawazier: reasonably suspected of plotting to overthrow Wahid but not easily proven guilty of his widely discussed corruption and tax evasion.

Against generals responsible for rampaging militias in East Timor: "These are things that have been jumped over and never touched by the reform process."[13]

Marzuki did not mention the most prominent cases—those against former president Suharto himself, whom a lower court had let off the hook for reasons of health; and the successful one against his son Tommy for a multibillion dollar land scam. The convicted man had then bribed his way out of surveillance when an arrest warrant was issued and was still in hiding. As a passing comment to the presiding Supreme Court judge who had sentenced Tommy, two men on motorcycles shot him five times at close range through the window of his car. The killing, coming a few days after Megawati's election as president, appeared to be a message to her about law enforcement in Indonesia. Maybe she didn't need it. Her husband, Taufik Kiemas, commenting on the prosecutions of the Suhartos, had told *Tempo* magazine that "this kind of suffering" should not be inflicted on the family.[14] A teachable Supreme Court appeared to complete the travesty soon after by reversing its conviction of Tommy for graft. A year later, nonetheless, a five-judge panel—too large, perhaps, to obliterate—convicted Tommy of ordering the killing of the judge, paying $11,000 for it, and supplying a handgun. He was sentenced to fifteen years in jail. Eventually he was sent to a safe and relatively comfortable island prison. There he joined Bob Hasan, who had developed a hobby of polishing gemstones and who shared his privileged polishing machine with other inmates.

President Megawati finally chose a career judge as attorney general—one who had headed investigations of human rights abuses in the Tanjung Priok killings by the military in 1985, as well as the fact-finding team looking for human rights abuses that followed the UN-sponsored ballot in East Timor in 1999. Neither report mentioned any high-ranking military leaders—the first to the incredulity of families of victims and the second to the consternation of the UN, whose investigators had made high-level accusations.[15] The pattern of scapegoating junior officers or men in the ranks while higher officers are unquestioned is well established in Indonesia. Lieutenant General (ret.) A. M. Hendropriyono had been a local commander in Lampung when scores of protesting Muslim villagers were massacred there in February 1989 after the hacking to death of an officer. Hendropriyono, an affable, energetic advocate of democratic free enterprise, became a personal advisor to Megawati in the early 1990s. Now she appointed him head of the State Intelligence Coordinating Body.[16]

The president expressed her taste for rigid protocol and tight security by appointing Bambang Kesowo as state secretary. He had worked for five years under Suharto as vice secretary in this key administrative ministry supporting the president's office. His return to power raised concerns that the corruption of an earlier era might revive, even though the distribution of power was now spread far more widely. In less than a year, a commission of parliament investigating the State Secretariat began to unearth old and continuing slush fund practices.[17]

Megawati strove to be upbeat. In her first eve-of-independence-day speech, she declared her intention to address corruption, among other goals calculated to unify the nation, rejuvenate the economy, and improve Indonesia's international standing. She apologized to the peoples of Aceh and Irian Jaya for inappropriate policies and for thousands of deaths and human rights abuses. She did not promise referenda like East Timor's (whose independence she at last publicly recognized); but she did offer special autonomy bills, already in the drafting. She verbally oriented herself to professionalizing the military and the police in their newly separate functions of national defense and law and order and to prosecuting human rights abuses where sufficient evidence existed.

With the stately gait of a parade horse, Madame Megawati pushed forward. Those watching were reassured that she was in control of the horse itself, the presidency, in contrast to her predecessor's attempts at blind acrobatics in the saddle. But her appointments already signified how unlikely it would be to realize her rhetoric opposing corruption and supporting human rights. Her close association with the military made it certain that national unity paid for in lives would prevail over Wahid's taste for support of regional ambitions. Autonomy of an administrative sort was galloping ahead everywhere: a rampant decentralization. Separatism, however, would be stiffly repressed. A likely formula from Mega and the military would be, on a wide front of issues, a combination of concessions and resistance that would effectively replace the phase of *reformasi* with one that could be called *restorasi*.

The evolving shape of the relationship between a sluggish, thuggish polity and the will of a more conscious but ill-coordinated "people" offered itself for presidential management. The optimism of the young Sukarno was needed, a new affirmation of the Indonesian identity he had done so much to shape, and an attempt to extend *reformasi* by the time of his centennial (2001), so that the nation might be inspired by a new and vigorous vision. Thus far, however, *reformasi* had probably not done much more than widen the circle of highly influential people from two hundred to two thousand, in a population growing far above two hundred million. A high proportion of the influential were not keen to discern the will of the people, let alone to educate it. In rage, it might express itself. Or some master puppeteers, in orchestrated riot and *peristiwa*, might choose to demonstrate to the media, and thereby to urban publics, what "the people" ought to be feeling.

Megawati shirked a great role in educating the people, the public, the *rakyat*, the masses. She cast herself narrowly as "mother," combining in that image a disdain for the media and contempt for the bureaucracy. The "public" was therefore left to be aroused, cozened, played-to by hungry media and political greed. The *rakyat*—the not-so-sovereign revolutionary "people" of Megawati's father—were sinking more quickly into myth, or even oblivion, than would have been the case with more sustained focus in national educational policy. Megawati herself thought they were with her, but polls after a year showed her seriously losing support. The Indonesian revolution was vanishing as a historical reckoning point far faster than the French, or even the Chinese, and not solely because a whole layer of consciousness within it had been killed: Tan Malaka and others in 1948 and D. N. Aidit with many, many others in 1965–66. A non-Marxist Indonesian trying to invent a genuine twenty-first-century progressivism would still be in danger of appearing to embrace their dishonored careers or suffering contamination by association.

As for the masses: Suharto had cultivated the peasantry in theatrical ways, admixed with sultanic distance. He used the urban underclass for short-term protest to intimidate the middle class whenever it might threaten his establishment. His "floating mass" theory of politics indicated how much he wished to keep as many of the people as possible unorganized, unanchored, ill-defined, drifting, manipulable every five years in engineered balloting. The time had long since arrived, as Sarwono Kusumaatmadja said, for a politics of interest groups, in modern communication and competition with one another. But this was slow to happen naturally. Megawati clung to a rhetorical and romantic use of the term *rakyat* in her father's tradition; and most of the politicians around her had not thought through or graduated from Suharto's notion of the "floating mass" with regard to the people at large.

While Megawati's personal steadiness was a welcome relief after Habibie and Wahid, her sense of proportion was often troubling. On her first visit to New York, she declined a pre-breakfast meeting arranged to reassure American businesses that had legal issues in Jakarta; she spent time shopping at Bloomingdale's and spent a six-figure sum in dollars to hire troupe and theater for an exclusive Monday-night showing of *The Phantom of the Opera* to her entourage.[18] Her minister of religious affairs went to Bogor with her blessing and began digging under a stone that bore a fifteenth-century royal inscription in Sanskrit. There, the minister asserted, a *dukun* had told him was enough buried treasure to cover all of the country's debt ($155 billion, at that point).[19] Her wishful thinking was basically little different from that of Wahid, also *dukun*-inspired, who as president had signed numbered letters and authorized meetings to track down gold bullion (estimated from $43.5 million to $15 billion) alleged to have been stashed by Sukarno in the

Different Pursuits in Papua

104. EXCAVATION. Digging west of Timika began by Freeport McMoRan in 1989 after a major discovery of gold. By 1996, continuing production yields this strange beauty of man-carved terrain at high altitude, and ecological/political problems with communities nearby. (Courtesy of Freeport McMoRan Copper and Gold)

105. PROSPECTING. Four of an exploration team survey a river for mineral sediment in the company's concession. From proven and provable reserves will come another 50–100 years of production. This American enterprise, Indonesia's largest taxpayer, cannot escape military-political tensions over Papuan moves for autonomy or independence. (Courtesy of Freeport McMoRan Copper and Gold)

106. PRESERVATION. A Dani tribal elder of the Baliem Valley displays a smoke-blackened mummy, complete with penis gourd. (Peter Schuyff)

107. FEATHER-GATHERING. Three Dani warriors on a feather-hunt rest and drink by a stream in February 2000. Their Stone Age way of life is under pressure from both modern industry and Javanese transmigrants. (Peter Schuyff)

1960s in Swiss and European banks. But there was no evidence to go on. The search collapsed in confused embarrassment.[20]

Such habits of the imagination have a regional resonance: in the Philippines there have been tales of General Yamashita's gold (where buried?) and even of General MacArthur's gold (where secreted?) and, in a lurid mixture of fact and fancy, searches for President Marcos's gold. Some $2 billion of illegally acquired assets had actually been recovered by the Philippine government by the year 2000. Imelda Marcos had not dampened appetite for recovery by asserting in 1998 that "we practically own everything in the Philippines"—referring to "trustees" who held about $11 billion.[21] Here we return to an elusive reality. Suharto was never boastful about wealth, but his kin and cronies were unrestrainedly greedy. There is much to be found, which should be distilled back into transparent public containers. Transparency, however, is precisely a major problem. Perceptions of government corruption among business people, academics, and risk analysts, as well as perceptions of access to official documents among journalists, are not favorable to Indonesia, according to assessments made in 2001 (Table 12).

"What is a political regime, when devoid of justice, but organized crime?"[22] The question came out of what is now Algeria sixteen centuries ago from the dark-skinned Bishop of Hippo, later known as Saint Augustine. On their own urgent premises, many Indonesians ask themselves similar questions. In 2002 an uphill effort by a group of legislators produced a carefully worked out set of constitutional reforms, including constitutional

Table 12. Opacity in government[a]

Transparency International Rankings (Corruption Perceptions Index: 0=highly corrupt; 10=highly clean), 2001[b]		Philippine Center for Investigative Journalism tabulation of "yes" answers to requests for 45 key government records, 2001 (%)	
Singapore	9.2	Philippines	56
Malaysia	5.0	Thailand	51
Thailand	3.2	Cambodia	42
Philippines	2.9	Singapore	42
Vietnam	2.6	Malaysia	33
Indonesia	**1.9**	**Indonesia**	**18**
		Vietnam	18
		Myanmar (Burma)	4

a. Based on rankings and ratings in Thomas Blanton, "The World's Right to Know," *Foreign Policy,* 131 (July/Aug. 02), pp. 50–58.

b. Neither Myanmar (Burma) nor Cambodia were covered for lack of adequate survey sources.

courts, which was eventually passed by the MPR. A group of retired generals led by Try Sutrisno made a show of forceful discontent late in the game, but they were unable to derail the amendments. After three years of work, the drafting committee under Jakob Tobing developed an esprit de corps that enveloped even its military/police members. The preamble of the constitution, binding to all, was preserved untouched. But the elements affecting the presidency that had led to arrogation of excessive executive power by both Sukarno and Suharto were removed. Likewise removed were opportunities for strangulation of the executive by legislative voting on the accountability speech, which had effectively ended both Habibie's and Wahid's presidencies. The unique Indonesian presidential system of the 1945 constitution was replaced by a system akin to that in the Philippines, many Latin American countries, and the United States.

Key formal aspects of change included direct election of president and vice president from the same ticket, with second-round voting if no one obtains 50 percent plus one, plus 20 percent in half of all provinces. There will be no more appointive members of any kind. That notably included no more military members—who actually appear to have concluded that it will now be better not to be encumbered with parliamentary roles. Implicitly they are confident that their territorial command system and large off-budget income will provide the essential powers they need. An entirely elected MPR henceforward will consist of two houses: the DPR as national legislature and the DPD (Dewan Perwakilan Daerah) as regional consultative assembly, a second chamber elected regionally whose concurrence is required on regional matters and whose consultation is enlisted on budget, tax, religion, and education issues, but not at all in foreign policy, defense, or security.

The Jakarta Charter, which was introduced again in 2002 but later withdrawn, has become a less likely psycho-political ploy. It requires a firmly backed petition of at least a third of MPR members—unlikely in a country whose Islamist popular vote in 1999 was less than half of that, unless globalized conflict changes public temperament.[23] In short, the Indonesian republic at its legislative apex moved in 2002 to an operating position far less vulnerable to being undermined by dictatorship, military control, or radical Islamism. All of that can be taken as a surprising and healthy opportunity for pluralistic democracy to learn how to work and to prove that it can. Those who observe that democracy and decentralization are too much to attempt simultaneously turn to the USSR and Yugoslavia to document their point. For Indonesia, however, the proper rejoinder is that its circumstances are unique. This success in patient, committee-based constitutional reform is a hopeful and potentially transformative achievement, and an eloquent rebuke to those who say that *reformasi* ended in 1999.

Business Culture in a Crisis Economy

Five years after the Asian financial crisis began, *The Economist* risked sounding like Adam Smith on steroids in asserting that much of East Asia seemed to be "doing fine." They reduced 1997–98 to a charted "blip" and graphically put South Korea at the head of a flock of flying geese. Indonesia did not strengthen the theme of the article, which was honest enough to mention its bad debts, weak banks, and governmental reliance on "aid money for life support."[24]

Indonesia is best understood, however, not as a laggard goose trying to follow South Korea's wingbeat, but on its own terms. A careful review of three decades of its per capita GDP shows a steady and even astonishing rise from 1970 through 1996. During the next five years it drops a sickening 40 percent. Indonesians, statistically speaking, still have incomes larger than in 1990, and three times as large as in 1975. But their economy does not yet show signs of returning to the heights of 1996. Foreign and domestic investment approvals in 2001 were at about one-fourth the level of five years previous.[25] Key indicators were sluggish at best (see Table 13).

Looking at the frontier of the business sector may suggest why recovery remained slow. The Lippo Group's $12 billion in assets and more than fifty private and publicly traded companies prompted them to call themselves "the GE of Indonesia." Mochtar Riady, the supreme strategic planner

Table 13. Key macroeconomic indicators, Indonesia, 1970–2001

Periodic levels	1970	1975	1980	1985	1990	1996	2001
GDP (US$, bn.)	8.84	30.47	72.50	87.47	110.92	223.51	146.97
Population (mn)	119.47	135.67	147.49	164.63	179.83	195.28	212.48
Per capita GDP (US$)	73.96	224.55	491.59	531.32	616.83	1144.58	691.68
Phases of real annual growth rates (%)		1970–1975	1975–1980	1980–1985	1985–1990	1990–1996	1997–2001
Population growth		2.58	1.68	2.22	1.78	1.38	1.35
Inflation (CPI)		19.53	14.61	9.72	7.46	9.11	21.90
Real GDP growth		8.05	7.92	4.74	6.25	7.27	(−1.30)
Real per-capita GDP growth		5.34	6.13	2.46	4.39	5.81	(−2.62)

Selected from Iwan J. Azis, "Incorporating Economic and Environmental Dimensions in Measuring Development Progress: The Case of Indonesia," in Fu Chen Ho, Hiroyasu Tokuda, and N. S. Cooray, eds., *The Sustainable Future of the Global System III* (Tokyo: The United Nations University and OECD, 2000), table 1, p. 300. Column for 1997–2001 specially provided here by courtesy of Dr. Azis.

among Indonesian businessmen, had invited me out to Lippo Karawaci, a tidy modern industrial village forty minutes west of old Jakarta, with a university, a hospital, and a new cyberpark. Back in May of 1998, a crowd estimated at 10,000 had torched and looted the town's supermall, the largest shopping center in the country, and 86 people had died. But now all looked hygienic and secure.

Dr. Riady apologetically declined to address my questions on the relationship of his Christianity to his business practices. He lectured me, with kindly authority, on his favorite American entrepreneurial strategists. I knew about them. I wanted to know him, but as he talked and I studied his face–that of a handsome, graying Confucian with an official smile—I realized that I would not hear any personal thoughts. When I asked him what he would do if he were made finance minister, however, I got a vigorous description of how he would gather the "one hundred people who hold power in Indonesia" and stem the "five bleedings" in the financial system. The economy, because of SOEs and IBRA, was now 90 percent under government control. He would solve that serious problem in the way that Emperor Han Wu Ti had done in China twenty-four hundred years ago: by abolishing state monopolies. In modern lingo, privatize. Sell Pertamina to Caltex, Garuda to Singapore Airlines, and so forth. "I don't want to beggar with IMF," he laughed. Pay off real debt (that not owed to Indonesians ourselves, or to the Japanese) and reduce corruption at the same time. A majestic solution, I thought. But a political mirage.[26]

A reporter for *Fortune* pursued operational questions with Mochtar's son, James Riady. His nearly twenty-year career in America had included a major interest in Arkansas' Worthen Bank—cited for improper overseas lending and later sold—and the Bank of Trade in California, which attracted federal cease-and-desist orders for "hazardous lending" and violations of money-laundering statutes. It was used for daisy-chain political contributions to Clinton campaigns (more than one million dollars from Lippo associates) before also being sold. James was the family leader in Across Asia Multimedia, whose initial public offering on Hong Kong's high-risk tech exchange made it the biggest ever in that bourse. His teammate was Jim Guy Tucker, the former governor of Arkansas who, after vacating office in 1996 upon two Whitewater fraud convictions, immediately joined up with Riady.

A key part of their plan was Kablevision, building a widespread Indonesian cable TV infrastructure. Despite theft of parts, graft of every sort, and hazardous wiring conditions, they built up 50,000 subscribers and supplied them with 45 channels before flattening out as an enterprise in 2000. Asian financial drag and Indonesia's own special tailspin made for tough business conditions. The Tucker-Riady friendship was not widely replicated, and there appeared to be Arkansas vs. Java cultural wars debilitating the enterprise. Having suffered three heart blockages by 44 years of age, James Riady decided to take time off to study divinity, while expanding the Christian private school system in Lippo Karawaci and hoping to open 1,000 schools in Indonesia's poorest villages.

The Riadys, father and son, unquestionably have vision, strategic acuity, and diverse successes. Indonesia needs such qualities. But they and the Lippo Group in the year 2000 were dealt one of the largest securities trading penalties ever administered in Indonesia, for artificially inflating the stock price of Lippo E-Net. And days before President Clinton left office in 2001, James Riady accepted a plea bargain to pay the largest political fine in American history, for illegally reimbursing Democrat campaign contributions.

Are Riady business tactics redeemed by their social vision? Despite the Christian schooling and community building, something doesn't jibe. When an American aide complained about a contractor who was endangering workers by placing cable too close to power transformers, James Riady replied, "People are cheap here. Labor is cheap here."[27] The family, in sum, appears to be an extraordinarily vivid example of split-level Christianity combined with split-level capitalism. They affirm elevated values in English while practicing *guanxi* ("connections") and the ultimate in Chinese-Indonesian opportunism. In *pribumi* and Islamic enterprises, the strategic business vision is less compelling. But analogous cultural schisms often appear.

Lippo is only one conglomerate. Turning to IBRA, however, gives one a swab on corporations, banks, and government all at once. Late in 2002 the agency that was supposed to make the economy healthy again was in flabby denial of that responsibility. It approached shareholder liability settlements by offering low interest rates to tycoon debtors—the same people who had enjoyed the high-interest returns guaranteed by the government in 1998 and who had violated the Maximum Credit Lending Limit. In accord with the banking law, said Minister Kwik Kian Gie, they should go to jail. He was alone in the cabinet in taking this stance.[28]

Against these behaviors some observers bravely noted that the small and medium enterprises growing in Indonesia might represent a different kind of business conscience: high ingenuity to maximize survival and less indifference to social damage. If true, they are prospective builders, with state and civil society, of a vigorous nation.

Some Demons of Comparison

Comparisons are the very devil. They involve flitting perceptions and shifting premises and may cloud the central focus. But without them, the prime point of interest may remain hidden by preconceptions. Indonesia, early in the twenty-first century, may be better understood by analogies to other *malhadado país*—"ill-fated countries"[29]—whose tragedies and greatnesses bear partial resemblances to its own.

One notably close comparison is with the Philippines, because of proximity, consanguinity, archipelagic nature, and social energies as well. The Philippines of 1986, against Marcos, bequeathed to Indonesia of 1998, against Suharto, the phrase "people power" as part of the dynamics of unseating a dictator. But people power cannot be bottled and is unpredictable. Both nations also opened the new millennium by impeaching a president. The middle-class demonstrations in Manila that brought "Erap" Estrada down in 2000, however, provoked powerful counter-demonstrations by the poor. Estrada would not be in jail awaiting trial on huge graft charges had not his vice president, Gloria Macapagal Arroyo, used both the supreme court and the army to establish her legitimacy as his replacement. People power in Jakarta gassed out much faster. Mobs were not critical against Wahid or for him. The legislature was overwhelmingly for change in midstream, and its military faction, steadfast in procedural niceties, was with the majority. Gus Dur was returned to life as an NGO activist leader, where his managerial deficiencies were not crippling.

Putting the Philippines and Indonesia under the same people-power/impeachment lens also reveals them as sharing split-level values in the widest sense: upfront voicing of Catholic or Islamic private morality and democratic free-enterprise public morality, while down deep acting upon cultural axioms of highly limited personal or group interest: "just among us" (*tayo-tayo*, Pilipino; *antara kita, diri-sendiri*, Indonesian). Such conflicts are of course universal, and in some countries even more acute; but Indonesia certainly experiences them as disabling to sustained and equitable development.

Indonesian intellectual and religious modernists readily employ the terms "mafiya" and "fascist" about behaviors they abhor among some of their powerful countrymen.[30] Such usage recalls the fact that early in his career Mussolini used street gangs, *squadristi*, to help exert his political will, just as the Suharto regime used Pemuda Pancasila, and after him General Wiranto employed Pam Swakarsa. It is important not to forget, however, that Mussolini as a fascist leader in power tried to suppress the *mafia* as a threat to order in his state. Such suppressive power in Indonesia, unfortunately, lies in a military which in itself contains much *mafioso* character.

The evolution of Spanish fascism, in contrast, is also enlightening. General Franco, in a dictatorship (1939–1975) that lasted longer than Suharto's, was able to defang his own Falange and motivate his bureaucracy to the point of generating an economic takeoff in the 1960s. When he died, de-

mocracy appeared and prevailed because he had allowed the basis of its political institutions to grow. Spain has no need now of threatening mottoes
or graffiti such as "Franco lives."

Some Argentines, however, cultivate populist Peronism and declare
"Evita triumphs." Others even write on walls that "Rosas lives!" evoking the
ruthless nineteenth-century military strongman whose gauchoesque style
overrode democrats like Domingo Sarmiento.[31] After balance and optimism
in the early 1990s, Argentina's condition in 2001–2002, with renewed hyper-
inflation, joblessness, riot, and emigration, worries many over a return
of military rule. Bad habits come back, and with them poor solutions.
Caudillismo lurks in Argentine history, as does the shadow of military fiat in
Indonesia. Peronism, *caudillismo* reified, continues to threaten excesses of
power.

Suhartoism by now may have crystallized as a similar recurring pattern
in Indonesia, differing chiefly in that it is anti-labor, whereas Peronism re-
lies partly on labor for its power. An ultimate irony could yet be that President Megawati becomes a kind of modern, nonflamboyant, dowager Evita,
combining elements of her father's populism with reliance on an unrepen-
tant and unreformable Suhartoite military. But her style, of course, will remain Javanese: nonconfrontational, with regally understated composure
and deliberate inattention to what she may choose not to see or seek remedy for.

In a world in which Indonesia both wishes recognition as a major nation
and hides in its insularity, two other structural comparisons may be noted:
Nigeria and Russia. Nigeria returned to a free national democratic election
in the same year, 1999, that Indonesia did, with a surge of hope. But its fed-
eralism has more antagonisms; several of its Muslim provinces are more di-
visively insistent on shariah law, and its generals have even less concept of a
national interest as distinct from a military mission. The late dictator General Sani Abacha pushed a "lootocracy" even more brazenly venal than
Suharto, amassing more than $3 billion in less than five years of rule. He
formed, through family and two former ministers, a shell company to purchase $2.5 billion of debt incurred to Russia for 20 cents on the dollar and
then ordered the Nigerian treasury to provide full payment of the debt. The
Nobel laureate Wole Soyinka said of Abacha that he has "no *notion* of Nigeria."[32] That could not be said of Suharto, who did believe in Indonesia and
tried, in his own sublime and bizarre way, to serve it.

Russia, too, evokes comparison and uncomfortable companionship. Neither privatization, nor proliferation of NGOs, nor freedoms in the media,
nor aspects of civil society, separately or together, have generated there a
due-process democracy. But, as many of its intelligent citizens say, "man-

aged democracy" is better than none.[33] Megawati's father had gone that route under vastly different conditions, but "guided" Indonesia into a deadly crash. His daughter's task is to manage toward incremental gains in justice—economic and social, for which rule of law itself is a vital underpinning. Without gains in rule of law, other gains will be reversible. An American founder of the Council of Institutional Investors had explained clearly, a month before the Asian financial crisis, why megabillion groups like his own held back from Russia. "A share of common stock is a remarkable contract, because it has no contractual language. Instead it is defined by an entire legal system." But where there is no rule of law, investors must charge a substantial risk premium, making the cost of capital very high. Still more so when "legal, contractual, banking, trading, judicial, corporate and governmental institutions themselves were subject to failure." In his letter, the writer did not mention Indonesia. But he did not need to do so. In these regards, in a later phrase, Indonesia was only "Russia with sunshine."[34]

With regard to state organization, Russia's asymmetric ethno-federalism has been successful, excepting Chechnya, in containing separatism. Indonesia has let loose its most irreconcilable province, East Timor, and may or may not succeed in enforcing national symmetry—with some bargained autonomies—elsewhere. Russia has probably less random crime than African "shadow states," because of a higher surviving level of state institutions. Indonesia can be posited as in between, still in need of building or regenerating institutions, while fixers, *squadristi*, rentier legislators, *mafiya* military, and auctionable courts are embedded in its history. An undigested past implics an undeliverable future. To the extent that Indonesia avoids truths and reconciliations about its national history, it cultivates clashing destinies instead of an integral hope.

An especially promising dimension of Indonesia's future emerges in comparison with Brazil and with its own past—in the current nature of its civil society. Tocqueville is a proper point of departure, reminding us that political institutions in the United States were the large schools where everyone learned the voluntary associations that they put into practice in numerous other ways. Such primacy is well to remember as a caution in regarding Brazil's civil society—very high in density and in recent years notably strong in labor union power, the landless peasant movement, and new neighborhood associations. At the same time Brazil remains low in institutionalization of its politics, suffers from extraordinarily high electoral volatility, and endures a state made dysfunctional by patronage and bureaucratic complexity. In such an environment, seven economic stabilization plans were launched and abandoned in eight years (1985–1993), and then an anti-political outsider, Collor de Mello, was elected president. He proved to be corrupt in majestic and sophistic ways. Despite improvement under Cardoso, Brazil remains subject to uncivil and violent social movements that do not consolidate democracy but threaten destabilization of regimes.[35]

Against this background, the Indonesia of the 1950s and early 1960s looks similar, regardless of its lower levels of income (unhealthy) and its higher levels of equity in distribution of income (healthy). The Indonesia of Sukarno's time was notable, despite poverty and illiteracy, for its flourishing labor unions, women's organizations, peasants' associations, and bodies for artists and students. These latter, however, could not enable democratic transition in 1965–66. That murderous passage was in great degree a function of *aliran* politics, each *aliran* a self-contained social universe disposed toward the negation of the others. When the PKI precipitated class politics, including unilateral land seizures, in this environment, the flow was regrettably easy from existing violence in August 1965 into mass murder after September 30. The other *alirans*, notably NU and PNI, joined the extermination sought by the military.

In the authoritarian regime that followed, a slow evolution proceeded, from GONGOs (government-organized non-government organizations) to "amphibians" (ICMI, a government attempt to coopt Islam in 1991, became a source of transmission of civil society ideas to the state) to a condition of profusion by 1996 in which 8,600 NGOs could be identified by the authorities. Most of them were development-oriented and therefore compatible with the government, but many others were sources of political criticism. This new element, in contrast to the late Sukarno years, was not ideological or oriented toward class struggle but centered upon lobbying the state, carving out domains for social initiative, and criticizing the regime from the vantage of impartial rule of law—all recognizable functions in the eyes of international sources that helped in funding and in making such Indonesian entities a part of a global civil society.

Indonesian civil society did not bring down the sultanic regime of Suharto, nor did it attempt any Brazilian style "pact" with it. Suharto was too strong to bargain had the NGOs wished to do so, which they did not. Their contribution was to shift the discourse under the ground of the government and to erode its ideological foundations. The converging crises of 1997–98 weakened Suharto, and when the society manifested its civil will and imagination in February–May 1998, he could no longer prevail.

In the general election that followed, both PKB and PAN reached out beyond their cores of *aliran* followers, and the only party insisting on an ideology of class conflict, PRD, got 0.1 percent of the vote. The first two post-Suharto presidents, Habibie and Wahid, endorsed *masyarakat madani* (civil society).[36] However beset with 'Hartoistic imitators and their habits, the Indonesia of the early twenty-first century is incomparably better equipped, in civil society terms, than that of the late Sukarno years to deepen and to widen democracy. Instead of its elements seeing one another as foes, they are much more likely to see the adversary as an overbearing state. Against it, the voluntary and cooperative energies of the civil imagination must hopefully, and continually, contend.

The New Strategic Environment

September 11, 2001, immediately changed America's understanding of itself and relations with much of the world. When they regained their balance, federal officials, including President Bush, distinguished Muslim peoples and nations clearly from the terrorists who had blasphemed Islam by indiscriminate killing of 3,000 civilians from 80 nations in the name of Allah.

Indonesia's Vice President Hamzah Haz, in a wholly different spirit, suggested that the attack, for the United States, was like a "cleansing of sins." The deposed Abdurrahman Wahid, in an apparent attempt to solidify new political ground under himself, said that America itself was a "terrorist nation."[37] Ambassador Robert S. Gelbard had been drawn into spats with prominent authorities and Islamists the year before and had briefly closed the American embassy because of "credible threats" of violence, including against himself. Now he charged again into verbal action, accusing Dewi Fortuna Anwar of anti-Semitic comments. (I myself thought it disappointing and crude for an intelligent woman to refer to the World Trade Center as "the symbol of Jewish financial influence in the U.S.") He charged Juwono Sudarsono with indifference to terrorism and criticized Indonesia's security forces for not moving against militants who threatened to kill Americans.[38] Later events would prove Gelbard's intelligence information valid. But his style was perceived as bluster by Indonesian officials who were at that time covering their eyes and ears against evidence of potential Islamic terrorism. Although announced vigilante "sweeps" against offensive infidels actually brushed no foreigners out, let alone injuring any, they surely deterred some tourism. That factor accomplished an interesting modification in Vice President Hamzah Haz: he admonished Ja'far Umar Thalib, head of Laskar Jihad, that Indonesia needed foreign investment and foreign exchange.

In this atmosphere, President Megawati determined to follow through on an invitation from President Bush to make a state visit to the United States, to show for the people of Indonesia "their deep sympathy and support for

108. PRESIDENT MEGAWATI AND PRESIDENT BUSH. At the White House in September 2001, a week after terrorists attacked New York and Washington, President Megawati follows through on her trip to the United States. (Courtesy of the Embassy of Indonesia, Washington, DC)

the Government and the people of the United States of America." In Washington she stressed to President Bush the desirability of resuming full military relations between the two countries. To a dinner of the United States–Indonesia Society, Megawati spoke personally, as one "who had experienced the bitter taste of tyranny," and during her political career as a member of the Indonesian parliament, "the sour and salty taste of politics." The culinary metaphors suggested strong personal conviction and expressed the unique outlook of one who told reporters that her model for running the nation was "the household." To recover from four years of financial crisis, her government had recently signed an agreement with the IMF that had been pending for eight months. President Megawati invited investors to Indonesia. She closed to standing and genuine applause, having expressed the shared national dreams of the United States and Indonesia, the desire of each to create "a great nation where all men and women are treated equal, where people of all races, ethnicity and religion live side by side in peace and prosperity as one."[39]

Megawati had spoken as the would-be Umayi of twenty-first-century Indonesia. But her people's deep problems and her own military had the power to re-manifest her as Durga. Megawati said she stood behind ad hoc tribunals to try violations of human rights. But what would the standards of evidence be? Challenges arose soon enough. In Aceh, GAM and TNI killings had resumed and would go on at a daily rate exceeding deaths in Palestine's chronic and continuing struggle with Israel.[40] On November 10, 2001, not long after a dinner with officers of Kopassus, the leader of independence for Papua, Theys Eluay, was found dead in his car, which had been pushed over a cliff. His blackened face and protruding tongue indicated that he had been strangled.[41] Suspicion focused on the military, and Police General I Made Mangku Pastika pressed forward professionally. An independent team of inquiry reported to President Megawati in 2002 that Kopassus was involved. Motives continued to be debated: was Theys obliterated in a controversy over a logging concession or exterminated as a warning to independence-minded tribal leaders? The trial of seven suspects from Kopassus by a military court in Java was progress, given past security atrocities in Papua, all unprosecuted.[42] A defense of "accidental asphyxiation" was incredible (the tongue of the dead Theys protruded 2cm from his mouth) but somehow saved all but the most junior officer, who took the rap. An Austra-

109. MASKED YOUTH AND OSAMA. Anti-American demonstrations at the U.S. Embassy in Jakarta reach a peak of 10,000 participants in October 2001, during American aerial bombardment of Taliban/Al Qaeda positions in Afghanistan. By Jakarta standards these are small demonstrations. For some youthful Muslim males, however, Osama bin Laden has become a poster hero, or more. (Kemal Jufri/IMAJI)

lian researcher claimed three steadfast sources who traced instigation of the murder to a retired general high in Megawati's administration, but his publisher, fearing a libel suit, suppressed the name.[43] In any case, critical focus on Kopassus was overdue. The days of its glory as a Special Forces unit created to oppose Darul Islam half a century ago have passed, and ordinary Indonesian citizens have seen it as stained with cruelty.

The interests of the Indonesian military in Papua are clear; its *modi operandi* are dark. They wish to reclaim their role as guarantors of national unity; and they are fully aware of opportunities for personal gain in this resource-rich province. They will never let it go like East Timor. An intelligence intercept in 2001, in the case of the murder of Willem Onde, a Papuan separatist associated with Theys, illustrates dreadful, if clumsy, determination. A military superior was overheard bawling out an inferior for botching the task: "Why didn't you remember to slit his stomach? Now the body will bloat and float!"

Murders of three civilians, two of them American schoolteachers, in a Freeport picnic caravan returning to Timika in August 2002, were traced by Police General Pastika and his successor to the military. A possible motive attributed to the armed forces by some observers was to get the Papua Independence Organization (OPM) categorized as a terrorist organization. But M16s, SS1s, and Mausers were used, and thousands of rounds were shot: OPM has no such wealth of munitions. Only the 650 army and police paid to defend the Freeport enclave were thus equipped. Some of them were apparently enraged enough by the company's idea of reducing their forces that they tried to stimulate preexisting policy by attacking those they were employed to safeguard.[44]

At a high level of policy, Megawati's commander of Kostrad, the strategic reserve, was Lieutenant General Ryamizard Ryacudu. In an interview with *Tempo* magazine about how to deal with separatists and disorder, he provided a simple and chilling prescription: "Exterminate provocateurs, shoot rioters."[45] Ryamizard, the son of a major general and the son-in-law of Suharto's general and Vice President Try Sutrisno, is deeply imbued with TNI tradition. But as an absolutist on security, he appears to cast back to Benny Moerdani, or forward to a new unity by force. The president in mid-2002 appointed him her new commanding general of the army.

In this mixed context of Indonesia's wars against separatism and America's war against terrorism, pressures built in Washington to relax the congressional restrictions on engagement with and training of the Indonesian military, passed after the 1991 massacre in Dili. The Bush administration's prominent hawk-on-Iraq, Deputy Secretary of Defense Paul Wolfowitz, was the best informed Washington voice on Indonesia. From his experience as American ambassador there in the senior Bush administration, he well understood several layers of reality: (1) that Megawati's challenge, in the words of one of her speechwriters, was "to provide democracy with strong authority in order to deal with instability. That is the main problem, not militant Muslims";[46] (2) that the Indonesian military was a powerful but flawed instrument, itself wholly capable of acts of terrorism. Any of its commanders-in-chief would be the real power behind the presidency, but that commander would be operating with many unreliable soldiers in an environment of many competitive and unaccountable power centers, including some retired and some active generals. (3) Irresponsibility and quasi-anarchy are endemic. As a former minister of defense, Juwono Sudarsono, observed of soldiers, "If you pay peanuts you get monkeys." And of national commotion and confusion in power: after the Suharto family there were now "300 mini-Suhartos" striving to take their place.[47] And (4) American policy had to discern clearly among secessionists, like GAM in

110. MEGAWATI AND MILITARY LEADERSHIP. In April 2002 Megawati is in the field with Lieutenant General Ryamizard Ryacudu, then commander of Kostrad. In June 2002, she will promote him to four-star general as army chief of staff. His father, Major General Ryacudu, is now said to have been ardently loyal to her father until Sukarno's downfall late in 1965.
(Beawirarta/Reuters)

Aceh, who were incidentally Muslim but primarily independence-minded; Islamist paramilitaries with a nationalist agenda, like Laskar Jihad (which itself "disbanded" in early October 2002); and genuine international jihadist terror groups, such as Jemaah Islamiyah (JI).[48]

In this environment, on the night of October 12, 2002, bombs went off in a vacationers' beach paradise, the town of Kuta on Bali. An explosion in Paddy's restaurant drove survivors out into a massive blast seconds later from the Sari discotheque across the street; 202 died and 352 were injured. Four months later there were still 200 body parts unidentified. The greatest number of fatalities were Australian—carefree college youth, older rugby heroes celebrating, husbands and wives dancing. The next largest number of dead were Indonesians, mostly employees. The rest were from all over the world, including several Americans.

Police General Pastika, a Balinese with brief international experience, was put in charge of the investigation, his reputation strengthened by his recent work in Papua. Now General Pastika followed what Professor R. William Liddle described as a "radical Sherlock Holmes approach," avoiding any reference to Al Qaeda and focusing instead on concrete evidence and to the linkages it suggested. Pastika's work took place in a doubting atmosphere. 14,000 media-aware Indonesians, early polled upon the Bali blasts, had by 82 percent ascribed it to the CIA. This distorted presumption resembled "causation" earlier imagined regarding the World Trade Center/Pentagon suicide attacks by hijacked passenger planes. The biggest tally then by far was for "Zionist terrorist plot." Osama bin Laden, who gloated over the event, got no more votes than "American terrorists" (was Timothy McVeigh imagined to be still on the loose, repeating Oklahoma?). Later Indonesian reaction to the American bombing of military sites in Afghanistan against the Taliban/Al Qaeda regime was 89 percent unfavorable.[49]

The resort island of Bali had precious little in the way of disaster equipment. White cloths covered the dead (no body bags). Chipped ice preserved them in the open (no morgue space). But local cultural resources went deep, and purification ceremonies for the dead were movingly sincere. Pastika said there would be no retaliation against the 10 percent Muslim minority. "Balinese will not blame others; they will blame themselves. When Balinese get angry they go to pray. To express opinion they will go to demonstration, and bring gamelan orchestra."

Pastika himself lacked vital police technology but quickly found ten nations from his region and the West willing to help, and to keep a low profile under his command. Pastika's team needed experts in DNA identification, and were provided them. They wanted chemical detection equipment, and were supplied it. They required technology for tracking cellular telephone calls, and again got help. They found metal fragments which—reassembled—could be identified as a Mitsubishi L300, vintage 1981–1983. A public transportation number was legible. Pastika's team traced it to the seventh owner of the vehicle, a handsome, unruly East Javanese named Amrozi, whose two brothers also proved to be deeply implicated. There followed five arrests around Banten, West Java, eight around Solo, Central Java, and fifteen in Kalimantan, including a Malaysian and a Singaporean. The local pride of a radical cell was manifest in Amrozi's defiant declarations of motive on TV (he wished they had killed more Americans) and in Ali Imron's TV demonstration of his technique for building a one-ton bomb. Imam Samudra, also involved in the Christmas Eve bombings of 2000, was commander of the Bali plot. Before capture, he sent a worldwide message of triumph from his website in Bahasa Indonesia and in English.

Even after thirty arrests, there were several men still wanted, including Hambali, JI's coordinator of operations for the whole region. The discovery in Solo of an entire book in Arabic on the organization and procedures of JI identified Abu Bakar Ba'syir as its "emir." Above him, Pastika's slide show identified Osama bin Laden as "spiritual leader." But hierarchy concerned Pastika less than the ground troops. The willing TV self-exposure of some culprits was important to show the public the threat and prepare them against its repetition. Leaders of government must act for the re-education of those brainwashed by misuse of Islam. Never *menaksir rendah*—Pastika sought audience help for the term —"never *underestimate* the frame of mind of shoeless villagers indoctrinated this way, or what they are capable of." Against the influence of radical *madrasas*, all other schools in their neighborhoods, secular or religious, should be given resources for counter-persuasion. Police work can only go so far. More basic is to draw influence away from schools that make apostles of *jihad* out of vulnerable youth.[50]

General Pastika had been able to make an announcement, on November 28, 2002, that the results of the Bali inquiry "should put to rest widespread doubts about whether JI exists in Indonesia." A low-key statement with probably low-density penetration—but, at last, the truth. The International Crisis Group then swiftly put out a study which used earlier trial documents, police information, and staff/consultant interviews to establish "How the Jemaah Islamiyah Terrorist Network Operates." From "dozens of deadly attacks" since 1999 across Indonesia, Malaysia, and the Philippines they showed how JI works through loosely organized cells with a changing structure. At the bottom rung are mostly young men from *pesantrens* or Islamic high schools, selected shortly before the attack for the dangerous work of surveying the target and delivering the bombs. Above them are field coordinators who supply money and explosives and choose a team leader for the local foot soldiers. All levels share to some degree or wholly in the convictions and traditions of those at the top: protégés of the co-founders, Abdullah Sungkar and Abu Bakar Ba'syir. Both had established an ultra-traditionalist *pesantren* outside Solo; both were arrested on subversion charges in 1978, fled to Malaysia in 1985, and returned to Indonesia after Suharto resigned. Sungkar, having founded Jemaah Islamiyah about 1995, died in 1999. Ba'syir carried on and helped found the Holy Warrior Council (MMI) in August 2000. After the Bali bombings, he sanctimoniously proclaimed his nonviolence but was arrested in mid-October 2002 for suspicion of involvement in terrorist activities. Singapore succeeded in its formal request of the UN, under Security Council Resolution 1267, to add JI to the list of terrorist organizations associated with Al Qaeda.

The histories and rebellious pedigrees gathered by ICG trace back to Kartosoewiryo's Darul Islam of the 1950s and '60s and fan across Sumatra and Java to Sumbawa and Sulawesi. They include involvement in bombing of Borobudur in 1985. They illustrate Afghanistan, the southern Philippines, and Ambon as three successive training grounds since then. They demonstrate that the Trade Center/Pentagon attack shifted Jemaah Islamiyah's focus. JI had killed Indonesian Christians on December 24, 2000, in revenge for Muslim deaths in Maluku. Now they were killing Westerners as part of a concerted international jihad.[51]

To Western observers and to many Indonesians, these men may look like murderous lunatics. But they are reminders of fundamental definitions in Wahhabi extremism and Salafi jihad: outside of the House of Islam there is only the House of War. Those who inhabit the House of War are evil and bent on destruction. To kill them is a holy act. Few Indonesians think this way. Extreme jihadists are only micro-sliver of the population. But they will not engage in dialogue, for they believe they possess complete truth. They are dangerous. And, as Pastika points out, further aroused they may act again.

A kite rises against the wind. In all its turbulence, Indonesia is nonetheless the promising home of constitutional reform, where new political parties are generating, and where civil society organizations are multiplying. Small- and medium-sized businesses are making steadfast growth through trial and error. And a police general points not only to better trained mobile brigades for national security, but to stronger and sounder education as even more basic.

There remains a drag, of course, from ill-handled debt, with a concurrent need for international aid as national budget support. There persists a heritage of violence which former General Prabowo, returned from exile and running his own private security service, justifies as inescapable, given Indonesia's variety of tribes and tongues and regions and religions. Are there fault lines in the military? He says they just reflect fault lines in the society. Have there been excesses committed by militias? Militias were the basis of Indonesia's revolutionary army and are natural to it now. Prabowo acknowledges the importance of winning the hearts and minds of the people—Nasution's guerrilla war theory at its best—but admits that Moerdani's approach (strike first; there is no substitute for fear) has prevailed for many years. He himself remains an example of the extremes in the latter style. Prabowo quotes General William Tecumseh Sherman with approval on the need for people to accept his army as a protector—apparently heedless of the hostile legacy in the American South from the destruction wrought by Sherman's army of occupation.[52] But the latest American ambassador reminds all that full restoration of military ties, resumption of non-lethal military sales, and restoration of full International Military Education and Training (IMET) depend on Indonesian progress toward holding accountable those responsible for past human rights violations.[53]

Unthinking reliance on force and preemptive use of privilege and power can only perpetuate disorder. Prolonged chaos could produce such disillusionment with the state as to draw people en masse toward a new ideology grounded in Islam, just as many people were drawn to communism in the 1950s and 1960s.[54] Against this possibility are ranged all the best hopes of progressive thinkers and moderate actors, Muslim and non-Muslim alike, who can be visionary without being perfectionist. They see history as a matter of repairing rutted roads and not of exploding open a route to paradise.[55]

How might the United States see and deal with contending destinies in Indonesia? It should recognize that the manner in which Suharto kept Indonesia quiet for foreign investors and his own cronies was not forever supportable. Not financially, not ecologically, not in any social dimension. Suharto's attempt to turn Pancasila into national *adat* is understandable in trying to band together a nation so complex, but so overreaching that it became repellent. It may be said of the United States that its citizens indeed desire to live by their own mantras of the American dream. But to try to turn our version of free-enterprise democracy into global *adat* is not likely to go well. America's geographic expanse and abundance of resources are nationally unique. American social mobility, high affluence, and consumer habits do not translate well into tropical climates and cultures.

As the continuing basis for a sound relationship with Indonesia, nonetheless, we must adhere to support of rule of law, democracy, civil society, transparent entrepreneurship, and monitored development aid. Counter-terrorism is no substitute for these elements of mutual growth, but a necessary complement to them. The new strategic environment for the United States was starkly revealed on September 11, 2001. But that date, for Indo-

nesians, precipitated very little. Its own new strategic environment began to
be defined by the Christmas Eve bombings of the year 2000 and took
clearer shape with the Bali blasts of October 12, 2002. Those dates, moreover, are only one kind of headline in a national saga that dates from August 1945 and its foregoing anti-colonial momentum.

Enduring Moral Tensions

The forces of Lenin are largely vanquished. But the foolishness of his
contemporary, Woodrow Wilson, lives on. His doctrinaire global agenda
spurred him to declare that "America had the infinite privilege of fulfilling
her destiny and saving the world."[56]

In an all too human way, after America arguably helped to save the world
twice, it went to sleep. The United States defeated fascism with concerted
alliances and won the Cold War with a classically imperial strategy—by sustained concentration of its power against the USSR. American administra-
tions of the 1990s, however, "thought they could have imperial domination
on the cheap, ruling the world without putting in place any . . . new military alliances, new legal institutions, [or] new international development organizations." According to Michael Ignatieff, this was "a general failure of
the historical imagination," an inability to grasp crises of order emerging in
countless areas where state institutions disintegrated in the face of urban
miseries. The poor, having looked up in envy and resentment at globalized
prosperity on café TVs, found, in Pakistan and elsewhere, protection and indoctrination in Islamic institutions funded from Saudi Arabia.[57]

Reinhold Niebuhr had warned America of just such hubristic errors almost half a century ago. The great eminence of Union Theological Semi-
nary in New York City saw tragedies that clearly could repeat themselves,
even if the Cold War were resolved and the antagonists changed. "We cannot affirm that the emancipation which western society has achieved from
. . . despotic conditions is the ultimate form of emancipation . . . The open
societies of the western world had cultural pluralism thrust upon them . . .
and different centers of economic and political power were developed, not
by design, but by the pressures of history." We have achieved a tolerable answer to community, Niebuhr said, by making freedom compatible with justice and stability. But "these virtues are more or less limited to the domestic
scene, and tend to evaporate in the heat of international competition." In
that larger environment, "Terrifying facts of modern history . . . [and] all
historic responsibilities must be borne without the certainty that meeting
them will lead to any ultimate solution of the problem, but with only the
certainty that there are immediate dangers which may be avoided and immediate injustices which may be eliminated."[58]

More recent, and far more sanguine than Niebuhr, is the comprehensive commentator V. S. Naipaul. He affirms that a universal civilization exists, at the heart of which is the pursuit of happiness. "So much is contained in it: the idea of the individual, responsibility, choice, the life of the intellect, the idea of vocation and perfectibility and achievement. It is an immense human idea. It cannot be reduced to a fixed system. It cannot generate fanaticism."[59]

I would like to agree with such assertive hopes, but I cannot soar so high. For firmer ground, and a final warning, Niebuhr again: "Among the lesser culprits of history are the *bland fanatics* of western civilization who regard the highly contingent achievements of our culture as the final form and norm of human existence . . . Our best hope, both of a tolerable political harmony and of an inner peace, rests on our ability to observe the limits of human freedom even while we responsibly exploit its creative possibilities."[60]

Niebuhr defined views that might keep Western democracies in balance as they struggled with Soviet totalitarianism. Now, the American problem of not-becoming-the-enemy, of not succumbing to spiritual horror and social rigidity, appears greater, insofar as the enemy expresses itself with an absolute ideology, suicidal conviction, and no capital city. And many of the people we would hope to help, even if within the circle of our better intentions, are beyond the reach of our media while within the range of our weapons. America's greatest new global problem is targeting—how to hit our enemies, and only them; how not to hurt potential friends, but to make some of our resources beneficial to them.

Meanwhile Indonesia-ness is being tested not only at the peripheries of that archipelago but in the hearts of its citizens and leaders. Can the largest Muslim nation in the world remain the most pluralist, by its own ideal design? Can a republic, founded in hope of justice and prosperity by revolution against a Western empire, now renew that hope by fairly mothering and mastering its own cultures, histories, habits, and resources? Indonesia is being tested as part of a world struggle to determine again that which any nation must endlessly re-resolve: What makes a livable society?

CHRONOLOGY

1942, February · In their "Holy War for Greater East Asia," the Japanese overthrow the Netherlands East Indies and install their own imperial structure

1945, May 28 · First meeting of the Investigatory Commission for Indonesian Independence

1945, June 1 · Sukarno's *Pancasila* speech

1945, July 16 · Draft of a constitution for the republic completed

1945, August 15 · Japan surrenders to Allied powers

1945, August 17 · "Proclamation of Indonesian Independence," signed by Sukarno-Hatta for the Indonesian people

1945, November 3 · Vice President Hatta proclaims right of the people to form political parties

1945, November 11 · Division commanders elect Sudirman as commander-in-chief of the revolutionary army

1945, July–1946, December · Negotiations with Dutch over a federation called the United States of Indonesia lead Dutch to create a State of East Indonesia

1947, July · Dutch pursue military operations to resolve differences by force

1948, September–October · Communist leaders launch revolt in Central Java to take over the revolution but are suppressed by troops of the republic

1948, December 19 · Dutch initiate "second police action" in Yogyakarta and capture most of the Indonesian cabinet

1949, December 27 · Pressure by the UN and the United States leads to Dutch transfer of power to the United States of Indonesia (USI)

1950, August 17 · With a new constitution endorsed by the USI and the federation dissolved, Sukarno is enabled to proclaim a unitary state, the Republic of Indonesia

1952, October 17 · Army indiscipline over command and support threatens the government and leads to suspension of General Nasution as army chief of staff

1948–62 · Darul Islam revolts begin in West Java and spread to other provinces; they conclude with the execution of Kartosoewiryo, its leader

1955, April · Asia-Africa Conference in Bandung attracts Zhou Enlai, Nehru, Nasser, Tito, and others; first conference of the Non-Aligned Movement

1955, September · Indonesia's only free general national election before 1999; support for the parties was widely distributed, with four obtaining 16–22 percent each of the vote and the remainder split among 24 parties

1957, March–1961, August · Regional rebellions in Sumatra and Sulawesi

1958, May 18 · Allen Pope shot down over Ambon, revealing American covert support of regional rebellions, and concluding the Dulles brothers' failure to subvert Sukarno's government

1950s/60s · Military articulation of doctrines of *dwifungsi* and *hankamrata:* of military role in sociopolitical development as well as security; and requirement that resources of the people be at the call of the armed forces

1959, July 5 · With the support of the armed forces, Sukarno dissolves the Constituent Assembly, reintroduces Constitution of 1945 with strong presidential power, and assumes additional role of prime minister, completing structure of "Guided Democracy"

1963 · National Parliament elects Sukarno "President-for-life"

1963, May · UN and Kennedy government press Dutch to yield West Irian (Papua) to temporary UN supervision

1963–65 · Sole years of the American Peace Corps program in Indonesia

1963–65 · Sukarno-led "confrontation" with Malaysia

1965, January · Indonesia withdraws from membership in the UN

1965, September 30/October 1 · Attempted coup fails; successful counter-coup leads to murder of perhaps half a million Communists and their sympathizers in the next several months

1966, March 11 · General Suharto forces delegation of acting presidential power to himself and proceeds to dissolve the Indonesian Communist Party

1967 · New investment law designed to bring in foreign capital passes; restrictions regarding Chinese status, names, and worship decreed

1968, March · MPRS confers full presidential title on Suharto; Sukarno now under effective house arrest

1968–71 · Period of the ambassadorship of Soedjatmoko to the United States and warming of bilateral relations

1969 · Papuan representatives, in coerced "Act of Free Choice," agree to join Indonesia

1970, June 21 · Death of Sukarno; followed by burial in Blitar, East Java

1970 · Young Muslim modernist, Nurcholish Madjid, begins to lay out religious developmental principles for Indonesia—"Islam, yes; Islamic party, no"

1971 · Mrs. Suharto, inspired by a visit to Disneyland, conceives a national cultural theme park

1973 · Forced fusion of Nationalist and Christian parties into PDI and Muslim parties into PPP, in a three-party system dominated by Golkar

1974, January · The "Malari" uprising in Jakarta against Japanese penetration of the economy, Chinese-Indonesian influence, and official corruption

1975, April · Mrs. Suharto dedicates vast theme park on outskirts of Jakarta: "Beautiful Indonesia-in-Miniature Park" (Taman Mini)

1975, August · Civil war breaks out in former Portuguese colony of East Timor

1975, December 6 · President Ford and Secretary of State Kissinger, returning from China, make hastily scheduled one-day visit to Jakarta

1975, December 7 · After departure of American official team, Indonesia launches long-planned invasion of East Timor

1976, March · General Ibnu Sutowo is "dismissed with honor" after a decade as head of his fiefdom, Pertamina, the state oil corporation

1976, July 17 · Suharto signs bill integrating East Timor into Indonesia

1976, November 19 · UN General Assembly rejects Indonesia's annexation and calls for an act of self-determination to be held in East Timor

1977 · United States surpasses Japan as Indonesia's biggest oil customer

1977, October · The trial of Sawito Kartowibowo for "subversion" begins

1978 · MPR elevates Pancasila to the status of compulsory moral education of youth and government officials

1978 · Suharto appoints B. J. Habibie state minister of research and technology

1979, December · Release of the writer Pramoedya Ananta Toer, after fourteen years of imprisonment on Buru Island, with hard labor

1980, May · The Petition of Fifty: a statement of concern to parliament about use of government power, propaganda, and presidential personality cult

1982–83 · Height of *Petrus*: "mysterious shootings" of thousands of suspected criminals by government security forces

1983 · Marriage of Prabowo Subianto, then a major in ABRI, to Suharto's daughter Titiek at Taman Mini

1984, September 12 · Tanjung Priok: Muslims demonstrate against security forces for insensitivities to Islam; many deaths in ensuing riot mark a new stage in Indonesian political consciousness

1984, December · In Situbondo, East Java, Abdurrahman Wahid (Gus Dur) is elected chairman of Nahdlatul Ulama, a position held previously by his father and grandfather

1985 · Indonesian government requires all associations of any kind to adopt *Pancasila* as their sole basis

1986 · *Challenger* disaster blocks Pratiwi's progress toward being an astronaut aloft with an American crew

1987 · Megawati Sukarnoputri becomes a member of parliament; President Suharto prohibits display of any images of former President Sukarno, which nonetheless appear frequently

1988 · Suharto elected to fifth term as president

1989 · Reemergence of GAM (Free Aceh Movement), first organized in 1976; suppression of its guerrilla activities leads to 2000 deaths by 1991 in Aceh province

1991 · Indonesia succeeds in winning presidency of the Non-Aligned Movement

1991, November 12 · ABRI troops fire upon demonstrative funeral procession in Dili; TV images of killings put East Timor high on international human rights agenda

1992 · Suharto successfully defies Dutch effort to link human rights to aid administered since 1967 by IGGI (International Governmental Group on Indonesia)

1992–93 · Capture by Prabowo, trial and sentencing of Xanana (Jose Alexandre) Gusmão, leader of East Timorese resistance

1993 · Suharto seeks a sixth term, despite having stated in his autobiography (1989) his inclination to retire; easily reelected by his rigged electoral system

1994, June · Suharto shuts down *Tempo* and two other publications for their critical reporting on Habibie's purchase of the fleet of the former East German navy

1996 · OPM (Free Papua Movement), which had arisen in the 1960s, hits international news by kidnapping fourteen scientists and foresters in Irian Jaya; after four months, abductees are rescued by a Prabowo-led unit in a bloody operation

1996, April · Ibu Tien Suharto, the president's wife of 48 years, dies of a heart attack

1996, July · Military-backed thugs burst into headquarters of PDI, Megawati's party, and evict her supporters as violent climax to government efforts to vitiate her party's popularity

1997, February · Suharto, alarmed by a *dukun's* warning that "the nail of Java has come loose," commands a massive *Ruat Dunia* ceremony (Cleansing of the World) near Borobudur

1997, June · Trade winds reverse over the Pacific, indicating onset of El Niño; severe drought hits much of Indonesia in ensuing months, with highly destructive fires, until rains of April 1998

1997, July · Collapse of Thai *baht* expands into an Asian financial crisis; Indonesia, the most severely afflicted, suffers a decline of equities and currency which, combined, slash asset values 91 percent by September 1998

1997–98 · Rising social firestorms in Indonesian cities, against Chinese, Christians, symbols of wealth, police, and bureaucracy—targets of violence varying by local circumstances

1998, February 23 · Women of *Suara Ibu Peduli* (Voice of Concerned Mothers) are arrested for public prayers on behalf of hungry babies; their demonstration indicates female and middle-class arousal against the regime

1998, March 11 · Suharto accepts unanimous election by the MPR to his seventh term; Habibie is his vice president

1998, late March · Student demonstrations against the regime rise to national prominence; on the whole they are peaceably sustained

1998, May 12 · Four demonstrating students at Trisakti University are shot dead by bullets from still unproven source

1998, May 13 · Memorial service for slain students leads to vandalism, arson, looting, and rape by roving mobs which continues, unchecked by army or police, until May 15, leaving nearly 1,200 dead

1998, May 20 · For National Awakening Day, Amien Rais pledges to bring a million protesters to demonstrate at the National Monument, but faced with barbed wire and massed troops, he calls off the rally to prevent bloodshed

1998, May 21, 9 AM · Suharto, deserted by his own cabinet and parliament, gives over the presidency to Habibie

1998, August · General Wiranto announces the discharge of Lieutenant General Prabowo from active duty, with full pension benefits—and without court-martial for abduction and torture of student activists (some of whom remain missing)

1998, November 10 · Megawati, Rais, and the sultan of Yogya, meet at Wahid's home in Ciganjur, issue series of reform statements, including demand for an end to the military's role in politics in six years

1998, November 13 · On last day of the MPR sessions, soldiers open fire on mass of protesting students, leaving at least fifteen dead and hundreds injured; killings are still uninvestigated

1998, November 22 · Violence erupts between Muslims and Christians in Ketapang, North Jakarta, and spreads to West Timor

1998–99 · Wahid, spurred by a contingent of "hidden *kiai*," undertakes seven visits to Suharto to emulate Qur'anic example of Moses confronting Pharaoh; but if the ex-president was a major source of "*wayang* wars" and destabilizing violence, Gus Dur's visits accomplished no change

1999, January 19 · Petty ruckus on the island of Ambon sets off Muslim-Christian clashes that escalate for three years in the province of Maluku: as many as 10,000 estimated dead, and 700,000 persons displaced—one-third of the province

1999, June 7 · First free and fair national election since 1955 takes place with minimal disruption and wide participation, but distribution of the vote among 48 parties leaves parliamentary election of president in doubt

1999, September · "Popular consultation," or referendum on the future of East Timor, is conducted under UN auspices, as promised by Habibie earlier in the year; four-fifths of the ballots are for independence rather than integration with Indonesia; pro-integration militias, trained and paid by ABRI, immediately resort to murder, abductions, and other violent tactics; on September 13, Habibie finally invites a UN peacekeeping force to restore order for transition to independence (accomplished in 2002)

1999, October · In a meeting of parliament, Habibie's accountability speech is rejected; Wahid, whose party had gathered one-eighth of popular vote, is elected president; Megawati, whose party drew one-third of the ballots, is elected vice president

2000, Christmas Eve · Coordinated bombings in more than three dozen sites in Indonesia, later proven to be planned by Jemaah Islamiyah in retaliation for Christian killings of Muslims in Maluku

2000–01 · President Wahid's administration is marred by failures to privatize or attract investment; by patterns of political favoritism and economic corruption reminiscent of pre-*reformasi* era; by inability to reform the military; by personal eccentricity and pettiness; by ineffectiveness in dealing with major religious violence in Maluku and Sulawesi, major ethnic violence (Dyaks vs. Madurese) in West and Central Kalimantan, and separatisms in Aceh and Irian Jaya

2001, July · Wahid is impeached, chiefly on grounds of incompetence; parliament elects Megawati president, 592–0; for the vice presidency, Hamzah Haz defeats Akbar Tandjung and Lieutenant General (ret.) Bambang Yudhoyono

2001, September · President Megawati visits President Bush a week after terrorist attacks on the World Trade Center and the Pentagon and speaks in New York and Houston, welcoming American investment; on return home, the Islamic right attacks her for cooperation in America's war in Afghanistan, and the nationalist left criticizes her for being too suppliant to foreign investors

2002 · Nahdlatul Ulama and Muhammadiyah, the largest Muslim organizations in Indonesia, issue joint statements critical of militant Islamists

2002, January · Floods hit urban centers, crippling Jakarta, Medan, and Palembang

2002, February · Peace talks in Malino, South Sulawesi, sponsored by Jusuf Kalla, Coordinating Minister for People's Welfare, appear to end three years of Christian-Muslim violence in Maluku and Poso

2002, July · Tommy Suharto is sentenced to 15 years in jail for illegal possession of arms, contempt of law, and masterminding assassination of a Supreme Court judge who had convicted him for graft

2002, September · House Speaker Akbar Tandjung is sentenced to three years for corruption

2002, October 12 · Bombs in Kuta, Bali, kill 202 people, the largest terrorist attack since September 11, 2001, in the United States; Indonesian police, aided by ten nations, subsequently track down Jemaah Islamiyah operatives whose Jihad had become international

2002, November · Eurico Guterres is sentenced to 10 years in prison for crimes committed following 1999 ballot in East Timor

2002, December · In Geneva, Indonesian government and GAM sign peace accord aiming to end decades of violence in Aceh

SOURCES

Books, Newspapers, Periodicals, and E-Sources

The best general history is M. C. Ricklefs, *A History of Modern Indonesia since c. 1200* (Stanford: Stanford University Press, 3rd ed., 2001). Anthony Reid's *Southeast Asia in the Age of Commerce, 1450–1680*, 2 vols. (New Haven: Yale University Press, 1988–1993), is invaluable for time perspective and regional context. Robert Cribb and Colin Brown's *Modern Indonesia: A History since 1945* (London: Longman, 1995) is short and soundly proportioned. Although not available in English, Shiraishi Takashi has also accomplished a short modern history with his *Sukaluno to Suhaluto: Indainaru Indoneshia wo Mezashite* [Sukarno and Suharto: Aiming for a Greater Indonesia] (Tokyo: Iwanami Shoten, 1997). Lontar Foundation will publish a history of the New Order, composed chiefly of contributions by Indonesian actors and observers and edited by Jeffrey Hadler.

John Legge's *Sukarno: A Political Biography* (New York: Praeger, 1972) has stood up splendidly since the death of his subject. Legge has recently pulled together short fertile essays by divers authorities, *Sukarno in Retrospect* (Clayton, Monash University Press, 2002). R. E. Elson's *Suharto: A Political Biography* (Cambridge, UK: Cambridge University Press, 2001) is a sound and valuable assessment. John Bresnan, *Managing Indonesia: The Modern Political Economy* (New York: Columbia University Press, 1993), is particularly good on the 1970s and '80s. Adam Schwarz, originally a correspondent for the *Far East Economic Review,* produced *A Nation in Waiting: Indonesia's Search for Stability* (Boulder: Westview Press, 2nd ed., 2000), which is unsurpassed for the 1990s. Another work of high journalism is Michael Vatikiotis, *Indonesian Politics under Suharto* (London: Routledge, 3rd ed., 1998). Donald K. Emmerson has assembled expert essayists, including his ever notable self, in *Indonesia beyond Suharto: Polity, Economy, Society, Transition* (Armonk, NY, The Asia Society and M. E. Sharpe, 1999). Leo Suryadinata, *Elections and Politics in Indonesia* (Singapore: Institute of Southeast Asian Studies, 2002), provides a half century of data and perspective. Kees Van Dijk, *A Country in Despair: Indonesia between 1997 and 2000* (Leiden: KITLV Press, 2001), is a compendious narrative of the subject. Kevin O'Rourke, *Reformasi: The Struggle for Power in Post-Soeharto Indonesia* (New South Wales: Allen and Unwin, 2002), has an intimate feel for the brief "reform" period, with a searching critique of the military.

All of Clifford Geertz's writings on Indonesian anthropology are awakening to read. His classic *The Religion of Java* (Glencoe: Free Press, 1960) is still a takeoff point for discussion of class, belief, and tones of feeling, by successors who offer different schema. Robert W. Hefner's *Civil Islam: Muslims and Democratization in Indonesia* (Princeton: Princeton University Press, 2000) uses both social anthropology and historical sociology in working to an upbeat conclusion.

Works of several other kinds are also helpful in asking why things happen as they do in Indonesia: Sartono Kartodirdjo, *Modern Indonesia: Tradition and Transformation* (Yogyakarta: Gadjah Mada University Press, 1991); William Liddle, *Leadership and Culture in Indonesian Politics* (Sydney: Allen and Unwin, 1996); and Damien Kingsbury, *The Politics of Indonesia* (Melbourne: Oxford University Press, 1998).

Corruption by power and corrosion through greed occur in all cultures and escape analysis by "–ism." On capitalism, Richard Robison, *Indonesia: The Rise of Capital* (Sydney: Allen and Unwin, 1986), and Jeffrey Winters, *Power in Motion: Capital Mobility and the Indonesian State* (Ithaca: Cornell University Press, 1996), are nevertheless interesting.

John Pemberton, *On the Subject of "Java"* (Ithaca: Cornell University Press, 1994), is stimulating on manipulation of culture by the New Order to form a "culture state." Among several recent works on violence, the greatest variety and historical depth is offered by essayists in Freek Columbijn and J. Thomas Lindblad, eds., *Roots of Violence in Indonesia* (Leiden: KITLV Press, 2002).

Anne Booth, *The Indonesian Economy in the Nineteenth and Twentieth Centuries: A History of Missed Opportunities* (New York: St. Martin's, 1998), and Hal Hill, *The Indonesian Economy* (New York: Cambridge University Press, 2nd ed., 2000), are both authoritative, the latter on the Suharto era only. For meaning and value in development statistics, two works are fertile: Amartya Sen, *Development as Freedom* (New York: Knopf, 1999) and United Nations Development Program and Arab Fund for Economic and Social Development, *Arab Human Development Report 2002,* (New York: UNDP, 2002).

The late Herbert Feith's magisterial *The Decline of Constitutional Democracy in Indonesia* (Ithaca: Cornell University Press, 1962) may be complemented by the provocative essays in David Bourchier and John Legge, eds., *Democracy in Indonesia: 1950's and 1990's* (Clayton, Victoria: Monash University Centre of Southeast Asian Studies, 1994). Feith, when asked why he never produced a sequel to his great work, is quoted as saying, "I suppose I didn't think I could bring myself to be fair to the Army." Harold Crouch achieved penetration and objectivity on the army's first thirty years in *The Army and Politics in Indonesia* (Ithaca: Cornell University Press, 1978; 2nd ed. 1988). His writings since include the excellent Jakarta dispatches, post-Suharto, of the International Crisis Group, available online. Sydney Jones took over and strongly sustained these responsibilities in 2002.

The late George McT. Kahin, like Feith, through heights of discipline and depths of benignity, enjoys a lasting productivity through his many students. To mention just two among their countless works: Benedict R. O'Gorman Anderson, *Java in a Time of Revolution* (Ithaca: Cornell University Press, 1972), and Daniel S. Lev and Ruth McVey, eds., *Making Indonesia: Essays on Modern Indonesia in Honor of George McT. Kahin* (Ithaca: Cornell Southeast Asia Program, 1996).

As a team using the Freedom of Information Act, Audrey R. Kahin with her husband George wrote *Subversion as Foreign Policy: The Secret Eisenhower and Dulles Debacle in Indonesia* (New York: The New Press, 1995). Paul F. Gardner tries to put that "costly 'covert' operation" into perspective with a history based on many interviews and State Department documents: *Shared Hopes, Separate Fears: Fifty Years of U.S.-Indonesian Relations* (Boulder: Westview Press, 1997). An abundance of other Indonesian, Australian, Japanese, Southeast Asian, Dutch, and other European, as well as American, expert writing in various fields can be tracked through my notes.

Newspapers and periodicals are invaluable for recent history. Foreign correspondence suffered a brief setback when David Jenkins's dispatch comparing Suharto to Marcos (1986) resulted in temporary expulsion of all Australian journalists from Indonesia. But such standards of vigorous inquiry and candid reporting prevailed over time in writers for the Sydney *Morning Herald, The Age* (Melbourne), *The* (Singapore) *Straits Times, The South China Morning Post* (Hong Kong); not to mention *The New York Times,* the *Washington Post,* regional papers like the San Jose (CA) *Mercury News,* and international services like Agence France Presse and Reuters. Among Indonesian dailies, *The Jakarta Post* and *Kompas* are outstanding, and *Republika* is trenchant from a Muslim point of view. Freedom for the press has expanded the field since 1998.

As a weekly, *Tempo* has been the leader since its beginning, despite its four-year suppression (1994–1998). The philosophy of its founding editor and the range of his subtle thinking are available in Goenawan Mohamad, *Sidelines,* Jennifer Lindsay, trans. (Jakarta: Lontar Foundation, 1994). Janet Steele is working on a history of *Tempo,* which promises to be a fine lens for review of its times. Of regional weeklies, *The Far East Economic Review, Asiaweek* (until its financial death in 2001), and *The Asian Wall Street Journal* are steadily revealing. All of these and other publications are culled by *joyo news service,* which nightly has generated three dozen or more articles as a public service to worldwide subscribers (joyo@aol.com). Professor Dr. Mohammad Sadli, in turn, has selected three or more *joyo* or other items daily for his own subscription list (sadli@pacific.net). Professor Edwin Aspinall manages an excellent electronic "I-discussion" on Indonesian issues. The *Van Zorge Report* has established a special niche as a candid biweekly on the political economy, with high-profile interviews and commentary. For relief from the fever of the quotidian, there are several scholarly quarterlies in the field and the indispensable biannual, *Indonesia,* published since 1966 by the Cornell Southeast Asia Program.

Interviews

In *The Blue-Eyed Enemy* (Princeton: Princeton University Press, 1988), I listed nearly one hundred Indonesians, Dutch, and Japanese I interviewed on colonial backgrounds and revolution. For the present book I have additionally interviewed the persons listed below. Titles are provided for time of interview, or highest previous position. Two asterisks indicate two interviews; three indicate more than that or continuing conversations. Only two persons contacted were "too busy" to be interviewed: former President B. J. Habibie, after seven weeks' notice, and former Secretary of State Henry Kissinger, after ten weeks' notice. I made attempts to interview Tutut Suharto, Mo. "Bob" Hasan, Liem Sioe Liong, and Prajoga Pangestu, but in each case well-placed intermediaries were unwilling to help. Confidentiality, when asked for, has been preserved and in several instances has been extended even when not requested. Numerous valuable in-conference dialogues may be cited in the notes but are not classified as interviews. Persons already thanked in the preface are not, as a rule, additionally included here.

Dir./Prof. Taufik Abdullah, Min. Tanri Abeng, Dr. Anggito Abimanyu, Petrus Alamet, Ali Al-Gadri, Desi Anwar, Dr. Dewi Fortuna Anwar***, Gordon Bishop***, Col. George Benson***, Mng. Dir. Carter Booth, Mochtar Buchori, Patrick Burgess, James Castle**, John G. Christy**, Dr. Harold Crouch, Robert and Maya Dakan**, Col. Joseph Daves**, Dr. Soedjati Djiwandono, Gov. J. Sudradjad Djiwandono, Min. Sumitro Djojohadikusumo***, Mark Dodd, Vaudine England, Fajrul Falaakh and Ratih Harjono-Falaakh, Prof. Herbert Feith, Amb. Robert S. Gelbard***, Ken Gibson**, Goenawan Mohamad, Dr. Edward Green, Aniseto Guterres-Lopez, S. H., Pres. Ismid and Chairperson Tini Hadad, Alamsjah Hamdani, Sultan Hamengkubuwono X, Col. John B. Haseman, Bara Hasibuan**, Lt. Gen. Abdullah Makhmud Hendropriyono, Sidney Jones, Prof. George McT. Kahin, Prof. Dr. Sartono Kartodirdjo**, Dir. Utama Aristides Katoppo, Everett Keech, Dra. Wahidar Khaidir, Exec. Dir. M. S. Kismadi, Marla Kosec***, Elizabeth Ary Krisnawati***, Rektor Dr. Nurcholish Madjid***, Omi Komaria Madjid, Min. Sarwono Kusumaatmadja***, Prof. Karlina and Dr. Ninok Leksono, Harvey Leve, CEO Budi Lim, Dr. Ir. Mochammad Maksum, Prof. Dr. Franz Magnis-Suseno, SJ***, Fr. Y. B. Mangunwijaya**, Teten Masduki, Rear Adm. A. A. Kustia**, Amb. Edward Masters, Amb. John McCarthy, Col. C. Don McFetridge, Gen. L. B. "Benny" Moerdani, Frank B. Morgan, Maj. Gen. Joko Mulani, K. H. Hasyim Muzadi, Gen. Abdul Haris Nasution, Buyung Nasution, S. H., Mark A. Nelson, Dir. Gen. Nugroho Wisnumurti, Yoke Octarina, Prof. Dr. Ong Hok Ham**, Col. William D. Patton, Dr. Pramoedja Rahardjo**, Pramoedja Ananta Toer, Aras Parura, Dr. Amien Rais**, Dr. Mochtar Riady, Amb. J. Stapleton Roy***, Amb. Sabam P. Siagian**, Min. Mohamad Sadli**, Dir. Felia Salim, Min. Emil Salim***, Dr. Selosoemardjan, Dr. Alexander Shakow, Dr. Nizar Shihab, Min. Alwi Shihab***, Maj. Gen. Sudi Silalahi, Min. Siswono Yudohusodo, Dr. Sjahrir, Soebadio Sastrosatomo, Pres. Dir. Soedarpo Sastrosatomo, Galuh Soedjatmoko***, Prof. Dr. Loekman Soetrisno**, Pres. Dir. Rini J. S. Soewandi**, Stella Maria, Endo Suanda, Min. Juwono Sudarsono***, Dr. Pratiwi Sudarmono**, Min. Laksamana Sukardi, Vice Pres. Megawati Sukarnoputri, Amb. Suryo Bambang Sulisto, Amb. Ilen Surianegara, Dr. Nasir Tamara**, Luis Varese, Jeremy Wagstaff, President K. H. Abdurrahman Wahid***, Chair/CEO Sofjan Wanandi**, Christianto Wibisono, Lt. Gen. Susilo Bambang Yudhoyono, Norma Zecha**, Dr. Mary Zurbuchen.

Photographs and Other Images

For the Japanese and revolutionary periods, I am immensely grateful to my late friend Niels Douwes-Dekker, who thirty years ago gave me a number of prints and negatives from his private collection. I subsequently persuaded him to donate the vast remainder of his holdings to Cornell University, where it is now splendidly catalogued and accessible in the Kroch Library, Division of Rare and Manuscript Collections. I have also benefited from the help of photo archivists at *Tempo*, Ipphos, and the Arsip Negara (National Archives). The Fairfax Photo Library in Sydney and Magnum Photos in New York (especially Malli Kamimura) were hospitable in like ways. Among skilled amateur photographers, Byron Black, Marla Kosec, and Jody Dharmawan have generously helped me open the reader's eyes to various Indonesian people and moments. Kemal Jufri took time out of his journalistic travel assignments to provide some splendid action shots of recent public significance. Photographers are individually credited next to the photo in every case when their names are known.

Anne Kinney, Helen Jessup, and Dirk Bakker advised me on classic statuary. For three decorative illustrations preceding parts of this book, I appreciate photographic permission of the Asia society, and from the owner of the original objects—The Museum Nasional of Jakarta. Sidup Damiri provided excellent transparencies of works of art and other subjects. John Briggeman of Wayne Motophoto scanned many dozens of images for me. Scott Miller of Sanchez Design was a patient technician and consulting advisor through several stages of preparing the whole program of illustrations. I commissioned two works of art especially for this book: the Sivaite Tetrad, designed and rendered by Kathë Chapman Grinstead; and the verses from the Holy Qur'an, in calligraphy and illumination designed by Achmad Haldani and his team in Bandung.

NOTES

Prologue: The Largest Muslim Nation

1. Quotations from interview with Dr. Nurcholish Madjid, 27 Oct. 98. A full story of what followed is in Chapter 12, below.

2. I am indebted to Robert Cribb's powerfully informative *Historical Atlas of Indonesia* (Honolulu: University of Hawaii Press, 2000). I have also drawn on *The Times Atlas of the World,* 7th and 10th comprehensive eds. (New York: Times Books/Random House, 1985, 2000). Tim Severin, *The Spice Islands Voyage* (New York: Carroll & Graf, 1997), has retraced the travels of Alfred Russel Wallace. Gavin Daws and Marty Fujita's beautifully illustrated *Archipelago: The Islands of Indonesia* (Berkeley: University of California Press, 1999) appreciates Wallace's place in intellectual history and is driven by concern for conservation of Indonesia's biodiversity. For anthropological data I have used Cribb, pp. 30–31, and William H. Frederick and Robert L. Worden, *Indonesia: A Country Study* (Washington, DC: Federal Research Division/Library of Congress, 5th ed., 1993), pp. 99, 354–356.

3. Julia Day Howell, "Sufism and the Indonesian Islamic Revival," *Journal of Asian Studies,* 60, 3 (Aug. 01), pp. 701–729.

4. Most notably, Robert W. Hefner, *Civil Islam: Muslims and Democratization in Indonesia* (Princeton: Princeton University Press, 2000); and essays in Nakamura Mitsuo, Sharon Siddique, and Omar Farouk Bajunid, *Islam and Civil Society in Southeast Asia* (Singapore: Institute of Southeast Asian Studies, 2001).

5. Jan Fontein, *The Sculpture of Indonesia* (Washington/New York: National Gallery of Art/Harry N. Abrams, 1990), p. 160.

6. Anthony J. S. Reid, "Political Tradition in Indonesia: The One and the Many," *Asian Studies Review,* 22, 1 (Mar. 98), pp. 23–38.

7. Characteristic tastes of these problems are available in: Onghokham, "The Inscrutable and the Paranoid: An Investigation into the Sources of the Brotodiningrat Affair," in Ruth McVey, ed., *Southeast Asian Transitions: Approaches through Social History* (New Haven: Yale University Press, 1978), pp. 112–157; Ingrid Wessel and Georgia Wimhofer, eds., *Violence in Indonesia* (Hamburg: Abera, 2001); Henk Schulte Nordholt shows the association of power and crime since the colonial period in "A Genealogy of Violence," Freek Colombijn and J.

Thomas Lindblad, eds., *Roots of Violence in Indonesia* (Leiden: KITLV Press, 2002), pp. 33–61; Daniel Lev, "Between State and Society: Professional Lawyers and Reform in Indonesia," Daniel Lev and Ruth McVey, eds., *Making Indonesia: Essays on Modern Indonesia in Honor of George McT. Kahin* (Ithaca: Cornell Studies on Southeast Asia, 1996), pp. 144–163.

8. Jaime C. Bulatao, S.J., "Split-Level Christianity," pp. 22–31; "Westernization and the Split-Level Personality in the Filipino," pp. 244–250; and "Another Look at Philippine Values," pp. 282–288, in *Phenomena and Their Interpretation: Landmark Essays, 1957–1989* (Quezon City: Ateneo de Manila Press, 1992), quotation, p. 22.

9. Fareed Zakaria, "The Rise of Illiberal Democracy," *Foreign Affairs,* 76, 6 (Nov./Dec. 97), pp. 22–43.

10. Clifford Geertz, "Soekarno Daze," *Latitudes,* 8 (Sept. 01), pp. 10–15, quotations, pp. 11, 10.

11. Extensive research discloses that such a statement actually came from a European contemporary of the great Chinese admiral Zheng He. The Venetian nobleman, Nicolò de Conti, travelled and traded in Asia, 1419–1444, and on return dictated his impressions to the papal secretary. Of Java, he said it "possessed the most cruel people in the world. They thought nothing of killing a man, and crimes went unpunished . . . The purchaser of a new knife tried it on the first person whom he met, and was not penalized." J.V.G. Mills, trans. and ed., Ma Huan, *The Overall Survey of the Ocean Shores* (Cambridge: Cambridge University Press, 1970), p. 64. I am grateful to Profs. Merle Ricklefs and Ben Stavis for directing me to the relevant literature.

1. Indonesia, the Devouring Nurturer

1. My inspiration for these thoughts is the novel by Y. B. Mangunwijaya, *Durga Umayi* (Jakarta: Pustaka Utama Grafiti, 1991). A splendid commentary on it is Michael H. Bodden, "Woman as Nation in Mangunwijaya's *Durga Umayi,*" *Indonesia* 64 (Oct. 97), pp. 53–82. On Siva: Stella Kramrisch, *The Presence of Siva* (Princeton: Princeton University Press, 1981), and *Manifestations of Siva* (Philadelphia: Philadelphia Museum of Art, 1981), passim. On Durga: Claire Holt, *The Art of Indonesia: Continued Change* (Ithaca: Cornell University Press, 1967), passim; Bodden, p. 67n49.

2. In these remarks on mandala history, I am inspired by O. W. Wolters, *History, Culture and Religion in Southeast Asian Perspective* (Ithaca: Cornell University Southeast Asia Publications, rev. ed., 1999; 1st ed., Singapore: Institute of Southeast Asian Studies, 1982), esp. pp. 11–67; quotations, pp. 27–28, 29 (I. W. Mabbett), and 39 (Paul Wheatley).

3. Paul Wheatley's brilliant geo-cartographical history from the early Common Era to the Portuguese conquest of Malacca contains helpful metaphors of other scholars about cities centroid to semi-states: "torches flaring and fading in political space" (Soemarsaid Moertono), and "suns to which their kingdoms were but haloes" (Theodore G. Th. Pigeaud): *Nágara and Commandery: Origins of the Southeast Asian Urban Traditions* (Chicago: University of Chicago, 1983), p. 429.

4. Anthony Reid, "Political Tradition in Indonesia: The One and the Many," *Asian Studies Review,* 22, 1 (Mar. 98), pp. 23–38, quotation, p. 29.

5. Ibid., passim, esp. pp. 29, 32–33, 34; Jane Drakard, *A Kingdom of Words: Language and Power in Sumatra* (New York: Oxford University Press, 1999), pp. 247, 262–267.

6. Wolters, *History, Culture and Religion,* pp. 139–142.

7. S. Supomo, "The Image of Majapahit in Later Javanese and Indonesian Writing," Anthony Reid and David Marr, eds., *Perceptions of the Past in Southeast Asia* (Singapore: Heineman, 1979), pp. 171–185. To allude to the images of a nationalist like Muhammad Yamin is not to concede his fantasies, but to recognize that late fourteenth-century Majapahit was an unusually strong power center. It was described by the poet-courtier Mpu Prapañca in *Deśawarṇana (Nāgarakṛtāgama),* Stuart Robson, trans. (Leiden: KITLV Press, 1995).

8. The phrase is from Wolters, p. 141.

9. Quotations from F. M. Schnitger, *Forgotten Kingdoms in Sumatra* (Leiden: E. J. Brill, 1964; 1st ed., 1938), pp. 30, 31. Suleiman, "Sculptures of Ancient Sumatra: Arca-Arca di Sumatra Pada Zaman Purba" (Jakarta: Pusat Penelitran Arkeologi Nasional, 1982). For the historicity of Adityavarman, see M. C. Ricklefs, *A History of Modern Indonesia since c. 1200* (Palo Alto: Stanford University Press, 3rd ed., 2001; 1st ed., 1981), p. 182.

10. Ricklefs, *Modern Indonesia,* chs. 11–13, esp. p. 189; Reid, "Political Tradition," passim.

11. Reid, "Political Tradition," p. 35.

12. Ricklefs, *Modern Indonesia,* p. 189.

13. K. M. Pannikar's *Asia and Western Dominance: A Survey of the Vasco da Gama Epoch of Asian History, 1498–1945* (London: George Allen and Unwin, 1953; rev. ed., 1959) is to some degree India-bounded, hence blinded to East Timor.

14. *Sukarno: An Autobiography,* as told to Cindy Adams (Indianapolis: Bobbs-Merrill, 1965), pp. 19–21. The process of composition of the autobiography and side-revelations are detailed in Cindy Adams, *My Friend the Dictator* (Indianapolis: Bobbs-Merrill, 1967). J. D. Legge, *Sukarno: A Biography* (New York: Praeger, 1972), assesses Sukarno's background, pp. 16–30, and gives balanced appraisal to Sukarno's assertions across the decades.

15. *Sukarno: An Autobiography,* pp. 22, 23.

16. Anne Booth, *The Indonesian Economy in the Nineteenth and Twentieth Centuries: A History of Missed Opportunities* (London: MacMillan, 1998), pp. 95, 100–101, 105–116, esp. pp. 113–114.

17. Ricklefs, *Modern Indonesia,* pp. 210–211.

18. *Sukarno: An Autobiography,* p. 39.

19. Ibid., p. 41.

20. Ibid., p. 82.

21. Ibid., pp. 24, 25, 121.

22. Ibid., pp. 110; 112–113.

23. John Ingleson, *Road to Exile: The Indonesian Nationalist Movement, 1927–1934* (Kuala Lumpur: Heineman, 1979), pp. 218–222.

24. *Sukarno: An Autobiography,* p. 92; Legge, *Sukarno,* pp. 101–102.

25. Theodore Friend, *The Blue-Eyed Enemy: Japan against the West in Java and Luzon, 1942–1945* (Princeton: Princeton University Press, 1988), pp. 82–84. *Sukarno: An Autobiography,* pp. 159–163.

26. *Sukarno: An Autobiography*, p. 164.

27. Friend, *Blue-Eyed Enemy*, p. 84.

28. Rudolf Mrázek, *Sjahrir: Politics and Exile in Indonesia* (Ithaca: Cornell University Southeast Asia Program, 1994), p. 384.

29. Friend, *Blue-Eyed Enemy*, pp. 191–193.

30. Ibid., pp. 193–197.

31. Ibid., pp. 162–166.

32. *Sukarno: An Autobiography*, p. 192; Adams, *My Friend the Dictator*, pp. 184–186.

33. Friend, *Blue-Eyed Enemy*, pp. 110–112, quotations, p. 110.

34. Ibid., pp. 113–114; Legge, *Sukarno*, pp. 185–187; Sukarno, *Autobiography*, pp. 197–199.

35. Friend, *Blue-Eyed Enemy*, pp. 117–120.

36. On the Japanese in Indonesia after surrender, Friend, ibid., pp. 218–222; on the Japanese in their homeland, John W. Dower, *Embracing Defeat: Japan in the Wake of World War II* (New York: W. W. Norton/The New Press, 1999).

37. Friend, *Blue-Eyed Enemy*, pp. 34 42.

38. Ibid., p. 240.

39. Ibid., p. 264.

40. Ibid., p. 265.

41. Interviews, Dr. Bahder Djohan, 14, 27 Mar. 68.

42. Interview, Pramoedya, 15 June 00. Pramoedya, *The Mute's Soliloquy: A Memoir* (New York: Hyperion East, 1999), describes living conditions under the Japanese: pp. 9–10, 36, 66, 181–182, 188–190, 193, 201, 250.

43. There exists a large literature on revolutionary politics and occasional combat in Java and on other islands. Without summoning it all here, I salute the masterly work of Benedict R. O'G. Anderson, *Java in a Time of Revolution: Occupation and Resistance, 1944–1946* (Ithaca: Cornell University Press, 1972). Also Robert Cribb, *Gangsters and Revolutionaries: The Jakarta People's Militia and the Indonesian Revolution, 1945–1949* (Honolulu: University of Hawaii Press, 1991). And for maps of changing conditions, Cribb, *Historical Atlas of Indonesia*.

44. This summary is condensed chiefly from Paul F. Gardner, *Shared Hopes, Separate Fears: Fifty Years of U.S.-Indonesian Relations* (Boulder, CO: Westview Press, 1997), pp. 75–94; Robert J. McMahon, *Colonialism and the Cold War: The United States and the Struggle for Indonesian Independence, 1945–1949* (Ithaca and London: Cornell University Press, 1981), pp. 251–328; George McT. Kahin, "The United States and the Anti-Colonial Revolutions in Southeast Asia, 1945–1950," in Yonosuke Nagai and Akira Iriye, eds., *The Origins of the Cold War in Asia* (New York/Tokyo: Columbia University Press/University of Tokyo Press, 1977), pp. 338–361; and Evelyn Speyer Colbert, *Southeast Asia in International Politics* (Ithaca and London: Cornell University Press, 1977), pp. 86–92. The most pronounced difference of opinion is between Kahin (quelling of Madiun revolt) and McMahon (second Dutch police action) as to the point in the Indonesian revolution where its fortunes turned to success. I believe that both these surges of American and international opinion, for the revolutionaries and against the Dutch, were necessary for the success of what was largely a diplomatic struggle.

45. Ricklefs, *Modern Indonesia*, p. 189, is the source for early twentieth-century data; Professor Pieter Drooglevers to Paul W. van der Veur, 27 July 98, generously for-

warded to me by the latter, 11 Aug. 98, for troops in 1947–48; and for total population at the latter time, in between widely separated censuses, I assign an estimate of 75 million, based on Ruth McVey, ed., *Indonesia* (New Haven: Human Relations Area Files Press, with Southeast Asia Studies, Yale University, 1963), table 1, pp. 14–15.

46. B. M. Diah, interview, 1 Dec. 83.
47. Sukarno, *Autobiography,* pp. 262–263.
48. Donald Petrie, interviews, 2 Sept. 99; 20 Aug., 1 Sept. 00.
49. Thomas Whiteside, "Upward and Onward with the Arts: Cable," *New Yorker,* 20 May 85, pp. 48–52, quotation, p. 48; Petrie interviews.
50. Robert Nathan, interview, 30 Nov. 99.
51. Dr. Sumitro Djojohadikusumo, interview, 3 Nov. 99.
52. Gerlof D. Homan, "American Business Interests in the Indonesian Republic, 1946–1949," *Indonesia,* 35 (Apr. 83), pp. 125–132, esp. pp. 126–128.
53. Alexander Shakow, "The Establishment of Indonesian Independence and Foreign Aid," ms. (1962), courtesy of Dr. Shakow; quotation, p. 5.
54. Sumitro interview.
55. Details from Shakow, "Independence and Foreign Aid," pp. 10–12; confirmed in general by Sumitro interview; quotation, Shakow, p. 13.
56. Sumitro interview.
57. Homan, "American Business," p. 131.
58. Shakow, "Independence and Foreign Aid," pp. 16–17.
59. Ibid., pp. 29–30.
60. Sumitro interview; Sudarpo Sastrosatomo interview, 29 Oct. 99.
61. Shakow, "Independence and Foreign Aid," pp. 29–31.
62. Salim Said, *Genesis of Power: General Sudirman and the Indonesian Military in Politics, 1945–1949* (Singapore: Institute of Southeast Asian Studies, 1991), pp. 3, 111–122, 130–131.
63. Sudarpo interview.
64. Shakow, "Independence and Foreign Aid," p. 31.
65. Sudarpo interview.
66. Sumitro and Sudarpo interviews. After I concluded my conversations with both men, their biographies were published: Aristides Katoppo, chief ed., *Jejak Perlawanan Begawan Pejuang* (A Champion Fighter's Resistance Trail) (Jakarta: Pustaka Sinar Harapan, 2000); Rosihan Anwar, *Tumbuh Melawan Arus* (Growth against the Tide) [A Biography, 1920–2001, of Soedarpo Sastrosatomo] (Jakarta: PDP Guntur 49, 2001).
67. Shakow, "Independence and Foreign Aid," pp. 41ff.
68. Sudarpo and Sumitro interviews; Nathan says that, net, Fox lost money; Homan, "American Business," p. 131n24.
69. Shakow, "Independence and Foreign Aid," pp. 58–60, quotations, p. 59.

2. Guided Chaos

1. Dr. Taufik Abdullah, "In Search of Democratic Order," 56-page draft (1999), pp. 3–13; interview, Dr. Taufik, 29 Oct. 99. See also Dr. Nurcholish Madjid, "The Potential Islamic Doctrinal Resources for the Establishment and Appreciation of

the Concept of Modern Civil Society," paper for Sasakawa Peace Foundation conference on "Islam and Civil Society, Messages from Southeast Asia," Ito City, Shizuoka, Japan, 5–6 Nov. 99.

2. Taufik, "Search," pp. 28–29, 32.

3. Ibid., pp. 43–44.

4. Ibid., p. 51, citing Herbert Feith and Lance Castles, eds., *Indonesian Political Thinking* (Ithaca: Cornell University Press, 1970), pp. 81–83.

5. C. L. M. Penders, ed., *Mohammad Hatta, Indonesian Patriot: Memoirs* (Singapore: Gunung Agung, 1981), pp. 241, 243, quotation, p. 241; Mavis Rose, *Indonesia Free: A Political Biography of Mohammad Hatta* (Ithaca: Cornell Modern Indonesia Project, 1987), pp. 124–125; Robert Cribb and Colin Brown, *Modern Indonesia: A History since 1945* (New York and London: Longman, 1995), p. 38.

6. Herbert Feith, *The Decline of Constitutional Democracy in Indonesia* (Ithaca: Cornell University Press, 1962), pp. 462–463, quotation, p. 463.

7. Ibid., pp. 428–431, quotation, p. 429.

8. Dr. Selosoemardjan, interview, 4 June 99.

9. Feith, *Decline*, p. 433.

10. Hildred Geertz, "Indonesian Cultures and Communities," in Ruth T. McVey, ed., *Indonesia* (New Haven: Yale University Southeast Asia Studies, HRAF Press, 1963), pp. 24–117, esp. pp. 48–49.

11. Feith, *Decline*, pp. 434–435, contains full election results.

12. Benedict R. O'G. Anderson, "Old State and New Society: Indonesia's New Order in Comparative Historical Perspective," in Anderson, *Language and Power: Exploring Political Culture in Indonesia* (Ithaca: Cornell University Press, 1990), pp. 94–120, esp. 98–102, quotation, p. 102.

13. David Bourchier and John Legge, eds., *Democracy in Indonesia: 1950s and 1990s* (Clayton: Monash University Centre of Southeast Asian Studies, 1994); Jamie Mackie, "Inevitable or Avoidable? Interpretations of the Collapse of Parliamentary Democracy," pp. 26–38, esp. p. 37; Harold Crouch, "Democratic Prospects in Indonesia," pp. 115–127, esp. p. 116.

14. Gilles Kepel, *Jihad: the Trail of Political Islam* (Cambridge: Harvard University Press, 2002), pp. 27–30, 292–298, and passim. Kepel discusses the Brotherhood in Afghanistan, Algeria, Jordan, Malaysia, Palestine, Saudi Arabia, and Sudan.

15. Dinas Sejarah, Tentara Nasional Indonesia, Angkatan Darat, *Penumpasan Pemberontakan DI/TII S. M. Kartosuwiryo Di Jawa Barat* [Extinguishing the Darul Islam Rebellion of S. M. Kartosuwiryo in West Java] (Bandung: Historical Section, Indonesian National Army Ground Forces, 1982), p. 142.

16. Cornelius Van Dijk, *Rebellion under the Banner of Islam: The Darul Islam in Indonesia* (The Hague: Martinus Nijhoff, 1981), pp. 28–29, 33, 41, 67–68.

17. Karl D. Jackson, *Traditional Authority, Islam, and Rebellion: A Study of Indonesian Political Behavior* (Berkeley: University of California Press, 1980), pp. 4–7, 128.

18. Van Dijk, *Banner of Islam*, pp. 4–9.

19. Jackson, *Traditional Authority*, p. 1, quotation, p. 17; Theodore Friend, *The Blue-Eyed Enemy: Japan against the West in Java and Luzon, 1942–1945* (Princeton: Princeton University Press, 1988), p. 242.

20. Sukarno, *Autobiography*, pp. 272–273; Sidney Jones, International Crisis Group, Jakarta, to the author, 28 Jan. 03.

21. Evelyn Colbert, *Southeast Asia in International Politics, 1941–1956* (Ithaca: Cornell University Press, 1977), pp. 311–333, quotations, pp. 331, 332.

22. Legge, *Sukarno,* pp. 263–266, quotation, p. 265; Evan Thomas, *The Very Best Men: Four Who Dared: The Early Years of the CIA* (New York: Simon and Schuster, 1995), p. 159.

23. Colbert, *Southeast Asia Politics,* ch. 12.

24. Audrey Kahin, *Rebellion to Integration: West Sumatra and the Indonesian Polity* (Amsterdam: Amsterdam University Press, 1999), pp. 178–183.

25. Ibid., pp. 184–186.

26. Pursued in detail by Audrey Kahin, *Rebellion to Integration;* Rose, *Indonesia Free;* and Barbara S. Harvey, *Permesta: Half a Rebellion* (Ithaca: Cornell Modern Indonesia Project, 1977).

27. Rose, *Indonesia Free,* p. 131.

28. Author's interviews with Hatta, Jakarta, 17 Feb. 68; Honolulu, 3 July 68.

29. Cribb and Brown, *Modern Indonesia,* p. 75.

30. Harvey, *Permesta,* p. 153, formulates this evaluation regarding Sulawesi, and I believe it applies to Sumatra as well.

31. Cribb and Brown, p. 80n13; see also Harvey, *Permesta,* p. 118n85.

32. Leonard Mosely, *Dulles: A Biography of Eleanor, Allen and John Foster Dulles and Their Family Network* (New York: The Dial Press/James Wade, 1978); Peter Grose, *Gentleman Spy: The Life of Allen Dulles* (Boston: Houghton Mifflin, 1994); W. Stephen Twing, *Myths, Models, and United States Foreign Policy* (Boulder: Lynne Rienner, 1998).

33. Audrey R. Kahin and George McT. Kahin, *Subversion as Foreign Policy: The Secret Eisenhower and Dulles Debacle in Indonesia* (Seattle: University of Washington Press, 1995), p. 75.

34. Ibid., p. 86.

35. Ibid., pp. 93–95.

36. Ibid., pp. 95, 97–98. The Kahins add the emphases in the quotation from p. 95. Allison's fate was like the detour suffered by the great Russian expert Charles Bohlen. Dulles mistrusted him and had him exiled as ambassador to the Philippines. There he conducted himself as a consummate professional. One of his admiring staff members said to me, even Dulles "can't turn a silk purse into a sow's ear." Personal conversations, Manila, 1957–1959.

37. PRRI = Revolutionary Government of the Republic of Indonesia (Sumatra); Permesta = Charter of Inclusive Struggle (Sulawesi).

38. Conboy and Morrison, *Feet to the Fire,* pp. 161–165.

39. Kahin and Kahin, *Subversion,* pp. 182–183; Conboy and Morrison, *Feet to the Fire,* pp. 145–146.

40. Kahin and Kahin, *Subversion,* pp. 179–182; Paul F. Gardner, *Shared Hopes, Separate Fears: Fifty Years of U.S.-Indonesian Relations* (Boulder: Westview Press, 1997), pp. 154–155. The incident is also touched on in Mosely, *Dulles Family,* pp. 437–438, and Grose, *Gentleman Spy,* pp. 453–454. "Life in secrets," Thomas, *The Very Best Men,* p. 380.

41. Kahin and Kahin, *Subversion,* pp. 206–208.

42. Conboy and Morrison, *Feet to the Fire,* pp. 35, 153, 157.

43. Harvey, *Permesta,* pp. 130–133. Sumitro, interview, 3 Nov. 99.

44. Kahin and Kahin, *Subversion*, p. 194, citing Daniel Lev, *Transition to Guided Democracy*, p. 171.

45. Y. B. Mangunwijaya, "The Indonesia Raya Dream and Its Impact on the Concept of Democracy," in David Bourchier and John Legge, eds., *Democracy in Indonesia: 1950s and 1990s* (Clayton, Victoria: Monash University Centre of Southeast Asian Studies, 1994), pp. 79–87, esp. pp. 82–86.

46. Salim Said, *Genesis of Power: General Sudirman and the Indonesian Military in Politics, 1945–1949* (Singapore: Institute of Southeast Asian Studies, 1991), p. 3. C. L. M. Penders and Ulf Sundhaussen, *Abdul Haris Nasution: A Political Biography* (St. Lucia: University of Queensland Press, 1985), chs. 1–2. Benedict R. O'G. Anderson, *Java in a Time of Revolution: Occupation and Resistance, 1944–1946* (Ithaca: Cornell University Press, 1972), pp. 245–247.

47. Quotations from Penders and Sundhaussen, *Nasution*, p. 29. Because the incident of the female guerrilla and the Gurkha's head appeared in Nasution's memoirs, published in 1982, it very possibly inspired the similar fictional incident in Mangunwijaya's *Durga Umayi*, published a decade later.

48. Anderson, *Java in Revolution*, pp. 292–295, 399–406; Said, *Genesis of Power*, pp. 57–62, quotation, p. 61; Penders and Sundhaussen, *Nasution*, p. 71.

49. Penders and Sundhaussen, *Nasution*, pp. 46–48.

50. Ibid., p. 49.

51. Loren Ryter, "Pemuda Pancasila: The Last Loyalist Free Men of Suharto's Order?" in Benedict R. O'G. Anderson, ed., *Violence and the State in Suharto's Indonesia* (Ithaca: Cornell University Southeast Asia Program Publications, 2001), pp. 124–155, esp. pp. 131–136; and Anderson, "Introduction," p. 16.

52. Quotations from author's interview with General (ret.) Nasution, 29 Oct. 98.

53. Said, *Genesis of Power*, pp. 112–113.

54. Ibid., p. 89n69.

55. Ibid., pp. 121–122.

56. Penders and Sundhaussen, *Nasution*, p. 85; Ulf Sundhaussen, *The Road to Power: Indonesian Military Politics, 1946–1967* (London: Oxford University Press, 1982), pp. 66, 75.

57. Penders and Sundhaussen, *Nasution*, pp. 86–90; Sundhaussen, *Road to Power*, pp. 71–76, quotations, pp. 71, 72.

58. Sundhaussen, *Road to Power*, quotation, p. 75; Harold Crouch, *The Army and Politics in Indonesia* (Ithaca: Cornell University Press, 1978), pp. 29–30.

59. Clifford Geertz, "Soekarno Daze," *Latitudes*, 8 (Sept. 01), pp. 10–15, quotation, p. 10.

60. Herbert Feith, "Constitutional Democracy: How Well Did It Function?" in Bourchier and Legge, pp. 16–25, esp. p. 19; Penders and Sundhaussen, *Nasution*, pp. 127–139; quotation, Sundhaussen, *Road to Power*, p. 86.

61. Legge, *Sukarno*, pp. 305–310; Sundhaussen, *Road to Power*, p. 137.

62. Shiraishi Takashi, *Sukaluno to Suhaluto: Indainaru Indoneshia wo Mezashite* [*Sukarno and Suharto: Aiming for a Greater Indonesia*] (Tokyo: Iwanami Shoten, 1997), p. 80.

63. Shiraishi, ibid., pp. 83–90, follows through all these implications.

64. Kol. A. H. Nasution, *Pokok-Pokok Gerilja: Dan Pertahanan Indonesia Dimasa Jang*

Lalu Dan Jang Akan Datang [Fundamentals of Guerrilla Warfare: And the Defense of Indonesia, Past and Future] (Jakarta: Pembinbing, 1953), esp. pp. 16–21, 53–76, quotation, pp. 65–66.

65. Ibid., pp. 74, 93–99, quotation, p. 102.

66. Ibid., pp. 102–105.

67. Penders and Sundhaussen, *Nasution,* p. 107.

68. Sundhaussen, *Road to Power,* p. 137.

69. Feith, *Decline,* economic phenomena, pp. 556–566; administrative and political, pp. 567–578.

3. Ego, Voice, Vertigo

1. *Sukarno: An Autobiography* (Indianapolis: Bobbs-Merrill, 1965), pp. 275–278; J. D. Legge, *Sukarno: A Biography* (New York: Praeger, 1972), pp. 270, 302, 304–309.

2. Paul F. Gardner, *Shared Hopes, Separate Fears: Fifty Years of U.S.-Indonesia Relations* (Boulder: Westview, 1997), p. 160.

3. Legge, *Sukarno,* pp. 292–293; *Sukarno: Autobiography,* pp. 272–274, quotation, p. 274.

4. *Sukarno: Autobiography,* pp. 284–285.

5. Ibid.; Anwar and Harsono Tjokroaminoto, author's interview, Mar. 68.

6. *Sukarno: Autobiography,* pp. 141–144, quotation, p. 142.

7. Legge, *Sukarno,* p. 334.

8. *"Bapak bisa bikin nasion, tapi tidak bisa bikin moral."* Shimizu Hitoshi, author's interview, 5 June 68. Legge, pp. 406–407, summarizes the divorces.

9. *Sukarno: Autobiography,* p. 139.

10. Dr. B. Kharmawan, interview, Feb. 68.

11. Theodore Friend, *The Blue-Eyed Enemy: Japan against the West in Java and Luzon, 1942–1945* (Princeton: Princeton University Press, 1988), Friend, p. 112; J. A. C. Mackie, *Konfrontasi: The Indonesia-Malaysia Dispute, 1963–1966* (London: Oxford University Press, 1974), pp. 19–23.

12. Gardner, *Shared Hopes, Separate Fears,* pp. 178–179.

13. M. C. Ricklefs, *A History of Modern Indonesia since c. 1200* (Palo Alto: Stanford University Press, 3rd ed., 2001; 1st ed., 1981), p. 327.

14. Remarks at the Asia Society, New York City, 22 Apr. 99, author's notes.

15. Quotation from author's interview with General Nasution, 29 Oct. 98.

16. Gardner, *Shared Hopes, Separate Fears,* p. 177, citing cabled instructions to Secretary of State Dean Rusk, 2 May 62.

17. Ibid., p. 173.

18. Ibid., p. 175.

19. Ibid., pp. 177–178.

20. Arend Lijphart, *The Trauma of Decolonization: The Dutch and West New Guinea* (New Haven: Yale University Press, 1966), p. 291.

21. Gardner, *Hopes, Fears,* pp. 179–181.

22. Mackie, *Konfrontasi,* pp. 255–256.

23. Ibid., pp. 296–297.

24. Ibid., pp. 260–261 quotation, p. 274n42.

25. Ibid., pp. 261–267.
26. Ibid., pp. 283–289.
27. Wm. Roger Louis, "The Dissolution of the British Empire in the Era of Vietnam," *American Historical Review*, 107, 1 (Feb. 02), pp. 1–25, esp. pp. 18–23, quotations, 19n.
28. Anne Booth, *The Indonesian Economy in the Nineteenth and Twentieth Centuries: A History of Missed Opportunities* (London: MacMillan, 1998), pp. 86, 259–260.
29. Ibid., pp. 62, 222, 312, quotation, p. 313.
30. Ibid., pp. 63–66.
31. Professor Dr. Sumitro Djojohadikusumo, interview, 3 Nov. 99.
32. Ricklefs, *Modern Indonesia*, 3rd ed., p. 325.
33. Soedarpo Sastrosatomo, interview, 29 Oct. 99.
34. Ibid.
35. Ibid.
36. Ruth McVey, "The Materialization of the Southeast Asian Entrepreneur," in McVey, ed., *Southeast Asian Capitalists* (Ithaca: Cornell University Southeast Asia Program, 1992), p. 19 and passim.
37. Charles A. Coppel, *Indonesian Chinese in Crisis* (Kuala Lumpur: Oxford University Press, 1983), p. 1, citing G. William Skinner; Leo Suryadinata, *The Culture of the Chinese Minority in Indonesia* (Singapore: Times Books International, 1997), p. 7.
38. McVey, "Materialization . . . Entrepreneur," pp. 16–17, 19.
39. Ricklefs, *Modern Indonesia*, pp. 120–121.
40. On the operation of Dutch defined hierarchies, I am indebted to conversations with Professor Dr. Onghokham; and for Surabaya in particular I am grateful to Ali Al-Gadri and Norma Zecha.
41. Coppel, *Chinese in Crisis*, pp. 5–6.
42. *"Rapport Korban Sakiter Tangerang Dari Tgl. 3/6–15/7 1946"* (Report on Casualties Around Tangerang, June 3–July 15, 1946) is a key enclosure among many from the Chinese Aid Committee for the Public Security of Jakarta to the Ministry of Foreign Affairs of the Republic of Indonesia; Box 32, envelope 9, Niels Douwes Dekker Collection, Kroch Library, Cornell University.
43. Box 19, envelope 11; Box 15, envelopes 6, 7; Douwes Dekker, ibid.
44. Dutch military report of 2 Sept. 47, Box 32, envelope 10, ibid.
45. Feith, *Decline*, pp. 481–487; Coppel, *Chinese in Crisis*, p. 37.
46. Robert Cribb and Colin Brown, *Modern Indonesia: A History since 1945* (New York and London: Longman, 1995), pp. 90, 115–116.
47. Bernhard Dahm, *Sukarno and the Struggle for Indonesian Independence*, Mary I. Somers Heidhues, trans. (Ithaca: Cornell University Press, 1969; 1st German ed., 1966), pp. 26–28; Legge, *Sukarno*, pp. 23, 56n, 83.
48. *Sukarno: Autobiography*, pp. 101–102, 142, 179.
49. Friend, *The Blue-Eyed Enemy*, pp. 75–78, 117.
50. James Sigel, "Revolutionary Stink and the Extension of the Tongue of the People: The Political Languages of Pramoedya Ananta Toer and Sukarno," *Indonesia*, 64 (Oct. 97), pp. 1–20; trans., p. 17.
51. Sukarno, "Genta Suara Republika Indonesia" (The Ringing Voice of the Indone-

sian Republic), 17 Aug. 63, *Dibawah Bendera Revolusi* (Under the Banner of Revolution) (2 vols., Jakarta, 1965), vol. 1, pp. 522–523, 527 (my translation).

52. Ibid., pp. 531–540, quotation, p. 540.

53. Ibid., pp. 542ff, esp. p. 545.

54. Ibid., pp. 581, 576.

55. Quotations, ibid., pp. 588–589, 593, 584.

56. Ibid., p. 582.

57. Ibid., pp. 593–597; "four hells," p. 595.

58. Legge, *Sukarno*, p. 370; quotations, *Sukarno: Autobiography*, pp. 297, 300.

59. Siegel, p. 20. For further perspective on Pramoedya see Keith Foulcher, "'The Manifesto is Not Dead': Indonesian Literary Politics Thirty Years On," Monash University Centre of Southeast Asian Studies, Working Paper 87 (Clayton, Victoria, 1994), pp. 5–6.

60. I saw this painting in the possession of Jack W. Lydman, then in Jakarta, March 1968.

61. Legge, *Sukarno*, p. 349; *Sukarno: Autobiography*, p. 283.

62. Alexander Shakow, interview, 11 Feb. 00.

63. Robert Dakan, interviews, 7, 8 June 99.

64. Robert and Maya Dakan, interview, 30 Oct. 99; Gardner, *Shared Hopes, Separate Fears*, pp. 179, 189, 191–192.

65. Robert Dakan, 8 June 99.

66. Alexander Shakow, 11 Feb. 00.

67. Friend, *The Blue-Eyed Enemy*, pp. 160–168, 264–265.

68. Booth, *Indonesian Economy*, pp. 65–70.

69. Ibid., p. 122.

70. J. A. C. Mackie, "Problems of the Indonesian Inflation" (Ithaca, Cornell Modern Indonesia Project, 1967), table 2, p. 96; chart 1, p. 100.

71. Ibid., pp. 1–4, 101, and passim; quotation, p. 2.

72. Feith, *Decline*, ch. 11; Mackie, "Indonesian Inflation," pp. 50–53, 62.

73. Mackie, "Indonesian Inflation," p. 62.

74. Ibid., pp. 67–68, 78, and passim.

4. Mass Murder

1. Global context is supplied by Ben Kiernan, "Genocide and 'Ethnic Cleansing,'" in Robert Wuthnow, ed., *The Encyclopedia of Politics and Religion* (Washington, DC: Congressional Quarterly Inc., 1998), and Stephane Courtois et al., *The Black Book of Communism: Crimes, Terror, Repression,* Jonathan Murphy and Mark Kramer, trans. (Cambridge: Harvard University Press, 1999; 1st French ed., 1997).

2. Professor Onghokham, interview, 21 Oct. 98. Ruth McVey has written profoundly on the attempt of PKI leaders to stress cultural compatibility: "The Wayang Controversy in Indonesian Communism," Mark Hobart and Robert H. Taylor, eds., *Context, Meaning and Power in Southeast Asia* (Ithaca: Cornell University Southeast Asia Program, 1986), pp. 21–51, esp. pp. 24–28.

3. On the "Fifth Force," J. D. Legge, *Sukarno* (New York: Praeger, 1972), pp. 379–

381, 382; M. C. Ricklefs, *A History of Modern Indonesia since c. 1200* (Palo Alto: Stanford University Press, 3rd ed., 2001; 1st ed., 1981), pp. 336–337.

4. Colonel (ret.) George Benson, at USINDO seminar on "Fifty Years of Indonesian-American Relations," Cosmos Club, Washington, DC, 7 Oct. 99, personal notes; interview, 1 Oct. 02.

5. C. L. M. Penders and Ulf Sundhaussen, *Abdul Haris Nasution: A Political Biography* (St. Lucia: University of Queensland Press, 1986), pp. 187–188.

6. For the preceding narrative, I have used many conflicting sources. Harold Crouch, *The Army and Politics in Indonesia* (Ithaca: Cornell University Press, 1978), ch. 4, best combines detail and judgment. Interpretations and emphases are my own.

7. Penders and Sundhaussen, *Nasution*, p. 179.

8. Benedict R. O'G. Anderson, "Petrus Dadi Ratu," *Indonesia*, 70 (October 2000), pp. 1–7 (translation of a review published in *Tempo*, 10–16 Apr. 00); first published in English in the *New Left Review* (London, May/June 00).

9. My view here is drawn from Colonel George Benson's personal knowledge of Suharto's solitary character (several conversations); from an assessment by Harold Crouch of Anderson's article in *Tempo* (email from Crouch to William Liddle, 17 Apr. 00); and from Crouch's account of engaging Latief (stroke-impaired) in a discussion attended by various PKI ex-detainees (email from Crouch to the author, 6 Jan. 01).

10. Interview of the Second Deputy Chairman of the PKI Njoto with *Asahi Shimbun*, December 2, [1965], *Indonesia*, 1 (Apr. 66), pp. 192–197. B. R. O'G. Anderson and Ruth McVey, *A Preliminary Analysis of the October 1, 1965 Coup in Indonesia* (Ithaca: Cornell University Modern Indonesia Project, 1971). An earlier draft of the latter was available to me in advance of my first trip to Indonesia, August 1966. On PKI in 1948 and 1965 "using troops under their influence to do the dirty work for them . . . [and] proclaim[ing] the upheaval to be an 'internal army affair,'" see Penders and Sundhaussen, *Nasution*, pp. 181–182.

11. Crouch, pp. 118–122. Chino Keiko, "The Night That Changed Asia," fourth in a series of articles, *Sankei Shimbun*, 11 Sept. 97, p. 6 (trans. by Komori Akiko), based in part on an interview with Dewi Sukarno, and *Dewi Sukarno Jiten* (her autobiography in Japanese). President Sukarno's actions, from the morning of October 1 onward, Dewi says, "were abandoned by god" *(kami ni mihanasareta)*, an expression that connotes being misdirected, counter-productive, and contradicted by fate.

12. Shiraishi Takashi, *Sukaluno to Suhaluto: Indainaru Indoneshia wo mezashite* [Sukarno and Suharto: Aiming for a Greater Indonesia] (Tokyo: Iwanami Shoten, 1997), pp. 129–133, esp. p. 131. Shiraishi (p. 130) makes the additional point that Suharto, by his silent nods, had persuaded the communist leader Darsono that he was with him in the July 4, 1946, incident, which turned out not to be the case. Two decades later Latief made the same mistake as Darsono, of not reading Suharto correctly and underestimating his guile.

13. Crouch, *Army and Politics*, pp. 142–154.

14. Geoffrey Robinson, *The Dark Side of Paradise: Political Violence in Bali* (Ithaca: Cornell University Press, 1995), ch. 11. With slight variations, that chapter also appears as Robinson, "The Post-Coup Massacre in Bali," in Donald S. Lev and

Ruth McVey, eds., *Making Indonesia: Essays on Modern Indonesia in Honor of George McT. Kahin* (Ithaca: Cornell Southeast Asia Program, 1996), pp. 118–143.

15. Quotations of Sukarno from Crouch, *Army and Politics,* pp. 162, 164, 163.

16. Quoted in Herbert Luethy, "Indonesia Confronted," part I, p. 82, in *Encounter,* Dec. 65, pp. 80–89; followed by part II, Jan. 66, pp. 75–83. Clifford Geertz criticized both pieces comprehensively, "Are the Javanese Mad?" and Luethy replied. Their eloquent exchange appears in *Encounter,* Aug. 66, pp. 86–90.

17. Carmel Budiarjo, *Surviving Indonesia's Gulag: A Western Woman Tells Her Story* (London: Cassell, 1996), pp. 48–50, citing Colonel Yasir's accounts published in the Jakarta press in 1980, 1983, and 1985.

18. Ali Al-Gadri and Norma Zecha, joint interview, Surabaya, 13 June 99.

19. Norma Zecha, interview, Pasuruan, 14 June 99.

20. Clifford Geertz, *After the Fact: Two Countries, Four Decades, One Anthropologist* (Cambridge: Harvard University Press, 1995), p. 2.

21. Ibid., pp. 9–10, 11.

22. Aristides Katoppo, interview, 24 Oct. 97.

23. Robinson, *Dark Side,* p. 273.

24. Adrian Vickers, *Bali: A Paradise Created* (Singapore: Periplus, 1996; 1st ed., 1989).

25. Robinson, *Dark Side:* on *puputan,* pp. 149, 279; on predispositions to violence, pp. 1–18, 235–273.

26. Ibid., pp. 296–303.

27. Ibid., pp. 299–302, and passim; quotation, p. 300.

28. Robert Cribb, ed., *The Indonesian Killings, 1965–1966; Studies from Java and Bali* (Monash University, Papers on Southeast Asia, no. 21, Clayton, Victoria, Australia, 1990), pp. 7–14; table, p. 12, all part of an excellent "Introduction," pp. 1–43.

29. Paul F. Gardner, *Shared Hopes, Separate Fears: Fifty Years of U.S.-Indonesia Relations* (Boulder: Westview, 1997), p. 232.

30. Robert Cribb, "How Many Deaths? Problems in the Statistics of Massacre in Indonesia (1965–1966) and East Timor (1975–1980)," Ingrid Wessel and Georgia Wimhofer, eds., *Violence in Indonesia* (Hamburg: Abera, 2001), pp. 82–98, quotation, p. 82.

31. Cribb, *Indonesian Killings,* p. 42, 42n.

32. Personal conversations, Toraja, South Sulawesi, Oct./Nov. 98.

33. See, in contrast, Helen Jarvis, "Documenting the Cambodian Genocide on Multimedia," Yale Center for International and Area Studies, Working Paper No. 4 (New Haven, CT, 1998).

34. Peter Dale Scott sees American involvement chiefly through the CIA as prominent, and a model for coups in Cambodia in 1970 and Chile in 1973; and for support of Central American death squads in the 1980s: "The United States and the Overthrow of Sukarno, 1965–1967," *Pacific Affairs,* 58 (Summer 85), pp. 239–264. H. W. Brands systematically discredits arguments for American responsibility for coup and killings in "The Limits of Manipulation: How the United States Didn't Topple Sukarno," *Journal of American History,* 76 (Dec. 89), pp. 785–808.

35. Ide Anak Agung Gde Agung, *Twenty years: Indonesian Foreign Policy, 1945–1965* (The Hague: Mouton, 1973), ch. 14, esp. pp. 188–189, 403–407. The ambassador's defence, "To Hell with Your Aid," ch. 8 of Howard Palfrey Jones, *Indonesia: The Possible Dream* (New York: Harcourt Brace Jovanovich, Inc., 1971), invokes

Sukarno's first such utterance, March 25, 1964, and avoids the much more angrily dramatic and still more public incident on August 17. See also Gardner, *Shared Hopes, Separate Fears*, pp. 185–192.

36. Gardner, *Shared Hopes, Separate Fears*, p. 207.

37. Ibid., pp. 213–214.

38. I did not hear this story in Jakarta in 1967–68, but by the time of my interview with Jusuf Wanandi and Harry Tjan Silalahi of the Center for Strategic and International Studies, Mar. 83, it was an archetypal tale.

39. Robinson, *Dark Side*, p. 284.

40. Ian MacFarling, *The Dual Function of Indonesian Armed Forces: Military Politics in Indonesia* (Australian Defence Studies Centre, 1996), seventh interleafed page between pp. 116–117, including quotation; interviews, Colonel George Benson, 12 Sept. 97, 1 Oct. 02.

41. Kathy Kadane, "Memo to Editors: From States News Service," July 1990, responding to *New York Times* story of 12 July 90 ("CIA Tie Asserted in Indonesia Purge") which questioned certain assertions in Ms. Kadane's States News Service Report on the matter. Accompanying the memo as rebuttal are extensive portions of Ms. Kadane's transcripts of taped interviews. The above are contained in David T. Johnson, "Indonesia 1965: Role of the US Embassy" (Center for Defense Information email to apakabar@access.digex.net, 5 Dec. 95).

42. Martens to the editor, *Washington Post*, 2 June 90, quoted in *Foreign Relations of the United States, 1965–1968* (Washington, DC: GPO, 2001), vol. 26, p. 386. Hereafter "FRUS."

43. FRUS, 13 Nov. 65. Preceding, surrounding, and subsequent documents declare that arms, material, and even nonmilitary aid to the generals "cannot be concealed" and were "politically unacceptable." Ibid., pp. 341–350, p. 374. In view of U.S. government suppression of publication, these documents were available through an NGO, the National Security Archive, on its website, in www.gwu.edu/~nsarchiv/NSAEBB/NSAEBB52/.

44. See notes 41, 42.

45. Dhani and Soebandrio are paraphrased by Terence Lee of the Institute of Defense and Strategic Studies, Singapore, in *Tempo*, 5 Feb. 01, rpt. in *Foreign Policy*, July/Aug. 01, pp. 91–92.

46. Ambassador Green to Assistant Secretary of State William Bundy, 2 Dec. 65, FRUS, p. 379.

47. Marshall Green, *Indonesia: Crisis and Transformation, 1965–1968* (Washington, DC: Compass Press, 1990), pp. 155–156.

48. Gardner, *Shared Hopes, Separate Fears*, p. 248.

49. David T. Johnson, Center for Defense Information, Washington, DC, cdi@cdp.UUCP, "Gestapu: The CIA's Track Two in Indonesia." He likens Indonesian events to CIA intervention in Chile, 1970, the Gulf of Tonkin incident, and the Reichstag fire.

50. Peter Zinoman and Nancy Lee Peluso, "Rethinking Aspects of Political Violence in Twentieth-Century Indonesia and East Timor," *Asian Survey*, 42, no. 4 (July/Aug. 02), "The Legacy of Violence in Indonesia," pp. 545–549.

51. Walter Russell Mead points out that toward the end of World War II, American

bombing raids killed more than 900,000 Japanese civilians (not including atomic strikes against Hiroshima and Nagasaki)—more than twice the number of U.S. combat deaths in all its foreign wars combined: "The Jacksonian Tradition and American Foreign Policy," *National Interest,* Winter 1999/2000, pp. 1–25, esp. p. 1.

52. *Terima* = acceptance; *menerima nasib* = to accept one's fate; *nrima* = Javanese colloquial compression of this idea.

53. Cribb, *Indonesian Killings,* pp. 33–34, quotation, p. 33. I am also helped on the concept of *amok* by Fr. Y. B. Mangunwijaya, interview, 29 Oct. 97.

54. Hermawan Sulistyo, *Palu Arit di Ladang Tebu: Sejarah Pembantaian Massal yang Terlupakan (Jombang-Kediri, 1965–1966)* [Hammer and Sickle in the Cane Fields: A History of the Forgotten Mass Killings in Jombang-Kediri] (Jakarta: Kepustakaan Popular Gramedia, 2000), pp. 231–235.

55. [General] A. H. Nasution, "Second Armed Forces Seminar, 1966," *Soeharto's New Order,* Jeffrey Hadler, ed. (Jakarta: The Lontar Foundation, yet to be published); advance copy, courtesy of the editor and publisher John McGlynn.

56. General Nasution, interview, 29 Oct. 98.

57. Mrazek, *Sjahrir,* pp. 464–465, 480, 485–486, 491–495; "tyranny," p. 495; Rose, *Indonesia Free,* pp. 199, 205; "suffering," p. 205.

58. Mary Margaret Steedly supplies rich context for practice of seance among these Bataks in *Hanging with a Rope: Narrative Experience in Colonial and Postcolonial Karoland* (Princeton: Princeton University Press, 1993), esp. ch. 8.

5. The Smile of Progress

1. Ruth McVey, ed., *Indonesia* (New Haven: HRAF, 1963), pp. 19, 33–35.

2. Benedict R. O'G. Anderson, "Scholarship on Indonesia and Raison d'Etat: Personal Experience," *Indonesia,* 62 (Oct. 96), pp. 1–18.

3. Details have been changed to protect Z's privacy.

4. Peggy Reeves Sanday, "Introduction," and "Androcentric and Matrifocal Gender Representations in Minangkabau Ideology," in Peggy Reeves Sanday and Ruth Gallagher Goodenough, eds., *Beyond the Second Sex: New Directions in the Anthropology of Gender* (Philadelphia: University of Pennsylvania Press, 1990), pp. 2–3, 143 (quoting Taufik Abdullah), and 163 ("rape-free").

5. I am indebted to conversations with Jeffrey Hadler on these subjects, 7 June 99 and 9 Nov. 00; to his review of van Reenen in *Indonesia,* 63 (Apr. 97), pp. 205–207; and his article, "Home, Fatherhood, Succession: Three Generations of Amrullahs in Twentieth-Century Indonesia," *Indonesia,* 65 (Apr. 98), pp. 123–154.

6. Joke van Reenen, *Central Pillars of the House: Sisters, Wives, and Mothers in a Rural Community in Minangkabau, West Sumatra* (Leiden: Research School CNWS, 1996), pp. 1–3 and passim. For perspective including and beyond Minang women: Jean Gelman Taylor, ed., *Women Creating Indonesia: The First Fifty Years,* (Clayton: Monash University Asia Institute, 1997), and Elsbeth Locher-Scholten and Auke Niehof, *Indonesian Women in Focus* (Dordrecht, Holland/Providence: Foris Publications, 1987).

7. Taufik Abdullah, "Some Notes on the Kaba Tjindua Mato: An Example of Minangkabau Traditional Literature," *Indonesia*, 9 (Apr. 70), pp. 1–22, describes *"the* state myth for the Minangkabau" (p. 22).

8. Field notes, conversations with Drs. Wahidar Khaidir, MLS; Padang, 25–26 May 99.

9. John Bresnan, *Managing Indonesia: The Modern Political Economy* (New York: Columbia University Press, 1993), ch. 3, esp. pp. 83–85.

10. Observations and quotations in this paragraph are largely drawn from R. E. Elson's excellent *Suharto: A Political Biography* (Cambridge, UK: Cambridge University Press, 2001), esp. pp. 4–5, 297–302.

11. Robert Cribb, "Nation: Making Indonesia," in Emmerson, ed., *Indonesia beyond Suharto*, pp. 3–38, quotation, p. 34.

12. Sukarno's thoughts during the revolution stressed "a system of economy suited to the genius of our people and the natural resources of our country. I am fully convinced that over-industrialization will not prove beneficial to us. We do not want to, nor can we hope to compete with the industries of the west." Photostat of personally signed speech, 28 Aug. 46; personal collection (gift of the late Niels Douwes-Dekkar, print 113-g-7, "Anti-Nederl, Propaganda").

13. Robert Cribb and Colin Brown, *Modern Indonesia: A History since 1945* (New York and London: Longman, 1995), pp. 115–116.

14. International Crisis Group, "Bad Debt: The Politics of Financial Reform in Indonesia" (Jakarta/Brussels: ICG Asia Report No. 15, 13 March 2001), p. 3.

15. John G. Christy, former CEO of IU International; interviews, 12 Oct. 97, 11 May 00.

16. Personal conversations with Professor Sumitro, 1967, 1997–1999; Dr. Salim, 1986–1990, 1997–1999; Dr. Sadli, 1990, 1997.

17. Dr. Salim, interview, 18 Oct. 97. Hal Hill, *The Indonesian Economy since 1966* (Cambridge, UK: Cambridge University Press, 1996), pp. 128–136.

18. Hill, *Indonesian Economy*, pp. 128–136.

19. Ibid., p. 136. Clifford Geertz, *Agricultural Involution* (Berkeley: University of California Press, 1963), is the classic statement of overpopulation and overintense cultivation, implicitly leading to ongoing marginal impoverishment. Hill, *Indonesian Economy*, pp. 124ff, refutes Geertz factually. On a theoretical level, Julian Simon ebulliently argues the irrelevance of entropy and monocropping, the nongeometric nature of population growth (Indonesia's birth rate declined 43 percent between 1965 and 1993), and the productive primacy of human imagination in a free society; chs. 4, 6, 22, 23, 28, esp. pp. 332, 407–408: *The Ultimate Resource 2* (Princeton: Princeton University Press, rev. ed. 1996; 1st ed., 1981).

20. Bresnan, *Managing Indonesia*, p. 55; Hill, *Indonesian Economy*, p. 136. Suharto uses the FAO event to launch his recollections; *Soeharto: My Thoughts, Words, and Deeds;* An Autobiography as told to G. Dwipayana and Ramadhan K. H., Sumadi, trans. ([Jakarta]: PT. Citra Lamtoro Gung Persada, 1991), pp. 1–4.

21. Peter Timmer, "Tensions in Indonesia's Food Policy," USINDO Brief, 17 Nov. 00, from USINDO@aol.com.

22. Bresnan, *Managing Indonesia*, p. 285; Hill, *Indonesian Economy*, pp. 206–207, 210.

23. Hill, *Indonesian Economy*, p. 212.

24. Januar Achmad, *Hollow Development: The Politics of Health in Soeharto's Indonesia* (Jakarta: Gramedia Pustaka Utama, 1999), pp. 179, 184.

25. Ibid., pp. 6, 150.

26. Ibid., pp. 11, 150, 152.

27. Ibid., pp. 156, 165, 171.

28. Dr. Robert Bernstein to the author, 7 Mar. 01.

29. *Asiaweek,* review of Achmad's book, 31 Mar. 00, p. 41.

30. Achmad, *Hollow Development,* pp. 156, 164, 174.

31. Dr. Bernstein to the author, 7 Mar. 01.

32. National Center for Health Statistics, "Health, United States, 1998," as reported in the *Philadelphia Inquirer,* 30 July 98, p. A1. Conversations and correspondence, Feb./Mar. 01, with Dr. Robert S. Bernstein, Senior Medical Program Officer, Office of Asia and the Pacific, Office of International and Refugee Health, Department of Health and Human Services.

33. Bresnan, *Managing Indonesia,* p. 1; World Bank, *World Development Indicators CD-ROM,* February 1997, "Indonesia Social Indicators," p. 1; Hill, *Indonesian Economy,* p. 207.

34. Rati Ram, "Forty Years of Life Span Revolution: An Exploration of the Roles of 'Convergence,' Income, and Policy," *Economic Development and Cultural Change,* 46, no. 4 (July 98), pp. 849–857; quotations, pp. 849, 851.

35. Ibid., p. 855.

36. Hill, *Indonesian Economy,* "Malthusian," quotation, p. 193; data, pp. 199–200.

37. Klaus Deininger and Lyn Squire, "Measuring Income Inequality: A New Data Base," Draft for Comment, 22 Dec. 95, provided by Professor Al Heston.

38. Hill, *Indonesian Economy,* pp. 195–196.

39. UNDP, *Human Development Report 2000* (New York: Oxford University Press, 2000), pp. 180–181. Figures are for 1998.

40. Hill, *Indonesian Economy,* pp. 198–199.

41. Ibid., 281 n. 13, citing A. Booth, "Counting the Poor in Indonesia," *BIES,* 29, no. 1, pp. 53–83, esp. p. 77.

42. World Bank, "Indonesia and Poverty," www.worldbank.org/poverty/eacrisis/countries/indon/pov/.htm (updated 3 Feb. 99).

43. Dewi Fortuna Anwar, "Indonesia: Domestic Priorities Define National Security," in Muthiah Alagappa, ed., *Asian Security Practice* (Palo Alto: Stanford University Press, 1998), pp. 477–512.

44. Ibid., pp. 480–489.

45. Ibid., pp. 506–507.

46. Ibid., pp. 498–499.

47. Ibid., pp. 490 and 492. Dr. Anwar's evolving concerns can be tracked through her essay, "Human Security: Intractable Problem in Asia," ch. 15 in Muthiah Alagappa, ed., *Asian Security Order: Instrumental and Normative Features* (Honolulu: East-West Center, 2003).

48. Theodore Friend, *The Blue-Eyed Enemy: Japan against the West in Java and Luzon, 1942–1945* (Princeton: Princeton University Press, 1988), pp. 187–188, 191–192. Anecdotes and personal impressions that follow are based on conversations with Soedjatmoko, his family, friends, and figures of his time.

49. Rudolf Mrázek, *Sjahrir: Politics and Exile in Indonesia* (Ithaca: Cornell University Southeast Asia Program, 1994), pp. 440, 488, 488n175.

50. John Legge, *Intellectuals and Nationalism in Indonesia: A Study of the Following Recruited by Sutan Sjahrir in Occupation Jakarta* (Ithaca: Cornell Modern Indonesia Project, 1988), pp. 130, 134, 136.

51. Soedjatmoko, Mohammad Ali, G. J. Resink, and G. McT. Kahin, ed., *An Introduction to Indonesian Historiography* (Ithaca: Cornell University Press, 1965).

52. Ibid., Soedjatmoko, "The Indonesian Historian and His Time," pp. 412–413.

53. All quotations in this section are from an 89-page typescript sent me in 1979 by Soedjatmoko, "Development and Freedom." All the themes may be pursued, with others, in Kathleen Newland and Kamala Chandrakirana Soedjatmoko, *Transforming Humanity: The Visionary Writings of Soedjatmoko* (West Hartford: Kumarian Press, 1994). They are brought to high moral focus in ch. 8, "Common Humanity: An Ethical Framework," based on a paper presented to the Independent Commission on International Humanitarian Issues, Stockholm, May 1986.

54. Ursula Fleming, ed., *Meister Eckhart: The Man from Whom God Nothing Hid* (Springfield, IL: Templegate, 1990), p. 96.

55. Soedjatmoko, "Development and Freedom." Ian Chalmers and Vedi R. Hadiz, eds., have compiled an excellent book of "contending perspectives" on *The Politics of Economic Development in Indonesia* (London and New York: Routledge, 1997).

56. Clifford Geertz, Foreword to Newland and Soedjatmoko, eds., *Transforming Humanity*, p. vii.

6. The New Majapahit Empire

1. Angus McIntyre, "Soeharto's Composure: Considering the Biographical and Autobiographical Accounts" (Clayton, Victoria: Monash University Southeast Asia Publications, 1996), passim.

2. Adam Schwarz, *A Nation in Waiting: Indonesia in the 1990s* (Boulder, CO: Westview Press, 1994), pp. 105–109; Soemarsaid Moertono, *State and Statecraft in Old Java* (Cornell University: Modern Indonesia Project, 1968), pp. 101–103, 109–111.

3. M. C. Ricklefs, *A History of Modern Indonesia since c. 1200* (Palo Alto: Stanford University Press, 3rd ed., 2001; 1st ed., 1981), pp. 20–21.

4. Sumitro Djojohadikusumo, interview, 28 Oct. 97.

5. John Pemberton, *On the Subject of "Java"* (Ithaca: Cornell University Press, 1994), pp. 177–181; quotation, p. 177.

6. Sumitro interviews, 28 Oct. 97; 9 Mar. 98 (quotation in response to dialogue).

7. Angus McIntyre, "Suharto's Composure," pp. 13–14.

8. Hamish McDonald, *Suharto's Indonesia* (Blackburn, Victoria: Fontana/Collins, 1980), pp. 1, 19.

9. Edi Sedyawati, "Three-Dimensional Art in Classical Indonesia," pp. 59–66, esp. pp. 62–63, in Staff of the National Museum, *Art of Indonesia: Pusaka* (Hong Kong: Periplus, 1998; 1st ed., Singapore, Didier Miller, 1992).

10. John Bresnan, *Managing Indonesia: The Modern Political Economy* (New York: Co-

lumbia University Press, 1993), pp. 157–158. Also excellent on Suharto and Javanese culture, pp. 48–50.

11. Ibid., p. 155.

12. Dr. Sjahrir, interview, 15 Nov. 02

13. Bresnan, *Managing Indonesia,* pp. 141–163; quotation, p. 144.

14. M. Bambang Pranowo, "Which Islam and Which Pancasila? Islam and the State in Indonesia: A Comment," in Arief Budiman, ed., *State and Civil Society in Indonesia* (Clayton, Victoria: Monash University Centre of Southeast Asian Studies, 1990), pp. 479–496; esp. pp. 493–494.

15. Bresnan, *Managing Indonesia,* p. 170; McDonald, *Suharto's Indonesia,* pp. 144–152. On other subjects I interviewed Nishijima in Jakarta, Feb. 67.

16. Bresnan, *Managing Indonesia,* quotation, McDonald, *Suharto's Indonesia,* p. 143.

17. Bresnan, *Managing Indonesia,* pp. 164, 171; McDonald, *Suharto's Indonesia,* p. 157; quotations, pp. 153–154.

18. McDonald, *Suharto's Indonesia,* pp. 160–161; quotation, Bresnan, *Managing Indonesia,* p. 186.

19. McDonald, *Suharto's Indonesia,* pp. 161–163; quotation, Bresnan, *Managing Indonesia,* p. 186.

20. Bresnan, *Managing Indonesia,* pp. 189–193.

21. Ahmad D. Habir, "Conglomerates: All in the Family?" pp. 168–202, in Donald K. Emmerson, ed., *Indonesia beyond Suharto* (Armonk, NY: MESharpe, 1999), esp. p. 189.

22. Richard Borsuk, "Markets: The Limits of Reform," pp. 136–167 in ibid., esp. pp. 146, 146n, 166.

23. McDonald, *Suharto's Indonesia,* pp. 194–196.

24. Bresnan, *Managing Indonesia,* pp. 96–100.

25. Coppel, *Indonesian Chinese in Crisis,* p. 109.

26. Ibid., p. 168.

27. Shiraishi Takashi, *Sukaluno to Suhaluto: Indainaru Indoneshia wo Mezashite* [Sukarno and Suharto: Aiming for a Great Indonesia] (Tokyo: Iwanami Shoten, 1997), pp. 150–152. McDonald, *Suharto's Indonesia,* pp. 198–199, highlights Harry Tjan and Jusuf Wanandi, under Murtopo. More recent books emphasize Harry Tjan Silalahi as diplomatic intermediary, sharing Indonesian secret plans with the Australian government and with Portugal: Don Greenless and Robert Garran, *Deliverance: The Inside Story of East Timor's Fight for Freedom* (New South Wales: Allen and Unwin, 2002), pp. 1–2; Desmond Ball and Hamish McDonald, *Death in Balibo, Lies in Canberra* (New South Wales: Allen and Unwin, 2000), p. 14.

28. McDonald, *Suharto's Indonesia,* pp. 198, 204.

29. Ibid., pp. 207–211. Ben Kiernan refocuses the sources and raises the level of charges in "Cover-Up and Denial of Genocide: Australia, the USA, East Timor, and the Aborigines," *Critical Asian Studies,* 34, no. 2 (2002), pp. 163–192.

30. Ibid., pp. 211–213; John G. Taylor, *East Timor: The Price of Freedom* (London: Zed Books, 1999; 1st ed., 1991), pp. 25–77, esp. p. 64. Greenless and Garran, *Deliverance,* pp. 12–14, are more detailed and emphatic about Ford and Kissinger. Although not precisely footnoted, their account appears to rely on published documents of the Australian Department of Foreign Affairs and Trade.

31. In addition to deaths, a huge percentage of the population was either interned (controlled refugees) or displaced (fugitive in fear or opposition); Taylor, *East Timor,* pp. 88–90. Also Shiraishi, pp. 152–153; McDonald, *Suharto's Indonesia,* pp. 213–215, and James Dunn, "The Timor Affair in International Perspective," pp. 59–72, in Peter Carey and G. Carter Bentley, eds., *East Timor at the Crossroads: The Forging of a Nation* (Honolulu: University of Hawaii Press, 1995).

32. Daniel Patrick Moynihan, *A Dangerous Place* (Boston: Little, Brown, 1978), p. 247.

33. Notable opportunities: Henry Kissinger, *White House Years* (Boston: Little, Brown, 1979); *Diplomacy* (New York: Simon & Schuster, 1994); *Years of Renewal* (New York: Simon & Schuster, 1999).

34. On Australia: this is the conclusion both of Paul Kelly, "Policy Failure: Our Legacy in East Timor," *The Australian,* 13 Sept. 00, and of Jamie Mackie, "Australia and Indonesia," *Australian Journal of International Affairs, 55,* no. 1 (2001), quotation, p. 141. They had freshly published records to consult: Wendy Way, ed., *Australia and the Indonesian Incorporation of East Timor in 1974–1976: Documents on Australian Foreign Policy* (DFAT and MUP, 2000).

35. Taylor, *Price of Freedom,* p. 64.

36. Mark Hertsgaard, "The Secret Life of Henry Kissinger: Minutes of a 1975 Meeting with Lawrence Eagleburger," *The Nation,* 251, no. 14 (29 Oct. 90), pp. 475ff; document published in full, pp. 492–493.

37. "Famine Relief for East Timor"; "Recent Developments in East Timor," hearings before the Subcommittee on Asian and Pacific Affairs of the Committee on Foreign Affairs, House of Representatives, 96th Cong, 1st sess., 4 Dec. 79; 97th Cong., 2nd sess., 14 Sept. 82 (Washington: USGPO, 1980, 1982).

38. Personal notes of the occasion, 17 May 01.

39. Robert Cribb, "How Many Deaths? Problems in the Statistics of Massacre in Indonesia (1965–66) and East Timor (1975–1980)," in Ingrid Wessel and Georgia Wimhofer, eds., *Violence in Indonesia* (Hamburg: Abera, 2001), pp. 82–98; quotation, p. 94. Cribb (2002) emphasizes that most of the violence was early in the occupation, and theorizes about Indonesian troops overreacting to "a form of tragic culture shock"; "From Total People's Defence to Massacre: Explaining Indonesian Military Violence in East Timor," in Columbijn and Lindblad, eds., *Roots of Violence in Indonesia,* pp. 227–241; quotation, p. 239.

40. Nikolai Berdyaev, *Slavery and Freedom,* R. M. French, trans. (New York: Charles Scribner's Sons, 1944), p. 171.

41. David Bourchier, *Dynamics of Dissent in Indonesia: Sawito and the Phantom Coup* (Ithaca: Cornell Modern Indonesia Project, 1984), pp. 22–28.

42. Ibid., 41, 41n; Elinor Clarke Horne, *Javanese-English Dictionary* (New Haven: Yale University Press, 1974), p. 336, on *lelana brata.*

Theodore Friend, *The Blue-Eyed Enemy: Japan against the West in Java and Luzon, 1942–1945* (Princeton: Princeton University Press, 1988), pp. 25, 76–77, and author's interview with Soedjono, 2 Apr. 68; Bourchier, *Dynamics of Dissent,* p. 32 n.

Bourchier, *Dynamics of Dissent,* pp. 40–45. See also Paul Stange, "The Logic of Rasa in Java," *Indonesia,* 38, Oct. 84, pp. 113–134.

Bourchier, *Dynamics of Dissent,* pp. 48–49.

Ibid., p. 22, 32–36.

47. Ibid., p. 81.

48. Ibid., pp. 82–86; quotation, p. 86.

49. Bresnan, *Managing Indonesia,* p. 207.

50. Elson, *Suharto,* pp. 229–232.

51. Bresnan, *Managing Indonesia,* pp. 206–208.

52. Pramoedya Ananta Toer, remarks at the Asia Society Forum honoring him, New York City, 22 Apr. 99, trans. John McGlynn; author's notes.

53. Bresnan, *Managing Indonesia,* pp. 209–210, 216–217.

54. Ibid., pp. 236–237; Robert Cribb and Colin Brown, *Modern Indonesia: A History since 1945* (New York and London: Longman, 1995), pp. 136–143.

55. Sjafruddin Prawiranegara, interview, 8 Feb. 68; Douglas E. Ramage, *Politics in Indonesia: Democracy, Islam, and the Ideology of Tolerance* (New York: Routledge, 1995), p. 35; Sjafruddin Prawiranegara to President Suharto, 7 July 83, translated as "Pancasila as the Sole Foundation," *Indonesia,* 38 (Oct. 84), pp. 74–83, quotation, p. 80 (originally in *Perihal: Pancasila Sebagai Azas Tunggal* [Jakarta, DDII, 1983?], pp. 3–14).

56. Mohammad Natsir, interview, 2 Dec. 83.

57. Bresnan, *Managing Indonesia,* p. 202.

58. Robert W. Hefner, *Civil Islam: Muslims and Democratization in Indonesia* (Princeton: Princeton University Press, 2000), pp. 121–122.

59. McDonald, *Suharto's Indonesia,* p. 229, 231n6.

60. Ibid., p. 216.

61. Carmel Budiarjo, *Surviving Indonesia's Gulag,* passim.

62. McDonald, *Suharto's Indonesia,* pp. 218–219.

63. Brian May, *The Indonesian Tragedy* (Singapore: Graham Brash, 1978), pp. 31–35; McDonald, *Suharto's Indonesia,* pp. 224, 227.

64. Pramoedya Ananta Toer, *The Mute's Soliloquy: A Memoir* (New York: Hyperion East, 1999), p. 42.

65. "Willem Samuels" [John McGlynn], introduction to *The Mute's Soliloquy,* xxi–xxii; Pramoedya Ananta Toer, author's interview, Utan Kayu, Jakarta (John McGlynn, trans.), 15 June 00.

66. May, *Indonesian Tragedy,* p. 38.

67. Pramoedya, personal remarks trans. John McGlynn, at "Pramoedya Unbound," Asia Society, New York City, 22 Apr. 99.

68. Keith Foulcher, *Social Commitment in Literature and the Arts: The Indonesian "Institute of Peoples Culture," 1950–1965* (Clayton, Victoria: Monash University Centre of Southeast Asian Studies, 1986), pp. 115, 119–123; Goenawan Mohamad, *The "Cultural Manifesto" Affair: Literature and Politics in Indonesia in the 1960's; a Signatory's View* (Clayton, Victoria: Monash University Centre of Southeast Asian Studies, 1988), pp. 6–7.

69. Michael Vatikiotis, "Unreconciled," interview with Pramoedya, *Far East Economic Review,* 15 June 00.

70. David Bourchier, "Law, Crime and State Authority in Indonesia," p. 186; in Arief Budiman, ed., *State and Civil Society in Indonesia,* pp. 177–212.

71. Ibid., 179–181. See also Robert Cribb, *Gangsters and Revolutionaries: The Jakarta People's Militia and the Indonesian Revolution* (Honolulu: University of Hawaii Press, 1991), passim; and John R. W. Smail, *Bandung in the Early Revolution, 1945–*

46: A Study in the Social History of the Indonesian Revolution (Ithaca: Cornell Modern Indonesia Project, 1964), passim.

72. Bourchier, "Law, Crime and . . . Authority," p. 179, fig. 1.

73. Joshua Barker, "State of Fear: Controlling the Criminal Contagion in Suharto's New Order," pp. 11, 17, *Indonesia*, 66 (Oct. 98), pp. 8–42. See also James Siegel, *A New Criminal Type in Jakarta: Counter-Revolution Today* (Durham: Duke University Press, 1998), pp. 105–106.

74. Barker, "State of Fear," pp. 18–19, 31–32.

75. Harsja Bachtiar, interview, 29 Nov. 83.

76. Soeharto, *Autobiography*, p. 336.

7. The Sound of Silence

1. Klaus H. Schreiner, "The Making of National Heroes: Guided Democracy to New Order, 1959–1992," pp. 283–284, 290, in Henk Schulte Nordholt, *Outward Appearances: Dressing State and Society in Indonesia* (Leiden: KITLV Press, 1997), pp. 259–290.

2. Photographs in *30 Years of Indonesia's Independence*, 3 vols. (Jakarta: State Secretariat, Republic of Indonesia, 1975), vol. 1, pp. 208, 215, 216, 218, 224.

3. Budi Lim, interview, 27 Oct. 98.

4. Shiraishi Takashi, *Sukaluno to Suhaluto: Indainaru Indoneshia wo Mezashite* [Sukarno and Suharto: Aiming for a Great Indonesia] (Tokyo: Iwanami Shoten, 1997), p. 158.

5. Ibid., p. 160.

6. Carter Booth, Managing Director, Asia-Pacific, Chase Manhattan Bank, interview, 1 Nov. 00.

7. Shiraishi, *Sukaluno to Suhaluto*, pp. 173–175.

8. Elson, *Suharto*, ch. 7, gives an interesting and differently accented account of the topic of "Ascendancy."

9. Bernard Lewis, "The Roots of Muslim Rage," *The Atlantic Monthly*, Sept. 90; Gilles Kepel, *Jihad: The Trail of Political Islam* (Cambridge: Harvard University Press, 2002; 1st French ed., 2000), passim.

10. John Bresnan, *Managing Indonesia: The Modern Political Economy* (New York: Columbia University Press, 1993), p. 239. Bresnan discreetly identifies this interview as with "a leader of the Nahdatul Ulama." I presume to ascribe it to Gus Dur himself. On the same point, see Ramage, *Politics in Indonesia*, pp. 37–38, and Hefner, *Civil Islam*, p. 263n63.

11. Bresnan, *Managing Indonesia*, pp. 222–225; quotation, p. 225.

12. Ibid., pp. 226–230.

13. Ibid., pp. 231–232; profile of Baraja, International Crisis Group, Asia Report no. 43, 11 Dec. 02, p. 32.

14. Ibid., p. 227.

15. Gen. Moerdani, interview, 22 Oct. 97.

16. AFP, Jakarta, 12 Oct. 93 <apakabar@access.digex.net>; Jakarta Post, 24 June 00 <sadli@pacific.net.id> <Joyo@aol.com>.

17. These indigenous terms were propelled into social science use chiefly by Clifford Geertz, *The Religion of Java* (Glencoe, IL: Free Press, 1960).

18. Aswab Mahasin, "The Santri Middle Class: An Insider's View," p. 140, in Richard Tanter and Kenneth Young, *The Politics of Middle Class Indonesia* (Clayton, Victoria: Monash University Centre of Southeast Asian Studies, 1990), pp. 138–144.

19. J. A. C. Mackie, "Money and the Middle Class," in ibid., pp. 96–122, provides analysis of data from Harold Crouch (pp. 100–105). I navigate my own path, relying on both of them.

20. Kenneth Young, "Middle Bureaucrats, Middle Peasants, Middle Class? The Extra-Urban Dimension," ibid., pp. 147–164; quotation, p. 162.

21. Aswab Mahasin, ibid., esp. pp. 141–144.

22. Mackie, "Power and Property in Indonesia," ibid., pp. 71–95; quotation from Mackie, "Money and the Middle Class," p. 118.

23. Onghokham, "Suharto and the Tradition of the Javanese Monarchs," ms. to be published in Jeffrey Hadler, ed., *Soeharto's New Order* (Jakarta: Lontar, forthcoming).

24. Juwono Sudarsono to Edward Aspinall et al., 21 Aug. 02.

25. Hefner, *Civil Islam,* p. 13.

26. I have compacted impressions from conversations with many people, including Cak Nur, and several with Gus Dur himself. For tapes of Om Khalsoum (or Um Khaltoum), I am indebted to my late brother, Charles Friend.

27. William Liddle, "The Story behind Abdurrahman," *Jakarta Post,* 9 Feb. 00.

28. V. S. Naipaul, *Among the Believers* (New York: Vintage Books, 1982; 1st ed., Knopf, 1981); quotations, pp. 320, 323, 324, 325.

29. Naipaul, *Beyond Belief* (New York: Random House, 1998), pp. 21–33; "stupefaction," *Among the Believers,* p. 325.

30. *Beyond Belief,* p. 29. Far more understanding in brief compass on this awakening is Mark R. Woodward, "President Gus Dur: Indonesia, Islam and Reformasi," paper presented at USINDO workshop, Cosmos Club, Washington, DC, 30 Nov. 99.

31. Nico Schulte Nordholt, "His Dream Came True," *Time,* 1 Nov. 99, p. 27. Intimates of Gus Dur, however, say that he gives out many variants of this story.

32. Hefner, *Civil Islam,* pp. 168–169.

33. Aburrahman Wahid, "Muhammadiyah dan Nahdhatul Ulama: Reorientasi Wawasan Sosial-Politik" [Muhammadiyah and Nahdhatul Ulama: Reorientation of Socio-Political Anxieties], undated article, pp. 49–59, quotation, p. 51. The source is a collection of 57 photocopied articles by Wahid from the period 1987–1993, apparently arranged for future publication, and inscribed "to Dr. M. Kosec, with affection and gratitude from the author." Ms. Kosec made the volume available to me.

34. Adam Schwarz, *A Nation in Waiting: Indonesia's Search for Stability* (Boulder, CO: Westview Press, 2000; 1st ed., 1994), pp. 162–163, 190–193.

35. Confidential interview, 13 June 99, with one who sat "only three metres away" from Wahid at this meeting in 1992. A subsequent interview with the host of the occasion drew no confirmation of these details and an allegation it was only a birthday party. The host had reason to suppress the motive of the gathering, because he was then seeking (3 Nov. 99) a post with Wahid's new government. He subsequently obtained it.

36. Privileged conversations with Wahid family confidantes.

37. Chris Manning, *Indonesian Labour in Transition: An East Asian Success Story?* (Cambridge: Cambridge University Press, 1998), passim, esp. pp. 64–82, 275–288. Elson, *Suharto,* counts four devaluations (p. 247), while also seeing labor in an integralist agenda (p. 242).

38. Douglas Anton Kammen, "A Time to Strike: Industrial Strikes and Changing Class Relations in New Order Indonesia," Ph.D. diss., Cornell University, May 1997, p. 126, table 4.1.

39. Ibid., p. 164, table 4.11.

40. Ibid., pp. 172–173, 197–198.

41. Ibid., p. 206n56.

42. Confidential interviews with an NGO leader and with a financier who alleged to have the facts directly from a former adjutant of the general. A third source, a foreign consultant, intimated that pinning down such facts on this man could lead to serious injury. So, at risk of the story being treated as a Jakarta equivalent of "urban myth," I leave the sources anonymous. They are unknown to each other, but their accounts dovetail from totally different sectors of society.

43. Kammen, "A Time to Strike," pp. 386, 388.

44. Ibid., pp. 14–23; quotation, p. 20; detail on site of the murder, confidentially conveyed, 198n41. Amplifications and contexts, pp. 31–38, 208, 385–390. See also Manning, *Indonesian Labour in transition,* pp. 214, 221.

45. Goenawan Mohamad, "Baldwin's Garment: Identity and Fetishism and Other Issues of Difference," *IHJ Bulletin* (International House of Japan), 18, no. 1 (Winter 1998), pp. 1–7; "After the Crackdown: Goenawan Mohamad on Politics and Journalism in Indonesia," *Journal of the International Institute,* 4, no. 2 (Winter 1997). Goenawan Mohamad, *Sidelines: Thought Pieces from Tempo Magazine,* Jennifer Lindsay, trans. (Melbourne: Lontar/Hyland House, 1994); Goenawan Mohamad, author's interview, 5 Dec. 00.

46. Schwarz, *A Nation in Waiting,* 1st ed., pp. 234 (quoting Suharto from the *Jakarta Post,* 18 Dec. 93), 240, 242–243.

47. *Van Zorge Report,* 23 Sept. 02, p. 38.

48. "Surat Dari Redaksi" (Letter from the Editor), *Tempo,* 6–12 Oct. 98 (inaugural issue, new series), p. 7 (courtesy of Janet Steele).

49. Ibid. Impressions of Hashim Djojohadikusumo from author's conversation with him on other matters, 12 Mar. 98.

50. This is a partial list of practices documented in HRW, *Academic Freedom,* passim. On a comparable "institutionalization of fear" in the late years of the Marcos dictatorship of the Philippines, Doreen G. Fernandez is highly instructive: "Artists, Writers and Intellectuals and the Culture of Crisis," paper for the Association of Asian Studies, Philadelphia, PA, 22–24 Mar. 85. Part of the unwritten code: "it is forbidden to criticize the family in Malacanang [the presidential palace] and Minister Enrile of National Defense" (p. 20).

51. Human Rights Watch, *Academic Freedom in Indonesia* (New York: August 1998), pp. 27, 55–57.

52. Elson, *Suharto,* p. 241.

53. Ibid., pp. 186–190.

54. Quotation from Hamish McDonald, *"Demokrasi!" Sydney Morning Herald,* 27 Mar. 99.

55. Sarwono Kusumaatmadja, personal interview, 2 Dec. 83.

56. USINDO Brief: "Open Forum: Election Watch," Washington, DC, 29 Apr. 99; personal notes.

57. Dwight Y. King, trans., intro., "White Book on the 1992 General Election in Indonesia" (Ithaca: Cornell Modern Indonesia Project, 1994), pp. 1–2.

58. Ibid., passim; quotation, p. 23.

59. Ibid., p. 45.

60. Ibid., King intro., pp. 2–3; report pp. 52, 57–58.

61. Ibid., p. 23.

62. Ibid., p. 60.

63. Gordon Bishop, interviews 20 Jan., 30 Jan., 19 Apr. 00, New York City, and 30 June 00, Villanova, PA; brochures and articles on the Javana Collection from Gordon Bishop.

8. The Last Years of Living Securely

1. One example of the theoretical literature: Margaret Levi, "The Predatory Theory of Rule," *Politics and Society* 10, no. 4 (1981), pp. 431–465. Dr. Min Xin Pei, now with the Carnegie Foundation for International Peace, has written both in German and in English on the Chinese state as a "parasite."

2. Mancur Olson, *Power and Prosperity: Outgrowing Communist and Capitalist Dictatorships* (New York: Basic Books, 2000), pp. 19–20.

3. Ibid., pp. 195–199.

4. Samantha F. Ravich nonetheless concludes that as in Taiwan and Korea, "marketization will slowly liberalize the government of Indonesia"; *Marketization and Democracy: East Asian Experiences* (Cambridge, UK: Cambridge University Press, 2000), p. 176.

5. John Bresnan, *Managing Indonesia: The Modern Political Economy* (New York: Columbia University Press, 1993), p. 243.

6. Who are "the eyes of the world"? Expatriate businessmen, transient globobureaucrats, and short-term foreign correspondents rarely question stability accompanied by increments of social improvement.

7. Harold Crouch, *The Army and Politics in Indonesia* (Ithaca: Cornell University Press, 1978), pp. 351–352.

8. David Jenkins, *Suharto and His Generals: Indonesian Military Politics, 1975–1983* (Ithaca: Cornell Modern Indonesia Project, 1984), p. 145, 145n.

9. Ibid., pp. 242–243, 247–248.

10. Ibid., pp. 186–187; quotation, p. 252n31.

11. Ibid., pp. 193–194.

12. Ibid., p. 187.

13. Crouch, *The Army and Politics in Indonesia;* Ian MacFarling, *The Dual Function of the Indonesian Armed Forces: Military Politics in Indonesia* (Australian Defence Studies Centre and University of New South Wales, 1996); Robert Lowry, *The Armed Forces of Indonesia* (St. Leonards, Australia: Allen and Unwin, 1996).

14. Bresnan, *Managing Indonesia*, p. 257. Jenkins spoke then of family assets of only $2–3 billion.

15. MacFarling, *Dual Functions*, p. 200, citing Prof. Michael Howard.

16. Ibid., pp. 203–204. Lowry, *Armed Forces,* p. 226, contends that MacFarling's observation is more true of the bottom end of the ABRI structure than of the top.

17. Guy J. Pauker, "The Indonesian Doctrine of Territorial Warfare and Territorial Management" (Santa Monica, CA: RAND Corporation, Memorandum RM-3312-PR, Nov. 63); "Indonesia: The Age of Reason?" (RAND, Feb. 68); "The Impact of Military Expenditure and Security Programs on Political and Economic Development in Indonesia" (RAND, Apr. 78); "Government Responses to Armed Insurgency in Southeast Asia: A Comparative Examination of Failures and Successes and Their Likely Implications for the Future" (RAND, June 85); "Indonesia under Suharto: The Benefits of Aloofness," in Daniel Pipes and Adam Garfinkle, eds., *Friendly Tyrants: An American Dilemma* (New York: St. Martin's Press, 1991), pp. 379–399. Pauker's change of heart comes in *Orbis* 40, no. 3 (Summer 1996), pp. 445ff, reviewing books by Adam Schwarz and Michael Vatikiotis.

18. Schwarz, *A Nation in Waiting,* pp. 117–119, 273, 283, 285–286.

19. Interview, Gen. L. B. "Benny" Moerdani, 22 Oct. 97.

20. Jeffrey A. Winters, interview with Ibnu Sutowo, 7 Mar. 89, in Winters, *Power in Motion: Capital Mobility and the Indonesian State* (Ithaca: Cornell University Press, 1996), p. 130n82.

21. James Clad, "The End of Indonesia's New Order," *Wilson Quarterly,* Autumn 1996, pp. 47–64; datum, p. 62.

22. David Bourchier, ed., "Indonesia's Emerging Proletariat: Workers and Their Struggles" (Clayton, Victoria: Monash University Centre of Southeast Asian Studies, 1994); Terence Hull, "Workers in the Shadows: A Statistical Wayang," pp. 1–18, esp. pp. 8, 14.

23. Schwarz, *A Nation in Waiting,* p. 301.

24. Ibid., p. 275.

25. Ibid., pp. 264–269; Michael Malley, "Regions, Centralization and Resistance," in Emmerson, ed., *Indonesia beyond Suharto,* pp. 71–105, esp. p. 104.

26. Quoted by Ariel Heryanto in *Far Eastern Economic Review,* 17 Oct. 96, p. 32.

27. Seth Mydans, *New York Times,* 27 June 96, p. A16; 20 June, p. A3.

28. Gordon Bishop, interview, 21 Jan. 00. Quotation of Ibu Tien Suharto from Sarwono Kusumaatmadja, interview, 8 Nov. 00.

29. I am aware of possible incredulity in some readers at this phenomenon. I have not personally seen such happenings but have heard them described in Bali and Java by persons with advanced Western educations who were witness to them. In the Philippines, a distinguished Jesuit social scientist finds extrasensory and suprasensory consciousness more pronounced than in the empirical cultures. He recounts numerous actions of poltergeists, carefully observed by himself and others. He also approaches in a scientific spirit other classes of paranormal phenomena, including hypnosis, trance, possession, exorcism, and faith healing. Jaime C. Bulatao, S.J., *Phenomena and Their Interpretations, Landmark Essays, 1957–1989* (Quezon City: Ateneo de Manila Press, 1992).

30. This account is condensed from interviews with Gordon Bishop in New York City, 8 Dec. 99 and 21 Jan. 00.

31. *Far Eastern Economic Review,* 11 July 96, pp. 19–20.

32. *The Economist,* 27 July 96, pp. 30–31.

33. Casualty figures from Schwarz, *A Nation in Waiting,* 2nd ed., p. 322; quotation of Wahid from Goenawan Mohamad, interview, 5 Nov. 00.

34. *Far Eastern Economic Review,* 8 Aug. 96, pp. 14–16; on rattan, my source is Col. (ret.) John Haseman.

35. *Far Eastern Economic Review,* ibid.; Kevin O'Rourke, *Reformasi: The Struggle for Power in Post-Soeharto Indonesia* (New South Wales: Allen and Unwin, 2002), pp. 12–15.

36. *Far Eastern Economic Review,* 16 Aug. 96, pp. 14–15; 22 Aug. 96, pp. 17, 20.

37. *MacLean's,* 19 Aug. 96, p. 30; confidential interviews, Nov. 97.

38. Seth Mydans, *New York Times,* 4 Aug. 96, p. A3.

39. Ibid.

40. Vice President Megawati Sukarnoputri, interview, 6 Nov. 99.

41. Schwarz, *A Nation in Waiting,* pp. 65–66; quotation from Hal Hill. For the themes of emerging tiger and emerging giant, see World Bank, *The East Asian Miracle: Economic Growth and Public Policy* (New York: Oxford University Press, 1993), and Hal Hill, *The Indonesian Economy since 1966: Southeast Asia's Emerging Giant* (Cambridge, UK: Cambridge University Press, 1996).

42. Vaudine England, "Rotten to the Core," *South China Morning Post,* 1 Aug. 99.

43. Confidential conversation, 3 Mar. 98.

44. Schwarz, *A Nation in Waiting,* p. 66.

45. The Castle Group, *Castle's Road Map to Indonesian Business Groups* (Jakarta: Java Consult Ltd., 1997).

46. Schwarz, *A Nation in Waiting,* pp. 109–110.

47. Ibid., pp. 122, 128–129. Schwarz, *A Nation in Waiting,* pp. 120–129, gives an excellent account of *pribumi*-Chinese struggles. Winters, *Power in Motion,* pp. 152–155, 159–160, evalutes Team 10 as a "solution" to the problem felt by *pribumis.*

48. Badan Pengurus Kemitraan Deklarasi Jimbaran Bali, *Laporan Pelaksanaan Perkembangan Kemitraan dan Prospeknya Dalam Masa Reformasi* (Jakarta: June 1998), pp. 1–2. I am grateful to Pak Sofjan Wanandi, Chairman and CEO, Gemala Group, for making this report available to me. Evaluation of its contents is, of course, my own.

49. Ibid., pp. 5–9; and appendices, "Rekap, Komitmen dan Realisasi Kemitraan, 1996–1997; Rekap Komitmen Realisasi 1997 Serta Komitmen 1998."

50. *Business World* (Philippines), "The Myth of Chinese Dominance of the Indonesian Economy," article forwarded by Joyo@aol.com and widely circulated, Jan. 99; conversations with Alberto Hanani.

51. Norma Zecha, interview, Pasuruan, East Java, 15 June 99.

52. Karl D. Jackson and Lucian W. Pye, *Political Power and Communications in Indonesia* (Berkeley: University of California Press, 1978), p. 37.

53. Nurcholish Madjid, paper for the Global Forum on Fighting Corruption, "Religious Values and the Struggle against Corruption: The Case of Indonesia" (Washington, DC, Feb. 99), esp. p. 2.

54. Richard H. Mitchell, *Political Bribery in Japan* (Honolulu: University of Hawaii Press, 1996).

55. *Yomiuri Shimbun,* 1, 2, 3, 7, 8 Apr. 99; unnumbered page clippings provided by Takeichi Sumio, trans. Ms. Komori Akiko. The quotation from Minister Hamzah Haz is 3 Apr. 99.

56. Murai Yoshinori et al., *Soeharto Family no chikuzai* [The Suharto Family's Accumulation of Wealth] (Tokyo: Commons, 1999), as reviewed by Murakami Saki and Morishita Akiko, *Kyoto Review of Southeast Asia,* issue 1 (Mar. 02).

57. Rosabeth Moss Kanter, "Using Networking for Competitive Advantage," Booz-Allen & Hamilton, *Strategy & Business,* 3rd. Quarter, 1996.

58. Samuel Huntington, *Political Order in Changing Societies* (New Haven: Yale University Press, 1968), pp. 62–71; quotation, p. 69.

59. The CEO referred to only by his nickname here, Top Gun, generously provided this interview 9 Dec. 98, and subsequent permission to publish it.

60. Peter Waldman, "Hand in Glove: How Suharto's Circle, Mining Firm Did So Well Together," *Wall Street Journal,* 29 Sept. 98, courtesy of joyo@aol.com, 31 Oct. 02.

61. Tempo Interaktif, 21 Mar. 98, Berita Hari Ini.

62. Richard Robison, *Indonesia: The Rise of Capital* (Sydney: Allen & Unwin, 1986), pp. 65–68, 82–88, and passim.

63. Andrew McIntyre, *Business and Politics in Indonesia* (Sydney: Allen & Unwin, 1991), pp. 244–251, 258–262.

64. Ibid., passim; Professor Sumitro Djojohadikusumo, interviews, 9 Mar. 98, 3 Nov. 99.

65. Yoshihara, Kunio, *The Rise of Ersatz Capitalism in Southeast Asia* (Singapore: Oxford University Press, 1988), p. 130.

66. Joshua David Barker, "Footprint of the State: Satellite Communications in the New Order," in Jeffrey Hadler, ed., *Soeharto's New Order* (Jakarta: Lontar, forthcoming).

67. Shiraishi Takashi, "Rewiring the Indonesian State," pp. 165–167, in Daniel S. Lev and Ruth McVey, *Making Indonesia: Essays on Modern Indonesia in Honor of George McT. Kahin* (Ithaca: Cornell Southeast Asia Publications, 1996), pp. 164–179.

68. Ibid., pp. 168, 174–178; quotation, p. 175, from Suharto, *Otobiografi,* p. 280.

69. Shiraishi, "Rewiring the Indonesian State," p. 175.

70. Ibid., pp. 178–179.

71. Ibid., pp. 170, 174.

72. Carl A. Serrato and Glenn Mennick, "The Indonesian Family Life Survey: Overview and Descriptive Analysis of the Population, Health and Education Data," RAND report prepared for United States Agency for International Development, Oct. 95, ch. 3, esp. pp. 68–74.

73. The following narrative and quotations are distilled and selected from interviews with Dr. Pratiwi Sudarmono, 6 Nov. 99 and 14 June 00.

74. www.forbes.com/tool/toolbox/billnow/net98.asp?condition+25,97.

75. Ibid., 25,98.

76. Confidential interview, 29 Oct. 86.

77. Berdyaev, *Slavery and Freedom* (New York: Charles Scribner's Sons, 1944; 1st. French ed., 1939), pp. 185, 187.

78. George Aditjondro, "Autumn of the Patriarch: The Suharto Grip on Indonesia's Wealth," *Multinational Monitor,* 19, no. 12 (Jan.–Feb. 98), p. 17.

79. John Colmey and David Liebhold, "The Family Firm," *Time Asia,* 24 May 99, p. 3. This investigation also exists in two other forms: a 19-page web version, available at egi.pathfinder.com/time/asia/magazine/1999/990524/cover2.html;

and the U.S. edition of *Time,* 31 May 99, "It's All in the Family," pp. 68–69. References will be to the first, above.

80. Colmley and Liebhold, *Time,* p. 3.

81. Other, and global, kinds of corruption are not only possible but extensive. On Osama bin Laden's and other terrorists' use of private relief groups and Islamic charities, see *New York Times,* 19 Feb. 00, p. A5 (nearly nineteen months before the attacks on the United States and subsequent freeze orders).

82. Ravich, citing *Warta Ekonomi Magazine* (1996), gives smaller and differing estimates; *Marketization and Democracy,* table 7.3, p. 168.

83. Colmley and Liebhold, passim; *Wall Street Journal,* 30 Dec. 98, p. A1; see also "Things Fall Apart," *Far Eastern Economic Review,* 13 May 99, pp. 10–14.

84. Shiraishi, *Sukalno to Suhalto,* pp. 174–175.

85. Marsillam Simanjuntak, "Democratisation in the 1990's: Coming to Terms with Gradualism?" in David Bourchier and John Legge, eds., *Democracy in Indonesia: 1950s and 1990s* (Clayton, Victoria: Monash University Centre of Southeast Asian Studies, 1994), pp. 302–312; quotation, p. 311.

9. Behind, Beyond, Beneath the Power Structure

1. Kathryn Robinson, "Women: Difference versus Diversity," is excellent on this (pp. 246–247) and other topics, in Emmerson, ed., *Indonesia beyond Suharto,* pp. 237–261.

2. Javanese maxim and translation from Dr. Soedjati Djiwandono, 2 June 99.

3. Interviews, Prof. Sartono Kartodirdjo, 30 Oct. 97; 7 Mar. 98. Among his chief writings on these subjects are: *The Peasants' Revolt of Banten in 1888: A Case Study of Social Movements in Indonesia* ('S-Gravenhage: Martinus Nijhoff, 1966); "Agrarian Radicalism in Java: Its Setting and Development," in Claire Holt, ed., *Culture and Politics in Indonesia* (Ithaca: Cornell University Press, 1972); *Modern Indonesia: Tradition and Transformation, a Socio-Historical Perspective* (Yogyakarta: Gadjah Mada University Press, 1984); and *Pesta Demokrasi di Pedesaan: Studi Kasus Pemilihan Kepala Desa di Jawa Tengah dan DIY* (The Festival of Democracy in Rural Areas: A Study of the Election of Village Chiefs in Central Java and the Special District of Yogyakarta) (Yogyakarta: P3PK, Universitas Gadjah Mada, 1992).

4. Y. B. Mangunwijaya, *Durga Umayi* (Jakarta: Pustaka Utama Grafiti, 1991).

5. Lindsay Rae, "Liberating and Conciliating: The Work of Y. B. Mangunwija," in Angus McIntyre, ed., *Indonesian Political Biography: In Search of Cross-Cultural Understanding* (Clayton, Victoria: Monash University Papers on Southeast Asia, 1998), pp. 239–262; quotation, p. 245.

6. Ibid., p. 249.

7. Y. B. Mangunwijaya, "The Indonesia Raya Dream and Its Impact on the Concept of Democracy," in David Bourchier and John Legge, eds., *Democracy in Indonesia: 1950s and 1990s* (Clayton, Victoria: Monash Papers, 1994), pp. 79–87; quotation, p. 83.

8. Fr. Y. B. Mangunwijaya interview, 29 Oct. 97.

9. Ibid., interview, 7 Mar. 98.

10. Soebadio Sastrosatomo, *Soekarno adalah Indonesia, Indonesia adalah Soekarno* [Sukarno Is Indonesia, Indonesia Is Sukarno], (Jakarta: "Guntur 49," 1995), p. 9.

11. Soebadio, *Era Baru—Pemimpin Baru; Badio Memo Cak Rezim Orde Baru* (Jakarta: "Guntur 99," Jan. 97). Subsequent political details are from the preface of the Australian edition, *New Era–New Leader: Badio Rejects the New Order Regime's Manipulations,* Sam Burg Foundation and Campaign against Militarism, trans. Perth, Joko Nofani Information Project, May 1997, pp. 5–9.

12. Soebadio interview, 26 Oct. 98.

13. Soebadio, *The Dosomuko Politics of the New Order Regime: Fragile and Making the Common People Suffer* (Jakarta: "Guntur 49," 1998). Soebadio's final shot before he died was published less than three weeks after Suharto resigned: *Manifes: Kedaulatan Rakyat* [Manifesto: Popular Sovereignty] (Jakarta: "Guntur 49," 9 June 98).

14. Among many sources on the subject, *Lordly Shades: Wayang Purwa Indonesia* is brief, authoritative, and well illustrated; eds. Pandam Guritno, Haryono Guritno, Teguh S. Jamal and Molly Bondan; subvention by Probosoetedjo (Jakarta: PT Jayakarta Agung Offset, 1984).

15. Aristides Katoppo interview, 24 Oct. 97.

16. Fr. Franz Magnis-Suseno, S.J., quotation from interview, 4 June 99.

17. Suseno interview, 4 June 99.

18. Katoppo, 24 Oct. 97.

19. Suseno and Katoppo interviews.

20. Katoppo interview.

21. Suseno interview.

22. Ibid.

23. Anne Booth, *The Indonesian Economy in the Nineteenth and Twentieth Centuries: A History of Missed Opportunities* (New York: St. Martin's Press, 1998), p. 179.

24. Jan-Paul Dirkse, Frans Husken, and Mario Rutten, eds. (Leiden: KITLV Press, 1993).

25. Booth, *The Indonesian Economy,* pp. 128–134.

26. Cited by Pronk in Dirkse, Husken, and Rutten, eds., p. 261.

27. Jan Pronk, "Looking Backward, Looking Forward," in ibid., pp. 257–267; quotation, p. 260.

28. Tim Kell, *The Roots of Acehnese Rebellion, 1989–1992* (Ithaca: Cornell Modern Indonesia Project, 1995), p. 84. Geoffrey Robinson argues forcefully that Suharto's Order was chiefly at fault for protracted violence: "*Rawan* Is as *Rawan* Does: The Origins of Disorder in New Order Aceh," in Anderson, ed., *Violence and the State,* pp. 213–242.

29. H. R. H. Prince Hasan M. di Tiro, correspondence with the author, 2000–01.

30. Kell, *The Roots of Acehnese Rebellion,* pp. 68–69.

31. Ibid., pp. 74–75.

32. Robert Gardner, "The More Things Change," *Transition,* 58 (92), pp. 34–66; quotations, pp. 39, 57.

33. Ibid., p. 42.

34. Ibid., p. 61.

35. AAP-AP photograph, Sydney *Morning Herald,* 14 Aug. 69 (Fairfax Photo Library, Sydney).

36. Human Rights Watch, "Indonesia: Human Rights and Pro-Independence

Actions in Papua, 1999–2000," III, pp. 2, 5n7, <www.hrw.org/reports/2000/papua>.

37. Helen and Frank Schreider, "East from Bali—by Seagoing Jeep to Timor," *National Geographic,* 122, no. 2 (Aug. 62), pp. 236–279, esp. pp. 276–278.

38. Robert Cribb, "How Many Deaths?" in Wessel and Wimhofer, eds., *Violence in Indonesia* (Hamburg: Abera, 2001), pp. 82–98. James Dunn offers data that make such a figure credible in "The Timor Affair in International Perspective," in Peter Carey and G. Carter Bentley, *East Timor at the Crossroads: The Forging of a Nation* (Honolulu/New York: University of Hawaii Press/Social Science Research Council, 1995), pp. 59, 67. Bishop Belo affirms that the total may have been 250,000 or more; Arnold S. Kohen, *From the Place of the Dead: The Epic Struggles of Bishop Belo of East Timor* (New York: St. Martin's Press, 1999), pp. 3, 89.

39. James Dunn, "East Timor: A Case of Cultural Genocide?" pp. 171–190, and Ben Kiernan, "The Cambodian Genocide: Issues and Responses," esp. p. 191, in George J. Andreopoulos, ed., *Genocide: Conceptual and Historical Dimensions* (Philadelphia: University of Pennsylvania Press, 1994); George J. Aditjondro, "Ninjas, Nanggalas, Monuments and Mossad Manuals: An Anthropology of Indonesian State Terror in East Timor," Jeffrey A. Sluka, ed., *Death Squad: The Anthropology of State Terror* (Philadelphia: University of Pennsylvania Press, 2000), pp. 158–188; Ben Kiernan to the author, 8 June 01.

40. Kohen, *From the Place of the Dead,* pp. 136–139; 203–204.

41. Ibid., 16–17, 29, 103–104, 127–129, and 259. Also author's personal observations in Poland, 1987, 1989.

42. John G. Taylor, *East Timor: The Price of Freedom* (London: Zed Books, 1999), p. 157.

43. Kohen, *From the Place of the Dead,* pp. 160–165.

44. Anicetto Guterres-Lopes, interview, Dili, 18 June 99; Kohen, *From the Place of the Dead,* p. 175; Col. (ret.) John Haseman, in an interview, 13 July 98, using identifiable individuals as a test, believed the count then stood at 21 killed, 46 missing.

45. Kohen, *From the Place of the Dead,* pp. 167–168.

46. "The Military Trials and the Truth behind the Dili Massacre," advance copy of TAPOL Bulletin No. 112, August 1992, apakabar@cdp.UUCP, 21 July 92; Kohen, *From the Place of the Dead,* pp. 170–171.

47. Privileged conversation, confirmed by confidential email.

48. Kohen, *From the Place of the Dead,* quotation p. 185.

49. Ibid., quotation, p. 216.

50. Personal observation and interviews, Dili, pp. 17–19, June 99; Kohen, *From the Place of the Dead,* pp. 225–226.

51. Kohen, *From the Place of the Dead,* pp. 243–244.

52. B. Wiwoho and Tribuana Said, eds., *Investment Opportunities in Indonesia's Provinces* (Jakarta: National Development Information Office, 1998), p. 320.

53. Ibid., pp. 311, 324–325.

54. The World Bank, *World Development Report* (New York: Oxford University Press, 1999), pp. 190–191. The per capita GNP of the Dominican Republic, which shares an island with Haiti, was at $1,670, five times as large.

55. The narrative that follows is based on field notes, 2–5 Nov. 97.
56. Sabam Siagian, interview, 4 Mar. 98.

10. Indonesia Burning

1. Robert G. Kaiser, "Forests of Borneo Going Up in Smoke," quoting the Asian Development Bank in *Washington Post,* 7 Sept. 97, p. A18.
2. James Schweithelm, "The Fire This Time: An Overview of Indonesia's Forest Fires in 1997/1998," World Wide Fund for Nature Indonesia Programme, Jakarta [1998] (no pagination), Section 3.1.
3. Schweithelm, "The Fire This Time," 3.4.2.
4. Charles Victor Barber, "Forest Resource Scarcity and Social Conflict in Indonesia," *Environment,* 40 (4 May 98), pp. 8–9.
5. Schweithelm, "The Fire This Time," 2.1.
6. Paul K. Gellert, "A Brief History and Analysis of Indonesia's Forest Fire Crisis," *Indonesia,* 65 (Apr. 98), pp. 63–85, p. 66.
7. Ibid., p. 77, table 2, p. 78.
8. Ibid., pp. 81–82.
9. Ibid., p. 82, 82n, citing Reuters, 30 Sept. 97.
10. Ibid., pp. 83–85.
11. David Lamb, "Fires again Ravage Indonesia's Forests," *Los Angeles Times,* 23 Mar. 98, p. A1.
12. Schweithelm, "The Fire This Time," 2.1.
13. Ibid., 2.2.
14. Prof. Douglas Fuller, interviews, 3 Feb. 98; 19 Feb. 99.
15. Quotations of Minister Juwono, Reuters, 14 Apr. 98; *Kompas* Online, 14 Apr. 98; *South China Morning Post,* 21 Apr. 98.
16. Schweithelm, "The Fire This Time," 2.3.1, 2.3.3.
17. David Glover and Timothy Jesup, eds., *Indonesia's Fire and Haze: The Cost of Catastrophe* (Singapore: Institute for Southeast Asia Studies, 1999), pp. 98–99.
18. Rona Dennis, *A Review of Fire Projects in Indonesia, 1982–1999* (Bogor: Center for International Forestry Research, 1999), p. 16; Charles Victor Barber and James Schweithelm, *Trial by Fire: Forest Fires and Forestry Policy in Indonesia's Era of Crisis and Reform* (Washington, DC: World Resources Institute, 2000), pp. 14–15.
19. Glover and Jesup, *Indonesia's Fire and Haze,* pp. 110–111. Certain disasters, it may be argued, are standard features of climate. The drought of 1988 in a third of the United States cost about $40 billion; Hurricane Andrew, 1992, between $25 and $33 billion; and the Mississippi Valley floods of 1993, $28 billion at most (William K. Stevens, *New York Times,* 25 Apr. 00, pp. F1, F4). But an advanced industrial society, while registering higher costs, also restores its losses more rapidly than an Indonesia.
20. Asian Development Bank study cited in Dennis, table 6, p. 18; Barber and Schweithelm, *Trial by Fire,* p. 15, table 3.
21. On Irian: Fuller, "Fire Distribution from DMSP-OLS (Aug.–Dec. 1997)," and personal note to the author, 27 Mar. 01.
22. Schweithelm, "The Fire This Time," 2.3.4; 2.3.5.
23. Schweithelm, ibid., 2.3.7, indicates studies under way.

24. Reuters, 14 Apr. 98.

25. "The Sky Flashes," Miami, 11 July 98, www.economist.com/archive/view.cgi

26. Fuller, interview, 19 Feb. 99. African savanna burns more broadly and frequently but without the degrees of species loss occasioned by fires in the wet tropics (Fuller, note to author, 27 Mar. 01).

27. Charles P. Kindleberger, *Manias, Panics, and Crashes: A History of Financial Crises* (New York: John Wiley, 3d ed., 1996; 1st ed., 1978).

28. Prijono Tjiptoherijanto, "Poverty and Inequality in Indonesia at the End of the 20th Century," *The Indonesian Quarterly, 25, 3* (Third Quarter 1997) ("Indonesia in the New Asia Pacific Order"), 251–275.

29. World Bank, Report No. 16433-IND, "Indonesia: Sustaining High Growth with Equity," 190 pp., May 30, 1997.

30. Ibid., pp. 61n10, citing *Foreign Affairs,* 1994, pp. 62–78.

31. A sage summary of these and other phenomena, tempering World Bank perspective, appears in Mark McGillivray and Oliver Morissey, "Economic and Financial Meltdown in Indonesia: Prospects for Sustained and Equitable Economic and Social Recovery," in Arief Budiman, Barbara Hartley, and Damien Kingsbury, eds., *Reformasi: Crisis and Change in Indonesia* (Clayton, Victoria: Monash Asia Institute, 1999), pp. 3–26, esp. pp. 5–10.

32. World Bank, Report No. 16433-IND, box 2.2, p. 44.

33. Ross Garnaut, "The East Asian Crisis," in Ross H. McLeod and Ross Garnaut, eds., *East Asia in Crisis: From Being a Miracle to Needing One?* (London: Routledge, 1998), pp. 3–27, esp. pp. 13–21.

34. I reflect on these and other phenemona in "The Asian Miracle, the Asian Contagion, and the U.S.A.," keynote address to annual dinner, Foreign Policy Research Institute, Ritz-Carlton Hotel, Philadelphia, 16 Nov. 98; published as FPRI *Wire,* 6, no. 6 (Dec. 98).

35. *New York Times,* 5 Sept. 98, p. C2.

36. Charles Wolf, Jr., "In the Eye of the Storm: The Impact of Asia's Economic Turmoil on 'Greater China,'" Nov. 98 (paper for FPRI Conference on "The Greater Chinese Economy," Philadelphia, PA, 16 Sept. 98), pp. 2–4.

37. Ibid., pp. 5–7.

38. McGillivray and Morissey, "Economic and Financial Meltdown in Indonesia," pp. 16–18.

39. Ibid., pp. 19–22.

40. As cited in McLeod and Garnaut, *East Asia in Crisis,* pp. 161, 227, and 321. For subsequent reflection, see Paul Blustein, *The Chastening: Inside the Crisis that Rocked the Global Financial System and Tumbled the IMF* (New York: Public Affairs Books, 2001).

41. Ross McLeod, "Indonesia," in ibid., pp. 46–47.

42. Titin Suwandi, "Indonesian Banking Post-Deregulation: Moral Hazard and High Real Interest Rates," Economic Division Working Paper, Research School of Pacific and Asian Studies, The Australian National University, 1995.

43. On handshaking style, several experienced testimonies. On "photo-op," Camdessus remarks at Council on Foreign Relations, "Asia Crisis: Lessons for the IMF and Wall Street," New York City, 6 Feb. 98. On impact of photograph, numerous Javanese commentators in person and in print.

44. Christopher Wood, *The Bubble Economy: The Japanese Economic Collapse* (Tokyo: Charles G. Tuttle Company, 1993), p. 8.

45. Friend, "The Asian Miracle," p. 3.

46. Website link and all source details withheld to protect the privacy and security of those involved.

47. Michael Richardson, "Intolerance in Indonesia," *International Herald Tribune,* 11 Jan. 97; TH, ANY, DM, "Tasikmalaya Riot: An Inter-Religion Conflict, An Effort to Encounter NU, or A Long Lasting Economic Disparity?" www.tempo.co. id~/harian/f_970107_1_e. See also Sarlito Wirawan Sarwono, "Situbondo dan Tasikmalaya: Bukan Ditunggangi," *Kompas* Online, 27 Jan. 97; replied to by Simuh, "Masalah Situbondo dan Tasikmalaya," *Kompas* Online, 7 Feb. 97.

48. Schwarz, 2nd ed., p. 332, citing Agence France Press, 19 Nov. 98. The figure is less horrific when compared to burnings, and other major vandalisms, of American places of worship in the same period. There was no systematic central count, or satisfactory breakdown by race and faith, but the number was clearly some hundreds. For data from several sources, I am indebted to Katie Gonos.

49. Pusat Penelitian Pembangunan Pedesaan dan Kawasan (Center for the Study of Village and Regional Development), Universitas Gadjah Mada, dengan Departemen Agama (Ministry of Religion) Republik Indonesia, *Laporan Akhir* (Final Report); *Perilaku Kekerasan Kolektif: Kondisi dan Pemicu* (Collective Violent Behavior: Conditions and Actors); Executive Summary (Yogyakarta, 1998), v.

50. Ibid., esp. p. 32.

51. Ibid.; analysis of evidence from the field, pp. 12–21; specific diagrams for each of the seven locales, pp. 33–39. See also Human Rights Watch/Asia, *Indonesia: Communal Violence in West Kalimantan,* 9, no. 10 (Dec. 97); U.S. Department of State, *Indonesia Report on Human Rights Practices for 1997* (released 30 Jan. 98), accessed by apakabar@clark.net, pp. 10, 13.

52. State Department, *Indonesia Report . . . Human Rights* (1997), p. 37.

53. P3PK, *Laporan Akhir,* pp. 22–25.

54. Prof. Dr. Loekman, Prof. Dr. Sartono, Dr. Ir. Mochammad Maksum, at P3PK, Universitas Gadjah Mada, Yogyakarta, interview, 30 Oct. 97.

55. Prof. Dr. Sartono, interview, 7 Mar. 98.

56. Former Minister Mo. Sadli, interview, 18 Oct. 97.

57. P3PK, *Laporan Akhir,* pp. 2, 5.

58. Prof. Dr. Loekman, interview, 30 Oct. 97.

59. Father Y. B. Mangunwijaya, interview, 29 Oct. 97.

60. Ibid., and Indonesian newspapers, Sept.–Oct. 97, passim. Nurcholish Madjid had also been openly sympathetic to Amien Rais' criticisms of corruption; interview, 21 Oct. 97.

61. Abdurrahman Wahid, interview, 26 Oct. 97.

62. Personal correspondence and field notes, Jan.–Mar. 98.

11. Forcing Out Suharto

1. Field notes, 4 Mar. 98.

2. Apakabar, Indonesia-L, Dec. 97, passim; *Economist,* 20 Dec. 97, p. 49; personal conversations, Jakarta.

3. *New York Times,* 10 Jan. 98, p. D1; *Philadelphia Inquirer,* 10 Jan. 98, p. A6; personal conversations, Jakarta.

4. Professor Hanke's article in *Forbes,* 6 Apr. 98, states his views and his defeated expectations. He persisted in believing that Michel Camdessus and the IMF were to blame for the Indonesian crash; testimony before the U.S. Senate Committee on Banking, Housing and Urban Affairs on "The International Monetary Fund and International Financial Institutions," 27 Apr. 00, and supplemental exchange with Senator Mike Crapo, 7 July 00. My judgments are based on travel and familiarity with key players in the 1990s in all countries mentioned and conversations in Jakarta, Mar. 98, including one with a member of "the family."

5. HRW/Asia, "Indonesia Alert: Economic Crisis Leads to Scapegoating of Ethnic Chinese" (draft, New York, Feb. 98), including statements from meeting at Sunda Kelapa mosque, 27 Jan. 98.

6. Adam Schwarz, *A Nation in Waiting* (Boulder: Westview Press, 2nd ed., 2000), pp. 346–347, 496n133; interview, Sofyan Wanandi, 21 Oct. 98 (Wanandi's own business card uses the old spelling "Sofjan," but I follow Western practice regarding use of his name, as pronounced).

7. Sofyan Wanandi, interview, 21 Oct. 98.

8. Soedradjad Djiwandono, interview, 27 Feb. 99. Ross McLeod criticizes Central Bank policy in "Indonesia's Crisis and Future Prospects," Karl Jackson, ed., *Asian Contagion: The Causes and Consequences of a Financial Crisis* (Boulder: Westview Press, 1999), pp. 209–240, esp. 210, 234–235.

9. Soedradjad Djiwandono, interview, 27 Feb. 99.

10. Ibid.

11. Multiple interviews, each man; Jakarta newspapers, Jan. 98, passim. Sumitro said that Suharto believed he had put the other two up to it, and for that reason was vindictive about his son. In approving Prabowo's reassignment to Bandung's staff and command school, Suharto told Wiranto, contemptuously, "He comes from an intellectual family anyway." Whatever the feelings between Suharto and Prabowo, each of his three former ministers had the independent integrity to oppose Suharto's reelection. They needed no cabal to speak from.

12. Interview, Professor Mohammad Sadli, 17 Oct. 97.

13. Interviews, 2, 3 Mar. 98, with business- and upper-middle-class families.

14. Interview, Karlina Leksono, 5 June 99.

15. Professor Dr. Franz Magnis-Suseno, SJ, interview, 5 Mar. 98.

16. Dr. Emil Salim, interview, 13 Mar. 98.

17. Ibid.; M. S. Kismadi, interview, 3 Mar. 98.

18. For the evolution of his views to that point, Margaret Scott, "Indonesia Reborn?" *New York Review of Books,* 13 Aug. 98.

19. I am grateful to former Ambassador Harry Barnes, now of the Carter Center in Atlanta, for subsequent discussion of this period in Chile's history, during which I had met him in Santiago.

20. Theodore Friend, "Timely Daring: The United States and Ferdinand Marcos," in Daniel Pipes and Adam Garfinkle, eds., *Friendly Tyrants: An American Dilemma* (New York: St. Martin's Press, 1991), pp. 201–219.

21. Amien Rais, interview, 4 Mar. 98.

22. Quoted in Schwarz, *A Nation in Waiting,* p. 350.

23. Suryo Bambang Sulisto, interview, 2 Mar. 98.
24. David Jenkins quotes Salim Said in "Vanishing Regime," *Sydney Morning Herald,* 18 Apr. 98, rpt. in *The Last Days of President Suharto,* Edward Aspinall, Herb Feith, and Gerry van Klinken, eds. (Clayton, Victoria: Monash Asia Institute, 1999), p. 35 (hereafter: Aspinall, et al.).
25. Schwarz, *Nation in Waiting,* pp. 353–354; Jenkins, "Vanishing Regime," pp. 34–37; "Security Tight as Indonesian Student Demos Repeated after Clashes," Surabaya, March 18 (Agence France Presse home page); "Clash at the Universitas Sebelas Maret, 25 Students Injured," Solo, March 18 (Kompas Online); interview, Professor Dr. Loekman Soetrisno, 24 Oct. 98.
26. Orville Schell, *Mandate of Heaven* (New York: Simon and Schuster, 1994), esp. pp. 74–96; personal travels throughout Eastern Central Europe, 1987, 1989–1992; interviews, Dr. Pavol Demes and Fedor Gal, founder of Eco-Glasnost, Bratislava, 6 Feb. 91.
27. Marshall Clark, "Cleansing the Earth," *Inside Indonesia,* 56, Oct.–Dec. 98, rpt. in Aspinall et al., pp. 37–40; Endo Suanda, interview, 13 Oct. 98.
28. Personal notes, USINDO Open Forum, 29 Apr. 98. See also Jenkins, in Aspinall et al., p. 36.
29. Personal notes, 29 Apr. 98.
30. These observations are a distillation of confidential comments to me by several prominent Indonesians who know Prabowo well.
31. John Pemberton, *On the Subject of "Java"* (Ithaca and London: Cornell University Press, 1994), pp. 177–181; quotation, p. 179.
32. "Surat Dari Redaksi" (Letter from the Editor), *Tempo,* 6–12 Oct. 98, p. 7; Schwarz, *Nation in Waiting,* pp. 161–162, 320, 490n35.
33. Schwarz, *Nation in Waiting,* p. 336.
34. Confidential interviews.
35. Schwarz, *Nation in Waiting,* pp. 336, 494n89.
36. Confidential interview, 9 Mar. 98.
37. Jenkins, in Aspinall et al., pp. 31–33; Schwarz, *Nation in Waiting,* p. 351; quotation, Jenkins, p. 32.
38. Testimony, Pius Lustrilanang, Hearing of the Subcommittee on International Operations and Human Rights, U.S. House of Representatives, 7 May 98; personal notes, 7 May 98; *New York Times,* 8 May 98, p. 3.
39. Stefan Eklöf, *Indonesian Politics in Crisis: The Long Fall of Suharto, 1996–1998* (Copenhagen: Nordic Institute of Asian Studies, 1999), p. 169n29.
40. Keith Richburg, "Indonesia's Unintentional Martyrs: Slayings of Four Students Transformed a Nation," *Washington Post,* 8 June 98, in Aspinall et al., pp. 45–50.
41. Professor W. Scott Thompson on NPR, *Talk of the Nation: Science Friday,* "Indonesia and the Internet," 5 June 98; printed transcript, p. 3; also www.sciencefriday.com.
42. Ibid., other commentators and callers, pp. 4–9.
43. Quotation from Dewi Fortuna Anwar, interview, 28 Oct. 98.
44. Gerry van Klinken, "The May riots," 29 May 98, in Aspinall et al., pp. 50–53.
45. Ibid., p. 50; Karlina Leksono interview, 5 June 99.
46. Schwarz, *Nation in Waiting,* pp. 380–381; Susan Berfield and Dewi Loveard, "Ten Days That Shook Indonesia," *Asiaweek,* 24 July 98, ibid., pp. 60–61. An opposi-

tion journalist experienced in casualty figures believed that the NGO rape numbers were exaggerated by procedural haste and double-counting; confidential interview, 5 Nov. 00.

47. Dewi Anggreani, "Exposing Crimes against Women," *The Age* (Melbourne), 21 June 98, in Aspinall et al., pp. 65–66. This incident appears to be the basis of the gripping short story, "Clara," by Seno Gumira Ajidarma, *Indonesia,* 68 (Oct. 99), pp. 157–163.

48. Confidential interview.

49. Soedjati Djiwondono, interview, 2 June 99.

50. Berfield and Loveard, "Ten Days," in Aspinall et al., pp. 57–58. These *Asiaweek* reporters relied on unnamed military sources and on a civilian who worked with the military.

51. "Classic tactics": Professor Dr. Onghokham, interview, 21 Oct. 98.

52. Dewi Fortuna Anwar, interview, 28 Oct. 98.

53. This is my distillation of several interviewers' and written accounts. Prabowo's own account of the Malang trip, as given to three Jakarta periodicals, is summarized in Kees van Dijk, *A Country in Despair: Indonesia between 1997 and 2000* (Leiden: KITLV Press, 2001), p. 193n. O'Rourke, *Reformasi,* pp. 104–112, is astute on military provocation and inaction.

54. Quotation, Berfield and Loveard, "Ten Days," p. 59.

55. Interviews: Lt. Gen. Bambang Yudhoyono, Maj. Gen. Joko Mulani, Maj. Gen. Sudi Silalahi, 9 June 99; Alamsjah Hamdani, 28 May 99.

56. Interview, Generals Bambang, Joko, and Sudi, 9 June 99.

57. Ibid. Fifty-four persons died in the riots following acquittal of white officers accused in the beating of black Rodney King. Police passivity in face of that rioting was later followed by revelations of deep corruption; Lou Cannon, "L.A.P.D. Confidential: America's Most Infamous Police Department Is in Trouble Again, Devastated by This Corrupt Cop's Confessions," *New York Times Magazine,* 1 (Oct. 00), pp. 32–37, 62, 64, 66.

58. Confidential interview.

59. Joint Fact Finding Team (TGPF), *Final Report about the 13–15 May 1998 Riot* (Jakarta, 23 Oct. 98). Excellent commentary is provided by Jemma Purdey, "Problematizing the Place of Victims in *Reformasi* Indonesia: A Contested Truth about the May 1998 Violence," *Asian Survey,* 42, no. 4 (July/Aug. 02), pp. 605–622.

60. Sofyan Wanandi, interview, 21 Oct. 98.

61. "Whither Place of Chinese Indonesians," article in *The Straits Times,* quoted by Ambassador Lee Khoon Choy, *A Fragile Nation: The Indonesian Crisis* (Singapore: World Scientific Publishing Co., 1999), p. 255.

62. Budi Lim, interview, 27 Oct. 98.

63. Ibid.

64. Indria Samego, et al., "Bila ABRI Menghendaki: Desakan-kuat Reformasi Atas Konsep Dwifungsi Abri" ["If ABRI wishes: Forcing Reform of ABRI's Dual Function Concept"] (Bandung: Mizan, 1998).

65. Dewi Fortuna Anwar, interview, 28 Oct. 98.

66. These and other theories are laid out in Schwarz, *Nation in Waiting,* pp. 357–358. Evaluations of each are my own.

67. Eklöf, *Long Fall,* pp. 180, 195–197.

68. O'Rourke, *Reformasi*, pp. 114–117, pointedly suggests that Wiranto tried to use pandemonium to bleed power from Suharto to ABRI and to himself.

69. Susan Berfield and Dewi Loveard, "Ten Days," p. 61.

70. Keith Loveard, *Suharto: Indonesia's Last Sultan* (Singapore: Horizon Books, 1999), pp. 351, 354.

71. Ryszard Kapuscinski, "A Voice for the Silent Masses," *New Perspectives Quarterly*, 14, no. 1 (Winter, 1997), p. 21.

72. Schwarz, *Nation in Waiting*, p. 358.

73. Nurcholish Madjid, interview, 27 Oct. 98.

74. I have put into direct discourse this account furnished by Schwarz, *Nation in Waiting*, p. 360.

75. Nurcholish Madjid, interview, 27 Oct. 98.

76. Schwarz, *Nation in Waiting*, pp. 362–363.

77. Ibid., pp. 358–359; Donald K. Emmerson, "Exit and Aftermath: The Crisis of 1997–98" in Emmerson, ed., *Indonesia beyond Suharto* (Armonk, NY, London: M. E. Sharpe, 1999), pp. 302–303.

78. Generals Bambang, Joko, and Sudi, interview, 9 June 99.

79. Schwarz, *Nation in Waiting*, p. 363.

80. Nurcholish Madjid, interview, 27 Oct. 98; Schwarz, *Nation in Waiting*, p. 363; Emmerson, "Exit and Aftermath," p. 306.

81. Abouprijadi Santoso, "Jakarta's May Revolution," *Inside Indonesia*, 56 (Oct.–Dec. 98), www.insideindonesia.org/edit56/tossi.htm.

82. Nurcholish Madjid, interview, 27 Oct. 98; Schwarz, *Nation in Waiting*, p. 364.

83. Schwarz, *Nation in Waiting*, p. 364.

84. Nurcholish Madjid, interview, 27 Oct. 98.

85. Emmerson, "Exit and Aftermath: The Crisis of 1997–98," in Emerson, ed., *Indonesia beyond Suharto*," pp. 309, 335.

86. Sarwono Kusumaatmadja, personal conversation, 26 Nov. 02.

12. Stroke

1. Adam Schwarz, *A Nation in Waiting*, pp. 367–369; Donald Emmerson, *Indonesia beyond Suharto*, p. 309; Kees Van Dijk, *A Country in Despair*, pp. 209–210, includes Prabowo's own later rationales.

2. Theodore Friend, "Indonesia in Flames," *Orbis*, 42, no. 3 (Summer 1998), pp. 387–407; quotation, p. 399.

3. K. Anthony Appiah, introduction to Soskia Sassen, *Globalization and Its Discontents* (New York: The New Press, 1998), p. xi; Anthony Giddens, *Runaway World* (New York: Routledge, 2000), p. 21.

4. Theodore Friend, "The Asian Miracle, the Asian Contagion, and the U.S.A.," keynote address, annual dinner of the Foreign Policy Research Institute, Philadelphia, 16 Nov. 98; published as FPRI "Wire," 6, 6 Dec. 98.

5. David S. Landes, *The Wealth and Poverty of Nations: Why Some Are So Rich and Some So Poor* (New York: W. W. Norton, 1998), p. 50.

6. These themes are well and repeatedly illustrated in Thomas L. Friedman, *The Lexus and the Olive Tree* (New York: Farrar, Straus, Giroux, 1999), and in John

Mickelthwait and Adrian Wooldridge, *A Future Perfect: The Challenge and Hidden Promise of Globalization* (New York: Times Books, 2000). For the privilege of reading the latter in unbound galleys, I am grateful to John Micklethwait.

7. John Gray, *False Dawn: The Delusions of Global Capitalism* (New York: The New Press, 1998), p. 215.

8. Hal Hill, *The Indonesian Economy since 1966: Southeast Asia's Emerging Giant* (Cambridge, New York, Melbourne: Cambridge University Press, 1996); Hal Hill, "The Indonesian Economy: The Strange and Sudden Death of a Tiger," in Geoff Forrester and R. J. May, eds., *The Fall of Soeharto* (Bathurst, Australia: Crawford House, 1998), pp. 93–103.

9. Paul Krugman, "The Myth of Asia's Miracle," *Foreign Affairs,* 73, no. 6 (Nov./Dec. 94), pp. 62–78. Krugman reviews and advances these and other themes in *The Return of Depression Economics* (New York: W. W. Norton, 1999).

10. Surjit S. Bhalla, "Domestic Follies, Investment Crises: East Asian Lessons for India," in Karl D. Jackson, ed., *Asian Contagion: The Causes and Consequences of a Financial Crisis* (Boulder: Westview Press, 1999), pp. 105–150, esp. pp. 110–111. See also Jackson, "Introduction," p. 9.

11. Ibid., p. 114.

12. Ibid., p. 146n6.

13. Ibid., pp. 125, 128, 144.

14. New York: Free Press, 1958, cited in Jackson, *Asian Contagion,* "Introduction," p. 24n1.

15. Such factors are overlooked, or at best understated, in the relevant essays in Joseph E. Stiglitz and Shahid Yusuf, eds., *Rethinking the Asian Miracle* (Washington/New York: World Bank/Oxford University Press, 2001); K. S. Jomo, "Rethinking the Role of Government Policy in Southeast Asia," pp. 461–508, and Joseph E. Stiglitz, "From Miracle to Crisis to Recovery: Lessons from Four Decades of East Asian Experience," pp. 509–526.

16. Toby Alice Volkman, *Feasts of Honor: Ritual and Change in the Toraja Highlands* (Urbana: University of Illinois Press, 1985), p. 22.

17. Ibid., pp. 22–26.

18. Aras Parura, interview, 7 Nov. 98; quotation from Volkman, *Feasts of Honor,* p. 28; Arrang Allo Pasanda, *Pong Tiku: Pahlawan Tana Toraja; Pejuang Anti Kolonialisme Belanda 1905–1907* [Pong Tiku: Hero of Toraja Land; the Struggle Against Dutch Colonialism, 1905–1907] (Jakarta: Fajarbaru Sinarpratama, 1995).

19. Arrang Allo Pasanda, *Pong Tiku,* pp. 177–178.

20. Volkman, *Feasts of Honor,* p. 38. Volkman errs (p. 28) in apparently believing that he received central and official designation. Pong Tiku's name does not appear in Klaus H. Schreiner's "Chronological Table of Indonesian National Heroes," pp. 288–290, appendix to his article "The Making of National Heroes: Guided Democracy to New Order, 1959–1992," in Nordholt, ed., *Outward Appearances,* pp. 259–287.

21. Volkman, *Feasts of Honor,* pp. 196–198.

22. Ibid, pp. 76, 100.

23. Ibid, pp. 98–99; quotation, p. 99.

24. Reflections on personal field notes, 4 Nov., 9 Nov. 98.

25. Volkman, *Feasts of Honor,* pp. 170–171.

26. Description, narrative, and evaluation in this section, where not otherwise noted, are based on personal field notes, 4, 6, 7, 9 Nov. 98.

27. Stanislaus Sandarupa, *Life and Death in Toraja* (21 Computer: Ujung Pandang, 1996; 1st ed., 1986), pp. 25–26.

28. Steven Radelet, "Indonesia's Implosion," Harvard Institute for International Development, 30 Sept. 98. See also Steven Radelet and Jeffrey Sachs, "The East Asian Financial Crisis: Diagnosis, Remedies, Prospects," HIID, 20 Apr. 98.

29. Personal notes, on-the-record discussion of "The Asia Crisis: Economic and Political Implications," Council on Foreign Relations, New York City, 15 Apr. 98.

30. *New York Times,* 15 Sept. 98, p. A1; *Financial Times,* 25 Sept. 98, special survey, "Brazilian Finance and Investment."

31. Quoted in the *New York Times,* 22 Sept. 98, p. A13. In an extended exchange of faxes, Aug.–Oct. 98, I gratefully received a variety of significant data from the Nomura Research Institute of the Nomura Securities Co., Tokyo. But then I asked what U.S. dollar values are given by the NRI to the LTCB liabilities and to the GNP of Indonesia, and what percentage of total Japanese banking system liabilities did the LTCB portion represent, The reply was "cannot be answered by NRI."

32. *New York Times,* 15 Sept. 98, p. A11; transcript of speech, p. A16.

33. Ibid., 24 Sept. 98, pp. A1, C11; 27 Sept. 98, Sec. 3, p. 1; *Financial Times,* 25 Sept. 98, p. 15; quotation from confidential conversation, 31 Aug. 00.

34. The World Bank Group (refutation), press release, "Indonesia and the World Bank," 28 July 97, www.worldbank.org/html/extdr/extme/1426.htm; Northwestern Newsfeed (reassertion), press release, www.nwu.edu/univ-relations/media/broadcast/winters.html.

35. Dennis de Tray and Jean-Michel Severino, "Battling Cancer of Corruption," *Jakarta Post,* 9 Sept. 98, p. 4.

36. Van Zorge Report, 18 Mar. 02, p. 33.

37. Minister of State for National Development Planning Boediono to Dr. Dennis de Tray, Country Director, Indonesia World Bank, 28 Jan. 99; Elizabeth McAllister, Acting Director-General, Operations Evaluation to Minister Boediono, 4 Feb. 99; both in "Country Assistance Review" (above); quotations, pp. 33, 36, 42. Document privately provided.

38. *Jakarta Post,* 14 Apr. 99, p. 6; <sadli@pacific.net.id> <Peter_McCawley @ausaid.gov.au>.

39. *New York Times,* 29 Apr. 99, p. A14.

40. Mark Landler, "Is It Morning in Indonesia or the End of an Eclipse?" *New York Times,* 2 Sept. 98, p. C2; and Christopher Wood of Santander Investments, cited therein.

41. Louis Uchitelle, "More Cash on Hand But Poorer," *International Herald Tribune,* 19 Oct. 99, p. 3.

42. Hill, *Indonesian Economy* (2nd ed.), pp. 203–204. Also Anne Booth, *The Indonesian Economy in the Nineteenth and Twentieth Centuries* (London, New York: McMillan Press and St. Martin's Press, 1998), pp. 128–131, table 3.7, p. 130.

43. Booth, ibid., pp. 132–134.

44. Emmanuel Skoufias, Asep Suryahadi, and Sudarno Sumarto, "The Indonesian

Crisis and Its Impacts on Household Welfare, Poverty Transitions, and Inequality: Evidence from Matched Households in 100 Village Survey," SMERU (Social Monitoring and Early Response Unit) [World Bank/AusAID/ASEM Trust Fund/USAID], Jakarta, Sept. 1999, p. 9. (Hereafter, "SMERU(1).")

45. Ibid., p. 16.

46. Duncan Thomas, Elizabeth Frankenberg, Kathleen Beegle, Graciela Teruel, "Household Budgets, Household Composition and the Crisis in Indonesia: Evidence from Longitudinal Household Survey Data," RAND, June 99, pp. 22–23.

47. Theodore Friend, "Indonesia in Flames," *Orbis,* 42, no. 3 (Summer 1998), pp. 395, 403; interviews with Marla Kosec and entourage of Abdurrahman Wahid, Mar. 98; Jakarta newspapers, Mar. 98, passim.

48. This remark is from a letter of Elizabeth Ary Krisnawati to me, 16 Oct. 99. All other information and quotations in this section are from our correspondence Apr.–Dec. 1998, and my field notes of 25 Oct. 98.

49. Anthony Reid, *Southeast Asia in the Age of Commerce, 1450–1680,* Vol. 2: *Expansion and Crisis* (New Haven: Yale University Press, 1993).

50. Benjamin Higgins, "Indonesia: The Chronic Dropout," in *Economic Development: Principles, Problems and Policies* (London: Constable, 1968), pp. 678, quoted in Booth, *Indonesian Economy,* p. 7.

51. Quotations and observations on the Netherlands from David S. Landes, *The Wealth and Poverty of Nations,* pp. 446–448.

52. Booth, *Indonesian Economy,* p. 260.

53. Ibid., pp. 263–264.

54. Syed Asif Hasnain, Shafiq Danani, et. al., UNIDO, "Foreign Direct Investment on Indonesian Manufacturing" (undated, year 2000, downloaded by email), concentrates on the high growth period, 1983–1999. The study finds that FDI contributed only 3–6 percent of total investment, employed a small proportion of the labor force, and contributed little to technological deepening of the manufacturing sector. Hasnain to the author (2 Jan. 01) observes that courting transnational corporations "may well be an exercise in futility, as they will come and go as part of their global . . . strategies, and they do not need any exceptional help from government to understand or realize their business prospects in Indonesia."

55. Martin Wolf, "A Miraculous Error," *Financial Times,* 29 Sept. 99, <sadli@pacific.net> <joyo@aol.com>.

56. *The Economist,* "Global Finance Survey," 30 Jan. 99, p. 8.

57. Paul Krugman, "Asia Has Not Learned Much From Crisis," *Time* magazine essay cited in *Business Times,* Singapore, 14 June 99, <sadli@pacific.net.id> <joyo@aol.com>; and Krugman, *The Return of Depression Economics,* passim.

58. Several confidential interviews across a three-year period.

59. Gray, *False Dawn,* pp. 215–218.

60. *New Perspectives Quarterly,* 16, no. 1 (Winter 1999), "DeGlobalization? From the Anglo-American Model to Market Pluralism."

61. Historical summary and crisis data from WFP staff draft document, untitled, courtesy of Dr. Lenard Millich of WFP, 9 Mar. 00.

62. Iwan Jaya Azis, "Why and How Institutions Matter in Indonesia's Episode of Economic Performance," draft, Dec. 99; I, "Introduction"; II, "Some Basic Con-

cepts"; III, "The Role and Nature of Institutions in Indonesia." (Because the pages of Prof. Iwan's lengthy drafts are unnumbered, references must be to their structure, focused upon tables and figures.)

63. Iwan Jaya Azis, "The Environmental Dimension of Economic Progress: The Case of Indonesia," draft, Mar. 00; III, Environmental Dimension: Sectoral and Spatial.

64. Ibid., IIIA; Urban Development, Welfare and Pollution. These figures obviously exceed those of SMERU (see note 44).

65. Ibid., figure 1.

66. Ibid., table 5B.

67. Ibid., table 6.

68. Ibid., tables 7A, 7B.

69. Ibid., IV: "Resource Accounting and Green GDP"; tables 9A, 9B.

70. For "little," see note 54.

71. Iwan, IV, "Why and How Institutions Matter." IV, "Modelling the Role of Institutions in Indonesia's Episode from Boom to Bust."

13. New Leaders, New Islam

1. Robert Hefner, "Islam and Nation in the Post-Suharto Era," Adam Schwarz and Jonathan Paris, eds., *The Politics of Post-Suharto Indonesia* (New York: Council on Foreign Relations, 1999), pp. 40–72, esp. pp. 41–45.

2. Hefner, *Civil Islam,* pp. 116–119; quotation, p. 117; Ramage, *Politics in Indonesia,* p. 116; author's conversations with Dr. Madjid, 1997–2000.

3. Hefner, ibid., p. 118; author's conversations.

4. Hefner, "Islam and Nation . . . Post Suharto," p. 48. Hefner develops similar points in a broader cultural context in "Religion: Evolving Pluralism," Emmerson, ed., *Indonesia beyond Suharto,* pp. 205–236.

5. Noorhaidi Hasan, "Faith and Politics: The Rise of the Laskar Jihad in the Era of Transition in Indonesia," *Indonesia,* 73 (Apr. 02), pp. 145–169, passim.

6. Olivier Roy, *The Failure of Political Islam* (Cambridge: Harvard University Press, 1998; 1st French ed., 1992); Gilles Kepel, *Jihad: The Trail of Political Islam* (Cambridge: Harvard University Press, 2002; 1st French ed., 2000); Azyumardi Azra, "Globalization of Indonesian Muslim Discourse: Contemporary Connections between Indonesia and the Middle East," in Johan Meuleman, ed., *Islam in the Era of Globalization: Muslim Attitudes towards Modernity and Identity* (Jakarta: INIS, 2001).

7. On the documents: Hefner in Schwarz and Paris, *Politics of Post-Suharto Indonesia,* pp. 61–62, 72n41.

8. Confidential interview; date withheld to protect identity of source.

9. Quoted by Mark Woodward, in USINDO workshop, "Sizing Up Indonesia's New Government," Washington, DC, 30 Nov. 99; transcript courtesy of USINDO.

10. Fazlur Rahman, the great Pakistani historian and interpreter of his religion, eventually concludes that Sufism is responsible for "superstitionism, miracle-mongering, tomb-worship, mass-hysteria and charlatanism" from which Mus-

lim society needs to be reclaimed. *Islam* (Garden City, NY: Doubleday, 1968), p. 305.

11. Alwi Shihab, interview, 26 June 98.

12. *Jakarta Post,* 24 July 1998, p. 1. A three-page organizational statement of the PKB (personal copy) affirms, among other things, that "NU will not be involved with PKB."

13. "Shihab seeks genuine harmony between different faiths," *Jakarta Post,* 14 Aug. 98.

14. Alwi Shihab, interview, 27 Sept. 98.

15. Quotations from personal notes, conversations with Marla Kosec, Mar.–Apr. 98, Apr.–June 98.

16. Ibid., 11 Aug. 98.

17. Quoted by Richard Borsuk and Rin Hindryati in the *Wall Street Journal Interactive Edition,* 25 Mar. 99.

18. Ibid. Deliar Noer is the author of *The Modernist Muslim Movement in Indonesia, 1900–1942* (Kuala Lumpur: Oxford University Press, 1973).

19. Nasrullah Nawawi, "Amien Rais, Orang yang Saya Kenal," <apakabar @saltmine.radix.net>1 May 99.

20. Margaret Scott, "Indonesia Reborn?" *New York Review of Books,* 13 Aug. 98, pp. 43–48; quotation, p. 43.

21. Ibid., p. 44, citing Rais, "The Muslim Brotherhood in Egypt: Its Rise, Demise, and Resurgence," University of Chicago, Dept. of Political Science, Mar. 81, p. 143.

22. Scott, "Indonesia Reborn?" p. 44.

23. Ibid.

24. Michael Vatikiotis, interview with Rais, *Far East Economic Review,* 25 Feb. 99, pp. 25–26.

25. Author's notes, USINDO and US-ASEAN Business Council, briefing for business leaders with Dr. Amien Rais, Washington, DC, 8 Mar. 99. Election data from Leo Suryadinata, *Elections and Politics in Indonesia* (Singapore: Institute of Southeast Asian Studies, 2002), pp. 106–107.

26. Angus McIntyre, "In Search of Megawati Sukarnoputri," Monash University Centre of Southeast Asian Studies, Working Paper No. 103, 1997, pp. 4–5; Mark McDonald, "Megawati: The Reluctant Heiress Apparent," San Jose *Mercury News,* 18 June 99, <sadli@pacific.net.id> <joyo@aol.com>.

27. McIntyre, "In Search of Megawati Sukarnoputri," p. 7; "hypnotized," McDonald, "Megawati," p. 3.

28. McDonald, "Megawati," p. 4; McIntyre, "In Search of Megawati Sukarnoputri," p. 7.

29. Istiadah, "Muslim Women in Contemporary Indonesia: Investigating Paths to Resist the Patriarchal System," Monash University Centre of Southeast Asian Studies, Working Paper No. 91, 1995, pp. 17–18.

30. Aung San Suu Kyi statement in 1991, quoted by McIntyre, "In Search of Megawati Sukarnoputri," p. 16.

31. Luisita Lopez Torregrosa, "Opposing Force," *Vogue,* Apr. 98, pp. 246–250; quotations, pp. 248, 249, 250.

32. *International Herald Tribune,* 9 Oct. 98, p. 4; *Japan Times,* 9 Oct. 98, p. 4.

33. Author's notes, American-Indonesia Chamber of Commerce luncheon for Laksamana Sukardi, New York City, 7 Jan. 99.

34. 15 Mar. 99, sent from Yogya, 20 Mar., sadli@pacific.net.id.

35. *Forum Keadilan,* 8, 30 May 99, pp. 28–32.

36. "Umweg über Lichtenstein," *Der Spiegel,* 15 Oct. 99, pp. 136–137; quotation, p. 137.

37. The first story is third-hand from a person present at the meeting. The second story is told by a friend of the chairman in question.

38. *Der Spiegel,* p. 136.

39. George Aditjondro, "Corruption Continues: More of the Same in Habibie's Indonesia," *Multinational Monitor,* Sept. 98, 19, i9, p. 25(3).

40. "Shoot the Criminals," *Newsweek,* 25 Jan. 99, apakabar@saltmine.radix.net, 19 Jan. 99.

41. *Jakarta Post,* 1 June 99, p. 1; *Far East Economic Review,* 3 Dec. 98, p. 16; various publications; sadli@pacific.net.id; <joyo@aol.com>. On other ramifications of corruption: Siswono Yudohusodo (cabinet minister, 1988–1998), "A Corrupt Regime Has One Alternative: To Stay in Power," pp. 14–16; and Teten Masduki (Coordinator, Indonesia Corruption Watch), "This Case Will Never Go to Trial," on ability to expose only 20 major cases of corruption a year from among 2000 annual complaints, pp. 17–18; both articles in *Van Zorge Report on Indonesia,* 22 (3 Sept. 99), hereafter, VZR.

42. "Habibie May Change, says Gus Dur," *Jakarta Post,* 22 July 99.

43. Ibid.

44. "A Look Inside the Student Movement: Moderates and Radicals," *VZR,* 1, 4 (27 Nov. 98), pp. 10–13.

45. Karlina and Ninok Leksono, interview, 5 June 99.

46. Schwarz, *A Nation in Waiting,* p. 375; Van Dijk, *A Country in Despair,* pp. 340–352.

47. Notes of telephone conversation with Alwi Shihab, 15 Nov. 98.

48. Van Dijk, *Country in Despair,* pp. 354–355.

49. Emmerson, *Indonesia beyond Suharto,* pp. 339–340, including quote from Wahid; "Season of Fear," *Asiaweek,* 4 Dec. 98, pp. 44–46.

50. Derwin Pereira, "Stroke Spurs Muslim Leader to Write More," *Sunday Times* (Singapore), 8 Nov. 98. In an article in an early issue of *Duta: Masyarakat Baru,* NU's new daily, Gus Dur is portrayed as sleeping whenever he chooses to do so, including during receipt of the treasured Magsaysay Award, and gathering material during sleep in an editorial chamber of his mind, "Bethoven dan 'Kentut' Habibie" (Beethoven and Habibie's Farts), 21 Nov. 98, p. 12.

51. This account is based on interviews with Alwi Shihab, 5 Apr. 99, and Nurcholish Madjid, 1 June 99. Interpretation of Gus Dur's motives and timing of the visits to Suharto is my own.

52. K. H. Hasyim Muzadi, Chairman of NU, East Java, interview in Surabaya, 13 June 99. Checking to corroborate the Qur'anic source, Professor Hafeez Malik, editor of the *Journal of South Asian and Middle Eastern Studies,* locates the following: "Go thou to Pharaoh, for he has indeed transgressed all bounds," which comes from Sura Ta-ha, xx, verse 24: *Al-Qur'an Al-Karim* [The Holy Qur'an, Eng-

lish Translation of the Meanings and Commentary] (Al-Madinah: King Fahd Holy Qur'an Printing Complex, 1410 A.H.), p. 883. Professor Malik confirms that this verse is used "when the occasion suggests," to correct errant leadership. Further discussion, with Dr. Nurcholish Madjid (4 Nov. 00), clarified for me that both texts apply. He kindly printed out variant English translations from his computer, the longer one cited by Malik and the shorter one indicated by Muzadi and used by the *kiai*.

53. For the short-term result of Wahid's seven visits to Suharto: "Gus Dur Gives Up in Battle against Riots," *Indonesian Observer,* 23 Mar. 99, <apakabar@saltmine. radix.net>. "Gus Dur warned that Soeharto still wields sufficient power to stage greater unrest than that which is occurring now."

54. Muzadi interview. After Abdurrahman Wahid's election as President of Indonesia, Muzadi was elected to succeed him as National Chairman of NU.

55. Ibid.

56. Alwi Shihab, interview, 5 Apr. 99.

57. Ibid.

58. *Indonesian Observer,* 23 Mar. 99 <apakabar@saltmine.radix.net>.

59. Author's notes, 25 Mar. 99.

60. Ibid., 7, 20, 28 Mar., 25 Apr. 99. Wahid's relationship with Yola is confirmed by two confidential sources; his with Aryanti in a variety of later newspaper articles.

61. Ibid., 19 May 99.

62. Ibid., 2 May 99; Paul Theroux, *Sir Vidia's Shadow* (Boston: Houghton Mifflin, 1998), p. 247.

63. Author's notes, 2 May 99.

64. Ibid., 20 Oct. 99.

14. Election 1999: Reds, Greens, Blues, Yellows

1. On these phenomena see Eric Bjornlund, "Democracy, Inc." *Wilson Quarterly,* 25, no. 3 (Summer 2001), pp. 18–24; quotation, p. 21.

2. Annette Clear, "International Donors and Indonesian Democracy," *Brown Journal of World Affairs,* 9, no. 1 (Spring 2002), pp. 141–155, esp. pp. 144–154. Two-thirds of the overall election costs of $300 million were borne by Indonesia's state budget.

3. Bjornlund, "Democracy, Inc.," p. 23.

4. The two most instructive color posters for public education were "Tanda Gambar, Nama dan Nomor: Partai Politik Peserta Pemilu, 1999; Gunakan Hak Pilih Anda Pada: Tanggal 7 June 1999" [Symbols, Names and Numbers of the Political Parties in the General Election of 1999: for your rightful use on June 7th]; and "Partai Peserta Pemilu, 1999" [Parties Contending in the General Election, 1999].

5. *Statistical Abstract of the United States,* 119th ed. (Washington, DC: U.S. Census Bureau, 1999), table 489, p. 301; 121st ed. (2001), tables 378, 403, pp. 233, 252. Emmerson, *Indonesia beyond Suharto,* p. 347; Suryadinata, *Elections and Politics,* p. 223.

6. Nurcholish Madjid, interview, 1 June 99.

7. Here, and henceforward, the source is my field notes of May–June 99, unless otherwise cited.

8. Sri Wahyuni, interview with Herbert Feith, *Jakarta Post*, 31 May 99, p. 3. A significant further historical source is Stephen Titus Hosmer, "The 1955 Indonesian General Elections in Java," Ph.D. dissertation in Political Science, International Law and Relations, Yale University, 1961. But Dr. Hosmer declined to let me read it, on the grounds that he was now preparing a book based on that long-sequestered research. All who care should wish him well in publishing his work.

9. Translation of Megawati speech in Magalang, 27 Mar. 99, *Van Zorge Report*, 13 (23 Apr. 99), p. 7.

10. Alwi Shihab, interview, 13 July 99.

11. Selo Soemardjan, interview, 4 June 99. Golkar eventually came in third in Central Java, behind PDI-P's 43 percent and PKB's 17 percent. But in West Sumatra Golkar's 24 percent actually beat both PAN (22 percent) and PPP (21 percent), in a province which was PAN's best nationally, and PPP's second best. Data from *Van Zorge Report*, 19 (23 July 99), p. 20; confirmed by Suryadinata, *Elections and Politics*, Appendix 1.

12. Author's field notes, June 99.

13. "Arrival Statement," Carter Center; personal notes, initial Carter press conference, 5 June 99.

14. Author's notes, 8 June 99.

15. "Statement of the National Democratic Institute (NDI) and the Carter Center International Election Observation Delegation to Indonesia's June 7th, 1999 Legislative Elections," Jakarta, 9 June 99; quotations, pp. 2, 3.

16. Author's notes, concluding Carter press conference, 9 June 99.

17. Elizabeth Ary Krisnawati to the author, 17 Mar. 99.

18. Ary to the author, 3 June 99.

19. "Hidup PDI-Perjuangan, Hidup Amien Rais," *Tempo*, 30 May 99, p. 19. *Tempo's* poll of 931 persons in 19 provinces was later shown, like other such polls, to suffer weaknesses of insufficient coverage and inherent bias—particularly in gross underrating of Golkar strength and gross overrating of PAN's.

20. Sultan Hamengkun Buwono X, interview, 10 June 99; his wife's dream, or vision, Professor Loekman Soetrisno, interview, 25 Oct. 98.

21. Allene Masters, "Letter from Yogyakarta," *Indonesia: Newsletter of the United States–Indonesia Society*, Autumn 1999, pp. 4–5.

22. Evaluation by Professor Loekman Soetrisno, interview, 25 Oct. 98.

23. PAN eventually received 17.3 percent of the vote in Yogya, a little less than half of what PDI-P received and just ahead of PKB and Golkar, tied at 14.3 percent. *Van Zorge Report*, 19 (23 July 99), p. 20; confirmed by Suryadinata, Appendix 1.

24. Sultan HBX, interview, 10 June 99.

25. Field notes, 11 June 99.

26. Ibid.

27. Ibid.

28. Dr. Pramoedja Rahardjo, interview, 1 Nov. 99.

15. East Timor

1. Peter Carey and Carter Bentley, eds., *East Timor at the Crossroads: The Forging of a Nation* (Honolulu: University of Hawaii Press, 1995), p. xii.

2. Field notes, Dili, 20 June 99.

3. John G. Taylor, *East Timor: The Price of Freedom* (New York: St. Martin's Press, 1999; 1st ed., 1991), p. xv.

4. Ibid, p. xvi. My source for the view of Minister Alatas is Dr. Dewi Fortuna Anwar, interview, 13 June 00.

5. Taylor, *East Timor*, p. xvii.

6. Dr. Dewi Fortuna Anwar, interview, 13 June 00. Interviews, Ambassador Stapleton Roy, 2 June 99; former Ambassador Sabam Siagian, 5 Nov. 99.

7. Ambassador Roy, interview, 2 June 99; confirmed by Dr. Dewi Fortuna Anwar, President Habibie's foreign policy advisor at that time, 8 June 99. The full text of Habibie's "muddled but high-minded sentiments" appears in Don Greenless and Robert Garran, *Deliverance: The Inside Story of East Timor's Fight for Freedom* (New South Wales: Allen and Unwin, 2002), p. 93.

8. Taylor, *East Timor*, p. xviii, citing Sander Thoenes, "Habibie Plays High-Risk Hand in Indonesia," *Financial Times*, 29 Jan. 99.

9. Greenless and Garran, *Deliverance*, pp. xiii–xv and chap. 5, passim.

10. Taylor, *East Timor*, p. xxi.

11. Ibid., pp. xxi–xxiii. Taylor gives Zacky Anwar Makarim's rank as lieutenant general. But this is not borne out in "Current Data on the Indonesian Military Elite, January 1, 1999–January 31, 2001," The Editors, INDONESIA, 71 (April 2001), pp. 135–173, esp. p. 141. Makarim's career in intelligence, covert operations, and trouble spots may be tracked in Tanter, Selden, and Shalom. *Bitter Flowers*, pp. 76, 168, 191–192, 197, 203–204n7, 204n16, 206n24.

12. Quotations of Galuh from field notes, Dili, 17–20 June 99.

13. Field notes, Dili, 17–20 June 99.

14. Aniceto Guterres-Lopez, interview, 18 June 99 (Galuh Soedjatmoko interpreting). These themes are developed from a female point of view in *Menyilam kemarau: usaha perempuan Timor Loro Sae menghentikan kekerasan, sebuah awal* [Ending the Dry Season: East Timor Women's Action to Stop Oppression; a Beginning], Forum Komunikasi untuk Perempuan Loro Sae [Timorese Women's Communication Forum] (Dili: FOKUPERS, 1999).

15. Aniceto Guterres-Lopez, interview.

16. Galuh Soedjatmoko, interview, 19 June 99; stories on Warda Hafidz, *Jakarta Post*, June 99, passim.

17. Galuh Soedjatmoko, interview, ibid.

18. Ms. Radhika Coomarraswamy, quoted by Louise Williams and Leonie Lamont, "Indonesian Soldiers Use Rape as a Secret Weapon, but Their 'Orphans' Bear Silent Witness," *Sydney Morning Herald*, 13 Sept. 99. Jill Hickson, "Women's Struggle in East Timor: An Eyewitness Report," *Green Left Weekly* (Australia), 7 July 99, <sadli/joyo>.

19. Field notes, Dili.

20. Ibid.

21. Carey and Bentley, *East Timor at the Crossroads;* Carey, "Introduction," p. 4; Dunn, "The Timor Affair in International Perspective," p. 59. Arnold S. Kohen, *From the Place of the Dead: The Epic Struggles of Bishop Belo of East Timor* (New York: St. Martin's Press, 1999), pp. 3, 89.

22. Taylor, *East Timor,* p. 169.

23. Articles by Agence France Presse, 12 Jan. 99; Hamish McDonald, *Sydney Morning Herald,* 13 Jan. 99; and esp. David Jenkins, "Why Not Open All E. Timor Files?" *Sydney Morning Herald,* 18 Jan. 99. <van zorge report/joyo>.

24. "World Urges Calm and Respect for Timor Vote," *Jakarta Post,* 5 Sept. 99 <sadli/joyo>; Donald K. Emmerson, "Moralpolitik: The Timor Test," *National Interest,* Winter 1999/2000, pp. 63–68.

25. Richard Tanter, "East Timor and the Crisis of the Indonesian Intelligence State," pp. 191–194, 203–204nn5–15, elaborates Makarim's involvement and choices. The essay is in Tanter, Mark Selden, and Stephen R. Shalom, eds., *Bitter Flowers, Sweet Flowers: East Timor, Indonesia, and the World Community* (Lanham, MD: Rowman and Littlefield, 2001), pp. 189–207.

26. "To address the allegations of foul play by UNAMET, a special investigative committee was brought in, comprised of three judges from South Africa, South Korea and Ireland. They found the allegations of UNAMET manipulation to be largely ungrounded." The Aksara Foundation Team, "Nationalism Versus Sensationalism? East Timor and the Press: A Quantitative Analysis" (Jakarta: Aksara Foundation, March 2000), p. 25. In certifying the results, the South African justice said, "Singly, jointly, put them all together, none of the irregularities could have affected the outcome." *Asiaweek,* 17 Sept. 99, p. 24.

27. *Far East Economic Review,* 16 Sept. 99, p. 10; Galuh Soedjatmoko email to friends, 30 Sept. 99.

28. *Far East Economic Review,* 16 Sept. 99, p. 14.

29. Ibid., p. 10. Taylor, *East Timor,* "Chronology," p. 228, says 3,000 refugees and uses the date Sept. 5. *Asiaweek,* Sept. 17, p. 29, says there were 5,000 refugees, of whom 30 were killed. Given anarchic conditions at the time, such reportorial discrepancies are unlikely ever to be authoritatively resolved.

30. Taylor, "Chronology," ibid.; *New York Times,* 8 Sept. 99, p. A1, 12. Quotation, *Far East Economic Review,* 16 Sept. 99, p. 13.

31. Transcripts of broadcast of "All Things Considered," National Public Radio (USA), 13 Sept. 99, relayed by Joyo@aol.com.

32. *Far East Economic Review,* 16 Sept. 99, p. 14.

33. *New York Times,* 9 Sept. 99, p. A8; *Philadelphia Inquirer,* 9 Sept. 99, pp. A1, A18; *New York Times,* 10 Sept. 99, pp. A1, A12.

34. *New York Times,* 9 Sept. 99, p. A1.

35. Ibid., 14 Sept. 99, pp. A1, 16, 22. A summary article, p. 16, chiefly credits Shelton's effectiveness with a culminating "ugly message," but a well-placed official American source in Jakarta says that brief and gentlemanly firmness by Admiral Blair was the turning point (confidential interview), 19 Oct. 99.

36. *Jim Lehrer News Hour,* Public Broadcasting System, 6 PM, 8 Sept. 99, on Cohen, followed by interview with Ramos Horta, personal notes. *Economist,* "The Tragedy of East Timor," 11 Sept. 99, p. 20.

37. Ian Martin, *Self-Determination in East Timor: The United Nations, the Ballot, and International Intervention* (Boulder, London: Lynne Rienner, 2001), pp. 121, 127.

38. USINDO report of a joint hearing of the House Committee on International Relations and Senate Committee on Foreign Relations, "The Political Futures of Indonesia and East Timor," 9 Sept. 99; *New York Times*, 13 Sept. 99, pp. A1, A6; Walter Russell Mead quoted in ibid., "Week in Review," 12 Sept. 99, p. 4. Data on InterFET: Alan Dupont, "ASEAN's Response to the East Timor Crisis," *Australian Journal of International Affairs*, 54, no. 2 (July 00), pp. 163–170, esp. pp. 166–167.

39. Richard Lloyd Parry, "A Chilling Audience with Dr. Strangelove of Jakarta," *The Independent* [London], 11 Sept. 99, <joyo@aol.com>; Taylor, "Chronology," p. 209; "Indonesia's Top General Sings of His 'Feelings' for East Timor," Associated Press, 12 Sept. 99 <joyo@aol.com>.

40. Tanter, "East Timor and the Crisis of the Indonesian Intelligence State," in Tanter, Selden, and Shalom, eds., *Bitter Flowers, Sweet Flowers*, pp. 189–207, esp. 193, 204n9–10. The point is substantiated by Hamish McDonald et al., *Masters of Terror: Indonesia's Military and Violence in East Timor in 1999* (Canberra: Australian National University, Strategic and Defence Studies Centre, 2002), and by Greenless and Garran, *Deliverance*.

41. *Financial Times*, 23 Sept. 99, p. 7.

42. Confidential interview, 19 Oct. 99; confidential correspondence.

43. Galuh Soedjatmoko, email to friends, 30 Sept. 99; Galuh email to the author, 3 Oct. 99.

44. Kemal Jufri, interview, 7 Nov. 00.

45. John Pilger, *Distant Voices* (London: Vintage, 1994; 1st ed, 1992), pp. 266–270; Desmond Ball and Hamish McDonald, *Death in Balibo, Lies in Canberra* (London: Allen and Unwin, 2000).

46. *The Independent* [London], 4 Sept. 99, <joyo@aol.com>.

47. "Remarks by Joyo for Laksamana-Mega," 5, 6 Sept. 99, and Joyo to Sukardi, 12 Sept. 99, copies provided to the author by joyo@aol.com, June 00; also Joyo to Siapa 2, 13 Sept. 99, ibid.

48. Eric Ellis, "Asia Buzz," *Time* magazine, 13 Sept. 99, provided with covering comment by ibid.

49. Nono Anwar Makarim, "Foreword" to *Nationalism Versus Sensationalism: East Timor and the Press: A Quantitative Analysis* (Jakarta: The Aksara Foundation, March 2000).

50. Ibid., quotations, pp. 9, 10, 13.

51. Ibid., "Foreword," pp. v, vi.

52. Desi Anwar, "The Games that Soldiers Play," 10 Sept. 99, for the *Jakarta Post, The Australian,* and the San Francisco *Chronicle*; <felia@cbn.net.id> to list of friends. This article is the more poignant coming from the sister of President Habibie's personal advisor on East Timor, Dr. Dewi Fortuna Anwar.

53. Colonel (Ret.) John B. Haseman, "East Timor: The Misuse of Military Power and Military Pride." This article has taken several forms. I quote from an email to me by Colonel Haseman, Sept. 99. A long opinion piece by Professor R. William Liddle accentuates incompetence and lack of political will on the part of

TNI Headquarters outside Jakarta, while finding mitigating factors to explain those conditions ("TNI dan Timor Timur," *Tempo* Interaktif, Kolom No. 31/ xxviii/04–10 Okt 1999). Professor Liddle stops far short of the civilian judgments of Ms. Anwar or the military judgments of Colonel Haseman.

54. This is a colloquial distillation of notes of a long confidential conversation (Jakarta, 19 Oct. 99) with two American official experts, whom I differentiate by the (changed) initials "K" and "L."

55. "Web-Only Interview [23 Feb. 00] with Juwono Sudarsono, Indonesia's First Civilian Defense Minister," Jason Tedjasukmana, *Time* Magazine, 28 Feb. 00. Email inquiry from author to Minister Juwono, 11 June 00.

56. O'Rourke, *Reformasi,* pp. 369–371, 390; quotation, p. 369; Juwono Sudarsono, interview, 8 Nov. 00.

57. David Jenkins, "To Stop the Dogs of War," Sydney *Morning Herald,* 27 Aug. 01, <sadli@pacific.net, joyo@aol.com>.

58. Samuel Moore (pseud.), "The Indonesian Military's Last Years in East Timor: An Analysis of Its Secret Documents," cites in this regard Usamah Hisyam, *Feisal Tanjung: Terbaik untuk Rakyat, Terbaik untuk ABRI* [The Best for the People; the Best for ABRI] (Jakarta: Dharmapena, 1999); *Indonesia,* 72 (Oct. 01), pp. 9–44, esp. 34–35, 39, 44.

59. McDonald et al., *Masters of Terror,* pp. 29–34, 52–57; quotations, p. 29.

60. Geoffrey Robinson, "The Fruitless Search for a Smoking Gun: Tracing the Origins of Violence in East Timor," in Colombijn and Lindblad, eds., *Roots of Violence in Indonesia,* pp. 243–276; quotations, pp. 245, 274.

61. Field notes, Dili, 19 June 99. For conversations on interventions in the 1990s, I am grateful to Dr. Harvey Sicherman and Professor Walter A. McDougall.

62. James Traub, "Inventing East Timor," *Foreign Affairs,* 79, no. 4 (July/Aug. 00), pp. 74–89; quotation, p. 74.

63. James Cotton, "Against the Grain: The East Timor Intervention," *Survival,* 43, no. 1 (Spring 01), pp. 127–142; quotation, p. 139. A five part series by GLOBO TV of Brazil, narration in Portuguese, conveys unforgettable images of conditions in early 2000; copy to the author, courtesy of Simone Duarte of GLOBO.

64. Galuh Soedjatmoko, email to the author, 9 Aug. 00; *New York Times,* 1 Mar. 01, p. A1.

65. Ian Martin, *Self-Determination,* pp. 121, 126–129; quotation, p. 126.

66. Jane Perlez, "Impoverished East Timor Exults over Independence," *New York Times,* 20 May 02, p. A6; Peter Carey, review of *Bitter Flowers, Sweet Flowers: East Timor, Indonesia, and the World Community, Indonesia,* 73 (Apr. 02), pp. 171–176, esp. pp. 175–176; Paddy Ashdown, high representative of the UN for Bosnia, in *New York Times,* 28 Oct. 02, p. A25.

67. Tina Rosenberg, "Designer Truth Commissions," *New York Times Magazine,* 9 Dec. 01, p. 66.

68. Vaudine England, "Accused Indonesian Generals True to Form," *South China Morning Post,* 16 Mar. 02, <sadli@pacific.net.id>; International Crisis Group, "Indonesia: Implications of the Timor Trials," Jakarta/Brussels, 8 May 02, <icg@crisisweb.org>; *New York Times,* 1 Dec. 02, p. A8.

16. Anarcho-Democracy

1. Van Zorge Report (hereafter, VZR), 21 (20 Aug. 99), pp. 9–11; *New York Times,* 10 Aug. 99, p. C4.

2. Yuri Sato, ed., *Indonesia Entering a New Era: Abdurrahman Wahid Government and Its Challenges* (Tokyo: Institute of Developing Economies, 2000), p. 6.

3. Conversation with Marla Kosec, 20 Oct. 99. The term *dukun* (meaning shaman or healer) when used informally by a foreigner may refer to someone whom an Indonesian might call an *ulama* or even a *kiai*. See Glossary.

4. Privileged conversation, some days later.

5. Sato, *Indonesia Entering a New Era,* pp. 6–7.

6. Nurcholish Madjid, interview, 21 Oct. 99.

7. Sato, *Indonesia Entering a New Era,* p. 7.

8. Privileged conversation with an American ophthalmologist who has examined Abdurrahman Wahid.

9. Personal notes, 31 Oct. 99.

10. Quotation from VZR, 26 (12 Nov. 99), p. 5.

11. O'Rourke, *Reformasi,* pp. 320–321.

12. Sato, *Indonesia Entering a New Era,* p. 8.

13. Confidential interview, 29 Oct. 99, with a source who had had recent personal conversation with Ma'sud.

14. Mohamad Sobary, interview, 31 Oct. 99.

15. Personal notes, "Indonesia Next" conference, Jimbaran, Bali, 24 Oct. 99.

16. Minister Alwi Shihab, interview, 7 June 00.

17. Notes of dialogue with President Abdurrahman Wahid, 7 June 00.

18. Minister Sarwono Kusumaatmadja, interview, 12 June 00.

19. Sarwono remarks to the Van Zorge-Heffernan conference, "Indonesia Next," personal notes, Bali, 24 Oct. 99.

20. Confidential interview, Jakarta, 6 Nov. 00; personal dialogue with President Wahid, Baltimore, MD, 9 Sept. 00.

21. Fullest account of the story: Louis Kraar, "The Corrupt Archipelago," *Fortune,* 24 July 00, pp. 200–204; see also van Dijk, *A Country in Despair,* p. 485n. Details on egregious corruption in Texmaco in the Suharto era, VZR, 28 (17 Dec. 99), pp. 17–22; on the loss of Sukardi as "an honest and progressive leader of outstanding integrity and credibility," VZR, 2 (8 May 00), pp. 16–18; on Sinivasan's role with Wahid in Sukardi's firing, confidential interviews.

22. World Bank and IMF v. IBRA on Texmaco, *Asiaweek,* 3 Nov. 00, p. 46. Sinivasan's political contribution, VZR, 3 (16 Aug. 01), p. 33. On Wahid's bizarre designation of the three untouchables, several journalistic reports.

23. Theodore Friend, "Indonesia's Year of the Blue Carpet: Plus Several Pathologies and Five Personalities," Philadelphia, Foreign Policy Research Institute, E-Note, 6 Dec. 00.

24. USINDO Briefs, Emil Salim, 4 May 01; James Castle, 14 May 01. International Crisis Group, "Bad Debt: The Politics of Financial Reform in Indonesia," *Asia Report,* 15 (13 Mar. 01).

25. VZR, 4 (18 Mar. 02), p. 33.

26. *Far East Economic Review,* 6 Apr. 00, p. 64.

27. Ibid., "Review 2000," 30 Dec. 99/6 Jan. 00, pp. 70–71.

28. Ibid., 10 Feb. 00, pp. 10–13; 17 Feb. 00, p. 57.

29. Privileged communications with three persons on the matter, 2000–2003; they in turn supported by still other sources.

30. Tanri Abeng, interview, 13 Mar. 98; "Episode Mimpi Tanri Abeng," *Strategi,* 4 (Apr. 99), pp. 20–28. Abeng was also a leader of Tim Sukses Habibie, entangled in the Bank Bali scandal.

31. Dr. Mochtar Riady, interview, 12 June 00.

32. McKinsey and Company, Investor Opinion Survey on Corporate Governance, June 2000, executive summary and passim; courtesy of Ken Gibson.

33. Jeffrey Sachs, cover story in *Far East Economic Review,* 25 Feb. 99, esp. p. 12. Two years later, Michael E. Porter, Jeffrey Sachs, et al. elaborated their formats in *The Global Competitiveness Report 2000* (New York: Oxford University Press, 2000). Adding a "startup index," in which Indonesia was midpack at no. 27, improved its "economic creativity" standing (pp. 32–35) and other rankings (pp. 154–155).

34. *Economist,* 5 May 01, p. 98.

35. Dow-Jones Newswires, 8 Dec. 99 <sadli@pacific.net.id> <joyo@aol.com>.

36. I have adapted this tale from one told conversationally by Bambang Harymurti.

37. Vito Tanzi, "Corruption around the World: Causes, Consequences, Scope, and Cures," International Monetary Fund Staff Papers, 45, no. 4, pp. 559–594, Dec. 98, pp. 1–3.

38. Dennis de Tray and Jean-Michel Severino, "Battling Cancer of Corruption," *Jakarta Post,* 10 Sept. 98 (news release of the World Bank Group).

39. *Jakarta Post,* 17 Apr. 01, quoting Minister of Industry and Trade Luhut B. Pandjaitan. Wardah Hafidz, coordinator of the Urban Poor Consortium, comments that, diverted from the poor, the loans only increased the debt problem; *Jakarta Post,* 21 Apr. 01, JoyoNews@aol.com. Also, *New York Times,* 10 Apr. 01, p. W1.

40. *Jakarta Post,* 18 July 00; Singapore *Straits Times,* 19 July 00, <joyo@aol.com>.

41. Gary Goodpaster, "Reflections on Corruption in Indonesia (Part 1), VZR, 3 (19 Mar. 01), pp. 22–32, esp. p. 25.

42. Goodpaster, ibid., Part 2, VZR, 3 (12 Apr. 01), pp. 27–33, esp. pp. 31–33.

43. Teten Masduki and Yoke Octarina, interview, 1 Nov. 99; and a supply of several of their supporting documents.

44. Notes of breakfast conversation, 13 Mar. 01, Washington, DC, at which were also present former Ministers Laksamana Sukardi and Ryaas Rasyid, and Professor Donald Emmerson.

45. Dr. Indria Samego et al., ". . . *Bila ABRI Menghendaki*": *Desakan-Kuat Reformasi Atas Konsep Dwifungsi ABRI* ["If ABRI Wishes": Reform Pressure upon ABRI's Concept of Dual Function] (Bandung: Mizan Pustaka, June 1998).

46. *Bila ABRI Berbisnis* [ABRI's Business Practices] (Bandung: Mizan Pustaka, Sept. 1998). See, by contrast, Arnoldo Brenes and Kevin Casas, eds., *Soldiers as Businessmen: The Economic Activities of Central American Militaries* (San Jose, Costa Rica: Fundación Arias por la Paz y el Progreso Humano, 1998).

47. *Tentara Mendamba Mitra* [The Army's Desire for Friendship] (Bandung: Mizan

Pustaka, 1999); *Tentara Yang Gelisah* [A Nervous Army] (Bandung: Mizan Pustaka, 1999).

48. General Wiranto, *ABRI Abad XXI* [ABRI in the Twenty-First Century] (Jakarta: ABRI Headquarters, 5 Oct. 98).

49. Ltg. Susilo Bambang Yudhoyono, "Indonesia in the New Millennium: Promises and the Price of Reform" (presented before the Temasek Society, Singapore, 17 May 99), pp. 11–12 and passim.

50. Agus Wirahadikusumah, MPA, ed., *Indonesia Baru dan Tantangan TNI* [The New Indonesia and Challenges for TNI] (Jakarta: Pustaka Sinar Harapan, 1999).

51. Confidential interviews; and John McBeth, cover article, *Far East Economic Review,* 9 Nov. 00.

52. Philip Yampolski, program notes, "Music of Indonesia 2: Indonesian Popular Music: Kroncong, Dangdut, and Langgam Jawa" (Smithsonian Folkways: SF 40056, 1991).

53. Ryamizard Ryacudu, "Konsistensi dan Komitmen TNI" [The Consistency and Commitment of TNI], in Agus Wira, *Indonesia Baru,* pp. 75–92.

54. The foregoing is informed by International Crisis Group, "Indonesia: Keeping the Military under Control," *Asia Report,* 9 (5 Sept. 00); VZR, 2 (25 Sept. 00), especially Dr. Salim Said, "The Indonesian Military Is in a State of Paralysis," pp. 15–19; confidential interviews and personal analysis.

55. Confidential interviews; both names and dates withheld.

56. Privileged conversation, 28 Oct. 99.

57. Quotation from VZR, 2 (25 Sept. 00), p. 14.

58. Salim Said, "Indonesian Military," p. 17.

59. Munir and Bara Hasibuan, investigatory conclusions as reported in *Indonesian Observer,* 21 Mar. 01 <sadli@pacific.net.id>; Bara Hasibuan, interviews, 18, 19 Dec. 02. Other working members of the FID group included Munir, Mar'ie Muhammad and Ratna Sarumpaet, in addition to founders Nurcholish Madjid and Emil Salim.

60. On *wayang* wars see O'Rourke, *Reformasi,* pp. 196, 369, 387–391; International Crisis Group, "How the *Jemaah Islamiyah* Terrorist Network Operates," *Asia Report,* 43 (11 Dec. 02); and privileged conversations.

61. *Tempo,* several reports, 28 Jan.–3 Feb. 03, including interview with Wiranto <sadli@pacific.net>.

62. Privileged conversation, 1 June 99.

63. Samantha F. Ravich, "Eyeing Indonesia through the Lens of Aceh," *Washington Quarterly,* summer 2000, pp. 7–20, esp. p. 11.

64. Gerry van Klinken, "What Is the Free Aceh Movement?" *Inside Indonesia,* 25 (Nov. 99), and riposte by M. Yusuf Daud, secretary general, GAM, 28 Nov. 99. <sadli@pacific.net.id>, <joyo@aol.com> 30 Nov. 99.

65. Ravich, "Eyeing Indonesia," pp. 15–18, and confidential interviews.

66. Edward Aspinall, "Sovereignty, the Successor State, and Universal Human Rights: History and the International Structuring of Acehnese Nationalism," *Indonesia,* 73 (Apr. 02), pp. 1–24.

67. Confidential interview, 3 Nov. 99.

68. AP (Geneva) 9 Dec. 02 and BBC, 8 Dec. 02<joyoIndonews@aol.com; personal

notes, USINDO and East-West Center Washington Conference, 1 Oct. 02, "National Integration in Indonesia: The Cases of Aceh and Papua."

69. Human Rights Watch, "Indonesia: Human Rights and Pro-Independence Actions in Papua, 1999–2000," www.hrw.org/reports/2000/papua.

70. Agence France Presse, Jakarta, 21 Dec. 00 <sadli@pacific.net.id>.

71. An incident well-analyzed in Octovianus Mote and Danilyn Rutherford, "From Irian Jaya to Papua: The Limits of Primordialism in Indonesia's Troubled East," *Indonesia,* 72 (Oct. 01), pp. 115–139.

72. International Crisis Group, "Indonesia: Ending Repression in Irian Jaya," Jakarta/Brussels, 20 Sept. 01, passim; personal notes, East-West Center Washington and USINDO conference, "National Integration in Indonesia: The Cases of Aceh and Papua," Washington, DC, 1 Oct. 02.

73. Peter King, "Morning Star Rising? *Indonesia Raya* and the New Papuan Nationalism," *Indonesia,* 73 (Apr. 02), pp. 89–127.

74. George Aditjondro, "The Tragedy of Maluku," 4 May 00; document courtesy of Ms. Cornelia Paliama.

75. Ibid., pp. 4–5.

76. Dr. Dieter Bartels, "Your God Is No Longer Mine: Moslem-Christian Fratricide in the Central Moluccas . . . After a Half-Millennium of Tolerant Co-Existence and Ethnic Unity," Ambon Berdarah On-Line, 9 Sept. 00, <www.geocities.com/ambon67>.

77. This narrative condenses points made in Bartels, "Your God Is No Longer Mine"; Paul Taylor, USINDO Brief, 13 Sept. 00; Professor Thamrin Tamagola, "In Every Corner of Indonesia, There Is Dry Grass Ready to Ignite," and Dr. Sahetapy, "If the Only Tool Is A Hammer Everything Becomes A Nail," VZR, 2 (18 July 00), pp. 16–20, and editorial summary, "War in the Malukus," ibid., pp. 4–15; also, personal familiarity with Ulster.

78. International Crisis Group, "Indonesia: Keeping the Military under Control," *Asia Report,* 9 (5 Sept. 00); Bara Hasibuan interviews, 18, 19 Dec. 02; senior American official, confidential interviews, 13, 24 Dec. 02. Amien at USINDO Open Forum, 30 Oct. 00, as reported in USINDO summary and completed by author's notes of the occasion.

79. Quotations from confidential interview, 4 Nov. 00. On social polarization in continuing consequence, *Economist,* 17 Mar. 01, p. 42.

80. Aditjondro, 10 Oct. 00, document courtesy of Cornelia Paliama.

81. Vaudine England, "Unpublished," email to the author, 12 July 01.

82. David Rohde, "Indonesia Unraveling?" *Foreign Affairs,* 80, no. 4 (July/Aug. 01), pp. 110–124; also *Economist,* 11 Aug. 01, p. 34. See also Lorraine V. Aragon, "Communal Violence in Poso, Central Sulawesi: Where People Eat Fish and Fish Eat People," *Indonesia,* 72 (Oct. 01), pp. 45–79.

83. International Crisis Group, "Indonesia: The Search for Peace in Maluku," *Asia Report,* 31 (8 Feb. 02); VZR, 4 (20 May 02), passim.

84. Donald L. Horowitz, *The Deadly Ethnic Riot* (Berkeley: University of California Press, 2001), p. 562; and personal notes, Professor Donald Horowitz seminar, "The Deadly Ethnic Riot," Foreign Policy Research Institute, 1 Mar. 01.

85. Horowitz, *Deadly Ethnic Riot,* p. 163n and passim.

86. Richard Lloyd Parry, "What Young Men Do," *Granta,* 62 (Summer 1998), p. 101.

87. Horowitz, *Deadly Ethnic Riot,* p. 419. Jamie S. Davidson and Douglas Kammen relate these murderous disturbances to the low-level PKI rebellion in West Kalimantan that ran from the early 1960s until 1974. They hypothesize but do not demonstrate causal connections: "Indonesia's Unknown War and the Lineages of Violence in West Kalimantan," *Indonesia,* 73 (Apr. 02), pp. 53–87.

88. O'Rourke, *Reformasi,* pp. 395–396; U.S. Committee for Refugees, "Shadow Plays: The Crisis of Refugees and Internally Displaced Persons in Indonesia" (Washington, DC, Jan. 01), 44 pp., passim.

89. Personal conversation with Colonel Benson, 13 Mar. 01.

90. O'Rourke, *Reformasi,* pp. 396–397, 413.

91. *Washington Post,* 17 Apr. 01, <sadli@pacific.net.id> <joyonews@aol.com>.

92. Ruut Veenhoven et al., *Happiness in Nations: Subjective Appreciation of Life in 56 nations, 1946–1992* (Rotterdam: RISBO, Erasmus University, 1993), pp. 121–123, 130.

93. Robert H. Frank, *Luxury Fever: Why Money Fails to Satisfy in an Era of Excess* (New York: The Free Press, 1999), pp. 72–73, 78–79.

94. Richard A. Easterlin, "Does Economic Growth Improve the Human Lot? Some Empirical Evidence," in Paul A. David and Melvin W. Reder, eds., *Nations and Households in Economic Growth* (New York: Academic Press, 1974), pp. 89–125, esp. pp. 118–119.

95. Ibid., p. 121; quotation from George C. Homans, p. 119.

96. Correspondence between the author and Professor Ruut Veenhoven, Erasmus University, Rotterdam, Mar.–Apr. 02.

97. Veenhoven, *Happiness in Nations,* p. 128.

98. Chua Beng Huat and Tan Joo Ean, "Singapore: Where the New Middle Class Sets the Standard," in Michael Pinches, ed., *Culture and Privilege in Capitalist Asia* (London: Routledge, 1999), pp. 137–158.

99. Jim Ockey, "Creating the Thai Middle Class," ibid., pp. 230–250.

100. Ariel Heryanto, "The Years of Living Luxuriously: Identity Politics of Indonesian New Rich," ibid., pp. 159–187.

101. Hans Antlov, "The New Rich and Cultural Tensions in Rural Indonesia," ibid., pp. 188–207.

102. Lizzy van Leeuwen, "Being Rich in Jakarta, 1994: A Mother and Two Daughters," Henk Schulte Nordholt, ed., *Outward Appearances: Dressing State and Society in Indonesia* (Leiden: KITLV Press, 1997), pp. 339–362.

103. Alfred W. McCoy, ed., *An Anarchy of Families: State and Family in the Philippines* (Manila: Ateneo de Manila University Press, 1994), identifies (p. 8) the anthropologist Robert Fox as originating the phrase "an anarchy of families" as descriptive of the Philippines in 1959. As a sometime drinking companion of Fox in Manila during that era, I respect McCoy's concluding essay, "Rent-Seeking Families and the Philippine State: A History of the Lopez Family," pp. 429–536. He illustrates a symbiosis between weak state and some enduring families (p. 517) far more manifest than any example yet in Indonesia. The two nations are alike in "subverting public institutions to promote private accumulation" (p. 518). Indonesia appears to me more anarchic, with greater family turnover.

104. Robert D. Putnam, *Making Democracy Work: Civic Traditions in Modern Italy* (Princeton: Princeton University Press, 1993); quotations, pp. 181, 184, 185. See

also Putnam, *Bowling Alone: The Collapse and Revival of American Community* (New York: Simon and Schuster, 2000), pp. 344–349, for comparative analysis of civic engagement.

105. Lawrence E. Harrison, "Promoting Progressive Cultural Change," pp. 296–307, in Harrison and Samuel P. Huntington, eds., *Culture Matters: How Values Shape Human Progress* (New York: Basic Books, 2000).

106. Ricklefs, *Indonesia since c. 1200*, pp. 49–56, 120–138.

107. "Squalid" quotation: Ricklefs, *The Seen and Unseen Worlds in Java, 1726–1749* (Honolulu: Allen & Unwin and University of Hawaii Press, 1998), p. 273.

108. Sartono Kartodirdjo, *Modern Indonesia: Tradition and Transformation* (Yogyakarta: Gadjah Mada University Press, 1984; 3rd ed., 1991), pp. 180–202, esp. 187–190. See also Franz Magnis-Suseno, *Javanese Ethics and World-View* (Jakarta: Gramedia Pustaka Utama, 1997; 1st German ed., 1981), pp. 155–157; and Niels Mulder, *Individual and Society in Java: A Cultural Analysis* (Yogyakarta: Gadjah Mada University Press, 1994; 1st ed., 1989), pp. 44–46, 149–154.

109. Dr. Mochtar Buchori, interview, 13 June 00. Laine Berman, *Speaking through the Silence: Narratives, Social Conventions and Power in Java* (New York: Oxford University Press, 1998), illustrates the linguistic point numerous ways, e.g. pp. 11–20. J. Joseph Errington, *Shifting Languages: Interaction and Identity in Javanese Indonesia* (Cambridge: Cambridge University Press, 1998), makes a powerful case for "flattening" in Javanese of personal pronouns in Indonesian (p. 189).

110. Pramoedya Ananta Toer, interview, 15 June 00 (John McGlynn, interpreter).

111. Regarding Romo Mangun, see Chapter 1 and Chapter 9, above.

112. Goenawan Mohamad, interview, 5 Nov. 00.

113. Dr. Franz Magnis-Suseno, interview, 9 Nov. 00.

114. Min. Sarwono Kusumaatmadja, interview, 12 Nov. 00.

115. Tu Wei-ming, "Multiple Modernities: A Preliminary Inquiry into the Implications of East Asian Modernity," in Harrison and Huntington, eds., *Culture Matters*, pp. 256–266; quotation, p. 265.

116. Post-Franco Spain obtained democracy with minimal civil society. Several scholars have pointed out that Weimar Germany marched toward fascism despite or even because of an abundance of Tocquevillean "voluntary associations." And of Robert Putnam it is well asked: How did Mussolini's fascism arise among the social compacts of Northern Italy? See especially Omar Encarnacion, "On Bowling Leagues and NGOs: A Critique of Civil Society's Revival," *Studies in Comparative International Development* (Winter 2002), pp. 116–131.

117. Quoted by Corey Robin, "The Ex-Cons: Right Wing Thinkers Go Left," in *Lingua Franca*, 11, no. 1 (Feb. 01), p. 32.

118. Quoted in W. H. Auden, *A Certain World: A Commonplace Book* (New York: Viking, 1970), p. 366, on "Tradition."

119. Theodore Friend, "Indonesia since Independence: Seven Unpopular Propositions," USINDO Brief of 5 Mar. 02, from presentation of 20 Feb. 02, Cosmos Club, Washington, DC. Author's version, edited from notes, conveyed to Aspinall I-discussion group, 8 Mar. 02.

120. V. S. Naipaul, "Our Universal Civilization," unedited transcript of address to the Manhattan Institute, New York City, 30 Oct. 90, courtesy of Harry A. Richlin.

Epilogue: Sukarno's Daughter in the Palace

1. Vice President Megawati Sukarnoputri, interview and field notes, 6 Nov. 99.

2. Privileged conversations, Jakarta and Washington, 2000.

3. Theodore Friend, "Indonesia's Year of the Blue Carpet," Foreign Policy Research Institute, E-Note, 6 Dec. 00; and "Power Vacuum in ASEAN: Indonesia, Regional Security, and the USA," ibid., 2 Apr. 01.

4. Personal conversation, Wimar Witoelar, 13 Mar. 01, Washington, DC.

5. Wimar Witoelar, *No Regrets: Reflections of a Presidential Spokesman* (Jakarta: Equinox Publishing, 2002), p. 112. Wimar's book is affectionately defensive of his boss. But after some months on the job he was quoted on "an uncontrollable president . . . I can say with all the honesty I can convey here that this man is a good guy. I can also say that my man does not have the competence to govern." Vaudine England, *South China Morning Post,* 9 Nov. 00, <sadli@pacific.net.id> <joyo@aol.com>.

6. Sympathetic treatment of these and other episodes is available in Greg Barton, *Abdurrahman Wahid: Muslim Democrat, Indonesian President* (Sydney: University of New South Wales Press, 2002), pp. 351–357.

7. Dino Patti Djalal, "President Megawati Sukarnoputri: Off to a Good Start," Indonesian Embassy, Washington, DC, Policy Views Series, no. 8, 30 July 01.

8. "Megawati's New Cabinet Accommodates Parties, Professionals," USINDO brief, 9 Aug. 01.

9. *Far East Economic Review,* 30 Aug. 01, pp. 40–43; quotation, p. 41.

10. Privileged conversations, Philadelphia, 15 Nov. 02 (AM); New York, 15 Nov. 02 (PM). Sadanand Dhume, *Far East Economic Review,* 29 Nov. 01; Tony Sitathan, *Asia Times,* 18 Jan. 03; Richard Borsuk, *The Wall Street Journal,* 28 Jan. 03; Tim Dodd, *Australian Financial Review,* 5 Feb. 03 <joyo@aol.com>.

11. *Jane's Intelligence Review,* 13, 4 (Apr. 01), pp. 33–37, on GAM; quotation on piracy, p. 44.

12. Quotations of Marzuki from John McBeth, *Far East Economic Review,* 24 June 01, pp. 20–21. Ginandjar's benefice in shares of Freeport McMoRan would appear to be one example, as reported in the *Asian Wall Street Journal,* 2 Sept. 98.

13. Marzuki, in McBeth, ibid.

14. *The Age* (Melbourne), 27 July 01, p. 9.

15. "Cabinet Profile: MA Rahman: Attorney General," Laksamana Net, 16 Aug. 01, <sadli@pacific.net.id>; "A Worrying Omen," Editorial, *South China Morning Post,* 16 Aug. 01, <sadli@pacific.net>.

16. Hamish McDonald, "Not Many Hangers-on, but One Real Shocker," Sydney *Morning Herald,* 10 Aug. 01, <sadli@pacific.net.id>; International Crisis Group, "Indonesia Briefing: The Megawati Presidency," Jakarta/Brussels, 10 Sept. 01, "C. Human Rights Violations" (unpag. transmission).

17. Kornelius Purba, "Bambang Kesowo's Return Revives Past Fear," Jakarta Post, 30 Aug. 01, <sadli@pacific.net.id>; "State Secretaries: Where the Money Went," Laksamana.Net, 15 June 02, <sadli@pacific.net.id>.

18. Privileged conversations, Indonesian and American sources, 2002.

19. *New York Times,* 25 Aug. 02, p. WK2.

20. John McBeth, "Wahid and Sukarno's Gold," *Far Eastern Economic Review*, 14 Dec. 00, pp. 34–35.

21. Alejandro Reyes, "Other People's Money," *Asiaweek*, 11 Aug. 00. Carmen Jardaleza has provided me a thick file on this matter, dating back to Pres. Corazon Aquino's freezing of Marcos assets in 1986 and turning chiefly upon the Presidential Commission on Good Government's efforts to retrieve ill-gotten and well-hidden wealth. The subject may be tracked on http://marcosbillions.com.

22. St. Augustine, *City of God*, 4.4, quoted in Gary Wills, *Saint Augustine* (New York: Viking, 1999), p. 117.

23. Jakob Tobing, interview, VZR, 4, 15 (2 Sept. 02), pp. 13–16; Andrew Ellis, "Constitutional Reform and the 2004 Election Cycle," USINDO Brief, 24 Sept. 02.

24. *The Economist*, 6 July 02, pp. 13–14, 65–67. Total CGI loans to Indonesia averaged a steady $5.2 billion for six years before a crisis infusion of nearly $8 billion in 1999. Thereafter they steeply declined annually to $2.7 billion for 2003. VZR, 5, 1 (27 Jan. 03), p. 27.

25. *Far Eastern Economic Review*, John McBeth, "Tentative Recovery," 13 June 02, p. 51.

26. Dr. Mochtar Riady, interview, 12 June 00. His full views appear in Dr. Mochtar Riady, *Mencari Peluang di Tengah Krisis* [Seeking a Way in Mid-Crisis] (Jakarta: Universitas Pelita Harapan Press, 1999).

27. Richard Behar, "The Year of Laying Cable Dangerously," *Fortune*, 124, 23 (July 01), <FT0119200011 MNS01–9>.

28. *Tempo Magazine*, 19–25 Nov. 02, <joyonews@aol.com>.

29. The phrase is from Mario Vargas Llosa's *El Hablador*, a novel about his inescapable Peru, brilliantly analyzed by Benedict Anderson: "El Malhadado País," in *The Spectre of Comparisons: Nationalism, Southeast Asia and the World* (London: Verso, 1998), pp. 333–359. Anderson, incidentally, derives his book title (p. 2) from a phrase of the great Filipino patriot and novelist Jose Rizal: *El demonio de las comparaciones*. But I take Rizal's *el demonio* more literally than Anderson does, because the Spanish word for spectre is *espectro*, or *fantasma*. Comparison is not "spectral" but real, even when partial or erroneous.

30. Interview, Dr. Nasir Tamara (a member of ICMI Board, and a leading spokesman of PPP, which Islamically-oriented party was fourth in the popular vote, 1999), 10 Nov. 00.

31. Edgardo Krebs, "Argentina: Wounded by Its Myths," Council on Foreign Relations, *Correspondence*, 9 (Spring 02), pp. 54–55.

32. William Reno, "Mafiya Troubles, Warlord Crises," and Mark R. Beissinger and Crawford Young, "The Effective State in Postcolonial Africa and Post-Soviet Eurasia: Hopeless Chimera or Possible Dream?" in Beissinger and Young, eds., *Beyond State Crisis? Postcolonial Africa and Post-Soviet Eurasia in Comparative Perspective* (Washington, DC: Woodrow Wilson Center Press, 2002), pp. 108, 119, 472n.

33. Personal notes, Eisenhower Exchange Fellowships and Eurasia Group, "Russia's Emerging Economy and Civil Society," University Club, New York City, 9 Nov. 01.

34. Roland M. Machold (then Director of the New Jersey State Pension Fund; later

Treasurer of the State of New Jersey under Gov. Christine Todd Whitman), to [name deleted] of Goldman Sachs, 16 May 97. Document courtesy of Mr. Machold.

35. I draw here upon Omar G. Encarnacion, "Civil Society Resurgence and Democracy: Cautionary Lessons from Brazil," draft, courtesy of the author.

36. In these remarks I am informed and guided by Edward Aspinall, "Civil Society and Democratization: From Aliran Struggle to Civil Society in the Countryside of Indonesia," paper presented to East-West Center conference in Phnom Penh, 24–28 Oct. 02.

37. Seth Mydans, "U.S. Lets Employees Leave as Indonesia Protests Mount," *New York Times*, 27 Sept. 01, B2.

38. Ibid.; and *Jakarta Post*, 15 Sept. 01, <sadli@pacific.net.id>. Dr. Anwar's comments appear in the *Jakarta Post*, 14 Sept. 01 <joyo@aol.com>.

39. Address by H. E. Megawati Sukarnoputri, President, Republic of Indonesia, at the USINDO Gala Dinner, Washington, DC, 19 Sept. 01.

40. Reuters; *Singapore Straits Times*, 22 Aug. 01, <sadli@pacific.net.id>; and author's notes on "Integration in Indonesia: The Cases of Aceh and Papua," USINDO conference, 26 Nov. 02.

41. Agence France Presse, 11 Nov. 01, <sadli@pacific.net>; *Wall Street Journal*, 12 Nov. 01, p. A19; *Economist*, 17 Nov. 01, p. 42; O'Rourke, *Reformasi*, pp. 412–414.

42. International Crisis Group, "Indonesia: Resources and Conflict in Papua," Sept. 02, pp. 3–5.

43. Confidential exchange of email messages, 2002.

44. Confidential interviews, (including "slit his stomach" quotation), senior American official, 13, 26 Dec. 02. Raymond Bonner, *New York Times*, 30 Jan. 03; Simon Elegant, Time-on-line, 6, 17 Feb. 03, p. 14.

45. John McBeth and Michael Vatikiotis, "An About-Turn in the Military," *Far Eastern Economic Review*, 25 Apr. 02, pp. 12–15; quotation, p. 15.

46. Rizal Mallarangeng, "The Future of Indonesia Depends on Our Friendship with the West," VZR, 3, 19 (5 Nov. 01), pp. 21–23.

47. Juwono Sudarsono, "Improving the US-Indonesia Military Relationship," VZR, 4, no. 11, 17 June 02, pp. 9–13; quotations, pp. 9, 10.

48. John Gershman, "Is Southeast Asia the Second Front?" *Foreign Affairs*, 81, 4 (July/Aug. 02), pp. 60–74.

49. USINDO Report, 5 Dec. 02, "Impact of the Bali Bombings . . . a Conference at the U.S.-Indonesia Society, November 26, 2002," and author's notes on the conference. Voluminous international dispatches from <joyo@aol.com> and personal notes, 2001–02; Donald Emmerson, "Whose Eleventh? Indonesia and America Since 11 September," draft to appear in the *Brown Journal of World Affairs*, 9 (1 Spring 02).

50. Personal notes, presentation by Police Gen. I Made Mangku Pastika to USINDO and guests, St. Regis Hotel Ballroom, Washington DC, 20 Feb. 03, and ensuing discussions; plus dialogue with Karl Jackson on the foregoing.

51. "Jamaah Islamiyah Operating in Indonesia: Police," *Jakarta Post*, 30 Nov. 02. International Crisis Group, "How the *Jemaah Islamiyah* Terrorist Network Operates," Asia Paper No. 43, Jakarta/Brussels, 11 Dec. 02, passim.

52. Prabowo Subianto, interview, VZR, *3*, 12, 26 June 01, pp. 24–29; remark on Gen. Sherman, p. 27.

53. Speech by Ambassador Ralph "Skip" Boyce on U.S.–Indonesia relations in context of U.S. security policy, 17 Dec. 02, relayed by American Indonesian Chamber of Commerce, NYC, 19 Dec. 02. Allen Nairn excoriates Generals Feisal Tanjung, Hendropriyono, and Prabowo as allegedly illustrious trainees of IMET; edited testimony before the International Operations and Human Rights Subcommittee of the U.S. House Committee on International Relations, 30 Sept. 99, printed in Tanter, Selden, and Shalom, eds., *Bitter Flowers, Sweet Flowers*, pp. 163–172, esp. p. 171.

54. Michael Vatikiotis, VZR Special Issue, 8 Dec. 01, p. 7.

55. *Jakarta Post* Panel of Experts, 31 Dec. 01, <sadli@pacific.net> <joyo@aol.com>. This is an extraordinarily rich product of discussion under Chatham House rules by thirteen panelists and two distinguished moderators, written up by a team of nine from the editorial board of the *Post*.

56. Walter LaFeber, "The Bush Doctrine," *Diplomatic History*, 26, 4, Fall 2002, pp. 543–558; quotation of Wilson, p. 551.

57. Michael Ignatieff, "Barbarians at the Gate?" review of Robert D. Kaplan, "Warrior Politics: Why Leadership Demands a Pagan Ethos," *New York Review of Books*, 28 Feb. 02, pp. 4–6; quotations, p. 4.

58. Reinhold Niebuhr, *The Structure of Nations and Empires* (Fairfield, CT: Augustus M. Kelley, 1977; 1st ed., New York: Charles Scribner's Sons, 1959), quotations, pp. 296, 294, 295.

59. V. S. Naipaul, "Our Universal Civilization," unedited transcript, 15 pp., address to Manhattan Institute, New York City, 30 Oct. 90, p. 15; document courtesy of Harry Richlin.

60. Niebuhr, *Structure of Nations and Empires*, pp. 298–299. Emphasis supplied.

GLOSSARY

Terms in Bahasa Indonesia

abangan · nominal Muslims; those whose beliefs and practices are a mixture of animist, Hindu-Buddhist, and Islamic (especially Sufi mystical) elements. Javanese: *abang* = red. See also *kebatinen; kejawen; santri.*

adat · tradition; custom with the implied authority of common law.

agama · religion.

aliran · literally, "current," descriptive of a major politicosocial group that expresses one's convictions, often in uncompromising competition with others. Per Soedjatmoko: "cultural solidarity groups . . . tied together by primordial loyalties of great intensity."

azas tunggal · sole guiding principle. In 1985 the MPR made Pancasila (actually, five associated principles) the *azas tunggal,* or only founding basis, of all associations of any kind.

bapak · father; abbr. *pak.* Substituted in the Suharto era for *bung* ("brother"), which in the Sukarno era conveyed the revolutionary flavor of citizen or comrade. Now, *pak* has a range of meanings from a neutral "mister" to "boss" or "protector."

becak · a trishaw for hire, pedaled by a driver who usually sits behind the passenger.

bulé · albino; now used as convenient and sometimes derogatory term for pale-skinned Westerners. Older usage, *londo,* was a corruption of *belanda,* or Dutch person, and was also applied to all Caucasians.

bung · brother; from 1945–1965, applied to Bung 'Karno and Bung Hatta as leaders of the revolution. Now a form of address to *becak* drivers and waiters whose name one does not know.

bupati · regent; one who governs a district *(kebupaten),* the next largest governmental subdivision after the province. In 1991 Indonesia had 241 districts and 40 city governments on an equivalent level of administration.

Cendana · street in Menteng area, Jakarta, of Suharto's personal residence. By extension, the nexus of family and crony power around him: "the Cendana gang."

cukong · Hokkien term for boss, referring to a Chinese-Indonesian businessman who collaborates with Indonesian state and military power.

cocok · fitting, agreeable, conforming. See also *rukun.*

desa · village, usually rural. For administrative purposes at the lowest tier, Indonesia in 1991 identified 66,979 villages.

dukun · seer, shaman, healer, sorcerer. Sometimes misused by Westerners to include any spiritual counselors to major political leaders, which advisors might in fact be *ulama,* or the most distinguished among those, *imam.*

dwifungsi · the doctrine of dual function of the military—defense/security plus social/political interventions. Presumptively discarded in April 2000.

gotong-royong · mutual help; as in villages cooperating to build a mosque or other project. Sukarno often idealized Indonesia as a *gotong-royong* society.

hadith · traditions regarding the words and deeds of the Prophet.

haj · pilgrimage to Mecca, as one of the five pillars of Islam, entitling one to be called by the honorific *haji.*

ibu · mother; missus.

imam · Muslim leader.

jihad · to strive; may apply to any spiritual effort from moral self-improvement to Holy War.

jilbab · garment adopted by many Indonesian women as part of Islamic resurgence, beginning in the 1980s. Clifford Geertz described it as a choice of "most especially educated young women, of Middle Eastern-style clothing: a long, loose-fitting, monochrome gown, reaching to the ankles, designed to conceal the shape of the body, and a long, winding scarf, usually white, designed to conceal the hair and neck . . . a sharp contrast to the form fitting low-cut blouse, tightly wrapped sarong, and carefully arranged hair the vast majority of Javanese women traditionally affect" (*Available Light,* pp. 180–181).

kampung · country village; cluster of buildings; or a definable quarter of a city with some rural characteristics and/or cohesion.

kebatinan · innerness; a comprehensive term for Javanese spiritualism.

kejawen · dedicated adherence to Javanese tradition; also referred to as *agama Jawa* (Javanese religion) or Javanism.

keraton · palace.

kiai · Javanese honorific for revered people, objects, and sacred relics; applied to the most highly venerated teachers of Islam.

krismon · contraction of *krisis moneter* (monetary crisis); coined in 1997 and followed in 1998 by *kristal.*

kristal · contraction of *krisis total;* referring to total crisis (financial, political, social, and so on).

laskar · soldier, warrior; most often, in titles of irregular militia groups; e.g., Laskar Jihad, an armed organization which emerged under Ja'far Umar Thalib early in 2000, was a name earlier used by other bodies.

Mahabharata · Indian epic, transformed over centuries in Indonesia, depicting the great Bharatayudha war between the related Kurawa and Pendawa families. Goenawan Mohamad says: "The battles in the war all relate to events that have happened in the past—to curses pronounced, favours and promises made, inter-family alliances, and they also connect with events that will occur in the future . . . The entire war is a tragic conflict between personal family loyalties and duty to one's kingdom . . . Fate . . . demands that certain actions must be carried out in fulfillment of destiny itself" (*Sidelines,* p. 233).

mandala · (Sanskritic) area or district; literally a circle, but, historically, a porous po-litical sphere. Also used symbolically, as when the Suhartos built Taman Mini In-donesia Indah (the Beautiful Indonesia-in-Miniature Park), 1971–1975. It was in-tended as a mandala of the archipelago, a binding microcosm of the newly ordered state, and a guarantee of its stability.

Muhammadiyah · founded 1912: second largest Muslim organization in Indonesia after NU (founded 1926); chaired by Amien Rais until the election of 1999. Muhammadiyah's "modernism" is Qur'anic—textual and anti-syncretist.

Nahdlatul Ulama (NU) · Renaissance of the Religious Scholars; large Muslim orga-nization founded in 1926; chaired by Abdurrahman Wahid (1984–1999), with an accent on deconfessionalization of politics, contrary to Muhammadiyah. NU's "traditionalism" involves accommodation between Islam and indigenous cultural practices.

nusantara · Sanskrit and Indonesian term for archipelago; as used to refer to the post-Dutch unitary and independent state, a more neutral term than "Indonesia."

Orde Baru (**New Order**) · self-styled description of Suharto's government, contrary to the *Orde Lama* (Old Order) of Sukarno.

pak · see *bapak.*

Pancasila · revolutionary ideology, voiced by Sukarno in 1945 and later dogmati-cally elaborated by Suharto's bureaucracy, consisting of five guiding principles: belief in a Supreme Being; nationalism; humanitarianism; social justice; consulta-tive democracy.

pegawai negeri · government official; or, in exalted analogy to Western civil service, "servant of the state."

pemuda · youth, with the connotation of "political youth"; used with reference to their actions and demonstrations of 1945–1949, 1965–66, and 1998–99.

peristiwa · incident or affair, with political connotations, applied to PKI revolt at Madiun in 1948; to the army's attempted showdown with Sukarno government, October 17, 1952, and so on. By continuing implication: a range of events from contrived confrontation to bloody clash, signifying irreconcilability, or lack of deliberative capacity to resolve issues of state.

pesantren · Muslim boarding school. (Less commonly used: *madrasah.*)

pici · male cap of black velvet adopted and advocated by Sukarno from the 1920s onward to show solidarity with the common man and support for an independent nation; in the New Order, it was also associated with Muslim identity.

preman · thug.

pribumi · native-born. Often used in contradistinction to Chinese Indonesians, whether recent immigrants or ancient arrivals from China.

priyayi · traditional Javanese aristocracy; especially court officials and highly ranked indigenous officials under the Dutch; now, by implication, a holder of power or status, but not hereditary.

Ratu Adil · the Just King. Associated in pre-modern Javanese mentality with upheaval and violent cyclical purification of society, focused on a charismatic leader who has received the *wahyu cakraningrat,* which implies its withdrawal from an established ruler.

romushas · Japanese term for "volunteers" during military occupation, 1942–1945. Actually labor conscripts, many of whom died overseas on Japanese projects.

rukun · a major Javanese principle of social solidarity. It stresses continuous harmony in social appearances and minimizes overt manifestation of any kind of social and personal conflict. See also *cocok.*

salafi · one who pursues extreme Islamic puritanism, Wahhabi (q.v.)-inspired, manifesting a return to seventh century (C.E.) standards by white clothing and enforced religious observances.

santri · orthodox Muslim; a practicing Muslim oriented to mosque, Qur'an, and perhaps to Islamic canon law. Sometimes called *putihan* (the white ones) as distinct from *abangan.* Very loosely: white turbans vs. rednecks.

saudagar · merchant. Among *priyayi,* a term of contempt for the business class, who were either Chinese or bazaar *santri.*

sawah · wet rice fields.

shariah · the way; Islamic canon law, regarded by some as a complete code of life.

supersemar · compression of *surat pemerintah sebelas maret* (government letter of March 11 [1966]), a document in which Sukarno was forced to devolve powers as Acting President to Suharto.

tiwikrâmâ · Javanese wayang term meaning to transform oneself into a huge giant. Suharto thus expressed his intention, out of office, to seek vengeance on those who deposed him. More contemplatively: to summon one's powers for a major purpose.

ulama · Muslim scholar.

Wahhabi · follower of the official school of Saudi Arabia, launched by Muhammad ibn Abd al-Wahhab (1703–87). His puritanical reformation of Islam seeks to rid it of "superstitious" traditions and indiscriminate Sufism. See also *Salafi*.

wahyu cakraningrat · mandate of heaven. See *Ratu Adil*.

wayang · a form of drama, of which the best known is *wayang kulit*–shadow theater using flat, ornate leather puppets enacting lengthy segments of the *Mahabharata* in its Javanese/Balinese adaptations. Also enacted with *wayang golek* (wooden puppets) and *wayang orang* (human beings).

yayasan · foundation; often suggesting, in the Suharto era, a philanthropic shell for business transactions and financial manipulations on the part of the first family and cronies.

Abbreviations, Acronyms, and Names of Politically Important Entities

ABRI · Angkatan Bersenjata Republik Indonesia: the armed forces. See TNI.

ASEAN · Association of Southeast Asian Nations.

Bulog · Badan Urusan Logistik: Logistic Affairs Agency.

CIDES · Center for Information and Development Studies.

CSIS · Center for Strategic and International Studies.

Darul Islam · House of Islam. Familiar name for the breakaway regime Negara Islam Indonesia (Indonesian Islamic State), founded by Kartosoewiryo and furthered by rebellion, 1948–1962.

DPR · Dewan Perwakilan Rakyat: People's Representative Council. The "lower" legislative house of parliament.

Falintil · armed wing of Fretelin (see below) and of East Timor resistance generally.

Fretelin · Revolutionary Front for an Independent East Timor; political party formed in 1974.

FOKUPERS · Forum Komunikasi untuk Perempuan Loro Sa'e. Communication Forum for Women of Loro Sa'e. An East Timorese NGO focusing on women's rights, minority rights, and victims' rights.

GAM · Gerakan Aceh Merdeka: Movement for Free Aceh.

G30S · Gerakan 30 September: Movement of September 30, 1965.

Gestapu · Condemnatory acronym for G30S.

Golkar · Golongan Karya: Functional groups; the Suharto government's "nonparty" party, used as an election vehicle and corporatist patronage organ for the state.

IBRA · Indonesian Bank Restructuring Agency.

ICMI · Ikatan Cendekiawan Muslim Indonesia: Indonesian Muslim Intellectuals' Association.

IGGI · InterGovernmental Group on Indonesia, established 1967 to coordinate multilateral aid. Succeeded (with Suharto's spiteful elimination of the Netherlands) by the Consultative Group on Indonesia (CGI), 1992.

IPKI · Ikatan Pendukung Kemerdekaan Indonesia (League of Upholders of Indonesia's Independence). Military-initiated political party; ninth largest vote-getter (1955); forced into fusion with PDI in 1973. Founding context for Pemuda Pancasila

Jemaah Islamiyah · radical Islamist organization devoted to establishing an Islamic caliphate in all of Muslim Southeast Asia. Although founded in 1995, its political heritage is traceable to Darul Islam.

KKN · Korupsi, Kolusi, Nepotisme: slogan of obloquy attributed to Christianto Wibisono in the *reformasi* era to attack the corruption, collusion, and nepotism of the New Order, by then both antique and riddled with crony capitalism.

KNIL · Royal Netherlands Indies Army.

Kopassus · Komando Pasukuan Khusus: Special Forces Command. Commando units first formed to oppose Darul Islam in 1952; prominent in operations to crush the PKI in 1965; in invasion of East Timor and continuing operations there; deployed for strategic intelligence and covert operations in Aceh and Papua.

Kostrad · Komando Cadangan Strategis Angkatan Darat: Army Strategic Reserve Command formed in 1960 for invasion of Irian Jaya. Usually, two infantry divisions and an airborne brigade with headquarters in Jakarta, with units expected to plug in to territorial commands for logistic support during short emergency deployments.

KPU · Komisi Pemilihan Umum: National Election Commission (1999).

LIPI · Lembaga Ilmu Pengetahuan Indonesia: Indonesian Institute of Science.

Malari · Malapeteka Januari: The January Disaster of 1974—anti-regime riots in Jakarta.

MMI · Majelis Mujahadin Indonesia: Indonesian Holy Warrior Council, founded August 2000.

MPR · Majelis Permusyawaratan Rakyat: People's Consultative Assembly. The "upper" house of parliament, rarely called into session by Suharto except for prescribed duties. Since 1999, in active contention for power with the executive branch of government.

MPRS · Same as above with addition of the word *Semantara* (provisional), as established in 1960 during Sukarno's guided democracy. "Provisional" was dropped when Suharto made it his legislative echo chamber.

NASAKOM · Sukarno's acronymic mantra for *Nationalisme, Agama* (religion), and *Komunisme,* which he declared to be the three main streams of the revolution. He used it intensively from 1960 onward, even to the end of 1965.

NGO · Non-government organization. What in the United States are called "not-for-profits" or "private voluntary organizations" are defined in much of the world in contradistinction to government. By the 1990s in Indonesia they were colloquially described by size—big, middlesized, and little—as BINGOs, MINGOs, and LINGOs. If government-organized, they were, oxymoronically, GONGOs.

NU · see Nahdlatul Ulama.

OPM · Organisasi Papua Merdeka: Papua Independence Organization.

PAN · Partai Amanat Nasional: Party of the National Mandate; political vehicle of Amien Rais and Muhammadiyah, 1999–.

PDI · Partai Demokrasi Indonesia: Indonesian Democratic Party; forced fusion of nationalist and Christian parties (1973).

PDI-P · Partai Demokrasi Indonesia-Perjuangan: Indonesian Democratic Party-for Struggle. Party led by Megawati Sukarnoputri after PDI was stolen by Suhartoites in 1996.

Pemilu · Pemilihan Umum: General Elections of 1999.

Pam Swakarsa · underclass/mass militia of opportunity first organized by ABRI in 1998, including Muslim elements (the latter in contradistinction to Pemuda Pancasila).

Pemuda Pancasila · Youth for the Five Principles. Ostensibly a youth organization for national morality, but in Orde Baru practice an ABRI auxiliary or Suhartoite muscle group for political pressure, infested with *preman*.

Pertamina · Pertambangan Minyak dan Gas Bumi Nasional: State Oil and Gas Company.

Peta · Pembela Tanah Air. Defenders of the Fatherland. Japanese-formed officers' training corps.

PKB · Partai Kebangkitan Bangsa: Party of the People's Awakening; political vehicle of Abdurrahman Wahid and NU, 1999–.

PKI · Partai Komunis Indonesia: Indonesian Communist Party.

PNI · Partai Nasional Indonesia: Indonesian Nationalist Party. The heritage of Sukarno's mass organization party dates back to 1928. It was the largest of the discordant elements forced into the PDI in 1973.

PPP · Partai Persatuan Pembangunan: Development Unity Party; forced fusion of Muslim parties (1973), continuing in strong numbers in 1999 and after, despite elaboration of other new Muslim parties.

SARA · Suka/Agama/Ras/Antara-golongan. Tribe/Religion/Race/Inter-Group Relations. Acronym devised by Suharto officials as comprehensive proscription against reporting or editorializing in those several sensitive areas.

SOE · State-Owned Enterprise.

TNI · Tentara Nasional Indonesia: Indonesian National Army. Revolutionary term of choice from August 1947 until later replaced by ABRI. With reorganizations of the year 2000, which included separation of police from other armed forces, the term TNI came back into use for the army in particular.

VOC · Vereenigde Oost-Indische Compagnie. Dutch East India Company.

INDEX

Page references to illustrations and tables are in italic.